Colony to Nation

A HISTORY OF CANADA

Colony to Nation

BY ARTHUR R. M. LOWER
C.C., PH.D., F.R.S.C.

Emeritus Professor of History,
Queen's University, Kingston
sometime Professor of History
and Political Science,
United College, Winnipeg

WITH MAPS BY T. W. McLEAN

McCLELLAND AND STEWART

To the Memory of My Mother

Contents

List of Maps and Diagrams

Preface to the First Edition

Most of those who see this book will probably decide without opening it that it must be a dull one. Few people read any history and fewer still read any Canadian history. Relatively few are interested in Canada. To outsiders Canada is not a country with intrinsic appeal. If it were internationally unreliable, it might attract as much attention as Ireland or Italy, but since it can invariably be counted on in advance by the powers to whom its conduct matters, it ranks as safe and sane, a successful mediocrity of a country, like Switzerland or Sweden. The main association which Canadians themselves have had with their own history has consisted in the terrifically boring stuff shoved at them in their school days.

The school teacher, however, is mainly effect rather than cause. If Canadians were able to realize themselves as a people and to lavish their profoundest political loyalties on their own country, instead of dissipating them in half a dozen different directions, then interest in their own past would come readily enough and the invincible determination to remain in ignorance of all except its superficial aspects would disappear. French Canada, it is true, finds in its history much of the spiritual sustenance that enables it to go on existing, but little of this can pass over to English Canada. There are, as yet, two Canadas, inhabited by two peoples who, as often as not, are at outs. In the strictest sense there can, therefore, be no History of Canada. There can be histories of French Canada and histories of English Canada. There can be *Histories of Canada* written by French authors or by English authors, which hardly seem to refer to the same country. There can be useful studies in economic or diplomatic or constitutional history. There can be accounts of this period or that region. There can be polite political history. There can be biography. The past twenty-five years have witnessed a remarkable output of these types of monographic material: it forms one of the most distinguished accomplishments of the Canadian intellect and a book like this certainly could not have been written without it. But since they have not been fused in life, for the historian to fuse all these elements into one integral substance is close to impossible. Writing Canadian history remains an act of faith, the substance of things hoped for.

Yet it is not lack of great themes that has prevented the history of Canada in this sense from being written, for the four centuries of the country's existence abound in themes which appeal not only to the analyzing intellect but to the imagination. If people find Canadian history dull, it must either be because they are dull themselves or because the Canadian historic scene has not yet been painted in its own bold colours. How could a history full of grandiose projects, startling contrasts, stark antitheses, be dull? How could significance be lacking in the story of a country whose very existence consists in a never-ending battle to accomplish the impossible?

There is matter enough in any one of a score of topics such as those set out below to relieve Canadian history of such aspersions.

The clash between backward and advanced cultures is an absorbing human problem: it finds its exemplification in the struggle between the Indians and the French.

The rush of the old world to seize the wealth of the new and the various geographic, political and economic patterns which arise in consequence, such as the staple trade, the colonial and imperial relationship, and the relationship of metropolis and hinterland, such subjects provide matter for endless investigation.

The never-ending conflict between the men and forces representing old-world attitudes of exploitation (which usually have also vigorously naturalized themselves) and those representing the settler and the soil, which symbolize the society being built, creates tensions that fill Canadian history with movement.

The antithesis, resulting from the English conquest, between two wholly different ways of life, in itself gives subject matter and to spare for the highest of high drama.

The antithesis between history and geography, as exemplified in the two separate English-speaking societies emerging from the American Revolution, is almost equally sharp.

Unique solutions, founded on unwilling tolerance have been reached by Canadians for these overwhelming problems of theirs. 'Responsible Government', the compromise between Imperialism and colonialism, or between dependence and independence, was worked out on Canadian soil and by Canadians: the Federal Union of 1867, which through mutual agreement to forgive and forget, opened a way to solving the problem of the conquest of 1763, was in itself one of the greatest acts of statesmanship in the nineteenth century; the bold defiance of geography contained in the national planning which was an essential aspect of Confederation, resulted in the integration of half a continent.

This book has been built about some of these great themes. The author hopes that a careful reading of his pages will help Canadians to some of that self-knowledge so necessary if they are to take their rightful place in the world, and still more, if they are to be a happy people, at peace with themselves. If he has not succeeded in this task, then someone else must take it up, for it is imperative. It may be performed by the statesman, by the novelist or the poet, or it may be performed by the historian. Certainly on no one is the duty of revealing to the people reasons for the faith that is in them more directly laid than on the historian, for by its history a people lives. This book is an attempt to discharge that duty.

A.R.M. Lower

Shining Tree
Lake of the Woods
Ontario
August 24, 1946

Preface to the Fifth Edition

After *Colony to Nation* had been declared "out of print", I received various suggestions to the effect that the book ought to continue to be available. Apart from whatever contribution it may have made to the study and interpretation of Canadian history, it has apparently become a document in its own right. I myself would like to think of it not so much as a "document", a piece of data, as a contribution to Canadian literature, since there is no good reason for excluding *history* from the category *literature*. Mr. Jack McClelland of McClelland and Stewart agreed with me and hence this fifth edition. The body of the text is not altered. I would like it "to stand on its own feet". But I have enlarged the "Prologue" to bring it, by means of a group of sketches added to the pertinent sections, down to date.

Let me mention the assistance I was given by Miss Nancy Bowes and my appreciation of Mr. McClelland and his firm in the services they have rendered in bringing out the book.

Arthur R.M. Lower

Queen's University
Kingston, Ont.
March, 1977.

Prologue

Up to the end of the Second World War, our history had unity and a certain logical quality, for it was, in essence, the story of how a new national state had come into existence. In the last thirty years or so Canada has advanced beyond the threshold of national life and that advancement, to my mind, puts us into a new stage, one which must be allowed to develop further before fundamental analysis of it can be undertaken. It is always possible to chronicle events, but the historian must select, and it is in the manner of his selection that he earns the title of artist. If he can join insight to artistic selection and discern the pattern of the endless cloth that history weaves, he may perhaps become a prophet, and if he can stir in his readers a sense of man's tragic destiny, then he has become a poet.

History is full of "lions in the path" that have proved to be shadows that merely looked like lions.[1] For example, the quarrel of Mitchell Hepburn with Mackenzie King at the beginning of the Second World War looked as if it might shake national unity. It did not. The method of history stands in jarring contrast to that of the journalist with his "spot news". Its study becomes an exercise in proportion, and this is one of its

[1] Our present plight may be a real lion (1977).

chief values. If men would only apply to affairs the time-scale which even their own single life-span (to say nothing of the centuries) puts at their disposal, we might be less worried at the sight of the lion in the path – if it is a lion! But how many of us can see even the previous dozen years in an ordered sequence and not as a mere jumble of disconnected events dimly remembered?

The life of the community expresses itself in certain broad classifications, and it is in these that I group the events of our current period; for the logical alternative, the reader is referred to the detailed chronologies published annually in the *Canada Year Book*. I propose to discuss Canada from 1945 to 1976 under these headings: politics, constitutional experience, administration, finance, economic affairs, demography, and external affairs. Naturally, within the scope of a few pages, none of these discussions can be definitive; nor can they be kept strictly within watertight compartments. And space forbids including at all many topics of current importance (the grand inquests into our national life conducted by the various Royal Commissions, for example), and the innermost "me" of a collectivity – up to the "make or break" of 1976 ff.

(A) Parties and Politics, 1945-1976

History is bound up with politics. What are we to say of the politics of Canada since say, the last World War?

Until 1957 we faced a phenomenon which had not presented itself to us before – the absence of an alternative federal government. After the Conservative defeat of 1935, the Liberal party went from strength to strength, and minor parties also appeared. The result was that the opposition became so divided, both in numbers, purpose, and geographical distribution,[2] that no group in it seemed within measurable distance of an electoral victory.

All the elections of the period[3] until 1957 went overwhelmingly in favour of the Liberals. The Conservative party suffered from frequent changes of leadership, much of it indifferent in calibre, and from something still more serious: it ceased to represent any distinctive idea or ideal. The historic coalition of 1854[4] had been based on schemes for the development of the country and amity between the two races. It had also

[2] None of the opposition parties was in a proper sense a national party, representation of each being mostly drawn from a single province. Thus the Conservatives were mainly an Ontario party.

[3] All tables in this Prologue are from the *Canada Year Book* or other publications of the Dominion Bureau of Statistics.

[4] See p. 291.

carried forward from the older Tory party the strong traditional elements of an emotional attachment to the British connection and to the monarchy, combining these with an unadmitted preference for a society of class distinctions. The intervening years made large developmental schemes common to all parties (no one, for example, was against the St. Lawrence Seaway), and by the irony of history, it was the Liberal party which fell heir to Sir John Macdonald's task of keeping the two races in step. More than that, the growth of national spirit in Canada after the war lessened the emphasis on the British connection and possibly on the monarchy too, while the spirit of the age became so strongly equalitarian that all parties paid at least lip-service to the idea of equality.[5] The major difficulty of Canadian Conservatism, and still more of its right, or Tory, wing was that the age seemed to have passed it by.

What was not anticipated was the continuing strength of the party which had conducted the war; as a rule, the electors lose no time in getting rid of a wartime government, but although the Liberals lost some seats in the election of 1945, their majority was not seriously threatened. Nor were the left-wing parties that had arisen as a result of the depression able to capitalize on war-time hardships. From the end of the war to 1957, the people of Canada seemed satisfied with the middle-of-the-road party that offered something to everybody and offended nobody very much; it is possible that its continued electoral success depended to a greater extent on the amazing prosperity of the post-war period than on its own merits. To this prosperity must be added just the opposite fortune from that of the Conservatives in the matter of leaders. In choosing St. Laurent to succeed King (1948) the Liberals chose a man who had a personality which won the confidence of everyone. As someone said, "he did not have to cross barbed wire" – but no one can deny the success of his charm and the breadth of many of the concepts which took shape under him. He appeared to be a true architect of nationalism. He was as characteristic as a Canadian can be, in that he was completely

[5] These words were written in 1963. The present footnote is added in 1977, fourteen years later. The interval has seen the spirit of equality driven even further. Little of the old ingrained feeling for *status* remains. The old "heroes", such as warriors and prime ministers receive scant respect (possibly because they do not have the stature to command it). When the Queen visits Canada, she is received with respect but no marked enthusiasm. In Quebec, the atmosphere is apt to be hostile. But new "heroes" are necessarily in the making. Among them, hockey "stars" are conspicuous. This marked transition probably indicates the important transition from "colony to nation", that is, to a community which is seeking to find its own symbols within itself, and necessarily floundering while it does so. For example, the Premier of Ontario ceased to be William Davis and became "Bill" Davis, just "one of the boys". Another symbol of the idea of equality was the reduction of the voting age from twenty-one to eighteen.

bilingual, had the blood of both peoples in his veins, and had a plain, lower-middle-class family background (his father kept a grocery store). More important, probably, in the eyes of the average citizen who saw him, he was a kindly old grandfather. His mere existence spoke volumes for that gentlemanly education and that genuinely Christian approach to men and affairs which the system of French Canada gives to the best of its sons.

One of the textbook maxims is that parliamentary government works best under the two-party system. A maxim harder to maintain would be that two-party systems are "normal". In Canada's case we have seldom had a simple two-party system for any length of time. There was never a period when we were farther away from it than after the Second World War, for in addition to the traditional parties, we had both Social Crediters and C.C.F.'ers (N.D.P.'s), each with a good-sized handful of representatives, and each in power in one or two provinces. The Social Credit party represented a new kind of conservatism. Social Crediters were not Tories, though some of them were reactionaries, and they did not have much interest in the historic traditions of Conservatism. But by nature, most of them were conservatives – with a small "c" – and that very naturally, for they represented the typical "little man" – the *petit bourgeois*, or lower-middle-class man, who feels himself threatened by the instability of the times and imagines that by singing hymns emotionally and voting for a new set of men, he is going to get things remedied. In Quebec, where the movement had been present for some years, but where it made little headway until 1962 when it suddenly flared up to the extent of sending twenty-six members to Ottawa, its class composition may have been somewhat more varied than in the West, including, as it did, groups of urban industrial workers. Mr. Stevens' "Reconstruction Party" of 1935 drew heavily on this lower-middle class, and many of the people in Alberta and British Columbia who voted for him in that year later on voted for Social Credit members. Social Credit might be termed "grass-roots conservatism". It would thus appear to be the first indigenous conservative party which this country has possessed, the historic Conservative party having represented old-country attitudes and traditions in a Canadian setting.

The fortunes of the C.C.F. waned and waxed and waned again in the period after the war. The patent difficulty with it was that the country was too prosperous to be bothered with theories of reform. It is one thing to present to the electorate such nice Christmas presents as Old Age Pensions,[6] for no one will quarrel with Santa Claus; but it is quite another to

[6] In 1952 the Old Age Security Act provided $40 a month for every citizen reaching the age of 70, regardless of his means. In 1957, this sum was increased to $55, in 1962 to $65 and in 1963 to $75. Since that year it has roughly kept pace with the increase in the cost of living.

get voters to understand "production for use, not profit". A collectivized society corresponds to a definite point in historical development – when people get packed together in a close community, then the state must act. But a loose, sprawling country like this is unpromising ground for theoretical schemes. Even decided measures of reform can only be taken when they appear to mean relief in hard times; the C.C.F. was not blessed with hard times.

It was in an attempt to make its appeal less abstract that this party in its Winnipeg Convention of 1956 abandoned most of its remaining elements of doctrinairism and virtually made itself into a reform party. This brought it not far away from what Mr. St. Laurent once dubbed it – "Liberals in a hurry". It is, however, sometimes well to have liberals in a hurry, especially when there are many old and fat men in the Liberal party proper. The performance of the C.C.F. leaders, men like Coldwell, Knowles, and Douglas, both in Parliament and in the government of Saskatchewan, showed that they were playing the historic role of reform groups, that of being the nation's conscience. To approach no nearer to power must have been disappointing to them, but they might take consolation in knowing that they were among the most useful, as they must surely have been the most industrious, public men of their generation. Their failure to make much impression on the electorate caused the C.C.F. party to turn in a logical direction and seek an alliance with trade unionism. In 1961 a new party, known formally as the "New Democratic Party", was formed, and for it a new leader was found: "Tommy" Douglas, who was at the time and for a good many years previously had been, the C.C.F. premier of Saskatchewan. It might be that with good leadership, the N.D.P. could bring back a sense of issue in Canadian politics, if it proved to represent "the wave of the future", and it had considerable success in 1962, but little prediction could be made as to the future of the new combination.

Most of this section on "Parties and Politics" was written about a year before the election of 1957. If it serves no other purpose now, it at least indicates how fallible the judgement of any one man may be, for since that time the Canadian political scene has changed almost unrecognizably. In the first place, the Conservatives secured for themselves, or perhaps it would be more correct to say, had thrust upon them, a new leader, John George Diefenbaker. Diefenbaker was a Saskatchewan man who had contested the leadership on a previous occasion, but without success. He had come down to Ottawa as a private member in 1940 and, at that time, had been almost as much repelled by the reactionary attitudes of the eastern Toryism of the day as had J.S. Woodsworth himself. It is questionable whether eastern Conservatism ever welcomed Diefenbaker's leadership. But he had already made a certain name for himself, not least in his advocacy of guarantees for civil liberties and in his strong opposition to ethnic origin as a distinction between citizen and citizen. This last may well represent experiences of his own, for it was often said that a man who had a German name could never become Prime Minister of Canada – this despite the fact that on his mother's side Mr. Diefenbaker was of unimpeachable Scottish descent.

George Drew, former premier of Ontario, had been the Leader of the Opposition for some time, and in that capacity he had fought several dogged battles against the Liberal government of the day, especially against that one of its ministers who came closest to embodying the public's idea of a reactionary Tory, C.D. Howe. That such a phrase can be used of a so-called Liberal Minister indicates how little ideological distinction existed by this time between the two traditional parties. Unfortunately for himself, Drew's hard fighting qualities, which were most useful to the country in that they prevented the ministry of the day from riding roughshod over Parliament, did not make him popular; they did not win elections. The best known example of Drew's efforts to oppose the measures of the government of the day was the so-called Pipeline Debate of the year 1956. The question at issue was whether the pipeline to carry Alberta gas to Ontario should be built by the government or by private enterprise, backed by public money. The debate was outstanding in its acrimonious nature. At one point, the authority of the Speaker was assailed and a scene of utter confusion resulted. It has indeed been alleged that the House of Commons on that day dissolved into something uncomfortably resembling a mob.[7] Drew himself was too far removed from the average Canadian voter to secure a large share of his favours. Moreover, he was primarily an Ontario man and did not succeed in making himself into a national figure. These shortcomings, joined to a severe illness, led to his resignation[8] and to the choice of Diefenbaker in his place.

Diefenbaker immediately demonstrated prominent, if somewhat unorthodox, qualities of leadership. He was able to appeal to "the little man", the very sector of society which had stood behind Stevens in 1934-35 and behind the later Social Credit provincial governments. Diefenbaker could make an impassioned, rhetorical speech, charged with high-sounding sentiment, delivered in semi-pulpit style. He won the confidence of the genuinely solid people who are the backbone of the traditional lower-middle classes and of the more evangelical sects. Moreover,

---

[7] See for vivid account of the debate and the scene, J.W. Pickersgill, *My Years with Louis St. Laurent: A Political Memoir*. (Toronto: University of Toronto Press, 1975).

[8] George Drew died in 1973.

he was "a natural" in the relatively new art of television campaigning.

Mr. St. Laurent had won his elections by himself, with his own personality. The present writer has never heard him seriously assailed: he always retained the respect of his countrymen. But he had little powerful help, and, in figures like C.D. Howe, positive handicaps. People get tired of the old actors and in democratic politics, few cries are more effective than "It's time for a change". Roughly speaking, it is always time for a change of administration, for men being what they are, it takes a relatively brief tenure of office to convince most of them that they are there by only a slightly diluted type of divine right.

So the voters thought in 1957, and to everyone's surprise, so the elections went. In May of that year, few thoughtful people anticipated any other result than the return of the St. Laurent government with a reduced majority. What happened was that the former large Liberal majority was wiped out: if Mr. St. Laurent had attempted to go on, he would have had to rely on the votes of Social Crediters and C.C.F.'ers.[9] The situation was similar to that which followed the election of 1925 when Mr. King found himself in a minority in the Commons. Mr. King at that time attempted to retain power by relying on the support of the minor parties and in the end he failed, thereby precipitating the crisis described on p.508 of this book. In 1957, the Liberals secured only 105 seats to the Conservatives 112. They could have carried on, hoping for support from the minor parties, but Mr. St. Laurent, to whom power in itself was much less important than it was to Mr. King, wisely decided to resign and leave to the new Conservative leader the task of forming an administration.

Mr. Diefenbaker duly took office, he in his turn now being in a minority position. His cabinet was not an impressive one and whether he could get through the session of 1958 was a matter of doubt. The Liberals themselves had been under the necessity of finding a new leader after Mr. St. Laurent's determination to leave public life, and their choice had fallen (1958) on L.B. "Mike" Pearson, a man who had made a considerable name as Mr. St. Laurent's Minister of External Affairs and as a diplomatist of international reputation. Mr. Pearson was shortly to be awarded the Nobel Peace Prize in recognition of his international services. He was a much respected figure of academic and clerical background, having for a short period lectured in history at the University of Toronto and his father and grandfather before him having been

[9] The party standings in the June, 1957 elections were as follows: Conservative, 112; Liberal, 105; Social Credit, 19; CCF, 25; Independent, 2; Independent-Liberal 1; Liberal-Labour, 1.

Methodist ministers. Mr. Pearson was to find that it was one thing, however, to address fellow diplomats and another to gain plaudits from an ill-informed, but highly equalitarian, democratic electorate. He did not succeed before the next election (March 31, 1958) in establishing himself as a national figure. Everyone recognized his *bonhomie,* but his public appearances were stolid and wooden compared with the shows that his rival was able to stage. He was simply no match for Diefenbaker either in the House or before the people.

Moreover, nothing succeeds like success. The result was that when Diefenbaker appealed to the country in the hope of ending his minority position, one of the most remarkable electoral swings that Canada has ever experienced took place. Diefenbaker secured 208 followers out of a total of 265 M.P.'s. The Liberal party was decimated and reduced to some forty hardy survivors. Most of its old warriors were eliminated. The C.C.F. party fared equally badly, and the Social Credit party was annihilated. The Conservatives had fought their 1957 campaign on the assumption that they might get a working majority outside of Quebec and in this they had almost succeeded. But in 1958 they got Quebec too. For the first time since the 1880's, that province returned a Conservative majority, and a vast one. This result has never been satisfactorily explained. Quebec's change of party allegiance was not to last. On the Prairies, Diefenbaker made another clean sweep.

How was all this to be explained? There were no hard times, and there was no overwhelming national problem. There is an anecdote that might help to explain 1957. An old and faithful servant decided to leave his master. The latter was nonplussed; conditions of work had been good, as had personal relations. Why was the servant severing this relationship of many years' standing? "To tell you the honest truth, sir," said the servant, "I'm sick of the very sight of you". That will do for 1957. 1958 is easier: it was mainly a case of "getting on the band wagon".

Diefenbaker made some gains among thoughtful people by his solicitude for civil liberties as expressed in his addition to the laws of Canada of a statute in the form of a Bill of Rights enumerating and underwriting our civil liberties. The constitutional effects of the Bill of Rights will not reveal themselves within a short period. Since it is a statute of the Federal Parliament, it can apply only to that constitutional area to which federal law applies; that area is large, and possibly elastic. It must remain for the future to evaluate the Bill of Rights. In the meantime it is a fair statement of what our state and nation stand for, an idealistic mark to shoot at, important not so much as positive law, but like a text of Scripture, enjoining on us a high code of conduct.

The Diefenbaker government was not outstandingly successful in handling the problems of the country's economy. Canada is a country in which economic progress has tended to go, as it were, by bursts: a period of excited prosperity has often been followed by a considerable period of marking time. Thus the decade of the 1850's was most prosperous and expansive, but it was followed by uncertainty and even stagnation for over thirty years. Then the period marking the settlement of the West, from about 1900 to 1930, was also a period of great economic advance (though punctuated by some considerable depressions), but it was followed by the greatest of all slumps, that of the 1930's. The late 1950's were extravagantly prosperous, but late in the decade, the pace of advance was slowing down, and in the early 1960's, various storm signals were appearing. Our prosperous periods have been based on readily identifiable factors, factors whose absence or relative absence helps explain the "flats" between the "slopes". Thus, in the 1850's, the Reciprocity Treaty with the United States, the Crimean War with its accompanying British demand for lumber and wheat, the building of railways with the consequent inflow of British capital – such factors satisfactorily explain that decade. The period of the settlement of the West, 1896-1930, saw two new provinces added, tens of millions of acres of new farmland opened up, two new transcontinental railways built (on foreign capital!) and the Great War with its enormous stimulus to industry. Canada found in the Second Great War an equal industrial stimulus; then at its end, she added enormously to her natural resources in oil, iron, and other metals. As before, capital rushed in from abroad.

Diefenbaker came into power when the current was beginning to slacken a little. It may be that another set of administrators could have managed things differently; it is anyone's privilege so to believe. There were other complications: as the elections of 1962 approached, the situation precipitated by the British decision to try to join the European Economic Community (the "Common Market") threatened to bring into discussion not only this country's fiscal relations with the mother country but also the much more fundamental question of what would be left of the Commonwealth. If Great Britain turned towards Europe in closer political relationship, if something like a European state should in time emerge, would Canada have to turn her back on her past and as a humble suppliant sue for favour from that other English-speaking union out of which the ancestors of many Canadians were once thrust? Or would closer economic relations among European states bring about in time closer economic relations and closer political understanding between the two sides of the Atlantic?

These were great questions, sufficiently great to have become the subject matter of a vast and dignified national debate. The country's most crucial problem surely has been that of its own existence vis-à-vis, first of all, Great Britain, and secondly, the United States. In the 1840's, when free trade had become the policy of Great Britain, many people in the colonies accused her of running away from her own Empire: The Montreal Annexation Movement in 1849 had been the result (p. 278). Now here in 1962 Great Britain was apparently doing something of the same sort – running away from the Commonwealth. One would think that Canadian public men would have risen to certain heights in placing the issues before the public. This they had done in 1891. They had done it again in 1911. This they failed to do in 1962. The election of that year did not stretch Canadian minds, it did not make public issues plain as pikestaffs, it did not make clear the distinction, if any, between the two historic parties. The plain citizen was puzzled to know whether the Liberals were conservatives or the Conservatives liberals, or what each, or either, was conserving or liberalizing – a quandary in which a good many of the party leaders also seemed to find themselves. As a result, the election seemed to turn not so much on policy as on methods of administration – which set of men could do the job best? From another angle, it may not have been much more than a popularity contest between John Diefenbaker and "Mike" Pearson, combined with enough secondary distractions to muddle the local clarity of the picture.

Among the great potential issues of the day were surely such matters as the change in the nature of the Commonwealth, the place of Canada in the international world with its unremitting threat of atomic war, the discernible local phenomenon of a class foundation for politics emerging. All these and others secured attention and discussion in university halls and other centres of thought, but they did not seem to bear perceptibly enough on a casual, more or less uprooted, only half-in-earnest electorate to secure reflexion in intelligent debate from political platforms. Canada, a mere constituent in the great, forming western world, could seem to the pessimist in the 1960's to be losing, not gaining, stature; and its political life, shrinking to the level of the municipal. Canadians having largely lost their old political moorings (which were firmly embedded in ancestralism, religion, and geographical section) and many hundreds of thousands of them being but recent arrivals in the country, seemed to be drifting and ready to go in the direction of any chance puff of wind.[10]

---

[10] Fifteen years later, 1977, this situation was just beginning to change. An issue, a deep issue, had arisen – the threat that an attempt would be made to take Quebec out of Confederation. Until the threat was dissipated, it would come to polarize Canadian politics more and more.

When returns were in, the Conservatives proved to have the largest single group of members, 166; with the Liberals not far behind, 100: a considerable quota of "N.D.P.", nineteen; and to everyone's surprise, twenty-six Social Crediters from Quebec, plus four more from western Canada. No wonder the next session of Parliament was marked by uncertainty. On one division, the government's majority sank to eight, and finally, the inevitable vote of want of confidence resulted. Parliament was dissolved, and the country was faced with still another election. This took place on April 8, 1963.

In the election campaign, while it was evident that Diefenbaker had lost a good deal of his personal popularity (along with a number of his ministers!), it was equally clear that the "man in the street" did not find Pearson much to his liking; he preferred professional hockey players. The outside observer could hardly have got the impression that Canada possessed an intelligent electorate, for our much vaunted school system seemed to have succeeded in producing a generation of youths whose idea of public debate – as many a large meeting showed – was howling the speaker down by sheer lung power. The mob seemed on the point of taking over. But the voting was surprisingly heavy and, everything considered, intelligent. Once more, no party had a clear majority, but the Liberals on election night could claim 128 seats out of the total of 265, and it therefore, seemed plain that they would be able to form a government if and when they were called upon. Mr. Diefenbaker had only ninety-six seats, and he could hardly rally behind him two such diverse factions as the Social Crediters and the New Democrats. He of course had the constitutional right to meet Parliament, but since the country had demanded strong government, it did not seem probable that he could long carry on. Nor could he have legitimately claimed still another dissolution. This appears to have been his own view, for he resigned, and Mr. Pearson formed an administration.

The election was also interesting in that it revealed a clear line between traditionalism (the rural east went Conservative) and what was possibly the greater alertness of the urban mind (which mainly voted Liberal). It also split the normally radical rural west from the urban areas of the country. What was not quite evident in 1962 therefore became clear in 1963 – the historic Grits were now the Tories, and the Tories, or the more dynamic sections of them, were the Grits. The political wheel had come full circle, and henceforth "Bay Street" and the "St. James Street Gang" would have to be denounced from the Tory strongholds of the wheat-growing west. (Written April 9, 1963.)

(B) Parties and Politics, 1963-1977

Few periods in Canadian history have had so much apparent political instability as the period from 1963 to 1977. It was a period marked by five general elections and by changes of leadership in all the parties. But political instability of this type is not necessarily identical with political chaos. In fact, it may well be no more than a surface phenomenon. Changes in party fortunes and tenure of office may well be no more than changes from the ins to the outs. Nothing occasions more sound and fury than party squabbling, but "party" does not necessarily affect the fortunes of the country very deeply. For example in the period from 1891 to 1911, it was only superficially a matter of Liberals *versus* Conservatives, Sir Wilfrid Laurier *versus* Sir Charles Tupper and R. L. Borden. The deep issue was Canada's alignment with respect to Great Britain, the United States and her own separate identity. Not even the decisive Liberal victory of 1896 and the equally decisive victories of the Conservatives in 1891, 1911 and 1917 settled this question. It is unsettled to this day, and will long remain unsettled, for it represents deep lines of cleavage in men's minds.

Examination of election results in our present period, 1963-1977, moreover, indicates clearly that shifts in party strength in Parliament need not reflect large shifts in public opinion, as registered by votes cast in elections. It is probably impossible fully to analyze any election results, for we are dealing with thousands of individual decisions made and taken under widely varying circumstances of time and place. The best that analysts of elections can do is to isolate "trends" and sometimes to equate results with the determining factors of race, religion, economic environment and family tradition. The attempt of political scientists to analyze election results by elaborate statistical processes must be considered a failure: what they have done is simply to abandon their role as political *scientists* for the much lesser one of "nose counters", with very inconclusive results – except the destruction of respect for their new version of "political science!"

If the reader will turn to the accompanying table, which shows the total results of the voting in the federal elections of the period, he will find that the Liberal percentage of the total vote cast only varied by eight points, from 39 to 47. The number of Liberal M.P.'s returned, however, varied from 109 to 155. The Conservative vote varied only three points, from 31 to 34, while Conservative membership varied from 72 to 107. Similarly with the minor parties. These simple findings should provoke serious meditation on the nature of our representative institutions and particularly on the meaning of the word *democracy*. It cannot be too emphatically stated that *parliamentary government* is not equivalent to *democracy* or *democracy to parliamentary government*. Parliamentary government is our Canadian system of government, the historic heritage of every year and generation since the middle ages. We rightly point with respect to the great "texts of scripture" such as Magna Carta, 1215, and the Petition of Rights, 1629, as the source of its strength and its virtue. Historically, democracy, one man one vote, majority rule, is a recent product, and our system of government by representatives of local interests – constituencies – is much older, and probably much more valuable. "Plebiscitary" democracy began with the French Revolution. It indicates how unstable "public opinion" whatever that is, can be. Napoleonic "elections" went about 99 per cent for the dictator, Napoleon, so did the plebiscites for his nephew Napoleon III in 1848-52, so did the "elections" held by Hitler in Germany, so do Russian "elections". It would be a strange government under parliamentary democracy that secured 99 per cent of the votes cast, and it would be one fatal to our liberties. In 1958, the normally Liberal Province of Quebec returned a phalanx of Conservative members, whereas in 1963, it was once more back in the Liberal fold. These two instances indicate how unstable "public opinion" can be and how tempting it is to vote for mere leadership. Parliamentary democracy is often weak and uncertain, because it represents a contest of wills, but it is out of such contests that freedom has come. "Her Majesty's Loyal Opposition" is not a meaningless phrase.

The above paragraphs should be kept in mind when studying the apparent instability of Canadian politics in the period. It is obvious that our system, if it is to work well, must grind out sufficient members who can work fairly well together, to furnish the administration with adequate support in the House of Commons. If it cannot find support, it must give way to another administration and unless the appeal in an election is to the primitive passions, such as racial or religious prejudice, the results will vary and possibly narrowly. It is an expensive way of securing a stable administration, but it results in some kind of equipoise and therefore free government. The alternative is the plebiscite, which opens a clear road to dictatorship. When Marsiglio of Padua in the fourteenth century spoke of "the voice of the people as the voice of a great beast" *(demos bellua est)*, he presaged the idea of the plebiscite (otherwise *referendum*) – a temporary, unstable, shifting gale of wind that decided nothing except in the most fleeting manner.

So much for the arithmetical aspect of electioning and government. A government is formed to govern and it is to be judged on its record. Since its record is comprised of innumerable details, great and small, which appeal to one person in one way and to another in another, it is difficult to evaluate the record of any parliamentary administration. Only occasionally, when a deep issue confronts the voter (such as Conscription in both world wars), is the "will of the people" clearly expressed and the government returned under such circumstances armed with a clear mandate to carrying out that will. The normal situation is uncertainty, to be settled by the long, tedious and often petty processes of debate in the House of Commons.

In the period from 1963 to 1977, government went on the uneven tenor of its way – a tax amendment here, a tariff amendment there, subsidies for this and that, political "handouts" and all the infinite detail of political daily life. But three issues struck to the depths. One was establishment of a Canadian flag – a symbol, rather than something important in itself. Another was the perpetual Canadian question of racial division: was Quebec a province like other provinces, crystallizes the attitude. And the third was the non-party debate on basic social issues, the attitude to be taken to deviant sexual relationships such as homosexuality, the attitude to be taken to abortion, and the attitude to be taken to capital punishment. These latter, simply because they struck so deeply, were by common consent, put outside the restrictions of party, and M.P.'s, as do American Members of Congress at all times, were given the privilege of voting as they thought fit, instead of voting "just as their leaders tell " 'em to".[11]

The Flag Question:

Whether Canada should have a distinctive national flag or not had been debated for many years, with sentiment gradually strengthening in favour. During and just after the War, Mackenzie King had gone so far as to decide that the Red Ensign, carrying the Canadian coat of arms, should be flown over the Parliament Buildings and other federal establishments. This had alienated both wings, those who objected to anything but the traditional Union Jack, and those who wished a

---

[11] The quotation is from Gilbert and Sullivan's opera, *Iolanthe* wherein the policeman on the door (of the House) soliloquizes in excellent political analysis:

> When in that House M.P.'s divide
> If they've a brain and cerebellum too,
> They've got to leave that brain outside
> And vote just as their leaders tell 'em to.

He goes on:

> But then the prospect of a lot
> Of dull M.P.'s in close proximity
> All thinking for themselves is what
> No man could face with equanimity. (etc. etc.)

completely new flag. Everyone worked out his own design for a flag and eventually Ottawa was flooded with three thousand separate designs. At last, Mr. Pearson constituted the invariable committee and this committee spent long hours in trying to select a design. The first proposal was a design showing a flag with three red maple leaves against a white background. The scoffers of the right immediately nicknamed it "Pearson's Pennant" and they succeeded in virtually laughing it out of court. The Committee eventually decided on the present national flag. It was based on a design submitted by George F.G. Stanley, then a professor of History at the Royal Military College and it was closely modelled on the institutional flag of that college. This design was accepted by the government and after an interminable debate in which every nook and cranny of the subject was investigated, the flag design was accepted by government and became the National Flag of Canada, as we know it today. The debate had been initiated by the Prime Minister, who in the course of introducing the bill, used among others, the following words:

'The Maple Leaf flag' will strengthen national unity and give us a deeper sense of national unity and national pride.

Mr. Diefenbaker, for the Opposition, replied in ritualistic party terms; the following quotation more or less summarizes his attitude:

If the government had calculated a means whereby division could be secured in this nation, they could not have gone about it in a more effective manner.

The debate on the flag consumed endless hours of Parliamentary time and many additional hours too. The subject being exhausted, to say nothing of the debaters, the new flag was ceremoniously hoisted. To the surprise of many, it was easily, even readily, accepted and little opposition followed. Of course the usual Canadian compromise was written into the arrangement in that the Red Ensign was to be used as the flag of the Commonwealth and the new design as Canada's own. The last stubborn seat of resistance lay in the Canadian navy, whose senior officers stuck out stubbornly for the traditional white ensign to be flown at the sterns of their ships. They bowed to direct orders and the Canadian flag appeared in that honourable position too.

The adoption of a Canadian flag symbolized still another stage in the evolution to complete national independence. French-speaking Canada accepted it because it carried no suggestion of imperialism and the rest of the country because, underneath the surface, there was a devotion to the idea *Canada* and a realization that the separate flag symbolized its own unity and its aspirations toward nationhood. For Anglophones the new flag carried no suggestion of a parting of the ways: Canadian hearts were still where they had always been, with English Canadians of British descent just as much convinced of the unity of the English-speaking world as ever, but seeing no "disloyalty" – a word that was rapidly altering its meaning, in concentrating their allegiance on their own country. Moreover, to Anglophones of non-British descent the difficult task of forgetting the homelands of their fathers and accepting the new was rendered easier. The adoption of a Canadian flag may be regarded as a major step forward to nationhood.

The other topics of debate lay in quite another area for they dealt with the very essence of humanity's life processes. Birth control and abortion at once confront us with the problem of life and death. In a Christian culture such as ours has been, is it right to refuse life to the unconceived through birth control? Is it not simply misuse and abuse of the gift of sexual reproduction that God has given to men. So spoke and speaks the historic Catholic Church, and many non-Catholics have asked themselves the same question. Still more grave the dilemma of a woman who has conceived a child and for some reason, good or bad, will not or cannot carry it through to birth. Again, the Church said and says, simply, "abortion is murder". And again, others, too, have had the same difficult question to face. The situation goes to the roots of belief, of criminality, of rationality. During the 1960's and 1970's, the newspapers bristled with "Letters to the Editor", for and against; Catholic pulpits thundered against and Protestant pulpits were "yea and nay" according to the convictions of their occupants.

Whatever the faith, or lack of faith, of the individuals concerned, it is evident that birth control became more and more accepted, even in the Province of Quebec, where the birth rate, from having been extraordinarily high from the beginning, fell year by year, until it became the lowest in Canada. Since abortion, as contrasted with birth control, was a serious criminal offence, statistics on its practice could not be collected, but the probability is that it became more and more prevalent, especially in large cities, where the breakdown in sex morals had long been evident and where it increased with the years: the increased incidence of venereal disease in itself illustrated the rapidity with which sexual restraint was being abandoned.

Nothing was done, or could be done, given the prevailing state of opinion, in changing the law about abortion until the Roman Catholic French-speaking Prime Minister Pierre Elliott Trudeau took office. Under him certain modifications to the criminality of the performance of abortion were made but the situation advocated by extremists – abortion on demand – has not yet been reached. One important incident in forcing people to face up to the harsh realities of life in their sexual aspects was the trial and condemnation of Doctor Morgentaler in Montreal, who made no secret of having performed and his intention to go on performing innumerable abortions. He was twice acquitted by a jury and twice was the jury's verdict overruled by higher courts. He was put upon his trial the third time but the new government of René Lévesque refused to proceed. The case probably opened the road in Quebec to "abortion on demand".

Apart from the right or wrong of abortion, the Morgentaler case revealed a serious flaw in Canadian criminal law. In some mysterious manner a section had been smuggled into the Criminal Code that opened a route by which a higher court could overturn a jury's verdict, order its reversal and impose punishment. This superseded the right of trial by jury, one of the historic and sacred rights of the citizen. The Morgentaler case revealed the flaw in the Criminal Code and a debate in Parliament resulted in its amendment. In future a higher court is precluded from altering the verdict of a court composed of judge and jury. The ancient right of "trial by one's peers" is thus restored. [12]

It was also the Catholic Prime Minister Trudeau who secured modification of the law respecting homosexuality. Homosexuality was mentioned in the laws of the Anglo-Saxons, dating from pre-Christian times, as a reprehensible and severely punishable offence. The offender was simply to have his face shoved into the mud and smothered.[13] While succeeding ages never lost the nominal attitude of severity, in practice in many European countries a good deal of homosexuality is known to have existed, especially among the higher social classes. Edward II of England, for example, is believed to have been a homosexual. But until quite recently no European, or "western" country has renovated its laws against the practice.[14]

In Canada, Mr. Trudeau, in the beginning of his administration, proclaimed quite frankly that what went on in the bedroom was nobody's business, and Canadian criminal law was renovated accordingly. But there certainly has been no widespread approval of homosexuality, though possibly some greater tolerance – in the abstract if not in the concrete. In the end, in 1969 an "omnibus" bill legalized homosexuality between consenting adults and also abortion when a committee of three

---

[12] Criminal Code of Canada, Part XVIII, Section 613 Subsection 4 (b) (ii). Non-jury verdicts of acquittal coming up from a lower court may still be reversed and punishment imposed.

[13] See Attenborough, F.L., *Laws of the Earliest English Kings*, (New York, 1963).

[14] The situation in certain Asiatic countries is quite different, where the practice has apparently acquired social acceptance and possibly approval – as it had done in ancient Greece.

doctors agreed that the mother's mental or physical health is in jeopardy.

The stiffest barrier to surmount in the matters of human life and death has lain in the question of capital punishment. Many years ago, there were innumerable offences for which death was the penalty, and even in Canada, hangings were relatively common. They were also public, and the crowd derived high entertainment value from a hanging. The last public hanging was just after Confederation. Thenceforth, the public taste – possibly we should say conscience, though the point is debatable – became more and more sensitive. Capital crimes were decreased in number until very few remained – murder, treason, rape, would comprise practically the entire list – and after the First World War, humanitarians attacked the institution in its entirety. As in the other cases, arguments flew back and forth, as to the effectiveness of hanging as a deterrent (to others) and as to its morality. "An eye for an eye" – did the old code hold? Modification was gradual. Sometimes life imprisonment was justifiably substituted. "Insanity" became a common defence. In the late 1960's government carried still further its practice of commuting the death sentence and the result was that hanging ceased. The Criminal Code was changed to retain it for certain special cases, but no executions took place under the newly amended law. Then in the 1970's the government, again Mr. Trudeau's, decided to allow a free vote of the House of Commons on the question of abolition. But the prime minister would not allow his ministers a free vote. The result was that abolition carried. If the cabinet of the day had been allowed the free vote it is probable that it would not have done so. It seemed quite certain at the time that the majority opinion of the day was not in favour of abolition. It cannot be disputed that over the years there had been a great growth in sentiments of clemency, that Canadians had become in the main steadily more humane. But the old blood lusts are hard to eradicate: they will never be entirely eradicated from mankind, for without them man would not be man, but they can be restrained. Restraints can easily be loosed, so that a few horrible murders might still be sufficient to restore the death penalty. Against that is the increasing squeamishness of men, not at all the same as humaneness. For the moment, the future seems to be for disappearance of the death penalty and various attempts, more or less successful, to reform offenders rather than punish them. The future depends on the swing of the pendulum, for our attitudes are based on our sentiments, rather than on the stern commands of a religious credo, as they used to be.[15]

[15] For a discussion of the other great topic of the period, racialism and the special position of Quebec, see p. XXXIX.

Constitutional Problems

By accident or design, the original British North America Act made no provision for its own amendment. In consequence each amendment since has been made by another British North America Act, passed by the Imperial Parliament. The procedure has been an "Address" of each Canadian House of Parliament to the Crown, requesting the amendment and indicating its terms. The British Parliament has then graciously consented to act as a rubber stamp. The procedure is unwelcome to all parties, but since no agreement has been arrived at for a general method of amendment, this makeshift arrangement has been resorted to. The provinces have always been free to amend their own constitutions, except with respect to the office of lieutenant-governor, that is, the position of the Crown. After years of inconclusive discussion, the federal government in 1949 secured an amendment to the original act by which the Parliament of Canada was given power to amend the Act in all matters that were purely federal in scope. These have yet to be precisely delimited by judicial interpretation. As an illustration of how little foresight there can be in even the highest matters – "by how little wisdom the world is governed!" the Latin saying has it – the amendment was introduced in terms so wide as to prompt a C.C.F. member, Mr. Stanley Knowles, to point out that they could be used to prolong the life of a particular Parliament indefinitely and also to avoid calling Parliament at all. On these "trifles" being brought to the government's attention, after a good deal of face-saving resistance on the part of the ministry (which seems not so much to have been opposed to constitutional safeguards as merely to have forgotten them), the amendment was reworded to make it read: "There shall be a session of the Parliament of Canada at least once each year, and . . . no House of Commons shall continue for more than five years . . .; provided, however, that a House of Commons may in time of real or apprehended war, invasion or insurrection, be continued, . . . if such continuation is not opposed by the votes of more than one-third of the members of such House". Mr. Knowles, who, like Woodsworth, in private life had been a Methodist minister, thus made a valuable stroke for Canadian liberties. It is regrettable that he should have had to do so; one would think that a government calling itself Liberal would be watchful of civil liberties, especially of the rights and liberties of Parliament. Unfortunately, that has not been the case: the wartime administration of Mr. King injured the tradition of liberty through its Defence of Canada Regulations, and when Mr. St. Laurent was Minister of Justice, his proceedings in confining suspects during the spy investigation of 1946 were of dubious legality and violated the spirit of our institutions.[16]

Parliament is not the powerful check on government which it formerly was, especially when a party has a secure majority in the House of Commons. Government may be drifting into the position of Charles the First in the 1640's – all government tends to do that – but the Long Parliament, Pym, and Hampden, have yet to emerge. For there is no such thing any longer in Canada as an independent Parliament – the calibre of the average M.P. is too low for that. What we do is to choose a party leader, and then if he can win an election bringing him a majority in the House of Commons and is not incredibly foolish, he is as securely in power for five years as is the American President for his four. Canada has almost changed from the British system of responsible government to the American system of presidential government, retaining some features of the British, but in general securing the poorer features of both systems and discarding the better. Not that the average Canadian cares; there seems to be little that the average man values less than his political liberty. If a free society is to be kept alive, it must be by the efforts of the few, not through the indifferent many.

Another move of a constitutional nature was also taken in December, 1949, when The Supreme Court of Canada Act was amended to secure the abolition of all future appeals to the Judicial Committee of the Privy Council. Appeals to the Privy Council had from time immemorial been regarded as appeals made directly to the King – as sentimentalists put it, "the right of the subject to lay his case at the foot of the throne" – and in 1833, the Imperial Act (3 & 4 Wm. IV C.41) systematized the procedure of appeal in the Judicial Committee of the Privy Council. It was this body which in the interval had constituted the supreme court of appeal for Canadian cases. Only persons with long purses had been able to resort to this distant court and, in practice, its main function had been in the decision of constitutional cases. Thanks to the apostolic succession of its judges and of the counsel before it, the tradition of "strict interpretation" had grown up within it, and its verdicts over the years since Confederation had trenched upon the original powers of the Dominion. It is not surprising then that persons wishing to see the national power ample for its purposes were against appeals to this distant court. As always in Canada, the question was cautiously approached and long debated. Criminal appeals had already been abolished, but it was not until after the war that the Liberal government summoned up enough courage to

---

[16] See on this subject the *Report of the Royal Commission appointed under Order in Council P.C. 411 of February 5, 1946* (Ottawa, 1946). See especially Section 11 (Law and Procedure), p. 649.

complete the abolition. No observable fissures in the earth's surface have since been noticed as a result, but a slow strengthening of the Supreme Court seems to be observable and since these men know the local scene, it is probable that their decisions will be better for the country in the long run than the abstract, "scholastic" judgements of a distant court.

A third topic is marginally constitutional: the inclusion of Newfoundland within Confederation (1949); at least, it presents certain constitutional features, such as the creation of six additional senators and some additional seats in the House of Commons. Newfoundland's inclusion, however, goes mainly under the political head. It had become apparent early in the war that the island would have to come under either American or Canadian influence. It was defended by both countries, and both secured rights there. If this embarrassing rivalry in protecting the lady had occurred in other parts of the world, the suitors would probably have come to blows. As it was, the Americans, having got all they needed in the way of defence facilities and probably assuming that they could go on getting them from Canada more easily than from a post-war Great Britain, made no objection to the completion of Confederation. The architect of confederation in Newfoundland was Joseph Smallwood.[17] The people of Newfoundland showed their approval by a small majority and in due course, the B.N.A. Act was amended in London to allow for the tenth province. With its unerring instinct for failure in matters of national symbolism, the Liberal government decided that the day of Confederation should not be marked in any particular way, but the people of Canada took the matter out of its hands, and it became evident that they found considerable satisfaction and a source of national pride in this extension of their country, even if it was, as everybody realized, mainly an economic liability.

Another side of constitutionalism was reflected in the accession of Queen Elizabeth II. Her pleasant, feminine personality would appear to have increased the popularity, if not the reality, of monarchy in Canada. Since her accession she has made many visits to Canada.

An indisputable area of constitutional conflict, always ready to gape open in a federal state, once more became visible after the war, namely, that of "provincial rights". In no federation is the centre of gravity ever in repose; it constantly oscillates between the centre and the component parts. Sometimes the swings are gentle, sometimes sharp, but they are always going on. In Canada, "provincial rights" became an issue the moment Confederation took place, and there have been few years since

---

[17] Smallwood (born 1900) became premier of Newfoundland after the confederation was completed and remained in office until 1971.

in which it has not been in evidence. At times it has been grave enough to threaten the safety of the state, as in the vast controversy during the 1890's over the Manitoba Schools Question. During our present period, 1947-1977, it presented itself in the form of quarrels over the division of revenue and, in the case of Quebec, extended into a touchy attitude over the whole question of "provincial autonomy". "Provincial rights" may thus also be considered under the general headings of finance administration or racial privilege.[18]

The Constitution and Finance

To take this sequence first on the plainest level, the financial, the point is simply that under modern conceptions of the functions of government, there is no longer room in Canada for eleven independent taxing and spending bodies. Each of these may enjoy a relatively free hand in good times, but let depression come and the weakest units will get into difficulties. This is what happened in the 1930's when the prairie provinces were virtually bankrupt, a situation that led to the searching investigation conducted by the Rowell-Sirois Commission and thence to the present position. In the 1930's much talk was heard of "have" and "have not" provinces, and the view was put forward that within a single nation, it was not fair for some communities to be on the edge of starvation and others to be "rioting in abundance". The only countervailing power to the natural forces of the economy (by which great metropolitan centres such as Montreal and Toronto tended to suck dry their distant hinterlands, to the benefit of the provinces within which they were fortuitously situated) was the political power – in other words, use of the federal government as a redistributor of income. This idea was tacitly, if not overtly, accepted, and the various schemes designed to secure more centralization of taxation (and possibly also of spending), such as "renting" certain tax fields, were the result. During the war, another equally potent factor was the additional necessity for mobilizing all the country's financial strength. After the war, easier conditions took the edge off the controversy, especially as the provinces accepted tax agreements of one sort or another. The position changed from year to year, but the provinces recaptured a good measure of their financial autonomy along with its precariousness.

It was only Quebec which made use of the argument of provincial rights, the others being interested in dollars, not abstractions. But Quebec, through its autocratic premier, Mr. Duplessis (d. 1959), professed to

---

[18] For constitutional considerations, see Lower, Scott, *et al., Evolving Canadian Federalism* (Durham, N.C., 1958).

fear for its special rights and privileges, for its language, religion, and way of life, if it should surrender the least trace of its rights under the Constitution; in fact, it went further and tried to claim a special position among the provinces. It began to call itself "L'État du Québec". There is no doubt that there is a strong feeling among the French-speaking people of Quebec against losing any of their rights. There is an honest and commendable distrust of a distant government and a sturdy determination, which Anglo-Saxons should admire, to "run their own show". It is equally clear that there is not so much distrust of the central government as Mr. Duplessis would have liked others to believe. He kept himself in power after 1936 (losing only the election of 1939) by appealing to chauvinistic elements and to the most conservative layer of his people – the country folk – and accomplished that through devices which they can understand even better than they can understand anti-English speeches. Though under Duplessis its political life was corrupt and its people had little interest in Anglo-Saxon concepts of constitutional freedom, Quebec nevertheless, in resisting the forces of centralization, may have been doing some service.

In the next thirteen years, 1963-1976, no outstanding new aspects of the situation have come into view, if we always except the formidable demand for "separation" so emphatically underlined in the provincial elections of Quebec, November 15, 1976. Until that period provincial premiers gathered with the Prime Minister in many bargaining sessions in which the size of their "piece of the tax pie" was the main matter of contention, as, indeed, it still is with the Anglophone premiers. In December 1976, Mr. Lévesque associated himself with this attitude, in exclaiming at the end of the conference on that occasion that "Quebec had been gypped". Of course it is always extremely difficult to determine just what fraction of the country's total revenues comes out of a particular province and therefore what should be given back to it is always a matter of bargaining. It is generally agreed that Ontario is the richest province (but shall we compare the palaces of Metropolitan Toronto with the log cabins of parts of Northern Ontario?) with British Columbia and Alberta in the next positions, but each province can always put in a good case for the poverty of large areas within it. Quebec seems to be the dubious case: rich or poor? Montreal's wealth against the poverty of much of the northern countryside? What is the balance? It seems generally agreed, however, that Quebec receives more from the federal government than it pays into it.

This quarrel about the "size of the piece of pie" has resulted in the emergence of what is almost an eleventh government: It has become the habit, each year, for the premiers of the provinces to meet with the Prime

Minister. Their session ended, the questions of detail are left to the appropriate ministers, usually the minister of finance, often the attorney-general. There is also an uninterrupted stream of discussion going on at other levels of government, mostly departmental. This can give a good deal of uniformity under the appearance of much diversity – notably in the administration of justice. But the conception is different indeed from the original Confederation idea of a Dominion Government attending to its own business and the provinces attending to theirs. It has sometimes been called "co-operative federalism". It illustrates the constant struggle in a federation between the centre and the composing units, with power swinging back and forth between them.

Since the 1950's, the conferences have been preoccupied with the problem of constitutional amendment (see above). This has lately blossomed out under the word "Repatriation of the Constitution", or, in abbreviation "patriation". The difficulty is that while everybody would like to see the power of amendment transferred to Canada, no agreement can be reached on the method. Two formulae have been devised, the one the "Fulton-Favreau" and the other the so-called "Victoria Charter". Under both, the method of amendment was intricate, but both were in their turn rejected. In 1968, Mr. Trudeau defined his government's position: if linguistic and cultural equality for French Canadians could be guaranteed, then in constitutional matters, Quebec could be treated as a province "comme les autres"! He accepted the principle of a total review of the constitution, with priority to the rights of the citizen and his linguistic rights. But Trudeau, evolving more and more into a strict federalist, opposed the notion of any special status for Quebec, beyond these guarantees. Here lay the great gulf between Trudeau and Lévesque. Trudeau stood for equality for Francophones throughout Canada, Lévesque stood for an independent Quebec state. At time of writing the issue is still pending.

It is unlikely that in any other province a serious movement for secession would arise, for the provincial-federal issues are merely financial, not bound up with linguistic nationalism. A seceding Quebec (as Lévesque has indicated) would demand control over immigration, banking, "the media" and foreign relations. A Quebec remaining in Confederation may still try to secure substantial control over all of these.

Quebec may also press for revision of the Supreme Court and of the Senate. It could claim that the Supreme Court is overweighted with Anglophones. Similarly, it could claim that since the inclusion of Newfoundland, with the addition of its six senators, the Senate is still more weighted against it than it was previously. There is also the slumbering feeling against the boundaries drawn by the Privy Council decision of 1912 between Quebec and Newfoundland. In any federation there is always enough dynamite lying around to cause an explosion, if it be not defused by a considerable amount of good will. It is on good will, mutual accommodation and trust that our string of ten provinces rests. Are they *federated* or *united?*

The "Racial" Question

The above discussion of federal-provincial relations leads directly to Canada's running sore, racial friction. In this field, although the years after the war were as free from quarrels as any period in Canadian history, and efforts to base provincial autonomy – a defensible concept – on fears for the race and the language were not convincing, yet groups were to be found which took extreme nationalist positions and which, if they could have, would have ended the association with the English. These groups did not have much importance until the rise of the separatist movement of the 1960's. Though they were correct in maintaining that there has not been brotherly love between the two races, they were wrong in professing to believe that they have nothing in common. The two races have many things in common, and among these, by no means the least are two centuries of history. Moreover, many good personal relationships have been built up over the racial wall. In this most difficult of relationships progress was being made, largely because English Canada was slowly coming to meet French Canada on a basis of mutual respect and a common Canadianism. Of this there were many signs.

When in the 1930's, surprised English Canadians found on their paper money strange words like *dix* and *cinq*, the horrid sight almost robbed the money of its value. But gradually, through such minor official channels, the French language has won a foothold for itself and there are now (1977) many English-Canadian elementary schools in which it is taught in the junior grades – a situation of which Quebec appears unaware. Within the 1940's and 1950's various institutions for making one people more familiar with the other, such as *Les Visites Interprovinciales* and the summer schools held at several universities, advanced the knowledge of the other language and of the people who speak it, and, more important, the view that it is not discreditable to know something about it. In this way, this most repugnant of ideas to a considerable section of a singularly provincial people, the English Canadians, the idea of a bicultural country with two official languages, made headway. English Canadians will never be widely bilingual, for to know a language a person must use it, and most of them have no opportunity to use French; but the number who are friendly to the use of both languages will increase, as will the

number of those who can use both in some measure. The progress in
understanding, both linguistic and in the wider sense, over the period
from 1940 to 1970 and possibly later was impressive, especially in a
group that may have predictive value, to wit, students. Canada may
some day take this last and most difficult of hurdles, racial division;
when she does so, we shall really be able to speak of "the Canadian
Nation".[19]

To return to the general subject of provincial rights, the period during
the war, and after, suggests that except for its racial aspects it is a field of
diminishing importance. In this troubled age internal divisions are lux-
uries that a relatively weak state like our own cannot afford. External
pressure, even more than sweet reasonableness within, must diminish the
weight of the provinces.

In the cold light of today, the words immediately preceding may
appear altogether too optimistic, for the present period has seen the
racial situation once more exacerbated by the movements within Quebec
for separatism, that is, for nothing short of the destruction of the Dominion of Canada. A brief account of the background of these movements
follows.

After Duplessis' death, his party quickly disintegrated, and this disintegration left the way open for the new Liberal administration under
Jean Lesage in 1960. The change in premiers represented more than a
mere change from outs to ins; it coincided with profound social movements in the province which affected nearly all aspects of life. Criticism
of the late administration appeared from many quarters, and it began to
be recognized that under Duplessis, Quebec had come close to a species
of fascist despotism.[20] Considerable self-examination resulted[21] not only
in the political field but in the educational,[22] cultural, and even to some
degree, in the religious. By 1963, this had become so evident and so
marked by spoken and written debate that people were beginning to
speak of the "revolution" going on in the province. This "revolution"
was marked by cultural achievements of a high order, and French
Canada's contribution to the novel, to drama, painting, television, and
other aspects of the arts was quite equal to that of English Canada and
in some fields surpassed it. Along with this cultural growth went a serious soul-searching, so that nearly every aspect of life in the province,

---

[19] See also below, page LXII.
[20] See especially Pierre Laporte, *The True Face of Duplessis* (Montreal, 1960). Laporte was
assassinated by a Separatist group in 1970: and Conrad Black, *Duplessis* (Toronto,
1977).
[21] See Abbés Gérald Dion et Louis O'Neill, *Le Chrétien et les éléctions* (Montreal, 1960).
[22] See *Les Insolences du Frère Untel* (Montreal, 1960) and *L'Ecole Laique* (Montreal, 1961).

including the church and its privileges, came in for critical examination. In the middle 1960's, French Canada was definitely "on the move".

It was inevitable that the intellectual eagerness of French Canada should extend into every field, including its relations with the rest of the country. To an extroverted people, self-knowledge must always be hard to face, especially when the convenient whipping boy, *les maudits anglais*, is always ready to hand. More specifically, despite the fact that he was of an old Tory *bleu* family and in that way had had and used the traditional Tory connections in the province, Duplessis had succeeded in posing as a French-Canadian nationalist. Then came the Diefenbaker election and a Conservative government at Ottawa in no sense dependent on the support of French Canada. A similar situation in 1917 had resulted in the Francoeur Resolution of 1918 (see p.470).

Séparatisme was the Francoeur Resolution re-armed and fortified with the stirrings of a renewed sense of racial identity. Why should French Canadians have to go on making all the concessions at Ottawa, especially in the matter of language? If Canada was to be a partnership, it must be a partnership, not a continuing game of bluff. The various separatist movements differed from each other. They formed part of the general ferment of ideas and emotions that marked French Canada and that were rapidly giving it an indigenous literary and artistic culture of considerable importance.[23] The old mould was being broken in the 1960's and *le vieux province de Québec*, where nothing ever changed and where ancestral voices were always heeded, was in fact changing very rapidly, losing its isolation and more or less taking its place in the dynamic modern world.

Even the most superficial student of Canadian history will understand that for three centuries along the short space of the shores of the St. Lawrence, a people has been growing up with its own special characteristics and an intense sense of its own identity. This could not have occurred without a powerful sense of the *group*, the *collectivity*, and many pages of this book refer to the phenomenon. It is one of the most interesting in the whole course of human affairs, this making of a new human group with its own characteristics and its own aspirations, and for us, it is one of the most vital.

The changes which had been becoming so obvious in Quebec during the middle twentieth century naturally did not stop short at the election

---

[23] See Marcel Chaput, *Pourquoi je suis séparatiste* (Montreal, 1961). *Les Creditists* specifically disavowed *séparatisme*, but they were strongly nationalist. See also Fernand Ouellet, "Le Fondements historiques de l'option séparatiste dans le Québec," *CHR*, XLIII (Sept. 1962), 185-203.

of 1963, which is the point to which the above pages have so far been brought. It remains to give a brief account of the leading points from 1963 to 1977. Many books have been written about this brief period and it is quite impossible to do more than touch here on the "highlights". Moreover, the story is far from complete. This writing is being done in 1977; it was on November 15, 1976 that the Parti Québécois government under René Lévesque procured a majority in the election of that date. Mr. Lévesque has declared in point blank fashion that Quebec, if he has his way, will be ripped out of Confederation.[24] It is quite certain that no country can be divided without a huge amount of friction. As Mr. Trudeau has said, it would be like cutting a human body in two. If and when the attempt is made at such a piece of surgery, keep as calm as we will, there is sure to be trouble. What kind of trouble? When the states of the Southern Confederacy tried to disrupt the American Union in 1861, civil war broke out. The writer's own opinion is that the same thing would happen in Canada. He hopes he is wrong. Not long after these words have been put before the public, the verdict will be given. It is a horrible prospect for Canadians, but other countries have faced these stern tests and have come through all the stronger for them. May Canada do the same!

It is not inappropriate to remind younger readers that their duty, their highest duty, is to the integrity of their country.

When the Liberal Jean Lesage took office in 1960, the fascist dictatorship of Maurice Duplessis was already being relaxed. Lesage was a Liberal of the Laurier pattern and had been a minister at Ottawa. He was a good Canadian, but a Canadian whose heart lay in "le vieux province". Moreover any premier of Quebec always has to put on a good show of opposition to Ottawa: otherwise accusations at once are made that he has become *un vendu*, a sell-out, virtually a traitor to his people. There is in consequence frequently a good deal of sheet lightning in Ottawa-Quebec confrontations. But in the 1960's there were elements which were virtually new – many men who were incipient rebels, ready to fight their way out of Confederation. Many, also, who were prepared to use the most extreme tactics in securing that end. These tactics duly came into play.

After the Second World War, came the great age of *decolonization*. In 1947 the British left India. Each year brought independence to some new part of the world. During the 1950's, France fought bloody wars in its Indo-Chinese colonies and especially in North Africa. Algeria had been a French possession since the 1840's and hundreds of thousands of

---

[24] He put his intentions down in writing and in the very reputable American periodical *Foreign Affairs*. See *Foreign Affairs*, (New York, July, 1976).

French people had made their homes there. The native Algerians developed guerrilla tactics and for years harassed the regular French army, working back into France in the form of persons who threw bombs, burned buildings and tried to assassinate prominent people. After France lost Algeria, there seems to have been some migration to Canada of persons who had acquired a taste for that stirring and bloodthirsty way of life. Not too much is yet known about this, but there are various indications that the more daring of the young Quebec nationalists learned their trade at the hands of these ex-Algerians, these *pieds-noirs* as they were called. At any rate, terrorist tactics began to appear in the Province of Quebec, centering in Montreal, arms were stolen from federal armouries and bombings occurred. Many frankly "independentist" groups arose. Some of these were simply formed to agitate for independence, others seem to have had terrorist purposes. When the Queen came to Canada in 1964, Marcel Chaput, former leader of *Le front républicain pour l'indépendance*, warned that she would come to Quebec at her own risk. Her reception there was hostile, at least on the part of the bystanders, many of whom turned their backs on her as she passed. Her route was heavily guarded.

The various *fronts* arose and fell with great rapidity, which is a well-marked phenomenon in the beginning of revolution. As a French writer once put it "en la révolution il faut d'abord, balayer les honnêtes gens" – in revolution, it is first necessary to sweep out the ordinary, moderate people. The revolutionary must mean business. He must be prepared to go the limit, whether that involves burning people in their homes, shooting them or otherwise advancing "the cause". The prospect of having to shoot a man in cold blood is too much for most people, so at each stage in the revolution, the less extreme are shaken out.

These aspects of revolution are common enough in many European countries, where political assassinations often have occurred, but they were unknown to Canadians of either language: the only precedent was the murder of D'Arcy McGee just after Confederation by a Fenian sympathizer, and that was really an introduction of Irish grievances, rather than coming from within. Consequently, most Francophones hastened to disassociate themselves from violence, notably René Lévesque, then still a Liberal member of the provincial parliament. But even Jean Lesage spoke in Toronto of the "transition d'une révolution tranquille jusqu'une révolution un peu moins tranquille". *L'Association de Jean Baptiste*, a private society that not unfairly could be compared to the Orange Order of Canada, quite definitely came out for Quebec as an associate state . . . Such words necessarily encouraged extremists.

On May 2, 1965, two Separatists were found guilty of the murder of an Anglophone gun shop proprietor in Montreal and sentenced to be hanged. The sentence was stayed pending appeal and eventually not carried out. More bomb outrages occurred in Montreal. In June *Le Monde Nouveau*, a journal loosely connected with Montreal's Faculty of Theology, expressed the opinion that good Catholics could be Separatists. The St. Jean Baptiste Society divided, the more extreme wing taking an out-and-out separatist position. Various other revolutionary groups kept appearing in Montreal. In 1966 the government in Quebec changed from Liberal under Lesage to *Bleu* under Daniel Johnson: both men had campaigned for Quebec nationalism ("Québec d'abord" and "Pour un Québec plus fort"). Neither had accepted separatism, neither had disavowed it. Arrests of alleged terrorists continued to be made. Suggestions for modes of constitutional amendment coming from Ottawa continued to be found unacceptable by Quebec.

In July, 1967 came the famous de Gaulle incident. President de Gaulle of France had been invited to come to Canada to join in the Centenary celebrations of Confederation. He arrived in a French cruiser and landed at Quebec. He spoke in the City Hall and was received by Premier Johnson as a distinguished visitor. On that occasion the present writer happened to hear him speak in an open air meeting in Quebec city: the large crowd was attentive but not ebullient.

It was different in Montreal, where de Gaulle had gone by motor along the North Shore, a journey apparently carefully organized to heighten his impressions of Quebec as a daughter of France. De Gaulle's Montreal speech included the words "Vive Montréal, vive le Québec, *vive le Québec libre*, vive le Canada français, vive la France". These words immediately hurtled about the country and were received in English Canada with indignation. Prime Minister Pearson issued a public rebuke. Without a word to Ottawa, de Gaulle cancelled his State Visit to Ottawa and went off on his cruiser back to France. This gratuitous interference by de Gaulle in Canadian affairs provoked something close to a breach in relations with France and it took careful diplomacy on both sides to heal the quite unnecessary split between the old wartime allies. A most stinging rebuke to the French was administered by Pearson who, at a time when de Gaulle's government was insisting on the other NATO powers taking all their men and supplies out of France, asked the French ambassador if de Gaulle would require the tens of thousands of Canadian soldiers' graves to be removed from France also.[25]

It is tempting to dwell on the details of the de Gaulle affair. De Gaulle was a great man and had rendered magnificent service to his own country. In a visit to Quebec during the war, he had been received in the

[25] Told to the present writer personally by Mr. Pearson.

streets of Quebec in a highly hostile fashion, since he was identified by the Francophone "man in the street" with the conscription issue. His patriotism, however, had put blinkers on him and he ended by antagonizing nations that had no desire for anything but the friendliest feelings for France. His visit must have encouraged the extremists among the separatists.

The hundredth anniversary of Confederation was enthusiastically celebrated throughout English Canada. The Queen visited us and was warmly received. Centennial Year proved an important milestone in consolidating Anglophone sentiment and reinforcing the concept of Canada as a nation. Its warmth, however, did not do much to heighten all-Canadian sentiment in Quebec: this was the year of "les anglophones", not that of "les francophones". One Francophone publicist had sourly remarked that the Anglophone idea of the partnership in Confederation was that of the horse and its rider. But Quebec was not a unit in separatism. In 1964, a barely known journalist, one Pierre Elliott Trudeau, had published "a brilliant, scathing denunciation of extreme nationalism". He argued that an independent Quebec would become a dictatorship – and of the right, not of the left. He was not the only Francophone attached to Confederation, but he was easily the most intelligent. So it is no wonder that Pearson kept his eye on him as a potential recruit for liberalism at Ottawa. Trudeau was shortly to enter Parliament as a Liberal and quickly to become a minister. This was probably Pearson's greatest domestic coup: recruiting not only Trudeau but also two other leading Francophones, all well to the left of centre, and giving them cabinet office.[26]

In 1968 Pierre Elliott Trudeau was chosen as leader of the Liberal party of Canada. The convention which chose him was replete with delegates with funny hats, gaily uniformed girls and all the other apparatus of a circus. It was entirely lacking in dignity, but filled with the raucous noises of the loud-speakers. It indicated quite exactly how completely American mass culture, with all its vulgarity, had overwhelmed Canadians, who, always quicker to imitate than to originate, took readily to the low level at which it was presented to them. This, too, was "democracy".

[26] The other two recruits were Gérard Pelletier and Jean Marchand. Each was elected to Parliament in 1965 and within a year or two each was given cabinet rank. Pelletier, after holding several cabinet posts, left the government to become Ambassador to France. Marchand held many ministerial positions. He had a somewhat stormy parliamentary career, but there is doubt of his weight. He resigned from the Trudeau government in 1976, contested a seat in the provincial election of 1976, was defeated and became a Senator. He formed a link with labour in the Trudeau government, having been for several years President of the Canadian National Trade Union (CNTU).

In the very month of Trudeau's choice, René Lévesque formed his Parti Québécois. His program was boldly enunciated: a unilateral declaration of independence, to be followed possibly by a conference with Canada on the continuing terms of the association, all immigrants to Quebec to be required to speak French, and similar racio-linguistic measures. He did not, however, speak of separation by violence and seemed to assume that separation would be easy and readily granted. Few French-speaking Canadians at the time supported these extreme attitudes. This apparently was confirmed by the provincial elections of April 29, 1970, in which the PQ only obtained six seats. It did, however, win 24 per cent of the total vote, mostly congregated in the Montreal area.

Meanwhile, Mr. Pearson had resigned the prime ministership and had been succeeded by Mr. Trudeau, who had won an easy victory in the federal elections of 1968. Trudeau followed up Pearson's efforts to make it clear that Canada, if it was to stay united, must recognize the French language on equal terms with English, and introduced and passed the "Official Languages Act". English and French were to be the two official languages of the country. French citizens must be able to do their business with the federal government in their own language. Hopefully, minority "islands" would have special rights for maintaining their language. In a book of this sort, it is important to correct the widespread apprehension that Trudeau was forcing everyone to learn French. That is ridiculous and can only be the belief of badly informed people. Canada will never be completely bilingual – the average English Canadian has far too unwieldy a mentality for that ever to come to pass – but surely citizens should not have to learn the other language in order to do business with their own government. Moreover Francophones are not really interested in bilingualism beyond the point of respect for their language and a reasonable ability to make their way with it in English-speaking Canada, without hostile reactions. It is even conceivable that they would resent the protecting shield of the French language being pierced by too many *Anglais*. In the meantime, they themselves remain one of the most bilingual communities in the world and their knowledge of two languages gives them many advantages over the Anglophones, though the Anglophones for the most part are too stupid to see that.

In October, 1970, occurred the incidents that brought separatism to a temporary apex. Bombings and other forms of violence had been going on throughout the summer but on October 5, the British senior Trade Commissioner in Montreal, James Cross, was abducted, presumably by the *Front de libération du Québec* (FLQ). Some very large demands were required for Cross's release. These the federal government declared unacceptable. René Lévesque dissociated the PQ party from the FLQ. Five days after Cross's abduction, Pierre Laporte, a minister in Robert Bourassa's provincial cabinet and the man who in the 1950's had written the book that denounced Duplessis as a tyrant, was abducted. This second daring abduction brought about a hysterical tension in the whole country, French and English. Bourassa demanded troops for protection of persons and places in Montreal and Quebec. This was his right as provincial premier.

Then on October 16, Ottawa proclaimed *The War Measures Act*, which sweeps ordinary law aside and gives government the powers of a dictator. On the next day poor Laporte was found murdered, strangled to death. *The War Measures Act* was employed under one of its clauses which gives government practically unlimited power "in the case of real or apprehended insurrection", etc. The pressure for this extreme measure is said to have come mainly from the Province of Quebec. Many people were dubious of its necessity. Some scoffed at the prospect of "insurrection". The truth has not yet been revealed. But the Trudeau government hastened to replace the War Measures Act (for the occasion only, the War Measures Act remaining on the books) with the *Public Order Act*. During the subsequent period, several of the murderers of Laporte were brought to justice, but none of them was executed.

The immediate effect of the events of October 1970 was without much question to put a stop to efforts to achieve independence in Quebec by violence. These efforts should be noted as coincident with the general bubbling and heaving in France, the United States and also in Canada, which produced clashes in the universities and the severe Negro rioting in many of the great American cities. The curious thing is that after 1970 all this rapidly subsided and North America returned to the even tenor of its way, its quiet only disturbed by the motor car slaughter on the roads, the bank robberies, and murders that seemed to be accepted as normal in the Republic. Little of this was experienced in Canada, where the racial question continued to be the major topic of disquiet. Mr. Trudeau won a couple of general elections and retained his place as prime minister without too much trouble and Mr. Bourassa won one (1973) in the Province of Quebec. This election secured for the PQ only six seats, but about 30 per cent of the vote. It was not until November, 1976, that the next election brought it to power with a large majority.

This election of November 15, 1976, may be interpreted in many ways. Had the province given a clear majority for independence and was Canada as a result to be dismembered? Or was the result simply a protest against bad government, corruption and the horrible burden of financial liabilities that the provincial government had built up? However it be interpreted, the election placed a devoted and determined separatist in power. He had fought his election on a programme of reform and had carefully abstained from making separation an issue. But he and especially the extremists who surrounded him were clearly determined to have a try for independence.

Lévesque had promised a referendum on the subject "possibly within two years", and in two years a government in power can do a great deal to influence its electorate. He had declared that he would found an associate state, establish a customs union with Canada, adopt measures to control the economy of the province, such as clipping the wings of the great banks, whether by expropriation or not, he did not say, cultivate good relations with the United States and more particularly France. He was chauvinist in all matters relating to the French language and French culture, but no more than well to the left in economic policy, at least to begin with. He quickly made a visit to New York, presumably on a money raising mission, but he apparently did not receive any warm welcome there for his separation goal.

It was up to that point, the end of 1976, that the scroll of history had rolled when this writing was done, so what is to happen in the future is a matter of conjecture. As conjecture, it can reasonably be inferred that the two ships Canada and Quebec, are on a collision course and that if one does not sheer off, they will collide with serious loss of property and of life. Trudeau took his stand for federalism and began a campaign to win the province to his point of view. This debate had not gone far by the time of writing, but it seems clear that the destinies of Canada are in the hands of these two men, Lévesque and Trudeau. If Canada at the moment had an English-speaking prime minister, the situation would be almost hopeless, for his every gesture would be interpreted by Separatists as evidence of prejudice and enmity. The chances for some kind of understanding being arrived at between the two Francophones are much better, though not bright. The issue for the present must be left to the good sense of the electorate of Quebec, for both men apparently are willing to abide by the results of the democratic process, and Trudeau specifically has asserted that he would not use force to keep Quebec in Confederation. But the issue has not yet become one of appeal to the passions.

In breaking up Canada, almost certainly incidents would occur that would shatter the peace. As has been said above, the nearest precedent and a horrible one it is, is the preliminaries of the American Civil War of 1861-1865. As hot blood took over, it might well be that both leaders would be pushed aside in favour of extremists, men who were not afraid to fight. Then Civil War might follow. We can think of no more dreadful fate for our country. The only sensible route for us to follow is to give deep heed to the slogan "Every accommodation to the French-speaking people of Canada: no special privileges to the government of the Province of Quebec". That is the road the prime minister has advocated, and it would bring us through. Being sensible, however, is no guarantee that it will be adopted.

The struggle between the two cultures, French and English, has been going on in America ever since the two cultures were introduced. Previous to that it had been going on in Europe, beginning shortly after the Normans conquered England in 1066. Most of the time it has taken the form of armed conflict and oceans of blood have been shed as a result. Luckily, since the days of Wolfe and Montcalm, we have averted armed conflict here, with the minor exception of 1837. It will be one of the tragedies of history if after two centuries of nothing worse than verbal war, we once more fly at each other's throats, in pursuit of ends that can invariably be settled by discussion.

This section might properly be ended by a slight rearrangement of de Gaulle's Montreal speech –

Vive le Canada!

The Social Service State

To external pressure are to be added, as forces of consolidation, several internal pressures, prominent among which is the idea of equality. Today the world presses towards equality among races of whatever colour, equality among nations great and small, equality among men rich and poor, educated and uneducated, wise and foolish. The domestic political expression of the idea takes the form of an infinity of "social services", dubbed collectively "social security". Today the state provides "family allowances" (1945), old age security payments (1952), allowances for the blind (1952), and other forms of direct aid; undertakes elaborate programmes of public health (National Health Grant Programme, 1948); gives grants to hospitals, to the prevention of this disease and that; and aids indirectly in an infinite number of other ways.

A hundred years ago, inequalities in wealth, opportunity, and fate were taken for granted, and if persons were unfortunate or afflicted beyond their owns means of remedy, the neighbours might help. Our urban life has weakened the notion of neighbourliness, but the notion that the state represents us all and that we are "all in the same boat" has grown greatly. It has therefore been natural to have the state act directly. It is clear that this immense extension of responsibility must be assumed mainly by the central government, rather than by that of each province, and that is the way the people of Canada, in their empiric way, have worked it out: at least, final responsibility rests upon the central government, though there are a number of devices which permit provincial administration.

The Problem of Bureaucracy

The consequence of the social service state, added to the many other responsibilities which the state has assumed, is the growth of the bureaucratic state. Both the term and the fact have been novel to Canadians, who in the past had been accustomed to think of civil servants as persons who had "landed government jobs" and were enabled to live happily ever after, free from both care and work. Down to the present century, the picture had a measure of validity, but it is no longer more than a cartoon. The civil servant today administers (that is, "runs") vast areas of our lives; he takes our money away from us and gives some of it back. If the laws do not suit his purpose, he contrives amendments to them, introduced into Parliament through the more or less mechanical medium of "his minister". Although the way in which policy is made and how its leading details are struck out must always be something of a mystery, it is, nevertheless, safe to say that with the suggestion and drafting of most leading measures, highly-placed civil servants have much to do; in the phrase of the day, they "sell" their ideas to cabinet ministers. Once measures are on the statute books, the same civil servants have the duty of carrying them out, and by interposing between the law and the citizen a maze of departmental regulations and interpretations, they may even make the law mean something it was not intended to mean. Parliament, with the low average competence of its members, is little protection against the civil servant.

Nor is the average minister, who has become the servant of his officials, responsible to them rather than to Parliament. For example, until 1971, our Income Tax Act did not provide for taxing "capital gains", but by a series of "interpretations" the income tax bureaucrats, so the writer is informed, almost succeeded in introducing the principle of the taxation of capital gain. There is one other aspect of this government by civil servants: today, and here again the Income Tax Act is the conspicuous example, the language in which the laws are written (which can hardly be said to be either English or French) is incomprehensible except to the initiate. This is so both by design and by the inability of the present generation to write clearly. A decisive step away from government of law and towards a government of men has been taken when the law has been made incomprehensible.[27]

Since there is so much more public work to be done, the number of civil servants has necessarily increased. Many other influences unite to promote this increase. The perfection of bureaucratic symmetry is never reached – there are always more files that might have been compiled, more agencies whose records might have been supplemented, and so on. Hence the multiplication of forms[28] and of persons to look after the forms. As our society becomes more and more socialistic, we shall have to maintain a strict guard against ending up as a community dominated by officials ensnaring each other and us in red tape.

The growth of the bureaucratic state has brought profound, but as yet not well-recognized, constitutional shifts. Under our system of responsible government, the appropriate minister of the Crown is alone answerable to Parliament for anything done in his department, and theoretically, if he offends, he can be brought to book by his fellow Members of Parliament, or the matter can be pressed further and the government turned out. At the time of writing, there had only been three cases since Confederation of the government of the day losing its majority in the House (1873, 1925 and 1963), so that this heroic measure is only likely under exceptional circumstances. Even where the government of the day does not have a majority of all the members of the Commons, it is in a fairly strong position, as Mr. Pearson's experience after April, 1963, suggests, for no one wishes to have the expense, toil, and confusion of a whole series of elections. Single ministers can shelter behind their government. Thus, in 1955 the Minister of National Revenue was the subject of strenuous attack for conduct which, to put the mildest construction on it, was injudicious, but he survived.[29] The government of the day, with a docile party majority behind it, is so completely in command that Members of Parliament are really responsible to it, rather than it to them: unless the multi-party system should become invariable, the incidence of "responsibility" has been reversed. To take the analysis a stage further, since ministers come and go and

[27] Those who doubt the deterioration of language in our law need only compare an older statute like the British North America Act with a current piece of legislation, especially taxation legislation.

[28] The present writer, in the course of some minor associations with a public agency, has on occasion signed eight different copies of the same form.

[29] He was accused of having revealed to the Premier of Ontario in an unofficial way certain secret information, drawn from the records of his department, about a political rival in his own riding, with the apparent intention of discrediting him. The Minister took refuge in silence, and rode out the storm. In a country with a nicer sense of honour, he would not have lasted overnight.

since they are "responsible" for areas of administration about which they often know little, it seems evident that our effective rulers are the heads of the permanent service, the so-called "mandarins" of Ottawa. Some branches have become virtually autonomous; Parliament has little control over the amounts of money they spend and the "responsible" minister not much more. The duty of the citizen of Canada becomes simply that of paying over the taxes which sustain them, without either knowing how they carry on or being in a position to learn, if he wished to do so (which he usually does not).[30]

To control such services it would take a much stronger type of man as minister than was forthcoming in the post-war period. The growth of administration as an almost autonomous branch of government is demanding more and more that the minister be not merely the head of his department, a kind of super-deputy-minister (which, unfortunately, several members of post-war cabinets seem to have been), but also a champion of the people against the administrators. But this is an aspect of our constitutional development which forms part of the history of our future, rather than of our past. It is a problem to be left with the younger readers of these pages.

Employment, Full and Otherwise

During the war, there was much discussion of "full employment". Towards its close, the coming demobilization of service men cast doubt over the future: would there be enough work to absorb them? War production had made it clear that our productive machine had vastly increased its powers. Was it not possible that a small amount of additional employment might give all the goods required and leave many men with nothing to do? An American economist said at the time that rather than take chances on widespread unemployment, "it would pay the United States to go on making tanks, even if it had to dump them in mid-Atlantic to get rid of them". All governments began to make their plans for reconstruction. Here was one of the lions in history's path that turned out not to be a lion at all, for what happened was an enormous increase in employment.[31] History seemed to turn a page in 1945, especially in Canada, and from that time for another fifteen years every machine hummed and the country grew at a pace that it had never before experienced. Why?

[30] A conspicuous example of apparent independence from ministerial and parliamentary control is the R.C.M.P.

[31] See diagrams showing the course of employment on pp. LXXVI-LXXVII.

No such movement can ever be simple, but there are clearly discernible factors in it. One is the huge "back-log" of wants in big things such as houses – the depression had virtually postponed house building from 1930 on.[32] The building programme was one of the mainstays of our prosperity. Another factor consisted in the social benefits, such as "mothers' allowances" which steadily return purchasing power to the economy. Still another lay in the spectacular discoveries of our natural resources: the oil and gas fields of the Prairie provinces, the iron of Ontario and Labrador, the copper, the lead, the nickel, and other such things, such amazing new supplies of which were found. These discoveries came at a time when the world needed them; they did not, like so many other Canadian treasures, languish for years until they could be utilized.

No national economy expands in a straight line upward; there are always swings and pauses. During the 1950's, Canada had taken in millions of immigrants from many countries. At the end of the decade, unemployment among both newcomers and native-born had become considerable; the Unemployment Insurance Fund was almost entirely depleted, and the usual Canadian accompaniment of domestic unemployment – attempting to get across the American border – apparently was again becoming marked. The American economy, for its part, was at last reaching the happy condition referred to above, for American employment was being sustained to an increasing extent by public expenditure on defence. In Canada defence expenditure also remained high, but we were not under the same necessity of employing idle hands in the same way as were our neighbours. Moreover, a renewal of severe drought on the Prairies brought back to farmers the bitter memories of the 1930's. The previous pace of economic expansion by 1963 was slowing down, though serious depression did not come and indeed the number of persons employed actually increased.

In general, the economic experience of the post-war years went in the direction of persuading the Canadian people that they could spend themselves into prosperity. Governments made little effort at old-fashioned budget-balancing, and private persons mortgaged their futures by buying everything – almost, it would seem, down to cigarettes – on the instalment plan. Old-fashioned thrift became sinful. Only at the very end of the period was it once more becoming apparent to the informed – not to the uninformed mass – that expenses cannot perpetually exceed income.

As with the other sections in this prologue, the reader must be cautioned that any attempt to write an account of relatively current events

[32] See diagram "New Dwellings Completed" on p. LXXVI.

is only tentative history and must leave out all but a bare skeleton of what actually happened. [33]

The "fifties" had been a decade of vast prosperity (as had the corresponding period in the nineteenth century which had ended up in the "big bang" of the American Civil War). The 1950's and early 1960's were a similar period of hectic prosperity, and luckily for Canada, they did not end up in the "big bang" of civil war. At least, they have not done so at time of writing. People began to expect the "good times" to last forever. They expected those days when large companies hired employment agents to hire employees, to go on indefinitely. Every university graduate expected to have an almost unlimited choice of jobs awaiting him. Were not new universities opening every day and private industrial companies ready and anxious to snap up the "trained brains" they assumed were being turned out from them?

Canadian economic life has never run in such channels for very long at a time: a much more normal condition is something like "scraping along", though not one of actual want. There is an easy explanation: Canada does not have the natural endowments that permit of constant expansion and the demands for its resources are geared closely to the demands of the outside world. If these flourish, Canada flourishes. It has neither the vast stretch of fertile land found in the United States, nor the climate that makes American acres more productive than Canadian. It is unfortunate in this respect that Canada, a country of modest endowments and as a rule of modest expectations, happens to be a neighbour to a country where expectations have always been immoderate, a country where traditionally "the sky's the limit". But what people ever yet learned from their history to cut their coat according to their cloth?

Just how complicated a short period is from a "front seat" can be estimated by the following list of some of its characteristics:

1963-1976 was a period in which the business cycle went through numerous short swings, rather than executing large, clearly marked "downs", "ups" and climaxes.

"Free Trade" so long the staple of Canadian economic discussion lost a good deal of its prominence.

Unemployment began to show up, sometimes in considerable quantity.

Many experiments in make-work schemes were tried out.

[33] The phrase echoes the conception of history enunciated by the great German scholar von Ranke, who declared that in writing history, he wished to see the past in terms of "what actually happened". But even our giant newspapers, some of which proudly proclaim that they "print all the news that's fit to print", do not in reality actually do better than print a fraction of it. Condensation and omission are the essence of historical writing.

These were in addition to the more formal measures such as Family Allowances and Old Age Pensions.

They all set going the never-ending debate on the form of the State – "free enterprise" or "socialistic"?

The State (federal and provincial) undertook a huge house-building programme. There was an unprecedented rise in interest rates, both for ordinary business purposes and for mortgages. "Tight money" was regarded as a necessary "brake" to the economy "overheating itself", that is, running into an old-fashioned "boom", to be followed by a "bust".

Federal government bonds gave a higher interest return than ever before in history, others accordingly.

"The developer" as a figure on the local landscape steadily increased in visibility.

Much argument went on as to the amount and wisdom of public interference with his projects. This underlay the great debate about "planning".

The debate on "planning" was loosely associated with the debate on the protection of the environment.

And this in turn easily led to prolonged debate on industrialism, the responsibilities of the industrial concern, the conservation of nature.

There were few activities in which the State was not concerned.

In Canada it provided the national air service.

It was a major provider of housing, as mentioned just above.

It maintained control of all developments in atomic power.

It took over the electrical systems of the leading provinces (except Alberta).

It got into the business of oil discovery and development.

The above list is short and only serves as a slight indication of the complexity of the Canadian economy. The question is as to how this complexity is to be regulated or directed. The historic political battles have been between "free traders" and "protectionists", passing more recently into the phase of "socialism" and "free enterprise". In general terms, "free traders" have tended to become "free enterprisers" and "protectionists" socialists. The antitheses are by no means as sharp as the terms indicate. Where, for example, is the "free trader" who is not ready to accept some "protection" for the product he has to sell in a "free market"? Where is the industrialist, manufacturing behind a protective tariff, who is also a "socialist"?

One prominent aspect of this struggle was the gradual realization of and concern over the fact that the tariff had had as one of its main effects, that of turning the Canadian manufacturing industry into a

mere "branch plant" economy. A prominent example of this is furnished
by the industry that has made and sustains the city of Oshawa – the
motor car industry. The McLaughlin Carriage factories of the 1890's
turned into the McLaughlin Car Factories of the 1900's and these in turn
into the plants of General Motors of Canada, a wholly owned subsidiary
of General Motors. In 1975-6 General Motors of Canada earned for its
parent company a sum of $76,000,000. This money all went to head
office in New York. This instance also brings up another equally prominent situation of the post-war period, the rise of the so-called "multinational" corporation. General Motors, like most of the multi-nationals
is in reality American. Another good illustration is furnished by Imperial
Oil, most of whose shares are owned by a former Standard Oil company,
now "Exxon". Imperial, all of whose directors are merely officers of the
company, also returns its quota of millions to the address of its major
shareholder. Some of the "multi-nationals" have made considerable
efforts to Canadianize themselves – except in the matter of ultimate control.

Analysis of the Canadian economy could go on in this way for volumes. Can the whole sweep of this interesting fifteen years or so be
classified and condensed into broad trends? It is not yet possible to do
this with much precision, but some tentative findings might be set out.

The major problem was how to prevent the crash in which the
"boom" of previous cycles so often had ended. The problem was haunted
by the ghost of the "super-depression" of the 1930's which had confronted the country with the suffering and hardships of that tragic decade. This must not occur again. But could it be prevented by allowing
the economy to go on expanding? And by using every device to maintain
unemployment at a manageable level. Mass unemployment could not
possibly be cured by the old simple device of leaving the unemployed to
look after themselves. One of the incentives to employment was "cheap"
money for business and industry. One of the brakes on too rapid expansion was "dear" money. This seemed to point to control of the financing
and banking arrangements of the country – to "management of the
money supply". The battle between the forces went on unceasingly, and
it was aggravated by the constantly increasing pressure arising from
injection into the labour market of tens of thousands of newly-arrived
immigrants. Pressure for more and more immigration was unremitting
on the part of many sections of the employing public, who saw in it a
more or less docile source of more reliable employees than the native
born, many of whom were benefiting rather easily, sometimes fraudu-
lently, by the efforts to "relieve unemployment". It sometimes seemed as
if people could live as well from public relief in various forms as from
work.

Under all these pressures, there seemed only one direction in which prices could go, and that was up. Year by year the "Cost of Living" index leapt upward. The dread of inflation, whose economic and social effects were understood by relatively few stared everyone in the face. Yet was there a human being who would not press at every possible moment for the direct benefit which an increase in prices seemed to offer him? Everyone always wants as much as he can get, does he not? Labour, now well organized, never ceased to clamour for "a larger piece of the pie". Employers, nothing loath, met this with increased prices for the goods already on their shelves.

In the midst of the turmoil, the Arab states, who controlled about half of the readily available oil supply of the world, took advantage of the situation, quite naturally, by greatly increasing the price of their oil. Were Canadian prices to follow suit by allowing freedom of export to the U.S. or was Canadian oil to be reserved for the use of Canadians? A sharp tussle took place with the government of Alberta, which predictably raised the question of "provincial rights" (the right, in this case, of a province to its natural resources). It was easy to contend that the drastic increase in oil prices would benefit mainly the American "multinational" oil companies, but it was another matter to convince the Albertans in general that their oil should not be sold at a high price in order that provinces "down east" might keep warm. "Let the bastards freeze" became a slogan in Alberta and it took more than patriotic sentiment to convince Albertans – or Albertan oil producers! The federal government stood between the Alberta oil or oil companies and the freezing or conceivable freezing of the eastern provinces. It was not a comfortable position and was more or less eventually avoided by illogical compromise which naturally pleased few. The energy crisis had burst upon the world, especially the North American world, with full force. It is not yet resolved. It may never be resolved.

The visible effect on these innumerable converging forces was "inflation": "double digit inflation" as it was termed actually was upon the country. How to avoid the catastrophic consequences (known to relatively few) as easily seen in similar experiences of the war-ruined countries of the 1920's and 1930's, France, Italy and emphatically Germany?

One statesman urged the remedy, Mr. Stanfield of Nova Scotia, leader of the Conservative Opposition. He fought the election of 1974 on the issue of the imposition of strict price and wage controls. He appealed to the intelligence of the electorate and he was defeated. He had induced his party to accept his policy but not the Canadian voter. Repudiated in three general elections Stanfield resigned party leadership and in about a year after, the Trudeau government which had refused to accept the idea of control of prices and wages, set up elaborate provision for the control of prices and wages! In defence of Mr. Trudeau's "stand pat" position, it could no doubt have been argued that there was no use adopting his opponent's suggestions until the voter had been convinced, by hard facts, that it was necessary. Even so, after the adoption of controls, unrelenting warfare was waged against the policy by labour, which still saw nothing involved but its rights to "a larger piece of the pie" and less openly by employers and manufacturers, who saw it mainly as an attempt to prevent their getting as much for their products as free enterprise would bring to them. This chapter of politics is not a happy one for students of Canadian behaviour, for it revealed an ill-formed electorate whose decisions were based not on any large-minded view of the future course of things, still less on public interest, but on short-run views and mere selfishness. "Every man for himself and let the devil take the hindmost"; the old point of view, seemed to have triumphed. It was the unfortunate man-in-the-middle, whoever he was, who was left to bear the consequences.

By 1977, the annual rate of inflation had been reduced, but the upward climb was by no means terminated. The question remained unanswered, with portentous consequences for the future: could a modern society, such as ours, with its tumultuous, contentious, often puerile debating, its "built-in" self-seeking, learn to manage its own fiscal affairs, and therefore, in broad terms, its destiny?

Governments, federal and provincial, found themselves caught up in the field of public welfare. In no field was this more prevalent than in housing. By a multiplicity of avenues, new housing was provided. Housing loans were made available, mortgage rates fixed for them and through the municipalities, actual housing provided. The index of "New Dwellings Constructed", tells the tale: in 1963, 128,191 new units of housing were built. This number rose irregularly year by year, reaching its maximum in 1974 with 257,243 new units. Housing of this order should have provided for some million people per year. While much of it was through private channels, most of it was made possible through the various loan and mortgage schemes made available under the authority established for that purpose, the Central Mortgage and Housing Corporation. Though strict repayment was required, the money provided could not but add to the National Debt and thus to inflationary processes. But the need was great, seemingly insatiable. And who would deny that this enormous number of substantial new houses had not added to the well-being of the population of Canada?

House building on this scale was basically made possible by the continuing productivity of the country. The cities of Edmonton and Calgary are testimony to the new wealth that was coming out of Canadian oil. Similarly, that great staple, the wheat of the Prairie provinces, was playing its accustomed large part in the country's economy. The average wheat crop for the years 1962-66 reached the impressive total of 673,-000,000 bushels. In 1966, the highest total on record was reached 829,-000,000 bushels. Succeeding years continued to be equally good: thus in 1969, the total was 671,000,000 bushels. In the period, there was only one bad year, 1970, when the crop was poor (331,000,000 bushels). For a region so subject to drought and blight as the Prairie provinces, this was a remarkable performance, a gift of a beneficent Providence of course but also a tribute to the energy and initiative of the wheat farmer. This huge store of golden grain could not but be a major factor in the economy of the country as a whole.

These illustrations of the Canadian economy and of its behaviour during the last fifteen years could go on indefinitely. They are also illustrations of the complexity of our day-to-day life. . . . In Canada as in every other social group, such complexities have always existed and will continue to exist. They are the backdrop of history in its more customary aspects.

The Change in Biological Behaviour

Most important of all the factors in the economy of the post-war period was the extraordinary turn in the birth rate. In the 1930's, the birth rate of the English-speaking section of this country touched bottom. This was in part deliberate – the deliberate attempt to offset hard times, which was reflected quite sharply in French Canada also. Then about 1939, a turn in the tide was observable. This trend increased year by year. In a period of return to relatively high birth rates throughout a large part of the world, Canada had one of the highest of all and one of the lowest death rates! From 1956 on, there were not far from half a million births a year in Canada.[34] The lowest number of births was in 1937: 227,454. 1937 was also close to the bottom of the depression. The largest single increase was in 1945, "the year the boys came home", from 24.4 to 27.2 per 1000. Since most of these were to non-French parents, "la revanche du berceau" was indefinitely postponed.

How can we explain this extraordinary change in biological behaviour? Here again, the answer is complex. Prosperity had much to do with it – jobs make men, men do not make jobs. A change in attitude affected it – young people getting married decided that a family was not a nuisance but was desirable, and they turned to thinking in terms, not of one

[34] See diagram showing births and deaths, and birth and death rates, on p. LXXV.

or two, but of four, children. The moral changes that began with the First Great War blew away the nineteenth-century attitude of parsimony, with its "take care for the morrow" morality, its honest desire to save before you spent, to lay away a bit for a rainy day, and to owe no penny you could not pay. A generation arose which was used to living on the instalment plan: it did not worry at living dangerously. As the sheriff of a certain county said to the writer: "Thousands of people in this county do not own the beds they sleep on". Some older people would not sleep very well on beds they did not own.

The decay of formal religion and the return to paganism must affect the situation, especially under the impact of war and its aftermath. War is always a pagan sexual stimulant. During war, woman takes again her ancient place as prize of the warrior. Moreover, after woman had fought for and won her freedom, man found out that she was just another animal like himself, and not merely "a vision of delight". So this business of begetting was seen in a more realistic light than in the early years of the twentieth century, and it ceased to be surrounded by pruriencies and, possibly, inhibitions. Whatever caused the change, change it was, and the arrival of several hundred thousand helpless new citizens every year in a country where provision of food and shelter depend only on the energy of the inhabitants in itself ensured full enough employment to the parents who had the job of rearing them, and to everyone else in the population.

But how fallible are predictions! This rosy estimate of the outlook or ambitions or intentions of the Canadian woman soon had to be sharply modified. Beginning in 1960 the birth rate fell by about one percentage point per year. The decline continued with little variation until about 1973: the last few years seem to have shown a tendency to stabilization at about fifteen births per thousand of population. At the same time there was a sharp increase in the death rate, which, however, soon stabilized itself at about eight and one half per thousand. Thus within the short space of some fifteen years, Canada's position slid from one of the highest birth rates in the western world to one of the lowest, and therefore to one of the smallest annual "home grown" additions to its population. A glance at the tables on these figures makes one wonder whether the two lines, births and deaths, may not actually cross in the not too distant future, and more people die than are born.

How is this last spectacular change in Canadian biological behaviour to be explained? It seems quite unlikely that it represents a change in sexual ardour: in fact, if the public press and the media be our guide, there never has been a time in history when sex has had more emphasis. No, the change does not come from the lack of ardour of Canadian males and females – unless our sex-ridden atmosphere be an index of mere "old man" satiety, but from their adeptness in managing everything respecting birth control, except the incidence of venereal disease, which is reported as on the rapid increase. The major factor seems to have been the discovery of "the pill": at least, this coincided with the precipitous fall in births that began in 1959. Abortion, secret or public, has added its considerable quota. If published statements and statistics are any index, it is now perhaps about as common and as little thought of as toothache.

Along with most of the western world, have the people of Canada discovered in birth control, how to have your cake and eat it, too, how to have your fun and escape its responsibilities? Many would say yes. They would be able to say that man in the past had secured a relatively stable population, roughly equated to the means of subsistence, by the painful agencies of war, disease and famine. They would probably be right, but the application of these means of limitation was once universal. Today it goes by localities and cultures, the more simple cultures standing at the points that parts of "The West" reached about two generations ago. The net result of "The West's" having its easy-going fling may thus well be its elimination by the pleasant route of natural death with no offspring left behind.

What or who will take the place of our western world? Here again we are in the dangerous field of conjecture. One change in biological behaviour might be succeeded by another. The air has vibrated of late with the battle cries of those who see nothing but "standing room only" left for humanity in a relatively short time, if it does not reduce its rate of increase to equal its deaths and thus obtain a stationary population, and of those who fear the weakening and diminution of their own people (notably Quebec: this is the ghost that haunts this once-highly productive province, whose birth rate is now the lowest in Canada), or those who unthinkingly bellow about "getting the country filled up", "developed".

"The developer" and his like are as powerful in some respects as once was the priesthood but for an ignoble end. People who think mainly in terms of "the high standard of living" are people subscribing to the materialistic philosophy which puts goods in importance ahead of life. They rise on their 'high standard' very often simply by taking advantage of the low standard of others. This is the *cheap labour* attitude. In Canada it sustains itself on the importation of people from all over the world who do not know Canadian conditions and who therefore are ready to take less or are more amenable to pressure. The "high standard of living" man simply goes up the scale and disappears, his place being taken by someone moving up from below. In this way, the older stock in most of the western countries is being replaced by people who in one way or another are willing temporarily to accept less from life. The process, of course, is a relatively slow one and may take a few generations to work itself out.

In our own day, the enormous intake of immigrant population into Canada has rapidly accelerated, so that already this country is virtually a new country, filled with new people who do not know the society they have entered. However quickly intermarriage and consequent adaptation might go on, it could never keep pace with the inflowing tide of new arrivals. In this way, the "old Canadian" with his tiny family, is fairly rapidly disappearing from view.

Since the newcomer comes to improve his lot, he must take things seriously and work hard. He has come to freedom and he often appreciates it more than the native. He finds that released from the strict discipline of the old-world family, he is often in a position to do much as he likes. He thus adds initiative at both ends of the scale, millionaires, and artists, at one end of the scale, criminals at the other. To a formerly rather old-fashioned, more or less rural society such as Canada's, the results are often upsetting.

This word *rural* may be the deepest of all the words to be used in discussing biological behaviour. The change from simple country values to the complexities and the sophistications of city life – sophistications of the streets as well as of the mansions – may be the hardest to which any people has to adapt itself. What the future of our country may be with most of its people locked up in great cities, who is to say? Once more, we are on uncharted seas.

The Canadian Community

Much interesting light can be thrown upon the nature of the Canadian community over the years by using the tables in the ten-yearly Census of Canada. Without a great deal of exploration of these formidable collections, the student can observe the relations of Canadians to one another and to the country in a great variety of categories. This section explores, but by no means exhausts, these data. It is designed to continue the pictures given by the diagrams.

The most acute problem we are faced with or ever likely to be faced with is the relationship of Canada's two peoples, the French and the English. French demographers watch with much anxiety the shifting balance in the totals of the two peoples and the language they speak. This concern is one of the deep underlying causes of Separatism. The

Census gives returns of "ethnic origin" and of "mother tongue", as well as of birth and death rates. From these, it is evident that the proportion of those who trace their descent to one of the two founding groups has in the last fifty years greatly decreased. These two sets of figures may be compared with those for "Mother Tongue". Since those who speak French as their mother tongue are fewer than those who give "French" as their ethnic origin, the difference may be regarded as representing the number of French who have been assimilated into the English way of life, and *vice versa*.

The same comparison could be made between those of "other" origins and those who speak "other" mother tongues. This is what has been attempted in the diagram on page 428. Mother tongue statistics begin only in 1941. The diagram on page 428 carries them to 1961. But the returns are available for 1971. The reader might be interested himself in extending the lines of the diagram from 1961 to 1971.

The Census data indicate that the range of the English language extends well beyond the original group of people who trace back to the British Isles. While it is probably inevitable that a person or group who speak a non-English or non-French language should sooner or later abandon their own language, the difficulty, as the French of Canada see it, is that in doing so, they usually learn English. For example, the number of Hungarians, Swedes, Germans, or what not, who speak French as their mother tongue is most limited, but of such groups, the number who speak English grows rapidly with each Census. The most debatable group is the Italian, whose language is closely related to French. But Italians, too, seem much more easily drawn into the English group than into the French. This is one cause of the linguistic squabbles in the City of Montreal, where there are many Italian immigrants. The French attitude towards English there is often misunderstood; there has been little official attempt to invade English constitutional and linguistic rights: the effort is concentrated on the immigrants.

The birth rate is another index which is always carefully watched. There was a time when French Canada had the highest surplus of births over deaths of any ethnic group in the western world. No wonder: a former Rector of the University of Montreal once declared himself to be the seventeenth child of a seventeenth child. Those days are over and there is no longer any hope of *la revanche du berceau.* Some of this precipitous fall in the birth rate of Quebec is probably to be attributed to the English group there (the Census does not provide data that allow birth rates to be allotted to "ethnic origins"), but even allowing for this it is clear that the large families of former days in Quebec are of the past. This, coupled with immigration, is regarded as a serious threat to the future of the race

and the language. As a matter of fact, it probably is not, for the decline
in births is general.

Closely related to these vital statistics are those that light up how
quickly Quebec has become an urban province. The following table tells
the tale.

The number of the population given as "urban" and "farm" for
Canada and for Quebec was as follows:

Urban and Farm Population of Canada
and Quebec

Urban	1966	1971
Canada	14,727,000	16,411,000
Quebec	4,525,000	4,861,000
Farm		
Canada	1,914,000	1,420,000
Quebec	494,000	305,000

This rapid decrease in the farm population was common to the entire
country. Nothing is more a commonplace than the decline of the farm
population. Farmers are replaced with machinery, so to speak. But as
long as his milk and meat lie in abundance on the shelves of the "super-
market", the town dweller does not worry about starving to death.

An aspect of the Canadian community to which little attention seems
to be directed is the obvious one of age. In a "natural" population, such
as existed in our pioneer days and still exists in such countries as Mexico
or Brazil, the number of children and young people is large. Until mid-
twentieth century, this continued to be true of Quebec. In any meeting,
for example, in which the two peoples were present, the greater youth of
the French was very much in evidence: the English furnished the grey
beards. Many often seemed tired, old men. The French were young,
quick and energetic in their movements. Probably some of the unrest in
Quebec comes from this greater youthfulness. Time will make this disappear and the two groups will grow old together. It will be left to the
immigrant to supply youthful vigour.

Quebec with no aid from French-speaking immigration held out very
well against the rest of the country. The "Age Pyramids" for all the provinces, Quebec included, have been shrinking at the bottom, but Quebec
held out fairly well until the 1960's, when the number of births began to
decrease rapidly. The diagram thus leads us back to the same deep cause
of fear – the shrinkage of the French race.

One topic that in former days was uppermost in Canadian consideration was religious denomination. As religious fires have slowly died down

this topic has receded in importance, but it is still prominent. The Canadian Census gives some exact information about it. Canada, for example, is steadily becoming more Roman Catholic. But this is not to be closely related to the Province of Quebec, for over many years, a heavy proportion, perhaps the majority, of immigrants from Europe has been Roman Catholic. The 154,000 Italians who lived in Montreal in 1971 or the 250,000 who lived in Metropolitan Toronto would be Roman Catholic almost to a man, at least nominally.

The latest Census figures show that the major Protestant denominations hold their own, but not spectacularly. They no doubt reflect the slowly rising numbers of the central English-speaking stock. The Presbyterians are almost stationary; the United Church increases slowly and the Anglican makes a considerable gain: this possibly reflects the large numbers of immigrants from the United Kingdom since 1950.

It is the minor Protestant denominations that have shown the heaviest increases – the Pentecostals, the Jehovah's Witnesses, the Mormons and various others. This situation is interesting: it probably reflects the desire of "the plain man" for an informal, emotional type of faith, for services of an evangelical nature, with plenty of hearty singing, and fervid preaching. The minor denominations no doubt appeal to those social groupings which are not sure of their status in a predominantly middle class society, to people not at the bottom of the heap but not as "well fixed" as the members of the more established and more traditional sectors of the community.

A classification that hardly existed half a century ago has come into prominence: in 1970, persons putting themselves down as of no religion numbered 939,000. This in itself reflects a considerable evolution in Canadian society, indicating perhaps the failure of the churches, but more probably the inability of the traditional religion to appeal to those who, either through apathy and negligence or through the inroads of secularism, aided no doubt by the undermining by knowledge and science, have ceased to be held by the idea of the supernatural.

Despite all this, however, Canadians, as compared with other English-speaking countries, still remain fairly faithfully attached to their churches, which while not as full as they once were, are far from being empty.

Those born in the United Kingdom still constitute the largest single group of the persons born outside Canada, but the proportion has steadily declined – from 52 per cent in 1921 to 28 per cent in 1971. Collectively, the persons born in Europe now far outnumber them, having increased from 23 per cent in 1921 to 51 per cent in 1971. Those born in the United States have steadily decreased in their percentage of the whole and this must reflect the cessation after about 1920 of American immigration to the new lands of western Canada. An almost new classification has lately appeared in that those born in Asia now number (1971) 3.6 per cent of the total born abroad. The "born elsewhere" – mainly the Caribbean – have also rapidly increased.

The Canadian population thus becomes more and more diversified. The job of the future is to make over these many newcomers into Canadian citizens.

To turn to the more distinctly economic side of the picture, the Census gives us much information on unemployment, houses built and incomes.

"Employment and Unemployment" are slippery terms. If a woman does a few hours a week "baby sitting" is she "employed"? If a man manages "to beat the game" by juggling his employed periods so as to get the maximum amount of Unemployment Insurance Pay, is he employed or unemployed? Then there is that large group, the retired people, who may secure an occasional bit of work to help out. It seems clear that for this essentially human situation, people cannot be reduced to mere statistics, and so all the various Unemployment indexes are to some degree fallacious. Nevertheless much effort is expended in making the returns as accurate and as representative as possible, so they may at least be regarded as broadly correct reflections of the actual situation.

For Canada as a whole, the outstanding point is that if we take the year 1961 as base and represent the "number" of Employed as 100, then we note year by year an increase in the index of number employed, so that when we come to 1976, the Index stands (first six months) at about 140. This means that there were about 140 jobs in 1976 to 100 in 1961, which was much greater than the increase in population. In Canada, as everyone must know, employment has wide seasonal variations, as well as variations from year to year. It is to ironing out these latter that so much effort, public and private, has gone.

Another index kept by the Census relates to income. The weekly income of "the work force" in 1960 averaged $70.20. In 1976 it was several times that figure and steadily rising. A rough idea of whether this vast increase meant anything in the way of actual "purchasing power" could be found by correlating weekly wage with "The Cost of Living" index. The finding would almost certainly be that wage increases, like other increased prices, are "fool's gold", with no one, or at least with only the "quick on their feet" type actually better off. This has been tacitly recognized by government in its practice of "indexing" certain public payments such as Old Age Pensions – that is, increasing them in proportion to the increase in the Cost of Living Index.

Since the depression of the 1930's many steps have been taken to prevent the recurrence of the suffering that then occurred. This constantly strengthened guard against "bad times" has saved the country from severe social upheavals of one kind or another (though greatly increasing the numbers and powers of the bureaucrats); so that despite the pessimistic reports often carried in the press, unemployment is not as serious a problem as it was a generation ago. It is a problem that can only be ameliorated and never solved, but the slow pragmatic approach probably gives much better results than would some grand design for an instant Paradise.

The Outside World and its Deplorable Deportment

The change in our biological behaviour is all the more remarkable when viewed against the background provided by the state of the world. Since 1914, there has been a succession of explosions, and since 1939, the violence of these has redoubled. Our own country, which in the nineteenth century was so securely tucked away from danger, has become more and more concerned in them. In 1939, we were in the war within one week after it broke out – we had already prepared our spirits for it – and subsequently there were many international imbroglios in which our membership in the United Nations involved us. To mention only a few, there were the Hungarian and Suez Canal crises of 1956, the truce-making arrangements in Indo-China and Cyprus, and the attempt to maintain order in the Congo.

Canada fought the Second World War, not as a "Dominion" (that is, a semi-subordinate state) but in her own right; she declared war on Germany and Japan in the name of her own King. Her separate statehood was maintained in her political and diplomatic relations, but her fighting forces had little more independence than they had in the First World War – with this difference, that in the first war, they were always parts of British commands, whereas in the second, they also at times came under the control of the Americans. Canada's split personality was glaringly underlined in 1945 when she was assembling a force for the war against Japan; this force trained with the Americans, used their methods and wore American type uniforms. Canadians, when with the British, were British, and when with the Americans, were Americans.

The Canadian contribution to the war, given the size of our population, was large, and once more our boys gave good accounts of themselves. Once more, as in the First World War, they seemed to find their own peculiar element in the air, particularly as fighting pilots. But it would be invidious, in the midst of so much devotion to duty, to pick up one service and enhance its prestige above the others. No Canadian need ever be ashamed of the record of his people as fighting men. But characteristically, as before, it was the plain fighting man, whether private or junior officer, who came in for his country's recognition. For generals, no popular taste developed; there could no more have been a General Eisenhower in Canada than a battleship afloat in Saskatchewan. This was possibly because none of our generals achieved great fame[35] and possibly because of the intensely egalitarian spirit of the country: men in high military places seem, to plain people, strange animals of whom they have had no experience and are not a little afraid. For the Canadian army, it had proved a hard war to get into. The Canadian divisions were distinctly unwelcome to the British and American commands in Italy, and it was not until they landed in France in 1944, after four years of marking time in England, that they began to play the role for which they imagined they had been cast.

After the war, a second experiment was made in internationalism – the United Nations. The preliminary meeting was held in San Francisco in 1945. Mr. King, then prime minister, made a good try at non-partisanship in foreign affairs by taking with him representatives of other parties, but he rather spoiled the effect by insisting on his own way, to the chagrin of the C.C.F. leader, Mr. Coldwell. The point was whether Argentina, then virtually a dictatorship, should be accepted as a member. The United States was for, Russia against. King felt it necessary to vote with the United States. Many felt that if Canada had not followed the United States, she would have shown her concern for free government and demonstrated her independence. As it was, the incident helped to confirm other nations in their view that Canada was a mere echo of the United States: what Mr. Gromyko, the Russian representative, later called her: "this boring second violin in the American symphony"! Whether on her own merit, or as providing a second member for the United States, does not appear, but in 1947 Canada was elected to one of the non-permanent seats in the United Nations Security Council.

At the first meeting of the United Nations Assembly, in London, January, 1946, the tactics which Russia long continued to employ were made clear, for she made every effort to isolate Great Britain and to drive a wedge in between that power and the United States. In this game she failed, but her effort continued to be the same, with variations in

---

[35] The generals are said to have fought a cautious, professional war, taking few chances. One of their German opponents compared their slowness of initiative unfavourably to that of the Russians. General McNaughton conceivably might have been an exception to the Canadian generals, if he had had the opportunity to command in the field. For McNaughton, see John Swettenham, *McNaughton*, (Toronto 1968-69).

detail – separate the two great English-speaking nations or if that could not be done, separate the western allies. Not until 1956, when the government of Mr. Eden suffered a sudden attack of insanity in its unprovoked attack on Egypt, did it seem possible that she might succeed, and by that time the alliance was too strong to be destroyed even by the folly of the Eden government.

It was clearly foreseeable, though only a few foresaw it, that once Germany and Japan had been disposed of, the war-time alliance between the two great world powers, Russia and the United States, would turn into an old-fashioned balance-of-power rivalry in which most of the world would be ranged around one or other of the two giants. It is this balance which has kept the world on tenterhooks ever since and whose delicate equipoise everyone dreads might be upset, especially now that to ordinary war the terrors of the hydrogen bomb, intercontinental missiles and other horrible devices of destruction have been added. Yet at least five times during the period down to 1963, the balance came close to breaking down into conflict.[36]

The first dangerous episode was the Russian closing of the routes to Berlin, which brought about the organization of the celebrated "air-lift" (1948) by which the city was supplied until the Russians accepted defeat and opened the roads again. This crisis did not directly involve Canada, but as a result of it and of the threatening situation in general, the western powers came together in the North Atlantic Treaty Organization – NATO (Canada's adherence, April 4, 1949). This organization bound us with our kindred and with like-minded powers in common defence arrangements. As a result of it, we maintained for some years the 27th Brigade (from May 4, 1951) as a fighting force in Germany, along with a considerable air force. That Canada after the Second World War meant business in defence is indicated by the amount of money she spent on it – in post-war years a sum equal to between one hundred and one hundred and fifty dollars for every man, woman, and child in the country. Unfortunately, the return in forces and armaments never seemed equal to the amounts spent on them.

There is reason to think that Canadian suggestions, made in the proper quarters privately and also in public by Mr. St. Laurent and Mr.

---

[36] See diagram, "National Defence Expenditures" on p. LXXVIII. By the 1970's China had attained a status approaching that of a great power. In terms of the balance-of-power concept of international affairs, this had the effect of giving world politics three "legs", as it were, to rest upon, rather than two. And by 1977, accuracy in intercontinental missiles had been attained to such an extent that one of them was (theoretically) capable of landing within thirty feet of its target.

Pearson[37] led to the idea of a western alliance being taken up by the United States. If this is so, the situation indicates the possibilities and the limitations of this country. More easily than most, our representatives can put proposals before the key men of the United States and use their influence as a friendly neighbour to get them to consider it. But if we were to introduce such a proposal as NATO on our own initiative, it would not get far, for the big powers would say that we were not the responsible party; moreover, questions of prestige – sheer jealousy, often personal – enter into these situations. NATO, nevertheless, is just the kind of arrangement that Canada could desire.

The second crisis was the invasion of South Korea by the Communist North Koreans, June 25, 1950. Luckily the Russians were "on strike" from the Security Council, so on American initiative, the United Nations organized a force to help the South Koreans. The war was a near thing, for the Chinese, whose government had by that time become Communist, came to the aid of the North Koreans. The Korean War was accepted by the Canadian people as a duty; there was no elation over it. It was a tough war, and it ended in stalemate. Our casualties were appreciable, but they were not heavy in comparison with the World Wars.[38] The Korean War was the first wholly professional war in which Canada had been engaged.

The third threat to the balance of power (apart from the constant growth in strength of Russia and her partner, Communist China) consisted in the complications arising from Arab nationalism, which led to the Suez fiasco of 1956 and from the rebellions in Russia's satellites, Poland (1956), East Germany (1953), and Hungary (1956), all of which were ruthlessly crushed.

The fourth threat is not an episode, but the constant danger of war, with all that war implies in this hideous atomic age of ours, contained in Russian efforts to crowd the allies out of the city of Berlin. Berlin became a symbol. If the western allies were to abandon it, their alliance would disintegrate.

The fifth threat occurred in the autumn of 1962, with the attempt of the Russians to place atomic rocket installations in Cuba. This was foiled by the energetic action of President Kennedy, an action with which most Canadians found themselves in agreement. As one young fellow said at

[37] On this point, see the following: Pickersgill, *op. cit.*, Thomson, Dale C., *Louis St. Laurent: Canadian* (Toronto, 1967) and Pearson, Lester Bowles (ed. Munroe and Inglis) *"Mike": The Memoirs of the Right Honourable Lester B. Pearson* (Three volumes, Toronto, 1972ff.).
[38] Canadians killed and died of wounds: First World War: 60,661; Second World War: 41,992; Korean War: 312.

the time, "I don't want to spend the rest of my life looking down the barrel of a loaded gun."

Yet despite these foreign clouds in the sky, Canada in 1962 was still a prosperous and relatively happy country. While she was not making remarkable headway in the things of the spirit, she was stronger materially than she had been before. Moreover as the first century of the country's existence drew to a close there was probably coming to her people some consciousness of their own identity. They were slowly discovering the fact of their own existence and might be beginning to believe that there was some merit and value in being Canadian. A Canadian had been at the head of their state as governor-general from February 28, 1952, and there were even daring spirits among them who looked forward to the day when Canada might have its own flag! Meanwhile, the average man was not worrying much about political symbols, whether flags or governors-general; he was working hard, earning good pay, raising a family, building himself a house, giving his children a great deal of schooling, if not much education, and generally getting on with the job. Probably with these humble efforts of the average man the future of the country was as secure as any future in these troubled days can be.

The fifteen years after the preceding pages were written might be properly described as "more of the same": that is, as far as Canada was concerned, no major change in the world position occurred. From a more general point of view, the period saw the rise in importance of the Arab states of the Near East: the prodigious quantities of oil beneath their soil put them in the position of being able to exert influence far beyond their intrinsic strength. It also saw the increasing consolidation of what came to be called "The Third World", that is to say, those peoples and lands that had formerly been European colonies or "possessions", notably in Africa. The world of the future will be a different world from that of the past, but it is as yet too early to predict its precise shape.

For Canada itself, the period was still within the neo-colonial era, that is, the influence of the long years during which the country had been under the wing of the motherland was by no means obliterated and the average Canadian was not yet facing the world entirely on his own as did the average Englishman or American. A slow sense of national identity was forming, but it still had a long way to go and it still had not bridged the gulf between the two peoples. It is paradoxical that while world communications had never been easier and world travel more frequent, Canadians seemed to be becoming more parochial, their interests more closely centred in themselves and perhaps even for their own country, with less sense of community than previously. Another way of putting this is to say that the country had lacked a focal point – it is huge in area and its people scattered about. Yet this sense of community could easily be reawakened; for example, when the best hockey team that Canada could assemble (in 1972) was on the verge of losing the world championship to the Russians, the whole country was caught up in a frenzy of uneasiness. Victory came that time but afterwards interest lapsed and hockey too became more parochial. It is probable that the subject of *separatism* will supply a focal point almost as concentrated as a hockey match.

It is a fortunate country whose outside threat is only to its prowess in hockey and this helps to explain our increasing parochialism. We are still fairly well tucked away under the protecting arm, no longer of Mother Britannia but of Uncle Sam. We do not "play in the big leagues". The best instance of our loss of interest probably is given by the action of the Trudeau government in the first year of its existence, 1968. This was the year in which the Russians finally conquered Czechoslovakia. As the Russians were marching on Prague, the Trudeau government drastically cut down the Canadian forces in Europe, thereby giving a wound to western solidarity. Mr. Trudeau talked some nonsense about home defense being our first consideration, as if we would have had any homes to defend if the European bastions fell. There was, however, no popular movement of resentment in Canada.

In the nineteenth century Canada had no foreign policy: her attitudes and actions were simply those of Great Britain. In the twentieth, the two great wars had shocked her into some conception of her own national interest, apart from those of the Mother country, and in the late twentieth century, she had come close to reversion to colonial status once more, with Uncle Sam playing the part of John Bull. By 1975 or so, the British had in popular parlance become simply "The Brits", foreigners among other foreigners. As trans-Atlantic crossings became easier, the ocean itself became wider. In part, this arose from the increasing weakness of Great Britain. Britannia no longer ruled the waves: rather, she was an aging woman, dependent on others for much of her subsistence. That picture could be easily overdrawn but however the matter is put, the importance of the Mother country steadily decreased (and to fewer and fewer Canadians was it still such, given their European countries of origin). *Sic transit gloria mundi.*

The United States by no means took the place of Great Britain in Canadian imaginations. "Uncle Sam" was a friendly giant, but he saw the world through his own eyes, and he was inclined to think that other people should see it as he saw it. The Canadian problem in external affairs came to be how to preserve whatever freedom of action the country had and assert itself as occasion offered. This meant considerable divergence. American law attempted to coerce the Canadian plants of American firms. This was greatly resented. American foreign policy, which in the 1950's saw a Communist under every bed, quite unnecessarily alienated Cuba. Canada did not follow suit. When the United States was drawn into its unsuccessful war to "contain" Communism in Vietnam, Canada did not participate: in this she may have been right or she may have been wrong, but it was quite evident that no Canadian government could have persuaded the Canadian people to fight that particular war. Similarly, Canada, after long hesitation, decided to recognize Communist China, whether the United States did or not. How sharply a country placed as ours could diverge from American foreign policy, no one knows. If our actions cut deeply across American interests and the American view of the world, we might find divergence had limits.

But that is a point not likely to arise, for since the two countries have the same culture and traditions, in any really serious threat they would be found standing together. This gives them the liberty to haggle over what in other parts of the world might be fighting matters but here are only domestic squabbles, or at most municipal arrangements. Instances abound: the constant fight against pollution of air and water, where negotiations are sometimes between government and government, sometimes between state and province. Or the use of boundary waters in hydro-electric power development, as the Arrow Lakes arrangements made by then Premier Bennett of British Columbia with the Americans. Canadian-American relations are not exactly "foreign relations": they are better under some such head as "internal development".

Yet every Canadian retains his old inherited guardedness against the powerful neighbour. "Uncle Sam" is a kindly giant, but you always have to keep your eye on him.

There are literally dozens of details in foreign relations to be discussed, but most must be passed over. One important exception will occur to the reader: the new law that is developing with respect to the sea and the sea-coast. Now that the ocean bed has been ascertained to have valuable oil and other minerals, its possession becomes a matter of much importance. There are also the increasing inroads on coastal fisheries lying outside the traditional "three mile line". The pollution of the very ocean itself by oil tankers becomes increasingly serious.

In response to such situations, the Canadian government enunciated its doctrine that the Canadian coastal waters, waters over which Canada intends to exercise jurisdiction, extend two hundred miles off shore. This takes it out across the Banks of Newfoundland and in most places off the Continental Shelf. Since other countries are also beginning to assert this claim, that of Canada may "stick"; if we were ever under serious attack by a great naval power, it is doubtful if we could retain it. Here again, the ultimate solution no doubt will depend on the United States. But when it is remembered that even the little island of Iceland dares to face up to Great Britain in defence of a similar claim, it may be realized how much a weak country can do if it plays its cards well. The obvious play in the modern world is to balance off the two giants, the United States and Russia, for each will accept a great deal of irritating action from the small powers rather than bring in the other to their aid. The successful manipulation of oil and oil prices by the Near Eastern states provides the best example of this.

In some respects the atomic threat to existence is similar: safety lies in stalemate. In the 1950's the atomic threat was taken with seriousness during the period of the Cold War. Today, while it is more dangerous than ever, we have convinced ourselves that stalemate may save us from its horrors. In any case, the average Canadian would probably say that since he cannot do anything about it, he will not lose his sleep over it.

*   *   *

This may be mere foolishness or a reasonable response to circumstances. At any rate, it illustrates how the point made in surveying the period down to 1963 applies to that since that year: Canada is still fairly safely tucked away from harm and can regard itself as a fortunate country.

Too fortunate, perhaps. Over-security brings on somnolence. English Canadians sometimes need waking up, need rousing from their parochialism and, the word must be used, from their ignorance. A peculiar word to use for a people who spend a high share of their money on schooling. *Schooling*, but it is to be feared, not *education*. An old slight against the Americans was to call them "the best half-educated people in the world". Canadians could fairly be called "the best quarter-educated". Every year there are thousands of well-trained and able young people turned out from our universities, but they do not seem to have much effect in leavening the mass. Part of the blame for this goes to the overemphasis on equality: the most rapid way in which a man can disqualify himself for public office is to be "different". This levelling down to mediocrity has increased with the years, not decreased: in the 1860's, Edward Blake, withdrawn, cultivated, aloof, highly intelligent, could be returned as M.P.P. for South Bruce. He would have no chance in South Bruce today. Is it a matter of "democracy" so-called being pushed too far? Thoughtful men have always said that civilization rests on the abilities and the public spirit of the relative few. If the services of the few be rejected, can we expect to get far along that road? "If the blind lead the blind, shall not both fall into the pit?"

It may be that the cloud rising as these very words are written, the cloud rising over Quebec, will set our ship off on a new course. Leadership we must have. Vision we must have – a prophetic vision. Men rise, the poet says, "on stepping stones of their dead selves".

May Canadians, Anglophones and Francophones alike, find this capacity!

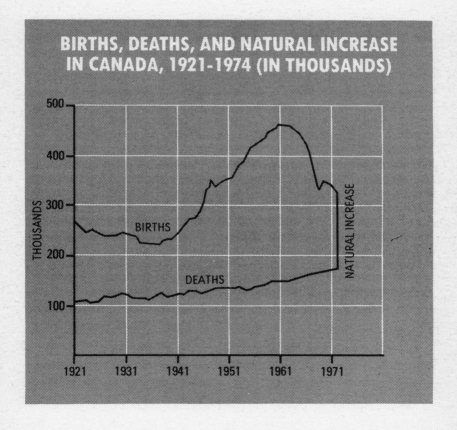

BIRTHS, DEATHS, AND NATURAL INCREASE IN CANADA, 1921-1974 (IN THOUSANDS)

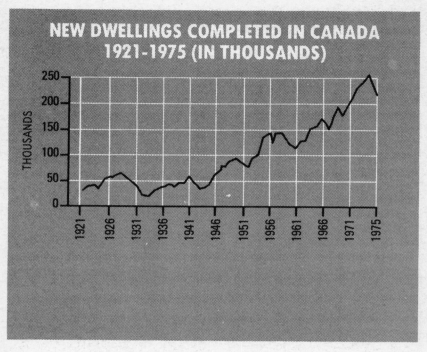

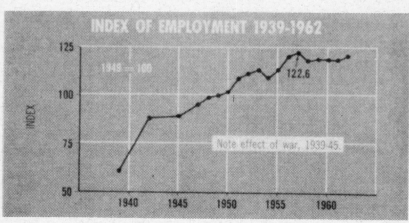

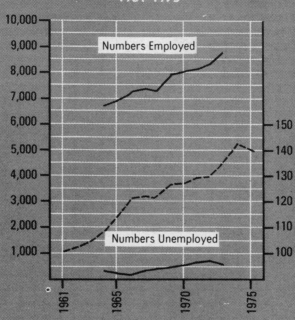

1964-1973
EMPLOYMENT AND UNEMPLOYMENT
IN ACTUAL FIGURES ——— ('000)
INDEX OF EMPLOYMENT ----- (1961 = 100.0)
1961-1975

Left-hand scale:
Actual numbers employed (top)
and unemployed (bottom) in
thousands depicted in solid lines

Right-hand scale:
Index numbers of employed persons,
1961 = 100.0
depicted in dotted line

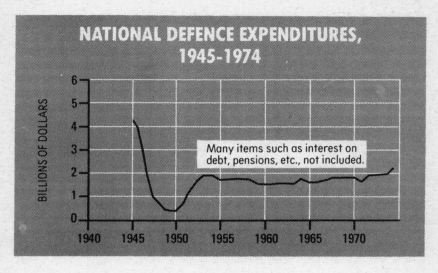

General References

Some references for "Additional Reading" have been placed at the ends of chapters following the Chronologies. Many of the books listed should be found in a good local library.

The following series will no doubt be found in practically all libraries, even the smallest. Though they are very old, they are still quite useful.

The Makers of Canada Series, London, 1926. 12 vols.

The Chronicles of Canada, Toronto, 1914-16. 32 vols.

Canada and its Provinces, ed. Adam Shortt and A.G. Doughty. Toronto, 1914-17. 23 vols. (This large series has a fair index volume which will enable items to be readily looked up.)

In addition there are for general reference the following:

The Canada Year Book. Queen's Printer, Ottawa.

The Dictionary of Canadian Biography. Stewart Wallace, compiler. Toronto, 1926.

The Encyclopedia of Canada. Ed. Stewart Wallace. Toronto, 1935-37. Supplement: Newfoundland, 1949.

Encyclopedia Canadiana. Ed. John T. Robbins. Toronto, 1963.

Canadian Annual Review. Ed. J.T. Saywell, Toronto. (Beginning in 1960, these volumes have appeared annually.)

The Canadian Annual Review of Public Affairs, Ed. J. Castell Hopkins. Toronto, 1901-1938.

A Historical Atlas of Canada, Ed. D.G.G. Kerr. Toronto, 1960.

The Canadian Historical Review (hereafter called *CHR*). Began publication in 1920. No student of Canadian history can afford to be without it, and without access to its files. The *Review* was preceded by *The Review of Historical Publications Relating to Canada* (Toronto, 1896-1922).

Canadian Historical Association (*CHA*) *Annual Reports.* Annual volumes as essential as the *CHR.*

The Canadian Journal of Economics and Political Sciences (hereafter called *CJEPS*). Mostly current economics, but has many articles of historical and political interest. In 1967, *CJEPS* was divided into two: *The Canadian Journal of Economics* and the *Canadian Journal of Political Science.*

Canadian Historical Association Booklet Series. These booklets are published from time to time and give good, brief treatment of specific subjects.

Some important books appearing since the above list was made, some bearing on the more recent period of Canadian history, are as follows:

Allen, Richard, *The Social Passion: Religion and Social Reform in Canada 1914-1928* (Toronto, 1971).

——, Ed., *A Region of the Mind: Interpreting the Western Canadian Plains* (University of Saskatchewan, 1973).

Beck, J. M., *The Shaping of Canadian Federalism: Central Authority or Provincial Right?* (Toronto, 1971).

Berger, Carl, *The Sense of Power: Studies in the Idea of Canadian Imperialism, 1867-1914* (Toronto, 1970).

Bernard, Jean-Paul, *Les Rouges: libéralisme, nationalisme et anti-cléricalisme au milieu du XIXe siècle* (Montréal, 1971).

Berton, Pierre, *The Last Spike: The Great Railway, 1883-1885* (Toronto, 1971).

Black, Conrad, *Duplessis* (Toronto, 1977).

Bradwin, Edmund, *The Bunkhouse Man: A Study of Work and Play in the Camps of Canada 1903-1914* (Toronto, 1972).

Brown, Robert Craig, *Robert Laird Borden: A Biography: I: 1854-1914* (Toronto, 1975).

—— and Ramsay Cook, *Canada 1896-1921: A Nation Transformed* (Toronto: 1974).

Buck, Tim, *Thirty Years: The Story of the Communist Movement in Canada 1922-1952* (Toronto: 1975).

Careless, J. M. S., *Brown of the Globe* (Toronto, 1959 ff.).

——, *The Union of the Canadas: The Growth of Canadian Institutions 1841-1857* (Toronto, 1972).

Cook, Ramsay, *The Politics of John W. Dafoe and The Free Press,* (Toronto, 1963).

——, *Provincial Autonomy, Minority Rights and the Compact Theory* (Ottawa, 1969).

Craig, G. M. *Upper Canada: The Formative Years, 1784-1841* (Toronto, 1964).

Creighton, D. G., *Canada's First Century, 1867-1967* (Toronto, 1970).

Dawson, F. McGregor, *The Conscription Crisis of 1944* (Toronto, 1961).

Dent, J. C., *The Last Forty Years: The Union of 1841 to Confederation* (Reprint, Toronto, 1972).

Diefenbaker, John G., *One Canada: Memoirs of the Rt. Hon. John G. Diefenbaker* (Toronto, 1975).

Fergusson, Bruce, *Hon. W. S. Fielding, I: The Mantle of Howe* (Windsor, Nova Scotia, 1970); *II: Mr. Minister of Finance* (Windsor, 1971).

Frégault, G., *Histoire de la Nouvelle France* (Montreal, 1967).

French, Goldwin, *Parsons and Politics: The Role of Wesleyan Methodists in Upper Canada and the Maritimes, from 1780 to 1855* (Toronto, 1962).

Graham, Roger, *Arthur Meighen* (Toronto, 1960 ff.).

Granatstein, J. L., *Canada's War: The Politics of the Mackenzie King Government 1939-1945* (Toronto, 1975).

Hodgins, Bruce W., *John Sandfield Macdonald 1812-1872* (Toronto, 1971).

Jamieson, Stuart Marshall, *Times of Trouble: Labour Unrest and Industrial Conflict in Canada, 1900-1966* (Ottawa, 1971).

Kilbourn, William, *The Firebrand* (Toronto, 1964). A Life of W. L. Mackenzie.

King, William Lyon Mackenzie, *Industry and Humanity: A Study in the Principles underlying Industrial Reconstruction* (Reprint, Toronto, 1973).

Laporte, Pierre, *The True Face of Duplessis* (Montreal, 1960).

Lévesque, René, *Option Québec* (Montréal, 1968).

Lower, Arthur R. M., *Great Britain's Woodyard: British America and the Timber Trade 1763-1867* (Montreal, 1973).

——, *My First Seventy-Five Years* (Toronto, 1967).

MacNutt, W. S., *The Atlantic Provinces: The Emergence of Colonial Society, 1712-1857* (Toronto, 1965).

Massey, Vincent, *What's Past is Prologue* (Toronto, 1963).

McKenty, Neil, *Mitch Hepburn* (Toronto, 1967).

McNaught, Kenneth, *A Prophet in Politics: J. S. Woodsworth* (Toronto, 1959).

Moir, John S., *Church and State in Canada West: 1841-1867* (Toronto, 1959).

Monet, Jacques, *The Last Cannon Shot: A Study of French-Canadian Nationalism, 1837-1850* (Toronto, 1969).

Morton, Arthur S., *A History of the Canadian West to 1870-1871* (Reprint, Toronto, 1973).

Morton, W. L., *The Critical Years; The Union of British North America, 1857-1873* (Toronto, 1964). # 12 in Canadian Centenary Series.

——, *Manitoba: A History* (Toronto, 1967).

Murrow, C., *Henri Bourassa and French-Canadian Nationalism: Opposition to Empire* (Montreal, 1968).

Neatby, H. Blair, *W. L. M. King, Vols. I, II, III* (Toronto, 1958-1977).

——, *The Politics of Chaos: Canada in the Thirties* (Toronto, 1972).

Neatby, Hilda, *Quebec: The Revolutionary Age, 1760-1791* (Toronto, 1966).

Neufeld, E. P., *The Financial System of Canada: Its Growth and Development* (Toronto, 1973).

Newman, Peter C., *The Canadian Establishment, I: The Great Dynasties* (Toronto, 1975).

Ormsby, Margaret, *British Columbia: A History* (Toronto, 1958).

Pearson, Lester B., *Mike: The Memoirs of the Right Honourable Lester B. Pearson 3 vols.* (Toronto, 1972 ff.).

Pickersgill, J. W., and Forster, *The Mackenzie King Record* (Toronto).

Pickersgill, J. W., *My Years with Louis St. Laurent: A Political Memoir* (Toronto, 1975).

Robertson, Barbara, *Wilfrid Laurier: The Great Conciliator* (Toronto, 1971).

Robin, Martin, *The Rush for Spoils: The Company Province, B.C. 1871-1933* (Toronto, 1972).

——, *Pillars of Profit: The Company Province, 1934-1972* (Toronto, 1973).

Rumilly, R., *Histoire de la province du Québec.* This many-volumed series now reaches up to 41 volumes.

Schull, Joseph, *Laurier* (Toronto, 1965).

——, *Edward Blake, Vols. I and II* (Toronto, 1975,1976).

Scott, J., *Sweat and Struggle: Working Class Struggles in Canada, 1789-1899, Vol. I* (Vancouver, 1974).

Sellar, Robert, *The Tragedy of Quebec* (Reprint, Toronto, 1973).

Smith, Denis, *Gentle Patriot: A Political Biography of Walter Gordon* (Edmonton, 1973).

Stanley, G. F. G., *Louis Riel* (Toronto, 1963).

——, *New France: The Last Phase, 1744-1760* (Toronto, 1968).

Stewart, Gordon and George Rawlyk, *A People Highly Favoured of God: The Nova Scotia Yankees and the American Revolution* (Toronto, 1972).

Thomson, Dale C., *Alexander Mackenzie: Clear Grit* (Toronto, 1960).

——, *Louis St. Laurent, Canadian* (Toronto, 1967).

Trudeau, P. E., *La fédéralisme et la société canadienne française* (Montréal, 1967).

Veilleux, Gérard, *Les Relations intergouvernementales au Canada 1867-1967* (Montréal, 1971).

Waite, P. B., *Canada, 1874-1896: Arduous Destiny* (Toronto, 1971).

Ward, N., *Party Politician: The Memoirs of Chubby Power* (Toronto, 1966).

Wood, Louis Aubrey, *A History of Farmers' Movements in Canada: The Origins and Development of Agrarian Protest 1872-1924* (Reprint, Toronto, 1975).

Colony to Nation

CHAPTER 1

The First Hundred Years of Europe in America

1. Expansive Forces Within Europe

The history of Canada must begin, as it were, pre-natally. The country of today was not born until generations of Europeans had tramped across the surface of the New World, had fought each other in its fastnesses, had given themselves in toil against the wilderness and had debated in their new homes the great questions that lie at the base of society. These men from overseas and that northern region into which they came, thrown together through four centuries of effort, brought to birth Canada, child of European civilization and the American wilderness.

All America might be said, in this sense, to have its fatherhood in that complex of European forces known as the Renaissance. A new and dynamic civilization had developed in medieval Europe. The scattered communities of feudalism had given way to great states. Some of the modern nations, such as England and France, had been built. Systems of law and administration had been formed. A money economy and intra-continental trade had taken the place of the barter and localism of manorial days. A middle class was growing up in the more advanced areas, the precursor of the capitalist class of later days. Considerable progress had been made in inventions and in the arts of life. Clothing, iron, and paper were all more abundant than a century or two earlier. Gunpowder had become an ordinary commodity; printing was common

Those who read the old Norse accounts of the Vinland voyages and compare them with the Columbian will see at a glance how much progress had been made in Europe in the five hundred years' interval: the Norse met the Skraelings on terms not far from equality, insofar as weapons went; but between the equipment of the Columbian discoverers and that of the natives, the gap was vast.

By the end of the fifteenth century, something like modern Europe had emerged. A similar way of life extended from the Mediterranean to the Baltic, from the Atlantic to the Vistula. In the north, Christianity had just pushed back the last of the heathen gods into the fastnesses of Karelia. In the east, Teutonic Knights, the outermost pillars of Christendom, were still engaged in wrestling from Slavdom souls for the Church and good lands for themselves. While the Turk remained seated firmly in the south-east, the other unbeliever, the Moor, had just been expelled from Spain. Europe, especially Latin Europe, was discovering its soul. Its energies were buoyant and youthful, fit for any task, ready for any adventure.

In the subtler aspects of civilization growth had been as marked as in the practical. The aridity of scholasticism was disappearing before the resurrection of the classical world. The intensity and passion of medievalism was mellowing and, in Italy especially, giving way to a tolerant open-mindedness that, like its counterpart, modern liberalism, passed over into elegant self-indulgence on the one hand and a scientific objectivity on the other. This objectivity permitted speculation upon the nature of man and the universe that would have been impossible earlier. Speculation led to observation, and observation led to extension of knowledge. All sciences grew rapidly, not least that group with which we are here primarily concerned, the astronomical and geographical. The conception of the earth as a sphere was becoming familiar to cultivated Mediterranean minds, and the old travel stories of the Polos about the marvels of a distant east were not forgotten. It may even be that echoes of the Norse voyages and of Greenland had been heard as far afield as Italy: there were few things that escaped the alert intelligences of Genoa, Florence, Pisa and the other northern Italian towns.

2. The Discoveries

The wider horizons of the spirit could not fail to evoke their counterparts in the physical world; consequently it may be said that the discovery of America lay in the logic of things. When the new civilization had grown to a certain point it burst its containing envelope, old Europe, and began to disperse itself throughout the world. If Columbus had not been the lucky man, there would soon have been someone else. America had to be discovered!

And it had to be discovered by an Italian, or at least a Mediterranean. Columbus brought his knowledge and his disposition towards scientific adventure from the most logical place; from a highly sophisticated Italian city state, where men had leisure for thought, uninhibited curiosity and a surplus of energy above mere subsistence. Like other great explorers, he came from a centre of civilization. He offered his knowledge and his skills in the most likely market, Spain, a rising state anxious to emulate the navigational feats of its neighbour Portugal. For the Italians, geographical science was interesting intellectual fare. For that marginal and maritime people, the Portuguese, it had been for a whole pre-Columbian century a matter of applied science in the interests of commerce. And now for the Spaniards, it was to be the occasion of dignity, power and profit. They were not long in realizing all three. Within less than a generation, the Atlantic coasts of both Americas had been laid open, and part of the Pacific coast too. The world had been circumnavigated. Gold, lands, and pomp had been obtained. Kingdoms had been conquered, cities founded. There remained only the tasks of detail such as the sketching in of local features, the penetration of the interior, the building of additional posts.

The discoveries rested on great individuals and on the organized power of states. Backward countries had little part in the process. The discovery of the New World represented no mass movement, no *Völkerwanderung*, such as had changed the face of Europe a thousand years before. It was aristocratic and classical, a new bud on the great Latin tree flung across the Atlantic.

3. The European Powers and America in the Sixteenth Century

If scientific curiosity and commendable personal ambition inspired the first great voyages, less worthy motives soon crept in. The New World became "a good thing". Greed awakened. A treasure house of riches stood revealed, and men hastened to possess themselves of them. Gold they had dreamed about, and gold, by great coincidence, they found. American gold changed the course of history. Peruvian gold destroyed the Peruvians, and by the habits it induced and the prices it set up, it almost destroyed the Spaniards for it encouraged all their worst characteristics. A people who had been fighting Moors in crusading fervour for seven centuries needed no inducements to cruelty; but when opposition was slight and greed great, cruelty mounted, and the natives were enslaved or extinguished. The backwash on Spain itself was sufficient to cripple native industry and to give the less fortunately situated northern races a chance to sell their wares in a luxury market. On rising Spanish prices, forced up by American gold, the English founded their new woollen export trade and flourished thereby, despite Spanish attempts to prevent the exportation of the imported gold. Spain moved into greatness on the wealth of her overseas possessions, but once the easy job of ruthless exploitation had been done, her progress stopped. As her empire expanded, she herself declined.

The lure of gold had led her men all over South America and over a good part of the north. Where no gold was to be found, they tried for other things. They had before them the example of the Portuguese and their spice islands; many good things, they knew, could come out of the heat of the tropics. And Europe hungered for good things. One of the best was sugar. Men everywhere have a sweet tooth, but before sugar became available, few there were who could satisfy their tastes. It was no accident that it was the queen who sat in the parlour eating bread and honey; ordinary people had to get along as best they could with beer and fat meat. Once sugar appeared, it added greatly to the joy of living and to the profit of the country that controlled the delectable lands from which the new supplies of it came—the West Indies, or "sugar islands".

With sugar, an agricultural product, came the need for labour. Lordly Spaniards did not go to the colonies to toil, so that it became necessary to find others to work for them. The native Indian seemed the natural solution, but he proved too proud or too tender and, consequently, as an alternative to slavery, died. A satisfactory substitute was eventually found in the African negro.

On gold, sugar and slaves, the Spanish and Portuguese colonies grew up. From Europe they were founded, and for Europe they existed. Those who came out to them sought fortunes, not homes; for almost all of them, the new world represented material gain. In America the exploitative attitude received from the first a strong emphasis.

One partial exception there was—the Church. In a religious age, the Church must have a large official place in the possession of a new world. To the credit of medieval Catholicism, its missionary instincts had never entirely faded, and with the prospect of new fields to conquer for the cross, they awoke to full life. In the Catholic world the evangelization of the natives, new souls for Christ, was always expressed as the foremost motive for overseas expansion. Nor did it remain merely a pious expression. Whether the discoverers and *conquistadores* wanted them or not, priests invariably accompanied the expeditions and devoted themselves to performing those rites that added souls to heaven. In the medieval Church, there was little incompatibility between the two types of men; for natives while being conquered could be conquered into the Church, and while being slaughtered could, by priestly miracle, be given entrance to the Christian heaven. But the latent humanitarianism of Christianity was bound to come to the surface, and it was not long before the Church was setting its face against the worst abuses. It became a moderating force and, true to Christianity's central concept that all men are equally the children of God, sought to shield its native converts from the white man. The results was a patriarchal attitude which, if it saved the natives from cruelty and death, tended to rob them of their own way of life and of their initiative. What neither aspect of white civilization—exploitative materialism or religion—would do was to leave the natives alone.

The division of the New World by the Pope between Spain and Portugal has often been decried in retrospect but it was quite a reasonable arrangement at the time. The Portuguese had been opening up new territories for a century and a half: they had already found the sea-route around the Cape to India. Spain had patronized the discoverer of America. They were the only two European powers that in a strict sense could be called maritime. They were the only two that had shown any interest worth mentioning in the discoveries and the problems growing out of them. The kings of France were more attracted by marauding expeditions into Italy. The English monarchy was absorbed in securing its own stability after the long anarchy of the wars of the Roses; Holland did not yet exist; and the Scandinavians, like the divided Italians, were too remote. Even the faint stir of interest shown by Henry VII of England when he made a gesture of assistance to the Cabots soon subsided. Spain and Portugal had a good case.

Since they naturally devoted their energies to the most profitable areas, they dismissed the coast of North America north of Florida with a cursory inspection. This left an opportunity for the more humble northerners, Englishmen and Frenchmen, to come in; but they were slow in availing themselves of it.

The Cabots, Italian geographers and navigators in search of patrons, had been fobbed off with a few pounds in England, most likely dismissed as innovating foreign nuisances. But the landfall they made in Newfoundland had results of its own, comparable almost to that of Columbus. For they found in those northern seas something that, to practical Bristol minds, was more valuable than gold: they found codfish.[1] To a continent that never had quite enough to eat, a new source of food supply was literally more valuable than gold. Consequently after

[1] See H. A. Innis, *The Cod Fisheries, the History of an International Economy,* rev. ed. (Toronto, 1954).

John Cabot's return to Bristol, others flocked out for the fishing, and the harbour of St. John's, Newfoundland, has never since been empty of ships. To the new southern staples on which Spain was building empires there was now added a northern, on which empires were some day to be built. Unlike the south, the north was not monopolized; nominally it was within the Spanish share of the tentative delimitation made by Pope Alexander VI, but to Spain it was of secondary interest. The delimitation, moreover, was indefinite and northerners did not regard it as law. None of them, however, had the organized power of a state behind them. They came as private parties, worked out their own arrangements on the spot as private parties and as private parties they departed. For nearly half a century no northern state took an official hand.

Among the fishermen there was no thought of settlement and permanent occupation; quite the contrary. Men who came to fish and remained to farm would be skilled hands lost to their employers. Worse, they might become business rivals, preparing and even marketing the fish without recourse to old country merchants. So whether the merchants who sent out the fishing expeditions were French or English, they were agreed in their hostility to any projects for settlement. Only gradually and reluctantly did they permit women to come out. Settlement in Newfoundland, based on codfish, came in time, but is was a long time. Meanwhile, French and English merchants from west-country ports brought home cargoes of the new food, or better still sent them down to Spain and Italy, where they sold them for Spanish gold. As their captains familiarized themselves with the opposite coasts, they went further afield, undertook more ambitious projects, and more especially, found that it paid to land their catch on a convenient shore and dry it.

The fishery in this way came to be divided into two halves: the green fishery—of cod caught off-shore, split and salted, and thence carried to Europe; and the dry fishery—of cod mainly caught inshore, cleaned, salted, and dried in the sun on the "flakes" still to be seen in any Atlantic coast village, and shipped to whatever market seemed best. Since northern Europe had its own abundant fisheries, it was the Spanish peninsula and the Mediterranean that provided the best consuming centres. Later on, after West Indian industry had become well organized and the slave population there had grown considerably, dried codfish from the north proved to be a cheap and economical food, so that another branch was added to this first northern staple trade. It was naturally the dry, or inshore, fishery that gave rise to settlement.

Within the limits of the sixteenth century, the codfisheries had not gone much beyond Newfoundland. In time all the Atlantic banks were exploited, and the exploitation was to be a factor in the occupation of the nearby coasts; but for the first hundred years, Newfoundland sufficed, and fishermen had little curiosity as to what lay round the next headland. Cabot had blazed a trail for them and that trail they were content to follow with little deviation. It is improbable that they had any contact of importance with the few natives of Newfoundland itself. On the other hand, some local products in addition to codfish may have come their way: sealskins and perhaps a few skins from inland like caribou and possibly beaver.

The next semi-public personage to come to northern waters, of whose voyage we have more than a mere mention, was Jacques Cartier. He seems to have kept his eyes open for valuables in fur, though his reason for coming was much the same as that of most other explorers: that is, sheer curiosity plus a bent towards adventure, cloaked in terms of science or of profit. Hailing from St. Malo, one of the French ports for the Newfoundland fishery, he would be familiar with its details, and in a subordinate capacity, he may have made the voyage before.[2] The hope of finding a north-west passage to the mysterious east or to those kingdoms from which the Spaniards were bringing back so much gold was a strong motive in his expedition.

Cartier's voyages have been made a great deal of in Canadian annals but the sum total of his achievements, viewed dispassionately, is not particularly great. Over parts of his route he had had two predecessors whose names are known, Jean Denys (1506) and Thomas Aubert (1508).[3] On his first voyage (1534), he followed a well-known route across to Belle Isle, ran down the Gulf past the Magdalens, and over to the Bay of Chaleur. Then he coasted the Gulf of St. Lawrence over to Anticosti Island, which may also have been known, and thence back to France. He had ascertained that the Gulf was no north-west passage, had erected a cross in a picturesque ceremony in Gaspé, had collected a short vocabulary of Iroquoian words, and had sailed a few hundred miles beyond the ordinary course of fishermen. His second voyage, the next year, was a little more ambitious: he penetrated the St. Lawrence up to the head of navigation at Hochelaga (now Montreal), wintered at Stadacona (now Quebec), and managed to keep himself and some of his crew alive during that very unusual experience. He returned to

[2] M. Gustave Lanctot, former Public Archivist of Canada, has offered convincing proof that Cartier, sailing with Verrazano, investigated the Atlantic coast of Nova Scotia and Newfoundland in 1524, ten years before the voyage heretofore recorded as his first, that of 1534. See his "Cartier's First Visit to Canada in 1524," *CHR, XXV* (Sept. 1944), 233-245.

[3] Lanctot, *op. cit.*, 241.

France in the spring, having in the grateful way of the times kidnapped a few of his Indian hosts as specimens to show off when he got home. His merit consists in his having been the first man to carry out a comparatively simple exploratory task and to record it in interesting detail.

His significance lies in his discovery that furs were to be had from the natives, and at the usual initial bargain prices, measured in trade goods. This discovery gave the French a second reason for their interest in what was already beginning to be called Canada, the lands about the Gulf of St. Lawrence, and although they did not follow it up vigorously, the connection Cartier had established was never entirely broken off again. We know that his heirs were granted some kind of trading rights, and they probably availed themselves of them to the extent of sending an occasional vessel to do a ship-to-shore trade. It has been conjectured that this obscure bargaining, possibly at the mouth of the Saguenay (where the Basques are supposed to have set up a whale fishery as early as 1544), may have set in motion Indian currents from the distant interior. Parties eager for French trade goods may at first have followed a difficult northern route to avoid the Iroquoian peoples on the St. Lawrence and at last have cleaned them out from their villages and rolled them back to where Champlain later found them. Whatever went on, little record remains, and official France stood aloof. It may be assumed that the long period from Cartier's last voyage or that of Roberval (1542-43) to Champlain's first (1603) saw the establishment in some form of what was to become the *raison d'etre* of New France, the fur trade.

If France displayed little interest in the New World, England until the reign of Elizabeth displayed even less. There are records of a few desultory private voyages that resulted in nothing, and that is all. The merchants of Bristol and other west country ports were doing well out of the new codfish trade, which took their vessels into the Gulf and perhaps a little distance up the river, but they were not interested in pushing on inland. When in Elizabethan times England began to get on its feet, the picture changed, at first through the efforts of buccaneers such as Drake. Voyages of exploration became numerous, especially into the North, and attempts were made at colonization. Then a group of colonial planners appeared, centring round men such as Hakluyt, Gilbert, and Raleigh, men full of big schemes for an English empire in the New World. These schemes were eventually to bear fruit, though not under the direction of their first proposers, but saving an abortive attempt at settlement in Newfoundland, none of them touched what is now Canada, and they do not concern us here. England does not come into the Canadian picture until long after Elizabeth was sleeping in the last of her famous beds.

The first hundred years of Europe in America close, insofar as what is now Canada is concerned, with relatively little done. The coastlines had become known in a general way; the St. Lawrence ascended as far as the first rapids; one staple trade and industry, the codfishery, had been strongly established; and another, the fur trade, just begun. To a great colonizing power like Spain, the northern part of the New World was an unconsidered trifle, and as such it was left to the somewhat barbaric peoples of the northern fringes of Europe.

Chronology

1492	Columbus discovers America.
1497	John Cabot's First Voyage.
1500	Newfoundland Codfisheries begin.
1524, 1534, 1535-6, 1541-2 Jacques Cartier's Voyages.	
1542-3	Sieur de Roberval's attempted settlement on the St. Lawrence fails.
1544-1600	Era of fishing and trading voyages to the St. Lawrence.
1584	Marquis de la Roche fails in an attempt to take a colonizing expedition to Canada; marks renewal of colonization interest on part of France.

Additional Reading

Biggar, Henry Percival. *The Voyages of Jacques Cartier*. Ottawa, 1924.

Brebner, J. B. *The Explorers of North America, 1492-1806*. New York, 1955.

Burpee, L. J. *The Discovery of Canada*. Toronto, 1944.

Innis, H. A. *The Cod Fisheries; the History of an International Economy*, rev. ed. Toronto, 1954.

Morison, S. E. *Admiral of the Sea; a Life of Christopher Columbus*. Boston, 1942. 2 vols.

Titles are not repeated from one chapter list to another.

CHAPTER 2

The St. Lawrence Portal

---

1. The French Background

The reason for the failure of France to take any significant part in over-seas enterprise during the sixteenth century is plain: during the first half of it she was remote from the new knowledge and uninterested, and during the second she was torn apart in the long agony of the Wars of Religion. Not until Henry of Navarre, as a former Protestant, had given toleration to the Huguenots[1] and had quieted his people by giving them good government, did the natural energies of France have opportunity to turn to the lands across the ocean.

Once order was restored, however, interest sprang up. At first it took the form of individual trading ventures based on an official grant of privileges. Most of these were directed to the region that was already vaguely becoming known as Acadia. The French had long been familiar with the southern coast of Newfoundland and Cape Breton Island: their fishermen had been landing and drying fish near the Gut of Canso, and some very probably had penetrated still farther west. In the interval since Cartier's day the coast of North America had become fairly well known. The advance to Acadia, therefore, represented no great feat of discovery. It was the natural place for the French to go; just beyond Newfoundland and removed a little from the land that God must have given to Cain, as Cartier had termed Gaspé and its neighbourhood.

[1] By the Edict of Nantes, 1598.

Many of the original concessionaires appear to have been Huguenots. This was to be expected, for Henry IV was not forgetful of his old co-religionists, and more than that, the Huguenots, like Calvinists everywhere, were linked closely with commerce and represented more than their numerical proportion of the trading energies of France.

Although they had few results of consequence at the time, these early trial trips of the Pont-Gravés, de Monts, de Chastes and others, did affect the future profoundly in that through them there were enlisted for France the services of Samuel de Champlain, a great imaginative intellect, a man of determination and vision without whom it is doubtful whether there would ever have been a New France in America. In his professional capacity of navigator and surveyor he accompanied the Sieur de Pont-Gravé on the latter's voyage of investigation up the St. Lawrence in 1603. The New World caught his imagination and he gave the rest of his life to it. Almost alone among these early Frenchmen he saw it in terms deeper than gain, deeper even than the extension of Christianity to the natives. He had a vision of empire and saw a new France in America. He is to be compared with that group of men who, in Elizabethan England, were dreaming the same dream in English terms and especially with one of them—Sir Walter Raleigh, the projector of commonwealths and the practical colonizer. Champlain's figure grows in retrospect, brooding over the portal to the distant interior that he uncovered, the city that he founded.

Even Champlain could do little until the confused situation in France was again resolved. There lay behind Acadian concessions a tangled web of religious jealousies, court intrigues and personal rivalries. Fear that the French Protestant faction might secure a hold on French America was evident from the beginning, and no less evident was the sordid play of selfishness around the court, based on the hope that some spectacular source of wealth would be discovered in the new lands. The example of Spain and its gold was too striking to be overlooked. Until something definite was known about the American lands and until the religious strife was stilled, little of significance could be accomplished overseas.

The religious problem was settled by the murder of Henry IV in 1610. Thereafter there was to be no question as to which creed was to be dominant in France and French possessions. Huguenot concession-aires soon disappeared and the New World was left to the old faith and to traders and explorers whose religious status was officially correct. The clarification of the question of faith meant a loss of commercial energy but this was compensated for by an access of religious zeal. As a result of 1610, the pace of exploitation was not to be so rapid in New France as it might have been; but the slow consolidation of a way of life was to be surer and deeper.

The first stone laid in this process, the corner stone of the whole French structure in America, was the building by Champlain in 1608 of the little post at the point on the St. Lawrence called by the Indians Quebec, "the closed-up place": the first point in from the sea where the big river narrowed down sufficiently to afford, in combination with a bend and an island (Orleans), a secure harbour for ships. All the effort involved in the founding of a people and in the exploration of a continent was to radiate from Quebec.

2. Opening Up the Continent:
Stages in Exploration and Routes to the Interior

The people, "les Canadiens", lay in the future: the task of exploration was immediate. The backers at home had to be given something for their money and it was now fairly evident that returns must come through fur if they were to come at all. The natives of the interior must, therefore, be sought out and induced to trade. The priests must also be given opportunity to establish contact with the Indians. But trade or no trade, Indians or no Indians, the great river would have had its way: no man with blood in his veins could have resisted the mystery of what lay beyond his sight, just round the next bend, and the next. The great river pulled men into the very heart of the continent and eventually, by the passage it gave, allowed them to follow the lure until they stood at last on the shores of the "Frozen and Pacific Oceans".[2]

Admittedly the fur trade served as the largest single component in opening up the continent, but the whole process was, for those engaged in it, a glorious game, the most enthralling of pursuits. Who would not today exchange all our mechanical gadgets, all our smooth way of living, for the chance to stand with Champlain and his companions there at the mouth of the French River when, first of white men, they gazed at the illimitable expanse of *la mer douce*, the "freshwater sea", Lake Huron!

The story of exploration is a large one, full of details which cannot be recounted here. Its various phases can, however, be distinguished and described so that an idea of it as a whole can be gained.

[2] Alexander Mackenzie, first man to cross the northern continent, called his book *Voyages from Montreal through the Continent of North America to the Frozen and Pacific Oceans in 1789 and 1793*. A standard work on exploration is J. B. Brebner, *The Explorers of North America, 1492-1806* (New York, 1955).

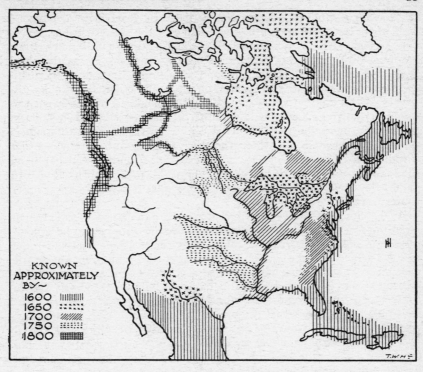

KNOWN
APPROXIMATELY
BY~
1600 ||||||||||
1650 ::::::
1700 /////
1750 ::::::
1800 ▬▬▬

A working distinction may be made between the discoveries and the explorations. The former word may be used to refer to the great sea voyages that brought the problem of a new world within the Old World's ken; the latter to denote the opening up of the interiors of the new lands, the filling in of details. In "discovery" in this sense, the French had little part; theirs was the work of exploration, and in North America they had the lion's share of this. Their work may be divided into four divisions, roughly chronological. The first includes the ascent of the St. Lawrence and the exploration of the Great Lakes basin, which was accomplished in about seventy years after the founding of Quebec, or say by about 1680. The second is concerned with the crossing of the St. Lawrence-Mississippi watershed (a feat that can easily be accomplished by portages of a few miles each at innumerable points from Lake Erie westward to Lake Superior) and the exploration of the Mississippi valley down to the Gulf of Mexico, a task associated with the immortal name of La Salle (1682). The main objective of this second phase, the

St. Lawrence-Gulf of Mexico connection, was reached in the second half of the seventeenth century, but many of the western tributaries of the Mississippi were not explored in their entirety until much later. Contemporary with this exploration there was going on as the third stage the establishment of a similar connection with the northern inland sea, Hudson Bay. Henry Hudson is usually credited with the discovery of this body of water in 1610, but it remained for the French to establish the route between it and the St. Lawrence. In their obscure journeys, around the middle of the century, Radisson and Groseilliers did not get down to salt water, though it must have been obvious that a route could be found.[3] In 1672, however (when Father Albanel made his journey overland up the Saguenay and down the Rupert River[4] to James Bay), the job was done, and in the next few years several other routes were also established.[5]

At the close of the seventeenth century, there remained—as the fourth large phase—only one outstanding task of exploration yet to be accomplished in North America and that was to complete the overland route to the Pacific. This the French never succeeded in doing, though in the next century, the eighteenth, they had a good try at it and one of their greatest names is associated with it. It was to be La Vérendrye's task to complete the water route west from Lake Superior to the western great lakes[6] and thence to reveal the prairies to the world. Whether his sons, who carried on his work, ever actually crossed the prairies and looked on the Rocky Mountains history does not say. Most probably not.[7] Before the French could go farther, Quebec had fallen and it remained to the English to finish their work.

Practically every expedition that added to knowledge of the interior, north, west, or south, had set out from Quebec, or its outpost, Montreal. Not without reason. When Europeans first gazed upon the North American coast, everywhere from Florida to Labrador, from tropics to arctic, they were confronted with a shaggy barrier of forest. They were forced into the openings that nature provided in the way of rivers, and once within the rivers, they felt the urge to ascend them. In this way it soon became evident that there were very few promising doors into the continent. The James River in Virginia, on which the English first settled, was wide at the mouth but its limitations as a road to the in-

---

[3] See Grace Lee Nute, *Caesars of the Wilderness* (New York, 1943).
[4] Not then so-called.
[5] Such as that used by de Troyes in his expedition against the English in 1686—up the Ottawa and down the Moose.
[6] Lake of the Woods is supposed to have been reached by Jacques de Noyon in 1688.
[7] They are supposed to have sighted the Black Hills of South Dakota.

terior were soon revealed when the "fall line"[8] was reached. Other rivers
flowing off the Appalachians were soon found to have the same feature.
Champlain was on the St. John early in the century, but though a large
river, it was a local watercourse, not a grand continental feature. The
Hudson proved more promising: from the seacoast it was tidal for
nearly two hundred miles, and that feature caused the Dutch to establish near the head of the estuary their post of Orange, now Albany.
Moreover, there flowed into the main stream an important tributary
from the west, the Mohawk, visibly leading between the mountains
which lay both to the south and the north. But in the gap and beyond
it lived the Iroquois Indians, friendly to the Dutch as long as muskets
and rum were forthcoming, but resolute in their opposition to the white
man's making a thoroughfare through their country.

In the distant north lay Hudson Bay. Its position in relation to the
St. Lawrence and to the interior would be plain from the first to any
good navigator, such as Hudson, who could keep track of his longitude.
Hudson Bay carried the sailor farther westward than any other body of
water north of the Gulf of Mexico.[9] The rivers flowing into it from the
west were numerous and large. One of them, the Albany, led westward
for hundreds of miles without a portage, but it came from nowhere in
particular. The only one that was really promising, the Nelson (and its
companion, the Hayes), the river that led back to Lake Winnipeg and
thence to the open prairies, was difficult of ascent. And then there was
the climate, the short open season. The Bay route was and is destined
to play a great part in Canadian history because it takes a ship into the
interior of the continent, but it has its handicaps, and for the seventeenth century, these were great.

At the other extremity, the Mississippi offered a channel of apparently
unimpeded navigation for thousands of miles in every direction above
its mouth, a natural highway of the most magnificent proportions; but
it too had its drawbacks. Floating down the rapid current to the sea
was easy, but it was a different story coming back. For canoe-travelling,
the Mississippi system was almost a one-way street. With the exception
of local expeditions up its lower tributaries, it did not provide the gateway to the interior that might have been expected of it, nor does it to
this day.

In all the vast stretch of coast line there remained only the St.

---

[8] The point at which the first rapids or falls occur up stream from seaward or
the rivers flowing off the Appalachians into the Atlantic coast. This "fall line"
occurring on nearly all these rivers, marks their western limits of effectiveness
for water travel.

[9] To about Long. 94°, W. as compared with Long. 98°, W. on the coast of
Mexico.

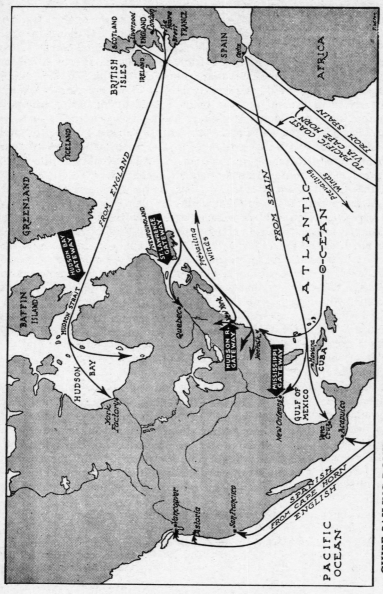

CHIEF SAILING ROUTES, EUROPE—NORTH AMERICA. CHIEF GATEWAYS TO THE INTERIOR

Lawrence. The magnificent stream and its great inland seas must have taken the breath away from those who first looked upon them. Nor did it offer many real difficulties of ascent: its rapids were strong and swift but not much portaging had to be done in the short trip of a hundred miles up to the head of the last of them (from Lachine to Prescott, in modern terms), and portaging soon came to be all in the day's work for the French. From the head of the rapids there was free sailing to Niagara Falls, and the Falls surmounted, there was easy ship navigation for a thousand miles.

As an alternative to the St. Lawrence with its rapids, there was another route. At Montreal, the Ottawa came in, a great river in its own right. Champlain's historic trip in 1615 established it as a relatively easy road to the upper lakes, a road that for almost exactly two centuries was to be taken in preference to the main river itself. The upper lakes themselves were not particularly dangerous for canoes. From French River to Pigeon River at the west end of Lake Superior there was an almost constant screen of islands along the north shore, and the prevailing north-west winds gave it the safety of a lee shore. On the south shores, easy portages led over the narrow height of land to water flowing southward: connection with the Mississippi system could be made almost anywhere.

For the period then, perhaps for all periods, the St. Lawrence and the lakes offered the most obvious and easiest of routes to the far interior, and it was for that reason that every exploration party of importance set out from Quebec and was French in its personnel. The French, having pre-empted the region around the Gulf, the St. Lawrence portal, had the key to the continent in their hands if they could but use it and keep it.

3. Clearing Out the Iroquois

French possession of this key was not to be without dispute: the history of Canada before the English conquest is a continual variation on the theme of contention for the St. Lawrence route and the prizes to which it gave access. From the beginning the French had to force their passage past the suspicious and hostile Iroquois, who were quite sagacious enough to see what the white man's game was. Before he came, they had ranged over a considerable extent of country, some of which they had subjugated, and they were by no means without trading experience of their own. As a partially sedentary group reaching the end of the fishing and hunting stage, they appear to have acted as "middlemen" between other tribes. From the first they seem to have been determined not to allow the whites direct contact with the peoples farther west, and it is probably for this reason, rather than from the accidental forays of Champlain against them, that they became inveterate enemies of the French.

Cartier had found an Iroquoian people as far down stream as Gaspé, and other Iroquois settled at Stadacona and Hochelaga. When Champlain came up the river, they were no longer there, probably having been pressed back by the up-country peoples anxious to take part in the ship-to-shore trade along the north shore of the St. Lawrence.[10] It was to be one of the main tasks of the French to press them back farther still. This involved several distinct operations. The St. Lawrence below Quebec was already clear of them, for the founding of Montreal in 1642 had secured the river between that post and Quebec. Champlain's inland voyage to Lake Huron, with the resulting relationships between French and Hurons, involved the adoption of the Ottawa route from the island of Montreal up, farther away from the enemy and not much longer. But the Iroquois disputed this route, and it was not made safe for the French until some years after the destruction of Huronia. The gallant stand of Dollard des Ormeaux at the Long Sault on the Ottawa (1660) must have impressed on the Iroquois the determination of their foes and contributed to the safety of the route.

The next step was to clear the St. Lawrence itself. This involved a long and difficult struggle lasting for over a generation and marked by such stirring incidents as de Tracy's campaign of 1666, Frontenac's building of Fort Frontenac in 1673, his subsequent invasion of the Iroquois' territory in 1690, and the Massacre of Lachine (1689), when the Iroquois carried fire and slaughter to the gates of Montreal itself. De Tracy, burning the villages in the Lake Champlain country and leaving the Mohawks to face a winter without provisions, taught a lesson that made the foe behave themselves for a considerable time. Frontenac was not so successful in his foray, but his building of the fort at the point where the St. Lawrence leaves Lake Ontario marked an extension of the French frontier from Montreal westward a hundred and sixty miles. This the natives were never again able to roll back. The Massacre of Lachine, though distressing, was only a temporary French reverse. This was the generation in which simple French settlers stood their ground against skulking Indian foes and won. It was the period of heroines like Madeleine de Verchères (1692), a period rich in the stuff of tradition, still vividly remembered by Canadians of French speech and the source of much of their spiritual strength today. English-speaking Canadians are the weaker for not possessing this trial-by-fire tradition.

[10] See p. 8.

By the eighteenth century the Iroquois barrier could be considered broken. The Iroquois Confederacy, having made a treaty of peace with the French, remained neutral throughout the weary length of Queen Anne's War.[11] There were no more serious raids on outlying French settlements, and by 1723 they had grown so weak as to permit the English to pass through their territory and establish Fort Oswego on Lake Ontario, an answer to Fort Frontenac. But it is to be noted that they did not allow themselves to be dispossessed of their lands. If they permitted the English troops and traders to pass through their territory, they did not yield to the English settlers until, having chosen the losing side in the American Revolution, they were dislodged and evicted once and for all.

4. The Wealth of the New World

The magnificent portal to the interior was almost too inviting. The French pushed in rather easily, found the natives (with the exception of the Iroquois) raising few difficulties, and in the fur trade hit upon a source of wealth which, if it was not as striking as the Spaniards' gold, did at least have the attraction that always attaches to high value contained within small compass.[12] Fur was a kind of mine product like Spanish gold, and it had much the same effect on those who sought it as mining does. It induced a hectic, gambling spirit which had its colourful side and threw off infinite incidental activity with all sorts of political repercussions, but it did not generate the plodding solidity of an agricultural society.

The fur trade was from the first based on the beaver. Beaver pelts could be "felted" and used for making the well-known beaver hats of the seventeenth and eighteenth century. These large, rich, and expensive hats, badges of social status to their wearers, were the foundation of the fur trade, furs for wearing apparel as they are used today being secondary in importance. Everyone in Europe with pretensions to "respectability" wanted a beaver hat, and when these had been furbished and refurbished through a chain of European owners, they could still be bought up and shipped out to South America to grace less particular heads. So close was the relationship between the fur trade and the beaver hat that when early in the eighteenth century fashion in Europe decreed that brims should be a little narrower, a crisis ensued in the backwoods of Canada.

[11] Or the War of the Spanish Succession, 1702-1713.
[12] The standard work on the fur trade is H. A. Innis, *The Fur Trade in Canada: An Introduction to Canadian Economic History.* (Toronto, rev. ed., 1956; also Canadian University Paperbacks, Toronto, 1962).

The first traders did not come in search of the beaver but stumbled upon it by accident. The Indians wore long fur cloaks made of beaver skin. For the traders, to see these was to covet them. The Indians wore little else but they traded in their cloaks all the same, and the traders found them smooth and sleek from contact with savage skins. The guard hairs had been worn away and a product usable at once had resulted. This was well named *castor gras*—fat, or greasy beaver, the choice article of the trade as long as used cloaks lasted. The beaver skins taken directly, *castor vert*, required more treatment before they could be felted but ultimately, in default of cloaks, came to be the mainstay of the trade.

The Indians were coaxed out of their cloaks by the usual assortment of trade goods. No one except the Catholic clergy had much conscience about the matter. The Dutch traded muskets to exterminate the Hurons and their Jesuit missionaries; Dutch, French, and later English traded hatchets, other tools and weapons, clothing, and above all liquor. Gaudy scarlet cloth (*écarlatines*) seems to have been one of the great desiderata and the records are full of French complaints about the cheapness of the English variety compared with their own. In liquor the French used brandy; the English, rum. Savage tastes were not particular, so that one was as effectual as the other in driving easy bargains and demoralizing the native. But rum was the cheaper, and the English had no Bishop Laval to rein them in. It was not long before the results of the competition were plain to be seen. Old and salutary habits of life were abandoned, independence and character lost, new diseases acquired and the whole structure of tribal life sent into decay. On the part of the French there is no evidence of the cruelty towards the Indian like that manifested by the Spaniard, and there was next to none of "the only good Indian is a dead Indian" attitude of the English. But whatever the attitude the consequences were much the same: whether the white man came to the Indian with Romanism or rum, bible or brandy, good intentions or bad, native life was shattered, borne down by the unfamiliar and complex civilization of the European.

The calamitous nature of the contact was one of the large factors in extending the area of the trade. When the beaver had been totally exhausted and the Indians completely exploited in one locality, it was necessary to push on farther and find new supplies of both. Thus the trade pushed its way across the continent, setting up a rhythm of its own as it went. At first the whole effort had been to induce the Indians to come down to the settlements with their furs. There a kind of annual fair would be held, at which trading, feasting, drinking and fighting would go on until the last skins had been handed over and the last Indian put out of commission.[13] For a variety of reasons, the next stage was to go up to the Indians. The traders wished to reach the Indians before the interloping English traders from Albany could get at them, and to head off their rivals. The Indians feared the Iroquois, began to realize their own bargaining power, and possibly attempted to preserve their own decency by keeping away from the posts. In this way many whites formed the habit of annual trips into the *pays d'en haut,* as it was coming to be called. There they felt as little restraint as the drunken Indians on the beach at Montreal, and it is not surprising that many of them did not come back to the settlers but, as *coureurs de bois,* "went Indian".

The third stage consisted in the establishment of posts in the upper country, either private ventures or government stations with an officer and a small garrison. These posts formed islands of security and order, and attracted neighbouring Indians. Again the Indian was coming to the white man. In the first outer ring of posts were such places as Niagara (1679) and Sault Ste. Marie (1670), but before the seventeenth century had ended, there were establishments all through the Great Lakes region and even well down the Mississippi towards the Gulf. The establishment of a post drew Indians from a certain radius; these brought in stories of still other Indians and still richer hunting grounds, so that one post begot another, until eventually—under the English— the continent was covered. As the post system extended, the problem of transportation down to Quebec increased in complexity; but as the extension was not overly rapid, there was time to build up a network that successfully served the fur traders down to the end of the era.

This system was based on the birch canoe, a gracious gift of the Indian to the white. The canoe had the advantage of ease of repair without tools, shallow draft, and extreme lightness combined with very respectable carrying capacity. Its crew carried it over the portages and it carried its crew over the lakes and rivers. With it the traveller could thread the wilderness as neatly as needle threads through cloth. The Indian canoes were soon adapted to the long trips of the fur traders; they became bigger, from two fathoms increasing to three, four, five, and eventually six. A six fathom canoe would carry its crew of six (bow- man, steerman and middlemen), along with five or six tons of goods, and could safely coast Lake Superior itself. A professional class sprang

[13] The saturnalian scenes that used to occur along the shore during the annual fur fair at Montreal have been vividly described by a contemporary, Dollier de Casson, in his *History of Montreal, 1640-1672,* ed. and trans. R. Flenley (Tor- onto, 1928). (This edition contains both French and English versions.)

up to man it, the *voyageurs*, skilled in the way of river and rapid, used to the bush and to the rough fare the bush necessitated. Trade goods became organized, neatly packed in bundles of uniform weight. On the return journeys the light and relatively fast canoes were well adapted to bringing back the precious bundles of furs, the be-all and end-all of the whole process.

The intrinsic nature of the fur trade compelled its return again and again to certain well-marked features. Of these the most conspicuous was monopoly, which had been readily established in marketing the furs but was more difficult to set up in buying them from the Indians. In New France, both before and after the English Conquest, new individuals were constantly obtruding themselves into the business but as constantly being shoved out. Since the supply of fur was never large in any given area, competition ran prices up at once and destroyed both the fur and the profits, thus forcing out the weak and bringing about combinations tending towards monopoly. Again, the vast distance to be covered from the ports to the interior and back necessitated careful organization, and the long period (three years or more) from the original investment to the sale of the furs, demanded substantial supplies of capital. This discriminated against the small man and favoured company organization. The delicately poised structure of the Canadian wheat trade, conducted over much the same route as the former fur trade, makes an instructive comparison in the study of our Canadian economy. The precarious nature of the fur trade, like the wheat trade, was forever causing endless inquiries, bitter internal feuds, perpetual re-organizations of control (mirrored in the innumerable trading companies in New France, some private, some co-operative, some under the authority of the state). There was the same suspicion of the outsider: just as Montreal today watches Buffalo and New York lest they drain off its wheat, so in the seventeenth century it watched the southerners lest they drain off the furs. This was a major factor in keeping the relations of the peoples concerned in a state of unrest that was never very far from the breaking point.

Montreal, in comparison with the English centres, Orange (Albany) and New York, was advantageously situated. It stood at the confluence of the Ottawa and the St. Lawrence and thus had two great natural highways leading down to it. And it was not far away from the Richelieu, which had a considerable basin of its own, including Lake Champlain. (The rapids on the way up to the lakes were not really major obstacles.) Orange, standing at the only practical water gap around the Appalachians, had the advantage of easy boat navigation from the sea to some distance up the Mohawk, but from that point, even if the Iroquois permitted, the traders had to carry their goods over a long trail through the bush until they reached a creek flowing down to Lake Ontario. Though their trade goods were cheaper than those of the French and the sea journey from New York easier and less expensive than that from Quebec, the English never managed to overcome Montreal's advantages, and in consequence that city remained the centre of the fur trade until the Hudson's Bay Company, with a salt water depot close to the best fur country, ran out the Nor'Westers in 1821.

Montreal's advantage, however, was never clear and decisive. The English were always a threat and when within fifty years of the original settlements, their colonies had grown to be thriving communities, they proved magnets to French traders, small and great. Ready money was forthcoming in the cities of the south, and despite threats and denunciations from government, furs often went down in exchange for it. Spanish dollars from the West Indies drifted up the Atlantic coast with the New England schooners and drifted into New France too from time to time. In an impecunious society, they were frowned upon and accepted. Neither English nor French could know that they were portents of the future—the forces of continentalism arrayed against the forces of the sea and of the blood. But they could be very clear as to what control of the fur trade meant, even though the size of that trade was in itself not impressive; it meant control of the continental interior—for those who had the eyes to see it one of the richest prizes then to be won.

Chronology

1589–1610 Henry IV King of France.
1610   Henry Hudson explores Hudson Bay.
1615   Champlain visits the Ottawa River, Georgian Bay, the Huron country and Lake Ontario.
1627   The Company of New France, or One Hundred Associates.
1631   Fox and James explore Hudson Bay.
1634–5   Lake Michigan discovered by Jean Nicolet.
1640   Lake Erie discovered by Chaumonot and Brébeuf.
1641   Raymbault and Jogues reach Lake Superior.
1645   Compagnie des Habitants succeeds Company of New France.
1659   Groseilliers and Radisson explore the country near Lake Superior.
1664   Canadian fur trade under the West India Company.
1666   De Tracy destroys the Mohawk villages.
1670   The Hudson's Bay Company founded.
1671–72 French expedition up the Saguenay to Hudson Bay.
1673   Fort Frontenac built by Frontenac.
1679   Dulhut visits the Sioux country.
1682   La Salle descends the Mississippi to its mouth.

1688   Jacques de Noyon explores the Kaministikwia route to Rainy River.
1689–90   Last Iroquois War.
1700   Compagnie du Canada formed in Canada for management of the
            fur trade.
1717   Compagnie d'Occident; granted twenty-five years monopoly of the
            export trade.
1723   Oswego founded.
1731   La Vérendrye begins his western explorations.

Additional Reading

Bishop, Morris. *Champlain, The Life of Fortitude.* New York, 1948.

Bishop, Morris. *White Men Came to the St. Lawrence: The French and the Land they Found.* London, 1961.

Bonnault, Claude de. *Histoire du Canada français, 1534-1763.* Paris, 1950.

Eccles, William John. *Frontenac, The Courtier Governor.* Toronto, 1959.

Groulx, L. A. *La Naissance d'une race.* Montreal, 1930.

Innis, H. A. *The Fur Trade in Canada; An Introduction to Canadian Economic History,* rev. ed. Toronto, 1956. (Canadian University Paperbacks, 1962).

Parkman, Francis. *Count Frontenac and New France under Louis XIV.* Boston, 1877. For New France, all of Parkman's books should be noted. His is a great "classical" history, fascinating in both matter and manner. Although published many years ago, it is still for the most part valid, subsequent research having changed only detail.

Salone, Emile. *La Colonisation de la Nouvelle-France.* Paris, c1906.

CHAPTER 3

The Faith and the Church

1. The French Counter-Reformation

The colonizing effort of France could not have begun at a moment more propitious for Christian missionary effort. The long Huguenot wars were over. The Catholic zeal generated by the struggle and stimulated by the results of the Counter-Reformation in Europe was mounting steadily. The Huguenots had never been more than a fraction of the population and now they were hived off by themselves in their own cities, well out of the main course of the nation's life. The new currents spreading through France represented the élan of a reviving French Catholicism but a Catholicism which was very definitely French and northern. It was not particularly intellectual; it was not particularly artistic. As intolerant as all fervent religions, it yet had little of the cunning subtlety or the cruelty of the true Latins beyond the mountains. It was enthusiastic, serious, moral, evangelistic, mystical. The Catholicism of the French Counter-Reformation was a warm faith, full of visions and of harmless miracles, strict in the standards of conduct it enjoined on its adherents. For those whose roots lie in nineteenth century Protestantism it diffused, save for its ritual and its sacramental basis, a religious atmosphere not too difficult to understand: it was a kind of nineteenth century Methodism in a seventeenth century Catholic setting.

Behind the church stood the power of a state fast rising to the leading place in Europe. The regency which followed Henry IV was congenial to piety, and in a few years the great Cardinal-statesman of France, Richelieu, was to mount into his place of power (1624). He did not share the transports of the zealots, but as a realist concerned in forcing the country into political unity and divesting the Huguenots of special privilege, he was glad to encourage enthusiasm in the faith, both at home and abroad. The French colony from the first was planned and managed by both state and church. A theocracy in as intense a sense as the Massachusetts Bay of the period 1630-1685, it was without the strong lay element of that colony and without its intellectualism.

2. The Missionary Movement

The revived religion was above all things missionary. It had reclaimed France, and Catholicism elsewhere had evangelized much of the outer world. There were great deeds and great men to emulate. Hence all enterprise in the New World had to wear an official Catholic character and to make provision for the evangelization of the natives. Traders and companies usually had to agree to take out priests on their ships and to afford them facilities in their labours. At first the missionary task was entrusted to the Récollets, but this order's lack of financial resources crippled its efforts and after ten years (1625) it gave way to the Jesuits. It was the Jesuits who constituted themselves *par excellence* the soldiers of the cross in French America. As educated men they were able to learn Indian languages and to make grammars and dictionaries for purposes of translation. The order was rich and could finance ambitious projects such as the establishment of the Huron missions. The zeal of its missionaries was unremitting. Many of them earned the martyr's crown and left to French Canada a record of unselfish heroism that constitutes one of its proudest and most vital traditions.

Missionary effort met with no marked success until the Huron missions were founded in the 1630's. The Hurons were among those Indians who had been bringing their furs for barter down to Quebec, and they were willing to accept white men to live among them. They may have had some idea that the presence of the strangers, with their guns and their magic rites, would afford them protection from the Iroquois enemy. For the Jesuits, their villages—fairly close together in what is now Simcoe County, Ontario—and their more or less settled way of life offered advantages over the nomadism of the Algonquin tribes. It is always difficult to judge of the success of missionary enterprise. Natives may conform to the white man's wishes easily enough in what to them may be the exterior things of attendance at a church service or participation in the rites, without having undergone any change of heart: even today while most Indians are nominal Christians, their Christianity is usually of a special Indian variety that does not involve any drastic break with the old beliefs. Confronted by problems of this sort Protestants everywhere have slid easily away from the simple problem of faith to efforts at creating an imitation of their own western way of life, trying to inculcate the same habits of conduct and morality in others that they themselves follow. Catholicism, being a sacramental religion, has been primarily concerned with Christianity as a species of legal status consisting in rites such as baptism and absolution. Since it is easier to administer the last rites of the church to a dying heathen and gain his soul for heaven than it is to persuade a young and healthy pagan to forsake his own way of life, Catholicism has had a numerical success in the extension of the faith that has not usually attended Protestantism.

The Jesuits had a good deal of this type of success among the Hurons and it is possible that in time they might also have brought them fairly close to the French way of life. But the opportunity never came, for the whole gallant endeavour went down to destruction in the Iroquois raids and massacres of the 1640's. Against the Iroquois with their Dutch muskets the Hurons did not have a chance; missions were destroyed, villages were burned, the Hurons as a tribe were reduced to a few survivors and driven from their lands. In that orgy of fire and slaughter the two most famous martyrs, Lalemant and Brébeuf, met their deaths.

After the destruction of Huronia, Jesuit missionaries ranged farther afield; Père Marquette, a Jesuit, was co-discoverer with Joliet of the Mississippi (1673). They even attempted (with modest results) the conversion of the Iroquois themselves. They were to be found wherever there was a French trading post, and beyond. Eventually many of the Indians became nominal Catholics (as they still are). The Jesuits were inspired in their task by the example of Paraguay, the Jesuit-Indian state of South America, a preserve of the Cross under the King of Spain, where white civilization was carefully filtered through the sieve of Catholic piety before it was allowed to enter. If something similar was their objective in North America, they never had a chance of realizing it, for the Indians were too scattered and the French authorities at no time showed any inclination to pursue other than a mixed secular and religious policy. In the end Catholic missionaries had to be content with their own piety and with humble native congregations; except for the tradition of devotion and valour they bequeathed to French Canada, they have had little effect on the history of the Canadian people.

They did have to their credit two specific accomplishments of the highest order. One was the publication in France of the annual volume of letters and accounts from the mission fields. The *Relations,* as they were called, coming out year after year, made absorbing reading and enjoyed a wide circulation.[1] Their effect in making the New World known in France and in directing towards it some of the current religious zeal was great, so great that there is an immediate connection between them and the next specific accomplishment, the founding of Montréal (1642).

Here was a deed than which there could have been none more significant and, at the time, more daring. Quebec was still a struggling little frontier post with a corporal's guard of men about it and hardly a permanent resident when Maisonneuve came out from France, bringing with him new priests, pious ladies, nuns and settlers, in a move that was to advance the frontiers of the Kingdom (in the minds of his company that word meant the Kingdom of Heaven rather than the Kingdom of France) one hundred and seventy-five miles farther into the realm of heathen night. All had been prepared beforehand, miracles had duly occurred and the site had been revealed to the faithful from on high. Everyone understood that the proximity of the Iroquois to the proposed settlement constituted a peril of the first magnitude, but to plant the cross defiantly in such a place was greater glory to God. Piety is not without its relation to shrewdness and certainly the founders of Montreal had chosen shrewdly.[2] At the head of navigation, at the junction of the two great alternative routes to the interior, not far from the route from Lake Champlain, on a large and fertile island, and with the amenities of natural beauty, the new settlement surely had a future. The metropolis of Canada, as it is today, bears witness to the wisdom of its founders. Their motives have sometimes been assailed, and it has been suggested that it was facilities for Indian trade rather than for the salvation of Indian souls that took them there. The indictment will not stand. The possibilities of trade could not entirely have escaped acute minds, but they were not the determining factors. Ville Marie de Montréal was founded "for a testimony". The glory of God came first, the advance of the fleur-de-lis next, money motives far behind.

Montreal and the Huron missions represented the climax of the mis-

[1] The *Relations* have been republished. See R. F. Thwaites, ed., *The Jesuit Relations and Allied Documents,* 73 vols. (Cleveland, 1896-1901). There is a fairly complete "run" of the original volumes in the Public Archives of Canada. An abridgment is *The Jesuit Relations and Allied Documents: Travels and Explorations of the Jesuit Missionaries in North America, 1610-1791,* selected and edited by Edna Kenton (New York, 1925).
[2] See p. 22.

sionary crusade. Much activity went on throughout the French regime,[3] but the spring-time fervour gradually cooled off, martyrdoms ceased and the evangelization of the Indian proceeded at a more plodding gait. If the French had shown the same zeal in colonizing as in missionary work, the racial situation in North America might have been different today.[4]

3. The Church in the Colony

In contrast with the growth of missions and of the knowledge of the interior, the colony grew slowly, and it was years before a church establishment for French settlers received much attention. Not until 1658, when François de Laval was appointed Bishop at Quebec,[5] did it receive formal organization: the bishopric of Quebec was not erected until 1674. The decision to maintain the colony as a preserve of Catholicism had long since been taken, and the church in one other respect had also been strongly founded. Through its orders, it had received numerous grants of land, some of them very strategically placed, such as that of the Sulpicians, who received the seigneury of the island of Montreal in 1663. When Laval landed, the Roman Catholic church was already strong in property.

It had as a matter of course assumed the ancient functions of the European church. The community that gathered round each country church soon came to have an organic unity about it. The parish became the natural subdivision of the countryside, comprehending most of the life of its people: their social occasions, their religious occasions, their marryings, their buryings, and their business went on within its bounds, and often within earshot of the church bell. The parish churches were a species of communal hearth: they became repositories for the parish records of births, marriages, and deaths; they became semi-public institutions, where public proclamations and notices were given out—a link between the central government and the countryside, as to some extent they still are. Within a few years, or by 1667, the parish curés were to

---

[3] And still goes on: French Canada today is said to support a missionary effort abroad many times greater in proportion to population than that supported by the wealthy Catholic population of the United States.

[4] See E. R. Adair, "France and the Beginnings of New France," *Canadian Historical Review*, XXV (Sept., 1944), 246-278. This article describes the whole complex of organization, piety, finance, and bigotry that lay behind the missionary effort and also explains the "miracles". Much of it turned on La Compagnie du Saint Sacrement, a "17th century combination of Oxford Group and Carnegie Endowment".

[5] Titular Bishop of Petraea.

get the right of tithe, one twenty-sixth of the grain harvest of the parish. Yet the church was not "established" in the English sense, for no formal act made it official; as in medieval Europe, church and state were obverse and reverse of the same coin.

The personality of Laval determined the nature of the church of French Canada, which has never deviated from the course upon which he set it. He was strong-willed, haughty, jealous of power, a Puritan in morals,[6] a zealot in faith, a genuine child of the French Counter-Reformation. His formative years had been passed under the tutelage of the Jesuits in the minority of Louis XIV, during the regime of Mazarin and the confusion of the Fronde. This and the zeal of *La Compagnie du Saint-Sacrement*[7] may have inclined him to look, not at the majesty of the French throne (not impressive during those years), but to the great centre of the faith beyond the Alps. He proved strongly ultramontane in his attitude, jealous of the privileges of the church as opposed to the state, jealous of his prerogatives as Bishop, jealous of his personal dignity in the presence of the Governor.

After Laval had left for the New World, division arose within the Church of France. Louis XIV was growing into a magnificent national king, against whose will the proudest of the prelates would hesitate to assert himself. It was natural that nationalism should be reflected in the Church. It took shape in the Gallican party whose contention for the so-called "Gallican Liberties"[8] would, if it had been successful, have gone far to make the church in France a French rather than a Roman Church. The division from within toned down the zeal of the French Counter-Reformation; the second half of the seventeenth century was cooler, more formal than the first, while the first half of the eighteenth was worldly. But this struggle within the church had little echo across the Atlantic. In distant New France, Laval, never faltering in his proper loyalty to his royal master, was laying the foundations of an ecclesiastical system that, within the general orbit of that loyalty, was to become as strong as the state itself.

From the first, education was in the hands of the church, as it still is.[9] During the continuance of the French regime no lay element of importance entered, except, towards the end, in one area—the teaching of medicine, not an overly significant occupation in a small colony. What

---

[6] He strongly opposed the first balls and the first dramatic offerings to be presented at Quebec. As his opposite numbers in Protestantism also held, they were works of the devil.
[7] See p. 29.
[8] Used by Louis XIV as a weapon in his quarrel with the Pope, 1682
[9] As it was everywhere else during the 17th century.

primary education existed was provided by the parish priest or by the monastic orders. As secondary education emerged, it too was the affair of the church. The crown of the edifice, the Seminary of Quebec, from which Laval University descends, was naturally a department of the church. Since there were few openings for bright boys in New France, it was little wonder that under the watchful eyes of the curés a high proportion of them entered the ranks of the clergy, which thus tended from the beginning to be a kind of élite, a chosen band with few limitations to its functions.

For many years natives of old France formed the bulk of the priesthood, but as the generations wore on, the proportion of Canadians steadily increased. This naturalization of the clergy had its advantages and disadvantages. The Canadian priests, drawn from the peasantry, were at one with their people: they were the natural shepherds of their flocks. They were also provincials, with little experience except in their own small corner of the world. Their culture was not as wide as that brought over from France by highly trained Jesuits and Sulpicians, but this lag in culture in the generation following the original immigrants is a familiar story in all new countries, a stage that must be worked through as a new society forms itself. It was as nothing compared with the priceless asset of the curé's closeness to his people. When the evil days of conquest came, he had been fitted by circumstance to become their natural leader, their comfort in tribulation. He retains his strength to this day, and he draws it from the same source and from the gratitude carried down from those troubled times.

This select body of men Laval welded into an order. With minor exceptions, none of which persisted long, they were never allowed to become independent incumbents of a "living" as had been the case in the Old World. Their charge was strictly the cure of souls, they were instruments of a purpose, and they were never allowed to develop any proprietary rights in the glebes and presbyteries they occupied. They were missionaries, fighting troops, to be moved about from station to station at the discretion of their commander, the Bishop. The instrument Laval fashioned, one of absolute authority after the Jesuit pattern, has proved its strength, for in Quebec it still endures.

In the latter part of the seventeenth century, churches began to rise in numbers along the banks of the St. Lawrence as new parishes were erected and as old frame buildings were burned. Some of those erected shortly after this period, in the first quarter of the eighteenth century, still exist. Today, with their good proportions and their bright white and gold interiors in the style of Louis Quinze, they are show places, beautiful monuments of an age that had taste even in a distant colony, strong contrasts to the pretentious ugliness of many of their modern neighbours. These solid stone churches signalized the transition from a stage of pure adventuring, when the very possibility of a colony was in doubt and when attention was mainly on the high calling of the missionary, to a day of assuredness. People had come to Canada to stay, their sons were succeeding them, farm house and manor house were rising in what was becoming a quiet countryside, and the parish church took its natural place as the centre of it all.

In Protestant settlement it has been the invariable experience that the more ritualistic (or more dignified) creeds have little success in the newer areas: the pioneer has demanded his religion simple and strong. Hence in North America the Anglican church has been weak in frontier regions, other denominations such as Baptist and Methodist strong. How does it come, then, that Roman Catholicism, the most ornate and sophisticated of all in its ritualism and symbolism, should have stood the shocks of frontier life so well?

For one thing, Roman Catholicism affords no series of alternative, as does Protestantism: the French pioneer could not leave one church and associate himself with another. Secondly, the authoritarian basis of Catholicism keeps its adherents together; Protestantism being individualistic, it cannot avoid shattering into innumerable sects. Individualism in this Protestant sense was entirely lacking in New France. The only place for the man who did not see eye to eye with his neighbours in matters of belief and behaviour was the forest, and to the forest he usually went, there to waste his non-conformism on the desert air and an Indian wife. A further and better reason for the survival of Catholicism in a frontier setting lies in the genius of the French, which differs entirely from that of the English. The English separate themselves from home and family with ease and cheerfulness; they dislike the cramping atmosphere of a small community. The French cling to the ties of mutual support. They dislike going away from the near and the familiar; they accept and enjoy the life of small communities. They, therefore, also accept the rules of the game, one of which is Catholicism. The success of Catholicism in meeting the disintegrating influence of the frontier has rested on simple traditionalism plus the faithfulness and intelligence of the average priest performing his duties in an environment with which he was thoroughly familiar and among people of whom he was one.

Catholicism, for these many reasons, suited the French. It suited and helped to form the society which they established in North America. A religion which placed its emphasis on life, not on the means of living, suited a simple peasantry close to the soil. Their business was not like the English to "make good", but to "make land" (that is, to clear it) and to "make land" many hands were necessary. Nature responded, as she always does. Practically all pioneer peoples are prolific, the transplanted French were especially so. There was lack of neither food nor function for every new child. A socially minded people saw no evil in being surrounded with their own, and in the swift, steady widening of the family connection. Quite the reverse. They found happiness in life, not in things. A new and larger house meant less to them than sons and daughters growing up in the neighbourhood. This other-worldliness, still so marked in the countryside of Quebec and not at all divorced from practical wisdom, was reinforced by the immemorial teaching of the church. Life was but a brief moment, a short prelude to eternity, and man's real life began hereafter. An intense belief in immortality works profound effects on the manner in which a people lives. Catholicism and the countryside, simple French peasant traditions as old as agriculture, and the French joy in human companionship came together into a strong complex which to this day has not given ground. Of the two branches of French religious effort in North America, the missionary, much the most spectacular to begin with, was destined to yield in importance to the social religion of the countryside, which endures to the present and, whatever the term may mean, makes of French-Canadianism a spiritual concept in the minds of the members of the race to be upheld at whatever cost.

Chronology

1534   The Society of Jesus founded.
1562–94   Huguenot wars.
1598   Edict of Nantes.
1615   Récollet mission established in Canada.
1625   Jesuit missionaries arrive.
1627   Huguenots excluded from Canada.
1639   Ursuline nuns and Sisters of the Hôtel-Dieu arrive at Quebec.
1642   Ville Marie de Montréal, founded by Maisonneuve and the Company of Notre Dame de Montréal.
1643   Father Jogues rescued from Iroquois by Dutch.
1643–61   Mazarin, chief minister in France.
1644   Father Bressani captured by Iroquois, ransomed by Dutch.
1649   Martyrdom of Brébeuf and Lalemant.
1653   Arrival at Montreal of Marguerite Bourgeoys, founder of the Congregation of Notre Dame.
1657   Sulpician priests arrive.
1659   François de Laval-Montmorency arrives at Quebec.
1663   Seminary of Quebec founded.
            The Seminary of St. Sulpice receives the seigneury of Montréal from the Company of Notre Dame de Montréal.

1665   Father Allouez establishes a mission on Lake Superior.
1669   Father Allouez establishes a mission at Green Bay.
1674–88 Laval, Bishop of Quebec.
1682   Quarrel between Louis XIV and the Pope, and proclamation of
         Gallican principles by the French Bishops.
1685   Revocation of the Edict of Nantes.

Additional Reading

Adair, E. R. "France and the Beginnings of New France." *CHR*, XXV (Sept.,
  1944), 246-278.
Frégault, Guy. *La Civilisation de la Nouvelle-France*. Montreal, 1944.
Gowans, Alan. *Church Architecture in New France*. Toronto, 1955.
Kenton, Edna, ed. *The Jesuit Relations and Allied Documents: The Jesuit Mis-
  sionaries in North America, 1610-1791*. New York, 1925.
Parkman, Francis. *The Jesuits in North America in the Seventeenth Century*.
  Boston, 1867.
———. *The Parkman Reader*. Boston, 1955.

CHAPTER 4

A Province of France Overseas

---

1. Government, Law and Institutions

The authority of the state entered the French new world much as it did the English.[1] There were at first ceremonial possession-takings (like that of Cartier), followed by individuals and companies that had obtained some kind of authority from the court, usually in the form of a concession or grant empowering them to do certain things, such as monopolize trade or maintain order and justice. These early documents were not as precise as those given in England; there was little in the French grants resembling the exact terms and legal formality of the charters to the Virginia Company and the Company of Massachusetts Bay. In part this arose from the ease with which the authoritarian French crown could change its arrangements. In part it was because there was in France (prior to the movement which resulted in the founding of Montreal) no such fund of knowledge, intelligence, and zeal for an overseas effort as in England. The Virginia Company represented a "promotion" of colossal magnitude for a small state like the England of 1606: in its combination of men seeking profit, visionaries of Empire, adventurers, it became a national project. In France there was nothing parallel. The early concessions were given and expressed loosely, and the colonizing

[1] For a general view of French colonial government, see Gustave Lanctot, *L'Administration de la Nouvelle-France* (Paris, 1929).

effort was limited to a few conventional objectives tacked onto the document. Usually priests were to be taken out, and so many colonists a year were to be settled. Needless to say, such conditions were rarely observed.

Richelieu's Company of New France (Company of One Hundred Associates, 1627) was an attempt to do things on a larger scale and in more precise form. The company had monopolistic trading rights, large powers of government, and the usual obligations. New France, however, like parts of New Spain, remained cursed with an easy staple, fur; and where wealth was to be got through the staple by the concessionaires, they would not bother much about the arduous business of building a new society. Moreover, fur and agriculture were incompatible, and the Company of New France, like its English counterpart of later days, would hardly cut its own throat by introducing settlers to drive away the animals. The colony remained in the doldrums until more active direction came from France. In 1661 Louis XVI's minority ended. Whatever history may make of that king's title to greatness, his energy and practical nature are not in dispute. He surrounded himself with efficient ministers, one of whom, Colbert, bears a great name in French history. The two men between them worked out policies designed to advance the interests, wealth, and greatness of France. The military and political schemes for the extension of French boundaries that involved him in wars with all his neighbours and finally in the great world war of the Spanish succession were the king's contribution, while Colbert furnished the housekeeping wisdom identified with his name, *Colbertisme*, a kind of early state socialism, a mercantilism of both an internal and an external type.

Colbert's idea for the colonies was reflected in his appointee as intendant, Jean Talon, the first Canadian administrator of note. The two of them tried schemes of all sorts, from promoting shipbuilding to promoting propagation,[2] in an effort to make something of the rather pathetic little establishments along the St. Lawrence River. The main expedient had to do with control. It was decided that New France would be brought directly under the Crown, much as Virginia had been in 1624, or Massachusetts Bay was to be in 1685, when the charters of those two colonies were rescinded and royal appointees sent out as governors. The colony was to be given the organization of a province of France. This involved considerable machinery of government, and for the constitutionalist it presents some nice problems in the delegation of power on the part of an absolute ruler.

---

[2] The famous *filles du roi* experiment that involved recruiting young women and sending them off to Quebec by the ship-load for marriage to the bachelors of the colony.

The provinces of France in the seventeenth century fell into two classe, *pays d'états* and *pays d'élection*: the former were those which had local *estates* or assemblies, the latter were those which had no trace of representative government. A king whose considered policy it was to avoid calling the States-General or even to allow administrative machinery to take on a permanent form could be counted upon not to add New France to the *pays d'états*.[3] The form of government chosen resembled the *pays d'élection*, on to which was grafted the more recent French administrative division, the *géneralité*. Both units in New France, though not in Old, coincided with the episcopal diocese. Since the great feudal appanages of the Crown had lost their semi-independent status, governorships of provinces were offices of great dignity but not of impressive power; they were often awarded in order to keep Richelieu's unemployed nobles from making themselves nuisances. But in New France, with the king 3,000 miles away, the governor was no mere *magnifico*. He soon realized his importance and tended to give himself viceregal airs,—something he had no right to do, for, as the Intendant Dupuy was to say later on, the king never delegated all his authority to anyone. From the governor there derived a little hierarchy of similar officials, delegates of his responsibility. There were governors at Montreal and Three Rivers and in the far interior, post commandants, all answerable to the governor at Quebec.

The office that had been one of the main instruments in the centralization and de-feudalization of the administration of France was that of the *intendant*, a term which will nearly bear the English translation *superintendent*. The official title gives an idea of the range of his functions: *intendant de justice, police et finance*—superintendent of the king's justice, of his peace, order, and good government, and of his income and expenditure. These powers were wide; in internal administration they were almost unlimited. The intendant was the great local Pooh-Bah. The range of his powers left the governor, the titular head of the colony, with little to do except in wartime when military exigencies placed him in command. But French law never clearly demarcated the spheres of the two officials, either in France or Canada. In France, they had been created as circumstances dictated and, in a despotic monarchy, were intended to get in each other's way. With something of the same over-subtle purpose the French government, fearful of placing too much power in the hands of a single distant official, instituted the

---

[3] Louis XIV was so jealous of anything of a representative character that he even objected to two of his noblemen coming to him on business together—two might constitute a delegation.

two offices in Canada: it could not understand the necessity of undivided responsibility in the struggling frontier colony.

Administration took on a hierarchical form in France, and the lower ranks were also set up in the New World where necessary. In Canada the intendant had his *sub-délégué* at Montreal, a local controller with limited local powers and functions. In Isle Royale there was a lesser version of the intendant known as the *commissionaire-ordonnateur*. The parishes were brought within the orbit by the system of *capitaines de milice*, local officials whose duty it was to act as general liaisons between their neighborhood and the king's government. The towns had their "syndics".

As government in France became more methodical there grew up the system of ministries which has passed into most modern states. Ministries were departments, and the French administrative departments were the first to be clearly and systematically set off in modern Europe. In contrast with the confusion of English colonial administration, where half a dozen branches of the home government had functions in the colonies, the French system was simple—the colonial government was under the Department of the Marine, with other departments having little place in the arrangements. The Ministry of the Marine, under the King, appointed the governor who, from the last quarter of the seventeenth century on, was usually a naval officer, and it was with the head of this ministry that nearly all the correspondence passed. Both intendant and governor appear to have had virtually unlimited right of correspondence with the minister.

The only lasting concession to representative government[4] appeared in the Sovereign (later, the Superior) Council, a body consisting of the great trinity of Governor, Bishop and Intendant, some minor officials, and a maximum of twelve citizens, the latter of course appointed, not elected. It would be hard to say whether this body was a provincial executive, an adminstrative agency, or a law-court, for in accordance with French history, its powers and duties were undifferentiated. In practice its functions were mainly those of a colonial supreme court, though for a supreme court it entertained remarkably small causes. Meeting once a week, it administered a swift, cheap, and honest justice, in marked contrast to the interminable delays and huge costs of the English courts. The *habitants*, with true Norman persistence, were

---

[4] Representation secured fleeting expression in the 1650's, in Frontenac's assembly of 1672 called to discuss liquor in the Indian trade (for which he received a sharp rebuke from the King), and in certain later meetings called to take the advice of the principal inhabitants on matters affecting the colony's prosperity.

litigious by nature and seemed to like the game of mutual prosecution. "The law" did not have for them the terrors that it has for us today. In such circumstances the Superior Council was an important and a useful body. In the course of its existence, the thousands of decisions it gave came to constitute a kind of elementary Canadian common law.

In Canada no question was more complex than that of the law. France had had an experience somewhat similar to England's in the growth of law; but it had come a century later, and that difference in time had had great import. It was in the twelfth century that the judges of Henry II began to work out general principles on cases that could not be brought under the law or custom of the neighbourhood where they were sitting. From their decisions arose the English common law, the law common to all England. In the twelfth century, France was far too decentralized for anything like that, hence every region developed its own law or custom. One of the earliest French law codes extant is the *Grand Coutumière de Normandie*, dating from the thirteenth century, a collection of the customs of Normandy at that period. A little later began the introduction of the revived Roman law from the south, the *lex scripta*. The lawyers of such kings as Philip the Fair (1285-1314), saw in Roman law with its emphasis on the maxim *Quod principi placuit, legis vigorem habet*—(the king's will has the force of law)—a powerful instrument for reducing anarchic feudatories to submission. As an instrument of absolutism such a doctrine could not be improved upon. Louis XIV's *l'état, c'est moi* three and a half centuries later followed as a natural deduction.

French law, therefore, contained three bodies of material: the old local customs, the principles of Roman law, and the concept of law as will—that is, of the unlimited legislative power of the Crown. Here again no clear and precise transfer was made to Canada. It was decided that cases should be tried "according to the Custom of Paris"—the clearest and most advanced of French regional laws.[5] But the king's will came into the colony uncurtailed, along with the general doctrines of Roman law. Since for France the so-called "commercial revolution" was pretty much in the future, French law as of 1663 was still the law of an agricultural, feudal state. Within a few years elaborate codification and extension of legislation was to be undertaken in the field of commercial law but these new codes were never introduced into Canada. Through the agency of Royal edicts and ordinances (for matters of first rate importance), of conciliar *arrêts*, of the ordinances and *arrêts* issued

[5] The *Custom of Paris* became the basis of colonial law in 1637, and was officially established in 1663.

locally by the intendant and his subordinates, and of the decisions of the Superior Council, a separate Canadian body of law began from the date of introduction of French law, but as decisions and local regulations were never printed, it was hard to know what the law of Canada was. This occasioned legal confusion and important political consequences in the generation after the Conquest, when a vigorous English commercial element had appeared in the colony.[6]

French law as introduced into and developed in Canada was the law of a rural people, living largely in terms of the family rather than the individual, and in a graded society. It had to do mainly with "property and civil rights"[7] which meant, substantially, property in land and the rights of inheritance under French law. "Civil rights" had no relationship with our English term descriptive of a free society—"civil liberties". Roman (and French) law has always had a place for the legal unit the family, English law has not. The family constitutes a well-recognized legal entity in Quebec today. The law of the family naturally has to do mainly with inheritance, especially with landed property. Here was the stuff of most of the litigation during the old regime.

The land law was perforce the law of France, a law developed in the country in which feudalism had received its fullest expression. English land law, too, is feudal in many of its aspects, but the course of English history and the individualism of the English character have reduced the feudal element to a matter of vocabulary and produced out of it the characteristic system of freehold tenure. Yet it was not until 1660 that the feudal tenures and incidents were abolished in England, just three years before the Province of New France was erected, and certain minor aspects of the old tenures, such as quit-rents, were actually introduced into the American colonies. It is no occasion for surprise that the land system of New France should have been feudal, or as it is usually termed, seigneurial. It could hardly have been anything else, for it was the only one the French knew. But like every other institution which has crossed the ocean, it was profoundly changed by its transplantation. Feudalism varied enormously in nature from district to district (it has been said that the only systematic aspect of the feudal "system" was its lack of system), every countryside having its own customs prescribing the relations of master and man, the terms on which land was held, the duties and privileges of lord and peasant. Necessarily, when the Crown gave its authority to the occupation of land in the New World, the patents it

[6] See p. 81.
[7] This old French phrase, in common use long before the Conquest, found its way into the British North America Act and has since by interpretation of the Judicial Committee of the Privy Council been enlarged beyond all recognition.

issued would not differ much from one another; and since most of the seigneurial grants were made within three-quarters of a century, there was not sufficient time for much variety to creep in. Feudalism in the new world really was something like a system.

The feudal anarchy in France that it had taken five centuries for the kings to overcome found no reflection in New France; from the first the secular power was as highly centralized as was the ecclesiastical. Seigneurs received no important grants of power along with their grants of land; none of them was ever in any sense a rival of the Crown. Because land was unlimited and the duties in return for which they were held were correspondingly light, the seigneuries set up were generous in extent. The Crown exacted the immemorial right of allegiance, ceremonially rendered in the act of homage; a few trifling payments, not nearly as heavy as the aids and reliefs of feudalism had originally been in Europe; and the customary obligations to bring a given number of followers to the levy, which were commonly found in European feudalism. Canadian feudalism stemmed off from the French at a period when the latter was breaking down. The day of the feudal levy had long since been over. In French Canada, when the call to arms came, it was much more of a national militia that answered than a collection of knights-at-arms and retainers. The obligation of court-service, heavier than military service at the height of feudalism—involving performance of duties as judges, counsellors, and administrators—hardly existed in New France, where a royal administrative system came into being with the province.

One of the most cherished privileges of the European feudatory was the right of justice. In England one of the principal irritants leading to the outbreak against King John (1215) had been Henry II's devices for drawing cases from the feudal courts to his own.[8] In France the Crown had never completely succeeded in depriving the feudatories of their rights of justice. But in Canada it was not disposed unnecessarily to extend a condition so unfavourable to itself. While the weight of tradition allowed right of *haute, moyenne, et basse justice* to creep into grants, these never became much more than formalities. "High Justice" involved judgment of life and limb, "middle" and "low justice" extended only to minor misdemeanours, and it was "low justice" alone that in practice was administered in Canadian seigneurial courts. The right of justice was a burden to the seigneur, not a privilege. He could not expect to exact heavy fees, and if he exercised his right, he had to maintain a court and a judge at his own expense, and the authorities at Quebec kept a sharp eye on him.

[8] Magna Carta provided for the non-issuance of the writ *praecipe*, by which the King took cases away from the feudal court.

In like manner some of his other grants, especially the *banalités*, were burdens. The right of *banalité* extended to a monopoly of mills and bake ovens. But the right-to-have soon became an obligation-to-maintain, and inured to the benefit of the habitants, not the seigneur. Similar was the stipulation that the labour be given by habitant to seigneur. In France the *corvée* (corresponding with the English "boon days") was one of the dreaded obligations, for it might mean as much as three days a week given to the lord without reward. It was the *corvée* which came closest to making the free tenant into a serf. But in Canada the legal limit of the *corvée* was six days a year—just about the same amount as the later device in the English provinces of "statute labour"—and its weight was lightened by the unfortunate seigneur's obligation to feed the workman. In French Canada the word *corvée* today means a "bee", that is, general community effort and get-together for a specific job in neighbourly spirit, sufficient commentary on the onerousness of the original obligation.

The seigneurs are hardly comparable with the feudal classes of France. No great noble was going to change his happy lot for a home in the Canadian backwoods. Although a number of younger sons did come out, most of the seigneurs were either from the *petite noblesse*—the small and inconspicuous men with nothing but their family dignity, who comprised so large a proportion of the French gentry—or were middle-class persons who achieved *noblesse* in the colony by patent from the King. Many seigneuries were held by monastic orders. Frontier noblemen, real or artificial, have always had a hard lot. What the frontier needs is not manners but muscle, which is something that the frontier gentleman, if he insists on remaining a "gentleman", is hardly in a position to give. Usually he shelves his order and turns into a hunter, a kind of forest beach-comber, or, when the chance comes, a warrior. The records of English Canada are even more replete than are those of French with examples of people of gentle blood who failed to "make good" as settlers. The French seigneur at least had an official position in society and an estate (of wilderness) in his name. Even so, his lot was frequently one of decidedly genteel poverty, unless he was rescued by war or was a merchant who had bought the seigneury to enhance his dignity.

The habitant, on the other hand, found everything in his favour. Labour is the imperative demand of all new countries. In New France, as elsewhere, the man who would actually go into the bush, clear, settle, raise a family and stay there, was the welcome man, the backbone of the colony. Whatever the legal formalities, practice everywhere turned in his favour. No governor was going to allow a good settler to be dispossessed because he failed to make some trifling customary payment to his seigneur. The peasants realized their position from the first and pressed their advantages hard, both by persistent default and by lawsuit, as in the well-known case of payment in money of Tours or money of Paris,[9] whose outcome in their favour gave them a decided reduction in money payments. If unwisdom did press them too far, there was always the bush, always the illimitable west and the Indian life to take to.

The peasants' legal obligations derived from the more general aspects of manorialism in France. Everywhere it was recognized as right that a man should pay some annual rent for his property—a survival from feudal days when no system of national taxation existed and public revenues were derived from feudal "aids", which in turn had to be obtained from manorial income. In New France this annual payment was known as the *rentes*. Combined with the initial or down payment when the grant was first made (tenure *en censive*), it was often referred to as the *cens et rentes*. And since feudalism nowhere recognized an absolute title to land, except that which resided in the Crown, a change of possession apart from direct inheritance was marked by a payment to the lord. In the old days in England this payment had been known as a *relief*. In France, its manorial equivalent was known as the *lods et ventes*. There were occasionally other obligations of payment, such as providing the seigneur with a fat capon at Christmas, but these were not much more than symbolical. All money payments were small from the beginning and as prices tended to rise became smaller in terms of value. Even so, in a land where nearly everything was on a barter basis the seigneur received little real money from his *censitaires*.

The seigneurial system was not without its merits. Since all the seigneuries were granted with river frontage, and were subdivided among the habitants also with river frontage, it kept the people close together along the banks of the great river. There was little scattering in all directions; it was favourable to communal life. The habitant never really abandoned society, as so many English settlers did. He never (except when he turned *coureur de bois*) got beyond the ordinary influences of the village and the curé. Once the initial shock of the transfer had been met, the change from being a craftsman in Normandy to being a settler in New France did not involve for him a complete dislocation of his way of life. He had been a social being, and a social being he remained.

The method of river front settlement under community leaders, seigneur and priest, meant that the French attacked the wilderness, not as individuals, but as groups. A new settlement was a new parish. For

[9] In money of Tours, the livre was worth 20 sous; in money of Paris, 25.

them this was and remains an eminently wise method. It had good results. The New England method, where the "church settlement" in a "town" was the characteristic method of pioneering and where the individual was never left completely to his own devices, affords an equivalent in English terms. The community settlement of New England and New France was a device which supported the individual, kept him within the pale of civilization, and provided him with neighbours, help, and advice. It involved far less human waste, far less lost motion, than the anarchic processes followed in the middle colonies or later on in Upper Canada, and probably resulted in a stronger countryside.

Naturally there were demerits. The river frontage system got into the blood of the French (for a century or more the river was their only highway) and this, combined with their distaste for moving out of the area in which they were born, produced exaggerated effects. Subdivision of frontage generation after generation at last meant farms of infinite length and no breadth. There is a tradition that at one point on the St. Lawrence, one great elm tree used to shade the frontages of three farms. The authorities tried to combat these extreme trends by prohibitions and occasionally went to the drastic point of pulling down houses, but to no avail: the humble habitant won in the end and today the north shore from Montreal downward is almost a countinuous row of houses.

The more serious charge might be made that this method of settlement encouraged the excessively paternalistic tone of French colonial life, leaving the habitant with too little self-reliance. That may have been true. He may have leaned on priest and seigneur, as he does today on priest, seeking from them advice and decision in matters which he should have faced for himself. The charge probably can be sustained, but the seigneurial system of settlement was only a reflection of the French system of society, which was authoritarian and paternalistic throughout. If judgment is to be pronounced, French society has to stand or fall as a whole.

2. Community in Its Own Right

That the French system had its merits is evident from the record of the colony once it got on its feet. Its beginnings admittedly were slow but after the stormy seventeenth century had passed, with its massacres, its martyrs, and its great adventurers, substantial progress was made. After the long trial of Queen Anne's War (1702-1713), the 2,000 people with which the province had begun in 1663 had increased to 20,000. The generation of peace that ensued (1713-1744), an unprecedented period of calm in a troubled history (which Parkman, for some peculiar reason wrote about under the title *A Half-Century of Conflict*), had marked effects in promoting growth; New France, under careful officials like the intendant Hocquart (1731-1748), enjoyed almost its sole period of prosperity. It had now had a history of a century, and some of its people represented the third generation born on Canadian soil: they were no longer French in the old sense. The colony had passed its pioneer days and was emerging into the "provincial" stage—that is, a community in its own right but dependent, comparable to the English colonies at the same period.

Relatively few people in early eighteenth century Canada had been born in France. The original immigrants had been few but amazingly fertile, so that there is hardly another case in history of a new people springing up so quickly from so few original progenitors. The total number of immigrants before the English Conquest was no more than 10,000 at the utmost (some authorities say 4,000), all of them French, most of them Normans.[10] From this handful came the 60,000 inhabitants of the colony at the Conquest and from it have descended the whole French stock in America today, perhaps as many as six million people. The race is therefore homogeneous to a degree entirely alien to the Anglo-Saxon imagination. The Canadians, like the Americans, responded to the stimulus of unlimited land, which meant the possibility of unlimited food supply and other means of simple livelihood, married young, and begot large families.

The 20,000 people of 1713 were settled along both banks of the St. Lawrence, from well down towards Gaspé on the south shore and from the Saguenay on the north, up to approximately the present boundaries of the province of Quebec. The eastern and western ends had few settlers. There were one or two seigneuries, such as Deux Montagnes, on the lower Ottawa, and a few reaching up the Richelieu to Lake Champlain. The bulk of the population lay between Quebec and Montreal and on the island of Montreal. Settled or semi-settled area corresponded to seigneurial area; there was no settlement outside the seigneuries, many outlying seigneuries having few settlers and some being empty. It was not until the 1840's, when the population of Lower Canada was approaching three quarters of a million, that the habitants found it necessary to go beyond the seigneurial area for new land.

The countryside of the eighteenth century had advanced beyond the first stages of pioneering. With the exception of the occasional crop failure, there were no large calamities. As a rule there was plenty of

[10] Estimates vary from 4,000 to 10,000.

maple syrup, bread, and pork available for all. *Fèves au lard* (pork and beans) and *soupe aux pois* (pea soup) became a national diet. Writers of the time point out how much better off the Canadian peasant was than the peasant of France: he had plenty to eat and though the country was cold, he had plenty of fuel—in contrast with the shivering winters of the French. His house was better and more commodious than that of most peasants. Those who go down the St. Lawrence today can see it, for the eighteenth century house survives in the hundreds. Wars and frontier disturbances had not prevented a fairly satisfactory rural life coming into existence before the English conquest: self-contained and rather primitive, with no bourgeois striving for style, no thought of ornateness, but altogether very fair material conditions for the times, good health, plenty of warm human association in simple social gatherings, and, for the preventing of mere animalism, adequate spiritual outlet through the church. If we can surmount our sterile middle-class philosophy with its pathetic belief that possession of things is the chief end of man, we may agree that rural Canada could not have asked of the eighteenth century a markedly better kind of society than it possessed.

Urban life contrasted sharply with rural. Quebec itself was a gay little capital, with more pretensions than the chief town of a province in France, for the Government represented the Crown in a much more direct way than in a province of the motherland. There were always soldiers about and romantic fur traders coming in from the interior. A smartish society grew up at an early date. From the standpoint of size the town continued to be trifling.[11] Montreal was smaller and probably duller, more of a frontier community, more given over to commerce than Quebec. Not that commerce amounted to much in either. As an English pamphleteer was later to figure out when arguing against the retention of Canada after the Conquest, one ship a year would have carried nearly the whole export trade of the country. But both places were centres of empire, and this redeemed them from complete backwoods obscurity. Trois Rivières, the only other settlement of any urban pretensions, was a centre for the countryside about it and no more. In Quebec and Montreal, there were most of the usual marks of Latin civilization: churches and schools, convents, monasteries, and officials. But there were no printing presses and few books. There was nothing of Latin culture, save for the occasional individual who embraced it within himself, nothing remotely resembling native creative growth in matters intellectual.

Industrial life was also feeble. A certain amount of iron was made

[11] Population, 1744: 4,748.

from the local deposits near Trois Rivières; the local iron works, *Les forges de St. Maurice* (1736), smelted bog iron with charcoal and worked it up into utensils for local consumption, especially into stoves. The Canadian stove had its origin in these iron works. Attempts had been made from Talon's time to establish a shipbuilding industry, but since there was no staple export to carry but furs and France could build its own ships more economically at home than in the colony, it never flourished. In the last generation of the regime however, some ships were built for the West Indian trade and then the French government was persuaded to give orders for some frigates. A few of these were built, the timber being cut upriver, some of it beyond the St. Lawrence rapids through which it was floated in rafts, and some of it as far away as Lake Champlain; but the dead hand of paternalism soon interfered and construction languished.

Some attempt was made to export lumber, the noted Sr. de Ramesay of Montreal, his widow and his daughter after him being pioneers in this, but again competition in the metropolitan market with the forests of France itself was impossible, and unless orders could be wheedled out of government, no export trade was possible. The West Indian trade fared a little better, but not much. In attempting to keep all colonial trade within the French empire, French mercantilism was much stricter than English and thus New France had the advantage over the American colonists of being able to trade legitimately with the flourishing French West Indies while the Americans could not. But the trifling Acadian settlements had nothing to send down, and the St. Lawrence was too far away. Experimental shipments of cattle, grain, and horses were made but no thriving exchange resulted, for the nearby Americans could always outbid the Canadians in prices and energy, two means that took them around official barriers.

Other industries were constantly talked of, such as hemp growing, extraction of tar and pitch, and tile making, but they never came to anything. The truth is that there was no natural resource except furs that could be turned into transportable wealth. Canada had to wait until the nineteenth century before she got another exportable product, timber, and that was only by the fortunes of war. Export overseas of the natural commodities Canada has had to offer has invariably been difficult because the commodities have usually been bulky. Not until the modern age of minerals and advanced technique has the country begun to approach industrial stability.[12]

---

[12] For example, Canada's huge forest of pulp wood had to wait for their utilization until a process was discovered by which they could be made into paper. Contrast Australian wool.

The worthwhile part of New France, it seems safe to say, was not the showy fur trade or the flashy insignia of French imperialism but the quiet countryside. It is this which has endured and in which a people with their own way of life, their own traditions, and supremely true to themselves, were being nurtured. Every year the French Canadians became less and less interested in distant France, more and more children of the soil, as they were later to dub themselves (*enfants du sol*), knowing no other home than Canada and with few other loyalties. Yet they continued to be pawns in the hands of France and in the high Imperial game then being played.

3. The Spirit of the New World

Into America were introduced the institutions of several European peoples, Spanish, Portuguese, English, French, Dutch, Swedes, Danes. Each was distinct from the others, but each met approximately the same set of wilderness conditions. Was "the spirit of the new world" sufficiently strong to bend them all in the same direction or did each retain its own genius? The original thesis of F. J. Turner[13] and his followers in the United States leaned strongly in the direction of rating the environment as all-powerful: reducing everyone who came into it to its own terms, levelling out all distinctions and differences, turning all Europeans into Americans. Turner's ideas were worked out within the English-speaking world of the United States and they did not reach sufficiently to the level of the universal; they were valid only for a limited time and place. If the problem is put in general terms—the effect of a new environment on persons coming to it from an old society—they must be modified. New Englanders and New Frenchmen have been living close to each other for over three hundred years now and in similar environments, but no one would assert that a New England Yankee was the same kind of person as a French Canadian or that the societies built up by each are the same. But while the New World has not had the power to make different things the same, it has had great power to modify: to change old institutions and give them new form and spirit. Many of the changes thus produced run parallel in different societies and tend to bring them closer together. New England and New France today are substantially closer than they were two centuries ago.

English settlement came from a land that as early as the day of the

---

[13] F. J. Turner, "The Significance of the Frontier in American History," *American Historical Association Annual Report for 1893* (Washington, 1894), 199-227.

first James had already acquired many of the features associated with the Anglo-Saxon way of life of today. The solid structure of English law had already been hammered out, and Englishmen from the first took out with them "the laws of England". Those laws were then conceived as including the institutional framework of government already built in England: Parliament, the right of self-taxation, and the liberties won from the sovereign over the centuries. In the year 1618, when Virginia had already become a going concern but while the Virginia Company still believed itself to be the sole source of power in the colony, "an assembly broke out", as the quaint phrase of the day had it, the second oldest parliamentary body in the English-speaking world; the genius of the people brushed aside the company's pretensions with relative ease. From that time on the institutions of the English-speaking people in the New World have gone on developing in the light of their own needs, but it is in detail rather than principle that they have diverged from those of England itself. Here is a nice example of environment modifying, but not completely changing, transplanted forms.

French settlement came from a land that had known little else but authority in church, state, and feudal domain. How could any other kind of conception have been taken across the ocean? Yet it is remarkable, and a tribute to the essential element of truth in Turner's analysis, that French life and society in America departed considerably from authoritarianism and in spirit approached English life and society in America. Where conditions were so uniform as in the settlers' attack on the forest, and where it was the worth of a man as a man—as an axe-swinging, forest-clearing, crop-sowing, animal—that counted, the same qualities came to the fore, the same scale of values tended to prevail. Men were measured by their abilities for the task in hand—the pragmatism of the New World emerged at once—and by their qualities as neighbours. There was not much room for differentiation in skills and still less for differentiation in social class. The gentleman and the scholar did not count for much when it came to stump-pulling. Nor could pioneering skill be bought. It could be and was freely given as among neighbours, but few could rise to wealth and greatness by securing land and hiring others to till it for them. That was why slaves were brought in. In all pioneer agricultural society, where nature was strong and man was weak, social equality was the rule, and a sturdy sense of personal values prevailed, an empiric rather than a traditional measurement of men's value. Slave societies were partial exceptions.

North American democracy was forest-born. It carried with it a stubborn attachment to the rights and privileges that come from an independent life and a disinclination to coercion that was a strong defence against arbitrary authority. In the case of the Americans this was carried so far as to induce suspicion of any kind of authority and brought them close to anarchy, but the French, in contrast, never had difficulty in giving all proper adhesion to legitimate authority. Yet the line between legitimate and arbitrary authority was clear to them, and their mode of meeting the latter effective. They met it not through rebellion but through passive resistance, and that has carried their point for them more than once, both before and after the Conquest. No governor could ever afford to be tyrannous; not even a bishop could lord it over his people. There were distinct limits to the nature of French authoritarianism. The *habitant* along the banks of the St. Lawrence was a very different kind of man from his brow-beaten brother in the France of the old regime. No contrast illustrates more aptly the essential falseness of the old Latin saying *Coelum non animam mutant qui trans mare in navibus eunt* ("they change their skies but not their minds who cross the sea in ships"), for it is this very change of mind that forms the deep chasm separating the New World from the old.

Much the same qualities, then, were educed by the forest in both English and French societies. The English already had political and legal institutions which encouraged these qualities; they were farther along the road than the French. The latter form a perfect test of the frontier thesis, for two tendencies quite opposite in character, tradition and environment, struggled to dominate them. The measure of their departure from the spirit of authoritarianism—and they departed a considerable distance from it—is the measure of the influence of the frontier upon them. If their history had been unbroken and the whole setting undisturbed by the introduction of English institutions after the Conquest, would tradition have re-asserted itself and would New France have become in spirit what it was in form, a province of France overseas? If the "divine-right monarchy" of France had continued, it might have: with the passing of the frontier, freedom would not have had the support of an institutional heritage. The English only needed to enlarge and revise theirs in order to advance towards the democratic state; in New France authority and privilege, by the slow pressure of a static community upon its weaker members, might well have won in the end. But that was not to be. History had decreed that in time the French would share the same set of institutions and accept much the same set of political ideas as did their English brethren.

Chronology

1637	The Custom of Paris in Canada.
1643–1715	Louis XIV King of France.
1665	Jean Talon, Intendant.
1667	Ordinance regulating civil procedure in the law courts.
1672	Frontenac summons a meeting of the "States-General" at Quebec.
1676	The principal inhabitants of Quebec make recommendations for the prosperity of the colony.
1685	First issue of Card Money.
1703	Reorganization of the Superior Council at Quebec.
1711	Arrêts of Marly. Uncleared lands may revert to seigneurs. Seigneurs not to exact more than customary dues.
1718–21	Redemption of Card Money.
1731–48	Hocquart, Intendant.
1731	Government begins shipbuilding at Quebec.
1734	Road completed between Quebec and Montreal.
1736	Forges de St. Maurice in operation.
1741	Sole occasion on which exports exceed imports.

Additional Reading

Frégault, Guy. *La Société canadienne sous le régime français.* (*CHA* Booklets No. 3) Ottawa, 1954. (Translated under the title, *Canadian Society in the French Regime.*)

Hamelin, Jean. *Economie et societé en Nouvelle-France.* Quebec, 1960.

Lanctot, Gustave. *L'Administration de la Nouvelle-France.* Paris, 1929.

Munro, William Bennett. *The Seigniorial System in Canada.* New York, 1907.

——. *The Seigneurs of Old Canada.* (Chronicles of Canada, Vol. 5) Toronto, 1915.

Parkman, Francis. *The Old Regime in Canada.* Boston, 1874.

Saunders, R. M. "The Cultural Development of New France Before 1760," in R. Flenley, ed. *Essays in Canadian History Presented to George Wrong.* Toronto, 1939. 321-345.

Trudel, Marcel. *Le Régime seigneurial.* (*CHA* Booklets No. 6) Ottawa, 1956. (Translated under the title, *The Seigneurial Regime.*)

Wrong, G. M. *The Rise and Fall of New France.* Toronto, 1928. 2 vols.

CHAPTER 5

The Great Duel

The long struggle between the French and the English in America began with the arrival of both and ended only with the conquest of Canada and the flare up of revenge taken by France in the War of the American Revolution. As early as 1613 Samuel Argall came up from Virginia and destroyed the little French post on Mount Desert Island in what is now Maine. Quebec itself had barely got its first permanent settler when an English expedition arrived and took it over.[1] It was handed back and left alone for sixty years, but in 1690 an attempt to take it, led by Sir William Phips, failed. The conflict between the two mother countries rose to its classical height in the middle eighteenth century, when fighting raged over almost all the world, engulfing America in its course.

The constant colonial warfare was partly a reflection of the long struggle between England and France and partly the outcome of local causes. The European powers began their efforts in the 1660's to restrain France from creating a continental hegemony and reached success only on the field of Waterloo. In each of the great wars, England, as the second power of Europe, was the centre of resistance, her field of action being the sea and the overseas world. No part of the British and French dominions could well escape being caught up into this epic encounter.

In the colonies themselves there were plenty of sources of friction that

[1] The semi-marauding expedition headed by David Kirke. Quebec remained in English hands from 1629 to 1632.

would have ensured continuous warfare, even without the added incentive from Europe. The main one was simply jealousy, the jealousy and fear of French and Catholic for English and Protestant, and vice versa. The secondary ones were competition in the Indian trade, the uninterrupted struggle of the St. Lawrence and the Hudson, Montreal and New York, embodied, in the eighteenth century, in increasing rivalry for the possession of the interior. The English countered the trader and the priest with the settler, whose slow, steady, onward march dismayed the French, who had no answer for it except wilderness forts.

There was a never-failing supply of frontier "incidents" to keep old wounds open and cause new ones. The Dutch and English armed the Iroquois; the Iroquois killed French missionaries. French Indians fell on outlying English farmsteads, burning and scalping. Persons of white skin were seen, or were alleged to have been seen, among the scalping parties. So it went on, one incident leading to retaliation and that to another, until the end. To this day each party has its legends of the fearfulness, treachery, and cruelty of the other. Religion played a much larger part than we today would care to think. There was no bridge between zealous seventeenth century Catholicism and stiff-necked seventeenth century Puritanism. For the Puritans Rome was the evil thing, to be blotted out whenever possible in the persons of its adherents. The Catholics hardly took so extreme a view: wholesale conversion, with some military persuasion, would have satisfied them.

1. Geography and Strategy

In the early eighteenth century the two "hereditary enemies" were extending their interests into every part of the world except the Pacific. The English, having no continental territories and no land frontier, were free to concentrate upon the sea. English sea power rose with the English overseas Empire. France, in contrast, was primarily a continental power and her statesmen usually thought in terms of extending her continental interests. The commercial point of view, which received expression through Colbert and which diverted some attention to the extra-European world, was a deviation from the normal; and until he came to the epic decision to accept, on behalf of his grandson, the crown of Spain, Louis XIV's chief interests lay in rounding out the boundaries of France. "Messieurs, il n'y a plus de Pyrénées," he is said to have exclaimed in announcing that event to his court. At a stroke, he seems to have thought, the entire Spanish overseas world would be laid open to Frenchmen, making an aggregation of power that no important European country could tolerate if it had any respect for its own future.

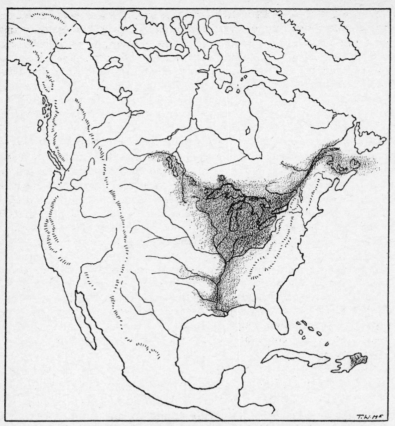

AREA EFFECTIVELY CONTROLLED BY NEW FRANCE ABOUT 1750

The War of the Spanish Succession followed, with its coalitions against France and all Marlborough's famous battles. At its conclusion, ascendant English sea power was reflected in the peace of Utrecht (1713), and by its terms the Hudson's Bay Territories, Newfoundland, and "Nova Scotia" passed to England. French access to the vast fan-like spread of the interior was now dependent upon the rabbit hole of the St. Lawrence, with the English dogs barking on either side of the entrance. At Utrecht France had suffered her first great defeat. She had tried to follow her traditional role as a great land power and make herself a great sea power at the same time. In both elements she had accomplished much, but the task was too great and triumph was to go to the nations whose attention was not so divided, to Prussia on land and England at sea. As Europe shrank and the great world opened up, English sea power became more and more of a universal force until it brought the whole oceanic world into the orbit of English metropolitanism, Canada included.[2]

"The Company of Gentlemen Adventurers", who in the years after 1670 had established their posts at the mouths of the rivers flowing into Hudson and James Bays, had had enough of French raiding parties burning their posts and killing their servants, so that using their not inconsiderable influence they saw to it in the peace of Utrecht that French claims in that region were surrendered for good and all. But the French made their own reservations about the extent of "The Hudson's Bay Territories", and for them they never included the lands on the distant head waters of the interior which La Vérendrye was soon to try to attach to New France. So with "Nova Scotia": the French had unexpressed reservations there, too, and tried later to whittle down the name to a small area in the western part of the peninsula. Here was a source of friction that was not eliminated until the expulsion of the Acadians on the eve of the conquest. The wide claims of the French were never made good, but they did save Isle Royale (Cape Breton) from the wreck. Had they not done so, their position in Canada would have been untenable, for they would have been at the mercy of an enemy who, holding the two sides of the Cabot Straits, would have been in a position to bottle them up.

The peace of Utrecht, in seriously weakening the French position, had revealed the decisive nature of sea power. Yet sea power, while important, was not the only factor in the fate of America and perhaps not the major one, for from the first the development of the English colonies went forward with an energy and assuredness that was absent from New France. This, added to their immensely greater area of fertile soil, better climate, and accessible position along the Atlantic coast, soon gave them population and wealth that New France could never hope to rival. By the time the curtain descended, there were thirty times as many English colonists as French. Except that the English colonies did not know their own strength and were hopeless in their efforts to organize it, given the antagonisms that existed from the beginning, the end was easily predictable. Only a smashing French victory in Europe could have changed the situation.

Geographically, considering the Atlantic basin as a unit, the English had great advantages: their colonies, full of ports and resources, spread out in an arc from Nova Scotia, or after 1713 from Newfoundland, to

[2] See Chap. 16, part 1.

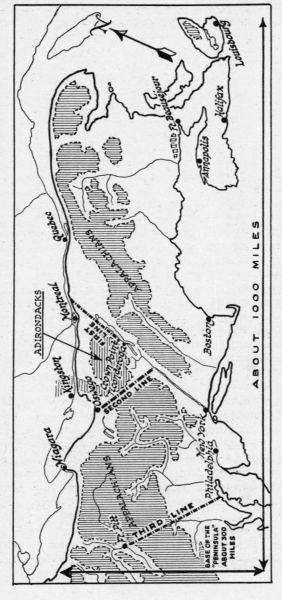

The Colonial Wars in relation to the Geography of
NORTH EASTERN NORTH AMERICA

Showing the various theatres of war.

The 1000 ft. contour line - - - - - - - indicates the approximate boundaries of the Appalachian and Adirondack Mountains.

Georgia, and thence on through to the West Indies. The French, on the other hand, had only one point to make for, the Gulf of St. Lawrence, and it was closed up half the year by ice. The English could drop down the coast of Europe in their ships until they struck the trade winds, run over to their West Indian islands and then come up the American coast on a fair wind well inshore, an easy voyage. The French had to buffet the westerlies of the north Atlantic straight across, or make two voyages, one to their southern islands and thence straight for Cape Breton. On the coast itself, the nature of every campaign was pre-determined. The French could hardly hope to operate westward of Nova Scotia against Boston and New York, but it was always open to the English to gather a fleet and army in the seclusion of their colonies and launch them against the French position in the Gulf. It was the opening move in all the campaigns, fully understood by both combatants.

Inland,[3] geography similarly imposed the plan of campaign upon both. The natural features of the continent provided three roughly parallel zones for the operations of armed forces. The Appalachians, running up parallel to the coast through New England and between the St. Lawrence and the Atlantic, terminating at the sea in Gaspé, imposed a strong barrier between the St. Lawrence basin and the English colonies. Only up country from New York was there an easy opening through them. Up the Hudson to Lake George and Lake Champlain, thence down the Richelieu, a great trench 400 miles long bordered by mountains, gave and still gives easy communication between the two cities at each end of it, the first natural cross-roads inland from salt water. It was up and down this natural highway that campaigns were to rage. Here were the famous forts—Ticonderoga, Fort Edward, William Henry, Frédéric, Crown Point, Carillon.

The second inland line of contact was formed by the Mohawk, the tributary of the Hudson coming in near Albany, and the route to Lake Ontario. Emerging on the lake at Oswego (founded 1723), this second line continued down the lake and river to Montreal, where it joined the first. It, too, was the inevitable scene of conflict, but not of major operations such as took place on the main route.

The third line, appearing late, lay across the mountains of Pennsylvania to the water flowing down into the Ohio. For the English, crossing the Appalachian Barrier through Pennsylvania was difficult, involving a long wagon route; but the French, holding the line of the St. Lawrence, could bring up their supplies by water to points on Lake Erie, make a short portage and thence embark them on the Ohio waters, which gave

³ See map, p. 56.

access to numerous points on the western side of the Appalachians Though far away from their base, they were able to put up a stout resistance to English efforts to consolidate the upper waters of the trans-Appalachian interior.

The whole theatre of operations may be conceived of as a roughly oblong peninsula jutting out to the north-eastward from a base line running between Lake Erie and Chesapeake Bay. This peninsula is about 1,000 miles long from south-west to north-east and about 250 miles wide, from south-east to north-west. It has water on three sides of it, the Atlantic on the south-east, the two lower Lakes and the St. Lawrence on the north-west and the Gulf of St. Lawrence around its north-east termination. Throughout its long diameter run the parallel Appalachian mountain ridges, ending in the sea at Gaspé and Cape Breton: these are cut through diagonally by a route up from New York which forks near Albany, one fork to Montreal, the other to Lake Ontario, and divides the peninsula almost in two.

The strategy of the Great Duel was imposed upon the combatants by this geographical base. Oceanic strategy dictated to the English the necessity of "containing", or blockading, the French Navy in order to have freedom of movement at sea; and to the French, weaker at sea than the English, the necessity of saving their fleets at any cost, of avoiding engagements and living to fight another day. Their use of their Navy was wise from their point of view: powers inferior at sea should and usually do keep their fleet in existence as a potential threat. It is the use which Germany in the two German wars made of her fleet, which Italy made of hers and which in 1942 England should have made of hers in the East Indies. It is only the power which has assured superiority at sea and relative safety from invasion that can afford to risk its Navy in the decisive task of "capturing or destroying the enemy".

On land, the nature of operations followed from the nature of the peninsula just described. Along the coast, the English aim was to seal up the Gulf, the French to keep it open. Louisbourg and Halifax are both monuments to these objectives. Inland, the English plan had to involve forcing the Hudson-Richelieu route, capturing Montreal and descending on Quebec. The French role necessarily was purely defensive: they were never in a position to take New York. Hence, to defend the Hudson-Richelieu route and keep back the English from the St. Lawrence by minor devices, such as raids on outlying settlements, was the sum total of French strategy in this all important central position. Farther into the interior, towards the base of the peninsula, water transportation enabled them to take a more positive attitude. The French tried hard to secure communications between the two Gulfs, St. Lawrence and Mexico, and to press eastward from such a line towards the mountains.

Here was a containing policy from inland, based on inland waterways: to drive up the rivers towards the mountains, build forts as close to the divide as possible, with Lake Erie and the Ohio at their back, became French interior policy. It failed, not because the English succeeded in crossing the oblong and cutting the water route but because the base on which it rested was itself dependent on that distant base in France from which English sea power succeeded in isolating it.

To sum up, the general line of the French was to hold what they had on the St. Lawrence and to expand in the interior. That failed because the St. Lawrence portal was too narrow and English sea power too strong. The object of the English was to strike at the enemy's centre, the St. Lawrence settlement, and destroy him. This they were able to do because of their immeasurably greater power.

2. The Campaigns

The actual campaigns fall into a natural sequence. Stage one involved the events of Queen Anne's War already referred to, the taking by the English of positions at the entrance to the Gulf, especially the harbour of Chebucto (where Halifax was later to be built) and Newfoundland. This was followed by the classical French reply, the building in the 1720's of the great fortress of Louisbourg, at the easternmost point of Isle Royale, commanding the whole of the Cabot Straits. The nearest English counter-position at the time was St. John's, Newfoundland, which was not maintained as a naval base and fortress. Matters drifted through the long interval of peace. Many were the complaints of fishermen of both parties in the zone of contact, along the Gut of Canso, at the aggressions of the other but the solid fact emerges that much of the supply of the fortress of Louisbourg itself was obtained from the New England schooners, which came up with food and took back with them whatever products had come down from the St. Lawrence. Louisbourg was becoming an entrepot for the Canadian-West Indian trade and New Englanders the middle men.

When the next war broke out, its threat to the whole American coast became apparent. Matters did not go too well in Europe for the English in this war (King George's War, or the War of the Austrian Succession) and if the balance of naval power had swung, as seemed likely at one time, the coast might actually have been in danger. A combined British and New England expedition under Admiral Warren and General Pepperell succeeded in reducing Louisbourg, 1745, though in unorthodox frontier fashion, but found itself unequal to the task of following this up with an expedition to the St. Lawrence. The next year a formidable armada under the Duc D'Anville, arriving in the harbour of Chebucto, filled the colonists with dread, for it appeared powerful enough not only to retake Louisbourg but also to threaten Boston itself. Fortunately for the English, it was destroyed by a storm and an epidemic. When the peace terms came out, French victories in Europe were reflected in the compromise by which Louisbourg was handed back in exchange for Madras in India.

King George's War was just a prelude to a greater struggle, as the years that followed it are an interlude. It was with the Seven Years' or French and Indian War, 1756-63, that the drama rose to its climax. No part of North American history has been more fully discussed, so a few words here will suffice. In 1749, the English replied to Louisbourg by building Halifax. This fort and base has ever since covered the entrance to the Gulf and, after the independence of the American colonies, the Atlantic coast too. Its strategic importance cannot be overestimated.

The French, for their part, true to their general view of things North American, proceeded to strengthen themselves in the interior. They sent Céloron de Blainville down the Ohio to assert, by formal ceremonial, the title of the King of France. As his means of keeping French possession rested on nothing more effective than lead tablets with inscriptions on them which he erected at the points of ceremony (these the Indians pulled down on his departure and melted up for bullets), his journey had little effect. Then the French began post-building inland from Lake Erie up towards the mountains and there occurred the famous clash in the woods between them and the young Virginia surveyor, George Washington, which led to the disastrous expedition under Braddock that was designed to assert English title to "the western waters", but which ended up in being destroyed by the "jungle-fighters" of that period.

The orderly nineteenth and early twentieth centuries would have assumed that the frontier clash in which hundreds of men lost their lives would precipitate war at once. The more chaotic later twentieth century knows that much bloodshed can occur without the irrevocable decision being taken. To the imperial centres of the eighteenth century, a distant affair of outposts did not seem cause for the rupture of good relations. That did not occur until Anson made his unprovoked attack on the French convoy which was entering the Gulf of St. Lawrence.[4] Such an onslaught could not be disregarded and hostilities once more broke out. The last act in the drama was at hand.

The Seven Years' War[5] (even more than the American Revolutionary

[4] See Julian Corbett, *England in the Seven Years' War* (New York, 1907).
[5] A standard reference work on the Seven Years' War is Lawrence H. Gipson, *The British Empire Before the American Revolution* (New York, 1936-61), 10 vols. to date. Gipson furnishes an extraordinary repository of detailed information, all meticulously arranged and indexed.

War) is the classical application in America of naval and military power to geographical background. Each position described above came into play at its proper time and received its appropriate weight in the total scale of the effort. The English first struck up the Hudson route for the French centre but, as usual in their wars, they had to get rid of their commanders before they could score. Loudon and Abercromby were failures whose incompetence enabled poor Montcalm, a master of tactical skill though harassed by the officialdom of Quebec and by inadequate resources, to put off the evil day for two years. It was not until the insight of William Pitt seized on the essential nature of the war as an amphibious conflict and co-ordinated sea power and land power that things began to move. The plan for the campaign of 1758, a move up the Hudson timed with an attack by sea and land on Louisbourg designed to take the fortress and to blockade the St. Lawrence, represented the proper co-ordination of all the factors. Even so, the Hudson valley campaign (except for Bradstreet's penetration of the Mohawk gap and capture of Fort Frontenac) ended in defeat at Ticonderoga and the siege of Louisbourg took so long that no advance could be made up the Gulf that season. The English fleet under Boscawen and the landing force under Amherst and Wolfe so outnumbered the defenders that the siege should have been short. As the French themselves said, "anyone else but the English would have taken the place in half the time". However at last it fell (July 28, 1758) and the English prepared for one more campaign the next year. The plans for this campaign testified to an even more complete appreciation of the geographical factors, calling as they did for expeditions up towards Lake Champlain and onward from Louisbourg by sea. Amherst was the commander-in-chief, with Wolfe designated for command of the Quebec expedition, and Saunders the admiral.

Again events moved slowly. It was not until June 26, almost two months after the river was normally free of ice, that the English expedition appeared before Quebec. Meantime Amherst was making slow progress up the central route. He did not clear it that year even though he did not have to meet Montcalm, who was absent in Quebec. Wolfe himself accomplished next to nothing until the last lucky stroke of that September night that took him up the cliffs onto the Plains of Abraham. It was his last chance: in those days, sailors were unwilling to take chances with the weather after September in that long bottle-neck, the St. Lawrence, and in a few more days the Admiral would probably have insisted on withdrawing. Luckily Wolfe blundered into success and in so doing earned immortal fame and accomplished one of the decisive deeds of history.

The battle, with the deaths of the two protagonists to give it the right sentimental atmosphere, has become so much the possession of the historical romanticists that it is hard to turn upon it or the campaign of which it was a part the cold light of critical analysis. Perhaps it is safe to assert that technically and morally the honours of the game had gone to Montcalm, a man of great ability and, for the age, nobility of soul; that Amherst was thorough but so slow as to cost his country an extra campaign (the operations should have been finished in 1758; the campaign of 1759 and still more, that of 1760, being really unnecessary); that Wolfe was a gallant officer without genius, a very lucky man to have secured what he did, lucky even in his death; and that the British conquered the French in America not so much by military skill as by the inexorable pressure of sea power combined with a good deal of main strength and awkwardness on land.

Chronology

1686	League of Augsburg formed against France.
1689	French plan for the conquest of New York.
1690	Sir William Phips fails to take Quebec.
1702	Grand Alliance declares war on France.
1704	Deerfield in Massachusetts destroyed by French and Indians.
1710	Port Royal captured by the British.
1711	British expedition against Quebec fails.
1713	Treaty of Utrecht.
1720	Fortress of Louisbourg begun.
1744	France declares war on Great Britain.
1745	Pepperell and Warren capture Louisbourg.
1746	Expedition of Duc d'Anville fails.
1748	Louisbourg restored to the French.
1749	Céloron de Blainville takes formal possession of the Ohio Valley.
1754	The French build Fort Duquesne.
1755	Braddock defeated.
	Vergor surrenders Fort Beauséjour in Acadia.
1756–61	Willian Pitt in control of the English Government.
1756–63	Seven Years' War.
1756	Montcalm sent to Canada; captures Oswego.
1757	Montcalm captures Fort William Henry.
1758	Montcalm defeats Abercromby at Ticonderoga.
	Amherst and Boscawen capture Louisbourg.
	Bradstreet captures Fort Frontenac.
	Forbes captures Fort Duquesne, renamed Fort Pitt.
1759	Sir William Johnson captures Fort Niagara.
	Amherst takes Ticonderoga and Crown Point.
	Battle of the Plains of Abraham.
1760	Vaudreuil surrenders Montreal and Canada to Amherst.
1763	The Peace of Paris.

Additional Reading

Casgrain, Henri Raymond. *Wolfe and Montcalm*. (Makers of Canada Series, Vol. 2) (London, 1926).

Channing, Edward. *A History of the United States*. New York 1905-1925. 6 vols.

Corbett, Julian S. *England in the Seven Years' War*. New York, 1907.

Gipson, Lawrence H. *The British Empire Before the American Revolution*. New York, 1936-61. 10 vols. (Two additional volumes in preparation.)

Graham, Gerald. *Empire of the North Atlantic: The Maritime Struggle for North America*. Toronto, 1950.

Mahan, A. T. *The Influence of Sea-Power on History, 1660-1783*, 12th ed. Boston, 1941.

McCardell, Lee. *Ill-Starred General: Braddock of the Coldstream Guards*. Pittsburgh, 1958.

Parkman, Francis. *Wolfe and Montcalm*. Boston, 1899. (Collier Paperbacks, 1962).

——. *A Half Century of Conflict*. Boston, c1899. (Collier Paperbacks, 1962).

Stacey, C. P. *Quebec, 1759: The Siege and the Battle*. Toronto, 1959.

Waddington, Richard. *La Guerre de sept ans; Histoire diplomatique et militaire*. Paris, 1899-1907. 3 vols.

CHAPTER 6

A French Catholic Province in an English Protestant Empire 1760-1774

1. Conquest

The gallant defence of the little French settlement on the St. Lawrence had proved of no avail. On Sept. 8, 1760 the Marquis de Vaudreuil signed the fateful capitulation and the *fleur-de-lis* was run down for ever. Today we study the classical operations that preceded the Conquest as if they were games of chess, but they were in themselves far less important than the results that flowed from them. For the British they were glorious victories, for the Americans they represented the removal of the threat from the north, and for France the loss of *quelques arpents de neige* ("a few acres of snow"). The heart of the French nation had never been in empire and it saw the vision of Champlain fade without regret or understanding. But the French had left children behind them in America, 60,000 people of French blood, French language, and Catholic faith. What of these, isolated now in the hostile Protestant English continent of the conqueror?

Among white and Christian peoples no two more complete opposites could have been found than French and English as they grew up in America. In the old world the two races met in the persons of diplomats, soldiers, aristocrats, and men of culture. Paris was London's cultural metropolis and France had given to England much of her civilization, her institutions and her language. In religion, Anglicanism, that *via media*, softened the contact between Catholicism and Protestantism.

Though the two peoples were traditional foes, the two civilizations had many bridges between them. But French culture had not emigrated to the New World, whereas the most extreme type of French Catholicism had. So it was with New England whose Protestantism was of a harsh and bigoted kind not representative of that of England. In New France there had been built up the myth of *les Bastonnois*, the dread Puritans from Boston who thirsted for all good Frenchmen's blood. The two races met in terms of frontier roughness, interpreted to each other not by spirits like Montesquieu but by the leader of the Indian scalping party.

The conduct of the invaders, whose slow year-by-year progress towards the heart of the colony must have endowed them with a peculiar terror, did not entirely bear out the myth, nor did it destroy it. They were not exactly fiends in human shape, although they did lay waste great tracts of land.[1] Yet no private plunder was allowed, their discipline was strict, and as individuals they did not seem sub-human. But these were the soldiers of the English king, not the ruthless hordes of Puritans, with death to the French in their hearts, who would pull down the churches out of sheer impiety.[2] New Englanders were at the very moment flocking into the lands from whence they had just driven the Acadians. If the colony fell, would it not be these, the dreaded Bastonnois, rather than the soldiers, who would shape its destinies?

At last the inevitable happened: French resistance collapsed, and the people were left unprotected. The bitter agony of Canada had begun.

It is hard for people of English speech[3] to understand the feelings of those who must pass under the yoke of conquest, for there is scarcely a memory of it in all their tradition.[4] Conquest is a type of slavery and of that too they have no memory, except as masters. Conquest, like slavery, must be experienced to be understood.

But anyone can at least intellectually perceive what it means. The entire life-structure of the conquered is laid open to their masters. They become second-rate people. Wherever they turn, something meets their

---

[1] Brigadier Murray's stern warning to the inhabitants to behave themselves or suffer the consequences may still be read in the church at Beaumont, opposite Quebec.

[2] As they had begun to do at Louisbourg in 1745. See Francis Parkman, *A Half Century of Conflict* (Boston, 1892), II, 153.

[3] Except those of the Southern States.

[4] Yet in the 19th century, English historians like Freeman drew a distinct line between the Saxon people, with whom he identified himself, and their conquerors, the Normans. In his writings the Saxons were always "we", the Normans "they". So with the 17th-century pamphleteer, Winstanley, who makes the same distinction. See his "An Appeal to All Englishmen" in *Works*, ed. G. H. Sabine (Ithaca, N.Y., 1941).

eyes to symbolize their subjection. It need not be the foreign military in force, it need not be the sight of the foreign flag, it may be some quite small matter: a common utensil of unaccustomed size and shape, let us say, taking the place of a familiar one.[5] And then there is the foreign speech, perhaps not heard often, but sometimes heard, and sometimes heard arrogantly from the lips of persons who leave no doubt that the conquered are, in their estimation, inferior beings. Even the kindness of the superior hurts. The educated may make their peace, learn the foreign language, and find many areas in common, but the humble cannot cross the gulf: they feel pushed aside in their own homes. Hence it is that the folk-feeling always lives long, even if not blazing up into fierce flame, in the hearts of the people, who maintain their own ways by the passiveness of their behaviour and little by little, as opportunity offers, edge forward into any chance space left vacant by their masters.

No one can suggest that the English conquest, as conquests go, was cruel or English government harsh. If the French in Canada had had a choice of conquerors, they could not have selected more happily than fate did for them. But conquerors are conquerors: they may make themselves hated or they may get themselves tolerated; they cannot, unless they abandon their own way of life and quickly assimilate themselves, in which case they cease to be conquerors, make themselves loved. As long as French are French and English are English, the memory of the conquest and its effects will remain. Not until that great day comes when each shall have lost themselves in a common Canadianism will it be obliterated.

2. A Conflict of Philosophies

The Seven Years' War gave rise to territorial changes on a scale hardly paralleled in history. To England went the territory in the three modern states of Florida, Alabama, and Mississippi, various islands of the West Indies, most of the French claims in India, and all but Louisiana in North America.[6] A surfeit of riches caused the English to give back to Spain Cuba and the Philippines, both of which they had

---

[5] A point of friction actually was later based on something like this. The Canadian peasants used a short one-horse sleigh that pounded and made pitch-holes —*cahots*—in the winter roads. The English began to object to this practice, but the more they tried to get the French to change, the larger the pitch-holes became.

[6] With the exception of the two little islets, St. Pierre and Miquelon, handed back out of magnanimity. These constituted a shelter for French fishermen, and recall the importance of the codfisheries described earlier.

conquered. And, strangely enough, considerable debate occurred as to whether they would return Canada to France. For a while it was balanced against the West Indian sugar island of Guadaloupe, but finally in the interests of a moderate peace, because of the pressure of rival sugar interests on government, and since colonial opinion would not have permitted the re-establishment of the French power in Canada, it was decided to let the French have back Guadaloupe, a richer prize in English eyes than the fur-trading wastes of the North.

After the capitulation of Montreal, all resistance in Canada had ceased, and until the definitive treaty of peace was signed (Feb. 10, 1763), the military were in charge. Just after the treaty came into effect, in the spring of 1763, the forces in America had to meet the challenge of Pontiac's great rebellion, an uprising inspired by what the change of masters might mean to the red men, and perhaps abetted by the French in the interior. Having suppressed the rebellion, the English were unchallenged masters of the continent from the Gulf of Mexico to the pole, from the Atlantic to the Mississippi. The rising hastened the publication of the well-known Proclamation of October 7, 1763, which set up new provinces out of the conquered territories and made certain provisions for their government. The peace establishment in Canada, now become the province of Quebec, took the transitional form followed in Nova Scotia after the conquest of that province, with a Governor acting under formal "Instructions", and an appointed council. There was also provision for the necessary courts. One of Wolfe's brigadiers, who had been acting governor during the *régime militaire*, General James Murray, became civilian governor and held his post until 1766. He then was recalled and Guy Carleton, a colonel under Wolfe, became lieutenant-governor for two years, then governor for ten (1768-78). It was during his governorship that the great winds of rebellion began to blow in the south. He spent four years (1770-74) of this long period in England, lobbying for the enactment into law of his solution of the Canadian problem. Just before the first bloodshed (1775) he returned to his post, bringing with him his prize, the Quebec Act (1774).

Probably no one in any of the countries concerned really grasped the magnitude of what had occurred in America. Changes of territory were common in Europe, and where no popular nationalism existed, they signified little. But the English had not held territory on the continent since the loss of Calais (1558), and their experience in dealing with alien peoples was limited to the Scots and Irish. After centuries they seemed, by the Union, to have solved the Scottish problem, and as for Ireland, it was far away and seldom heard of. Now the crown of England was to take under its wing a type of alien that it knew nothing about, and these foreigners were so distant that their fate must be left to the few men directly concerned. It could have been argued that the insertion of a miserable 60,000 French into a colonial empire of some two million English Protestants was no great event and should not have occasioned much disturbance, but the truth would be otherwise. A century and more of colonial strife could not be erased from the colonists' memories, even if it had never touched Englishmen. Now that the great threat to the north had gone, they were determined that it should never in any form come back; and what is more, its removal gave them a sense of relief, of freedom and of independence that they could never have previously had. The New Englanders had never been over-fond of England anyway, and now they did not feel even the need of her protection. The balance in America and in the world had been profoundly disturbed.

Moreover, the problem was not merely 60,000 new subjects, for the conquered people formed a strong society in a habitat of crucial geographical importance. The problem, therefore, consisted in associating a new and very different kind of community with old ones which were nearly all of a piece. The English colonies were all self-governing and extremely sensitive about their rights. Could New France be made over at once? If it were not and if authoritarian government were continued, would that not generate suspicions and antagonisms towards the Imperial power? Here was an immediate political dilemma.

Another and sharper problem was to arise in time, as members of the two societies met in the new province of Quebec. How were two such different families to live in this one house? Was there a point that they had in common? In addition to the differences in language, faith, and institutions there were many others, stemming from the same root, equally intractable. Once Canada became an English possession there emerged the profound antithesis, the vast conflict in philosophies, which ever since has kept the country divided and which, in presenting it with a problem of such proportions, constitutes the principal theme of Canadian history.

The French peasantry of the St. Lawrence valley were a chip off the old European block: they duplicated on North American soil the pre-Reformation peasant society of the Old World; they represented the very essence of the medieval, rural, Catholic way of life. To the Catholic everywhere, especially to the rural Catholic, life is more than livelihood. It is a series of ritual acts such as being born, coming of age, marrying, begetting, dying, each of which, properly performed, brings its satisfactions and its reward. There is little need for striving, little occasion for the notion of progress. The rural life harmonizes well with this conception: man is subject to nature and to nature's moods; he learns to acquiesce in the drought and the flood, the good years and the bad. As his animals and plants grow and come to harvest, so he grows and comes to harvest, a creature of nature and of nature's God. It is the simplest and oldest of all religions, Catholic almost by accident.

Into this unchanging world, there comes bursting the hurly-burly of the English man of business. He has long since cut his associations with the soil. He is in a hurry. He wants to get things done. He has ends to gain. He has an object in life. That object is one comprehended only remotely by the peasant. From the first, the New World had released in men the passion of greed. Greed the peasant can understand well enough as an ordinary human quality, but not greed erected into a way of life and fortified not only with the majesty of law but also the sanction of a religion. Yet no set of men have so systematically set up acquisition as an object in itself and made it the centre of a cult, a new god Mammon, as have the men of business of the English-speaking world. In 1760, the new creed had not gone as far as it has today; it has almost swamped us now, especially in the New World,[7] but in 1760, the older elements in English life like feudalism in its eighteenth century form of aristocracy and the more traditional elements in the Church of England still resisted it. It was in the fighting and governmental services that these elements found their strongest expression. It was, therefore, these that were to have the best relations with the conquered Canadian Catholics. The weight of the English thrust into the new province was not, however, to consist in them but in men representing that new way of life which had already appropriated for itself a theology by which its conduct was justified and rationalized.

The connection between Protestantism, and the especially close connection between Calvinism, and material achievement has been the subject of much investigation.[8] Wherever Calvinism has prevailed societies largely committed to the commercial and industrial way of life have arisen.[9] The coincidence seems logical, for although the spirit of acquisition is as old as humanity, Calvinism subtly reinforces it. Its doctrine of "the elect" has led directly to the attempt on the part of the individual to reassure himself that he is one of the elect; and what more visible sign of election unto salvation could God give him than by prospering him? In this and many other ways, Calvinism accentuated the motives of action having to do with success and accomplishment. Everywhere it found its most congenial soil in urban areas, among the middle classes,

[7] Though newer social dynamics are beginning to offer strong resistance to it.
[8] Especially by Max Weber, Ernst Troeltsch, R. H. Tawney, etc. See bibliography in G. Harkness, *John Calvin, The Man and His Ethics* (New York, 1931).
[9] Holland, New England, Scotland, and Canada form examples.

and nowhere more so than in the New World. For there, in communities of English or Dutch origin, traditions that might have held the success motive in check were weak: most people had come to the New World to improve their lot, and, with their middle class and Calvinistic background, improvement almost necessarily meant material improvement. There had logically developed an ethic quite unlike the older Catholic code, with different standards of value, and despising the older ideal with all the intolerance that the new and the moving invariably shows for the old and the static. This ethic of material success passed over easily into success in terms of accomplishment or of power and in these forms afforded that driving energy which has mainly made America. In so doing it reduced to its own utilitarian terms most elements in society, such as education, for example, and even life itself, for deep in the heart of Puritanism there is a denial of life. The dynamic of the commercial ethic has transformed the world but it has left little room for the things of the spirit, and where societies have been completely dominated by it, they have been societies of attenuated art and meagre culture, above all societies whose parsimoniousness with life has made them hollow at the centre.

If Canadian history is to be understood at all, it is necessary first of all to be able to understand and apply to common situations these two ways of life: the static Catholic-rural, careless of well-being, not over-burdened with social responsibility, prodigal of life, welcoming many children, not grieving too intensely if many die and others live misshapen; and the dynamic Calvinist-commercial with its devotion to acquisition and its haunting fear of animal "robustiousness".[10] They touch every corner of the national structure,[11] and there is not a person

[10] "Hawthorne watched with a New England shudder the loud romping and horseplay of the working classes. . . . In New England life was rarified; the Oversoul had been conceived at Brook Farm. In old England, life spewed forth in excess." (*New Statesman and Nation*, London, 24 Oct., 1942, p. 275). The same note is struck in *Notre Milieu, Aperçu général sur le province de Québec* (Montreal, 1942, p. 97 ff. The English population of the Eastern Townships "est devenue une population de vieillards . . . qui ayant vendu leurs biens à des Canadiens-Français, vivent en retraites dans les villages. Ces villages ont, comme on dit, 'l'avant goût d'une nécropole' ('the foretaste of a cemetery')".

[11] The correlations that may be made between the two outlooks on life and their physical manifestations are innumerable. As an example, take the 1941 Census Bulletins on the Blind and the Deaf-Mutes. (This table does not appear in subsequent censuses). 43% of the deaf-mutes in Canada (the total was only 7,000) were French and 56% Catholic. These two elements constituted about 30% and 45% of the total population. Correlations for the blind were similar. These figures represent a whole economic, social, and philosophical complex. The greatly increased Protestant birth rates of the years following the Second World War may in part be attributable to the sharp decline in Puritan attitudes.

living or who has lived in Canada who has not been affected by the antithesis between them, for it has determined the very essence of the country's politics, religion and society. It is not a simple task to reveal it, as it should be revealed, on every page and in every incident.

Close analysis of the antithesis between commercialism and agrarianism pushes it beyond race and religion. There lurks in it some basic contrast in the attitude towards life. On one hand stand those who are close to the soil, irrevocably committed to the land in which and by which they live; and on the other those who simply regard Mother Earth as a source of good things, who cut down its forests and tear out its minerals regardless of its future and then, if opportunity offers, rush off to pleasanter places. This selfish and hostile attitude towards the earth by which man lives gives one pole of modern history: the driving, ambitious, accomplishing, mechanistic pole. It gives us the opportunists, the exploiters, the men with no past and little future. The other attitude gives the pole of acquiescence, acceptance, harmony with life. It produces the custodians of society, the fathers of the race. These attitudes, crystallized in the contrasting figures of the business man and the settler, but not confined to either, are writ large on every page of Canadian history, and they, as well as their racial and religious manifestations, must be understood if Canadians are to understand themselves as a people and their country as a nation.

3. Makeshift Government

In 1763 no one saw the problem in such fundamental terms; for both sides it was a matter of specific rights and privileges, of what was done or not done. Yet in almost every decision taken the fundamentals can be seen mirrored.

True to their genius, the English had no considered policy for their new possessions. There was no clearly charted course in respect to government, to trade, or to religion. The proclamation of 1763 seemed to envisage large-scale immigration and the erection of another colony like the rest, but it was in general terms and not applicable to Canada alone. It apparently saw Canada mainly in terms of the fur trade and the French, for the boundaries of the new province of Quebec which it set up drew a line around the French seigneuries but left a narrow corridor to the upper country.[12] Of penetration into the actual conditions implied by the existence of an alien community it was innocent. In the important matter of the laws that were to apply in Canada it spoke with uncertain voice. It assumed that the English-speaking immigrants who were

[12] See p. 133.

expected would bring with them, as they had done wherever else they had gone, the laws of England. Did that mean that they would have representative government? If so, would the French, mostly illiterate, participate in it? And if they did, would the laws of England that prevented Catholics from taking part in public life be changed for their especial benefit? Or would the English incomers run the country, with the French shoved aside? Would these English have their land-grants in free and common soccage? Would that upset existing French grants and the seigneurial system of tenure? Would the French be stripped of their own laws? If so, the Conquest would have proved harsh indeed. In like manner, would they be stripped of their religion? The Treaty of Paris provided that they should retain freedom to practise their religion and then added the obscure rider, "so far as the laws of England do permit". Strictly interpreted, the laws of England probably would not have permitted of the practice of the Roman religion at all; certainly they would have allowed it and its adherents no privileges, public or private. Was the new province to become another Ireland, with the religion of its people proscribed? These thorny questions the Proclamation did not face. Nor did any English government down to the time of the Quebec Act squarely face them.

England's intentions towards her new colony have often been debated, but that it is impossible to determine them should be plain from the simple reason that England as a political unit did not have any. Various politicians and officials in London had various intentions and these found expression now in one document and now in another, as often as not contradictory. Little knowledge is needed for the state of English politics in that fateful decade of the 1760's with its six ministries in ten years and the party from which all but the last of them was drawn split into as many fragments, to understand how impossible was any consecutive or logical policy. Instability in England, with its deduction, a colonial policy that had little consistency, gave to the obscure new province makeshift government. For all the colonies, and certainly for Quebec, it was not ill-will but ignorance and lack of responsibility that was creating the tempest to come.

Under the circumstances, the local authorities had to act largely in accordance with their best judgment. Murray and Carleton, the English governors during the period, who were in the aristocratic rather than the commercial tradition, tended to make common cause with the gentlemen they found among the French—the seigneurs—and to try and protect the ordinary *habitant*, whom they found a likeable person, from the rapacity of those English who had accepted the invitation of the Proclamation. These men, fly-by-night traders from New England, demobilized soldiers, and other rather irresponsible types, were loud in their insistence on their rights as Englishmen. One of these seemed to be to swindle the innocent *habitants*: they bought up for a song the discarded paper money of the French regime, knowing that an effort was being made to have the French government redeem it, and in the legal confusion after 1763, they successfully trumped up lawsuits to deprive Frenchmen of their land.

Protection for the French should have been found in the courts that Murray had set up, but there were difficulties there—the time and place of meeting, the English system of fees, the language, and also the extraordinary personnel. Chief Justice Gregory had been taken out of the debtors' prison and given his appointment, and Adam Mabane, who became a judge, had begun life as a surgeon's mate in Saunders' fleet. They were just two examples of the odd fish that so frequently drift to a frontier backwater. More important, was the law to be the law of England or the laws of Canada? If the latter, who knew what the laws of Canada were? They had never been printed and most of the experts in them had gone home with the French army. Long research by Attorney-General Masères failed to find out what they were. There was no agreement on such a fundamental as the seigneurial rights of the Crown and these went partially unpaid, as did the services owed to the seigneurs by the *habitants*. The tithing right of the priesthood may have been known, but since the clergy were in no position to enforce collection, it too went by the board, the *habitant*, nothing loath, being freed of both these obligations. Masères himself recommended in place of these very indeterminate "laws of Canada" a code based on usage and on English principle. If his code had been adopted much confusion would have been saved. But there was the promise of the protection of the laws of England constantly standing in the way and made much of by the English group. One point, at least, seemed clear: when it came to commercial matters, the laws of Canada were singularly incoherent.

The religious problem provides the neatest example of the English *ad hoc* method of government. It became not so much a matter of principle as a matter of bargain. Whatever notions anyone in England might have entertained of a grand campaign of evangelism and repression for making the French into Protestants were soon given up, and "the liberty of practising their religion", insofar as church services, marriages, and other rites went, was not interfered with. But there was the momentous question of the priesthood (because many priests were still French-born), and of the consecration and ordination of priests. Were newcomers to be allowed to come from hostile France? Or was a bishop to be allowed to have his old place? Few things could have been more obnoxious to stiff English Protestantism than the idea of a Romish bishop, especially as the introduction of even an Anglican bishop was enough to set Puritan colonists by the ears. Yet it seemed a hardship to allow the ranks of the priesthood to empty for lack of a bishop to ordain candidates, and anyway priests would be smuggled in!

The English colonial authorities were willing to compromise on an individual who should be known as the Superintendent of the Romish Church, and be approved by them, but the Catholic clergy pointed out that that did not solve the problem of ordination and that approval by a Protestant king was after all rather peculiar. Eventually, they ventured to elect to the bishopric of Quebec the Breton, Jean Olivier Briand, hoping that somehow he would find both consecration and English approval (1764). This is just what happened, for he went to England trying to find the approval, and while waiting for it, it was suggested to him that if he could get himself consecrated, nobody was likely to say very much. So he slipped off to France, and the ceremony took place (1766). He then went back to Canada and began to exercise the office of bishop over his flock, and after a long interval was officially recognized as such. In this subterranean way the French church got back its head again. It is a characteristic proceeding of the period: the English Government is ready to do justice, provided that not too much fuss is made; everything can be compromised with everybody.

4. An Apparent Solution—The Quebec Act

Eventually some new kind of system, more or less satisfactory to all parties, would probably have been worked out, for the forces in the colony were of no great pressure and need not have caused an explosion. Events elsewhere, however, brought about a formal attempt at a solution. It was the shadow of the American Revolution that brought forth the Quebec Act.

Guy Carleton, an Ulsterman of rigid and humourless mentality, got on as badly with his English-speaking fellow-subjects in Quebec as had Murray before him, and almost as well with his French-speaking fellow-aristocrats. It seemed clear to him that there was little likelihood of the colony ever becoming Anglicized, and realistic thinking, he believed, should make the most of that fact. Already scenting disturbances to the south, he saw in the French, won over by concessions, a means of helping to keep the southern colonists in their place and hinted that the province might provide troops to take the old Richelieu-Hudson road should there, by the worst of misfortunes, supervene "a catastrophe too shocking to think of". When he went to England on what turned out to be a four-years' absence (1770-74), it was some such view as this that he urged upon the Tory Government of Lord North. Not much in detail is known about his activities during the four years, but it may be supposed that as long as things were reasonably quiet across the Atlantic— which they were from 1770 to 1773—the government would be loath to disturb sleeping dogs. Once the pot began to boil again in lively fashion, with Boston tea parties and committees of correspondence, Carleton's proposals for Quebec would get a better audience. There was also the question of the interior, left since the Proclamation of October 7, 1763.[13] In the interval it had become plain to English traders and officials alike, that the St. Lawrence was the easiest way into it.

So, suddenly, in 1774, the government brought down the Quebec Act. It was numbered by the American colonists, with the other coercive acts of that year, as one of the "Intolerable" Acts and it was opposed by what was left of the English Whig party (men like Fox and Burke) as unnecessary and suspicious, as "squinting at tyranny". But a Tory majority, not opposed to coercion and arbitrary measures, forced it through and it became law, ready for Carleton to take back with him to his government. He had had his way.

The main objections of the English colonists, which had the support of their Whig friends in England, were three: the act set up non-representative and arbitrary government in America; it was the first instance of Parliament legislating a colonial government into existence and was beyond the powers of that municipal assembly; and it "established" the Roman Catholic religion.

Non-representative government of the governor and council type was set up by the Quebec Act, but Parliament surrounded this with safeguards by giving to it virtually no power of taxation. That was contained in another act, its silent partner, the Quebec Revenue Act, 1774, which gave to the new colonial government, as its chief source of revenue, the old dues and fees of the King of France, now the right of the King of England. As to the parliamentary right to legislate for the colonies in every respect, that had been asserted in the Declaratory Act of 1766, and if the Americans refused to accept this view of the British constitution, then so much the worse for them.

The truth seems to have been that by 1774, George III, Lord North, and a large section of the Tories had determined to settle the issue with the Americans and had not much patience for colonial constitutional arguments. The new law itself, in its relation to the Province of Quebec, seemed an act of justice for the 99 per cent of the province's inhabitants

[13] See p. 67.

who were French and Catholic: it decided that in civil matters resort
should be had to the laws of Canada, that the priests should again have
their tithes and the seigneurs their dues[14] and that the oaths obnoxious
to Catholics and which therefore debarred them from public office need
not be taken by them.[15] There was no mention of the question of lan-
gauge and thus no guarantee for French. But on closer inspection,
most of these provisions were seen to apply to the favoured classes,
clergy and seigneurs: the *habitants* certainly had no desire to resume
payment of the tithe and seigneurial dues. "The laws of Canada" related mainly to the land law, that is to seigneurialism. Did the Act,
then, represent justice or expediency? Was it expected to secure the
"natural leaders" of the French, and thus the people too, in the evil day?

There is now no means of answering these questions. As it turned
out the Act did not secure the active loyalty of the *habitants*, who
showed themselves singularly indifferent to the quarrel among *les sacrés
Anglais* and did not appreciate the restoration of their symbols of servitude. But French Canada was still a stratified society and if its natural
leaders accepted and appreciated the act, that was perhaps enough.
This the natural leaders, those whom a modern French Canadian would
term their *élite*, did; and since they were the literate classes, the tradition soon formed which still obtains, of the Quebec Act as the Magna
Carta of French Canada, the great enactment which gave back to the
province its religion, its laws, and its institutions. Extreme eulogists will
even maintain that it ensured the survival of the race itself, whereas
English extremists, who would like to anglicize Quebec, continue to
assume that without the Act the French language would have passed
away.[16] On the contrary, the race with its language would have survived
by its own indomitable will, without the help of English Acts of
Parliament.

The Act was not a complete restoration of the old regime and there
were various escape clauses in it which could have been used to employ
it as an instrument of renovation. It did not restore the old French
criminal law with its secret trials, its lack of confrontation of witnesses
with the accused, its absence of cross-examinations and of juries, and its
refusal to give to the accused the right not to testify against himself.
It did introduce English criminal law, "because of its greater leniency"—
there being only some 100 capital crimes on the English statute book at
the time! English methods of trial, with their attention to the rights of

---

[14] The Quebec Act did not in so many words re-assert seigneurial rights, but it did
restore "the laws of Canada" of which they were a part.
[15] A much milder one being substituted.
[16] "As it has in Louisiana", they are apt to say, forgetting that it has not passed
away in Louisiana.

the subject, made the change a gain, but it is a gain which the English-speaking part of Canada has been too ready to take for granted. The "escape clauses" would have permitted the introduction of the *habeas corpus*, of certain categories of English civil law, and even of English freehold tenure in certain circumstances. Owing to the outbreak of the Revolution, however, there was no chance of their being used. The grievances of the English-speaking, therefore, mounted.

Whatever the state of mind and intentions behind the Act, it must be regarded as a great constitutional landmark in Canadian history and the history of the British Empire. In the province of Quebec, it gave the French assurance of the British Government's good will and apparently of its sense of justice. In North America, it gave the Americans, in equal measure, assurance of its ill-will and sense of injustice, and hastened the Revolution. In the Empire as a whole, it marked a clean departure from the older method of setting up colonial governments by prerogative acts of the Crown and inaugurated the era of parliamentary supremacy in Imperial affairs. Following it, all the great constitutional instruments, such as the Constitutional Act, British North America Act, Commonwealth of Australia Act, Union of South Africa Act, Act of Westminster, were put in the form of Imperial statutes. The second Empire grew up in the system of parliamentary supremacy and accepted it naturally; the first broke up under the controversy over the authority of Parliament to enact fundamental legislation for a colony. A century and a half later, the second Empire hit upon the solution for that contest and produced the "Commonwealth" idea, which represents the point in constitutional thinking attained by the Americans on the eve of their Revolution.[17] Only in our own day has the wheel come full circle. The two conceptions have been reconciled[18] and that by the usual piece of illogicality: by keeping the full dignity of the theory of Parliamentary supremacy and reducing its reality to a ritualistic formula.

Chronology

1760–63 The "Régime Militaire".
1763   Feb. 10: Peace of Paris.
        Oct. 7: The Proclamation, constituting the Province of Quebec.
1763   Pontiac's Rebellion.
1764–68 James Murray, Governor.
1766–68 Guy Carleton, Lieutenant-Governor; 1770: Governor.
1773   "Boston Tea Party".
1774   Quebec Act.
        Quebec Revenue Act.

[17] One very clearly understood and described by John Adams and other leaders of the Revolution.
[18] By the Act of Westminster, 1931. See p. 489 ff.

Additional Reading

Burt, A. L. *The Old Province of Quebec.* Toronto, 1939.
——. *Guy Carleton, Lord Dorchester, 1724-1808.* (*CHA* Booklets, No. 5) Ottawa, 1957.
Chapais, Thomas. *Cours d'histoire du Canada, 1760-1860.* Quebec, 1919-1934. 8 vols.
Clark, S. D. *Movements of Political Protest in Canada, 1640-1840.* Toronto, 1959.
Coupland, R. *The Quebec Act.* London, 1925.
Creighton, D. G. *Commercial Empire of the St. Lawrence, 1760-1850.* Toronto, 1937. (rev. ed., *Empire of the St. Lawrence,* 1956).
Graham, G. *British Policy and Canada.* London, 1930.
Kennedy, W. P. M. *The Constitution of Canada, 1534-1937; An Introduction to its Development, Law, and Custom. . . ,* rev. ed. London, 1938.
——, ed. *Statutes, Treaties, and Documents of the Canadian Constitution, 1713-1929,* 2nd ed. Toronto, 1930.
Martin, Chester. *Empire and Commonwealth.* London, 1929.
——. *Foundations of Canadian Nationhood.* Toronto, 1955.
Peckham, Howard. *Pontiac and the Indian Uprising of 1763.* Princeton, 1947.
Tawney, R. H. *Religion and the Rise of Capitalism.* London, 1929. (Penguin Books, 1938).
Wade, Mason, ed. *Canadian Dualism: Studies of French-English Relations.* Toronto, 1960.
Weber, Max. *The Protestant Ethic and the Spirit of Capitalism.* New York, 1958.

CHAPTER 7

The Disruption of the English Race

1. Quebec and the American Revolution, 1774-1783

In its direct aspect the American Revolution enters the story of Canada only through a few military incidents, such as the invasion of 1755 and the departure for the south of Burgoyne's army in 1777. Indirectly there is the whole tremendous problem of the relation of Canada to the United States, to say nothing of the immediate specific effect, the Loyalist immigration. For subsequent generations the Revolution has been in the English-speaking world what the Reformation has been for the Christian world: those on one side of it have rejoiced at the new nation and its strength and have held in disapproval and contempt the old mould out of which they burst; those on the other have seen in it the great tragedy of history, the breaking of the unity of the race, the driving of those of like blood apart—just as the Reformation broke the unity of the faith.

There have been few in the United States who have looked backward, sighing for the return of a vanished past,[1] and probably not many in Great Britain either, busy with her own new life ever since. But Canada is the child of the Revolution: many of its people are Americans who

[1] Those who did have never thought of a renewed colonial status, but they have been fond of Anglicizing themselves in various ways, just as a wing of Protestantism also looks back with regret and approaches Catholicism in its ritual.

did not break the tie with England, and they feel more than any others the tragedy of the cleavage. They are the children of divorced parents and they know the bitterness that comes of a broken home. In the heart of the Canadian of English speech there will be found, if he will confess it—as he often will—one profound spiritual wound, the division in the race, the American Revolution.

For the American colonists, the period after the conquest of Canada was one of freedom and irresponsibility: the threat to the north removed, they could go ahead with their own abounding life, heedless of the world beyond their doors. When the British Government sought, not in a very wise way, to impose on them responsibility for their own continent, they would have nothing to do with the proposals. Perhaps William Pitt had been too clever in his conquests: perhaps a united empire would have been better served by more blundering commanders-in-chief, not fewer. That day, however, was over. And now it seemed natural to systematic and efficient men like George Grenville to overhaul and tidy up the great edifice that had been built. England had managed her colonies in the eighteenth century on the principle of salutary neglect. There was much that needed to be attended to, but in peace it was best to let sleeping dogs lie, and in wartime reform was not possible. The situation had been like the Irishman's roof: when it was not raining it did not need mending, and when it was raining it could not be mended. George Grenville undertook to mend the roof, and before he and his successors had finished their work, there was neither roof nor house.

"We had always governed ourselves," said an old colonist, "and then they began to interfere with us." That surely is explanation enough of the Revolution. Once there was no foreign threat to coerce them, people who had always governed themselves could not be coerced. If the pace had not been forced, the colonial system or absence of system—with its place men in offices, its structure of prohibitions, preferences, bounties, and regulations that went by the name of mercantilism, and all its other anachronisms—would have held up for a long time by mere force of custom; but to attempt to alter it in the direction of centralization, as did the politicians of the England of the 1760's and 1770's was to shove it over. The day for recriminations has passed, but surely history has seldom witnessed the like of the blind and stupid conduct by which British ministers destroyed an empire and split the race. Nor was it for lack of men who told them plainly where they were going. Both the Earl of Chatham (the elder Pitt) and Edmund Burke, to name only the two most prominent, were well aware of where the course being followed by the Tories of the day must lead. It must be agreed that the Tories had the weight of British public opinion on their side. But whom the gods wish to destroy, they first make mad!

For the French people of Quebec, learned and unlearned alike, the subtleties of constitutional doctrine in this domestic quarrel among the English must have been incomprehensible. But everyone knew what a rebel was and could see the simple issue of subject versus king. When, however, the rebel subjects invaded his countryside in 1775, the *habitant* could hardly be expected to behave like a British partisan; he had no emotional attachment to a distant English and Protestant king, and the rebels were near at hand. No surprise then that some urge of the moment—perhaps personal grievances, American inducement, or, in an occasional case, understanding of the principles at stake—drew off to the rebel camp a few hundred Canadian recruits. On the defeat of the Americans these became refugees, the first in the procession from the conservative north to the less constricting atmosphere of the "States". To the average *habitant*, it seemed best to let the English fight it out. The rebels' proclamations he probably never saw, nor would he have understood them anyway, but the rebels' money he did. While coin was forthcoming, so were supplies. When, however, payment began to be made in paper, that was another story. He had had enough of the French king's worthless paper. So he found another reason for holding aloof, a reason doubly strong after the collapse of the American siege of Quebec (1755).

With priests and seigneurs it was a different story, especially with the priests. They knew the ideas of *les Bastonnois* about Catholicism; they knew their bread was buttered on the side of the Crown. So did the seigneurs (some of whom were Scotsmen who had found it compatible with romance to acquire a seigneury by first acquiring its heiress). Hence Guy Carleton need not worry about the classes. But the masses, in spite of all he thought he had obtained for them, stood aside. "The most ungratefullest wretches," he wrote home in his indignation.

There was another group in the colony who watched proceedings with a wary eye—the English-speaking people of the non-official class. They were concentrated in Montreal and Quebec. Their reputation for "respectability" had been rising, particularly since they had been joined by substantial merchants from Albany, and since some of those who had rushed into the colony after the conquest had departed. But many of them had affiliations southward, and a rebel success might have freed them from onerous obligations. Moreover, had they not been denied their rights as British subjects? They were not likely to get any enlargement of their privileges, any more of the "rights of Englishmen", out of Carleton.

Division of race and interest made the position of Carleton, as the man responsible for the colony's defence, almost impossible. He deserves the credit history gives him for getting out of a tight place. His avoidance of capture at Montreal was a good piece of work and his rout of Montgomery at Quebec a little later,[2] a decisive victory. He had not destroyed the colonial force; but by spring it was so weak that it had to withdraw, and with its retreat the last siege of the old city had ended.

Once the war had become more than a matter of midnight sieges, both sides organized for a large-scale effort. In 1776 Carleton, perhaps because he considered there might still be opportunity for reconciliation, had shepherded the rest of the Continentals out of the province, when he might conceivably have captured them all and gone on towards New York.[3] But the time to stop the quarrel had passed, and next year the advance in force began. A large army, consisting of some English troops and of German mercenaries, was sent out from England. Carleton was out of favour with the authorities probably because he had allowed the American besiegers of Quebec to escape and it must have been with chagrin that he saw the command go to Burgoyne, especially as it was to be his favourite strategy that was to be followed. This consisted in an advance up the Richelieu and down the Hudson to meet General Howe and cut the colonies in two, the normal manoeuvre for all wars in eastern North America—or the Seven Years' War in reverse.[4] Burgoyne's southward march ended in his being entrapped and forced into surrender at Saratoga (1777). This brought in France and thus indirectly lost the war for Great Britain. The same year Carleton, having made himself cordially disliked by his senior officials for his arrogant ways, went home and was replaced by an honest but not singularly brilliant Swiss soldier of fortune, General Haldimand, who saw the war out in Quebec and remained for a year of peace. Haldimand was equal to the military duties laid upon him, which were defensive and protective, but not very well fitted for his civil responsibilities as governor. Before he retired he had alienated the English merchant class, though, French in speech if Protestant in religion, he had got on well with the native Canadians.

2. The Revolution Settlement

It was during Haldimand's regime that the fateful conclusion of the family quarrel was reached. Great Britain was forced to acknowledge independence of the colonies and make peace. The settlement, the

---

[2] Dec. 31, 1775.
[3] A. L. Burt, *The United States, Great Britain and British North America from the Revolution to the Establishment of Peace After the War of 1812* (Toronto, 1940), pp. 10-11.
[4] See p. 60.

Treaty of Paris, 1783, ranks with the Treaty of Paris of 1763 and the British North America Act as one of the great fundamental documents in Canadian history, for it severed the old empire from the new, and declared the boundaries between the old and the new British North America.

The diplomacy of the settlement forms too intricate a story to be given here and belongs to Anglo-American history rather than to Canadian. Canadians are interested in that side of it only as a young man would be in negotiations that his father conducted before he was born and that resulted in his inheriting a shrunken estate. What happened at Paris was not entirely a credit to any of the parties. Whereas American representatives have sometimes been accused of breaking faith with their French allies and the French did not have the purity of motive towards the Americans which they professed, the British showed the most amazing confusion of purpose and an astonishing incompetence in negotiation. The reality is that the European powers, England included, did not have vital interests in America; and when they had to deal with men who were making a nation, whose whole future was centred on the kind of bargain they could drive, they were at a disadvantage, and a settlement favourable beyond the wildest American dreams resulted.

For the British, the sun of England's glory seemed set when "America", meaning the thirteen colonies, was lost, and there was no point in prolonging the fratricidal struggle or quarreling about the way in which it was to be ended. Since Elizabethan days few Englishmen had seen the colonies in any light but the commercial, and in the eighteenth century, with its cold rationalism, this view had swallowed up all others. The colonies had been "empty spaces, out there", "plantations", places where the Moll Flanders of the day went for England's good; above all they had been markets. There was little conception of a great race bestriding the Atlantic, little emotional sanction for empire. But the Revolutionary War had pressed in on Englishmen a good deal of new information about America, and now that it was too late, the nation woke up to what it had lost. In the moment of their departure the Americans became children and blood brothers. Here was one cause of indifference to the settlement. If they must go, get the parting over with, and as generously as possible, so that reconciliation might follow. To people who knew nothing about America, even from a map, what did a few square miles more or less of wilderness matter? The French, who had had twenty years to think over their own losses, made the jibe that "England does not make peace, she buys it". Rather, England was winding up the whole affair, writing it off as her most colossal failure.

The Revolution had broken out when the old conception of Empire, the mercantilistic, was wearing out and before the new, the sentimental idea of Empire, had been formed. The old "markets" conception, product of purest mercantilism, was, for the best minds, losing it validity. Adam Smith had published his deflating *Wealth of Nations* in 1776, and he is supposed to have advised Lord Shelburne, on the latter's becoming Prime Minister (1782), that the best way of ending the dispute would be to give up everything in America, to clear out and let the colonists have the whole continent: they, he argued, would develop it vigorously and they would need English capital to do it. That would mean English goods and the "benefit" of America to England would be greater than ever. Benjamin Franklin made the same proposal to Oswald, the first British negotiator, who seemed to be as much on the colonial side as Franklin himself, and Oswald recommended it to London. Shelburne himself was in favour of a generous boundary settlement because he believed that magnanimity would tend to heal the wounds and bring the two parties together again. The main question remaining unanswered in respect to the negotiations of 1782-83 is why, with such views paramount, the British retained any territory at all in North America. To say that they had to look after the interests of the fur traders and find homes for the Loyalist *émigrés* is to give no explanation at all, for neither point seems to have got much consideration at Paris: authorities knew well enough that the fur trade was small in terms of pounds and shillings and that other areas of settlement could have been found for the Loyalists. Factors of possibly greater weight than these were the settlements in Nova Scotia, the fishing interests of that province and of Newfoundland, the strategic harbour of Halifax, and the renewed confidence given by Admiral Rodney's great naval victory of 1782. The diplomatic triangle which developed between France and Spain (the two European allies), the Americans, and the English, is also to be allowed for. Neither Americans nor Europeans really desired the British out of America. The French wished to keep the Americans dependent upon them, which could best be done by keeping the British on the St. Lawrence. The Americans, in their turn, had no desire to see the French back on that river.

Perhaps all these factors together suffice to explain why certain colonies remained in British control. Collectively, as a small stake on the American continent, they were not a large liability and might at some time come in handy. Or perhaps the explanation is simpler and lies in Adam Smith's statement—"no nation willingly surrenders territory".

Whatever the explanation, the British kept their toe-hold in America. None would be more surprised than the men responsible for doing so to learn that the successors of those they had left clinging so precariously to it had succeeded in securing their position and enlarging it into modern Canada. Nor would they have been prepared for the criticisms and recriminations so often directed at them for their bungling settlement. In 1783 the English were fighting for England, not for stretches of American wilderness, of which not even accurate maps were available. The boundary lines agreed upon reflected both the lack of interest and the lack of knowledge. The settlement gave to the Americans territory upon which no American had ever set foot[5] and it described parts of the boundary in impossible geographical terms.[6] The boundary provisions of the Treaty were to provide the most prolific area of contention between the English-speaking peoples: the disputes arising out of them were not all settled until the twentieth century.[7]

If they desired to have any territory at all left under their control in America, why did not the British contend for a better settlement? They probably did about as well as could have been expected in the eastern area from the Atlantic to the intersection of the St. Lawrence by the 45th parallel: here they were arguing the old French case, while the Americans were arguing the former English case. But from that point west, the French case was surely in their favour, and possession gave them nine points of the law. Why the British did not insist on the boundaries according to the Quebec Act, or at least some compromise between them and the line actually settled on, something that would have given them a water connection to the Ohio and the possession of Lake Michigan, it is hard to understand, except on the suggestion advanced in the preceding paragraph or on the hypothesis that the American offer of freedom of trade and travel across the boundary seemed as good as political possession.[8]

A memoir of the time, submitted to government by a firm of fur traders, argues for the Lake Erie-Upper Ohio line, the boundary laid down by the Quebec Act.[9] If this be found impossible, it says, retreat to the next, the western Lake Erie-Maumee-Wabash line, thence to the Chicago-Illinois River, thence to Green Bay, thence to the connections between Lake Superior and the Mississippi. The final line, it contends, upon which there is any point in standing, if any road is to be kept open to the upper country, is "the water connection between Lake

[5] Modern Wisconsin and Minnesota.

[6] The boundary of the Lake of the Woods region was to run "to the said point thereof and from thence in a due west course to the River Mississippi". The Mississippi lay due *south* of the Lake of the Woods.

[7] The last was the arbitration held under the treaty of 11 April, 1908, over small islands in the mouth of the St. Croix.

[8] On boundaries see A. L. Burt, *op. cit.*, pp. 20-27, where he suggests that actual boundaries were not considered as such but as mere adumbrations of boundaries.

[9] See p. 75.

Superior and the Lake of the Woods". This was the line agreed upon, though since the Grand Portage lay to the south of it, it was later found impracticable and a line still farther north had to be found by the fur traders. The fur traders did not have much influence in the settlement, but apparently government was anxious to keep open some kind of connection with the west. Why then did it keep the least favourable of all? The mystery remains unsolved. In practice it accepted one of the two alternatives offered by the American commissioners, both based on expediency—either the line of 45° right through to Louisiana[10] or the "natural" channel through the river and lakes. This latter was chosen, "natural" being interpreted to mean not the middle of Lake Michigan but a line drawn well to the north in Lake Superior around Isle Royale, which almost blocked the British from access to the western end of the lake.

The line that had been agreed upon made any coherence of British territory almost impossible: it separated what is now New Brunswick from the St. Lawrence settlements, and when the details were later on filled in, it gave the main channels of navigation in the St. Lawrence and the lakes (above the point of intersection of 45° with the river) to the Americans, rendering the rising British colonies dependent on their good will. With remarkable precision, it divided the fertile country of the south, save for the peninsula of southern Ontario, from the muskeg and rock of the Canadian shield. For a future of significance, what remained to Great Britain in America was unpromising in the extreme.

3. Parting in Bad Blood

Of greater moment than the boundary settlement was the parting itself. Here surely was the profoundest depth of the Revolution. For the parting had been in bad blood. The race was broken. Neither Englishmen nor Canadians, especially Canadians, have realized to this day what Revolution really means, how wide and enduring is the gulf that it opens between the winning and the losing sides. In Canada there is much American influence, but no instinctive understanding, except on the part of individuals here and there, of what the Revolution did to the older society. From the beginning, Canadians have been emphatically on one side of the gulf and Americans on the other. Environment and language have given them much in common, but throughout their histories the gulf of Revolution has been a mental reservation with them all, keeping them from complete understanding, and precipitating dif-

[10] The watershed of the right bank of the Mississippi.

ficulties and misunderstandings which have gone far deeper than their apparent causes. Quarrels about a particular bit of land in a boundary settlement predicated, though they did not express, a principle which each party was doing its best to uphold, the one that the American Revolution had ushered in the New Jerusalem, the other that it had been a foul and treasonable occurrence. In England there was little understanding of the spirit of America but much generous appreciation of the Revolutionists and their ideals. In Canada the spirit of America came spontaneously but there was little understanding of the essential nature of the Revolution and still less sympathy with the breadth of the ideals that had partly inspired it and which it in turn inspired.

Canadians lived on the lost cause, hoping in the bottom of their hearts that some day their side would win. Americans for their part were sure that they represented triumph. Theirs was the rising sun. Each party from the beginning leaned over backward in its effort to assume the erect posture of its principles. The "Yankees", whenever they had dealings with the British, became exaggeratedly "Yankee". The Canadians, in every contact they had with the "Yankees", tried to show how "British" they were. For the vast majority of Americans, except those along the northern border, once the War of 1812 had been passed, Canada became only a half-heard whisper, but no Canadian could forget the United States. So for generations each side consciously strove to get farther away from the other.

The American Revolution bore not one but two nations in its womb —the American, its obvious offspring, and a more obscure progeny, the Canadian. Here, for the lands north of the border, was to be the Revolution's highest interpretation: it gave rise to a second American country, Canada, the offshoot of the losing, conservative side of a great racial upheaval.

Chronology

1775   Montgomery and Arnold capture St. John's and Montreal.
       The Americans defeated at Quebec and Montgomery killed.
1776   Carleton expels the Americans from Canada.
       Declaration of Independence of the United States of America.
       Adam Smith's *Wealth of Nations*.
1777   Burgoyne surrenders at Saratoga.
1778   Alliance between France and the United States.
       Butler's Rangers attack western frontiers of New York.
1778–84 Haldimand, Governor of Quebec.
1782–83 Earl of Shelburne, Prime Minister.
1783   Peace of Paris.
       Independence of the United States of America.

Additional Reading

Bemis, Samuel F. *The Diplomacy of the American Revolution.* Bloomington, Ind., 1957.

Bradley, A. G. *Lord Dorchester.* London, 1926.

Kerr, W. B. *The Maritime Provinces of British North America and the American Revolution.* Sackville, N.B., 1941.

Ryerson, Egerton. *The Loyalists of America and their Times.* Toronto, 1880.

Stanley, G. F. G. *For Want of a Horse* (being a journal of the Campaigns against the Americans in 1776 and 1777 by an officer who served with General Burgoyne). Toronto, 1962.

Talman, J. J., ed. *Loyalist Narratives from Upper Canada.* Toronto, 1946.

Van Tyne, C. H. *The Loyalists in the American Revolution.* New York, 1902.

Wallace, W. S. *The United Empire Loyalists.* (Chronicles of Canada, Vol. 13) Toronto, 1914.

Wrong, G. M. *Canada and the American Revolution.* Toronto, 1935.

CHAPTER 8

The Arch without a Keystone: British North America after the Revolution

1. The Old Colonial System: The Atlantic Trading Unit

The first British American Empire at its time of greatest extent, 1763-1776, might have been likened to an umbrella. The end of the handle was grasped by John Bull in the British Isles, who was holding it out open in front of him. At the top side of the frame was Labrador and at the bottom, the Leeward Islands. In between lay all the continental colonies and Newfoundland.

To make the umbrella had taken just a century and a half. The great additions had come in 1713, when the Hudson's Bay territories, Newfoundland and Nova Scotia, were added, and in 1763, with the conquest of Canada, Acadia, the islands in the Gulf of St. Lawrence and the Floridas. The great subtraction came in 1776, when the keystone of the Atlantic arch of colonies and a good part of each wing fell out: every colony from Massachusetts to Georgia took itself off and the Spaniards regained the Floridas. The smiling lands of New York and Pennsylvania, the wealth of the plantation states and the wide-ranging energies of the New Englanders were gone. These jewels no longer shone in the British Crown. To shine in their stead, with lacklustre light, there remained the fogs and codfish of Newfoundland, the barren rocks and pine trees of Nova Scotia, and the St. Lawrence with its furs and its Frenchmen. King George now in bitter truth reigned in the place of King Louis and a poor place it was. No wonder that Englishmen felt that the world had come to an end, that "Britain's glory had departed". Well might they, when their thoughts turned to the millions of fellow-subjects who, but for a foolish king and as weak a set of ministers as Great Britain has ever had, might still have been with them, reasonably satisfied with the regime under which they had grown up.

The Old Colonial System, as that regime is usually designated, is a convenient short-hand phrase for the jumble of charters, statutes, orders, rules, and regulations, political or commercial in tenor and administrative or executive in purpose, which came into existence in the seventeenth and eighteenth centuries. Politically, it involved everything from the high theories of society governing the relations of colonies and mother country, to the miserable small change of colonial patronage. Economically, it extended from great regulative policies to the minutest details of customs administration.

Until the Quebec Act, 1774, every British colonial constitution had proceeded from the Crown, rather than from Parliament. In the eighteenth century, prior to the conquest of Canada, two new continental goverments had been set up—Nova Scotia the thirteenth colony, and Georgia the fourteenth. Neither of these constituted a departure from the old rule. The Crown, directly or indirectly, also appointed the more important colonial officials, such as the judges. It kept in its hands the old royal right to refuse assent to legislation; when colonial acts reached London, they could be disallowed within a given period, usually one year. Unless disallowed, they were operative. The right of final appeal to the King-in-Council was part of the colonial heritage, the law of England.

In England, machinery for the superintendence of empire developed gradually, growing out of that central tree of all English institutions, the Privy Council. At first this body threw off a committee, then one of the King's two Secretaries of State[1] assumed nominal oversight, assisted by a salaried *Committee for Trade and Plantations*, whose chairman, *The President of the Board of Trade*, might or might not be a member of the Council. The last Presidents of importance were Lord Shelburne, April-September, 1763 and Lord Hillsborough, who issued the proclamation of October 7, 1763.[2] In 1768, American affairs had become troublesome enough to warrant the creation of a third Secretaryship of State (Secretary of State for America). This office lasted until 1782 when it was abolished on the ground that there was no longer any need for it, decisive testimony to what Englishmen believed the Revolution

[1] The Secretaries of State in 18th-century England corresponded more or less exactly to the modern Secretary of State for Foreign Affairs.
[2] See p. 67.

had done to the Empire. After that year, the colonies were the Cinder-
ellas of English government, drifting about from department to department until they found haven with the Secretary-at-War, where they
remained. A separate Colonial Office gradually developed during the
early nineteenth century, but there was no separate Colonial Secretaryship until 1854.

In addition to the Secretary and the Board, half a dozen other
imperial departments had authority in the colonies. The Treasury,
through the Customs, appointed and controlled customs officials, as well
as their receipts. The army, through several offices, controlled movements, disposition, and payment of the land forces. The Admiralty,
through its senior officer on the American station, exercised considerable
jurisdiction in maritime law and in shipping and maritime regulations.
Senior officers on the spot took no orders from each other.[3] All the
departments were in competition with one another, and fought vigorously for their share of the colonial patronage, which, considerable item
though it was, was not nearly large enough for the vast army of the
somewhat well-born. Neither before nor after the Revolution was any
attempt made to bring order out of this chaos.

The administrative agencies in London had as their functions the
appointment and recall of governors and other officials, the issue of
commissions and of formal "instructions", and correspondence. Correspondence included everything from the simplest routine to the gravest
decisions of policy. In general, the imperial administrative system,
though it often commanded the services of able men, was cumbersome,
inefficient, and saturated with favouritism, absenteeism, and corruption.
But as George Grenville found, that is why it worked.

To discern how policy was made is more difficult. The Secretary of
State himself made fairly large decisions. The Duke of Newcastle's
decision, when he was pressed about the defence of Annapolis Royal,
was typical of that noble fumbler: "Annapolis must be defended, to be
sure Annapolis must be defended. . . . Where is Annapolis?" The great
campaigns of the Seven Years' War were planned by William Pitt, Secretary of State. The Stamp Act was introduced by the Prime Minister,
George Grenville, after he had offered the colonies opportunity for hear-
ings on his proposals. It was repealed by the Prime Minister, Lord Rock-
ingham, after a formal inquiry had been made into its operation. The
"Intolerable Acts" were introduced by Lord North's government, after
the King had made his notorious remark as to the die being cast and
the colonies having either to triumph or submit. George III himself

---

[3] An admiral took no orders from a colonial governor.

must bear responsibility for the leading decisions that drove the colonies out of the Empire; Lord North confessed as much at the end of his ministry. The Quebec Act was introduced by government, but it is legitimate to infer that Guy Carleton had a great deal to do with it. Day-to-day policy seems to have been departmental, with graver decisions the responsibility of Cabinet.

High policy, although determined by government, naturally had to be formulated within the prevailing assumptions about colonies. These altered from age to age. The Elizabethans had expected colonies to be "other Englands", extensions of the race, while the Puritans had determined that their settlements would be shrines of their God. As the seventeenth century wore on, however, and the tide of staple products began to flow out of America, commercial considerations swallowed up all others. As tobacco, sugar, and rice poured into England, manufactured goods poured out. The plantations in the forests and islands of America proved insatiable in their demands and from the latter half of the seventeenth century on, English exporters had a continuous seller's market in the New World. The pressure upon production invited short cuts, and, necessity being the mother of invention, ways of supplementing hand labour were devised; the great industrial machine inventions of the eighteenth century were the result. America, by the natural wealth it supplied and the necessities its exploitation demanded, had been a major factor in ushering in the machine age and the Industrial Revolution. Colonial policy in consequence became predominantly commercial.

As men of business multiplied in numbers and wealth, they spoke more loudly in governmental circles. In a day when statesmen were seldom men of business, the chance often came to the business man to get legislation practically on his own terms. This government by business men for business men, which has often been called the mercantile system, was not systematic in its means but in its end, which was simply to secure for the merchants of England the greatest possible benefits out of every given situation. Adam Smith neatly indicated the spirit of mercantilism in his remark to the effect that what every merchant wanted was some device that would compel the customer to come into his shop. Every man of business secretly craves the blessings of monopoly. So does every nation. Mercantilism, as an attempt to use the power of the state to secure advantages for the home merchant and deny them to the foreign competitors, is with us always.

The mercantile system as applied to the historical phenomena of the colonial world of the seventeenth, eighteenth, and nineteenth centuries, was virtually identical with the great body of regulations making up the "Old Colonial System". Among the most famous of these on the English

Statute Book (and all nations having colonies manifested the same exclusive spirit and the same desire to make profits out of them) were the Navigation Acts (of which the two principal were enacted in 1651 and in 1660), which gave a monopoly of trade within the English Empire to English ships.[4] Such acts have been judged successful both in creating an English mercantile marine and in providing a basis for naval power, the merchant navy constituting in the phrase of the day, a "nursery for seamen". They lasted two centuries, 1649-1849, and were replaced by less conspicuous legislation, British and Dominion, whose object has not been materially different. They are the best example in the colonial system of statesmanship joined to vested interests, the vested interests securing profits and the statesmen securing defence. Adam Smith condemned them as commercial arrangements but commended them for their national value in his dictum that defence is of more importance than opulence.

The Navigation Acts were but a fraction of the whole body of government enactment, which extended in every colonial and commercial direction. Early in the eighteenth century, in an attempt to develop an alternative supply to timber from the Baltic, the Timber Bounties were instituted. Later on came the Molasses Act of 1733, the Hat Act,[5] the Iron Act of 1751, new timber legislation, the system of "enumerated articles", and the innumerable port and shipping regulations. Some of this legislation rested on relatively broad ideas of national interests; some of it even represented a great imperial design; but most of it was merely a response to the individuals or groups who were able to gain the ear of government: the "Old Colonial System", or "the mercantile system", when analyzed reveals the features of a familiar modern friend, the pressure group.

The shipping interest soon became and remained the most important of pressure groups. It spanned the oceans, and by the time of the Revolution, half as many ships were being built and operated in New England as in Old. But the centre of pressure remained in Great Britain, maintained by shipping associations of various types. A second type of influence was that of organized merchant groups in the principal ports, especially London: "The merchants of London trading to North America" took an active part in some of the decisive incidents both

---

[4] The term included colonial ships.
[5] The Hat Act affords a good example of pressure, for it was practically dictated by the hat industry. See M. G. Lawson, *Fur, A Study in English Mercantilism, 1700-1775* (Toronto, 1943). See also L. H. Gipson, *The British Empire Before the American Revolution*, III, 237-242; and J. F. Crean, "Hats and the Fur Trade," *CJEPS*, XXVIII (August, 1962), 373-386.

before and after the Revolution. A third group consisted in English manufacturers; they do not appear to have been as powerful as either of the preceding, but the Iron Act of 1751 indicates their rising influence. A fourth group, the West Indian sugar planters, most of whom were born in England and expected to return there, maintained a powerful lobby in London for generations and as early as 1733 secured the Molasses Act. In 1764 they secured the Sugar Act, directed against the continental colonies' importations from the foreign West Indies. The West Indians remained strong until the abolition of slavery in 1833 and the adoption of free trade in 1846 reduced the islands to minor importance in the scheme of Empire. The continental colonies were the least influential; some of them maintained agents in London to keep an eye on their interests, but the pre-Revolutionary agent did not accomplish much. In contrast, post-Revolutionary agents, such as Bliss of Nova Scotia, sometimes had influence in helping to prevent the repeal of legislation favourable to the colonies.

The "Old Colonial System", in the eyes of the theorists favourable to it, rose to a highly idealistic conception of Empire. The all-wise counsellors of the King, brooding over these mysteries in London and gazing out over the world-wide expanse of Empire, deftly revolved the colonial planets around the metropolitan sun in ordered harmony. The Empire was a planned and co-ordinated body and transcended mere commercial concepts such as mercantilism. Needless to say, such fine-spun notions were not very close to reality. But the Colonial System did become well enough defined to be recognized as the special English type of imperial organization, not systematic in a precise sense but well enough understood in its general features, which were embodied in such slogans as "Ships, Colonies and Commerce", "The Privilege of regulating Colonial Trade", "The Regulation of Trade in return for Protection", or "the Western Ocean as a 'Nursery for Seamen' ".

2. The Atlantic Trading Unit

The pre-Revolutionary Empire was essentially an empire of the North Atlantic: it might conveniently have been called "The North Atlantic Trading Unit". Its metropolitan centre, Great Britain or London, that is, in practice, held all the threads in its hands. In London were concentrated finance and political influence, the business relations with Europe and with America, the internal industrial connections; and from the British Isles went out the factors for the branch houses abroad, whether fur factors for the "factories" of Hudson's Bay, tobacco factors for Virginia, or slave factors for the west coast of Africa. There was no doubt about John Bull having firm hold of the umbrella handle.

In America each geographical area had its appropriate staple, such as codfish from Newfoundland or rice from the Carolinas. Most of the produce went to England but where surpluses existed, their export elsewhere was usually permissible. One of the striking contrasts between the first Empire and the second was the great place of the West Indies in the first. "The Sugar Islands", with their sugar, molasses, rum, spices, pimento, cotton, and slaves, weighed as heavily in the mercantilistic scale as all the continental colonies put together.

On the ocean, ships followed well-understood routes. Large vessels from England with manufactures for the West Indies ran across the Bay of Biscay and dropped down the Trade Winds to the Leeward Islands. Returning, they might run up along the coast of the continent and call in at some southern port for cotton, tobacco or rice. Other ships left English ports with holds filled with cheap trade goods, such as rum, muskets, and axes; ran down to the West Coast of Africa and there picked up cargoes of slaves in exchange and carried them across to America, either to the British Islands or the Spanish main; then returned to England with West India wares. This was a version of the so-called "triangular trade".

The most successful of all the Atlantic trades was conducted by New England, old England's competitor within the Empire. By the eighteenth century, in addition to their codfisheries on the Banks, New Englanders were drying and pickling all kinds of fish, and were making clapboards, shingles, lumber, "knock-down" door and window frames, ready-made houses, and some of the ingenious gadgets for which the Yankee was to become famous. The Banks schooners (bankers), small ships manned by light crews, cheaply operated, fast, of shallow draft, and able to get into any West India creek, which meant almost to the doors of the plantations, were ideal for the island trade. They were used for fishing on the Banks in season and then in autumn and winter could be employed for West Indies voyages. On the way south, with cargoes made up of small parcels of the things named above, they might slip into a port of the middle colonies and pick up a few chickens, a cow or two, or a horse. When they arrived in the islands the crews peddled their cargoes from plantation to plantation, taking in return Spanish dollars (whence the currency of today) and island products, chiefly molasses for local New England distilleries, which made from it a peculiarly obnoxious brand of rum. This rum came in handy for the African trade: cheap rum and trade goods to Africa; slaves to the West Indies; molasses, sugar, and rum to New England. This was the second version of the "triangular trade". New Englanders were not particular whether their cargoes went to or came from the foreign West Indies; smuggling was easy, an innocent offence, and profits the main consideration. Once

their violent reaction to the Molasses and Sugar Acts, especially when
these were enforced.

All eighteenth century roads led to the West Indian Islands, those
givers of good things; they were the pivots of empire. The Old Colonial
System was a West Indies system, a sugar, rum, and molasses system.
Regrettable but true, the old Empire was largely built on rum and
slaves. But it worked well and brought prosperity all round, except to
the slaves.

3. The Old Colonial System in the New Empire and the Failure to Reconstitute the Atlantic Trading Unit

The Revolution, by tearing the continental colonies out of the Empire,
tore up the Old Colonial System. Could it be reconstructed? On that
question there developed a controversy which raged for two generations.

The Treaty of Paris (1783) was designed as only part of the settlement between motherland and colonies. The other part was to have
been a generous trade arrangement which would have left the old system
more or less undamaged: control from the centre would have been
replaced by control by agreement, and the Atlantic Trading Unit would
have continued. But the Prime Ministership of Shelburne, originator of
the idea, was brief, a period of confusion in English government followed,[6] and when William Pitt took up the plan, opposition proved
powerful enough to wreck it. The commercial and West India groups
were aligned against the shipping interests, which feared the competition
of the American mercantile marine, and had the good luck to find a
champion in John Holroyd, Lord Sheffield. Sheffield, posing as a disinterested student of trade, contended that the Americans, having made
themselves foreigners, should now be treated as foreigners. His books
gained a wide audience, for they went beyond economic discussion and
struck a high patriotic note. All was not lost! England could live without the Americans! Sound principles would build a wealthier empire
than before! Sheffield and the shipping interests won the day. The Shel-
burne-Fox-Pitt policy of healing was laid aside, and militant mercantilist
practices resumed. American ships and goods were to be excluded from
the West Indies and from the remaining continental colonies, and in
England itself they were to be put under all possible disabilities.
Generosity disappeared; reaction reigned.

The objective was to re-establish the Atlantic Trading Unit on what

---

[6] A hiatus of a month in the winter of 1783 during which there was no ministry,
then the 'infamous coalition' of Fox and North, April-December, 1783.

remained of the Empire. The old trade routes would have to be shifted to run not from New England but from Nova Scotia or Canada. A glance at the map would suggest that Nova Scotia could step into New England's shoes without too much difficulty, for it is no farther from the West Indies and nearer to the source of slave-food, codfish. But there were other factors.

Nova Scotia (the name then including New Brunswick) was the poorest and least populated of the continental colonies. It was an extension of New England, but not New England over again. It did not have a good enough climate, enough soil, enough trading initiative or capital for the task of supplying the West Indies. It did have dried codfish and a variety of other fish, but it had no grains. It had some lumber and shingles, but not enough, and it did not have skill in making these things. It had none of the Yankee's knock-down houses. Its schooners would not be allowed to call in at American ports and complete cargoes on the way down: they would be able to get no grain and cattle and none of a commodity still more essential, the humble white oak barrel stave.

The wooden barrel is the ancestor of the modern tin can. The barrel, under its various denominations of kegs, firkins, hogsheads, pipes, and tuns, was the ordinary container used by our forefathers, the only effective way they had of carrying and preserving not only wet goods but dry goods. Goods in wooden ships ran constant risk of wetting: the barrel kept them dry. The barrel preserved salt pork, salt beef, salt herrings, and the barrel held molasses and rum. Now there was only one way to make a barrel and that was out of white oak staves. These staves ranged up to a dozen feet in length and three inches in thickness. They were made by hand with the drawknife, and stave-making formed a large winter industry in the provinces possessing good supplies of white oak near salt water, that is, in all from Massachusetts Bay southward. They afforded convenient "dunnage" for schooners with a few cubic feet of space still left in their hold, and there was a never-failing demand for them in the islands, to which they were literally a matter of life or death.

Unfortunately Nova Scotia had no white oak. That should have settled the matter. Unless American vessels were permitted to enter West Indian ports there would be no barrels. The result was that for half a century the islands remained pawns in the mercantilistic struggle between Great Britain and the United States. At times temporary arrangements allowed the Americans to supply them; at others this had to be done surreptitiously. Whether the islands were starving (Americans kept out) or supplied (American goods allowed in), one thing stared everyone in the face: Nova Scotia could not take the place of New England in the Atlantic Trading Unit, nor could Canada. In the latter province there were both food and white oak, but there were also the winter closing of the St. Lawrence and the thousand miles of additional sailing up a dangerous river before ships could get to the supplies. Nor were there the ships. So the West Indies slowly died on the altar of the self-contained mercantilistic empire. When such conceptions had been swept away, Nova Scotia and the St. Lawrence, and later the Dominion of Canada, never succeeded in securing much of the island trade, although Canada subsidized it heavily. If history teaches anything, it surely teaches that as against geography and resources, artificial devices will not foster the Canadian-West Indian trade.

4. A New Phase of Mercantilism: The Timber Trade

The failure to reconstitute the "arch of Empire" did not involve the abandonment of the Old Colonial System. What was left of Empire in America was so weak that decision and policy centred more than ever in London, whence a stream of orders and regulations continued to issue. Yet there was much less to regulate. There was no substitute for the rich list of staples from the south. The remaining colonies had little beyond fish and furs to export and, therefore, could import little. It was to take them many years to get on their feet, and as they did so, a revised version of the old colonial system evolved which was to change its incidence and to last until the whole edifice was swept away in the 1840's by Sir Robert Peel.

The province of Canada had just escaped out of the dreary mercantile prison of the French Empire and begun to bask in the sun of a continental and Atlantic polity when the Revolution blew the clouds up once more and the province found itself shut up within a new British Empire that seemed little less narrow than the old one of France. From 1763 to 1776 and later, the province was being aligned to some degree with the continental economy, but after 1783, the southern door was closed and some other outlet had to be found. The West Indies were not available. There remained Great Britain. But what was to be exported? Furs? They were small in amount and hardly concerned the inhabited province itself, which, since the *habitant* lived a self-sufficient life, had never had an export market of consequence and had never missed it. But the English mercantile class had to live, and in terms of export trade. Since 1763 it had lived successively on the French, on fur, and on the war. Now where was it to turn?

It seemed almost mere luck that opened a new door. The wood

bounties have already been mentioned. They had not sufficed to enable colonial merchants to export to England profitably against high trans-Atlantic freights, but one branch of the industry, mast-making, had gone fairly well. The Revolutionary War had cut off the British navy from its best source of masts, New Hampshire, and this had been a factor in its loss of control of the sea to the French.[7] An alternative supply had been sought and before the war was over a moderate mast industry had been established on the rivers of what is now New Brunswick.[8] This industry called into existence a small subsidiary lumber industry, the lumber being sent down to the West Indies. It helped support some of the early Loyalist settlements.

But lumber could not yet cross the ocean profitably, for although a small preference was extended to colonial wood by Great Britain, only the choicest grades could stand the freight. Then in 1793 war broke out with France. As more and more countries were drawn in, the British import problem increased in difficulty, and efforts were made to get needed supplies from the colonies. It was in this period that the first wheat was exported from Quebec, and before the century had closed, this export had become quite considerable.[9] The additional shipping arriving for the wheat provided further facilities for shipment of other things, among them wood manufactured into the shape then demanded in England, square timber.[10] Meanwhile the preference on colonial lumber over that from elsewhere (which in practice meant the Baltic) was being increased a little each year until by the end of the century, it stood quite high. This allowed rather more export to take place from the colonies to England. In the first years of the new century, English firms began to send out representatives to buy timber for them. In this they were handicapped by the long-standing Imperial policy of reserving for the needs of the navy the pine timber on Crown lands, granted or ungranted.[11] The navy made its purchases through one agent and this firm did not welcome private competitors. However, ways can always be found round a monopoly, and by 1806, there appear to have been a number of Englishmen buying timber up country from Quebec.

In 1808, the second piece of colonial good luck occurred. Napoleon,

[7] See R. G. Albion, *Forests and Sea-Power* (Cambridge, Mass., 1926).

[8] The main mast of a ship of the time reached the size of 112 feet by 40 inches. To get a large enough pine tree out of the woods intact was a feat, and the mast in the port of shipment became valuable, worth about £1 per foot.

[9] H. A. Innis and A. R. M. Lower, *Select Documents in Canadian Economic History, 1783-1885* (Toronto, 1933), pp. 209, 261, 265.

[10] Logs squared on four sides with the broad-axe.

[11] See Albion, *op. cit.* This reservation is still made in deeds issued by the province of Ontario.

in perfecting his continental system, had just concluded his agreement with the Czar of Russia, which closed all the Baltic ports of that country to English shipping. He was in occupation of Prussia, so her ports were also closed. Denmark was forced in and then Sweden. The ring was complete, and Great Britain could hardly buy a stick of timber or a pound of hemp anywhere in the Baltic. Timber, hemp, and tar in those days were as essential to war as gasoline is today. The British navy, therefore, had to depend on limited supplies of English oak and was forced to turn to America again. Some sort of bargain was struck between the government and the timber dealers of England,[12] by which the dealers undertook to send out agents, employ capital to exploit colonial forests, and secure ships to bring the timber back, in return for an engagement by government to double the preference and give a guarantee for its continuance.

The preference was duly doubled (1810), and the attack on the Canadian forest began. Since then it has never ceased, and year by year timber of every type has gone over to Great Britain. The preference had been made great enough to equalize, and rather more than equalize, the difference in freight between Baltic and British American ports. As wartime prices increased, and as the Baltic embargo was lifted (in its most intense form it only lasted for one year), the government was persuaded to increase the preference until by the end of the wars (1815), it had reached fantastic heights. It had served its immediate purpose and had created a large forest industry in Canada devoted to the production of square timber and, to a lesser extent, of "deals"[13] in sawmills erected for the purpose.

This new forest industry, which proved capable later on of standing a reduced preference and still later (from 1842 on) of getting along with very little and eventually none, was to be the colonies' salvation, for it gave to them the only means of growth they could have had—their third staple, timber. Timber could support far more people than both the other two, fish and fur. Upon this third staple Saint John grew up, Quebec received a second lease of life, and later on, interior towns such as Ottawa were built. Canada, in many senses, has been hewn out of her forests.

As the timber industry became more firmly established, a new set of vested interests was built up. Colonials saw their harbours full of ships, they saw men hiring lumberjacks, and merchants selling goods to those

[12] A completely unscrupulous lot who did not hesitate to imperil their country for their own profits. See Albion, *op. cit.*, and A. R. M. Lower, *The North American Assault on the Canadian Forest* (Toronto, 1938).
[13] English term for three-inch planks.

lumberjacks when they came out of the bush in the spring, they saw and appreciated all the bustle and business that the new trade was bringing. They became firmly convinced of the benefits it conferred, and whenever the preferences were attacked in England, all the vocal elements in the colonies rose as one man to their defence. The British merchants who had established branches in the ports and who were sending out their sons and nephews to superintend them were getting deeper and deeper into the colonial world. Their fortunes were linked with it, and they, too, were valiant defenders of the "differential duties", as the preference came to be called. No one wasted regrets over the wanton destruction of the Canadian forest.

The timber trade was a godsend for the most effective pressure group of the time, the ship-owners of England, who, because of the cheaper wages and the superior shipping of Baltic countries, could not get their ships into the Baltic timber trade. But the colonial trade was a closed trade, for under the Navigation Acts no foreign vessel could enter a colonial port. They could, therefore, exact freights up to the very last farthing of the preferences. The English ship-owners were the principal beneficiaries of the preferences. As the ships engaged in "superior trades", such as those of the East and West Indiamen—the aristocrats of the ocean—became older, their owners could shift them into bulkier and rougher cargoes, until at last they came down, as it was termed, to timber. Ships that were too slow to carry silk would carry sugar, those too old to carry sugar could carry cotton, and those that could not carry anything else could carry wood. Anything that would float would carry timber; the Canadian timber trade became the last refuge of all the battered hulks on the Atlantic. No money was needed for upkeep, insurance, or depreciation. If they were wrecked, as they often were, little but sailors' lives was lost. They were the ship-owner's joy and the sailor's tragedy. The ship-owners' associations of England were, therefore, the strongest supporters of the new system of duties.

These duties forced Canadian wood on to the English market at high prices, which handicapped the English in everything from factory-building to furniture-making. The differential duties were a dead weight on England and the only possible arguments for them were not economic at all but political: they did keep open the alternative source of supply, which would be useful in case of another war, and they were an indirect if peculiar subsidy to the colonials. Whatever the incidence of the mercantilism of the first Empire had been, and it is usually taken to have fallen mainly on the colonies, there is no question where the incidence of the second fell; it fell squarely on the people of England. Mercantilism in its second, post-Revolutionary phase operated

first for the benefit of a limited number of shipowners, second for that
of an even more limited number of timber importers, and thirdly for
that of the colonists. It was a strange reversal of conception: England
now exploited for the benefit of her own Empire. A far cry, this, from
the stark metropolitanism of the eighteenth century, when everybody
would have admitted that the colonies existed for the benefit of the
mother country.

Additional Reading

Albion, R. G. *Forests and Sea Power: The Timber Problem of the Royal Navy,
1652-1862*. Cambridge, Mass., 1926.

Crean, J. F. "Hats and the Fur Trade." *CJEPS*, XXVIII (August, 1962),
373-386.

Easterbrook, W. T. and H. G. J. Aitken. *Canadian Economic History*. Toronto,
1956.

Innis, H. A. and A. R. M. Lower. *Select Documents in Canadian Economic
History, 1783-1885*. Toronto, 1933.

Lower, A. R. M. *The North American Assault on the Canadian Forest*. Toronto,
1938.

——. "The Trade in Square Timber," in University of Toronto Studies (History
and Economics) *Contributions to Canadian Economics*, VI (1933), 40-61.

——. *Settlement and the Forest Frontier in Eastern Canada*. (Canadian Frontiers
of Settlement, Vol. IX). Toronto, 1936.

CHAPTER 9

The Thirteenth Colony: Nova Scotia

1. Nova Scotia and Its Settlers

When the movement for independence began, there was little except youth and poverty to distinguish Nova Scotia from the other colonies. Its population was small but mostly of Yankee origin. The constitution of the province was of the familiar governor, council, and assembly type, deriving from Virginia. Its sentiments towards the mother country were the same as those of other colonies. It had been a colony longer than Georgia, and went back to the period when there was only one colony of Carolina. One of the intriguing questions in colonial history is why this province did not follow the other thirteen into independence.

Until shortly before they came together in Confederation, the British North American provinces lived in separate worlds, and it is, therefore, impossible to furnish them with a common history. None of the colonies was further removed from the Canadas than Nova Scotia, not even the islands Prince Edward and Newfoundland. The only bond between the colonies which remained British after the Revolution was the adjective: they were "British". All of them were tied to the metropolitan centre that sent them their goods and their governors and which took from them, if convenient, the products they had to offer.

Nova Scotia was the scene of the earliest of all the attempts at the colonization of the Gulf of St. Lawrence region. Annapolis (1605), called Port Royal by the French, proudly claims an older foundation than Quebec itself (1608). For almost two generations the history of the peninsula consists in the squabbles of traders and grantees who lived there but built up no community. This period of casual concessionaires was interrupted by the episode of the Nova Scotian baronetcies. Sir William Alexander, the Scottish grantee of Nova Scotia, left no other mark on the peninsula than the name, some empty titles at home, and a provincial flag (still flown). Meanwhile French fishermen were coming ashore on Isle Royale, or Cape Breton, from the off-lying banks (Canso, Misaine, Artimon, Banquereau and others) and living in the coves, especially around Canso (about 1607). On the other end of the peninsula, east from Port Royal and along the Minas Basin, French peasants were settling; these were the Acadians,[1] well if not historically known to persons susceptible to romantic poetry in the lines of *Evangeline*.

By the Peace of Utrecht, "Nova Scotia", or Acadia, became English. The French, however, clung obstinately to their interpretation of the term, which placed the eastern part of the peninsula, the Isthmus of Chignecto, Cape Breton, Isle Royale, and all the continent across to the St. Lawrence and down to the boundary of New England (wherever that might be) outside the territory surrendered. They still tried to exercise authority over it, its Indians, and those Acadians who lived near its debatable margin. From 1713 until the Conquest, the authorities at Quebec attempted to maintain their hold, especially over the Acadians, whether within or without Nova Scotia. The English insisted that the Acadians had become British subjects and, therefore, must do their duties as such, to the point, if necessary, of serving in the English militia against their former compatriots. The French from Quebec threatened them with fire and scalping if they took oaths of allegiance to the British. This placed the poor Acadians between the hammer and the anvil. In their extremity they worked out their own conception of "neutrality". Serve against men of their own flesh and blood they would not. Go to the extremity of losing their lands they would not. For over forty years, guided and urged by priests from the St. Lawrence (the notorious Father LeLoutre was the best known), they temporized. When the Seven Years' War threatened, with the restoration of Louisbourg still fresh in memory, powerful persons in Boston and elsewhere demanded a resolution of the quandary. The answer was the celebrated deportation of 1755,[2] which scattered most of the Acadians up and

---

[1] Population of Acadia in 1671: 392.
[2] The estimated French population of Acadia, Isle Royale, Isle St. Jean, and the mainland before the deportation was 19,300; after it, 13,000. The population of the peninsula decreased by 7,000; that of the mainland and Isle St. Jean increased by 500 each.

down the Atlantic coast and left their lands vacant, ready for the occupation of others. "Neutrality" had been drastically terminated.

In the twenty years of war with which the French regime ended, conflict around the Gulf and its bordering lands followed certain beaten paths. The conventional English move up the coast[3] from Boston had as its result, in addition to the cessions of 1713, the two captures of Louisbourg. These operations were naval, with military addenda. Then there was an inner line of operations, rather more military than naval, which centred on the Isthmus of Chignecto. The French built Fort Beausejour there in 1750, on a magnificently chosen site commanding wide views across the Isthmus and out to the sea over the Cumberland Basin, and the English took it away from them in 1755, renaming it Fort Cumberland. Its fall severed the maritime French from their brethren up the St. Lawrence, and in 1758-60 these too were conquered.

Nova Scotia, the English province, had by now already had 45 years of life. At its little capital, Annapolis, there had been gathered since 1713 its governor and garrison, a few officials, and a tiny group of settlers. Most of them were from New England, and Boston was their metropolitan centre,[4] as it still is for the western end of the peninsula. A Canadian historian well named his volume on this phase of history "New England's Outpost", for pre-Revolutionary Nova Scotia most certainly was the outpost of New England.[5]

As counterpoise to Louisbourg and to secure the harbour of Chebucto, the British government in 1749 decided to found a post on that body of water. Catholic Irish settlers were brought up from the continental colonies and from Ireland, and about an equal number of Protestants from the old colonies and out of the army. This approximate proportion between the two religions has held ever since. The new post was named Halifax, in honour of the then President of the Board of Trade, Charles Montagu Dunk, Lord Halifax. As it was made the capital instead of Annapolis and had an important garrison, the little town became the centre of peninsular life. It attracted a mercantile community, which in the nineteenth century was to become rich and powerful. Many of its members were Anglicans, and, as so often happens, when they attained place and power, they experienced some difficulty in distinguishing between church and state. Through them Halifax became the centre of

---

[3] See p. 57.
[4] A comparison of the monuments in the graveyard of Annapolis with those in the old cemetery at Concord, Mass., shows how the mottoes and figures came up from New England, the centre of dispersion for grave stones, as for governors.
[5] J. B. Brebner, *New England's Outpost: Acadia before the Conquest of Canada* (New York, 1927).

Anglicanism in Nova Scotia, with a strong outpost at Windsor (where King's College was founded in 1793).

Four years later, 1753, in an effort to make the British position more secure, the English induced a number of German Protestants to come over. Some of them (said to be from Alsace and thus French subjects) did not like the conditions they encountered and ran off to the French at Louisbourg, but most of them stuck it out and made their settlement sixty miles west of Halifax. Fortunately for them they had the only area along the south coast which contained a good amount of arable land. Though they were of inland origin, they soon turned themselves into fishermen, frequenting the Grand Banks of Newfoundland. Their descendants have made themselves famous as hardy "bankers" (fishermen on the Banks) and builders of "bankers" (ships on which the "bankers" sail to the Banks). The ship on the Canadian ten-cent piece, the schooner *Bluenose* (built but not designed by Lunenburgers) was their crowning achievement. Lunenburg county and town is their monument. With the exception of the founders of Halifax and a few settlers around Annapolis, these Germans of Lunenburg, who early lost their language, are virtually the oldest English-speaking Canadians.

The local legend is that after the Acadians were deported Germans made their way up the LaHave river valley and across to the empty lands, secured some of the cattle wandering about ownerless and brought them back with them. A little later these empty lands were advertised in New England. The prospect of a ready-made farm, complete with cattle, brought plenty of response from the Yankees. Men from frontier settlements in Connecticut and Massachusetts decided to make another move, on farther into the bush. In proper pioneering style, they brought their families and began life in the new surroundings. Yet it was not quite pioneering, for most of the clearing was done, and an established government was at hand. The new settlements in the Annapolis valley quickly got on their feet, and, as in old New England, within a year or two, schools, town-meetings, and churches had made their appearance.

These New Englanders, from the newer towns, had been washed by the wave of religious revivalism then sweeping the back country from Massachusetts to Georgia and known as the "Great Awakening". The frontier did not take kindly to the stiff and intellectual Congregationalism of the original Puritans, and in the Great Awakening, it formulated a more emotional religion, one more to its taste. Followers of Wesley and Whitefield became Methodists, others Baptists. In New England, the more fervent areas became Baptist. It was this denomination that overtook the settlers in Nova Scotia. Today, the Annapolis Valley is one of the Canadian strongholds of the Baptist Church. The Valley is so well-defined between its North and South Mountains that it forms its inhabitants into a distinct community within the distinct community of Nova Scotia. They have their own University, Acadia; their local industry, apple-growing; and their own traditions. When asked about their origins, it must not be suggested to them that they are "Loyalists"; they are of an older breed: "Pre-Loyalists", they will proudly say.

This little extension of New England into New Scotland brought up a vigorous and wide-awake group of people, among the best immigrants that Canada has ever received. Their long role of famous men (Bordens and Fieldings and Tuppers) bears this out. From the first, they gave the province weight and ballast and the reality of a democratic tradition. As New Englanders, they were not the people to accept a Governor's will; they insisted on the rights of Englishmen, one of which, inherent in an English community and not the gift of a kindly monarch, was an elected Assembly. This they demanded even before they came, and in 1758, the authorities in England ordered the unwilling Lawrence, the Governor at the time, to summon one. This Nova Scotian Legislative Assembly is the oldest Canadian representative body.[6] The Assembly, meeting at Halifax year after year, gave a centre to the province; at it representatives, with their local knowledge, discussed common affairs and made arrangements best suited to local conditions. Nothing could have drawn the scattered communities so effectively together into a genuine body politic—not even the church, whose various denominations would have hindered it from doing so.

The year of the first assembly was the year of the second surrender of Louisbourg. Wolfe's army left behind in Cape Breton a few of its men, but there were no other distinct groups coming into the province after the Pre-Loyalists until the early 1770's, when some people from Yorkshire settled in Cumberland county, on the Isthmus of Chignecto. These people had become converts to John Wesley's new faith, Methodism, before coming to America. They were the first settlers in what is now Canada to call themselves by the then new name, Methodist. They must have been sturdy and competent for their legacy lies in such towns as Amherst, with its distinguished sons, and Sackville, where one of their number years after (1839) founded the university that bears his name, Mount Allison. Their Methodism, now merged in that of all Canada and that in turn in the United Church, wore a different hue from that

---

[6] Because called pursuant to a Royal Instruction, it was not parliamentary in origin. This allows the pundit to argue, if he so desires, that since Nova Scotia does not derive its institutions from Parliament, the doctrine of Parliamentary supremacy does not apply to it.

which was later brought up from the backwoods of the United States to Upper Canada: it was less emotional, more formal and conservative.

Just a little later than the Methodists, there arrived in the harbour of Pictou, on the Gulf coast of the peninsula, the good ship *Hector*, bringing the first Highland Scots (but not the first Presbyterians) to Nova Scotia. They and their descendants filled in the lands on the Gulf coast. Other Highlanders, some Presbyterian but many of them Roman Catholic,[7] worked their way up into the fastnesses of Cape Breton. That island was to become another Scotland whose very speech was Gaelic as, in many districts, it still remains today. In this way, the eastern third of Nova Scotia including Cape Breton became veritably New Scotland. The Scots proved a formative element, especially the Presbyterians around Pictou, and eventually they too secured their educational centre, Pictou Academy.[8] It was not until much later that the Catholic Highlanders made their impression on provincial life: today they too have their University, St. Francis Xavier at Antigonish.

During the Revolution, scattered individuals and families seeking to avoid the storm in New England, made their way to Nova Scotia; these people are still remembered by the Pre-Loyalists, who were mostly republicans, and by the Loyalists, who were not. They fall between two stools and are referred to, somewhat contemptuously, as "refugees". They do not share the badge of honour which has been claimed by the Loyalists, thousands of whom came to Nova Scotia in 1783, among them men of substance, position, and education. How many remained of those who came is another matter. The settlement of Shelburne, where a town of seven or eight thousand rose out of the bush overnight, only to subside just as quickly because there was nothing but rock under the forest cover, is rather typical of what happened to Loyalism in Nova Scotia. Nearly all those camped on Halifax Common in the winter of 1783-84 went over to the St. John in the spring, to form the basic stock of the present province of New Brunswick. A few went up to Cape Breton, a few to Prince Edward Island. Shortly afterwards, a steady drift set in back to the United States. It is, therefore, impossible to say how many were left. Statistical evidence would indicate relatively few, perhaps less than 6,000 out of the peninsula's population (in 1790) of about 30,000. Everything considered, Nova Scotia cannot be put down as a Loyalist province. It is primarily pre-Revolutionary New England, a statement borne out by the appearance of its houses and villages and by the energy of its people, their avidity for higher education, and their religious denomination. Secondarily the province is Scottish (partly

---

[7] Antigonish and Cape Breton counties are the chief Highland Catholic areas.
[8] Dalhousie University, founded by a Scottish governor, Lord Dalhousie, was under strong Scottish influence from the first, but was not denominational.

Presbyterian, partly Catholic) and thirdly Acadian, German, or Catholic Irish. The Loyalists come well down in the list, not more numerous than the Ulster Irish, English, and other miscellaneous people who came into the province in the nineteenth century.

The influence of the Loyalists, or at least of the outcome of the Revolution, was another matter. If the Revolutionary movement had been successful in the province, Nova Scotia would have become another New England state, only slightly different from Maine. As it was, it took on another complexion, which could not be called British, still less English, in anything but political sentiment, but was observably different from New England. The difference arose from an isolated position, continuing association with the Atlantic world, and from the colonial and class traits which the Loyalists imposed. Within fifty years after the Revolution, New England was turning inland, becoming more and more part of the continent. Nova Scotia remained part of the Atlantic region until after Confederation and has never rested very easily in Confederation because she still feels the pull of the Atlantic basin, the islands up and down the western side, and the metropolitan islands to the east.

The Loyalists reinforced this anti-continentalism by their strongly colonial point of view: they had been forced to leave the old colonies because they would not take part in a movement for independent nationhood, and they naturally emphasized their ideals among the people to whom they came. As they came with the prestige of those devoted to a cause and as Nova Scotia remained a colony, the colonial point of view was strengthened. The pre-Revolutionary class structure, which appealed to the Loyalist leaders, served to reinforce colonialism, for it was frankly anti-democratic. In some respects the Revolution had been a contest between the classes and the masses; the classes lost, but their broken remnants, which established themselves again in America, looked for a continuation of the kind of society for which they had fought. No surprise, then, that not long after the immigration, the exclusive little clique which was to appear in all the provinces emerged in Nova Scotia, too. Educated men being rare in the new settlements but relatively abundant among the Loyalist exiles, their influence went a long way and it was in the directions indicated. Nevertheless Nova Scotia was never made over into a Loyalist province. It remained dominantly New England and Scottish.

2. Why Nova Scotia Remained a Colony

If built on a New England base, why did Nova Scotia remain a colony? It was no more isolated from Revolutionary ideas than Georgia or the

back country of the Carolinas. Its American population had been born
in New England. They were democrats as surely as they were Christians
and Puritans. They began their settlements with the town meeting.
They were non-conformists as opposed to the state connections of
Anglicanism. They were frontiersmen as opposed to urban privilege.
Every reason existed for their seceding.

It may be that the heady ideas of Sam Adams and others down in
Boston were strained out a little by the intervening leagues of sea and
forest and that, as simple people, the settlers had some difficulty getting
excited over the abstract wrongs of their brethren in Massachusetts.
Halifax, too, we know, was a counter-Revolutionary influence, though
not a large one, for it was small and its merchants' interests, it is said,
did not extend much beyond the Bedford Basin.[9]

One good reason for the province not seceding was that secession was
tried and failed. An attempt to raise the American population in 1776
failed and the few rebels who appeared before Fort Cumberland were
outnumbered by the garrison and dispersed in a midnight skirmish. No
further risings were attempted, though the province was full of American
sympathizers. Why? The explanation is simple: British sea power. Nova
Scotia, as almost an island, was beyond succour from Continental
armies, and the British with their base at Halifax could move men to
any threatened point, as they had done to Fort Cumberland, when the
rising occurred. The Nova Scotians had to accept the British connection
whether they liked it or not. Probably most of them were indifferent.
They instinctively took the same position as had the Acadians years
before and attempted to represent themselves as neutrals. That was
logical. Most of them still had their family connections in New England
and were averse from joining the British in a strife which might bring
them into conflict with their own flesh and blood. Yet they could have
had no wish to match themselves aimlessly against superior British power.
Neutrality and acceptance of their fate was necessarily their line, and
they followed it. With his usual skill, Brebner, the historian of this period
has hit off the situation in the title of his book, *The Neutral Yankees of
Nova Scotia*.[10] The author brings out nicely the marginal position of the
peninsula: it constitutes the termination of the Appalachian Barrier to
the north-east, but part of it is on the Barrier's Atlantic side and lies
open to Boston and New England. The rest of it, the eastern end, Cape
Breton and the Gulf coast, is drawn into the orbit of the St. Lawrence
through the sea, around the end of the Barrier. The two halves together

---

[9] J. B. Brebner, *The Neutral Yankees of Nova Scotia. A Marginal Colony during
the Revolutionary Years* (New York, 1937).
[10] Brebner, *op. cit.*

are marginal, wobbling between the forces streaming out of the St. Lawrence, that is, Canada, and those streaming up from New England. As with all areas which stand at a point of convergence of forces originating outside themselves, the tendency has been to call into existence on the peninsula feelings of impatience at the outside, local patriotism, the "curse on both your houses" attitude.[11]

An isolated position, the pull of outside forces, a fairly long and undisturbed history, have been sufficient to make of Nova Scotia a genuine political community. Her people today are Nova Scotians before they are Scottish or Pre-Loyalist, and, it is to be suspected, before they are Canadians. Time and the beloved environment of a beautiful peninsula, well separated from the rest of North America, have done their work, erecting over the various original communities of this very diverse province, a common structure, the Province, and a common sentiment, Nova Scotianism. These deep realities are merging into a general Canadianism only as Canada itself becomes a political community, a nation with a life and soul of its own.

Chronology

1598 Settlement on Sable Island.
1604 de Monts at Ste. Croix.
1605 Port Royal founded.
1611 Jesuit mission in Acadia.
1621 "Nova Scotia" granted to Sir William Alexander.
1631 Charles de la Tour builds a fort at the mouth of the St. John River.
1670 The English forts in Acadia surrendered to the French.
1710 Port Royal captured by the British.
1713 Hudson Bay, Newfoundland, and Acadia confirmed to Great Britain by the Peace of Utrecht.
1721 English settlement at Canso.
1744 The French destroy Canso.
1749 Foundation of Halifax.
1750 The French establish Fort Beausejour.
1755 Expulsion of the Acadians.
1758 The first legislative assembly of Nova Scotia meets at Halifax.
1763 Islands of St. John (P.E.I.) and Cape Breton added to Nova Scotia.
1767 The lands of Isle St. John granted to absentee proprietors.
1773 Meeting of the first legislature of Island of St. John.
1778 Loyalist refugees begin to arrive.
1782 Loyalist settlement begins in New Brunswick and Nova Scotia.

---

[11] As Canada itself, which so painfully feels the tug of Great Britain and the United States, plays one off against the other and hopes against hope that out of the balance its own survival may be possible.

Additional Reading

Beer, G. L. *British Colonial Policy, 1754-1765.* New York, 1907.

Brebner, J. B. *The Neutral Yankees of Nova Scotia; A Marginal Colony During the Revolutionary Years.* New York, 1937.

——. *New England's Outpost: Acadia Before the Conquest of Canada.* New York, 1927.

——. *North Atlantic Triangle: The Interplay of Canada, the United States and Great Britain.* Toronto, 1945.

Saunders, S. A. *Studies in the Economy of the Maritime Provinces.* Toronto, 1939.

CHAPTER 10

A Second Chance for Empire

---

1. The Meaning of the Revolution

Great Britain, having lost one empire by the American Revolution, managed within a year or two to find another.[1] Few countries have had such a second chance. In North America, the loss of the Thirteen Colonies assured the survival of British power. Canada, the modern version of the former British North America, is a by-product of the American Revolution. It originated in a lost cause, the other side of the Revolution. To understand Canada it is as necessary to understand the two philosophies underlying that upheaval as the two associated with French and English. This materialistic continent rests upon idealistic foundations: upon the strong religious convictions of New France and New England, which give the primary antithesis, Catholicism as against Puritanism; and upon the almost equally strong political convictions which give the second antithesis, monarchy and republicanism. It is out of all four of these major creeds that modern Canada is built.

Just as the gulf between English and French represents a deep division over the nature of man, so the American Revolution represented a deep division over the nature of society. The Revolution stood for the environment as against the forces of history from across the sea; for a measure of democracy as against the idea of an ordered hier-

[1] The first settlements in Australia were begun the year after the peace, 1784.

archical community; for relative freedom from privilege as against a world in which privilege had nearly everywhere triumphed. The view of society that won had been nurtured by the circumstances of colonial life and from conspicuous elements of the English tradition. By 1776, though there was no rigid uniformity in the way of life over the long line of the Atlantic arch, a fairly distinct American pattern of society had emerged. The common American way of life arose out of the common attack on the wilderness environment. Its outstanding traits were individualism, freedom of a rather anarchic type, and the sense of equality. There might be many rich men in America, like George Washington, but the poorest men did not feel that they had to remain poor; they were not called upon to be content with that estate in life unto which God had been pleased to call them, but rather to prove the favour of God by rising to a better estate. Thomas Jefferson, when he drafted his Declaration of Independence, enunciated sentiments to which nearly all colonials could subscribe: "We hold these truths to be self-evident, that all men are created equal . . .".

The Declaration was born not only from the American environment but from English history as well. The "natural rights" philosophy of the age arose from the teachings of the political philosophers, especially from those of the great philosopher of the English Revolution, John Locke. Locke, and others like him, saw in the upheavals that had expelled the Stuarts one dominating principle, government by the consent of the governed. The old divine-right conceptions, by which God placed over subjects a monarch responsible to none but Himself, had been swept out of seventeenth century England, never to return. If the Puritans of old England had made the Great Rebellion, the Puritans of New England inherited its principles and results.[2] Few indeed must have been the colonials who did not hold to the principle of government by consent.

Yet it would be misleading to represent America as entirely of a piece. Although it could not have been soil in which "the magic of monarchy" would flourish, it was productive of a fair harvest of privilege. There was plenty of privilege in Virginia, and even in Massachusetts. But it was privilege that could be escaped by the simple act of moving west, and, for the most part, privilege that was instinctively resented. Privilege, in some provinces, was the major factor in provoking the Revolution. Providing the term be used cautiously, the prevailing American way of life may be summarized as one of political and social democracy.

[2] All the New England colonies had been founded before the second, or "bloodless" revolution, 1688; all had been deeply influenced by the first, 1642-60.

What was the way of life to which it was opposed, the clashing view of life that led to war? Would it be fair to describe it as the English way? In part. The English way of life has always been difficult to depict because it is a great mass of custom and tradition collected over the centuries, differing from locality to locality and still more from class to class. In the English constitution there are elements of almost every kind of government, as Edmund Burke idealistically contended when he claimed it to be a nice mixture of monarchy, aristocracy, and democracy. There was, in the English tradition, something for almost everyone. But its major contrast with colonial life was (and to a high degree is still) the amount of privilege and differentiation of rank which it contains. The seventeenth century revolutions had not destroyed the old English way of life; they had merely placed a new type alongside it. Puritanism and commercialism came in, but the Cavalier tradition did not go out. England merely became two nations. The Cavalier-aristocratic-Tory tradition remained immensely powerful and, to as great a degree as the newer Roundhead-middle-class urban tradition, determined the tone of English life.

England in the eighteenth century still presented a nicely graded hierarchical society, where nearly everyone from the king to the beggar was neatly tucked into his appropriate niche, that of his ancestors and descendants, with everyone very much aware of the rights inhering in that niche. Those rights, as they evolved over the centuries, were mostly hard property rights. They were the concrete rights of ownership, control, and conduct, earned by struggle and competition: they did not concern themselves with the philosophical abstraction, freedom. They carried with them many devices intended to protect them: all that body of law roughly called civil liberties, such as the right of freedom from arbitrary arrest, the right to a fair trial by one's fellows, the right of reasonable freedom of speech and of assembly. It was this body of rights and liberties, together with the right of representative government and self-taxation, that colonists usually meant when they spoke of the law of England or the rights of Englishmen. English rights were quite compatible with a society based on privilege, for there was nothing to prevent you from having very few rights and me from having a great many. Since the man who had many rights was the most likely to make a fight for them if they were threatened, English law was, in fact, a guarantee of privilege.

Privilege had not been buried at sea as English institutions crossed the ocean, but the atmosphere of the New World was uncongenial to it. In America, privilege was on the defensive and barricaded itself in that area of society most immediately in contact with the Old World, that is to say, in colonial government. The governor was appointed from England, together with a long list of other officials. From the powers of his office came many good things, like land grants. Around him circulated a little knot of office-holders, would-be office-holders, and other persons looking for favours. Added to these were others whose natures imbued them with respect for authority or who found pleasure in basking in official sunshine, those who itched to be "in the know", those whose egos were inflated by association with the great, those who liked to be considered among the best people: all whom history comprises under the term courtier.[3] With time these groups strengthened themselves: sometimes they were able to pass on their privileges to their children and, if the Revolution and the limitless West had not upset things, they might have become a colonial aristocracy, a real privileged class.

The members of this incipient aristocracy did not have the same chance of becoming Americans as the ordinary people subject to the full stress of the environment. They advanced easily enough to the provincial stage, which meant that they had accepted their province as their place of residence and probably had for it the love that our homes evoke from us all. But they could not rise to the spiritual concept which is America. They could not make the entire surrender to the New World which is necessary if, in the fullest sense, it is to become ours and we its. Sir John Wentworth was a New Hampshire man born and bred. His family had controlled the province for nearly a century. He was its governor, as his father had been before him. His wealth and his heart were in it but, on the Revolution breaking out, he found that his place and status had predestined him for the King's side. He was repudiated by his fellow provincials and went to England. Later on, still within the charmed circle, he became governor of Nova Scotia and after that retired to England, where he lived the rest of his life. He and his family had been typical provincials, but they never became Americans.

Men who have obtained privilege and an entrée are soon set apart from their fellows. They have something that others do not have, not only property, but place and the power that goes with it. They bulge with mysterious secrets. They are not likely to surrender these things without a fight.

In the key province of Massachusetts Bay, privilege was the very centre of the controversy. Some arrogance might be permitted to an Englishman as governor, but not to a native, not to one of the home-bred Boston boys. Thomas Hutchinson, last royal Governor of Massa-

---

[3] See G. P. Gooch, *Courts and Cabinets* (London, 1944).

chusetts, had four generations of New England born behind him, but his temperament and his associations with government, his fondness for privilege, served to keep up that subtle link with the Old World which prevented his becoming an American in the deep meaning of the word and retained him in the ranks of colonials, men whose ultimate, if sometimes secret, centre of reference was still across the seas in the distant metropolis. All the objectionable features of the governmental system were concentrated in this province-born governor, upright man personally as he appears to have been, and so crucial was the personal situation thus created that it has been asserted that if this appointment could have been avoided the Revolution might not have occurred.[4]

Just outside Hutchinson and his group in the prosperous province stood other men with not quite as good a social standing, men such as John Adams or John Hancock or especially Samuel Adams. One can hardly read the history of the Revolution in such provinces as Massachusetts Bay without feeling that it was more a domestic quarrel between the privileged and the not-so-privileged than a struggle over a fundamental difference in allegiance. The former invoked traditional sentiment and raised the loyalty cry, the latter used class appeal and fanned the resentment of the men on the bottom of the heap towards those in place and power. It is a common pattern of revolution.

In most provinces the privileged lost[5] and the not-so-privileged won. Samuel Adams became governor of his native state and John Adams president of his country. The American view of life, with which the not-so-privileged had had to associate themselves, whether they liked it in its entirely or not, had triumphed over the English. The notions of equality, of a formless, *laisser-faire* society with the fewest of trammels and the least possible degree of authority, which Thomas Jefferson refined into a philosophical concept of democracy, had won over the idea of privilege, and the new nation started its career with its faith plighted to it.

2. Why Men Became Loyalists

The Revolution had cast up party terms—Tory and Whig. Tories, the privileged, were similar in most respects to their English counterparts but lacked the wide popular approval that centuries of feudalism had given to an aristocratic system. Whigs based themselves on that same body of political philosophy popular in Whig circles in England, the

[4] See R. V. Harlow, *Samuel Adams, Promoter of the American Revolution* (New York, 1923).
[5] Virginia was a partial exception.

doctrine of natural rights, but lacked the great magnates who led the English Whigs and drew their main strength from intuitive native conceptions of equality and individualism. The family quarrel had left little room in the new country for the Tories, the ex-privileged. They were faced with hard alternatives: they either had to conform and demonstrate their loyalty to the Revolutionary cause, lose themselves in the crowd, or else get out. They could take their choice of the distant mother country which most of them had never seen, the southern island colonies, or worst of all, the northern wilderness, there to face life all over again.

Many Tories took the plunge and came out on the side of revolution, others managed an obscure neutrality, still others stuck to their guns and at the end of the war were proscribed by the victors. These latter it was who formed the élite of those people who, when they had once more settled down on British soil, were allowed to use the description *United Empire Loyalist*. Needless to say, a change of residence did not work a change of philosophy. In its new wilderness home and its new aspect of British North Americanism, colonial Toryism made its second attempt to erect on American soil a copy of the English social edifice. From one point of view this is the most significant thing about the Loyalist movement: it withdrew a class concept of life from the south, moved it up north and gave it a second chance. There it worked itself out in an environment similar to the old, and with not dissimilar results. This historical process gave to English Canada a body of sentiments and traditions, an outlook, and a certain social tang, which cause it to differ from the United States.

The process by which the ordinary plain man found himself a Loyalist must have been complex. When society is rent in twain, it becomes difficult for its members to avoid making decisions as to which side they will join. Yet to avoid decision, to keep out of the storm, is just what most people try to do. The average man does not have decided political views or an exact conception of the pros and cons of a given situation. In ordinary times he may resolve his indecisions by following a leader or may bury them by living a non-political private life. When civil conflict is breaking out, he becomes confused and he is disinclined to follow extreme leaders, if for no other reason than that he does not know which side will come out on top. His natural instinct is to leave it to the men active in affairs to settle between themselves.[6] But as the situ-

[6] See F. Landon, *Western Ontario and the American Frontier* (Toronto, 1941), p. 177 for a perfect illustration. When half a century after the Revolution, the crisis of 1837 came, "the men of Eramosa . . . met, discussed the situation, and resolved—'that we return home, remain neutral, and mind our own business'. . . . But the men of Eramosa were not left alone. Armed Loyalists descended upon the settlement. . . ."

ation becomes tense, the men of affairs put pressure on the ordinary individual and attempt to force a decision out of him. Most men will fall in readily with the side uppermost in their neighbourhood, as the safest and easiest thing to do. The number of persons who make their decision on pure political principle, or even on emotion based on tradition, must necessarily be small.

It is, therefore, wrong to believe that the Loyalists could have been chosen spirits, resolved to die rather than submit to a political philosophy of which they disapproved. There were relatively few such men. There were far more whose place in society had singled them out as "Tories" and who were repudiated as such by the new society. But the majority of them must have been plain, bewildered people who found themselves on the losing side for obscure reasons. They had just happened to put their money on the wrong horse. Allegiance is not readily changed, and it is now generally agreed that the American Revolution, like other revolutions, was made by one minority of active spirits, that the masses were in varying degrees passive, and that another minority was actively loyal. The passive many would take their allegiance to the Crown for granted, but that in itself would not be a cause of exile, for which more conspicuous behaviour of a compromising nature would be necessary. Suspicion would fall at once on the people of communities in which active Loyalism was dominant, perhaps because of dominating local personalities, such as the family of Sir William Johnson in upper New York.[7] Persons who, from whatever reason, openly espoused the King's side would be driven out. The irrevocably compromising step was to take the King's shilling. Whatever their reasons for enlisting (and men enlist for dozens of reasons, among which the pure fire of faith in the cause is usually secondary) the King's soldiers could not stay in the rebels' territories. A large proportion of the Loyalists, especially among those going to Nova Scotia, were soldiers, members of the various Loyalist corps that had been raised during the war.

3. The Loyalist Migrations

The main body of this eastern group of Loyalists, made up of Tories, soldiers, soldiers' families, and others, sailed from New York to Halifax in the late summer and fall of 1783, on board the ships Sir Guy Carleton had assembled to take away those who thought it best to leave. There were two other distinct groups, both farther west. The one moved up

[7] See p. 126.

the Hudson Valley by Lake Champlain and down the Richelieu to Sorel, where an encampment was made in the winter of 1783-84. The other consisted of those persons who, during and after the war, made their way over the Niagara frontier. Scattered individuals and families also crossed the border at other points.

Each of the groups had their own characteristics. Among those coming up to Halifax were a good many people of birth and education, gathered from nearly all the former colonies, such as the Winslows and Chipmans and Robinsons, names still well known in Canadian life. But the majority were plain people, private soldiers who had been simple farmers or townsmen before the great decision had to be made.

It was this Halifax group that formed the foundation of New Brunswick, still the most conspicuously Loyalist province in Canada. The most likely area of good agricultural land in that vicinity was in the valley of the St. John River, then unoccupied. These lands, above the river mouth, up to the neighbourhood of the modern town of Woodstock, were settled corps by corps, with colonel and officers taking up land along with their men.[8] New Brunswick received a strong Loyalist start, and its history afterwards illustrated the Tory conception of society. The province, at its origin, was given representative institutions and the ordinary rights and privileges of English law. But old Thomas Carleton (brother of Sir Guy, Lord Dorchester), governor from 1783 until 1817, conjoined with the grandees among the Loyalists to prevent the ugly spectre of American democracy from showing itself. A little knot of men at the centre directed the affairs of the province and they managed to confine the Assembly to safe limits, sometimes by rather strong arm methods.[9] The spirit of the continent finally destroyed privilege in New Brunswick as elsewhere, but privilege engrossed place and power for many years, and when it did disappear before responsible government, it left an unfortunate heritage in a certain failure of political capacity as contrasted with the republicans, a failure to rise as boldly to the challenge of self-government.

Of those who came to Sorel[10] the majority were simple frontier farmers from the province of New York, and many were from the estate of Sir William Johnson, the great land-owner of the region around Schenectady. Johnson had died[11] before the full storm of the Revolution

---

[8] Outside the St. John Valley, the modern province is not conspicuously Loyalist in stock.

[9] See *Canada and Its Provinces*, XIII, 158ff.; also see Alfred Bailey, "Personalities in the History of New Brunswick," in C. H. McLean, *Prominent People of New Brunswick* ... (Saint John, 1937).

[10] 5,576 persons received rations there in 1784.

[11] 1774.

broke, but his son and nephew, Sir John and Colonel Guy, secured for the Crown the services of the Mohawk Indians under their great chief Joseph Brant, brother of Sir William's Molly, and held the Mohawk Gap, principal gateway to the west until 1777, when the Americans weakened the barrier in the battle of Oriskany. The Johnsons rallied to the Royal cause many of the recently arrived Catholic Highlanders whom Sir William had brought out to settle on his estates, together with a number of Ulstermen, embodying them in the "Royal Greens".[12]

It was these "Johnsonians" and their associates who formed the camp at Sorel in the winter of 1783-84. Others from the old province, who in one way or another had been caught up on the losing side, were also there—Hessian mercenaries adrift from their regiments, ordinary New York farmers, Germans, and Hudson Valley Dutchmen. They formed the largest single group of Loyalists to come to the Province of Quebec and their varied origins suggest that those of English speech[13] and Anglo-Saxon origin may actually have been in the minority among them.[14] When they were distributed to lands along the upper St. Lawrence, care was taken that the people of the different groups should be kept together. We can picture the processions of barges that set out in the spring of 1784: settlers, animals, supplies, tools, all piled in together, for the attack on the wilderness in the new townships surveyed between the last French settlements and the Bay of Quinté. The convoy would move slowly along, sailing, poling, rowing, and as it came to the spots decided on, some of the barges would drop off, leaving their occupants to face the woods that were henceforth to be their home. Highland Catholics were the first to land, adjacent to the outlying French settlements; there they would be next to their co-religionists. Next came their Presbyterian brethren, so that all the Scots could be together in what was to become their county of Glengarry. Then the Germans, also Protestants, were assigned their sites in Stormont County, where German names and Lutheran churches still are to be found. Lastly came the miscellaneous Dutch and English, along the river up to Kingston and the Bay of Quinté.

It may seem strange that so many people of origins other than English should have become Loyalists, especially in that many New York Dutch had shown a dubious loyalty during the previous war. But those with whom tradition is acquired are often apt to be more tenacious of it than those with whom it originated, to whom it is familiar and perhaps threadbare: cultures originate in a centre and disperse to circumfer-

[12] The Royal Regiment of New York.
[13] Many of the Highlanders spoke Gaelic.
[14] One-third, Hessian mercenaries included, were said to have been German; see E. C. Guillet, *Early Life in Upper Canada* (Toronto, 1933).

ences, where like old fashions in clothing, they may flourish after they have disappeared from the centre itself. So apart from specific reasons, such as the lack of political interest among the Germans, which would incline them to accept things as they were and the King along with other features of their colonial life, it is not strange that the United Empire Loyalists should include so many non-Anglo-Saxon elements.

The third stream coming into British territory crossed the new frontiers along the Niagara River and there slowly "sprayed out" into the Niagara peninsula, along the shores of the two lakes: along Lake Ontario in the direction of what is now Hamilton, and along the north shore of Lake Erie. There were not more than a few hundred of them, and to an extent probably greater than the other two groups, they were Loyalists by circumstance rather than by conviction. Most of them had been frontier Dutch and English in neighbouring New York, and a few in Pennsylvania. Niagara stood directly in the line of march of the westward-moving pioneers, and it is improbable that a recently established political boundary would have been as serious a deterrent in deflecting them as the river which marked it. So they came trooping into the Niagara peninsula, looking for land, and just as well pleased that they would escape the responsibilities of re-establishing order and making a new society, content to leave those tasks to authorities of a type to which they had long been accustomed.

Some of them, like other Loyalists, had no choice. Influential personages in western New York, such as Colonel John Butler, had raised among the settlers various corps of "rangers" who fought, as a rule, under the name of their commanders. Butler's Rangers, recruited mostly from Loyalist refugees at Niagara, became celebrated for their courage on the one side and notorious for their foul deeds on the other. Men who had, as was alleged, assisted in scalping parties directed against their old neighbours had to keep their distance, whatever the truth was.

The question is invariably raised as to how many Loyalists actually came to British North America, and it is one impossible to answer in exact terms. The most generous allowance, arrived at by taking the top figures of all estimates, would give a total of some 49,000 persons. A more moderate figure, but a fairly liberal one, would be about 35,000.[15] Of these many returned to their homes in the states, but a substantial nucleus was left and from it comes the present-day Canadian population of Loyalist descent. This population is scattered from Atlantic to Pacific, but the bulk of it still lives in the areas of the original settlements. While

[15] The available statistics are gathered up in the *Report on the Manuscript Lists relating to the United Empire Loyalists* (Public Archives of Canada, Ottawa, 1909).

its moulding force cannot be over-estimated, all in all, no one would claim that it forms any considerable proportion of the total Canadian population.[16]

4. Loyalist Influences in Canadian Life

Results of the migrations in terms other than numerical were of the first magnitude. Two new colonies, soon to become provinces, furnished the first visible and tangible result. The St. John valley settlements formed the nucleus of the new province of New Brunswick when it was set off from Nova Scotia in 1784, and the St. Lawrence and lake region settlements became Upper Canada in 1791. In addition, enough Loyalists went into Prince Edward Island and Cape Breton to affect, to some extent, the tone of those two colonies. Many of the new settlers had been pioneers, at home in the bush; these brought to their new abodes the adaptiveness and initiative common to the frontiers they had left. The old soldiers among them were not so adaptable. Loyalists of urban origin were not relatively numerous, but among them, especially in the Maritimes, there was a good proportion of educated men; many graduates of Harvard College came to Nova Scotia. This influx must have had some effect on the cultural level of the new settlements and on the amount of ability available for the tasks of citizenship. Though a good many of the leaders, to the detriment of their attachment to their new country, tried hard to make of Great Britain a spiritual home, the Loyalists, whatever their standing in life, constituted an English-speaking population that could have no other real homeland than British North America.

The intangible results of the migrations were the greatest. The anti-republican animus of all the Loyalists, great and small, made it certain that there would be a second group of English communities in North America and supplied for them a common bond, the primary expression of which was anti-Americanism and the secondary, strong sentiments of loyalty to the conception "British". The nature of this conception is revealed by the term they were allowed to append to their names, "United Empire": they disliked seeing a large empire made into a small one (although they put the blame for that on the wrong people); they shrank from breaking the unity of the English-speaking world. It is this deep-seated desire for the unity of the race which would seem to be their weightiest bequest to their descendants and to other Canadians.

[16] On a purely mathematical basis of natural increase, generation by generation, it could not exceed three or four hundred thousand at the utmost.

The common bond which hatred of the successful rebels constituted, negative though it might be, proved sufficient eventually to make all the English-speaking colonies realize that they had a common destiny. In this way, the Loyalists, by their stubborn determination to set up new, non-republican communities in the wilderness, gave birth indirectly to Confederation and thus to the Canadian nation. Mere settlement without a strong emotion behind it would not have been enough to resist the terrific draw of the advancing nation to the south. This emotion the Loyalists supplied. Down through the years they and their children nursed their wrath to keep it warm. The nationalism of the United States is founded on violent repulsion from England, that of Canada originally rested on repulsion from the United States.

Since Loyalist leaders sought to erect in the new homes the same kind of society they had enjoyed in the old, the new British North America started off with a curious mixture of aristocratic pretension and homespun frontier qualities. Aristocracy, having no natural basis in pioneer communities, retrogressed until it came to represent mere snobbery and the selfish interests of cliques; but monarchical attachment, encouraged by the fact that the monarch was a long distance away, survived. Canada today, partly owing to the original Loyalist conception, is strongly monarchical in sentiment and strongly republican in practice. The attempt to stem the tide of continental forces was bound to be a failure. Democracy, a word that two revolutions were to make stink worse in the nostrils of our ancestors than the word Bolshevik in the period after the Russian Revolution, might be reprobated for years by name but the fact was making steady progress; and Canada in time came to be almost as deep a popular democracy as the United States itself, though a much more conservative one; for a country founded to preserve the old order against the new must necessarily be conservative.

The aspect of conservatism that died hardest was colonialism. For many of the Loyalists, especially those of education, the new forest homes were places of last resort. Having been cast out of heaven, men could not at once give their hearts to hell. What they did was to erect a kind of imaginary heaven in compensation and to ascribe to it the qualities of far-off fields. This imaginary heaven was placed in the distant metropolis, the mother-country, the heart of empire. To preserve their *amour-propre*, the Loyalists called an old world into existence to redress the balance of the new. This they endowed with qualities not always corresponding to the actuality. They exalted British successes in arms and British "greatness", but they were not overly understanding of the lasting contributions of England to civilization: her devotion to freedom and the great edifice of law, custom, and spirit that Englishmen had built up to preserve that freedom. It was a partial and one-sided English tradition that the Loyalists cherished, a drum and trumpet tradition of mere "Britishism".

The Loyalists, many of them, added to the ordinary nostalgia of the colonist for his old home so great a resolve to make out of the mother-land a counterpoise to the republic that they got things out of proportion and were almost blinded to the greatness and beauty of the task that lay at hand, the creation of a new society with a way of life its own.[17] Yet though they gave a pattern to colonial life which it never lost, their leaders did not succeed in erecting what they might have regarded as perfect colonial societies, duplications of the semi-feudal structure of rural England, because the lowly among them responded to continental forces in much the same way as their republican brethren and because newcomers, plain Americans from the old colonies, began to make their appearance among them at once and ended by outnumbering them.

5. A Period of Confusion

The coming of the Loyalists and other settlers necessitated changes in political organization. These turned in part on the official English inter-pretation of the Revolution. Officials like William Knox[18] credited the success of the rebels to the ease with which they were able to combine in Continental Congresses and took the view that small separate colonies would show less independence than large ones. It has been the tradition that New Brunswick was set off from Nova Scotia because the St. John was so far away from Halifax, making for great inconvenience to the settlers, but probably as strong a motive for setting off not only New Brunswick but also Cape Breton from the parent province was *divide et impera*. Before the year 1784 was out, there were five colonies in the maritime group where previously there had been three, all of them prerogative colonies, deriving their form of government directly from the Crown.

On the St. Lawrence, the Revolution was followed by renewed ad-ministrative confusion. Haldimand, the Swiss, saw no reason for relaxing strong government on the coming of peace and resisted the demands of the English merchants for the accustomed legal rights of Englishmen, which he himself did not understand very well: he had seen nothing wrong with popping one or two of them, whose principles were dubious,

---

[17] Honourable exceptions naturally were many; Egerton Ryerson stands as their type for all time.

[18] Under-Secretary of State for the Colonies, 1770-1782.

into jail without a trial. The remainder of his term[19] was filled with quarrels with the merchants. After the war, there was the usual lapse from wartime prosperity, and many men were caught with large stocks of goods, bought at wartime prices. During hostilities, there had crept in an extraordinary practice of financing private bills of exchange with government funds (government acted as banker to the importers), and when the war boom broke, most of the merchants owed the government large sums that they could not meet. The situation reflected on Haldimand's supervision of finance, something of which the old soldier was patently ignorant, and he started a series of lawsuits to get back the public money. If successful he would have bankrupted every business man in the colony. Their natural recourse was to defend themselves by taking the offensive, and this they did by attacks on Haldimand himself, on the judges, and on the confused state of the colonial laws.[20]

The personnel of the bench was, to say the least, peculiar, with men upon it like ex-Naval Surgeon's Mate Mabane, a man with no pretensions to legal training,[21] and the confusion in the laws was evident to the least discerning eye. No one was much clearer on "the law of Canada" than he had ever been, certainly not the judges. Yet the merchants had to do business under it. Now the whole situation was shown up by the suits that Haldimand launched. A period of petitioning and counter-petitioning began, the object being to get English law and representative institutions introduced. An extension of the right of trial by jury was obtained in the last year of Haldimand's regime, and under his successor, the more liberal-minded administrator, Henry Hamilton, 1784-85, the English Habeas Corpus Act, with some modifications, was made part of the law of the province. But this was hardly enough, and the agitation went on.

The Loyalists up river had been cited by the merchants as English-speaking people who would certainly demand an assembly, but Haldimand had rather shrewdly observed that they had probably had all they desired of assemblies in the old colonies. He may have been right, for as it turned out, they did not show much concern at the lack of representative institutions and left it to the merchants of Montreal and Quebec to do most of the fighting for them. When, in 1786, Guy Carleton, now Lord Dorchester, was again sent out as governor, his chief duty was to end the

---

[19] He returned to England in 1784.
[20] For the whole incident see A. R. M. Lower, "Credit and the Constitutional Act," *CHR*, VI (June, 1925), 123-141.
[21] See p. 73; also see Hilda Neatby, "The Political Career of Adam Mabane," *CHR*, XVI (June, 1935), 137-150, and her *Administration of Justice under the Quebec Act* (London, 1937).

legal and administrative confusion in the province and find a reasonable way out. He brought back with him as his Chief Justice and adviser-extraordinary, William Smith, a characteristic Tory in that he had been Chief Justice of the province of New York, as had his father before him. Smith was determined to establish his mastery over the judiciary and probably had little sympathy with the formless "laws of Canada". Finding in the Quebec Act no express abrogation of the traditional right of Englishmen to the law of England, he began deciding cases on pure English law! This was confusion worse confounded, and arrayed the French in defence of their old laws. But Dorchester refused to accept the merchants' contention that the up-river population necessitated English institutions and thought that for the time a county organization would be sufficient for them. He admitted that the Revolution had changed the situation and that his old ideas about the country remaining French forever were no longer valid. The loyalist settlers could not be expected to hold their lands under the seigneurial tenure but should have grants in freehold. Meantime, the home authorities were inclined to think an Assembly would, through its powers of taxation, relieve them of the financial burden which the colony involved. But the French opposed an Assembly for this very reason: they equated it with increased taxation. How to reconcile the very diverse interests in the colony was the problem.

6. What the Revolution Seemed to Have Taught: The Constitutional Act

Under the circumstances it was decided in England to take the plunge and endow the colony with representative institutions, regardless of its religious or racial complexion. Since the Quebec Act could only be amended by another Act, a parliamentary rather than a prerogative basis for the St. Lawrence settlement was dictated. The government, then headed by the younger Pitt, introduced the Canada Bill, which was to become known in Canadian history as the Constitutional Act, 1791. This was the Act which determined the general shape that government was to assume in Canada and in all succeeding white colonies. There was to be a governor and a legislature, the latter consisting of appointive council and elected assembly, relations between the three being left to work themselves out. Herein lay "the very image and transcript of the British constitution" which, William Pitt explained, they were erecting in the American wilderness. There were other aspects of the Act which made the image even more realistic, but what English statesmen did not understand was that images and transcripts are not exportable. Certain elements of the British constitution could come and flourish; others at once died in the North American climate. If a new England in very truth could have been built in the forests of the St. Lawrence valley, then the Constitutional Act might have worked very well. As it was, it was hopeless to expect the "very image and transcript" to fit French Catholics and backwoods colonials who had hazy ideas, if any, of the English way of life.

The English statesmen of the day, in making a constitution for Canada, were anxious to avoid the evils that had occasioned the American Revolution, but their interpretation of that event led to the ultimate failure of their work. The Revolution had been caused, so the thesis went, by too much democracy, lack of sufficient aristocratic elements in the colonies, lack of an established church, not enough firm rule on the part of the home government, insufficient supervision of colonial governments, the weak position of the governor, his dependence on the legislature for money: the colonies, in short, had rebelled because they had been too free. That defect was now to be remedied. Democracy was to be confined within reasonable limits by the appointive Legislative Council and especially by the creation of a colonial nobility, with hereditary right to seats in the Council, which was to be a colonial House of Lords. Republicanism, which had especially marked colonial governments like Connecticut, was to be avoided by such devices as the suspensory veto, under which colonial acts referred to England did not come into force until approved by the Crown (in the old colonies they had become law unless subsequently disallowed), and by the continuation of the office of Governor-in-Chief of British North America (1786) with a Lieutenant-Governor for each colony.

One of the bones of contention in the old colonies had been the matter of a colonial episcopate. The Episcopal Church had been established in Virginia, New York, and certain other colonies, but no colonial bishopric, thanks largely to New England Puritan opposition, had ever been erected.[22] With the objecting colonies out of the way, the step could be taken. The Revolution had hardly ended before the diocese of Nova Scotia had been set up (1787); within a few years that of Quebec followed (1793), as an integral part of the arrangements of 1791. The Act itself was designed to strengthen the church, although it did not establish it. Yet it went a long way in its introduction of those apples of discord, the *Clergy Reserves*. Under this title one-seventh of all land granted was to be reserved for the benefit of a *Protestant Clergy*. How

---

[22] Except the Catholic bishopric of Quebec, 1766. See p. 74.

this curious word *Protestant* crept in can only be conjectured. It may be that it is to be accounted for by the presence in the ministry of a Scottish Presbyterian, Henry Dundas, close friend of Pitt. *Protestant Clergy* could be stretched to cover the colonial ministers of both established churches. It is possible that it was this factor that prevented an Anglican establishment.

Not the Act but the spirit of post-Revolutionary colonial administration (which could not learn that it was the weight of regulation from London under which the old Empire had sunk) was to ensure that the governor should be tied more closely to London than in former days. Correspondence and instructions grew to be endless until governors hardly felt free to do anything without "referring it home": the result was something approaching stagnation. The governor, in his turn, was strengthened against the legislature. He retained the veto, to which was added the suspensory veto of reservation, and had more financial elbow room than in the old colonies; no post-revolutionary governor ever had to go without his salary because he would not consent to Assembly bills. It was not until after the War of 1812 that the increased cost of government began to press on non-executive sources of income and force requests for legislative grants.

The grand scheme for an image and transcript was wrecked before it was launched. Canada, with its dominant Catholic population, would have been an unfortunate field for experimenting with a state church of the type which is so integral a part of the constitution of England; and in a few years it was to be plain that among the English-Canadians, the dissenters were in the majority. The plan for a colonial aristocracy was never, thanks to the good sense of the authorities, put into execution. As Robert Gourlay a few years later was to write, it would have been an amusing but unavoidable sight in a country where there was little wealth and little other basis for distinction in rank, to see men doing the haying along a country road and on inquiry to find that the man on top of the load was the Marquis of Erie while the other, pitchfork in hand, was the Duke of Ontario. The wilderness killed artificial aristocracy, as it was to kill local attempts to secure official privilege. The biggest thing the Constitutional Act introduced was representative government. That granted, all else would in due course follow.

A second chance for Empire, yes, but upon colonial terms. If England's statesmen of the 1780's misread the lessons of the Revolution, circumstances were to prove too strong for statutes, and in the end, the spirit of the New World had its way, leaving in the new colonies, as a heritage of the great upheaval, only shadows of the philosophy of privilege that had occasioned it.

Chronology

1782–84 Loyalist Migrations.
1784   New Brunswick and Cape Breton made separate provinces.
1784   End of Haldimand's governorship.
1786   Lord Dorchester (Guy Carleton), Governor.
1791   The Canada or Constitutional Act.

Additional Reading

Burt, A. L. *The Evolution of the British Empire and Commonwealth*. Boston, 1956.
Bruchési, Jean. *A History of Canada*, trans. by R. W. W. Robertson. Toronto, 1950.
Neatby, Hilda M. *The Administration of Justice Under the Quebec Act*. London, 1937.
Reid, J. H. Stewart, Kenneth McNaught, and Harry S. Crowe. *A Source-Book of Canadian History*. Toronto, 1959.
Wade, Mason. *The French Canadians, 1760-1945*. Toronto, 1956.

CHAPTER 11

The Undivided West, 1760-1783

1. The Government of the West

In 1763, Great Britain fell heir to the territorial claims of the French Crown. In contrast to South America, no longer was there a France to play Portugal to Britain's Spain. By the Peace of Paris, all the immense territory from Cape Breton to the distant Mississippi, from New Orleans to Fort Maurépas[1] became hers. The British flag waved without lawful rival from the southern tip of Florida along the full stretch of the Atlantic coast to the Arctic wastes beyond the Hudson's Straits, from the Gulf of Mexico to the twilight zone out beyond Lake Winnipeg. A few Indians remained to be brushed aside and a few thousand French-speaking "new subjects" along the banks of the St. Lawrence slightly modified the linguistic harmony of the whole. But these were trifles. Once the authority of the Crown had been asserted, there would lie at the disposal of the English a vast continental expanse; in it they would be able to build a structure such as the mind of man had never before conceived.

Many peoples would have shown some imaginative reaction to such a situation. Its potentialities would perhaps have awakened their poets and, almost certainly, their planners. Not so with the English of either world. They had rejoiced in their victory and then proceeded to forget all about it. When, a few months after the peace, a plan for the ad-

[1] At the mouth of the Winnipeg River.

ministration of the new acquisitions was produced which, for so empiric a race, was large and imaginative, the English of the Old World hardly heard of it and the English of the New found in it mainly occasion for complaint. True to their genius, both halves of the race were following their noses, meeting specific problems as they arose, not indulging in great sweeps of continental planning; such idle dreams could be left to the French, who had failed.

The immediate things to do were to put down Pontiac's Indian rising and to work out some form of government for the conquered territories. Of these the chief was New France. But what was New France? It is impossible to say. Céloron de Blainville had taken possession of the Ohio country for France. De Lauzon had long before proclaimed the King of France at Sault Ste. Marie, and LaSalle along the Mississippi. La Vérendrye had represented him on the banks of the Missouri and the Saskatchewan. Was all this New France? The English could show some legal right, too. The grant of 1670 by Charles II to the Hudson's Bay Company gave title to all lands on the Hudson's Bay watershed. After their surrender of 1713, the French could not dispute the English right to "The Hudson's Bay Territories"; insofar as the interior went, they could merely ignore it, as La Vérendrye had done in building his posts on the waters flowing north.

To the west of the settled colonies, another set of English claims cut into "New France". Under the colonial charters, Massachusetts Bay, Connecticut, and Virginia could all claim extensive lands across the mountains. Massachusetts and Connecticut were entitled to narrow strips running clear across to the western ocean, and Virginia had its well-established but highly indefinite charter right to a slice of land that, by one interpretation, would have comprised most of the interior. These cut across the French claims and as soon as the English had the continent, they became worth something. Were the French titles, based on a show of occupation[2] and now, inherent in the British Crown, better than colonial claims which with partial exceptions, had not been pressed for a century and a half? Matters were not made simpler by the French handing over to Spain their unconquered colony of Louisiana, which comprised all their claims on the right bank of the Mississippi from the Gulf to the farthest northern extent of its watershed.

The French had disputed the right of the English king to grant lands across the mountains to the Ohio Company but that right was now

[2] There were a few little French settlements in "the west" around the fur posts and forts, such as Vincennes, Terre Haute, Caskaskia, etc. Some of these, such as St. Louis and St. Genevieve, lay on the right bank of the Mississippi and therefore in Louisiana.

established by the most indisputable of instruments, conquest: between the Crown in England and the Crown in Virginia or other colonies, the right now lay. Colonies would find it hard to assert their conflicting charter claims to these interior lands. Yet the schemes that began to be mooted within a few years for the erection of one or more new provinces across the mountains seemed logical enough to secure the support of prominent men like Benjamin Franklin, especially when they contained such brilliant prospects from the proceeds of land speculation. In one way or another colonial claims would have been adjusted, the conflict of jurisdiction ended, and the west opened to settlement.

The question became pressing even before the Peace of Paris, for frontiersmen and fur traders began to make their way westward as soon as the French generals surrendered in 1760. There had to be some authority in the wilderness if law and order were to be maintained. When the whole interior burst into the flame of Pontiac's rebellion, some considered plan for the government of the west became imperative. The Proclamation of October 7, 1763, was the first step. It was decided to try to keep settlers from going beyond the mountains until the Indian titles could be extinguished and order restored.[3] The new governments erected, Quebec and East and West Florida, did not include any of the interior, plans for the government of which were to be made separately: these were to be of such a nature as not to injure the sensibilities of colonies whose claims might be involved. The new province of Quebec was a much compressed version of "Canada", for it included little more than the seigneurial area and the corridor along the Ottawa to Lake Huron.[4] The British government, in thus shifting boundaries about, did so under its own right, killing the old French title to which it had fallen heir.[5] A Board of Trade Memorandum of 1764 was designed to carry the plan farther. It called for two Superintendents-General of Indian Affairs, answerable directly to the Imperial Government, one for the north and one for the south, and under them various Superintendents and Commissaries, who were to act as go-betweens with whites and

[3] There was no suggestion of permanent exclusion, as is sometimes alleged. See L. H. Gipson, *The British Empire Before the American Revolution*, IX, Chap. 3 for a good discussion of the Proclamation. The latest word on it is in Jack M. Sosin, *Whitehall and the Wilderness: The Middle West in British Colonial Policy, 1760-1775* (Lincoln, Neb., 1961). Sosin claims that the dealings in western lands, even of George Washington himself, were not marked by complete integrity.

[4] See p. 71.

[5] See A. L. Burt, *The United States, Great Britain and British North America*, p. 18.

Indians, administer the law in the back-country, and, in particular, have the responsibility of securing the extinction of the Indian titles.

Such a scheme would cost money. There was also necessity for protecting the colonies against further Indian risings. This involved troops. The armies sent out to fight the French had not all been recalled; several thousand men remained, under General Gage as Commander-in-Chief. The scheme involved the use of some of these troops as frontier garrisons. The degree of centralized authority implied by the continued residence in the colonies of the Commander-in-Chief would soon have offended suspicious colonial particularism, and any justification of the general plan in the west on the ground of keeping order beyond the settlements would have received scant attention; the colonies took disorder more easily than the English government, murders and fights out there being incidental in the rough and tumble of frontier life. When the question of payment for the grand scheme came up, there was not interest enough among colonials to procure the representations against it for which George Grenville was careful to offer opportunity. Silence giving consent, he went ahead and enacted the measure which destroyed the whole experiment, the Stamp Act (1765). Once colonials realized that the money was to come out of their pockets and by the fiat of a distant authority which had never tried to do anything of the sort before, they began to protest that the west could look after itself, that danger from Indian risings was nil, that troops were unnecessary, and that anyway they would pay no taxes without representation. So on colonial particularism and on George Grenville's lack of imagination (for if he had known the colonists, he could have predicted the event), the scheme for the west broke down and for nine years that region was left to itself, bereft of any pretense of law and order.

It was not until the Quebec Act was passed (1774) that the British government again tackled the problem of law and order in the back country. This time it had a little more experience. The natural way into the interior lay through the St. Lawrence and the lakes and nearly all the people going into it went through this gateway. Most of those who did not drifted across the southern Appalachians, and down the Cumberland and Tennessee, eventually to form the new states of Kentucky and Tennessee. They would have been looked after if the project for an interior colony had come to anything: the scheme might have become the southern counterpart of the Quebec Act. It was clear that settlers could not be restrained within the Proclamation line,[6] but north of the Ohio it had not been the settler so much as the trader who had oc-

⁶ See p. 133

casioned the necessity for a government: this factor added to the logic of the Quebec Act in its provision for extending the boundaries of Quebec to its ancient hinterland, the country between the lakes, the Ohio and the Mississippi. In the Act was a provision which expressly safeguarded other colonial claims, but to that no attention was paid, and the extension of the boundaries of Quebec was added to the other reasons for assailing the measure.

2. The British Fur Traders

The west that lay north of the Ohio (the old North West, as the Americans call it) remained under the government of Quebec until the end of the Revolutionary war, when the present boundaries were drawn. From 1775 to 1783 small British garrisons were maintained at Oswegatchie (now Ogdensburg), Oswego, Detroit, Michilimackinac, and some interior posts. Some of these latter were surprised and cleared out by George Rogers Clark during the early years of the Revolution, but his prowess had no bearing on the cession, and the American diplomats at Paris made no claims based upon his deeds. The war ended without a rebel having set foot in the greater part of the territory north of the Ohio. It had been held by the British while the eastern war was raging just as it had been held by the French in previous eastern wars, and communications from its eastern gateway, Quebec, through the St. Lawrence and the lakes, to the depths of the interior, had been maintained without interruption.

The going and coming had been confined to officials, soldiers and fur traders. These latter had begun to make their way into the west shortly after French resistance had been broken. By 1765, Thomas Curry had penetrated west of Michilimackinac, and by 1767, he had got beyond Lake Winnipeg. By 1768, the Frobishers had reached Portage du Traite on the Churchill River. Peter Pond, demobilized New England soldier, crude and acute, an outstanding example of many of those who rushed into the trade after the fighting, quite on his own, after having in previous years traded farther east, had got out as far as the Athabaska river in 1778. James Finlay, Forest Oakes, Maurice Blondeau, were other examples of traders who had gone into the west almost before the ink on the treaty of cession was dry.[7] By the 1770's such men, with their French assistants, were tapping the Hudson's Bay Company's trade at some of its sources, especially on the Saskatchewan River. References to "the pedlars from Quebec", began to go home in factors' letters, indicat-

[7] See A. S. Morton, *A History of the Canadian West to 1870-71* (Toronto, 1939).

ing what "the Bay" thought of them and how scanty their resources were.[8] Nevertheless, since they obtained the Indians' furs fairly cheaply because they saved them the long trip down the Nelson and the Hayes to York Factory,[9] these men made the old company wake up and give over its practice of "sleeping by the Bay"; thenceforth it had to send its men into the interior too, and compete for furs on the spot. From that time until the amalgamation of 1821, the Indians enjoyed their "palmy days": they had the choice of more than one purchaser for their furs, and many of them were shrewd enough to take advantage of this.

3. Competition's Consequence: The North West Company

The St. Lawrence depot lent itself admirably to the kind of control the Imperial government decided should be exercised over these men. Every trader had to have his licence, specifying the number of canoes he was taking and the amount of his trade goods. Since everyone had to leave by the river there was no possibility of evasion: all goods went over the road from Montreal to Lachine, there to be embarked in the six-fathom canoes for the *pays d'en haut*, and at Lachine everything could be checked and supervised. This system did not procure complete order in the west, but by tying individuals down it gave government a check on them and prevented the interior from becoming a mere no-man's land.

It did not take long for the fur traders in the old post at Albany to appreciate the advantages of the newly-won base of Montreal. Albany traders had competed with the French for over a century, yet although their goods were cheaper, geography and the more imaginative attitude of the French towards the Indians had kept the balance weighted in favour of the St. Lawrence. After 1760, the French were gone, but the Iroquois remained, still something of a barrier to easy trade from the Mohawk across to Oswego and the Lakes. So it was not long before the solid Scots, into whose hands most of the Albany trade by that time had come, were shifting their establishments north to Montreal.[10] This shift was to inaugurate a new period in the St. Lawrence fur trade. A much needed sense of responsibility was introduced and greater financial

[8] W. S. Wallace, "The Pedlars from Quebec," *CHR*, XIII (Dec., 1932), 387-402.

[9] Further east, north of Lake Huron and Superior, these "pedlars" did the same thing, cutting off fur supplies just over the height of land, at posts on such rivers as the Metagami, the Missinabie, and the Albany.

[10] See R. H. Fleming, "MacTavish, Frobisher and the Company of Montreal," *CHR*, X (June, 1929), 136-152.

resources. Since some of the new merchants had their London connections, the old trans-Atlantic chain could be reforged. This would complete the restoration, under English auspices, of the old French system—by canoe and ship from the far west to the capitals of Europe.

For the canoe half of the trip, the Scottish merchants depended entirely upon the previous French arrangements. The *voyageurs* had willingly signed on with their new masters and had placed at their disposal all that skill with paddle and pack-strap upon which the whole system rested. One hundred and eighty pounds a man over a portage, twenty hours travelling a day if necessary, salt pork, corn-meal, dried peas and pemmican, infinite amounts of strong tobacco: these were the pillars of internal exploitation. The men who did the bargaining, the traders themselves, had, in the astuteness, driving power, and the "poker-face" of the typical trader, much more ordinary skills to offer and, as usual, got bigger rewards for them. In the fur trade, as later in lumbering and other activities, the Scottish and French, as masters and men, formed an irresistible combination.

The *voyageur* system had a definite relationship to the geography of the interior. The basin of the St. Lawrence led into the heart of the country. To the south were the illimitable woods of the Continental Plain, to the north the vast extent of the Canadian Shield with its trees, its rocks, its muskegs, its lakes, and its beaver. Farther west, still other waterways flowed along the edge of the Shield: Rainy River, the Lake of the Woods, Winnipeg River, Lake Winnipeg. The Saskatchewan and Churchill rivers touched and penetrated it. Farther north and west along the margin of the Shield, still buried in their northern recesses at the period with which this chapter deals, were Lake Athabaska, Great Slave Lake, Great Bear Lake, and the Mackenzie River itself, all among the world's largest bodies of fresh water, all leading along the edge of the interminable Shield. It was the Shield from which the best furs came. But conveniently adjacent to it was country that would grow food either naturally, as the western plains grew their buffalo, or through agriculture. The fur trade was supported by the fertile country with food bases at intervals along the route; many, such as Detroit, Michilimackinac, and Sault Ste. Marie, developed in French times. After the Conquest these increased, and when the exploitation of the far west began, the exploitation of the buffalo began with it. The buffalo-pemmican system, which is more pertinent to the next chapter, carried many Scotsmen and Frenchmen across the prairies and eventually beyond the mountains.

At Montreal, more important Scots soon appeared, with longer purses, who could bring in trade goods from Great Britain and let the men of the upper country have them on long credits. These port merchants themselves were usually "carried" by some exporting house in a British port. The chain was long and complex. If the Montreal merchant got his mail off by the last ships in, say, 1770, he would get his goods out in the spring of 1771. With luck, these would reach the head of the lakes by late summer and the Saskatchewan by late fall. The winter of 1771-1772 would be put in by the traders awaiting the results of the fur season. In the spring with the arrival of the Indians, trading would begin. Then the furs would start their long journey at express-train speed for those days: sometimes a good canoe would cover seventy miles in a day.[11] Again, with luck, they would be in Montreal for the last autumn ships and reaching London, would be prepared for the trade and put on the market in the new year, say, 1773. If everything went well, the London house's money was "out" for two years, and if anything in the chain went wrong, it might well be three. An accident to a canoe might make it fail to return at all. The time element, to say nothing of the risks, meant an expensive and difficult trade, one in which every detail had to be treated so as to reduce time and expense. Only a high degree of organizing, technical, and bargaining skill could have made the long six thousand mile chain stretch and hold.

The worst danger of all would be cut-throat competition, and nothing was more certain to develop. No trader was going to go a journey of thousands of miles and come back empty-handed: he had to get furs, regardless of price. There were also plenty of other dangers: the great expense of the long journey and the risks of lake and rapid, which often extended to life and limb; starvation and freezing; the financial burden on the small man, his uncertain standing and difficulty in getting credit, with resulting high interest rates; the high prices he himself had to pay for his trade goods. All these things pointed in one direction, which was the road the French had previously found themselves forced to follow, that is, combination.

Combination in the form of partnerships apparently began almost at once but it was not until the 1770's that it became conspicuous. Individual adventurers were disappearing and men were drawing into groups. A very considerable partnership was effected in 1779, about which year the phrase the "Gentlemen of the North West", "*Les Bourgeois du Nord-ouest*", began to be heard. By 1783, monopoly of practically all the trade out of Montreal was effected, when all the partnerships came together into one big partnership, the North West

[11] There are records of light passenger canoes covering the 700 miles from Sault Ste. Marie to Montreal in just over a week.

Company. This concern was not a chartered or limited company like the Hudson's Bay, but a series of partnerships embracing Montreal middlemen and up-country traders. These latter, since most of them did not come down to Montreal in the fall, became known as the "wintering partners". Because they had a direct and proportionate interest in profits and were not employees, the system worked excellently, and provided a degree of energy in exploitation that has never been surpassed. With the appearance of the powerful organization that monopoly rendered possible, the foundation was laid for the resurrection of the fur trader's dominance over colonial life. The great river had reasserted its sway and the way had been opened to the second edition of "The Commercial Empire of the St. Lawrence".[12]

By the period of the amalgamation of 1783, traders from Montreal were all through the lakes region, down south towards the edge of profitable fur country in the Ohio Valley, through what is now Wisconsin, Minnesota, the Dakotas, Manitoba, along the Saskatchewan, and one of them had even got onto the upper waters of the Churchill, ready to take that all but final plunge which would have brought the fur trade to the confines of the continent. But in that very year, 1783, the empire that might have had an unbroken continent at its disposal was rent in twain and the illimitable west was divided. A chapter had been closed.

Additional Reading

Alvord, Clarence W. *The Mississippi Valley in British Politics*. Cleveland, 1917.

Campbell, Marjorie Wilkins. *McGillvray, Lord of the Northwest*. Toronto, 1962.

———. *The North West Company*. Toronto, 1957.

Davidson, Gordon G. *The Northwest Company*. Berkeley, Calif., 1918.

Fleming, R. H. "McTavish, Frobisher and Company of Montreal." *CHR*, X (June, 1929), 136-152.

Morton, A. S. *A History of the Canadian West to 1870-71*. Toronto, 1939.

Rich, E. E. *The History of the Hudson's Bay Company, 1670-1870*. London, 1958. 2 vols.

Sosin, Jack M. *Whitehall and the Wilderness: The Middle West in British Colonial Policy*. Lincoln, Neb., 1961.

[12] Donald Creighton, *The Commercial Empire of the St. Lawrence, 1760-1850* (Toronto, 1937); (rev. ed., 1956: *Empire of the St. Lawrence*).

CHAPTER 12

The Hinterland of Montreal, 1783-1821

1. The Western Posts: Jay's Treaty

In the moment of their amalgamation the fur traders, thanks to the bargain made by the diplomats at Paris, lost half of their kingdom. Or rather two-thirds of it, since that proportion of the annual trade (some £200,000 out of a total of £300,000) was supposed to have come from the American side of the new boundary. The imposing individuals who cut such figures in frontier Montreal, who were able to defy a governor and whose agitations were within a few years to secure a change in the form of colonial government, found that they did not count for so much in the capital of the Empire. The politicians and the diplomats had other matters to consider besides North America: France, Spain and Holland were all enemies, and the Baltic supplies, so vital to England in that age, were being threatened by the Armed Neutrality of the North. Mere fur traders represented only a minor colonial interest, and the imaginations of great men in London were in no danger of being fired by the vision of an empire of canoes and fur posts extending over some thousands of miles of howling wilderness. The boundary settlement of 1783[1] left to the fur traders only the very northernmost of all the entrances to the far west. They had lost the easy territory to the south and would have to draw more and more on the distant north-

[1] For the boundary settlement of 1783, see p. 85.

west. More than ever, efficiency and economy would be necessary. In those days when people talked of trade as if it were an object that could be handed about in a box from one person or nation to another, it was assumed that the Americans would automatically take over on their side of the line. Montreal, base for efforts flung over half a continent, would lose much of its hinterland. Politics would dominate economics.

Yet, at the moment, few of the advantages lay with the Americans. Their outermost western settlement was only a few miles beyond Albany. They had no access, except on British sufferance, to the lakes and the great region beyond them. Only by slow degrees were they able to enter into the inheritance with which audacity on the one hand and indifference on the other hand endowed them.

They had taken their first step during the Revolution when they had broken the power of the Iroquois.[2] After the battle of Oriskany the Iroquois could not prevent the Americans penetrating up the Mohawk in the direction of Lake Ontario. But when the war closed, they had not reached the lake and Oswego remained in British hands. Not until the 1790's was the tide of settlement, the real American conquest of the west, to roll up the valley and out towards the lake.[3]

Further political advance westward on the part of the Americans was prevented by the British refusal to give up the so-called "Western Posts", Oswegatchie (Ogdensburg), Oswego, Niagara, Detroit, Michilimackinac, each one at a strategic point on river and lake. Not for another thirteen years, until 1796, could the Americans take possession of the southern side of the lakes. British apologists have usually stated that the western posts were retained because the American states would not fulfil the conditions of the treaty relating to the Loyalists and the debts owing to private merchants. Americans have always asserted that this was only an excuse and that the British hung on to the posts in order to continue enjoying the fur trade. But the profits from the trade would not have paid the cost of maintaining the posts.[4] Insofar as a single reason will explain any historical decision, they were retained because of the Indian situation or perhaps, beyond that again, because of the reluctance to keep the bad bargain of 1783 as long as any chance remained of retaining the territories then ceded. The Treaty of Paris had involved the British in a breach of faith. In 1768 they had made

[2] See p. 19. The Mohawks became Loyalists at the end of the war, and most of them removed to Upper Canada, where they still are.

[3] The Genessee Tract, whose centre was the city of Rochester, was settled by an English landowner in the 1790's.

[4] See A. L. Burt, *The United States, Great Britain and British North America*, pp. 83-85.

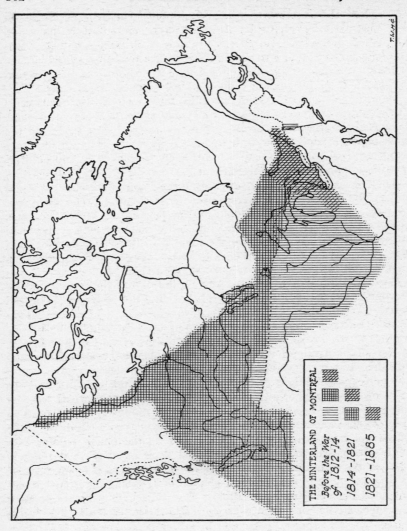

the treaty of Fort Stanwix with the western Indians. The Indians had
surrendered everything between the Proclamation Line, 1763,[5] and the
Ohio and Allegheny rivers and in return the country north of the Ohio

[5] The Appalachian Watershed.

and west of the Proclamation Line, extended by an irregular area in New York and Pennsylvania, was to become a vast Indian reserve. Now, fifteen years later, the British surrendered this region without consultation with the other parties to the treaty, the Indians. Pontiac's rising was fresh in everyone's memory. It had been provoked partly because the French had sold out the Indians to the English. Now the English had sold them out to the Americans. The Indians had come to believe in the justice of the distant Imperial government but they were well aware of what to expect of their hereditary enemies, the colonists. Would the English surrender provoke another Pontiac's rebellion?

This was what General Haldimand thought would happen, so he held on to the posts, not revealing the surrender to the Indians until they could be reconciled. He converted the home government to his plan. Neither the Indians nor the Americans could be informed of it, so the Loyalist argument was used as the most effective counter to American demands for possession. As time went by, it became more and more difficult to break the unpleasant news to the Indians, who assumed that the solemn engagement of 1768 was being observed. When the truth did come out, the response was just what Haldimand had expected: an Indian confederacy was organized and a good, plucky fight made against the Americans, who, in Indian eyes, were violating the Treaty of Fort Stanwix and invading their territory. From this fight the British were absent. The British in 1783 most likely could not have got the Indians' consent to the abrogation of the Treaty of Fort Stanwix, but they might have done better than make a surrender of land that was not theirs.

Meanwhile, conquest by settlement was creeping westward. Settlement began on the Ohio immediately after the Revolution. It had already crossed the Fort Stanwix line in New York and Pennsylvania, and was ready to roll along the southern side of the lakes. Quite apart from high political considerations, it would in itself have forced a "show-down" in "the old North West".

It was this situation, together with other matters in dispute, such as the question of trade between the United States and the British West Indies, that led to the Treaty of 1794, known as Jay's Treaty, from the name of its principal negotiator, John Jay, later Chief Justice of the United States. The war with the ancient enemy, France, was giving American good-will value in British eyes, a factor which may have hastened the settlement. Conditions in the west had been going from bad to worse. American military expeditions that were cutting into the territory restrained themselves with difficulty from disturbing the British-held posts, while the Indians gathered ominously for a stand. Permanent good relationships could never be established until the posts were surrendered. Jay's Treaty provided for this: the British agreed to hand them over in return for settlement of the private mercantile debts still pending from Revolutionary days and for a promise that the boundary would remain open for the fur traders. Given American sovereignty and the speed of American settlement, the illusory nature of such a promise must have been foreseen easily enough by the acute individuals behind the Montreal fur trade: not that that helped matters, for their interests got no more consideration from the British government than did those of the Indians. The treaty coincided with General Wayne's victory over the Indians at Fallen Timbers (1794), near the south-west corner of Lake Erie; if the surrender had not been made, this victory, which broke the Indian power, would have led to an American attempt to expel the British too, and thus to a second war. As it was, the situation had generated much bad blood; the stock American accusation was that the British incited the Indians to resist, furnished them with muskets and ammunition, and fought among them in disguise. The British, in their attempts to keep faith with both sides, found their faith unfaithful keeping them falsely true, a position from which the politicians in London, if not the men on the spot, were only too glad to escape, leaving the Indians to make their peace as best they might. American accusations of secret aid through John Graves Simcoe, lieutenant-governor of Upper Canada, have never been quite refuted.

Though the fur traders were to be free to come and go across the border, American jurisdiction involved limitations. The American garrisons at the posts might not be unfriendly, but they were not British. Nor was the law. Foreseeing difficulties, some of the trading companies —by 1786, the North West Company had suffered various ruptures and a few new men had come in—abandoned the southern route, through Detroit, and tried for a share in the northern. Among them were Forsyth, Richardson and Co. of Montreal, who as general merchants and traders had been powerful in the country from Montreal to Detroit and on through into Michigan. Their shift was one of the factors in causing the most serious of the breaks in the monopoly. This was the formation of the Nor' Westers' rival, the X Y Company.[6]

Such incidents reveal a more decided concentration on the northern route than hitherto. After 1783, a nominal change in an un-run boundary line had not had the expected effect of causing the transfer of the

[6] Formed 1800 between Sir Alexander Mackenzie, Forsyth, Richardson and Co., and the Ogilvy firm. See Morton, *A History of the Canadian West to 1870-71*, 343ff.

fur trade from British to Americans, but now a real change was coming and there were preparations to meet the storm. No withdrawal seems to have been contemplated from Michilimackinac, which point gave entrance to Green Bay, Lake Michigan, and thence by an easy route to the upper Mississippi, but more business was undertaken west of Lake Superior. The usual route to the west left Lake Superior at Grand Portage, surmounting the wall of rock down which the Pigeon River tumbles by a "carry" on the south side of that river some fourteen miles in length. This was the *grand* or big portage, which led over to the headwaters of Rainy River, down which the canoes proceeded to the Lake of the Woods. After 1796, Grand Portage grew in importance until, one day in 1800, the fur traders coming down from the west with their season's take of skins found an American customs officer at the end of the portage, demanding duty on the furs transported through American territory. They discovered that freedom to continue the fur trade in American territories was freedom to continue it under American conditions, one of which was a good stiff duty on goods going across American territory. The Americans were blasting the Montrealers out of their second line. While the original peace treaty was being made, fur traders had pleaded with Shelburne in vain, to secure a boundary that would give them easy access to the west through British territory. The western territory had been kept, but why, under these conditions? It seemed to be loaded with as many disabilities as could be conceived.

The result of the customs incident was the abandonment of Grand Portage by the Nor' Westers and a shift to the north-east, where they found a river, the Kaministiquia, that avoided the fourteen mile portage to the Hudson's Bay watershed, but which involved a longer and much harder route to the Rainy River. At its mouth they built a post (1803), Fort William (the original of the present city), named after one of their "Big Bourgeois", William MacGillivray. Here they established their most elaborate half-way house to the west, a fur traders' capital to which men from all over the west gathered every year for counsel and jollification. It was at this point that transfer was made from the six fathom lake canoes (*canots de maître*) to the smaller three and four fathom western canoes (*canots du nord*), more suitable for the smaller waters and frequent portages encountered on the route to the prairies.

After the surrender of the posts, it became an object with the Americans to place as many handicaps on the Canadian fur traders as possible, in order to confine the privilege of entry to the narrowest compass. The American point of view was that the country was unconditionally theirs under the treaty of 1783 and that the "international servitude" involved in free entry was an indignity that they had had to accept for the sake of peace. This legalistic paring away of an international engagement was reinforced by the deterioration of relations between the two countries arising out of the Napoleonic wars. Jefferson's embargo (1808) at first included the stoppage of the fur trade, and when relief was secured under Jay's Treaty by representations at Washington, local customs officials carried on in the spirit of the embargo. For example, the Michilimackinac Company[7] had a large part of its season's supplies—eight bateaux out of twenty, over £6,000 of goods— seized in American waters off Niagara in the spring of 1808, as they were on their way up the lakes. The company, it is said, never entirely recovered from this blow which played a direct part in crushing the British trade through Lake Michigan. The commercial emperors of the St. Lawrence were being shown that there were stronger forces in life than business efficiency. About that time the North West Company itself began to use the short cut across Upper Canada rendered available by the building of Yonge Street north from Lake Ontario to Lake Simcoe. Thenceforth it did not need to enter American waters on the lower lakes and by going across via Lake Simcoe to the Georgian Bay, saved much distance too.[8]

It was only the potency of North-West Company influence over the Indians and its supreme efficiency in management that enabled Canadian traders to operate anywhere in American territory. As long as American authority refrained from interference, North-West qualities were more than a match for American competition, and down to and during the War of 1812, the Company continued to monopolize the fur trade through Lake Superior to the Mississippi, as far south as Rock River.[9] Through it, the British government had control of that region and of the Indians. But at Ghent in 1814, as at Paris in 1783, the fur traders found themselves abandoned by the peacemakers. If the fur traders had been able to think in terms other than commercial and if diplomats had been inclined to think more in terms of the St. Lawrence and of Empire, the two in conjunction might have forged a veritable "commercial empire of the St. Lawrence". As it was, to diplomats, fur traders remained minor colonial merchants. Further, when the British government displayed some intention of demanding from the Americans the terms which the situation seemed to warrant, it found its guns

---

[7] Organized by the Montreal traders as a subsidiary to carry on the American part of the trade. See Burt, *op. cit.*, p. 257; Morton, *op. cit.*, p. 487.

[8] This route was not used much after the War of 1812, when the American trade was lost.

[9] Where the present city of Rock Island, Ill., is situated, or well south of the latitude of Chicago.

spiked by no less a person than the Duke of Wellington, gave in at once, and signed a peace based purely on the status quo.[10] The Peace of Ghent, like the Peace of Paris in 1783, left the Nor' Westers to the mercy of the American authorities. After the war (which was taken as abrogating Jay's Treaty) the American government, by special legislation, ousted the fur traders from the unsettled area, therewith ending British influence and laying once and for all the ghost of the Indian problem.

2. The Map Unrolled: The Arctic and Pacific

The conflict over the "western posts" and the fur trade on American territory did not greatly impede exploration and expansion in remote areas. Under the driving lashes of profit and curiosity, penetration of the west had been rapid from the first. By the middle 1770's, English traders had got out into territory never before touched by white men, well beyond the limit of the La Vérendrye journeys. Among this early group none did more to unroll the map than Peter Pond, that daring and unscrupulous old Yankee heathen; from the upper Saskatchewan, he succeeded in crossing over through the Cumberland House district and reaching the Churchill. From that river, he got to Lake Isle-à-la-Crosse and from there to Methye Lake. He crossed the Methye Portage to Clearwater River, which leads into the Athabaska, and descended it (after wintering on it in 1778-9) almost to Lake Athabaska. Although he did not see the lake itself, he had found water flowing north and opened the attack on the great valley of the Mackenzie.[11]

His geographical successor was a young Scot, Alexander Mackenzie, nominally a fur trader but actually a man under the spell of the beyond, an explorer and a man of science. Mackenzie's is the greatest non-French name in the annals of North American exploration and either one of his exploits would have made him a famous man. Having made the Methye Portage and established posts on the northern waters, Mackenzie decided to follow them down to the sea and in 1789 he made the journey all the way to salt water, to "The Frozen Ocean", as he called it, at the mouth of the great river that he had discovered, soon to be called after himself, the Mackenzie River. He had made a great exploration but had suffered a great disappointment in that it was now clear, from the position of the mountains which ran parallel with the great river almost to its mouth, that no easy water route led down to the Pacific.

A few years later, Mackenzie began his most daring adventure, a try,

[10] See p. 178.
[11] See H. A. Innis, *Peter Pond, Fur Trader and Adventurer* (Toronto, 1930).

in default of a river passage, for an overland route across the mountains to the long-sought Western Ocean. He went up through the mountains by the Peace River and then on down the other side for some distance by the Fraser, and leaving that river, struck overland for the coast. He reached it in Bella Coola Inlet, where he daubed on the rocks his famous "Alexander Mackenzie, from Canada, by land, 22 July, 1793". He was the first man, north of Mexico, to cross the continent from ocean to ocean, thirteen years before the Americans sent Lewis and Clarke west to have a look at their new possessions.

Mackenzie could not claim to have faced the unknown in the absolute sense of the earlier Spanish and French discoverers. He knew that there was a western ocean and approximately how far he had to go to get to it. He might even have expected to find the ships of compatriots on the coast, for the trade route via the Horn had been opened just a few years previously. Captain Cook had been there in 1778, and English and American private traders soon followed him. It had been the seizure of an English trading expedition by the Spaniards at Nootka Sound in 1789 under their omnibus claim to the whole Pacific coast, that had led to the destruction of Spanish pretensions to sovereignty in that region, for when the news had got back to England, William Pitt had given Spain some very straight talk, the offer of a war, in fact, and she had backed down. Thenceforward the way was clear and the Pacific Coast maritime fur trade (the basis of which was not the beaver but the sea-otter) could go on. A year before Mackenzie arrived by land, Captain Vancouver had circumnavigated Vancouver Island. He was still there in 1793, at work on his coastal survey but he and Mackenzie missed each other in Bella Coola Inlet by about a month.[12]

3. From Fort William to Astoria

Mackenzie's trip blazed a trail for successors who were to open up the whole transmontane region. Yet, since the fur trade, wrecked on the rocks of strong personalities and individual jealousies, had suffered one of its periodic relapses from monopoly, it was a decade before anything more was done. To personal clashes, Mackenzie had contributed a generous share. Like many another explorer he tended to think that the fur trade was just a device for furthering exploration, whereas the traders proper looked on exploration as a humble hand-maiden of exploitation. The main secession took shape in "The X Y Co.". The old evils manifested themselves at once in high fur prices and too many

[12] Vancouver heard of Mackenzie's visit from the Indians.

drunken Indians. That way destruction lay, so a few years later, 1804, the rivals buried the hatchet.

Two men stand out in the western trade, Simon Fraser and David Thompson. Fraser took up Mackenzie's trail (1807), following the river from which Mackenzie had struck overland and which he had supposed to be the Columbia. This river, the Fraser, led to the sea many miles north of the Columbia, giving Lewis and Clarke a chance to get to the mouth of that river before the English. Yet no considerable weight rested on this feat when title to the country came to be decided.

The work of David Thompson went a long way to counter-balancing any claims based on prior discovery by the American pair. Thompson was a surveyor disguised as a trader. He mapped each foot of his way. It was in 1807, too, that he got across the mountains on the upper waters of still another great river. This, in 1811, he followed to its mouth: it turned out to be the Columbia. He mapped the whole Columbia system and turned aside from the vocation of his heart only long enough to establish a solid system of posts, on which he built up an equally solid trade.

The continent at last was bridged and furs from the farthest ocean could roll across it now, down the long St. Lawrence watershed to Montreal and across to London, seven thousand miles of tenuous communications resting on the sailing ship and the canoe. Not even this conquest of distance was enough, however. Across the Pacific lay China. Cargoes of sea-otter had already gone there and now the Nor' Westers began to think of developing this rich market further. However, the monopoly of the East India Company extended to China, so no other British ships could enter Chinese ports. This limitation the Nor' Westers avoided by employing American ships, which, being no longer under the British flag, did not suffer the disabilities of British ships.

The generation just passed had witnessed a race across the continent between British and Americans; to be specific, between Nor' Westers and the German-American John Jacob Astor, whose American and Pacific Companies had attempted to challenge the Nor' Westers in Wisconsin, in Minnesota, farther west, and at last on the Pacific. Although he had enticed a number of the Nor' Westers' men to serve under him, Astor had come off a poor second best. A traveller of the time in describing his trip down Rainy River tells how his party came to a North-West Company post, were well, even sumptuously, received, and then looking across the river saw some badly kept buildings and a gaunt, decaying man. This, it was explained to them, was the local representative of the American Fur Company. The Nor' Westers had such a hold on the Indians that the American agent was getting neither fur nor food. The story appears to have been similar at the mouth of the Columbia for, on the eve of the war of 1812, Astor sold his post there— "Astoria"—to the North-West Company; thereby, since a British ship arrived ten days later, avoiding its capture. Like the rest of the west, the Pacific coast had become a British fur preserve.

4. Red River Cross-Roads

The nodal point in the vast North-West Company system was the confluence of the Red and Assiniboine Rivers in what is now Manitoba. This obscure spot was the junction of routes, a bottleneck through which all traffic from east to west had to pass. By canoe, it could be reached by the Winnipeg River from the Lake of the Woods. Overland, a short trail led from the point on that lake, afterwards called "The North West Angle", to the edge of the bush, where the Red River flowed. Westward, the Assiniboine led up to a point only some dozen miles from Lake Manitoba, Portage la Prairie, the prairie portage: this cut some hundreds of miles off the water route to the far west. Near the confluence could be found the eastern outliers from the immense buffalo herds of the prairies. Here was food enough and to spare for all. The location of various North West and Hudson Bay forts near the junction of the two rivers was to testify to the advantages of the spot. Some of the voyageurs settled down there, doing a little desultory farming in odd moments but mainly engaged in the more exciting work of slaughtering the buffalo and making pemmican out of the meat for the fur traders. The Red River thus became the great food base, supporting the trading system clear across to the Rockies, near which another one, Edmonton, was beginning to be built up in the last years of the eighteenth century.[13] The confluence was what the city, Winnipeg, which was afterwards to grow up there on another extractive industry, the wheat trade, also was —the gateway to the west. It was so because nature had made it so. The city remains a concrete testimony to the fact that Canadian trade does not flow naturally north and south, but east and west.

At the confluence of the Red and Assiniboine Rivers, this east-west route, which was destined to become the backbone of modern Canada, was crossed by a natural line of communications running north and south. The Red River rising in central Minnesota flows north to Lake Winnipeg, and, three hundred miles farther north, the Saskatchewan-Nelson system leads down from the lake to Hudson's Bay. Ten miles to the east of the mouth of the Nelson along the coast lies

[13] Edmonton House, 1797.

the Hudson's Bay Company's York Factory, then and now the "capital" of that northern Mediterranean world.[14] By the new century, the Hudson's Bay Company had some posts in the interior, but it had not shown the aggressiveness that characterized its rival, nor had it evinced interest in the far-off Red River region, a portion of its domain that lay pretty well out of the fur regions. Now, thanks to the actions of Lord Selkirk, a gentleman whose interest in fur was secondary, and contrary to all fur-trading principles, it was to be precipitated into an experiment in settlement and the bitterest of all its contests with the Nor' Westers.

The years of the Napoleonic wars were hard on producers of luxury goods like furs, particularly hard when the measures of the belligerents closed the European market to English exporters. For the Nor' Westers hard times meant that every individual partner had to go with less; for the Hudson's Bay they meant a drastic fall in the price of its stock. The old company was not far from failure when Lord Selkirk came along and, to further his social and philanthropic aims, induced his relatives to join him in buying a controlling interest in it at bargain prices.[15]

Selkirk, as a Scottish land-owner, had seen the sufferings of the Scottish peasantry when their landlords (formerly their clan chieftains) began to find more profitable uses for land than allowing crofters to live on it in small holdings. With the harsh English land law behind them, the landlords turned out men and put in sheep. People starved. Selkirk, unwilling to drive his own tenantry away, devoted his best years and most of his money to trying to form colonies for them in North America. He had brought out several hundred to Prince Edward Island and some to Upper Canada in 1803 and 1804, and now he was to essay the daring feat of a colony in mid-continent, removed by hundreds of miles from the nearest settlement.[16] The prospective settlers came out through York Factory (1811). How, with all their possessions and animals, they ever got up the Hayes River and across the portages is a mystery. Arriving in Red River in 1812, too late to put in crops, they had to face the winter as best they could. Then it was discovered there were worse adversaries than the climate. There were the Nor' Westers. As fellow fur traders, the Hudson's Bay men could be tolerated, but all the ancient enmity of the fur trader flared up at once against settlers. To the Nor' Westers, there could only be one motive in the settlement, and that was a deliberate attempt to cut their line of communications with the west.

[14] York Factory lies on the Hayes River, a stream that parallels the Nelson and is easier for canoes than its mightier sister.
[15] For Selkirk, see J. P. Pritchett, *The Red River Valley, 1811-1849: A Regional Study* (Toronto, 1942).
[16] In 1811, the closest was Detroit.

Superficial appearances bore them out, for the settlers were to be planted squarely across their line of march, and already the Hudson's Bay governor was ordering the stoppage of the pemmican trade, really to save food supplies for the colony, but according to the Nor' Westers' way of thinking, to starve them out.

A deliberate decision was arrived at to destroy the settlement. In this job, the Nor' Westers were sure of the willing assistance of the half-breed population, the *Métis*, nothing loath to scare away these Protestant and foreign newcomers. At first persuasion was used to dissuade them, and a good many were induced to leave for Upper Canada (1815). Then terrorism, in the form of horse stealing and house-breaking, was resorted to against the rest. Still more settlers left, in canoes gladly provided for them by the Nor' Westers, and found their way to Upper Canada. By the summer of 1815, the Nor' Westers could consider the colony destroyed. But at Norway House the remnant was joined by a fresh body of emigrants, and once more they advanced to the Red River. Robert Semple, the new governor (1815-16), proved aggressive, if not too wise, and used his authority as representative of the sovereign power, the Hudson's Bay Company, to arrest the Nor' Westers' leader, Duncan Cameron, seize his mails, and then take his post, Fort Gibraltar. This precipitated a show-down. A band of *Métis* was gathered, a collision occurred, guns went off, and twenty-two men, including Semple, were killed. "Vingt-deux anglais de tués," one of the *Métis* was heard to shout, making clear his own particular motive for his acts. This was the famous Massacre of Seven Oaks (1816), on the northern limits of the present city of Winnipeg.

Lord Selkirk had realized that strong measures would be necessary to make his position good, and he was then on the way west (by the lakes) with a force of disbanded Swiss soldiers, the de Meurons. At Sault Ste. Marie he heard of the massacre and hastened on to Fort William, and here he committed a tactical error by seizing the post. For this he had no authority. This mistake proved his undoing, for later on when the whole series of incidents was being aired in the courts of Lower Canada,[17] his adversaries matched his unlawful act against their own. Selkirk's actions, however, saved the colony. He had discovered enough written evidence in captured Fort William to convict the Nor' Westers of the most serious and premeditated of crimes. Going on to Red River in the spring of 1817 with his force, he restored order, re-established his colony for the third time, and devoted the summer to nursing it on to its feet. In this he succeeded, but at the cost of most of

[17] The West was attached for judicial purposes to the Canadas.

his remaining fortune. The colony was not interfered with again, but when Selkirk went east that fall to prosecute his adversaries, they had their revenge on him personally. His evidence was ample to convict, but so great was their power in the Canadian fur-trading metropolis, Montreal, that they managed to pervert the course of justice itself. Accusation was met with counter-accusation until it became plain that there was no justice to be obtained against a Nor' Wester in a Canadian court. Selkirk went back to England to carry on the fight there, but with as little success, for the Nor' Westers' influence reached into the depths of the British Colonial Office. Then, broken in health and purse, he retired from the struggle, to die worn out a year or two later. His colony, however, went marching on and remained after Nor' Westers were forgotten.

5. The Triumph of "The Bay"

The sequel was the most curious of all these stirring events. Out of the blue, one day in 1821, it was announced that the North West Company had amalgamated with the Hudson's Bay Company. Every effort was made to dress the transaction up as a reasonable compromise, but the bitter truth was, as the wintering partners were soon to find out, that the old company had triumphed and the Nor' Westers had had to surrender in order to avoid bankruptcy. The wintering partners were chagrined to find that they now had the option of getting out of the fur trade or becoming employees of their late enemies. The fog of lawsuits that ensued did not better their position, and most of them accepted the inevitable, bringing to their new allegiance, strangely enough, all the loyalty that had marked their association with each other. Over the whole vast region of the Canadian northland, no matter what his conditions of livelihood or his treatment, the Hudson's Bay man has not existed who has not been as loyal to the Company as a Jesuit to his order.

The old Company had won; or rather, geography had won. The Nor' Westers' long, tenuous line of communications could not stand the accumulating strains of twenty-two years of war followed by years of depression. The old Company could, for its annual ship could come into the Bay, land its cargo at York Factory and other points at prices no higher than in Quebec, and then send them up country with all this great initial advantage. The Nor' Westers had tried hard to avert the calamity, but to no avail. In the first decade of the century they had applied in London for a charter, which would have given them the same rights of sovereignty over the North-West Territories, that is the

area outside the Hudson's Bay Company's domain, as their rival possessed over Rupert's Land. The charter had not been forthcoming.
Then during the war of 1812, when on one occasion they nearly lost
their furs to American ships in Lake Huron and only saved them by
taking a long detour through the islands of the North Shore, they had
petitioned the old Company to allow them to take them out by the Bav.
This had been refused. If they had not been short-sighted, they might
have prolonged their life by encouraging the settlers rather than destroying them, for the colony would soon have provided plenty of food for all,
and better food than pemmican, too. But the settler always made the
fur trader "see red", so they went ahead to their own destruction. Not all
the skill and drive of one of the most efficient trading organizations ever
erected could upset the elemental fact of distance. The old Bay came
into its own, the North-West Company ceased to exist and fur trade and
fur traders disappeared from the metropolis which their efforts had
largely built.

Additional Reading

Bemis, S. F. *Jay's Treaty: A Study in Diplomacy and Commerce.* New York,
    1923.
Gailbraith, J. S. *The Hudson's Bay Company as an Imperial Factor,* 1821-1869.
    Toronto, 1957.
Martin, Chester. *Lord Selkirk's Work in Canada.* London, 1916.
Pritchett, John P. *The Red River Valley: A Regional Study.* Toronto, 1942.

CHAPTER 13

The Canadas Between Two Wars

1. French Canada Introduced to Representative Government

By the close of the American Revolution only a small part of the St. Lawrence basin had been settled. At the end of the period with which this part of the book deals, 1783-1867, the scattered provinces had come together politically and had established their grasp on all the territory from the sea to the head of Lake Superior, the best parts of which were under the plough. The occupation and settlement of the St. Lawrence Lowlands, that fertile band of soil bordering the St. Lawrence and the three lower lakes, upon which there lives today sixty per cent of the population of Canada, may be regarded as the dominating activity of these eighty-four years.

It has been the fate of this definite geographic unit to be severed into two sections by factors stronger than geography itself, that is, race and religion. The north-eastern half of it had long been French and Catholic before the Loyalist migration made the south-western English and Protestant. Seven years of confusion and experiment after the peace settlement of 1783 made it evident to the Imperial authorities and their representative in Canada (Lord Dorchester, formerly Guy Carleton) that no one solution for the problem of government could be applied to both parts. It seemed best to leave each to work out its own salvation. Moreover, two small provinces would be easier to handle from

London than one large one. The Constitutional Act (1791) made provision for the separation, and on its proclamation at Quebec, the province was divided into Upper and Lower Canada. The only people seriously put out were the Lower Canadians of English speech, among whom the fur-traders and the business men who had supplied most of the pressure for the new Act had been the most vocal. They had expected the Act would give them the support of their recently arrived brethren in Upper Canada in getting rid of French law. Now they found themselves still under French law and with every prospect of being under a French Assembly too. They could see little reason for the division of the province and the Montreal group could not understand why Montreal should not have been included within Upper Canada, for there was little French settlement above it and the English were dominant within it. The annexation of Montreal to Upper Canada as a solution to the troubles of Montreal merchants was to be urged constantly for the next half century. The authorities, however, chose the old, rather accidental seigneurial area to determine the boundary line. such a boundary may have been a reflection of Lord Dorchester's old dislike of business and a desire to secure the most favourable terms for "gentlemen" (the seigneurs). Montrealers argued that the new province would be without a seaport, the first in British experience of empire to be completely inland. All to no avail; the Constitutional Act took the commercial men of Montreal out of the frying pan and put them into the fire.

Quebec remained the seat of government. Lord Dorchester, as Governor-in-Chief of British North America, ranked as vice-royalty, being in quite another realm of dignity from the lieutenant-governors of the provinces. But fate and geography were not to permit of this attempt at imperial state becoming impressive, for within five years, the Governor-in-Chief had lost all control of the affairs of the other provinces and had been reduced to a status practically the same as that of the lieutenant-governors.

In Lower Canada, the perennial spectre of racial difference made its appearance in the first Assembly. To the French *habitants*, this novel business of telling the government how to govern was a puzzle, but they had the guidance of their leaders and though they did not return as many members as their numbers would have entitled them to, the weight of numbers was strongly on their side.[1] This majority was used to reject an English proposal that debates be in English. The battle of language began early.

[1] 36 French; 14 English.

During the remainder of the 1790's the new institutions do not hold the centre of the historical stage, that being reserved for the gusts from the great world that swept into Canada from the south. It was the day of the French Revolution: the Fleur-de-lis went out and the Tricolor came in. Would the ferment in the old mother country affect its daughter? A struggle began for the *habitant's* soul. It was plain to the clergy that the Revolution was the antithesis of every notion that they had about life. "Fear God and honour the King", a dictum from which the Roman Catholic church has never departed, did not find much sympathy in Paris. While the church has never entirely committed itself to monarchy, there is a marked affinity between a monarchical state and a hierarchical church, especially when the king of that state is "the eldest son of the church" and "His Most Christian Majesty". Republicanism, democracy, social equality, a Pelagian list of "rights of man" as a foundation for society, a deism close to atheism—these could hardly win the favour of the Catholic church. Nor would the confiscation of the lands of the church of France evoke much approval by the church in Canada.

Yet the Revolution was vital and dynamic, and could not wholly be kept out of Canada. It penetrated by channels difficult to trace, through mysterious strangers from the south, leaflets scattered through the countryside, and news of the great deeds of Frenchmen on the battlefields. The *habitant* had shown an unwelcome independence in those years in which he had been free of tithes: might he not do so again? The situation was difficult, for the United States was the former ally of France and her ports were wide open. For some years, evidence of propaganda coming from the States, designed not so much to win converts as to cause trouble for the English enemy, was abundant, and it was effective propaganda. Liberty is an intoxicating word. If it means getting out of payments imposed by an unwelcome law, it becomes doubly intoxicating. The church in French Canada was perhaps in greater danger in those days when *habitants* were comparing the new and the old than appeared at the time. When efforts from the south stopped, discontent stopped. Not, however, until a man had gone to the scaffold were the dangerous influences extirpated and the ancient ways secured.[2]

2.   French Canada's Discovery of Itself

By the end of the century, it was clear that the French Revolution was not coming into Quebec. The two French vessels had parted company,

[2] In July, 1797. See A. L. Burt, *The United States, Great Britain and British North America,* p. 179.

sailing on opposite courses. In New France, people could look back at forty years under an alien flag without excessive reason for complaint. They had their own laws, their system of landholding, their church. French members sat on the council, where the French language was used more than the English. And now they had an assembly. At first seigneurs had not wanted it, and *habitants* had never heard of such things, but now both were beginning to discover its uses. It was bringing the leaders of the people together. They were talking over their situation and discovering something of the first importance, that is to say, themselves. The discovery came as a great light. The more they contemplated their experience, the more miraculous it seemed. They had borne the stormy wind of conquest and had survived. They had met their fate with dignity and had preserved their institutions without alienating their conquerors. The miracle of French Canada had occurred. This period, 1760-1800, has never ceased to be a source of inspiration and its essence has been caught in a single word—*la survivance*—survival!

After the Conquest, France turned her back on her American children and forgot what little she had known about them. In their worst days, when all the terrors of the unknown confronted them, when the rumour was going about that the English were going to make them all become Protestants, simple people had turned, not to the seigneur, who could no longer fight for them, but to their curés, who could at least pray for them. The curés heartened their people, exhorted them to stand fast, advised them in difficult situations, became in many ways the practical men of the parish, its natural leaders. While the gratitude of the peasantry did not extend to an undue anxiety to pay the tithe, it was real, and to the priest now went not only spiritual respect but the honour due to a leader of the race. Forty years of this new life gave to the "new subjects", as they still were called, the supreme gift of faith in themselves. They were getting to know their strength. Now with the Revolution, old France was gone. There was no motherland. They were alone. Dawning self-consciousness meant that they would see themselves as a separate people, not French in the old sense, but what they had long been calling themselves, Canadians, and as a people set apart, chosen by God to some high task—if someone could be found who would tell them so.

The prophets to proclaim the gospel were not far to seek. No Canadian village had been complete without a notary to draw up wills and deeds. Like the curés the notaries and advocates (*avocats*) were of the people, with their education alone marking them off. When the seigneur receded in importance and in popularity after 1774, the advocate edged forward. It was to him that the Assembly was revealed as an especial blessing. As the local man of affairs, the man who knew about government and could speak, he was the natural person to send up as member. The Assembly of Lower Canada soon came to have in it a disproportionate number of advocates and notaries, able men whose education, especially in legal acumen and philosophical grasp, was good. Like lawyers everywhere, they were fond of debate for the sake of debate and, unlike their English colleagues, not interested in getting on with the job. The basic Canadian antithesis soon came out through the clash of wills in the Assembly. The English appeared to have just one idea about life—improve on nature and put the proceeds in their pockets; this they called progress. To the French, this philosophy was distasteful and immoral. For themselves, they wished dignity, honour, and security, the ability to make a great speech that would earn the applause of their fellows, the importance of being the founts of local patronage, pleasant posts under government with reasonable pay, no excessive amount of work or responsibility, the dignity and safety of an official position. For their people, they coveted the right to be left alone, to be themselves, to go on in the old way, not to have to pay unnecessary taxes towards new-fangled English schemes for changing the face of the world.

The combination of assembly, advocates, and the peculiar English habit of letting everyone say and print whatever he saw fit, produced the inevitable in the first years of the new century. The Canadians discovered themselves as a people, and they received a voice. A century and a half of history was coming to life. They were beginning to remember their martyrs, their heroes and their battles. The chrysalis was opening. The Canadians would probably have admitted the relative lightness of the English yoke, the liberties of the English system. Nor was there religious oppression as such, though there was plenty of mutual suspicion, and a struggle, political rather than religious, for power and prestige.[3] For years the Anglicans of Quebec actually held their services in a Roman Catholic chapel, and this degree of mutual tolerance seems to have been typical. For a people who had been conquered, it was a relatively happy situation, but there was one insuperable hardship that could not be overcome: the trouble with the English was that they were not Frenchmen.[4] In making a people, if there are no grievances, it is necessary to create them. The mere presence of the foreigner in an emerging French society was grievance enough.

[3] As when the Anglican bishop of Quebec claimed the right to be the sole bearer of such a title while expressing the utmost desire to see the Catholics have complete liberty of worship.

[4] Unnecessary to add; the English found the corresponding fault in the French.

The creation of grievances was the appointed task of the first genuinely French-Canadian newspaper, established in 1806, *Le Canadien*, a journal whose "tone was energetic, if not indeed violent".[5] Its programme was contained in the slogan on its "masthead": *Notre langue, nos institutions, nos lois.* The threat made to the language had been successfully met in the first session of the Assembly. The only threat to institutions had been the proposals of 1801 for education, contained in the Act establishing the so-called "Royal Institution".[6] This Act set up a corporation to which was given the power to hold and dispense public moneys and to make rules and regulations subject to the sanction of the governor for the "direction, conduct and government of free schools of Royal foundation". The governor was given power to erect free schools in parishes or townships and to name local trustees for them. The local church wardens were to be trustees for the erection of the school and the division of the expenses among the residents. The rights of existing religious institutions and private schools were specifically preserved (Section IV). The governor was to name the masters of the schools and fix their salaries. The Royal Institution is held up by many French-Canadians today as an example of the "tyranny" to which their ancestors were subject, another English attempt to anglicize and proselytise[7] them. Complete purity of motive need not be attributed to the authors of the project, but a reading of the Act in the spirit of English parliamentary institutions suggests that it contained little that could not have been used by French and Catholic people to their own advantage. Too much power was given to *The Governor*, yet as early as 1802 those words had some similarity to *The Crown*. The first membership of the Institution was far too heavily weighted with English and for that (a condition common to every phase of government in the province at the time) there is no defence. Yet if the French people had taken the Act and worked it, as they afterwards worked Responsible Government, they would sooner or later have brought matters to the same point of democratic control and would have had a system of free elementary education long before they actually obtained it. The difficulty lay not so much in the Act as in French misunderstanding of the genius of English institutions, especially of the great part of government that resides in convention rather than in law; and it lay still more in the opposition of bishop and clergy, who, not finding themselves given specific mention and place

[5] Jean Bruchési, *Histoire du Canada pour tous* (Montreal, 1939), II, 91.
[6] Acte pour l'établissement d'écoles gratuites, et l'avancement des sciences dans cette Province: 12 août, 1802.
[7] See Bruchési, *op. cit.*, pp. 76-80, ". . . sa fin primordiale qui était de défranciser et de décatholiciser les Canadiens. . . ."

under the terms of the Act, believed they were shouldered out of the all-important field of education. But they too, a reading of the Act would suggest, could have found their place in the scheme, if they had desired it. They did not desire it; they thought in terms of a church which should have a position in society independent of, if not superior to, the state, not of a church subject to the general law of the land. The charge of tyranny would seem to have little foundation when levelled against an act carried in an assembly of which the great majority were French and Catholic.

Apart from the Royal Institution, the largest bones of contention that the historian digs up belong to small animals. Of these, one was the controversy over the project of building jails, wherein a land tax was turned down by the French, as it would have been by any agrarian group, in favour of increased customs duties. It was the intangibles of the French-English situation that were the real difficulties. The English in government circles were *"orgueilleux et arrogants"*, "thought only of their own advancement", "were turbulent and powerful favorites"; while the French in the Assembly were "jealous of their rights and not anxious to be kept in the shade, determined to have their influence and rebellious at a subordinate role".[8]

It was a fortunate turn of the wheel for the objectives of *Le Canadien* which brought to the governorship, Sir James Craig, an eighteenth century martinet of the type that once made the British so well beloved in India! Egged on by his secretary, Herman Ryland, a man who had Germanic notions on race and religion and the necessity of "co-ordinating" the unorthodox, he took *Le Canadien* too seriously, regarded it as a threat to British rule, arrested printers and proprietors on charges of "treason", and, under a special war-time act, suppressed the newspaper. This act opened a struggle for control of the province that was not settled until the grant of responsible government. It is wrong to see in these embryo Canadian nationalists disloyal subjects. They perhaps carried to extremes the recent English gift of freedom of speech, but they had no objection to being British although they had no intention of becoming English, for they had discovered themselves to be French and they were determined to maintain their little French world. They were *les enfants du sol* and they intended to see that their soil should continue to belong to its children, and that they, the French, should control the society which they had formed. That accomplished, there need be little debate about the over-riding British allegiance.

Sir James Craig must be considered one of the founders of French-

[8] Bruchési, *op. cit.*

Canadian nationalism. In 1809, he dissolved the Assembly because it would not get on with business but spent its time bickering about what seemed to him trifles, such as attempts to debar judges from sitting in the legislature. It was the kind of quarrel that had been common in the old colonies, but it was new in Canada, and aggravated by the racial difference. Sir James supplied the necessary "persecutions". He was not the first old soldier to be rewarded with a job in the outer Empire, and not the last, but he was rather more typical of those who were to come than of those who had preceded him, so one irritant in the relationships of the two peoples would continue to be supplied. There were many other points of friction, but with or without them, the decree *nisi* of 1763 between France and New France having been made absolute in the 1790's, some such consequence as the semi-revolutionary national awakening of the 1800's could have been predicted.

3. The First British Province Inland: Upper Canada

The new inland province of Upper Canada stretched on westward from the last French seigneuries for some five hundred miles. In 1791 its water areas, the Great Lakes, were already well known, but the interior was still a wilderness. For practical purposes, the province consisted of the banks of the upper St. Lawrence and those of Lakes Ontario and Erie. This was "The Front", as it came to be called by the inland dwellers later on. Lake Huron and Lake Superior still lay a little beyond vision. Upper Canada, though inland, was so dominated by the lakes that it might have been called a maritime province.

In the new province there were several fairly distinct regions, such as the St. Lawrence, the lower and upper lakes, and the interior. The St. Lawrence section was broken into three by a band of pre-Cambrian rock about fifty miles wide which crossed the river into New York State, forming the "Thousand Islands". Below this point lay a district of good soil and good rainfall, destined to become a fine dairy region. In the pre-Cambrian band, the hard granite ridges rendered settlement unattractive. From Kingston, where it ended, to what is now Belleville a thin layer of soil lying over flat limestone beds made farming precariously dependent upon rainfall. Beyond that the soil gradually deepened and good country was continuous to the south-western tip of the peninsula. From Lake Ontario south-westward, new species of trees were encountered, winters were mild and the environment genial. The great bodies of water on three sides moderated summer heat and winter cold: in some districts southern fruits like the peach and the grape grew well. The neck of land between Lakes Erie and Ontario, the

Niagara peninsula, was particulaly favoured by nature and also best known.

The interior of the new province was relatively unknown. The courses of the main rivers, such as the Thames and the Grand, were familiar, and the portage across from a place then called Toronto, the one good natural harbour on the north shore of Lake Ontario, to Lake Simcoe and then to Georgian Bay, was sometimes used. Champlain's old route from Lake Simcoe via the Kawartha Lakes to the Bay of Quinté was still followed by fur traders. The Ottawa river route to Lake Huron was thoroughly known. But the western peninsula was still mostly unpenetrated hardwood forest and swamp. Rough country was known to lie back from the St. Lawrence but few suspected that the readily available land ceased abruptly, in places as close as twenty miles away, and that everywhere to the north lay a wilderness that could never be settled. To the men of the time, Upper Canada seemed a not unworthy substitute for what had been lost and carried with it no idea of limitation: it could become the foundation for another great empire, inland of course, but easily entered through the St. Lawrence portal.

4. The Upper Canadians

In 1783 this region, save for a few Indians, had been empty. By 1812 it contained seventy or eighty thousand people, all of them strung along "the Front" from Soulanges to Amherstburg. In that thin line of settlement there were still gaps, such as along the north shore of Lake Ontario west of the Bay of Quinté, and on Lake Erie west of Long Point. Hardly anywhere were farms far from the water's edge. Of these 70,000 people, 20,000 at most were of Loyalist stock, the rest miscellaneous. In the east part of the province, some Glengarry highlanders had come in from Scotland, the sole group of "old countrymen" to enter the province before the war of 1812. The only other tight-knit community of non-Loyalist settlers consisted in the Mennonites who, towards the end of the century,[9] had come up from Pennsylvania. Crossing at Niagara, they had gone on out beyond Hamilton to land they had bought deep in the bush. Within a few years their settlements had begun to take on some of the comfort and prosperity that they had left behind them. Waterloo county and other German districts of central Ontario stand as their monument. These Pennsylvania Dutch formed a valuable element in the country's population: they were models of sobriety, industry, and

---

[9] The first Mennonite settlement was at Twenty Mile Creek, Lake Ontario, in 1786.

good agricultural practice. They were lacking, however, in political interest, and were content, like so many Germans, to leave the conduct of public affairs to other people. Like them, in their Quietist attitudes, was the little band of Quakers who went up north from York, along Yonge Street towards what is now Newmarket. These two humble sects formed the first settlements of consequence away from "the Front".

The rest of the newcomers came as individuals. After the original Loyalist lists had been closed, many people came over to join their relatives, attracted by good reports on the lands and climate of the new western settlements. Others came because they liked the old ways best. After the dead-line of 1783[10] they could not call themselves United Empire Loyalists, but their political sentiments must have differed little from those of the originals. People of this type kept drifting in for a good many years. Their descendants are firm in the faith that their ancestors were "U.E.L.'s".[11]

As the Revolution receded into the distance, political sentiment became of less importance than the prospects of good land, so that before the end of the century, those coming in were hard to distinguish from ordinary American backwoodsmen. The Niagara district of Upper Canada stood in the stream of the westward movement through the Mohawk valley, and many of the people who came into it were just making another move westward, crossing the river rather than going on round south of the lakes. Similarly, in the Eastern Townships of Lower Canada, people kept making their way up from New Hampshire and Vermont, at first men with decided views on politics and then just ordinary Americans. It would have been difficult to draw a line between the two groups, for men's allegiance had not as yet had time to harden, and the adults who came to Upper Canada up to 1812 had been born British subjects.[12] A man might easily decide that he was a monarchist one day and the next change his mind and become a republican. Political views probably had rather a high correlation with success or failure in the new environment.

Some distinction might be made between Americans who came to settle and those who formed the less fixed elements of the population, such as tavern-keepers, teamsters, pedlars, "school-masters", and wander-

[10] Governor Simcoe in that year ordered the registration of all "who had adhered to the unity of the Empire" before the Treaty of 1783. Only they or their descendants were to be entitled to the letters "U.E.".
[11] See B. P. and C. L. Davis, *The Davis Family and the Leather Industry 1834-1934* (Toronto, 1934) for an example. They are sometimes referred to as "Late Loyalists".
[12] As every American President had, down to Van Buren, 1836-40.

ing specialists of every description, from saw-sharpeners to preachers. Nomadic people, of bourgeois rather than rural type, they were more apt to have "views", "half-baked" of course, and also more apt at expressing them. Outside the very small circle of the educated, they supplied most of the limited intellectual stir in the province. Very likely their tone was republican, in some cases offensively so.

The counter to republicanism lay in government circles and in the few successful merchants living in the villages of Kingston, York, Hamilton, or Niagara. At Kingston, Richard Cartwright established his business of importing and exporting about 1785 and became one of the earliest "forwarders" on the St. Lawrence. He founded a family of which his grandson, Sir Richard Cartwright, Minister of Finance, 1873-78, was the best known member. Hamilton was called after a merchant of that name, prominent around the western end of Lake Ontario. Some substantial people such as the Merritts and Keefers came into the Niagara region from New York in the 1790's. The province's most portentous import, without question, was a certain impecunious young Scotchman, who arrived in 1799 and discovered a remarkable shortage of Church of England clergy. Adding together the views and personalities of those in authority, he became convinced that duty, to say nothing of opportunity, called in the direction of Anglicanism, and at the first convenient moment he blossomed out in Holy Orders.[13] He opened, at Cornwall, U.C., a "school for the sons of gentlemen". Thereafter his feet were in the way, and he became a power in the land, an Anglican of Anglicans. Unnecessary to say, his pupils in the Upper Canada of 1800 were few, but their families were influential and as flattered by the appellation of the school as the young Scot was to receive them. His name was John Strachan.[14] He was only one among many Scots who have formed their careers by carrying the Episcopalian banner in colonies too poor to attract their English brethren.

5. Democracy, Religion, and Governor Simcoe's Schemes

The most paradoxical component of the Upper Canadian situation was supplied by the first governor, Colonel John Graves Simcoe, the first and the last real personality the province was to have as governor. Here was a man who, in his reactionary convictions, his overwrought professions of loyalty, his love for monarchy, aristocracy, and the Church of

[13] He had studied theology at St. Andrews.
[14] Executive Councillor, 1818-1836. Legislative Councillor, 1820-1841. Archdeacon of York, 1825. Ex-officio President of King's College, 1827-1849. Bishop of Toronto, 1839-1867.

England, his contempt of everything democratic and republican, was Tory to the tips of his fingers and who yet had the gift of creative enthusiasm. Simcoe felt upon himself the weight of a mission, no less a one than to reverse the American Revolution, if possible by keeping from the United States its western lands; if not, by founding in the wilderness a replica of England, one so excellent that it would do by example what force had been unable to accomplish. His ideal was the old squire-and-parson countryside: a squirearchy to give a lead, to maintain correct ideas, to prevent democracy growing up; a loyal and contented following, looking up to its leaders, trained to military service; a clergy inculcating from the pulpit sound doctrine and independent of its parishioners through its endowments in land, embodying the old Tory view of religion as a good thing for preventing "dangerous thoughts".

Yet Simcoe encouraged republican immigration! He tried to "handpick" it as best as he could by examination into character, by exacting, what was lightly given, an oath of allegiance, and by attempting to keep it away from the immediate frontiers and out of contact with old temptations; but these devices could have had little effect. Simcoe, the ultra "Britisher", flooded Upper Canada with American settlers. The reason lay partially in his zeal for the progress of the province. It was people that it needed, and people could only be obtained from "across the line". He was willing to take a chance on their republican principles, realizing that with settlers land weighs heavier than political attachment. What he did not understand was that whereas republicanism was a matter for debate, democracy was in their blood, and on it his little dream of another English countryside must be wrecked. Simcoe served Upper Canada well and ill. His efforts put the colony on its feet, but his old-country ideas gave encouragement to a social outlook that within half a century led to bloodshed. There were only too many people who were ready to volunteer for membership in a privileged class. Many such shared Simcoe's outlook, others were merely "on the make". British allegiance and the desire for an English type of society became so intertwined in Upper Canadian life with economic mastery and exploitation that the two conceptions were never completely unravelled and the one can still to a limited extent be used as a powerful support for the other.

After Simcoe left, his system degenerated. The future of Empire received less emphasis, opportunities in land, more. As in Lower Canada a period of riotous land-grabbing followed, in which officials played leading parts and even governors did not hesitate to share. Speculators advertised their wares in the United States, and no pretence was made of conserving the province for those of tested principles. The only persons who found it difficult to get good land with clear title were *bona fide* settlers.

Simcoe's plans were wrecked on the frontier, with its urge to democ-racy. No better illustration exists than in the field of religion. It was assumed that the Loyalists and other settlers were Anglicans. They were not. The Anglican church made little effort to reach them, and when it did, its formalism and class characteristics made no appeal. Many, far away from the influence of the church in their old homes, continued to be strangers to it in the Canadian wilderness. To illustrate: the western half (or "head") of Amherst Island, near Kingston, which had been granted to Sir John Johnson as one of the rewards of his loyalism, and later passed to Lady Bowes, who gambled it away at cards, was settled by Loyalists from the "back-country" of New York. A generation later, the eastern half (or "foot") was taken up by God-fearing Ulstermen. These latter used to look askance at the wild men of the "head", who drank whiskey in amounts excessive even by Irish standards and indulged in horse-racing on the Sabbath. It was not Anglicanism but Methodism which tried to fill this vacuum. In the year 1791 the first circuit-riders, sent by the Methodist Church of the United States, landed at Hay Bay on the Bay of Quinté. There a little church, which still exists, the mother church of Methodism in Canada, was built. Year by year as these men made their circuits through the settlements, they drew the people after them.

It was primitive "hell-fire and damnation" that they preached. The camp-meeting[15] with its exciting hymn singing, its fervent preaching, its hysterical conversions amid the flickering torches in the intimacies of the silent woods, gave to the lonely pioneers the only emotional outlet alternative to a spree or a fight that they could find, and in drinking and fighting their womenfolk could not engage. The substitution was all to the good. The participants went away emotionally purged. They had become attached to a group and were to find that there were other things in Methodism besides ecstasy. True to the strong social gospel of the founder, no circuit rider neglected man's duty to his neighbour. The Methodists became a people with a deep social conscience, the leaders in all movements of social progress. Though they might not then realize it, that road led straight to politics, and if they were to be true to their faith, to the left wing in politics. Some interesting phenomena in Cana-dian life spring from this.

The leading example immediately comes to mind, a man who can hardly be kept out of a single page of Upper Canadian history. Egerton Ryerson[16] was the fifth in a family of six sons born to Col. John Ryerson,

[15] Introduced from "the States" in 1805.
[16] 1803-1882. The standard work on Ryerson is C. B. Sissons, *Egerton Ryerson, His Life and Letters,* 2 vols. (Toronto, 1937-1947).

a Loyalist of remote Dutch descent, who had gone first to New Brunswick and later moved up to the Long Point settlement on the north shore of Lake Erie. The father, as a man of some status, was an Anglican, but in the year 1815 three of his sons, in attending a camp meeting near his home, "got religion", and two of them announced their intention of becoming Methodist ministers. The father promptly turned their pictures to the wall. Egerton was by far the ablest of the family, and he shortly followed his brothers' example. Throughout his life, he fought the battle of his church; this, a battle against privilege, shoved him leftward, and he probably always considered himself something of a radical. His zeal for education put him in the van of movements of public progress. Yet he was of Loyalist stock, and this his blood never allowed him to forget. On two crucial occasions he came down heavily on the side of the governor and the monarchy, against the popular cause.

Here is the anomaly resulting from the Loyalist settlers' conversion to Methodism. Loyalism made them strong monarchists and Tories, Methodism reinforced their natural democracy and sometimes made them political radicals. The resulting combination was a curious Tory radicalism that has had marked effects. Many Methodists who have gone up the economic scale have had their Toryism emphasized to the point of reaction. If they have not broken with the faith, the price of conformity has sometimes been a strong tendency to hypocrisy. Their last stage, on occasion, has been to scale the social summits and become Anglicans. Others have been driven by the spirit of their creed into humanitarian careers: for them, it has been an easy move to radicalism in politics. If men of strong convictions, their eventual fate has sometimes been to leave the church and, in the twentieth century, to embrace the political religion of socialism.

Methodism gathered in the humble. It did not touch the privileged, and in the Upper Canada of the early nineteenth century, privilege was rapidly fortifying itself. In a pioneer community men sufficiently educated to carry on the public service are rare, and anyone with an acceptable personality may get his chance. John Strachan was one example. There were many others, of whom a minority were Loyalists and a majority old-countrymen. Such men found easy entrance into the public service and after they had drawn together into a little oligarchy, the name "Family Compact" was invented for them. Though they were an improvement on the queer characters who had come out to run the original province of Quebec in the 1760's, they could hardly have escaped being tender of their own interests in place and land. Not outrageously corrupt according to the standards of the time, they yet managed for half a century to secure for themselves, their relatives, and their church almost a monopoly of political patronage and public office, along with a huge proportion of the best land in the province. The settler long remained too busy with his daily tasks to know what was going on, and it was left to one or two unimportant troublers in Israel to denounce the offenders. Denunciation did not get far: the public life of Upper Canada before the War of 1812 was unexciting.

By that fateful year, settlers and circumstances had made Upper Canada into just another American colony. Its problems closely paralleled those of late seventeenth-century Virginia or eighteenth-century New York. It was top-heavy with officialdom in church and state. The usual accompaniments of officialdom, favouritism and administrative confusion, were superimposed on a natural but rather anarchic democracy that did not recognize abuses until it felt them and then was liable to turn rather savagely on the perpetrators. But that time was still a long way off.

Chronology

1785   Trial by Jury introduced into Quebec.
1786   The Habeas Corpus Act introduced into Quebec.
1786–96 Lord Dorchester Governor-in-Chief of British North America.
1786–93 William Smith Chief Justice.
1791   Constitutional (or Canada) Act.
        Methodist Circuit Riders come to Canada.
1792   First Legislatures of Upper and Lower Canada.
        "Citizen" Genêt Ambassador of French Republic to the United States
        and channel of communication with French Canada.
1792–99 John Graves Simcoe Lieutenant Governor of Upper Canada.
1793   Bishop Mountain, first Anglican Bishop of Quebec.
1794   Simcoe founds York, Upper Canada (Toronto).
1799   John Strachan opens his school at Cornwall.
1801   Lower Canada statute incorporating the Royal Institution.
1806   Founding of *Le Canadien*.
1807–11 Sir James Craig Governor-in-Chief.
1809   Craig dissolves Assembly of Lower Canada.
1810   Craig imprisons Pierre Bédard for seditious publications.

Additional Reading

Christie, Robert. *A History of the Late Province of Lower Canada.* Quebec, 1848. 3 vols.
Creighton, Donald G. "The Struggle for Financial Control in Lower Canada." *CHR,* XII (June, 1931), 120-144.
Cruikshank, E. A. "The Administration of Sir James Craig; A Chapter in Canadian History." Royal Society of Canada, *Proceedings and Transactions,* 3rd series (1908-9), II, No. 2, 61-87.
Manning, Helen Taft. *British Colonial Government after the American Revolution, 1782-1820.* New Haven, 1933.
Mills, Audrey. "Administration of Sir James Craig, 1807-1811." (Unpublished M.A. thesis, Queen's University), 1959.

CHAPTER 14

Canada's War of 1812

1. Causes

The War of 1812 was not a quarrel of British North America's making. The colonies were pawns among the players and did not prepare their own fate. The war was begun by others, largely fought by others, and settled by others; what the colonists did was to suffer and profit from it. Its causes lay in great world events, the great duel then taking place in Europe and the heritages from the American Revolution, chief among the latter a bitterness on the part of the Americans towards Great Britain that produced unaccommodating dispositions and an over-anxiety to win every negotiation, and on the part of the British an arrogance that former colonials found hard to endure. How these attitudes have shaped action, every page in the relationships of the two states from then to now bears out. They did not in themselves cause war but, given other conditions looking in the direction of war, they made peace hard to maintain.

There were many other conditions pre-disposing towards war. The running sore of the Indian question and the west had been reduced in importance but not eliminated by Jay's Treaty. The old American grievance about exclusion from the West Indies rankled. The undetermined portions of the boundary made for difficulties in the regions affected. The French, under Napoleon, made unremitting efforts to cause bad blood. Above all the United States as the most important neutral, at times the only neutral, occupied an impossible position: the republic was to have its first experience of the hard saying "He that is not for me, is against me".

The wonder is that the conflict did not break out long before it did. In the first two years of the Anglo-French war (1793-95), when French ambassadors such as Genêt were openly making trouble for Great Britain in the United States, there was provocation a-plenty. Those were the very years when Indian confederacies, prompted, the Americans insisted, by the British, were being formed in the west. At Fallen Timbers (1794) the British in Fort Miami were almost within gunshot of the battle field, and afterwards the American victors passed right under the fort. The slightest accident might have set the guns firing. Luckily, John Jay in London managed to negotiate the situation, and peace was, for the moment, saved. Its preservation was aided by the reaction to Jay's Treaty in France, where it was considered as a piece of treachery and was followed by such indiscriminate seizure of American ships that an undeclared maritime war ensued between the erstwhile allies. This was hardly over before half-time sounded in the great Napoleonic match, and the Peace of Amiens (1802) was signed.

In the interval, Napoleon, to prevent a British occupation, sold his newly acquired Louisiana to the United States (1803). The sale had the calculated effect of deflecting the American current from flowing towards England, as it surely would have done if the French had returned to New Orleans. When war began again (1803), everyone knew that this was the final round and no combatant could afford to be indulgent to mere neutrals. But the French, losing their navy at Trafalgar, could not interfere with neutral rights as the British could. American displeasure once more swung against the British. Yet it was mainly British purchases that were making the war, like all European wars, a good thing for America —and British North America is to be included in that term. Prices were sky-rocketing, and demand for everything was insatiable. Anyone who had a ship that would float could be sure of handsome profits, perhaps a fortune; and cargoes that got through the blockade paid for those seized. For maritime America, whether New England or Nova Scotia, it was a time to be remembered. Prosperity was so great that if men like Thomas Jefferson had not been intent on "the principle of the thing", the situation might have dragged on, with nothing more than mutual recriminations, until the great wars ended. New England merchants and shipowners could overlook the impressment of an able seaman if the voyage brought profits.

But Jefferson was a man of principle and of peace. He attempted to reconcile the two with his embargo, a "too proud to fight" gesture, by which American ships were all to be kept in harbour and the combatants to be made to feel the wrath of the great neutral by being deprived of her supplies. The embargo did not have decisive effect on the combatants, but it annoyed the New Englanders and created an American disunity that delayed the outbreak of the war. For a time, the likelihood of war receded, particularly in 1809. In that year the British minister to Washington, Erskine, had practically completed an agreement by which the United States was to except Great Britain from its Non-Intercourse Act, the successor to the Embargo, and she in turn would lift her obnoxious Orders-in-Council from American shipping. This would have amounted to the United States' deserting Napoleon's Continental System, to which the Embargo had been tantamount to an adhesion. But George Canning, then British Foreign Minister, for reasons not yet discovered, repudiated and recalled Erskine. Just at the moment when good relations seemed in sight, his action destroyed all prospect of them. For a time the United States tacitly accepted British dictation at sea, thereby coming very close to sinking to the position of satellite. Never has there been a period in American history in which that country was in a more unhappy condition, disastrously divided against itself, weak beyond words, with no army and no navy worth mentioning, its people possessed only with desire to avoid war at any price. The two years 1939-41 do not exceed the period prior to the war in 1812 in vacillation and indecision, in hopeless turnings and twistings to escape ineluctable fate.

President Madison, a man of peace, at last rescued his country from its unhappy state by declaring war in the very climax of the European struggle, when Napoleon was on his way to Moscow and England was fighting for her life and Europe's liberty. There were many Americans who refused to be parties to conduct which they did not hesitate to call by what they believed to be its right name. Taking a view of the war based on the ethical principles underlying it, as well as on long-range considerations of national interest, these, who comprised the majority of New Englanders and many men of position and education in other sections, believed their country was making itself a party to the enslavement of mankind and a satellite of the enslaver. It was as if the isolationists of 1939-41 had succeeded in getting the United States into the Second World War on the side of Hitler.

The War of 1812 is usually explained on the basis of international law. The United States, it is said, fought to uphold its conception of the rights of a neutral, briefly expressed by the phrase "the freedom of the seas". It fought for "sailors' rights", to prevent the British stopping its merchant ships and removing not only British deserters but American sailors too. It fought, in part at least, to efface the insult of the attack on the *Chesapeake* (1807) by the *Leopard*. It fought to prevent the widening of the category, "contraband of war", beyond all reason. It fought to prevent one powerful nation asserting its sovereignty, and that harshly, over the very spaces of ocean themselves. That is the traditional thesis. It is borne out by examination of the American Civil War, the Great War of 1914-18 and the Second German War. In the American Civil War, when the position as to neutrality was reversed, each power astutely manoeuvred to maintain all the rights it had formerly asserted and enjoy all the advantages it had contended for. In the Great War, until the United States entered in 1917, she took the same attitude as before 1812: Secretary Lansing hardly needed to do more than re-despatch notes of his predecessors of a century earlier. One of Wilson's *Fourteen Points* (1918) upon which the new world was to be built, provided for "the freedom of the seas". The legal position in the second German war was identical, but American opinion was so soon mobilized on the allied side that it was never pressed. The long discussion of the rights of neutrals is still open, though it will always turn, not upon legal argument, but upon the power of the neutral.

Another explanation of the war, not based on "the rights of neutrals", suggests that it could be regarded as another aspect of the American westward movement, that it was pioneers on the look-out for cheap land who precipitated the struggle in an effort to seize Upper Canada. To pioneer land-hunger and intransigence could be added the constant fear and irritation in the American mind caused by British relationships with Indians within American territory. This explanation rests on Turner's so-called *frontier thesis*.[1] More generally, it assumes the war to be an aspect of what later came to be called "Manifest Destiny", or that today would simply be termed American imperialism: a piece of expansionism that was written in the stars, the forces of American life being such that only one direction could be followed: the advance throughout the con-tinent until the frontiers of ocean were reached.[2] The War of 1812, it could be fairly said, was the first of the many American efforts at west-ern expansion by armed force. And it was the first and only failure. It was to be succeeded by the conquest of Florida, of Texas, of New Mexico, California and the south-west, by the annexation of Hawaii, the conquest of the Philippines and by the incorporation into the American empire of various lesser island groups in the Pacific. Only

---

[1] Discussed above, p. 48.

[2] The proponent of this explanation, J. W. Pratt, did not flout the older ideas; he simply called attention to neglected phenomena which he thought carried some weight. See his *Expansionists of 1812* (New York, 1925).

British North America succeeded in resisting the wave of American conquest, and that is why there is a Canada today. It seems pretty hard to interpret, as popular American historiography has done, this result as a "victory".

This expansionist thesis of the War of 1812 has been emphatically rejected by an author[3] who, turning back to the traditional view, refuses to give the West much weight in the causes of the conflict. The war, he claims, had to occur, given British use of naval power in assertion of extreme belligerent rights and given American insistence on the rights of neutrals. From the beginning of the struggle between England and France, the only question was not "would the United States fight", but "whom would the United States fight?" Logically, it would seem, she should have fought both France and Britain, for each violated her rights and with about equal hauteur. That being impossible, she "wobbled", now protesting to one, now protesting to the other. She fought France, after a fashion, in the last years of the eighteenth century. In the nineteenth, she finally turned against the power that, by reason of its supremacy at sea, was inflicting upon her the most injury, Great Britain. Had Great Britain not been so successful in smashing the French navy, the equipoise might have continued to prevent war or the Americans might have fought the French. As against this re-exposition of the older thesis, it must be remembered that the major part of the American war effort was devoted not to the war at sea but to the attempt at inland conquest of Canada.

It seems wisest not to lean too heavily on either thesis. The War of 1812 was a complex, like other historical events. It was a complex of the historical relations of the two countries that fought it, of the judgments and ambitions of men, of the logic of international law, and of the historical situation in the west. Among all these factors, the greatest weight should perhaps be attached to the international situation at sea and its derivatives. No country of the pretensions of the United States could accept the dictation of another. The pressure from the West screwed the courage of principle to the sticking point, and so war followed. It was to give to the United States its first lesson on the impossibility of isolation, a position with which insistence on "sailors' rights" and the freedom of the seas accords. That lesson the Americans did not learn, and it was to take two more wars before the republic would understand that no nation, no matter how far removed or strong it may be, can play a lone hand.

[3] A. L. Burt.

2. Campaigns

The war itself was satisfactory to all parties in that both sides won it: the American tradition is one of glorious victories and so is the Canadian. The British, who did most of the fighting and whose navy was the major instrument in ending the war, have no tradition at all, and there are few English people who have ever heard of it. The war was no fight to the death, and it produced no Marlboroughs or Nelsons. It was a succession of timorous advances and hasty retreats, of muddle-headed planning and incompetent generalship, interspersed with a few sharp actions and adroit manoeuvres which reflected credit on a few individuals and discredit on many. Except for the uninformed and for the professional patriots, time has almost turned its melodrama into farce.

There had certainly been enough examples of how a war between Canadians and Americans ought to be fought. Sea power must be used to contain the adversary within his own coasts and the army then employed to cut him in two along the vital St. Lawrence-Hudson highway.[4] Strategy was just the same for both parties, excepting that one marched south and the other north. The side that had no navy must march all the more quickly. If it had no army, it must use its navy that much more vigorously. The British had a navy, but no army worth speaking of in Canada; and the Americans had little navy, but a relatively inexhaustible supply of manpower. Since the British navy was busy all over the world, it did not really get round to blockading the American coast until 1814. Part of the delay was to be ascribed to policy, for internal division within the United States gave the British a trump card and it would have been foolish to throw this away by rigorous naval action upon the coasts of New England, where sentiment was strongly against the war. The Americans, who should have been able to take Montreal in 1812 as Montgomery had done in 1775, did not undertake a serious offensive against that decisive spot in the entire struggle but, instead, devoted most of their efforts to outposts whose possession could settle nothing.

The key points of Canada, in order of importance, were Quebec, Montreal, Kingston, Niagara, the Detroit River. The order in which the Americans attacked was Detroit River, Niagara, Kingston, Montreal. Without a navy, they could not get at Quebec from the sea, but a mild degree of competence would have given them Montreal, from which they would have had a fair chance at Quebec. As it was, they aimed for the fingers and toes, not the heart. They did not really do much harm

[4] See p. 57.

to fingers and toes. This may be explained on two counts. The first lay in sheer military incompetence and in the inability to grasp the strategical situation (which must have argued great ignorance of history). Strategical ignorance was associated with neglect of primary objects. The American Secretary for War, General Armstrong, seems to have contemplated the taking of Montreal but to have let himself be distracted by objectives in the interior. The second explanation lay in the state of that American community, Upper Canada: it was so American that it would surely welcome the invaders. This the British authorities as well as the American expected, and it explains Hull's easy-going operations around Detroit on the opening of the war. He believed that his proclamation would win the war, without any fighting.

What changed the whole situation was that classic of the Canadian school-room Queenston Heights (October 14, 1812). The doggerel verse, sung by generations of young Canadians, in which that "dark October day-y-y" has been celebrated, has possibly detracted from the significance of the occasion. As a battle, it was just a big skirmish "and ere the setting sun, Canadians held the Queenston Heights", thanks in large part to British regulars.[5] Yet by showing that the British were going to make a fight for it, that they could hit hard, and that things might not be a walkover for the Americans, Queenston Heights changed the whole picture, confirming the doubters in their allegiance, strengthening the wavering, and forcing the pro-Americans to change their tune. There is nothing like a good display of successful force for making people decide which side it is their patriotic duty to support. After Queenston Heights, there was little danger of fifth columnism swinging the province into the Republic. Isaac Brock, the only commanding officer on either side to show any marked ability throughout the war, who was killed in the gallant but injudicious charge up the face of the Heights, as every school child knows, deserves his monument there at Queenston. Without him, Upper Canada would have been taken.

In the campaigns of 1813 and 1814, the Americans displayed more military efficiency but not much advance in co-ordination and in generalship. The main effort was still directed at Upper Canada, its points of departure being Sacket Harbour and Oswego on Lake Ontario, Niagara, and the harbours of western Lake Erie. The military achievements of

[5] The Canadian militia, both French and English, once it got some training, fought well during the war, but in British North America in 1812, there were only a few thousand trained Canadians available and 4,000 British regulars. See William Wood, *The War with the United States* (Vol. 14 of *Chronicles of Canada*), 36ff., and C. P. Stacey, "The War of 1812 in Canadian History," *Ontario History*, (Summer, 1958), 153-159.

either side, apart from the occasional brilliant incident, such as Col. Fitzgibbon's at Beaver Dams or such engagements as Chrysler's Farm and Chateauguay, were inconsiderable and inconclusive. The only engagement of the war to be fought out in hard blows, with credit to both sides, was at Lundy's Lane, July 25, 1814. In this battle British losses were heavier, and it might be called a tactical victory for the Americans; but as they afterwards withdrew, and the battle prevented their campaign against the Niagara district from coming to anything, it amounted to a British win.

The decisive aspect of the struggle was not military but naval: the side which could secure and hold control of Lakes Champlain, Ontario, and Erie, in the order named, would be able to dominate the St. Lawrence valley; the side which could control the Atlantic coast would win the war. In 1814, the Americans had the stronger forces on Lake Champlain, but with the opportunity in his hands to alter the situation, General Prevost, the British commander, with characteristic ineptitude let it slip. On Lake Ontario the two fleets remained fairly evenly matched throughout the war, causing both commanders to take the view that discretion was the better part of valour; there was no decisive engagement on that lake. On Lake Erie was fought the only freshwater engagement of the war (and one of the few in history) that amounted to anything, when Commodore Perry, with half a dozen ships built on the spot, met the British in the battle of Put-in Bay, Sept. 10, 1813, and destroyed them.[6] This naval victory gave the Americans command of Lake Erie and was followed by Harrison's march into Upper Canada and his victory at Moraviantown, Oct. 5, 1813. The victories came at the wrong end of the line and decided nothing, except that the Americans sat in Amherstburg instead of the British sitting in Detroit. The American invaders did not even cut communication with the west, for a new route was improvised overland from York to Nottawasaga and thence by boat and schooner to Michilimackinac, which port had been taken by the British at the beginning of the war and was held throughout.

It was British sea power that decided the war. As Napoleon's giddy career drew to a close, British ships were able to give more attention to the American war. The arrival of some thousands of veteran reinforcements in the St. Lawrence (who were to be mishandled at Plattsburg, Sept. 11, 1814, by Prevost) was followed by an intensified blockade of the American coast, culminating in the burning of Washington in

---

[6] Perry's ships were manned by saltwater sailors, those of the British by the sailors of the backwoods; the result was not in doubt.

August, 1814, an act which had no military significance and whose only
excuse was the previous American burning of Newark and York. The
British would have acted more sensibly and much more effectively if
they had taken and held New York. Some territory they did seize: that
part of Maine adjacent to New Brunswick, down as far as the Penobscot.
There they required the inhabitants to take an oath of allegiance and
it is related that "they showed no unwillingness to remain permanently
British subjects".

The vast weight of her sea-power, as it stood in 1814, would have
enabled Great Britain to do almost anything she wished in the United
States, short of actual permanent conquest of the inhabited areas. Her
statesmen were not unaware of this. If peace was to be achieved, it
looked as if the Americans would have to eat humble pie, and for peace
they were most anxious. Two years of unsuccessful war following upon
the frictions of the previous period had gone far towards disintegrating
national unity. New England was talking of secession. Victory was impossible; defeat close. In negotiation lay wisdom. The American government had arrived at this conclusion as early as the winter of 1813, after
one campaign, when it accepted the Czar's offer to mediate. Thanks to
the European situation, the British at no time desired to go on with a
war which had been forced upon them and from which they neither
expected nor desired anything. They refused to accept mediation but
showed no indisposition to direct negotiation. Madison accepted their
offer of November, 1813, with alacrity, and peace preliminaries may be
considered as commencing with the New Year, 1814.

3. The Peace of Ghent

The Peace of Ghent, concluded over a year later, was the outcome. No
country could have had the ball more completely at its feet than Great
Britain. Yet when the treaty was published, it was revealed as based
entirely on the status quo. In the words of a French wit, it may be
described as "the peace that passeth understanding".[7]

It was not farsightedness or mere goodness of heart that let the
Americans off so lightly. The proposals of the British had no punitive
purposes or any inflated notions of aggrandizement, but they plainly
displayed an intention to prevent a recurrence of such an attack and,
up to a point, to rectify the unfortunate treaty of 1783. The original
British plans (not presented in definitive form to the American com-

[7] A. L. Burt, *Great Britain, The United States, and British North America* is
illuminating on the Peace of Ghent.

missioners) were that the Indian buffer state, so often attempted, should be erected in the west, the Treaty of Greenville line[8] being the boundary; that all the islands in Passamaquoddy Bay should become British; that a "solid land connection" between New Brunswick and Lower Canada should be ceded out of Maine, the 47th parallel being mentioned as the northern boundary; that Michilimackinac, key to Lake Michigan and the west, should be ceded; that a strip should be ceded on the *east* side of the Niagara river; that the boundary should be drawn straight from the Lake of the Woods to the Mississippi; that the northern limit of Louisiana should be so determined as to leave the British on the Columbia river; and lastly, that the international servitude contained in the American liberty to take and dry fish on the shores of Nova Scotia should cease. Three items in this programme were impracticable as they stood: the Indian buffer state, the cession of the Niagara strip, and of Michilimackinac. The Americans would never have accepted the idea of the buffer state and the loss of all territory west of the Wabash river. Nor would they have suffered the cession of the two strategic points for long, for they both stood within American territory. There would have been a better chance to change the boundary from the centre of Lake Superior to that of Lake Michigan than to isolate Michilimackinac alone.

The question is, why were these intentions watered down until nothing was left of them? The military and naval situation improved for the British in about the same proportion as the American commissioners whittled down the British terms. Their argument that British insistence on this or that point would cost them more than it was worth because of the resentment that it would rouse in the United States is not sufficient to explain the British diplomatic defeat. It was the Duke of Wellington who destroyed British resistance to a defeated foe in his dictum of November, 1814. The British had not been able, he said, to carry the war into the enemy's territory, and had not cleared their own. He took no note of eastern Maine. They could not claim territory except in exchange for other advantages, which they did not possess. His implication was that victory might be potential but not actual, that the war, to warrant cession of territory, would have to go on.[9] For continuation of an obscure war about obscure objects in the American wilds neither the British government nor people had any heart. When the treaty was signed it was on the basis not of *uti possidentes*, each taking

---

[8] Made after the American victory of Fallen Timbers, 1794, and involving Indian surrender of the lands east of the Wabash River.

[9] See Dudley Mills, "The Duke of Wellington and the Peace of Ghent in 1814," *CHR*, II (March, 1921), 19-32.

what he had at the moment, but on that of *status quo*. All conquests handed back and not a word said about impressment, freedom of the seas, the right to navigate the Mississippi, or the liberty of taking fish on the shores of Nova Scotia! If to have failed in all their objectives was to have won the war, then the Americans had won it!

The peace of Ghent was only an armistice. The real peace came three years later in the conventions and agreements of 1817 and 1818. By the Rush-Bagot agreement of 1817, the lakes were de-militarized, and no naval forces were to be maintained upon them. This arrangement, which has conduced so greatly to permanent peace between Canada and the United States, sprang from no sentimental or idealistic base. The Americans could always outbuild the British on the lakes: they knew it. From the standpoint of expense, it was their interest to have no British navy there. It was still more the British interest to have no American navy there, since they could not hope to have one equal to it. The other matters, the western boundary and the fisheries, as settled in 1818, continued the British diplomatic defeat. In the event, the 49th parallel from the Lake of the Woods to the Rockies was accepted: in the exchange, the Americans got the rich Red River Valley and the British, the sage brush and rattlesnakes of southern Saskatchewan. The British right to navigate the Mississippi disappeared, but the liberty of taking fish in Nova Scotia was sold by the Americans for a good, high price— the liberty of taking and drying fish on certain other shores and also privileges on the coast of Nova Scotia. These fisheries clauses, with the inclusion of American privileges in British territory, remained to trouble the relationships of the two countries for nearly a century.[10]

It is difficult to resist the conclusion, borne out by examination of many peace treaties, that British diplomats suffer from a chronic paucity of constructive ideas, which serves them badly at the conference table. They are agile and adept at bargaining over specific points, but they seldom seem to possess large, far-sighted plans. Their diplomacy after the War of 1812 showed no lack of aggressive qualities, but it let slip the chance of building a second great power in America. But did any British statesman ever wish to build such a power? Was not every British mind divided against itself when it came to negotiations with the United States, on whether to fight with the prodigal son or surrender to his wishes? Or does the succession of diplomatic defeats grow inseparably out of the impossible case which Great Britain left itself in 1783? Whatever the explanation, history may have a rough justification for what it has brought forth in that it is probably better that there

[10] They were not completely settled until 1905.

should be one overwhelmingly great power on the continent, capable of defending it, than two (or three, since a large Canada might also have meant later on an independent South) balanced against each other and divided in their counsels.

4. Effects of the War on the British American Colonies

On the parties most intimately affected, the British North Americans, passive recipients of the blows struck in other peoples' quarrels, the war left deep effects. In a material way, not a single province was worse off, and nearly all were better. Even in Upper Canada, where most of the war's destruction had occurred, the large British military expenditures probably balanced private war losses. In Lower Canada the story was the same, and there was to be added to it the clandestine trade which went on with the Americans, who sometimes supplied the British forces with stores and were supplied in turn with British industrial products. Under the smiles of the God of War, Montreal prospered greatly; New Englanders said that the city should erect a monument to President Madison, for no place had profited more from his policies. The border districts of New Brunswick had the same experience; for them and for the port of Saint John high prosperity reigned throughout the fighting, and their good relations with their neighbours were hardly fluttered. In Nova Scotia, there were the adventures and fortunes of privateering, intense naval activity in Halifax with its usual Haligonian concomitants of high prices and hard drinking, and good times everywhere. The Americans had received news of the peace with rejoicing and relief, but the colonists, even in Upper Canada, had not welcomed it. The war was just beginning to go well for them, they were about to get their own back, and they had no fear of another campaign or two, with the attendant cash. They did not see what might lie ahead of the brittle prosperity of war.

In addition to the deeply ingrained legend that "war brings good times", Upper Canada was left with the uneasy heritage of the alien question, which was to trouble the province for another half generation. All who could not prove themselves British subjects could be presumed to be aliens. As such they could be (and for a time, were) declared incapable of owning land. This meant that the thousands of old settlers not technically Loyalists might be deprived of their farms. A settlement was finally arrived at, but the agitation was bitter while it continued, and burning hatred of the southern foe continued to be evinced in the province. Many a quiet settler, who had happened to come over the line after 1783, had to think out this problem of allegiance; and when he made his decision to secure some tangible evidence of British citizenship, it must have meant a cutting of all ties with the old homeland. In this way, the war and its aftermath turned Upper Canada from an American province into a British colony peopled by Americans.

The effects were not so sharp in the other colonies. French-Canadians had fought valiantly in the war and inserted an additional martial leaf which they have never forgotten into their French tradition. To the Maritime provinces, the economic aspects had been the most significant. The War of 1812 is not a very formative tradition in Maritime life; not the basis of community, as it became in Upper Canada.

The most important aftermath of the war lay not in boundaries but in psychological effects. For the Americans it became, in retrospect, a second war of independence; they had at least shown that if trampled on too frequently they would eventually turn. The conflict strengthened the sentiment of anti-Britishism, on which American nationality had been founded, and caused the courses of the two nations to deviate more widely.

For Upper Canadians it did the same thing. The sense of Canadian nationality, which has radiated out from Upper Canada, or Ontario, through all the west and to some degree into the Maritime provinces, dates from the War of 1812. It gave to Upper Canada an official tradition of military glory. It did not matter that this was rather insecurely based; people believed in it, and it influenced their loyalties. It accentuated Upper Canada's dominant hatred, whose incidence it changed slightly, from hatred of "republicanism" to hatred of "the Americans" or "the damn Yankees". Before 1812, Loyalist sentiments of dislike for the republicans prevailed. But the war saw Americans on Canadian soil, it saw purposeless raids, shading into mere brigandage, houses burned, property destroyed, relatives and friends abused. Nothing makes one's patriotism mount to greater heights than having the enemy burn his house over his head. Acts of violence were thenceforth associated not so much with the original homeland and the Revolutionary War but with Canadian soil and the invader from the south. Upper Canada emerged from the War of 1812 a community, its people no longer Americans nor solely British subjects, but Upper Canadians. The essence of the War of 1812 is that it built the first storey of the Canadian national edifice.

Chronology

1794   Jay's Treaty. Battle of Fallen Timbers.
1795   Treaty of Greenville.
1796   Surrender of the Western Posts.

1802   Peace of Amiens.
1803   Renewal of Napoleonic War.
         Louisiana Purchase.
1806   Napoleon's Berlin Decree directed against English export trade.
1807   The British reply: the Orders-in-Council prohibiting neutral trade with
           France and her allies.
         Napoleon's counter: the Milan Decree.
         H.M.S. *Leopard* fires on U.S.S. *Chesapeake,* seizing deserters aboard
           her.
1808   Jefferson's Embargo.
1812   June 18: U. S. declares war.
1815   March 9: Peace of Ghent formally ends war.
1817–18 Rush-Bagot Convention and other British-American settlements.

Additional Reading

Horsman, Reginald. *Causes of the War of 1812.* Philadelphia, 1962.
Mills, Dudley. "The Duke of Wellington and the Peace of Ghent in 1814." *CHR,*
    II (June, 1921), 19-32.
Pratt, J. W. *The Expansionists of 1812.* New York, 1925.
Richardson, John. *War of 1812.* Brockville, Ont., 1842. (Reprint, ed. by A. C.
    Casselman, Toronto, 1902).
Stanley, G. F. G. *Canada's Soldiers: The Military History of an Unmilitary
    People,* 2nd ed. Toronto, 1960.
Weekes, William M. "The War of 1812: Civil Authority and Martial Law in
    Upper Canada." *Ontario History,* XLVIII (Autumn, 1956), 147-161.

CHAPTER 15

A New Cycle of Growth, 1815-1865

---

1. The Second Wave of English Immigration, 1820-1850

After the War of 1812, and with the settlement of the Napoleonic problem in Europe, a new cycle of life began for British North America and especially for the St. Lawrence colonies. It was a reflection of the Industrial Revolution and of that movement's secondary result of large-scale emigration, in combination with the virgin soil of the New World. British North America received only a fraction of the immigration that came to the continent, and it had only a small bit of the good soil. Nevertheless, though its expansion could not compare with that of the United States, it was considerable, and for the half a century from 1815 to 1865, the period during which new free land was available, the colonies forged ahead.

In 1815 the total population of the British North American provinces was about half a million; in 1865 it was three and a half million. New land meant more life, life by way of immigration and of the cradle. In all the provinces the cradle gave a good account of itself, as it invariably has done in pioneer communities where young and vigorous people face life with hope in their eyes and every additional pair of hands is a blessing. English-speaking people in those days were not constantly gazing with apprehension on the number of children that played about the doors of their French neighbours. The race was young, not decaying at the bottom.

Among the provinces, Upper Canada easily led. Its expansion was rapid from the beginning. Its population increased by leaps and bounds, from nothing in 1783 to a quarter of a million in 1831, half a million in 1843, a million in 1853. In 1850-51 it passed Lower Canada, which shared little of the influx. Population expanded in periods of no immigration, such as 1815-1825 or 1836-1840, during which the increase of the province was also much greater than that of Lower Canada. In the five years 1816-21 Lower Canada increased at the rate of 2.94 per cent per annum, Upper Canada at 6.40 per cent, with no immigration of consequence into either.[1] In the years of relatively heavy immigration, such as the period 1831-36, the disparity was much greater: 11.16 per cent per year in Upper Canada, but only 1.88 in Lower Canada. Immigration contributed to the growth but mainly in the periods when economic and political conditions were good. The rate of growth slowed down in periods of depression or disturbance: thus in both Lower Canada and Upper Canada, the rebellion period registered the lowest rate on record.

After 1860 growth tapered off quickly in all provinces. In Canada, settlement by that time had reached the rocks of the Canadian Shield: in no province was there much more available land. Other industries, such as lumbering and shipbuilding, though prosperous, could not compensate for the lack of room, so after 1860 the young people began to go away and the population of the colonies increased only slowly. The resulting feeling of frustration produced efforts among the more far-seeing to gain more elbow room by the political device of Confederation.

Within a decade of the War of 1812, which had made them suspect, Americans in considerable numbers were again coming into western Upper Canada. Because of their type they were important out of proportion to their numbers. Many ministers, doctors—the medical profession was pioneered by them—teachers, printers and other professional and technical men were comprised in the later American immigration. The major improvements in nearly all the arts from education to agriculture seem to have come into Canada by this route. A high proportion of it came across what might be called "the Niagara bridge", a pathway of cultural progress as important for Canada as the Paris-Calais-Dover-London route was for old-time England.

As long as their lands lasted, the colonies had a place in the vast nineteenth century movement of the peoples, one of the greatest phenomena in recorded history. Beginning with the people farthest to the

[1] Compare the increase of all Canada 1931-41, 1% per annum, or 1951-61, 3.5%.

west, the Irish, the Old World sent over to the New millions upon millions of its children; the flood did not cease to roll until it had drawn in migrants from the far recesses of eastern Europe. The colonies had a modest share in it for a generation, from about 1822 to 1850, and then as their empty lands were taken up, the flow was diverted from them, not to be resumed until the Canadian west was opened. Canada partook only of the beginning and the end of the immigration movement.

Though there were many examples of public or private aid to emigrants during the "Great Immigration" of 1820-1850, not all of them wise, most settlers came to Canada at their own expense. The ocean voyage was cheap, the fare being usually around thirty shillings, plus food and bedding. It was just as nasty as it was cheap. Emigrants were herded down into the holds of the oldest type of ship, those sent out to bring back cargoes of timber. Men, women and children were all mixed up together, with the most primitive of sanitary arrangements, and very limited supplies of fuel, food and water; enough water to wash in was a luxury rarely enjoyed. The stormy Western Ocean voyage might take six weeks or it might take sixteen. If the latter, many who started out were left in the ocean *en route*. The westward crossing was a trial by fire.[2]

In 1820, there were a few hundred immigrants; in 1825, a few thousand, and in 1830, 28,000. A peak was reached in 1832 when 52,000 landed in the St. Lawrence, bringing with them the cholera. Hundreds died. Then the disease spread to the shore and up river, from Quebec to Montreal, Kingston, Toronto. In reduced proportions it reached the western limits of Upper Canada. The epidemic of 1832, repeated again on a lesser scale in 1834, checked emigration and had grave political consequences. Those were the years when the storm clouds of rebellion were massing in Lower Canada. The French had disliked the idea of immigration from the first because of the threat in it to their majority, and especially they resented the newcomers being settled on lands in Lower Canada, for did not these lands belong as of right to *les enfants du sol*, "the children of the soil"? To this dislike the cholera added bitterness; the more extreme and credulous asserted that it was an English ruse to kill them off. But it is more pleasing to recall that the priests and nuns of the French church showed their Christian spirit in the devotion with which, often to their own death, they tended the sufferers.

The second cholera outbreak was followed by the disturbed years of

[2] The return passage east was often made in 18 days.

the rebellion period, during which outbound emigrants avoided Canada, and the stream was not renewed again until the 1840's. Here a second and higher peak was also crowned by an epidemic. In 1846 there occurred the notorious Irish "potato" famine.[3] The Irish having in the eighteenth century been introduced to the potato, proceeded in true Malthusian fashion to breed up to the limits of potato subsistence. The humble vegetable gives so much in return for so little that population in the course of half a century rushed up from 4,500,000 to over 8,000,000 on 32,000 not too fertile square miles, nearly all living on potatoes and nothing else but potatoes. In 1846, the crop failed, and Irishmen began to die like flies. Those who could, fled from the smitten island, and of the refugees some one hundred thousand came to the shores of the St. Lawrence. They had died on the way across, and they continued dying on arrival. Thousands reached the St. Lawrence only to die a miserable death upon its shores. The Irish famine immigration of 1846 was the bitterest example of human misery in all Canadian history.

This movement was not repeated. The English corn laws were repealed, and thenceforth surplus Irishmen were liquidated on a more orderly basis. Immigration to Canada soon slackened. The great movement had lasted just about a quarter of a century, and had added directly some three hundred thousand persons to the population of Upper Canada, with smaller amounts to other provinces.

The Great Immigration completely changed the nature of the British North American colonies, swamping the old Loyalist and American communities with Irishmen, Scotchmen and Englishmen new to the New World and its ways. Of these the English are the hardest to find and describe. They did not settle in blocks, as the other two did, and it took only one generation for them to lose their distinctive traits, whereas many of the others retain theirs to this day. Census returns of racial origin do not help much because "English" is an omnibus term that gets more elastic as people forget their old-country origins. Many English came in by the Canadian front door, the St. Lawrence, and went out by the back, to the States; some came into Canada by way of the States. Land opportunities and government being better in new states such as Illinois than in Upper Canada, men with some capital tended to pass on. Upper Canada was known as "a poor man's country".

There is one stratum of English which consists in "persons of quality", half-pay army and navy officers and other small "gentry": among these the names of Moody, Strickland, Trail, are well known, and there are

[3] See Cecil Woodham-Smith, *The Great Hunger* (New York, 1963).

scores of others. All over Ontario today (usually in what was once good "huntin' and fishin' " country) there are traces of this class of person, often descendants who live in large decaying old houses that they cannot afford to keep up but with family traditions which still keep them apart from the ordinary run of people. Mazo de la Roche's fantastic novels come vaguely out of this background.[4] In general, the English reflected the class structure of their native land, sending out aristocrats, intelligent middle class people of some means and education, and some irresponsibles from the bottom of the heap.

Lowland Scots melted almost as readily as English. But the Highlanders are still conspicuously visible. Many came. They filled up Cape Breton, which is today one of the world's strongholds of Gaelic, filled parts of the mainland of Nova Scotia, completed the occupation of Glengarry County in Upper Canada, formed some settlements in Lower Canada such as in Argenteuil and numerous others in western Upper Canada, those in Oxford and Bruce counties being among the most continuous. Many Highlanders could speak no English and had no acquaintance with English ways. Most of the Scots were Presbyterian, but a number, especially among those going to Cape Breton, were Roman Catholic, a religion which, it has been contended, is better fitted to the dreamy, poetic genius of the Highlander than dour, matter-of-fact Presbyterianism.

It was the Irish who left the plainest marks on modern Canadian life. Careful distinction must be made between northern Irish and southern, between Saxon and Celt, Protestant and "Papist". It is now impossible to determine the proportions of the two in the immigration of 1820-50, but it was clearly the Protestant who remained in greatest numbers.[5] The Catholics were among the poorest of the poor and when they landed, they took the first available job, which meant loading timber at Quebec, to be followed by a winter in the lumber camps, from which the labourer might graduate to pick and shovel work on the canals. Thence he would drift to a city as casual labourer. This story is plainly written on the face of Canada today: there are few rural Irish Catholics[6] but in the ports—Halifax, Saint John, and Montreal—they are relatively numerous. They form the largest group in the small English-speaking community of the city of Quebec. The majority must have been drained off to the cities of the United States, for the Catholic

---

[4] See Anna Brownell Jameson, *Winter Studies and Summer Rambles in Canada* (London, 1838; reprinted Toronto, 1923, 1943) for interesting descriptions.

[5] In 1941, Protestants constituted 68% of all those of Irish origin. Later figures are not available for this correlation.

[6] In 1931, 147,000 out of 385,000.

Irish of Canada today are a relatively small group[7] whose growth has almost stopped.

The Ulster Protestants, on the other hand, almost turned Upper Canada into an Irish community[8] and left their mark heavily on New Brunswick, too. In the latter province, they completed the occupation of the St. John valley and infiltrated through the older settlements. In Upper Canada, they went in behind the original settlers all along "the Front", taking up the second and subsequent tiers of townships and penetrating out to the water's edge where land remained, as in Peel. Some counties of Ontario today are almost wholly of North of Ireland descent. A little "hall" by the roadside with "L.O.L." over the doorway indicates an Ulster countryside, except where Loyalist communities have increased the range of their prejudices by adopting Orangeism. For over a hundred years[9] the Orange Order has been one of the largest and most powerful of political forces and pressure groups.[10] Ulstermen came into a society already conservative to the point of Toryism, and perfervid in its Britishism. They brought similar qualities. They re-inforced the Toryism and Britishism of the Loyalist, and added to Loyalist prejudices another, that of religion.

Before the Irish immigration, religious strife had been uncommon in Canada.[11] Once that immigration had got well under way, the country was never again free from it. The Irish, Catholic and Protestant, introduced into Canada memories of persecution, bigotry, and contention treasured up in their native land. At first they confined the ancient battle to each other, but it was not long before Orangemen discovered that the French were Papists too, and after that their persecution became continuous. This constant religious squabble, which has penetrated every nook and cranny of Canadian life and is one of its most typical features, does not rest primarily on the antithesis between French and English, since after the Conquest the country was free of it for some seventy years; it is in large part the ancient Irish quarrel transferred to Canadian soil and flourishing there because of the antithesis.

Irishmen did not limit their activities to religion. Elections became occasions for a fight and a spree. That Donnybrook atmosphere still not entirely dissipated in the public life of Ontario is attributable to the

[7] In 1941, 404,000.
[8] Of all Ontario people of Irish origin in 1961, a rough estimate would make about 30% Catholics.
[9] 1st Grand Lodge founded Brockville, 1830.
[10] There is no satisfactory account of Orangeism in Canada. Perkins Bull, *From the Boyne to Brampton* (Toronto, 1936) may be mentioned.
[11] See p. 159.

Orangeman.[12] The coming of the Irish completed the great Trinity of Protestant Upper Canadian (or Ontarian) hates: hatred of the "Yankees", hatred of the French, hatred of the Pope of Rome.

2. Settlement and the Disposal of the Public Lands

With all these varied people pressing into the colonies year by year, most of them poor, the one thing needful was a quick and efficient mode of getting them on to the land. In the United States every year hundreds of thousands were placed on land, with clear and valid titles. Unfortunately if there was one aspect of colonial government which was not quick and efficient, it was the public land system. It is wrong to use the word system, for there was none. There was simply confusion. No account of the muddle, the favouritism, and the mismanagement of the Crown lands could be exaggerated. When in 1817 Robert Gourlay sent out his famous questionnaire, his concluding question was "What, in your opinion, retards the improvement of your township in particular, or the province in general, and what would most contribute to the same?"[13] Every answer was the same: the difficulty of securing clear title to land.

In the new empire, as in the old, free grants were provided for ex-servicemen, varying in size with rank, from the 50 acres for a private to some thousands for general officers. A considerable number of these grants were claimed, though the results of the settlement made on them were not impressive. Next came the provision in the Canadas for the Clergy Reserves: one-seventh of the land granted and of quality and situation equal to other grants. The fraction was awkward in itself and made still more so by the necessity of setting off Reserves near the other grants. No settlement being possible on the Reserves, they remained bush lots, accumulating the unearned increment from the improvement of private holdings nearby. The Crown Reserves, set up by order-in-council, not by act, were also to be of one-seventh and were subject to the same objections. But here the intention was frankly to profit the Crown from the unearned increment (rendering it less dependent on the legislature). The Clergy Reserves contained an abuse of quite another

[12] See the account in J. C. Dent, *The Last Forty Years: Canada Since the Union of 1841,* 2 vols. (Toronto, 1881) of the Orange "bludgeon men" who drove Lafontaine's supporters away from the polls in 1841, thus securing his defeat. See also the illuminating account of the Montreal election of 1844, Jacques Monet, S. J., *"La Crise Metcalfe* and the Montreal Election, 1843-44," *CHR,* XLIV (March, 1963), 1-19. Father Monet shows, however, that in the mob battles of the election, a good many "Irlandais" had French names!

[13] Robert Gourlay, *Statistical Account of Upper Canada,* 2 vols. (London, 1822).

order, the grant to a *Protestant Clergy*,[14] a phrase interpreted by authority to mean the Anglican ministers without question and ministers of the Church of Scotland grudgingly. These two churches being confined to a minority of the people, the amount of denominational heart-burning set going by the Clergy Reserves may be imagined. The Clergy Reserves question disordered public life in Upper Canada for sixty years.

Another method of alienating Crown lands was by direct grant in large blocks to individuals or groups who could wheedle such gifts out of government. The number and size of some of these grants staggers the imagination. "To General Robert Shore Milnes, (Lieutenant Governor of Lower Canada, 1797-1808), 48,067 acres, to Elmer Cushing, 58,692 acres, to John Richardson, 36,400 acres, to James Cowan, 43,000 acres," so the list ran.[15] There was not the slightest pretence that the individuals so favoured had done anything to deserve their good luck; they were officials, friends of government, or persons who held out vague promises of putting in settlers. All of them procured their grants because they expected to be able to sell them privately after having expended the minimum of effort in development.

Related to these large individual grants were those to the "Township Associates", a type of alienation practised mainly in Lower Canada, where an enterprising individual would suggest to a number of others that they club together and put in for a township. Some of the grants first made in this way were genuine enough, forming the foundations of settlements in the Eastern Townships, though the collective title remained to plague the heirs of the grantees for two generations; but they soon shifted over to pure speculation. One man would produce a number of collusive "associates", whom he immediately bought out at a nominal sum; he then had the township to himself. In the 1810's William Price, founder of the well-known Quebec lumber firm, then a young man fresh out from England, went about getting up a list of "associates", backed by some London timber importers who could see a good speculation in 50,000 acres or so of good forest land. This corrupt favouritism, nearly all of it for the benefit of the English, was another factor of weight in the rebellion.[16]

Down at the bottom of the list came the ordinary settler who, if he had asked for it, might or might not get his 100 acres. For years the plan was to issue to him a "location ticket" under which he went and

[14] See p. 128.

[15] See Camille Bertrand, "Concession des terres du Bas-Canada, 1796 à 1808," *CHA Annual Report for 1928,* 73-77.

[16] Bertrand's study, referred to above, still reflects the French indignation at this English greediness.

found his lot and began to live on it. Sooner or later a title might issue, though this was somewhat problematical and was surrounded by red tape and fees. More settlers may have got their lands from private holders than from the Crown. Not until the colonies got self-government was improvement effected.

There are always persons ready to believe that they can make colonization pay cash dividends, but it rarely has, for capital has to be literally dumped into a new country before it begins to make returns. However, in Canada, as elsewhere, optimists had a fling with the colonization company. The two principal ones were *The Canada Company* in Upper Canada and *The British American Land Company* in Lower. The former secured over a million acres from the Crown in the Huron Tract (the country bordering on Lake Huron) and began a lavish programme of road-building, town-site development (Guelph, Galt, and Goderich are among its monuments), school buildings, even harbour improvement. It was half a business venture, half a romantic idyll under the direction of that rare bird, a business man and poet, the Scot, John Galt. The Company brought in many immigrants and did a fair job of settling them, but it neither earned their gratitude nor a dividend.

John Galt founded a Canadian family. His son Alexander Tilloch Galt, destined to bear a great name in politics and commerce, became as a young man first secretary and then commissioner of the British American Land Company, which had a large block in the Eastern Townships. Its lands were too far away from transportation to be attractive and lay unused for nearly twenty years, until the railway age began. Then, at the end of the half-century, Galt got the backing of Montreal and Portland capital for a railway, the St. Lawrence and Atlantic, between the two cities, which would give Montreal an open winter port only 300 miles away and, incidentally, go through the B. A. Company's lands. The railway opened and the lands went rapidly, but not to immigrants; they were sold mostly to French Canadians from the seigneuries. When the Company was formed, about 1832, the French had been bitterly hostile to it as an English device for giving their province away to strangers. Ironically enough, it turned out to be the device by which the French began shoving the English population out of the Townships, for in "developing" its holdings, the Company started that ingress of French which has converted the Townships into a French countryside.

There were other and still more surprising methods of alienating the public lands, such as the extraordinary devices associated with Colonel Talbot in the Lake Erie country. This eccentric, crabbed, and reactionary ex-officer received grant after grant in the years following the

war, tens of thousands of acres, on the understanding that he would
turn it over to settlers.[17] His lands did fill up, but titles did not issue
except at his will, and sometimes a man would be "dismissed" after
years of occupation. Talbot was a dictator; only acute land hunger
could have made his methods go. His settlement, illustrating in itself all
the evils clustering round this vital area of government, was a focal point
of rebellion.

3. The Pioneer Community and Its Traits: Society, Politics, Religion, Education

The British North American colonies in their pioneering stage were like
other such communities, raw, vigorous, and indiscriminative. Yet history
had given each a particular twist which furnished it with local character.
What was true of the individual colony was also true of the group.
Some time before Confederation, "British North America" had become
more than a mere geographical expression. It was distinct from the other
American community. As Durham noted, the pace of life was less rapid
and sure, the tone of life less exuberant and less generous than in the
republic. In the Maritimes, a habitual pessimism reigned. "If their
neighbours persist in seeing all their geese as swans, it is equally true
that the Bluenoses see all their swans as geese", said an acute observer
of the 1840's.[18] "Nothing can prosper here" was the alleged attitude.
Traces of it still remain. In Upper Canada, the typical pioneer community of the period, the energy that should have served the state was
diverted into miserable squabbles over Clergy Reserves, churches, and
schools, the favoured few against the many, with the natural result of
apathy, sloth, and backwardness. A traveller of the 1830's noted that
Canadian hotels were "badly conducted, from the stage-coach to the
preservation of butter which, instead of being as in the States, hardened
by means of ice, was an unclean fluid".[19] The mere presence of "the
States" continuously thrust a painful contrast on men's notice, intensi-
fying every grievance. In Lower Canada there was the perennial racial
cleavage; in Prince Edward Island, that relic of eighteenth century
English corruption, the absentee proprietorships.[20]

In all the provinces there was poverty, poverty severe enough to stunt

[17] In 1832 it was claimed that Talbot had received over 60,000 acres as his own
personal property.
[18] J. F. W. Johnston, *Notes on North America* (Edinburgh, 1851).
[19] Patrick Shirreff, *A Tour Through North America, 1825*; quoted in F. Landon,
Western Ontario and the American Frontier, p. 136.
[20] See p. 356.

the growth and constrict the spirit. On the British side of the line, narrow circumstances and the individualism of the New World produced a materialism less inviting than the sheer delight in things which marked the American. Private poverty produced public poverty—every province was slow in undertaking necessary public works and fumbling in their execution—and public inefficiency produced private poverty. A government whose centre was across the sea failed to generate the same healthy public spirit as existed across the border, where self-government prevailed; a certain lack of responsibility towards public affairs ensued. In Canada to this day, "the government" sometimes seems to be a thing apart, not proceeding out of the people as it does in the United States.

In every province, local society, except for the representatives of the old country classes mentioned above, was equalitarian to a degree. Every countryside was knit together in a semi-communism: the great virtue was neighbourliness, manifesting itself in bees, barnraisings, logrollings, in exchange for work and for draft animals. New blood-communities soon formed through intermarriage, and the huge networks of rural family clans so conspicuous today came into being. The different racial settlements soon began to melt along their edges, Highlander to marry Lowlander, or Lowlander Ulsterman, making the eastern provinces genuine communities or groups of communities, their people bound together by ties of blood. The inhabitants, for the most part highly Puritan in their morality (the French included), exhibited the copy book virtues of industry, thrift, honesty, and fortitude. But not sobriety; the tradition, no doubt exaggerated, is that outside every log-cabin door stood an open barrel of "green whiskey" with a tin dipper in it. Whiskey was everywhere. No barn was "raised" without it. It hovered on the edges of the camp-meetings. Whiskey represented an escape, but often a catastrophic escape.

In politics it cannot be said that the British-American colonials exhibited any remarkable degree of acumen. There was nothing parallel to the public intelligence marking the first days of Massachusetts. The economic, political, and denominational abuses practised in Upper Canada would not have been submitted to in most of the northern American states. None of the British provinces give the impression of a citizenry as alert or as capable of taking wide views as the average northern state then being settled, such as Ohio or Illinois. Such qualities could not be expected under government from the top.

There was also another good reason. The Americans who pioneered the old North West were at home in their own institutions; they had their own tradition behind them in addition to the general traditions of the English. Most of them were English in descent. In British North

America, great numbers, whether French, Germans, Irish, or Highland Scots, lived in an acquired tradition. Only the pre-Loyalists, some of the Loyalists, later Americans, the English, and the Lowland Scots in part, had the English institutional tradition in their blood, the tradition of parliament and the English law. The French had no political memories but authoritarianism tempered by the frontier. Both Scots and Irish came from the outlying regions of the British Isles: neither of them had ever lived in the full stream of English civilization. The Highlanders had been scarcely touched by the English tradition: they were as remote as many "New Canadians" today. Lowlanders were much closer to it, and they also had the fine representative tradition of the Presbyterian General Assembly. The Catholic Irish had none of the English tradition; the Ulstermen not a great deal. Ulster was itself a colony, the plantations of the seventeenth century having been formed as an Anglo-Scottish projectile against Papistry, and it was an anti-papist, Catholic-fighting tradition, narrow and bitter in its intolerance, that came to Canada with the northern Irish, a colonialism reinforced by removal to another colony, very different from the metropolitan English heritage. Parliamentary institutions and "the rights of Englishmen", by which the New Englanders had set such store, have left a deep mark on the American constitution, and they form the unique English contribution to civilization, but they were an acquired taste for most of the people of the remaining British colonies. These miscellaneous backgrounds, after they had shaken down together, gave rise to new political communities which differed materially from the original English prototype, and often not for the better. The task of preserving the classical English inheritance of freedom based on compromise and adapting it to Canadian usage is one upon which we are still engaged. All honour to the many men not in the direct English tradition, to the Baldwins and Mackenzies, the Lafontaines and Blakes, who fought so valiantly to that end.

The religious inheritance of the newcomers offered a contrast to their political, for it was a self-conscious aspect of their own culture and proved influential in the new land. The Anglican church, prior to the Great Immigration, had been the church of the classes and mostly urban, but many of the English and Irish among the newcomers belonged to it and made it a rural church also, though not a very strong one. Wherever the countryside is strongly Ulster and Orange, there will usually be an Anglican church in the community and a Tory member in parliament. Although it lost many of its people to the Methodists, the Anglican Church finally woke up to the fact that it would get farther by taking a leaf out of their book than by merely struggling for an official and a privileged position. By the middle of the 1830's, Anglican travelling ministers were tending their wandering flocks as Methodist circuit-riders had long been accustomed to do. This was the first departure from strict officialdom, the first tentative step of the Church of England towards naturalization on Canadian soil. However, it still remained the most colonial of the churches.

With the exception of Nova Scotia and of the fur-traders' St. Gabriel Street congregation in Montreal, Presbyterianism before 1830 was American in origin, several varieties having come in from New York State via Niagara to Upper Canada. American Presbyterianism was Calvinism eroded by frontier forces down to a level not far removed from Methodism: it used the familiar frontier devices of vigorous hymn singing, revivalism, and other forms of emotionalism. Until the Rebellion of 1837, it remained the prevailing form of the denomination in Upper Canada, but after about 1840, the Scottish and Irish immigration altered the situation. Although many of the Ulster Irish were Presbyterians (Presbyterianism ranked after Anglicanism and before Methodism among them), they did not dominate, and the Presbyterian churches in Canada came to be characteristically Scottish. Scottish Presbyterianism brought those qualities with which Calvinism has everywhere been associated: the steady, sober, efficient, reliable, and career-building qualities, the dependability, the self-restraint, the concealment of emotion, the matter-of-factness of the average Canadian, his precautionary slowness to act, and possibly his censoriousness, with the lack of imaginative daring coupled to it, and his heavy-handedness.

By the nineteenth century the Presbyterian church had shed some of the rigours of its Calvinism (though it gave us the Canadian Sunday) and had taken on some of the characteristics of the more evangelical types of Protestantism. It had become strongly missionary, a phenomenon which had never distinguished Calvinistic churches in their heyday: the Presbyterian Church in Nova Scotia had the honour of sending abroad the first Canadian missionary, the Rev. John Geddie, who went to the New Hebrides in 1847. In the cities and towns Presbyterianism soon became marked by a high concentration of successful men, not the rulers of the land who, under the old government, remained mostly Anglican, but the prosperous middle and professional classes.[21]

The only denomination that had sprung up on the spot, in answer to the needs of the people, was the Methodist. This church had an ultimate English origin, but it was shaped to American conditions on the frontiers of the republic, and when its circuit riders came into

[21] By 1840 Presbyterians were obtaining official recognition. The first Legislative Council of United Canada had, of 24 members, 8 Anglicans, 8 Presbyterians, and 8 Roman Catholics.

Canada, they brought a religion that suited the simple people to whom it was preached.[22] Methodism cut a wide swath, first among the original American population, then among the Ulster people. Within a generation after its introduction, it was the strongest denomination in Upper Canada. Until 1824, Upper Canada remained a part of the New York, later Genessee, Conference. This fact, and the American origin of its first preachers, subjected it to the constant accusation of being an agency of republican seduction rather than a religion. "Republicanism" at that time seemed a more sinful failing than drunkenness or adultery. Methodism, to be sure, seduced many away from their original denomination, but accusations of disloyalty have never been proved. In 1824, to secure a better position of defence, separation from the New York Conference took place, and the Canada Conference was set up. In 1828, this body became an independent church organization, the first Canadian church.

The original preachers had landed on the Bay of Quinté and worked westward. The church they built became centred in western Upper Canada, around York, later Toronto. Meanwhile there had come in by sea the Wesleyan Methodist Church of England, which was as colonial a church as the Anglican, and like the Anglican mainly urban, its charges running from Montreal to Brockville and for a while as far as Kingston. It was in competition with the Canada Methodists from its introduction and received the blessing of the authorities, for it was regarded as an effective instrument in snatching the allegiances of the Methodist faithful from republicanism. The quieter character of the Wesleyan Church probably suited the urban congregations somewhat better than the other brand of Methodism, and it made most of its appeal to solid lower-middle class citizens, whose creed it had been before their arrival from England.

One of Egerton Ryerson's[23] tactical moves in the battle with Archdeacon Strachan was to engineer a union between his own church and the Wesleyans (1833). Union meant accepting inclusion in the Wesleyan, in order to rid Canadian Methodism of the charge of republicanism. But the union did not prove successful, for Anglo-colonialism and Canadianism would not mix, and in 1840 each went back to their original independence. The differences were fundamental, though indicated mainly by surface ripples, such as the split over the attitude towards the Anglican Church. The English Wesleyans were ready to accord it the character of an established church. This was to kick over the Canadian Methodist hornet's nest. Minor frictions developed over clerical garb

[22] See p. 167.
[23] See p. 167.

and type of service, but the main rift between the two was that which the Atlantic Ocean had put there. After 1840 congregations of the same faith, Canadian Methodists and Methodists from Great Britain, dwelt side by side, distinct and often hostile. Not until another thirty-four years later (1874) did all Methodists come together in one great national church.[24]

The only other denomination to gain markedly from the Great Immigration was the Roman Catholic. There was little or no English-speaking Catholicism in Canada until the Irish came (Scots Catholics were Gaelic in speech). By the middle of the century, however, most towns in Upper Canada had an Irish congregation, and in the Maritimes, a third or more of the population in the cities of Halifax and Saint John were Catholic. The Catholic church, while not "established" even in Lower Canada, enjoyed a status in official eyes not shared by the non-Anglican Protestant bodies, for, after all, a bishop was a bishop.

The qualities of a pioneer community come out strongly in the field of education, in addition to that of religion. The people of the provinces appreciated "schooling", for the advantages of being able to read and write a little were easily grasped. Except, however, in occasional communities, of which, possibly, the pre-Loyalists of Nova Scotia formed one, having behind them the intellectual traditions of New England, desire for education for its own sake must have been rare. "I'm going to see that my boy gets a better chance than I had" would express the bulk of popular Canadian educational philosophizing.

The offset to pioneer materialism lay, like so much else in civilization, in the Christian church. An educated ministry had always been insisted upon by Presbyterians and Anglicans, and at the height of circuit-riding, it had not been lost sight of by the Methodists. It was they who founded in Upper Canada the first institution of higher learning actually to operate—the Upper Canada Academy (established by Royal Charter 1836), later Victoria University. They were soon to be followed by the Presbyterians with their college at Kingston, Queen's University (1841).

Education, like everything else, became an issue in the running Upper Canadian sore, denominational strife. Archdeacon Strachan, with skill, pertinacity, intrigue, and misrepresentation, tried to establish a provincial university, which he called King's College, under the auspices and control of his own sect. He was defeated largely through the vigilance of Egerton Ryerson. The foundation of Victoria was a by-product of the struggle, but not before the province had been split on the subject and

---

[24] Space will not permit of remarks on the smaller Protestant denominations, of which Baptists and Lutherans were most numerous.

some additional grains of salt rubbed into the community's wounds. This attempt of Strachan's constituted a phase of the constant struggle going on in Canada between privilege and democracy, between the Old World and the New, between history and geography. The establishment of the non-sectarian University of Toronto in 1849 marked a compromise which was not readily accepted by any of the warring elements but which was destined at long last to provide a solution, for when about 1890, the various denominations agreed to federate their colleges with the University, Ontario received that educational centre and impetus, which, in the early days, it had been unable to find.

4. The Economic Basis

In pioneer areas, subsistence agriculture had to be practised. That meant no exportable surplus of importance, a high degree of dependence on the plot of soil on which a man lived, and on his own labour. The main way out was through one of the staple industries, which in the Maritimes were fishing, timber-making, or ship-building, and in Canada, timber-making and wheat growing. The fisheries provided comparative wealth for a few merchants but no more than subsistence for the fishermen. Timber was the same, save that it gave to the employees a sense of adventure that may in some measure have compensated for economic well-being. Shipping and ship-building could and did build up not only capital but also a small middle class of ship-captains, officers, and artisans. In Canada, lumbering built many large fortunes and more small ones; it gave a great deal of part-time employment which was not altogether to the country's benefit, and was extensive enough to support a fairly large mercantile class. It was an important factor in building the community.

The main dependence in both Canadas was on wheat, which has been the usual pioneer crop in the northerly parts of the continent. Lower Canada should have been out of the wheat stage before the nineteenth century began, but conservatism retained it there almost as long as in Upper Canada. Wheat was almost the only cash crop the Upper Canadian could grow, the only means by which he could get his hands on a little money. It was also the most suitable first crop after clearing, being sown, hit or miss, between the stumps. An exportable wheat surplus had appeared in Upper Canada within a few years after the first settlements, and by 1850, production had grown to nearly thirteen million bushels, which was far more than could be consumed locally. Wheat farmers had become group-conscious as early as the 1830's, at which period they were making attempts to secure protection against

American wheat. Wheat as an Upper Canadian staple had its best days between 1845 and 1865; after the latter year, it began to decline in importance before dairying, therein again repeating the experience of neighbouring areas.

In pioneer communities, such as the Canadas, until home demand could be satisfied there was not much surplus for export overseas and not much foreign exchange with which to purchase imports. Without striking natural resources and with no great extent of soil, the arts of life could develop only relatively slowly. Their society reflected its economic base. Except in a few urban centres, merchants and settlers saw little ready money. Yet no man need starve; there was plenty of food and fuel for all, and all could have a healthy life if not a spacious one. In such a society it was the poor man's homespun virtues that met with approval. Things were simple and ostentation frowned upon. Everybody was religious, if not pious. Wit and wisdom were close to the soil. Nearly everything was measured by a narrow utility, too often by the dollar yardstick. This did not make for the rapid development of communal feeling and attachments, for men were too ready to change for the sake of improving their lot. Except in French Canada, there was not much attachment to the countryside or the country. In contrast with the United States, there was little imaginative conception of the future. But if progress was slow and obstacles many in those formative years, perhaps Canada would be no worse off in the long run, for men were striking their roots into deep soil and slow growth makes the hardest wood.

Additional Reading

Clark, S. D. *Church and Sect in Canada.* Toronto, 1948.
———. *The Social Development of Canada.* Toronto, 1942.
Cowan, Helen. *British Emigration to British North America: The First Hundred Years.* Toronto, 1961.
Dent, J. C. *The Last Forty Years, Canada Since the Union of 1841.* Toronto, 1881. 2 vols.
Gourlay, Robert. *Statistical Account of Upper Canada.* London, 1822. 2 vols.
Jones, Robert L. *History of Agriculture in Ontario, 1613-1880.* Toronto, 1948.
Lower, A. R. M. *Canadians in the Making.* Toronto, 1958.

CHAPTER 16

New Avenues of Exploitation

1. Metropolitanism

The two threads, exploitation and settlement, are twisted together throughout the history of Canada, sometimes smoothly, more often not. Exploitation of natural resources has been part of that world-process which began with the discoveries and which consisted in the Old World trying to seize and use the wealth of the New. At this game England proved the most successful, and it was by Englishmen that most New World staples were developed. The colonial staple product was the reflection of English metropolitan demand. London, as the capital of the country which was pioneering and dominating overseas trade, became a metropolis in the fullest possible sense of that word. No other European city and no colonial city came within measurable distance of it. In it were houses specializing in every type of traffic, handling the most commonplace and the most exotic products, importing them from some centre of supply, exporting them to some centre of demand. These houses had their members and juniors in the supply areas, men willing to reside abroad for a lifetime, learning the customs and language of the country. In time an extraordinary fund of knowledge and experience was built up in the metropolis. There could be found in London not only ex-Hudson's Bay factors who could speak Ojibway or Esquimo, but also sandalwood men who understood Polynesian, ex-slave dealers from the coast of Africa who knew exactly the right type of bangle to appeal to the chiefs at Cape Coast Castle, or men who, like the ancestor of the Pitts, had made fortunes from jewels "acquired" from Indian temples.

The mercantile houses made London the centre of the world's shipping interest and the ship-owners of England came to constitute one of the most powerful political lobbies in existence. Close to them, often with interlocking memberships, were the financial houses, banks, brokers, and insurance men. On top of them all rested English naval power, English world-politics and the edifice of English civilization and culture, drawing into itself the wealth gathered from the ends of the earth and the ability of half a world. All this was tied together into one great whole, termed *English national interests*, by the institutions that commercial interests did so much to elaborate, parliament and the law. From the sixteenth century on, the English nation had been thoroughly organizing itself for dominating the raw materials of the world, and consequently, much of the world's life. After it had disposed of France in the eighteenth century, no further serious rivals were to appear until the last third of the nineteenth century.[1]

In this vast edifice of metropolitanism, far wider than the British Empire, the British North American colonies were fully caught up. To disregard for the moment their political and cultural experience, nothing about their commercial development can be understood if it is not realized that trade and development, the utilization of natural products, the organization and connections of commercial houses—the whole process here termed *exploitation*—were only small parts of the vast machine operating from and for Great Britain. The job of the men-on-the-spot who worked the local phases of the system was to transmute the natural wealth of the locality into figures in a London bank account. The methods used might be wasteful, the natural product in question might be exhausted, the inhabitants used up, exploited, or enslaved, the country might at last be squeezed dry and thrown aside like a sucked orange, but "the business" had to go on.

Metropolitanism, if it were to go to its logical conclusion, would sooner or later drain down all the significant life of the world into one centre (as Rome did in the ancient world). Since the metropolis as a rule has had its choice of supply areas and since supply areas have depended on one or two staple products and on the metropolitan market, the only defences they have been able to oppose have been political in nature. If the area of exploitation were an old civilized country, it might fight and try to throw out the intruders, as China did. Or it might be

[1] From about 1880, when Bismarck's Germany began to expand overseas.

conquered, as India was. Or, if it were a settlement colony like Canada, it might attempt by petition, representation, or agitation to turn the edges of the exploiters' blades so as to secure something for itself of its own natural wealth.[2] The American colonists objected to English mercantilism, cast it overboard in the Revolution, and then began to hit back with protective tariffs, navigation laws, and other political devices, all in a conscious and successful effort to build up a metropolitanism of their own. The British North American colonies found it difficult to combat metropolitanism, but as soon as they had received self-government, they too followed the same road as the United States. The province of Canada moved toward a protective tariff in the very year it got some control of its own tariff policy, 1846, thus beginning the development of a local metropolitanism. Fiercely competing metropolitan centres all over the world give us our own troubled times. When the exploited country obtains some measure of self-government, it immediately makes efforts to prevent metropolitanism from sucking it dry. If such efforts become immoderate, they may go on to the whole programme of autarchy, with its Sinn Fein accompaniments in small countries and its Nazi philosophies in large. The struggle for self-government is the initial political phase (not necessarily carried to insane lengths) in the conflict between exploitation and settlement, metropolitanism and localism.

2. The Battle Between Montreal and New York

The commercial structure of the St. Lawrence, with its English branch houses in Quebec, its merchants in Montreal, its financial and shipping relationships between these cities and Great Britain, was closely oriented to England. The shifts and changes in the exploitive process, having nothing to do with local well-being, sometimes caused dislocations in colonial life, as in the overnight removal from Montreal of the fur trade, thanks to the agreement made in England in 1821. The end of the fur trade seemed to be just one step more in that shrinkage of Montreal's hinterland which had been going on since 1783. Up to that year, the whole interior of the continent had been open to the merchants of Montreal. Then it was cut down by the peace treaties, given a precarious restoration through Jay's Treaty, and, a little later, sliced in two through the War of 1812. Now in 1821, with the disappearance of the North-West Company, the British west itself was removed from the city's purview.

Fortunately, the fur hinterland was not the whole story. As settlement

[2] See pp. 100-101.

crept up both sides of the river and lakes, the St. Lawrence, it was found, could be used to carry more than skins. The northern districts of the border states could not be supplied direct from American ports on the Atlantic seaboard; their imports had to come in from England through Montreal. Every pound of nails needed by new villages in the Genessee tract contributed to the prosperity of Montreal. Upper Canadian timber and flour shippers attempted, from time to time, to have taxes levied on American shipments down the St. Lawrence, thus inviting retaliation, but Montreal interests successfully averted the peril; at all costs the route to the west must be kept open. For the first decade or two of the nineteenth century, it looked as if the St. Lawrence might recapture what it had lost in 1783.

Montreal, however, was not the only place to understand the significance of the interior. Every American Atlantic port lived on its upcountry trade: its growth was in proportion to the tract of country that could be laid under tribute. But in every case except one nature had imposed a sharp limit, for not far away from all of them—Charleston, Norfolk, Baltimore, Philadelphia, Boston—the Appalachian Mountains lay athwart the route. Only in the case of New York was there a natural gateway. New York had already had 150 years of stiff competition with its northern rival, and although the Revolutionary War had greatly improved its position, its ultimate victory was not assured: there were still miles of primitive bush road between the upper reaches of the Mohawk and Lake Ontario, the highway to the west. The heavy freight costs on this stretch deprived New York of control over the supply trade of the west, and gave Montreal a fair chance.

The rivalry was one of rivers rather than of cities: it was the Hudson versus the St. Lawrence. The Hudson, through the Mohawk, reached out towards the lakes but did not quite touch them. Through Lake George it reached out towards Lake Champlain and the Richelieu but did not quite touch them either. The St. Lawrence, with some portages, did reach the lakes. Both rivers were closed in winter, but the Hudson for a shorter time, and at its mouth was year-round open water. In accessibility, depth, shelter, and spaciousness, the harbour at the river mouth could not be excelled. After leaving their moorings opposite the warehouses of the city, ships within an hour or two could be upon the open sea, free of all banks, reefs, fogs, or currents. The St. Lawrence presented some hundreds of miles of difficult navigation, commencing with the fogs on the Banks of Newfoundland, continuing with the dangerous islands in the Cabot Straits, and then presenting to sailing ships the long funnel from Gaspé to Quebec, a funnel that narrowed down to a channel studded with islands and shoals between which strong currents swept. In autumn, there was the danger of being caught with east winds and frozen in; in spring, the perils of drift ice. Above all, there was the long closing from November until some time in May. The Hudson easily had the better of it seaward. Whether its margin would counterbalance that of the St. Lawrence inland, time would tell.

The urban centres upon each of the two rivers reflected these conditions. The good harbour at the mouth of the Hudson had produced New York. Quebec represented the head of sailing ship navigation up the long estuary of the St. Lawrence. But above each city the rivers were large and tidal, and navigation was not reduced to boats or barges. In the unimproved state of the St. Lawrence, a vessel drawing some ten feet could get up to Montreal, and less than a century ago this was a respectable draft. On both rivers there was an intermediate stretch, an estuary on the St. Lawrence from Quebec to Lachine Rapids (173 miles) and from New York to Albany on the Hudson (190 miles). At the end of the estuaries another pair of urban centres had grown up. Albany had become the fur trading centre of the original English colony as Montreal had been of the French, but after 1763 its vitality had been sapped by Montreal. Moreover New York harbour had too many advantages to permit of Albany becoming the dominant partner. On the St. Lawrence, priority between the two river ports was settled only after a long struggle. Quebec, as seat of government and as depot of the new timber trade, remained the centre of colonial life until well after 1850. Later, the development of canals and the deepening of the channel up to Montreal caused it to lose ground. Quebec did not have as many advantages as New York; Montreal had more than Albany. On the St. Lawrence it was the upper city which won.

Of the two rivers it was the Hudson which won, and this because it managed to overcome its faulty link with Lake Ontario. When DeWit Clinton began to build the Erie canal in 1815, every St. Lawrence merchant should have flung himself into the task of securing an equally effective scheme for the rapids portion of his river. That was not done. In ten years, by 1825, the Erie was opened. New York, from being merely an Atlantic port, became the Atlantic port, leaving Boston and Philadelphia far behind. In a few years it had become the metropolis of America, the main new world substation of the metropolis-in-chief, London. The Erie canal enabled the produce of all the west tributary to the lakes to be brought down to Buffalo, there trans-shipped to barges and taken on to New York, to be trans-shipped to vessels. The canal barge, though small (the first canal gave only four foot draft), was large enough to turn the scale as against the rapids of the St. Lawrence.

From the completion of the Erie Canal, the never-ending duel between the two routes has been fought in terms of new techniques of transportation. The southern, with its greater supply of capital and energy, has always been the first to secure these, and no sooner has the northern equipped itself with them than the southern has found another means of outdistancing it. This duel, which began with the founding of Quebec and Manhattan, had its most spectacular phases in the nineteenth century. While the Erie was being built, the Americans rushed through the Lake Champlain canals, which gave navigation from all of Lake Champlain to New York and tore away from the St. Lawrence its commercial sway over Vermont and part of New York (1822). Then the Oswego Canal was completed, running from the Erie to Lake Ontario and tying in the country upon that lake with the New York system, except insofar as it was conserved to Montreal by law.

The next step was for the Canadians to reply by building the Welland Canal. This great work was the project of William Hamilton Merritt,[3] an able man of affairs, endowed with imagination, public spirit, and pertinacity, like whom there were many in the United States but few in Canada. Merritt went at this immense project privately, with a group of his neighbours. It involved nothing less than bringing ships down a small mountainside. When they had exhausted their own resources, they had to ask provincial assistance, but by 1830 the canal was through and schooners had proceeded from one lake to the other.

The Welland was only one link in Merritt's grand scheme, for since ships could now come down to Oswego and there trans-ship for New York, that city would benefit rather than Montreal. Another twenty years of his life were devoted to the completion of his plan, nothing less than the canalization of the whole St. Lawrence from Lake Erie to the sea. Some of the canals were on the Upper Canada portion of the river and these he induced that province to embark on. Over-elaborate canal programmes had driven new states like Michigan to repudiate their public debts. Upper Canada, drawn into the same current, did not have the same credit standing in London as insecure Michigan and found it difficult to borrow. Its fate was in the hands of great London banking firms like Baring Brothers, whose strong American connections predisposed them to regard the states more favourably than the colonies. However, some loans (at high rates) were obtained and construction began.

Upper Canada bankrupted itself in building the St. Lawrence canals, tried to get help from Lower Canada, which would draw large benefits

---

[3] 1793-1862. The founder of St. Catherines, Ont., M.L.A., and later a Minister of the Crown.

from them, and failed.[4] Lower Canada, its legislature controlled by men from the lower river who had no interest in the port of Montreal, would not undertake the necessary canals through its portion of the river, nor would it adopt a generous attitude in dividing the customs revenues collected in its ports on goods many of which went to Upper Canada. The upper province felt itself imprisoned, bound hand and foot to a partner indifferent to its interests. It was not until after the two had been manoeuvred into Union (partly as a result of the promise of an Imperial guarantee for a canal loan) that the great scheme could be proceeded with. At last, in 1849, it was completed, eight feet of water on the sills, and Canada had schooner navigation all the way from Lake Huron to the sea. Within the next few years a dilatory Montreal, which had stood half-jealous of the project that was to bring it greatness, found within itself citizens who could rise to their city's destiny by tackling the deepening of the natural channel to the sea. Every foot it was sunk brought the fate of Quebec that much closer.

Hardly had the magnificent series of canals been completed than the march of invention seemed to have rendered it obsolete. It was in 1853 that a series of short railways in the Hudson-Mohawk Valley was linked together to form one continuous run between New York and Buffalo— on the "New York Central Railroad". Not only that: it was not to be long before railways were pushed through the equally easy country south of Lake Erie and across to Chicago. New York had reached the heart of the continent, and on a grade of less than six inches per mile. Montreal and the St. Lawrence seemed farther behind than ever.

Canada replied, belatedly for lack of finances, with the building of the St. Lawrence and Atlantic across from Montreal to Portland[5] (this line gave Montreal a winter outlet to the Atlantic) and then the Grand Trunk Railway, which as its name indicates, was to be as large a scheme as the canals had been. After many efforts the Grand Trunk was finished, stretching all the way from Rivière du Loup below Quebec to Sarnia on distant Lake Huron. Again the St. Lawrence had grappled to it the Canadian portion of its hinterland. Later on, in the 1870's, when the Grand Trunk was extended to Chicago (last link, the St. Clair Tunnel, 1890) it could carry the war into the enemy's camp and make a bid for the hegemony over the American interior which the Erie canal and the New York Central had conferred upon New York. By that time it was

---

[4] The canal-building projects were factors in creating the rebellion situation in 1837. See p. 234.
[5] Completed 1853.

too late: the American railway net was too efficient, American finance too strong, American politicans and business men too watchful, to permit of the old chain being forged again. The Grand Trunk secured some of Chicago's trade, and other portions of it were drawn off through the lakes to connecting ports in Ontario,[6] but it never became more than one among many of the agencies competing for the great prize.

After the railway phase of the duel, the situation was stabilized until Canada's canals, deepened to fourteen feet by 1898, threw out another challenge. New York state replied with a deepened Erie but American railroads were too efficient[7] for the Erie to take its old place. Another piece of technique was, however, in the offing, the automobile and the motor road. Here again superior financial strength brought an American triumph: each new road knitted the interior more securely to centres leading down to the great metropolis on the coast. Canada again replied in kind, only to find that while she had been building motor roads, the Americans had been projecting airways. The last phase of the great transportation duel is the St. Lawrence Seaway.[8] The new Welland Canal, with a depth of 30 feet, enables the largest ships to come down as far as Kingston or Prescott. With the canalization of the St. Lawrence completed, large ocean-going vessels are able to go up to the head of the lakes and the large lake ships to come right down to Montreal, as their ancestors, the little lake schooners, were able to do for the first time in 1849. Montreal itself has always imagined that it would be ruined by these efforts to take the ships past its wharves. Instead, each succeeding improvement, including the Seaway, has added to its prosperity.

Montreal has become the metropolis of Canada, and Quebec is only an outlier down river. But there is a still greater metropolis 400 miles to the south at the other end of the Richelieu-Hudson trench.[9] To it Montreal is bound by canal, by many lines of railway, by motor roads, air-routes, and all the intimacies of business and finance. While Montreal is still a rival of New York (both of them way stations on the road to Europe), New York, which by the middle of the twentieth century was beginning to overshadow the ancient metropolis-in-chief, London, has become so great in its own right that Montreal's ties with it are a shade short of glorious: they are the ties of subordination, and Montreal, like Toronto, is a kind of distant suburb of New York.

[6] That is, Collingwood, from which lumber went to Chicago and wheat returned.
[7] The New York Central alone had four lines of track between Buffalo and New York.
[8] Completed about 1959.
[9] See p. 57 and map, p. 56.

3. Montreal's Subjugation of Upper Canada

Perhaps those Montrealers who witnessed the last fur brigade depart also saw a steamer crossing Lake St. Louis with immigrants for Upper Canada on board. They could have seen in such a steamer a portent of the years at hand, when their city was building up what was left of its hinterland. Down stream lay the fertile farming country on the lower St. Lawrence, already well-peopled. To the south, in the valley of the Richelieu, was more good country. The Eastern Townships to the south east were fast filling up with an energetic English-speaking population. The main hope of salvation, however, was upstream, in Upper Canada, which by 1821 was beginning to go ahead. On the upper river there was also the remnant of the American supply trade. Altogether, the St. Lawrence might still be expected to care for its children. The greatest threat was the energy with which the Americans were pushing their canals.

The future depended on the resource with which the river was used. Thanks to the energy of Hon. John Molson,[10] member of one of the families whose initiative made Montreal, there had been a steamboat, *The Accommodation*, plying between Montreal and Quebec since 1809. After the War of 1812, others followed it and within a few years, there was a chain of these boats along the river and on the lakes: the journey up to York or Niagara became easy. On the Ottawa, points 300 miles above Montreal could be reached by steamer. There was nothing poor about the accommodation offered; travellers testify unanimously to the high standards of the inland steamers. They carried first class passengers in their cabins, immigrants on their decks, and package freight in their holds. At the portages the first class rode, the immigrants walked, and the freight was teamed across, to be loaded into another steamer. Some immigrants and freight still went up by bateaux,[11] which could be poled and tracked up the rapids, saving a trans-shipment for the goods.

The "forwarding business", as this was called, grew to importance in the up-river traffic. It was an aspect of the middleman role for which its geographical position had cast Montreal, and was linked with the importing system of the city, the whole following a well-marked routine. The importing merchant of Montreal sent his orders to his London cor-

[10] 1764-1836. An Englishman, in Canada from 1784. Founder of Molson's Brewery. President, Bank of Montreal, 1826-1834. M.L.A. and Legislative Councillor.
[11] A *bateau* is a sharp-ended boat with a flat bottom, like an overgrown dory. The "pointers" used by lumbermen are *bateaux*.

respondent, with the first ship off from Quebec in the spring, or prefer-
ably through New York in the winter. His goods, a miscellaneous
assortment of everything from iron spikes to ladies' hats, came out to
him in the course of the summer. At Quebec they were transferred from
one of the few "fast-sailing, copper-fastened" vessels that sufficed for
the superior trade and were brought up to Montreal on the steamer.
They were then sent to upcountry correspondents at Kingston, York,
or Hamilton and, again distributed, sooner or later reached a retailer.
At each change of hand, personal notes were given for long terms and
at high rates of interest, for not until the settlers had got their harvest
in could they begin to make payment. This mostly took the form not of
cash but of potash, wheat, salt pork, boards, shingles, staves, and various
other odds and ends. The retailer took everything that came and disposed of it to some forwarder (such as Richard Cartwright of Kingston)
who combined it all into large lots, sending the wheat and potash down
stream on a timber raft or forwarding it by bateau or Durham boat.[12]
When the consignment reached Montreal, its suitable components
were exported. The retailer settled with the wholesaler or forwarder
with a minimum of cash, and so payment went on down the line
until the Montreal importer had himself satisfied his London correspondents.

The long chain was almost as tenuous as the fur trade had been, and
it was more individualistic. Restricted channels of occupation forced up
the numbers engaged in distribution. Competition, high interest rates,
long credits, and the uncertainties of the settlers' returns made for many
business casualties. The result was high prices in Upper Canada and, on
the part of the Montreal merchants, an unpleasant insistence on payment of debts, combined with an over-sharp eye for profits, which made
them thoroughly detested by the people of the upper province. This
creditor-debtor relationship was crucial in the conflict between metropolis and hinterland and it had political results: in an effort to defend
themselves, and in order to avoid excessive tolls to Montreal, the western
merchants strove to get the colonial system modified so as to enable
them to import direct via New York. The Montrealers regarded proposals to import via New York as treason; they raised the loyalty cry
against this trafficking with the devil. Not until the destruction of the
old colonial system in 1846 did they have to submit to this crowning
indignity and see their own preserved share of the hinterland, British
soil itself, laid open to the enemy from the south.

[12] An improved canal barge, on different lines from the bateau.

4. The St. Lawrence System at its Height

Growing mercantile strength brought other forms of power. A merchant, if prominent enough, could always pry out a good big grant of land from the government. A successful middleman position and the sale of land held for speculation brought money into Montreal; capital began to accumulate. Already this had had its reflection in the first bank. The Bank of Montreal (1817) at first represented the North West Company and the fur trade interest: it was founded by men close to the fur trade like Hon. John Richardson[13] but it fitted well into the new middleman position and became the rallying point for mercantile Montreal. It was soon well-established with numerous branches, rivals not appearing for some time.[14]

The views of the mercantile community found reflection in the English-language newspapers. The most interesting among these today, since one of them still survives,[15] are the *Montreal Gazette,* founded in 1785, and the *Montreal Herald* (founded 1811). To read the *Gazette* of 1963 is to read the *Gazette* of 1843 or of 1793, for then as now, it was the voice of the mercantile interests of Montreal; its doctrines and its attitude remained unchanged, those of complacent, commercial Toryism. When in 1813 James McGill[16] left part of his fortune to found a University, the mercantile community consolidated its educational base; the official relationships of this institution with Montreal business have paralleled those of the newspapers.

Business organization, money, banks, newspapers, and university—all these plus historical continuity (some of the original families of the Montreal business group as it began in the eighteenth century are still prominent, and others have had long associations with it) produced a compact block of power in Montreal which necessarily found political expression. Because of the French, it was impossible to dominate the province directly through the elected assembly, so the group entrenched itself within lines that votes could not assail, the legislative and executive councils. As in Upper Canada, a relatively small body composed the corps from which the councillors were selected, and family or business relationships were common within it. The group that controlled the administration of the province was known as the Chateau Clique, or Scotch party.

[13] 1755-1831. Arrived in Canada shortly after the Conquest. Member of Forsyth, Richardson and Co., and of North-West Company. M.L.A., Legislative and Executive Councillor.
[14] See p. 353.   [15] 1963.
[16] 1744-1813. Emigrated first to American colonies, thence to Montreal. Partner in North-West Company, M.L.A., and Executive Councillor.

The men who were the bearers of the commercial state were mostly "old country" in origin: a few of English descent, most of Scottish. There was an occasional American; such as Horatio Gates, the prominent merchant of the 1820's and 1830's. By 1821 a good many must have been native-born, but few of them, native-born or not, would have considered themselves "Canadians", a term of opprobrium which was reserved for the French. They were still Englishmen and Scotsmen overseas—colonials—and their living as a kind of garrison in a semi-hostile sea of "natives" accentuated their colonial psychology.[17]

5. A Third Staple, Timber

The group of English-speaking people who dominated the commercial life of Quebec had somewhat different characteristics from those of Montreal. From the beginning of the century, Quebec became the timber and ship-building centre of British America; its fortunes were linked to wood. Unlike Montreal (but like modern Winnipeg), it was a one-commodity town, exhibiting all the phenomena of committal to one great staple. The timber merchants who established branch houses after 1800, a number of which remained in business in Canada for over a century, came mostly from Liverpool. Younger sons and nephews sent out to carry on the branch went home frequently on business and kept up the family connections. A firm like that of Sharples and Co., established about 1830, continued to bestride the Atlantic on this family basis for three generations. Towards the end of the century when the timber trade was disappearing, many of the members of such firms "went home" to stay, where they, or their sons, are still to be found buying and selling wood imported from other sources.

The timber merchants, with few exceptions, remained middlemen and did not go into the production of lumber. Their job was to buy square timber and deals from the timber-makers and the lumbermen, and ship them to England. The main branch of their trade was in square timber. It saved cargo space to load a ship with square timbers rather than round: the typical English import for centuries, first from the Baltic and then from America, had been square timber. "Squaring" wasted the best timber in the tree, the litter it left in the bush caused forest fires, and since squaring often revealed internal defects, it was prodigal in the number of trees cut down to get good timbers. But Canadian pine was in such demand in England that the industry ran

[17] An actual, though extreme, example of the Montreal colonial liked to tell of the four generations of Montrealers behind him, but refused to call himself a Canadian; he was a "Yorkshireman".

like a bush fire up the banks of the St. Lawrence, the Ottawa, the St. John, and other streams, devouring the best of the white and red pine, of the white oak and other hardwoods. By the 1830's lumbermen had worked up the Ottawa as far as Lake Temiscaming and up the St. Lawrence to Lake Ontario. Niagara Falls itself hardly stopped them. The native lumbermen had no more consideration for the forest than the English merchant, but the former at least came to see that it paid to cut up a log into planks and boards rather than square it, and when they got a chance to get into the American market, they turned away from square timber to sawn lumber. In the presence of an "inexhaustible" natural resource such as the Canadian forest, no one seemed able to remain sober very long: the main task was to pitch in and destroy it, grabbing as much of the proceeds as one could. Lumbering illustrates the exploitive spirit at its worst.

The communities built upon the wood staple were like the seed cast on stony ground that sprang up quickly and sometimes as quickly wilted. A staple trade brings ready cash when the market is good, but staple markets are always precarious, and a dealer may be a millionaire one day and a pauper the next. This was especially true of the timber trade with Great Britain, for prices there varied greatly, and on the Canadian side there was no means of knowing the variations until engagements had been entered into. If a merchant had bought timber when it was "up", only to find that it was "down" when it arrived in England, he was ruined. The timber-maker was similarly situated. He might go into the bush in the fall, having bought supplies and engaged men on the expectation of a good price, only to find when he came out in the spring that something had depressed the market in England. The trade reflected and magnified English commercial crises: in a bad depression its sufferings paralyzed the colonial economy. It induced a speculative spirit and a flashy type of living on the part of those engaged in it, especially the producers and their employees.

At first the timber trade held the field almost alone, but before the War of 1812 some mills had been put up for making "deals" (three-inch planks) for the English market. A mill was built at Hawkesbury, on the Ottawa River about 1804; it passed into the hands of the Hamilton family, who operated there for over a century, an example of continuity and stability in a precarious industry. Such mills soon increased in number, and by mid-century, much sawn lumber was going across to England. But it was not until the great American market opened in the 1850's that the day of the sawmill really arrived in Canada. By that time, a good part of the economy of every colony except Newfoundland and Nova Scotia was already resting on the forest. Timber-making and lumbering were supporting most of the population in the St. John and other New Brunswick river valleys and in the Ottawa valley. Quebec and Saint John had been built on square timber. Bytown was growing rapidly on a wooden foundation, Toronto derived much of its wealth from forest exploitation, and lesser places like Pembroke and Peterborough were building themselves up on it exclusively. In all, the lumber trade was furnishing the Canadas and New Brunswick with over thirty per cent of their exports.

The timber trade, like other metropolitan activities, was conducted without reference to colonial interests, and where it influenced national policy, that too was adjusted without much thought for the distant producing areas. The celebrated parliamentary inquiries of 1820 and 1821 into the trade of England were so far-reaching that they set going the current which did not stop until the old system of protection was washed out (1846), but the evidence submitted to them by persons who claimed to know the colonies did not ring quite true and the inquiries themselves were in exclusively English terms. They revealed the internal division of the English wood trade between the group importing from the Baltic countries and the ship-owners and timber merchants interested in British North America. They resulted in some reduction in the preference accorded colonial wood over that from the Baltic (the so-called "differential duties"); thenceforth, though often assailed by the Baltic and free trade interests, the preference stood unchanged for twenty years, giving the colonial timber trade a long chance to entrench itself firmly in the British market. No clearer insight into mercantilism is to be obtained than in the contests between the two groups of timber merchants and ship-owners to determine English policy. Their arguments were invariably put in the high terms of patriotism, or at least of the nation's economic well-being, but a little analysis reveals the cloven hoof of self-interest.

Of such was mercantilism; of such is metropolitanism composed. Although the exploitive process in Canada has cast off many incidental benefits, it is built on the hard rock of business self-interest, with its undignified philosophy of "grab"; and during the period here discussed, it was cemented tightly into the larger and still harder rock of British, or metropolitan, commercialism.

Chronology

1603	East India Company.
1670	Hudson's Bay Company.
1694	Bank of England.
1783	North West Company.

1785   Montreal *Gazette* founded.
1793–1813 English preferences on colonial timber established.
1804   Hawkesbury (deal) Mills begun.
1809   Steamer *Accommodation* between Quebec and Montreal.
1817   Firm of William Price established at Quebec.
               Bank of Montreal founded.
1820–21   British Parliamentary Inquiries into Trade and reduction in Colonial Timber Preference.
               McGill University opened.
1822   Champlain Canal.
               First Proposals of Upper Canada to trade with England directly through New York.
1825   Erie Canal opened.
1828   Oswego Canal.
1830   Welland Canal.
               Sharples and Co., representative timber merchants at Quebec.
1830's   Square Timber being made on Lake Temiscaming.
1842–45   Further reductions in colonial preferences.
1846   Free Trade in England and virtual end of the Colonial Preferences on wheat and timber.
1849   St. Lawrence Canals completed.
1851   New York Central Railroad between New York and Buffalo.
1853   St. Lawrence and Atlantic Railroad opened to Portland.
1853   Grand Trunk Railway begun.
1879   Grand Trunk Railway completed to Chicago.

Additional Reading

Aitken, Hugh G. J. *The Welland Canal Company; A Study in Canadian Enterprise.* Cambridge, Mass., 1954.

Glazebrook, G. P. de T. *A History of Transportation in Canada.* Toronto, 1938.

Keefer, Thomas C. *The Canals of Canada.* Montreal, 1894.

Whitford, Noble E. *History of the Canal System of the State of New York.* Albany, 1906. 2 vols.

Willoughby, William R. *The St. Lawrence Waterway: A Study in Politics and Diplomacy.* Madison, Wisc., 1961.

CHAPTER 17

An Unstable Community: Lower Canada, 1815-1837

1. The Elements of Friction

Self-consciousness had come to French Canada a few years before the War of 1812. The presence of the English in the province had hastened, but did not cause, the process. The English were a foil, a reminder that the homeland had to be fought for every day if it was to be possessed, that no advantage was too trivial to be sought in the great goal of *survivance*. The English served as models to be avoided. They stood for a kind of life which the French could not understand or, if they did understand, disliked: they stood for restlessness, change, a striving after wealth that they often did not know how to use, for a kind of bearish individualism. About even the most agreeable of them there was an air of superiority which many did not trouble to conceal. Their arrogance, that besetting English sin, wounded sensitive French souls, to whom it meant being considered second class. Yet some strange blindness in the English had prevented them from foreseeing that insistence on their own institutions would give the French the weapons with which they themselves might be fought. What more could a conquered people ask than a representative assembly with the powers of debate and taxation?

On the average French Canadian, English domination did not sit heavily. Unless he happened to live in Montreal or Quebec, or worked in one of their timber camps or shipyards, he seldom saw Englishmen. He was under no obligation to learn their language. The main change from the old way of life was that now every few years there would be an election, with crowded meetings where a man could argue and joke with his friends, and at which candidates would make exciting speeches. Since there were not many ridings in which the electorate was of both races, an election for the *habitant* meant speeches by rival French candidates, vying in eloquence with each other, trying to outdo each other in telling how they would stand up to *les sacrés Anglais*. That was platform enough. Elections were fought by persons and by oratory, not by platforms. *Les sacrés Anglais* became a stereotype: how they took the lands *les enfants du sol* should have, how they wanted to impose direct taxes, how they monopolized all the *postes*, the well-paid, dignified jobs in the government service, how rude and important they were, how, worst bogey of all, they might come and take the young men off to serve in English ships-of-war. The "damned English" were the best of whipping-boys, nightmares to feed a Frenchman's fancy and win an election for his representative.

When encountered, the "damned English" did not seem such bad fellows. They were not very courteous, but sometimes kindly in a rough way and often generous. They paid very good wages in their camps. The French Canadian river drivers came to trust the wisdom and courage of their English-speaking boss and to look to him for leadership in everyday affairs. The old song has it that "Jack Boyd, notre grand foreman, nous emènera" (will lead us on). That mythical Scotchman, Jack Boyd, led many a Frenchman on, encouraging him on the "drive", setting the example in cutting log-jams, and seeing that he got hot food at night.

An example of good relationships was furnished by William Price, the English immigrant who pioneered the Saguenay country. All his work people were French. In a semi-feudal, paternalistic way, he seems to have dealt justly with them. When he died he was remembered affectionately as *Le Père du Saguenay*.

There was little friction in the area of society in which most might have been expected, religion. Between English Protestant and French Catholic there was practically none. The major disturbance was between the two Catholic groups, the French and the Irish, who from the first disliked each other.

Where, as in lumbering, English and French met on an employer and employee basis, an association which suited the qualities of each, things went well. It was the contest for power that produced bad relationships, and these were, therefore, most in evidence in the legislature and in public life generally. Some of the bones of contention between the two peoples were large, others small, and it seemed to be the small things that irritated most, as the long trivial contest over the establishment of Registry offices indicated. The French had always left their deeds, wills, and other legal papers with their local notary. The English wanted the new device of a public registry office. This was enough to make the French oppose it, and the battle raged in consequence. English-language newspapers of the day reveal a contempt which had slumbered while the French had been good enough to keep in their place but which became conspicuous when they began to thrust forward to equality. Plenty of points of ridicule could be found: the habitants were absurd rustics who wore long stocking caps even in summer, and shod their feet, not in honest English boots, but with cowhide made up after the fashion of the Indian moccasin (shoe-packs). So ignorant were they, that for generations they had been carting their manure over the edge of the river bank and letting the winter ice take it down the St. Lawrence, instead of placing it on the fields. If they would use more intelligence, they could double their yield of wheat and would then have a little cash to buy clothes (from the English importers), instead of wearing a ridiculous kind of homemade cloth. They might even learn to write, these *Chevaliers de la Croix* ("knights of the cross").

On the opposite side, there was the converse of the same attitude. The time-honoured jokes on the superior with which the inferior salves his subordination, the fits of sullenness or passion that came over French leaders, their non-co-operative, suspicious attitude, the tempestuous and unmeasured utterances in press and legislature, all were easily recognized phenomena of a sense of inferiority.

Was there any remedy? The distant Imperial government never understood the real nature of the cleavage until shortly before the rebellion. It thought it was an ordinary constitutional struggle, such as had dragged on during the eighteenth century in most of the former colonies. Lord Durham said he came expecting to find a contest of principles and was shocked at finding "two nations warring in the bosom of a single state". Durham prescribed remedies: many have since been adopted, but in fundamental outline the situation has not changed. The two "nations" still struggle, sometimes in polite form, sometimes openly. Under favourable conditions, understanding based on a common Canadianism develops between the more sympathetic spirits of the two peoples but there is no sign of amalgamation. Such wars never end: there is no constitutional formula that will solve them.

The system of government in Lower Canada could not have been more skilfully contrived to promote friction if such had been its design. Under it, only one result was possible; 1837 was implicit in 1791. The

Governor-in-Chief of British North America (who in practice was merely Governor of Lower Canada) was an overshowy figure on an insecure pyramid of dignity, yet clothed with great powers. He could veto or reserve all bills. He could prorogue or dissolve the legislature. He was commander-in-chief of a not inconsiderable British army, and had at his disposal for emergency use the Imperial funds from which it was maintained. The reservation to the executive of revenue arising from the Crown lands and other sources made him to some degree independent of his own legislature, an independence that resulted in his being all the more dependent on London. After the Revolution the Colonial Office kept a tight hold on colonial governors. Nearly everything had to be "referred home", with the result that the wheels of government often stood still while sailing ships were taking their interminable way across the ocean and leisurely London clerks were writing innumerable memoranda. Often files were lost, and the subjects dealt with, however pressing, could not be proceeded with. Sometimes literally years went by before simple points could be decided.[1] What was needed was a viceroy; what the colony had was an agent.

The governors of Lower Canada were superior to the lieutenant-governors of the other provinces in their rank and usually in their personalities. They were well above the average of governors in the old colonies. Lord Dorchester (1791-96) was followed by one or two nonentities, then by Sir James Craig (1807-11), the old soldier whose memory is still hated in Quebec.[2] General Prevost, the governor during the War of 1812, was a poor soldier, but partly because as a French Swiss, he understood French people, he was rated *"un gentilhomme qui avait su comprendre les Canadiens, dont le tact, la prudence et l'ésprit de justice les avaient conquis"*.[3] Sir John Sherbrooke (1816-18) was wise and conciliatory, but his successor the Duke of Richmond (1818), a broken-down nobleman, soon antagonized everyone. His death brought as successor Lord Dalhousie (1820), a cultivated man but one of set opinions. Both Dalhousie and Sherbrooke had been Lieutenant-Governors of Nova Scotia before being transferred to Canada. Sir James Kempt (Administrator, 1828-30), who attempted to placate the French, was labelled an appeaser by the English. Lord Aylmer (1830) and Lord Gosford (1835) were both estimable, but in their regimes the situation had become impossible, and probably no one could have rescued it. Lord

---

[1] As with the timber slides on the Ottawa River, where "reference home" began in 1831, and was still going on in 1839.

[2] See p. 161.

[3] Bruchési, *Histoire du Canada pour tous*, p. 113.

Durham's[4] ability put him in a class by himself, but he was in Canada only five months (1838). The office of the governor should have kept him above local issues, but that was difficult, for only the occasional strong personality like Durham could avoid falling under the sway of his councillors, the men-on-the-spot who knew local conditions and were carrying on the day-to-day work of government.[5]

In all the colonies there was friction between the Legislative Council,[6] the stronghold of privilege, and the Assembly; but in Lower Canada there was the additional difficulty of race. The proportion of French members in the council, fairly large at first, gradually declined. The same was true of the executive council, which interlocked with the legislative to an unhealthy extent. In 1827, 18 out of the 27 members of the Legislative Council were receiving salaries or pensions from government, and all of these 18 were English. Of the 18, seven were members of both councils. The conciliar system in itself would have caused revolt sooner or later, as it did in Upper Canada.

The Anglican Bishop of Quebec sat in the Councils from the beginning, as did some of the judges. Twenty-seven years later, in 1818, the Catholic Bishop was made a member of the Executive Council. It was in an attempt to prevent the judges being councillors that the Assembly had its first brush with the executive, during the regime of Sir James Craig. The Assembly was to return to the attack year after year, without much success. Like everything else, the sound proposal to divorce the judicial from the other branches of government became the subject of racial strife, for the Councillors took the attack on the judges (most of whom, before 1830, were English) as an attack on the ruling race.

Perhaps the conquerors would have been more astute if they had refused to shut themselves up in conciliar citadels, for such prominent targets were sure to invite attack even had the behaviour of the Councillors been exemplary, which it was not. Favouritism was rife. The spoilation of the public lands was only one of many areas of abuse; there were frequent charges of plurality and absenteeism in office-holding and of monopolization of posts by the English. In 1827, of eleven judges, three were French; of some thirty judicial appointments,

---

[4] See Chap. 19.

[5] The Executive Council, a non-statutory body, advised the governor, but in no sense constituted a ministry. It had a number of resemblances to the American cabinet.

[6] The Legislative Council, statutory under the Constitutional Act, was a second chamber of the familiar, appointive type, modelling itself, as far as it could, on the House of Lords.

1800-1827, ten had been French. In 1834, although they constituted over three-quarters of the population, the French held less than a quarter of the public places. This was a serious grievance to a people who did not have the commercial outlet of the English and looked on governmental posts as major goals. The Jesuit Estates had been confiscated to the Crown and their proceeds were being applied to state education through the Royal Institution[7]: through French eyes that looked like Catholic money being spent on Protestant education. In 1822 there was the resounding defalcation of the Receiver-General, Hon. John Caldwell, who was found to be some £100,000 short in his accounts. Here was English finance, said the French. The *enfants du sol*, it was contended, had been cheated of their birthright by an English government which allowed the Eastern Townships to be settled by English-speaking people. French extremists even professed to regard the whole immigration movement, cholera epidemics and all, as a carefully planned manoeuvre to outnumber them. French grievances, real or fancied, were endless.

Had the councillors been angels from heaven, their race and power would have earned them accusations. Angels among them, however, were few, but hard-boiled business men or cynical self-seekers, many. Anglo-Saxon superiority stuck out of them all. Among them were men of personal integrity; most of them were energetic and many were able. But they were also aggressive, self-centred, proud, devoted to the commercial way of life, taking so narrow a view even of their own interests as to ensure their ultimate loss.

The French members of the Assembly had the qualities calculated to provoke the maximum of dissension with persons of this type. They had the characteristics of their race: sensitive vanity, egotism fed with the applause of their fellows, love of oratory and of argument for its own sake, powers of expression too picturesque and too energetic for unimaginative Englishmen to relish, the logical approach which finds it so hard to compromise and raises everything great and small into a principle. Their education had as its guiding tenet the medieval scholastic philosophy; this caused their approach to everything to contrast sharply with the purely empiric attitudes of the English. Each year found them more conscious of their history and of their numbers, less disposed to put up with attempts to keep them "in their place". Colonial institutions encouraged irresponsibility, for the Assembly was a debating society with few constructive functions but with the great negative power that lay in the right of taxation. In such a strategic position no body of men,

[7] See p. 160.

certainly not French Assemblymen,[8] could have been expected to have refrained from pressing their advantages.

For every French grievance there was a corresponding English complaint; the English could build up just as formidable a list as the French. They supplied most of the energy and initiative of the province, but they had to submit to antiquated French law. They had to carry the dead weight of French conservatism on their shoulders. They were chronically under-represented in the Assembly, which year after year had refused to give members to the new English settlements.[9] They were loyal subjects of the Crown, and opposed *in toto* to the attempt to build *la nation Canadienne* under the subterfuge of a nominal allegiance. The province belonged to them as much as it belonged to the French; it was part of an English Empire and would have to become English.

The list could be extended indefinitely on both sides but it always comes down in the end to the one simple fact, the central fact of Canadian history, to the English conquest. In the last analysis, the English based their claims on the conquest, the French on the effort to obliterate the conquest. Such being its essence, the situation unrolls according to well-worn formulae until it reaches the logical end, armed conflict, after which there is opportunity for a new start.[10]

2. The Medium of Friction: Representative Government

In Lower Canada, there are three distinct aspects of the struggle leading up to the Rebellion, all of which at the appointed time fuse into one: the racial cleavage, with which may be included the economic cleavage between static and dynamic conceptions of society, the clash of personalities, and the constitutional struggle. The racial cleavage gives driving power to the other two.

Of the personalities, Louis Joseph Papineau, who became speaker of the Assembly in 1815, towered above all others. His gifts of eloquence and tactical ability at once made him the leader of the French party,

[8] There was never more than a handful of English in the Assembly.
[9] See also p. 238.
[10] For the period 1815-37 in detail, see W. P. M. Kennedy, *The Constitution of Canada, 1534-1937*, 2nd ed. (London, 1938), A. De Celles, *The "Patriotes" of '37* (Vol. 25 of *Chronicles of Canada*) and A. De Celles, *Louis Joseph Papineau* (Toronto, 1926), and Thomas Chapais, *Cours d'histoire du Canada*, 8 vols. (Quebec, 1919-34), especially III and IV. For Papineau, see Fernand Ouellet, *Louis-Joseph Papineau, Un être divisé*, (CHA Booklet No. 11) Ottawa, 1960, his *Papineau, Textes choisis* (Quebec, P.Q., 1958), and his Louis-Joseph Papineau dans la Révolution de 1837-38," *CHA Annuel Report 1958*, 13-34.

and, in this capacity, it was his fate to clash with all the governors. Governors came and governors went, but Papineau went on, comparatively speaking, forever, and each contest gave him more experience for the next. A timely recognition of his abilities would have made him a useful servant of the state; as it was, he was always on the outside, and from at first knocking at the door, he came to kicking it open. Eloquence, ability, charm, learning, Gallic verve and tempestuousness, not too much ballast—all joined to bitterness, made Papineau the bearer of Revolution. Other men were secondary. Hardly a single name on the English side, except those of the governors, is remembered today, perhaps because nearly all acute and generous minds sympathized with the French. On the French side, scholars still talk of the Bourdages and Quésnels but already these are the names of historical ghosts, even as compared with those of the inevitable English sympathizers, of whom Neilson, Nelson, and O'Callaghan were the chief.[11]

The constitutional struggle in Canada runs until about 1832, after which Papineau becomes so intransigent as to warrant the belief that he did not wish a solution. The Imperial government, which had been drawn into the colonial troubles at a comparatively late stage in their development, maintained constitutional attitudes until 1837, the year of the report of the Gosford Commission,[12] when Lord John Russell's Ten Resolutions, the sequel to the report, closed the door to negotiation.[13]

The constitutional period may be divided at the year 1822. Previous to that date, the early phenomena of revolution can be discerned: these consist in skirmishes on points of detail and the growth of a sense of identity within the two groups. This period was marked by the pre-war struggles with Sir James Craig, which gave to the French the necessary memories of persecution (they still call his governorship "the Reign of Terror"), and by the academic presentation of constitutional points: M. Bédard's long speech of April, 1809, on the liberty and independence of the Assembly, in which he touched on the desirability of a ministerial form of government, provides an example. Other points of controversy

---

[11] John Neilson: Editor of the *Quebec Gazette* from 1797. M.L.A. 1818-34. Took the moderate side from an early date. Wolfred Nelson: English doctor in the French countryside. Warmly sympathetic with habitants. Successfully led rebels at St. Denis, 23 Nov., 1837, against British regulars. Later amnestied and re-entered public life. O'Callaghan: Irish doctor. M.L.A. Editor of the *Vindicator*, English-language Reform journal.

[12] Lord Gosford, governor, 1835-38, headed a commission of inquiry into the affairs of the province; its recommendations were inconclusive.

[13] The Ten Resolutions offered one or two concessions, but rejected "responsible government", and authorized a limited payment of governmental expenses without vote of the Assembly.

also arose, such as the presence of the judges in the Legislature, or the appointment of a colonial agent in London. In Sherbrooke's regime, finance, the heart of the constitutional question, was reached. Assembly leaders like Papineau were well up on their English constitutional history and quite aware that the powers of the House of Commons were founded upon the one great rock of control over the purse strings: by refusing to vote supply the representatives of the people could starve out king and ministers, prevent payment of armed forces and bring the wheels of government to a stop. In the old Empire, the struggles of colonial assemblies to capture full control over finance had merged into Revolution. In the new, the process began again. Before the War of 1812 Assembly demands for control had been more or less academic, but during Sherbrooke's governorship the question began to go beyond that phase, and each year saw more insistence on it.

The contest took much the same form as it had in English history. First there was the demand for the right to inquire into the expenditure by the Crown of money voted by the Assembly. Then began the tussle to secure control of all revenue and supervision of all expenditure. At first the Crown would not hear of surrendering its revenues to the Assembly, but then it began to modify its position: it would surrender some conditionally, the main condition being "a permanent civil list". The experience of the eighteenth century, when governors dependent on the Assembly for their salaries had had to do its will, was still remembered. "A permanent civil list" at first meant that the salaries of the governor, chief justice, and other officers of state, great and small, were to be voted in perpetuity and not to come up for an annual consideration. This had been the desideratum of the Crown in the eighteenth century, and there is no record of a single colony ever having been induced to accord it. In face of this unbroken record of failure, the Colonial Office began the old struggle over again and with no greater prospect of success. The story becomes familiar: impressive refusals of concession on the part of the Imperial government, followed by increased demands from the Assembly; further refusals and greater increase in demands; at last the Crown concedes everything in return for nothing, and the Assembly secures complete financial control.

Bargaining went on with Lower Canada from about 1822 to the eve of the rebellion. The stipulation for a "permanent civil list" was first reduced to a list for the lifetime of the king, then to a list for a limited number of officers. In 1831, the Colonial Secretary offered all the Crown revenues to the Assembly, with the exception of the Casual and Territorial, in return for a Civil List of high officials only during the king's lifetime. This was refused. Next he reduced his list to five officials and made some other concessions; all were refused, the Assembly demanding absolute and unconditional control of revenue. In 1836, Lord Gosford offered to hand over all revenue in return for a small permanent list. This was refused. Rebellion ensued, and in the new world which followed, the Crown did hand over all revenue and did not get any permanent civil list.

In 1822, a project for a union of the two Canadas was launched upon an unsuspecting colony. The bill calmly proposed a return to English as the sole official language, along with a property franchise so high that most Frenchmen would be debarred from voting, to say nothing of Crown control of the revenue and some limitation on the freedom of the Roman Catholic church. Here was anglicization again, after sixty years, and in a more hideous form than ever before. The political imbecility of those who cooked up the measure, mainly the Montreal group of merchant politicians who saw in it a way out from French domination, could not have been more clearly revealed. They did not know the French, who buzzed out at the bill like a nest of hornets. The British government dropped it very precipitately,[14] but the mistrust aroused by it went into the general bill of French grievances which has been presented at intervals ever since. The Union bill of 1822 marks the transition in Lower Canada from light skirmishing to fairly heavy fighting, but fighting still on constitutional lines.

Papineau had gone over to London to get the bill dropped; it indicates the elementary stage of the revolutionary process in 1822 that he could come back and pour out praises of English institutions. When he reached home, he found the country in the midst of the Caldwell scandal. Then occurred his breach with Dalhousie over the latter's threat to use the Crown's revenues whether the Assembly voted expenditure or not. From that time on, Papineau's conduct became less rational, more violent. In every revolution violent men are needed, men of *l'ideé fixe,* fanatics with strong passions and able minds, Robespierres and Trotskys. After 1822, Papineau fast turned into that type.

Matters dragged on, with much petitioning to London and the "showdown" coming when the governor refused to accept "the tribune", (as Papineau had now become to his admirers) any longer as speaker of the Assembly. Dalhousie was recalled, and for two years (1828-30) relative peace reigned under Sir James Kempt. As a result of the quarrel, a committee of the British Parliament made an elaborate inquiry into the condition of Lower Canada: this was the first echo of the struggle in

---

[14] The bill was transmuted into the Canada Trade Act regulating the division of the customs revenue between the two provinces.

England. The Committee, which could detect only an ordinary struggle for constitutional reform, brought in recommendations favourable to the popular side, but its report received little attention, and the government did not act on it. Here was a not unimportant aspect of the situation: the Canadas were so inconspicuous in the British scale of things that their affairs were invariably neglected.[15] The opportunity to compromise did not recur.

By 1831, the Assembly had become intransigent. It had to be all or nothing. This was the year of Lord Goderich's conciliatory financial offers, both of which were rejected.[16] Papineau and Neilson refused offers of seats in the Executive Council. The Assembly now had a programme, a programme aimed at the conquest of power, with no place for compromise; this included complete control of all revenue and, with the American Senate as a model, an elective Legislative Council. A forward surge of the American masses in 1828 had carried Andrew Jackson into the Presidency in a victory that marked the high point of faith in the elective process: many French intellectuals, basing their political philosophy on democracy and the rights of man, were coming to share that faith, and, incidentally, an elected council would give them almost complete control over government.

The year 1832 stood out as the year in which the struggle widened from the few to the many. This was the year in which the troops fired on an election crowd in Montreal, killing three young Frenchmen, in a duplication of the Boston Massacre. As long as it was matters of fine-spun principle that were being fought over, the strife was above the heads of the masses. But now English troops had killed three Frenchmen, and that was language which everybody could understand. The crowd could also appreciate the vilification with which Papineau was beginning to denounce the moderates, driving them to take sides. The true revolutionaries, as always at such times, were learning to stand together, and the half-hearted, the Laodiceans, the liberals, were beginning to flee. The Assembly was more tempestuous than ever, carrying a vote in favour of an elective Council and refusing to vote supply. This action brought sharp condemnation from the Colonial Secretary who still, however, believed it to be an aspect of a rather radical agitation for constitutional reform. This was the time that Papineau, in his alienation of the church on the minor question of church wardens and parish accounts, made his first grave error: he proposed to extend

[15] Sherbrooke suggested to the minister that Papineau be named to the Legislative Council. The minister agreed in principle, but three years passed before the offer was made; then the time had passed, and Papineau refused it.
[16] See p. 224.

popular participation in such aspects of church government and managed to get a bill to that effect through the Assembly. If democracy raised its hand against the church, so much the worse for democracy: the majority of Papineau's partisans among the clergy now deserted him.

By 1834 the bounds of constitutionalism were being reached. The 92 resolutions, that enormous document which contained every charge and complaint that could be thought up, some valid, some foolish, became the touchstone of virtue. Those Assemblymen who were not for the Resolutions were against the Reformers; further middle-of-the-road men were sloughed off. The ranks closed and the semi-party name, *Les Patriotes*, began to be used. The next year, 1835, the British government, slowly becoming aware that all was not well, sent out the Gosford commission. Lord Gosford, by his social gifts, weaned away still more adherents from Papineau, whose band was thus left more closely integrated than ever. The assemblymen from Quebec, centre of conservatism, had left him, and his support now lay mainly around Montreal and in the Richelieu valley, always the uneasy section of French Canada. But his party had plenty of strength left, and he knew how to make the most of his political opportunities. In 1836, the premature revelation of the Imperial intention to refuse an elected Council enabled him to turn his wrath against Lord Gosford as the author of the recommendation, and thus prevent that official's forthcoming report from finding acceptance by Canadians.

The Gosford Report took its stand on the basis, not of wholesale reconstruction, but of reform. Many of the objectives of the French party had already been achieved: there were now more French in the Legislative Council than English, more French judges than English; several officials who had been found wanting had been dismissed; and the Executive Council was in process of reorganization. But there was to be no elected council, something far too contrary to English ideas, and no concession of ministerial government, for which, it is to be emphasized, the *Patriotes*, who never understood it well, had not pressed very hard. In finance, another bargain was offered: the "permanent civil list" this time was to be for £19,000 per year in exchange for surrender of all Crown revenue. There was no chance of this being accepted. The Report became in part the basis of Russell's "Ten Resolutions" (March, 1837),[17] which projected the Imperial Parliament itself into the fight against the *Patriotes*. The Resolutions at once engaged the sympathies of English Radicals. Just as before 1776 Whigs like

[17] See p. 223.

Burke and Fox were firmly on the side of the colonial agitators, so now were radicals like Hume and Roebuck.

The Ten Resolutions drove the *Patriotes* to another well-recognized stage in the making of a revolution: they began to organize large and excited public meetings throughout the country and turn argument into passion. Nearly all the clergy had left the revolutionaries and were warning their flocks to remember that "the powers that be are ordained of God." The session of August, 1837, the last session of the Assembly of Lower Canada to be held, lasted only a week, for Papineau still commanded a majority and would vote no supplies. Mass demonstrations began in the Montreal area: the governor was burned in effigy, the captains of militia refused to read his proclamations, and "Sons of Liberty" were organized in Montreal. It was with difficulty that the English, or "Constitutionalists", were held in check; they wished, as the extreme right wing always does under such circumstances, to "teach them a lesson".

3. The Inevitable Explosion: Rebellion

By the fall of 1837, the *Patriotes* had reached the position to which the logic of their programme carried them. They were finished with compromises, finished with English rule. They were out for independence as a democratic republic and, it must be presumed, were willing to fight for it. A meeting held at St. Charles on October 23, called itself an Assembly and went some distance towards organizing a provisional government. Papineau, who for all his fieriness was not of revolutionary stuff, now began to waver and to counsel constitutional means again instead of inflaming his audience. However, matters had gone beyond him, and sterner spirits were in control. At last, November 22, 1837, at St. Denis, bloodshed occurred and in exactly the same way as at Lexington sixty-two years before: a column of troops sent to arrest offenders (in 1837 Papineau himself was one) encountered a band of patriots, and shooting began. But there the parallel ended. For Lower Canada, whose leaders had taken a course that would require an army but who had not had the cold precision of purpose that would have organized one, St. Denis was not to be the opening of a long hard struggle crowned by victory, but of a brief and unsuccessful armed rebellion. The rebels fought well, but after a few sharp encounters the affair was all over, and the *Patriotes* scattered, never again to come together as a party.

The Lower Canadian revolution had failed. It had failed not only because of the division of the province into French and English, but also because of divisions among the French themselves and of the type of men who had attempted to make it. To upset a regime requires more than oratory. It requires more than the prophetic fanatic, such as Papineau was. It requires careful organization, military experience,[18] money and the support, or at least acquiescence of, the masses. The *Patriotes* had none of these. The cry of *à bas les Anglais* was no substitute for the positive programme needed to rally a shrewd and cautious French peasantry, nor had the rebels succeeded in securing any degree of unanimity among other classes of the population. In any Catholic country it has always proved hard to effect political changes, for the church instinctively fears reform, and still more it fears revolution. Any Catholic population will normally be split at such periods, the upper clergy and many of the faithful standing aloof, neutral at best, some actively in support of the powers that be. Only among the lower clergy, intimate with the people, will there be found an element willing to risk disobedience and join the movement. The Lower Canada of the 1830's illustrated these conditions exactly. There was an additional reason: reform among Catholics often involves a break with the Church. This, too, was the case in 1837. The movement had got into the wrong hands: American influences, so visible during the ten years prior to the outbreak, might perhaps have been tolerated, but Papineau and some of his followers had taken another, and the wrong, turning: they had been influenced by European liberalism. The nature of that enemy was well-known: it meant intolerance of authority, anti-clericalism, free-masonry, confiscation of Church lands—and atheism! Papineau himself was a rationalist, strongly under the influence of advanced French ideas, much impressed with the July Revolution in France. By 1836, he was lumping the clergy along with the moderates as betrayers of the people's cause, and at about the same time, his followers were spreading a work condemned by the Church and whose circulation had been forbidden by the Canadian bishops, the gospel of the liberals of old France, Lamennais' *Paroles d'un Croyant*.

The Rebellion of 1837 as a military movement may have been a flash in the pan, but as an incipient revolution it struck deep. While most of the French themselves deserted the Revolutionaries, there were none among them who did not recognize the justice of the cause. If many turned back, it was because Papineau was offering them not the re-establishment of the *ancien régime* but something very much like the free-thinking, anti-clerical First Republic. To the majority of the French, much more representative of French Canada than the Papineau group, the way to salvation seemed to lead not through revolution but through

---

[18] Among the rebel leaders, Dr. Wolfred Nelson was one of the few with military experience. See note 11 of this chapter.

compromise, acceptance of the English regime, and use of the weapons of constitutionalism which the English had obligingly furnished. After all it was not the metropolis that was the enemy; the enemy were within, they were few, though powerful, and could be fought. They were *"les vrais coupables . . . ces fanatiques, ces bureaucrates, ces favoris du pouvoir qui, depuis 1763, sournoisement ou à ciel ouvert en prenaient à tout ce qu'il y avait de français et de catholique."*[19]

Chronology

1815-36 L. J. Papineau speaker of the Assembly.
1822   The Union bill, for uniting Upper and Lower Canada. Transmuted into The Canada Trade Act.
1823   Receiver-General Caldwell's defalcations.
1827   Dalhousie's refusal to accept Papineau as speaker.
1828   The "Canada Committee" of the British Parliament.
1829   Representation of Eastern Townships provided for.
1830   Proposal for an elective legislative council.
1831   Major Crown revenues transferred to Assembly.
          Judges removed from Legislative Council.
1834   The 92 Resolutions of Grievances.
          Committees of Correspondence.
          Papineau party win general election.
1835   Lord Gosford Governor-General.
          "The Constitutional Association" of Montreal and Quebec, formed in opposition to Papineau.
1836   Assembly refuses supplies.
1837   The Gosford Report.
          March 6: The Russell Resolutions.
          August 26: Assembly prorogued after two-day session.
          Revolutionary mass meetings begin.
          November 23: Rebellion in Lower Canada. Engagements of St. Denis, St. Charles, St. Eustache. Papineau flees to U.S.A.

Additional Reading

Audet Louis Philippe. *Le Système scolaire de la province de Québec.* Quebec, 1955.
David, L. O. *Les deux Papineau.* Montreal, 1896.
De Celles, A. D. *Papineau.* London, 1926.
———. *The "Patriotes" of '37.* (Chronicles of Canada, Vol. 25) Toronto, 1916.
Manning, Helen Taft. *The Revolt of French Canada, 1800-1835.* Toronto, 1962.
Ouellet, Fernand. *Louis-Joseph Papineau: Un être divisé.* (*CHA* Booklets No. 11) Ottawa, 1960. (Translated under the title, *Louis Joseph Papineau, A Divided Soul*).
———. *Louis-Joseph Papineau: Textes choisis.* Quebec, 1958.

[19] Bruchési, II, 162. "Those really responsible were the fanatics, the office-holders, the favourites of power, those who, since 1763, secretly or in the open, had been trying to put down whatever was French and Catholic."

CHAPTER 18

Privilege on a Frontier: Upper Canada, 1815-1837

1. Privilege in Church, State, and Affairs

The long line that stretched from London up the St. Lawrence carried with it more than trade goods: it carried institutions of society and government. Governor Simcoe's effort to duplicate the English countryside in the wilderness of Upper Canada[1] had been an aspect of that same whole of which the timber trade, the Church of England, and the railway builders of the 1850's were other parts. They were all varying aspects of metropolitanism. Contrasted with them were the forces growing out of the soil: the absorption in local and familiar things, the resentment against the abuses in land-granting and against government in the interests of the few, a debtor psychology, hostility towards the attempt to impose religious practices from above. The antithesis between exploitation and settlement did not have, it is true, the sharp edge which racial difference lent to it in Lower Canada, and Upper Canadian farmers were constantly passing into the commercial classes, yet the two strands in the community were only too clearly visible and the problem was plain: was Upper Canada to be for the favoured few or for the many on the land?

In the thirty-five years between the organization of the province and

[1] See p. 166.

the beginning of the new immigration which was to change its character, or from 1791 to 1825, privilege had deeply entrenched itself. The movement for an established church had proceeded on every front. Ten years after the war of 1812, land set aside for the support of "a Protestant Clergy" already amounted to two million acres.[2] A few years later on (1836), Sir John Colborne, then governor, invoking an unused clause of the Constitutional Act, endowed from the Reserves forty-six Church of England rectories. Other privileges which the law gave the Anglican Church were strenuously defended. Its clergy were the only ministers, apart from Roman Catholics, who as a matter of course, were entitled to solemnize marriage. "Calvinists" had been admitted to this right by statute (1798) and while this term was stretched to comprise obscure sects such as the Tunkers,[3] it was not allowed to include the leading Protestant denomination, the Methodists, who had to wait until 1831 before the predominantly Anglican Legislative Council condescended to extend it to them. In education, the effort of the Church of England to secure, in King's College and Upper Canada College, a monopoly of higher education (including large public endowments) failed only after a bitter struggle which deprived the province of the benefits of a University for some twenty years.[4] In the area of government, Archdeacon Strachan retained his seat in the two councils by virtue of his official position. The clergy of the Church of England sought and obtained a semi-official and social status to which no others could aspire.[5] Yet, despite all these efforts and despite the favour of successive governors, the Church of England never became an established church.

In the state, privilege was more invidious than in the church, for it had no moral basis to rest on. It was because of this that the little group of individuals who managed to keep the good things to themselves, the so-called "Family Compact", were so sensitive on the question of allegiance. The only warrant for their conduct was the King's will; they, therefore, were unremitting in their attempts to maintain themselves as the sole channels of royal grace and in efforts to make it appear that those who challenged their authority challenged the throne. Because it rested on this unstable foundation, privilege in Upper Canada took on a special *hauteur*, a high intolerance.

The members of the little governing body, as a rule, won their places

---

[2] Population 1824, 150,000. Average area under field crops in "old" Ontario today, about 9 million acres.
[3] F. Landon, *Western Ontario and the American Frontier,* p. 123.
[4] See p. 198.
[5] The Catholic bishop of Kingston was made a Legislative Councillor in 1831, but no other denomination was ever so represented.

by bringing the right family connections into association with some ability. A young man, such as Peter Robinson,[6] brother of the Attorney-General and later Chief Justice, Sir John Beverley Robinson,[7] might begin life by securing a seat in the assembly, where he would always be sure to vote on the side of the powers that were. He might be advanced to the Legislative Council and, if *persona grata* to the governor, he might be suggested for an office in government service. This might be a small one, but he might advance until he had secured one of the big prizes, such as Surveyor-General or Receiver-General. He would then be an official member of the Executive Council, close to the governor and with a part in the determination of policy. He would be in receipt of a salary, large for the time and place, on which he could keep up a considerable establishment.[8] He would have opportunities to share in whatever good things might be going, such as speculation in the public lands, flotation of banks or other financial companies, or in the 1830's, canal contracts. Much of this sort of thing must be present in any government. We tolerate a good deal of it today, but the essential reservation, that government may be turned out through an election or on the floor of parliament, prevents it from biting into us as it did into our ancestors. It was the spectacle of a privileged group whose title to privilege no one could ascertain that irked, even more than the privileges themselves.

These, however, were substantial. In addition to lands and salaries, there were pensions to be "wangled" and above all, patronage. The mere fight over the loaves and fishes may not have been the whole story, but considering circumstances at the time and the eternal nature of politics, it must have been a great part of it. In the Canada of a century and a quarter ago, "a government job" meant dignity, security, and social status. For the masses, who did not get "government jobs", it usually signified little work and much play. In the days of irresponsible government, not only was patronage within a narrow circle but it was always conferred in the same direction, upon the safe and loyal people, upon "friends of government", upon Tories.

Privilege in politics can never be separated from economic privilege.

[6] M.L.A., 1817. Commissioner of Crown Lands, Executive and Legislative Councillor, 1827-36. He was found short in his accounts, and resigned. His brother undertook to make the shortage good.
[7] 1791-1863. Prominent Family Compact leader. Attorney-General, 1818. M.L.A., 1821. Chief Justice, speaker of Legislative Council, and President of Executive Council, 1830.
[8] Sir John Beverley Robinson, it is said, used to ride around Muddy York in his coach and four.

There was a close association between the "Family Compact" and the more ambitious business schemes of the time, notably the Bank of Upper Canada, which came to be regarded as the fortress of the "government men". When in the panic of 1837, it refused to suspend specie payments, the allegation went out that it was trying to break the smaller banks in order to monopolize financial power. This may not have been wholly just, but it accentuated the atmosphere of discontent.

There were similar dissensions over the great public works that were undertaken in the 1830's, the St. Lawrence canals.[9] The canal system was an integral aspect of the commercial state, the link between metropolis and hinterland. Its immediate services would have been to vessel-owners, forwarders, and merchants, but not much foresight should have been required to see its vast indirect benefits to the producers. The Upper Canadian farmer was no more remarkable for long views than other settlers, and the cry soon went up that the province was being ruined for the benefit of a few contractors, linked to the "ruling class". Agitators made the most of the situation, which nevertheless was, as they described it, an area for Family Compact patronage,[10] and one of the soundest of all the current economic conceptions was made to add to the prevailing dissensions and discontent.

2. A Growing Society and a Static Conception of Government

If those in control had given progressive and efficient government, the ordinary man might have put up with privilege indefinitely. But instead the province had to suffer the evils of ineffective and unimaginative administration. In some respects the situation was the reverse of that in Lower Canada: there a minority in control was too active and aggressive for the conservative majority, but in Upper Canada, everyone would have welcomed "progress".

The land question, already discussed, was the major example of inefficiency. It is hard to see what greater evil there could have been than the settler's inability to get quick and sure title to his land. Often he could not even be sure that he was located on a specified piece of land, for surveys were notoriously bad.

Another area where antiquated notions or actual privilege touched the settler closely was that of local institutions.[11] The original American

[9] See p. 206ff.
[10] See C. P. Lucas, ed., *Lord Durham's Report on the Affairs of British North America* (Oxford, 1912), II, 189.
[11] See J. H. Aitchison, "The Municipal Corporations Act of 1849," *CHR*, XXX (June, 1949), 107-122.

Loyalist settlers had brought with them that admirable New England institution, the town meeting, but its introduction had caused alarm to Governor Simcoe, familiar with the way Sam Adams had kept the flames of revolution fanned with it ("the very serpent's head of rebellion", he called it) and although it had been legalized, he had reduced its powers to trifles. Most of the duties of local government went to an artificial body patterned, like other ideas of Simcoe's, on English usage, the Board of Quarter Session. This body consisted of the magistrates of the district, who were appointive. Simcoe had gone on to create County Lieutenants, imitating the English system of Lord-Lieutenancies but because they, like municipal councils, might subtract from the power of the Crown, the Colonial Office had forbidden them. The magistrates soon became mere local extensions of the Family Compact. The most numerous class among them was the half-pay officer. It was as if in early twentieth-century Western Canada the "remittance-men" had been appointed from Ottawa to govern the countryside. Such men were out of touch with their constituents, had little insight into the needs of their districts, and introduced English class conceptions repellent to the genius of the New World. They must have represented just so many centres of grievance, sore spots ready to be inflamed when the troublous times came along.

In the Boards of Quarter Sessions rested practically all local government: roads, bridges, drains, dams, the peace, and institutions of correction. The gap between them and the countryside, joined to the absence of a system of local taxation, had results ranging from unsatisfactory to deplorable. Roads and bridges could not be built on the basis of statute labour alone: consequently, as a rule, they were not built. The community naturally sought relief through the local member of the Assembly, thus projecting parochial affairs into a parliamentary body. Members tried to serve the interests of their constituents by obtaining cash grants towards this local project or that: thus was built up the famous practice of "log-rolling". Just as the neighbours got together to roll up the newly-cut logs from a clearing into piles for burning, so the members "rolled up" each other's financial logs. Before the Act of Union (1840), any member could introduce a resolution for a money appropriation (there was no such thing as "a private member"). Since there was no chance of one vote going through if others were voted down, what usually happened, in the dying days of the session, was a swift orgy of unanimous money votes, each moved by the member for the benefitting constituency and supported by the others.

The provincial government was no more successful in dealing with Lower Canada than in supplying good municipal institutions. The

Assembly of Lower Canada imposed for revenue purposes a duty of five per cent on all imports. Upper Canada, to which many of the imports went, was not very successful in getting its share of the amount collected. This did nothing to increase the government's popularity.

The conditions out of which the rebellion grew stare us in the face. All of them were accentuated by the constant painful contrast afforded by the good government and prosperity of the neighbouring states. The explanation for all afflictions, whether public or private, was naturally ready to hand: it was "the government". But it is a long step from discontent to armed violence, a step that needs explanation.

3. The Emergence of Parties

The political evolution of Upper Canada possesses one marked contrast with that of Lower Canada in that in the one there emerged a party system and in the other only a division of race. In Upper Canada, the absence of racial differences prevented issues from becoming quite as clear-cut. Persons whose sympathies or affiliations were with authority were not, as tended to be the case in Lower Canada, automatically deprived of the chance to gain seats in the Assembly. At times they possessed an actual majority. When they did so, as in 1830 and 1836, harmony could reign among Assembly, Councils, and Governor. Unfortunately for their own interests, the group which at these times was in undisputed possession of power and which stood for privilege could evolve no popular and constructive programme, so that its defeat in due course was assured. Yet such members in the Assembly could always claim to represent the popular will; they thus acted as a cushion between the privileged class and the people.

Those who were opposed to privilege lacked the infallible rallying point of race, and were often divided among themselves. In reform movements there are apt to be as many groups as there are opinions. This was true in Upper Canada, where several distinct interests were pressing for their own reforms. Reforms in Upper Canada never had the cohesion that, right up to the fighting, race gave it in Lower Canada. Nor could there be the same singleness of leadership. Where in Lower Canada one powerful personality (Papineau) dominated, in Upper Canada various individuals held the stage. In Upper Canada the revolutionary tendencies were muffled by the prospect of constitutional reform, and the revolutionary group ultimately was smaller and less representative. For Upper Canada the prospect of adjustment through reform never disappeared, but in Lower Canada no reform could make the clash of race disappear. Good government in Upper Canada would have prevented the rebellion but in Lower Canada good government would have been of no more avail than it was in modern India before independence.

Save for such differences, the movement of events in the two provinces was not unlike. There was the same period of conflict during which the lines were formed, the same phase of constitutionalism, the same radical agitation headed by a dominating, narrow-minded, and highly intense personality, passing into efforts to rouse the masses through great public meetings, surrender of hope of reform, organization for coercion of authority by threat of violence, and then the embracing of the ultimate remedy, a new regime through revolution. In both provinces the moderates fell away, though later in Upper than in Lower Canada, leaving the movement in the hands of those resolved to win through at any cost. Eventually and logically, armed outbreak followed.

It was in 1817 with the arrival in Upper Canada of Robert Gourlay that the contest really began. Gourlay, like the Mackenzies, the Macdonalds, and the Browns, was one of Scotland's gifts to Canada of whom, whatever else can be said, mere sane mediocrity cannot be alleged. He was a natural trouble maker, a disputatious person to whom it was "the principle of the thing" that mattered. Gourlay had been a misfit wherever he had lived.

In compiling his *Statistical Account of Upper Canada* Gourlay encountered the land problem. His widely-circulated questionnaire[12] was enough in itself to mark him out as dangerous but when he went on to call a convention (a word of ominous ring in "loyal" ears) to discuss grievances, the situation became intolerable to those in authority (whose conduct might not have stood much investigation). Gourlay had to be crushed, and crushed he was by as sorry a manipulation of the law and the bench as ever disgraced a British country. "British justice" did not mean much (the case of Lord Selkirk is comparable[13]), when it touched the private interests of the very "British" persons affected, who never tired of ringing the changes on the word but were so blind to its essential significance. Gourlay was driven from the province a broken man,[14] but his case had brought the situation sharply before the public.

One year after Gourlay's arrival, Upper Canada received a contribution from another sector of British society in the person of Sir Peregrine Maitland, the impecunious soldier who had eloped with the daughter of the Duke of Richmond. When the young couple were duly forgiven,

[12] See p. 190.
[13] See p. 152.
[14] 1819.

the Duke, who was coming out as Governor-in-Chief, packed up Sir Peregrine along with his other baggage and brought him along with him as Lieutenant-Governor of Upper Canada, a post he was to hold for ten formative years.[15] Sir Peregrine was a Tory after Simcoe's cut but without Simcoe's energy and imagination: he was crammed with the pet prejudices of religion, flag, and caste, the perfect Colonel Blimp. To the provincial administration he must have seemed a gift from heaven, especially when he proved willing to give behind-the-scenes impetus to the Gourlay prosecution. A good deal of the leftward movement of events during the 1820's can be chalked up to Sir Peregrine's score.

After the expulsion of Gourlay, the authorities kept grievance alive by their refusals to redistribute seats in the Assembly. Here was a common phenomenon in colonial government, encountered regularly since the seventeenth century: the older areas in control were invariably reluctant to decrease their own influence as the country filled up by extending proportionate representation to the new districts, especially as these were invariably discontented and sure to be "agin' the government".[16] In the Upper Canada of the 1820's the newer settlements in the western peninsula were predominantly of American extraction and very much suspect; that part of the province was to remain the stronghold of pioneer agricultural radicalism for many years.

It was partly by its vote that in 1824 an Assembly was elected which contained a number of "reformers". The name was beginning to be used loosely for all who did not approve of things as they were, but was not yet a party label. The "reformers" of 1824 lacked cohesion and a platform; they formed only a loose opposition group, not an official opposition. Yet they were the fathers of the Reform party and through it of the Liberal party. The reformers of 1824 supported a bill to allow Methodist ministers to solemnize marriage. This was thrown out by the Council. Here was an issue sufficient in itself to press together two major aspects of reform, political and religious. In the same year the necessary ferment was stirred into the reform mixture in the shape of another unballasted young Scot, William Lyon Mackenzie,[17] who made his debut as editor of the celebrated *Colonial Advocate*. His paper at once signalized the arrival of a new force in public life: a man of ability, rash courage, a biting tongue, an over-facile pen, a burning sense of justice, and no over-weight of common sense—just the mixture needed for

[15] 1818-28.
[16] See, for Lower Canada, p. 222.
[17] 1795-1861. Canada, 1820. Editor, 1824. M.L.A. for York, 1828. Expelled for "libel", 1831. Re-elected and expelled five times. First mayor of Toronto, 1835. Rebel and fugitive, 1837.

quickening the pace by keeping every one on edge. His articles, aspersing the private lives and ancestry of some of the leading members of the Compact, earned him the destruction of his press (1826) by Compact believers in direct action, but he snatched victory out of this defeat by a suit for damages that set him on his feet financially.[18]

In 1828, the Reformers had so far gained ground as to have a majority in the Assembly, included in which was now Mackenzie. In those days a majority availed little, for its proposals, no matter how good, were almost certain to be turned down by the Legislative Council. Those that did run the gauntlet might be vetoed by the governor, or "referred home" and forgotten. The session of 1828 constituted a drastic example, 58 Assembly bills being killed in the Council. Though they may have appeared radical, the proposals of the Reformers were strictly constitutional. They were also indicative of the various groups pressing for reform. The Methodists and other "dissenters" were advocating secularization of the Clergy Reserves, the proceeds to be devoted to education; Mackenzie radicalism would have taken part of them for road building. Other reforms, advocated by individuals or small groups, consisted in the removal of judges from the legislature, their independence,[19] some reform of the council, and a vague suggestion of "responsible government".

It was the battle between Anglicanism and Methodism, between Strachan[20] and Ryerson,[21] which raged most fiercely. Hitherto, Methodism had been on the defensive and had accepted the scorn and sneers of Anglicans without retort, for it was still under the cloud of republicanism. Now, however, in the person of young Egerton Ryerson, whose political principles, as son of a Loyalist and born an Anglican, could not be traduced, it had found a David to advance against the Goliath of ecclesiastical privilege. Strachan's furious blast against Methodists and republicans, in his sermon on the death of Bishop Mountain[22] in 1825, received the rejoinder it deserved in the form of an able and devastating pamphlet, written and printed by Ryerson within a few days. Ryerson's pamphlet made Methodism a political force, a powerful wing of reform. No more could Strachan mislead the home authorities at will with his counterfeit "Ecclesiastical Charts" and other such

[18] He collected £625. Joseph Howe's victory in Nova Scotia (1835) is a parallel case.
[19] Until 1834, colonial judges were appointed during pleasure, not during good behaviour.
[20] See pp. 165, 198, 232.
[21] See pp. 167, 197.
[22] First Anglican bishop of Quebec, 1793-1825.

documents:[23] if the Anglicans possessed influence and many of the educated, the Methodists had numbers, for by 1825 they were the largest denomination in the province.

Demand for an elective council did not come until the 1830's, when Jacksonian democracy was making itself felt in Upper Canada. The words "responsible government" had not become popular currency, and there were possibly only two men in the province who really understood what they involved, Dr. William Baldwin[24] and his more famous son, Robert.[25] It was in 1829 that these two submitted a memorandum to the Duke of Wellington, then Prime Minister of England, explaining the term and urging that the form of government indicated be given a trial in Upper Canada. What they had in mind was simply ministerial government, in which the executive would at all times have to maintain a majority in the popular house or resign. The mechanism was simple and was to prove a solution for colonial difficulties, but in 1829 it was almost revolutionary. The Duke resigned shortly afterward, and the memorandum received no attention. But when Robert Baldwin entered public life, the project of responsible government entered with him, and when he left (1851), it had been accomplished. To Baldwin, far more than to Lord Durham, must go the credit for having sponsored the only device capable of retaining the colonies in the Empire and of reconciling Imperial and local interests. He soon gathered about him a strictly constitutional group, Baldwin reformers, as they came to be called.

In the elections of 1830, the authorities called on "friends of government" to rally to it, the never-failing device of "flag-waving" was employed, and an Assembly was returned in which reformers were in a minority. The reform movement was, however, in no danger of dying, for William Lyon Mackenzie was coming to the front as its leader, and his resource in finding fuel for the fire was inexhaustible. In the House he followed the tactic of moving for inquiries into abuses, outside of it he kept the quarrel going in his newspaper. It was the increasingly bitter controversies of the four years of the "loyal" Assembly that resolved the situation clearly into its constituent elements, preparing the way for

[23] Strachan had computed the number of Anglicans by the simple process of adding up known adherents of other denominations and subtracting the result from the total population of the province.

[24] 1775-1844. M.L.A. 1824-30, 1841-43.

[25] 1804-1858. M.L.A. 1829-30. Appointed member of Executive Council, 1836. Resigned over differences with Lieutenant-Governor as to constitutional functions of Executive Council. Similar experience with Governor Sydenham 1841. Formed semi-responsible Council with Lafontaine under Governor Bagot, 1842. 1848-51, the Baldwin-Lafontaine "Great Ministry", the first responsible government.

the ultimate test of strength. Mackenzie's sharp tongue and sharper pen earned him a personal assault, and the repeated expulsions from the Assembly that made him a popular hero. After five re-elections, his cup of satisfaction was filled by his election as the first mayor of the new city of Toronto. That it was a contest between privilege and a somewhat noisy though constitutional reformer was made evident by the governor's[26] coolness to the method of expulsion used against him and by Mackenzie's favourable reception in England where Lord Goderich,[27] who was anxious to penetrate the situation obtaining in both provinces, gave him a cordial hearing. Had Mackenzie been able to use one word instead of three, he might have got farther still, but no busy minister could be expected to read the interminable pages that the reformer proliferated.

While in England Mackenzie built up his connections with the left wing of the Whig party, then known loosely as "the Radicals". These men were the intellectuals of the day. They shaded out from the empiricism of progressives like Charles Poulett Thomson to the doctrinaire radicalism of men like Joseph Hume. Disciples of Adam Smith or Jeremy Bentham, they were believers in *laisser-faire* and the other articles of the Utilitarian creed. The antagonism of Radicalism to monarchy and aristocracy easily came *en rapport* with what it understood to be American democracy (though its exponents, as scholars and gentlemen, would have found it hard to endure the reality) and its insistence on equality in church, state, and society, and on republicanism. Mackenzie's visit to England, which had been preceded by a trip to Washington, 1829, where he had had an interview with President Jackson,[28] came at a time when the tide of Jacksonian democracy in the United States was at the flood and beginning to spill over into Canada. Just as French Liberalism and American democracy converged in Louis Joseph Papineau, so in Upper Canada, the two channels of thought, English radicalism and American democracy, united in Mackenzie.

Mackenzie was not the only Canadian to appear in London. Egerton Ryerson, over there on the business of freeing his co-religionists from charges of republicanism by uniting them with British Wesleyanism,[29] also heard about Hume, Roebuck, and Grote, and what he heard was not to their credit. He had a place for them in his analysis of parties, which under the title of *"English Impressions"* he printed in the

[26] Sir John Colborne, Lieutenant-Governor, 1825-35.
[27] Colonial Secretary, 1830-33.
[28] Landon, *op. cit.*, 153.
[29] See p. 197.

Christian Guardian on his return (1833). For high Tories he had bitter words, for moderate Tories moderate words, for Whigs, words of commendation; but he had discovered that the Radicals were atheistical, and that was the label he pinned on them in Canada. This was defaming Mackenzie indirectly: and what kind of defamation could have been more effective in the highly religious province? Mackenzie at once made a characteristically vituperative denunciation of Ryerson (October 30, 1833) and the ensuing break between the two divided the reformers; there were now Methodist reformers, Mackenzie radicals, and the looser body of constitutional reformers looking to Robert Baldwin. From 1834 on, Methodism became more conservative: it could no longer be considered on the side of political progress in general but only zealous for its own special interests (such as equitable disposition of the Clergy Reserves).

The battle was left to the other two, who in 1834 succeeded in reversing the verdict of 1830. Mackenzie was apparently now determined to reach a solution one way or another, for he drove harder than ever at his task of discrediting the provincial government. As Chairman of the Special Committee of Grievances, he dug up innumerable points of abuse and suggested remedies: his purview included patronage, salaries, pensions, public lands, title deeds, roads, surveys, Clergy Reserves, and the privileges of the Church of England. Among his suggestions now appeared an elective legislative council, in part imitative of the demands of Lower Canada, in part derived from American practice, and in part resulting from the logic of frontier democracy. To the list was added "responsible government", though it has yet to be proved that Mackenzie had grasped in any satisfactory way what was meant by the term. In all this there was nothing that suggested anything but constitutional reform.

Meanwhile, Sir John Colborne had been replaced by Sir Francis Bond Head,[30] one of the most extraordinary appointments ever made to public office. The legend goes that the letter of appointment reached the wrong man. That is perhaps as plausible an explanation as any. Head was the first non-military appointee. He had had no experience of public life and in temperament was unfitted to deal with a colonial assembly. He had had some business experience in South America; possibly it was this "American" experience that secured him the place. He was a figure of sound and fury, without dignity, convinced that American democracy was the great enemy and British constitutionalism the robe of spotless purity. When men like Baldwin took him at his

[30] Lieutenant-Governor, 1836-38.

word and attempted to secure just that, a British constitutional government, Head discovered that a colony was a colony after all and not
entitled to the robe.

Head began well. For a moment it looked as if Baldwin was to win
through with his idea of responsible government. The authorities in
England were anxious to see a contented province and had no desire to
sustain a mere clique in its privileges; they were ready to relinquish to
the Upper Canadian Assembly, as to the Lower, practically all Crown
revenues. Head was in tune with them when he offered Baldwin and
two of his colleagues seats in the Executive Council. As Baldwin could
secure a favourable vote in the Assembly, surely this must mean a
ministerial government. Disillusionment came quickly. The governor
refused to be bound by the advice of his councillors. Therefore, they
did not have his confidence. They resigned, and the semi-responsible
ministry promptly ended.

4. The Approach of Rebellion

Baldwin's constitutional approach to self-government had failed, as
Mackenzie's tactics of agitation had failed, and now Assembly and
Governor were in direct opposition. The province was in an uproar, all
shades of reformers being thrown together, meetings being held, and
organization taking place. The Assembly voted want of confidence in
the new executive, asserted that "responsible government" was already
part of the constitution, which of course it was not, and withheld
supply. Head met the challenge by the time-honoured expedient of a
dissolution and added a typical twist of his own, reserving all the money
bills of the session in an attempt to throw responsibility for the confusion on the Assemblymen. In the election campaign he himself
virtually got out on the stump, making bombastic speeches, raising the
Loyalty cry and shouting anti-Americanism. It was a rare spectacle for
a representative of the Crown to afford.

Nevertheless his tactics succeeded, as they have never failed to succeed, in Ontario. Tories damned reform and reformers by calling them
"American" and "Republican". "The object of the nasty republican trio,
that is to say of the hypocrite, the atheist, and the Deist . . . is to
wheedle weak and sinful souls into the path of rebellion. . . ."[31] Where
verbal denunciation was not enough, violence was added. As a result of
the election, Head got a compliant Assembly, which voted him supplies
and a civil list. Three factors had been uppermost in his victory. The

[31] Quoted in Landon, *op. cit.,* 157.

eastern part of the province was passing out of the frontier stage and not as much touched by current abuses as the west; the vote of its Loyalist population went consistently in support of government. Secondly, Egerton Ryerson had been cooling off since his discovery that Mackenzie radicalism had atheistic associations, and now in the crisis, his Loyalist and Tory side got the better of the dissenting and liberal. He had never been much interested in forms of government, and his main concern was now not political reform but Methodist interests. When cheers for King William were going up, Ryerson could not refrain from joining in. His influence turned many a Methodist vote.

The third factor was the recent heavy immigration. The claim was made by a Tory paper that the immigrants "exceeded in numbers, property and knowledge" all the rest of the population.[32] "Knowledge" may be queried: that seemed to manifest itself chiefly in the brawls of Irish shillelagh-slingers. Numbers, however, reactionary sentiments, and readiness to resort to physical force may be allowed. "The Orange mob is worse every election, so that it is impossible for any honest, peaceable reformer to give his vote for a member of parliament without the fear or realization of having his head broken."[33] In the elections of 1836, Ulster and Orangeism vaulted into the Upper Canadian saddle and for many a year they were not dismounted.

The election of the "loyal" assembly of 1836 ended the period of constitutional agitation. Not even the vote was effective against the will of the authorities, and reformers, if abuses were to be remedied, would have to take sterner measures. Mackenzie again was in the lead, with the moderates like Baldwin, true to their type, drawing back at this point and talking compromise, which to Mackenzie meant knuckling under. Mackenzie's new paper, *The Constitution*, which appeared July 4, 1836, contained articles close to the line: it began to sound a revolutionary note. The mass meetings throughout the province, organized by both sides, showed that the public temper was approaching the breaking point. Matters were not improved by the systematic Tory attempt to show that every Reformer was a republican traitor. While Reformers were influenced by American models, as Canadians are in everything, few of them wished more than reform. It was the impossibility of securing reform that drove a number of them to think in terms either of independence or of annexation. Even so, only a minority was prepared to go to extremes, and in the eastern part of the province, disaffection was slight. In the west it was much more widespread: from Toronto to Lake Huron, whether a man shouldered a musket or not, the

[32] Landon, 162.
[33] Quoted in Landon, 159.

chances were about two to one that his sympathies would be with the reformers and, in most cases, with the rebels.

The rebellion itself, when it finally came in December, 1837, was a far slighter affair than that in Lower Canada. Militarily, both sides behaved in the best traditions of comic opera. What strikes home today is not the fighting but the light the rebellion casts on what happens to a society that is rent in twain. As in the American Revolution, the number of active spirits was small, the number of sympathizers larger, and the number of people who tried to avoid decision larger still. Until a few years ago, it used to be supposed that the suppression of the rebellion was a decent proceeding all round, conducted with magnanimous desires to heal the wounds and involving only two executions, but today we know that triumphant Tories were guilty of cruelty of a kind hard to associate with Canadian life.[34] Such conduct widened the gulf. Far from deciding the political and social question, the Rebellion of 1837 in its failure and suppression, introduced into Canadian life fundamentally divisive issues which are still with us.

William Lyon Mackenzie, ill-starred leader of an ill-starred revolt, may yet not be lightly dismissed. Fanatic though he was, he was also something more. Although he cannot be hoisted into the position of the impeccable hero, on the plane of other rebels who have had better luck, it is also impossible to dissociate him from the cause of Canada. He stood for the plain man, for the many against the few, for democracy against privilege. He had the wit to discern what was wrong with his province and the courage to battle against it. Canada has had few men of rash courage and inflexible principle, and those few have each cut a wide swath. Mackenzie was one of these, a man whose many faults are lost in an essential integrity, a crusader for what he deemed the right and for what subsequent generations have approved as the right, and therefore a man to whom Canada owes much; more than to the ordinary politician and far more than to those she has as a rule preferred, the merely successful railroad builders, lumber kings, mining magnates or business men. Without Mackenzie, Upper Canada would have continued locked in its dreary provincial prison, but after he had brought it to the point of revolt, that was no longer possible: self-government was on the horizon, and just beyond it, national life.

[34] E. C. Guillet, *Lives and Times of the Patriots* (Toronto, 1938), especially Chap. 19. Tory conduct and the general hopelessness of the situation, which was deepened by the commercial depression of 1837, induced a purge of forward-looking elements from Upper Canada which went far beyond the actual rebels. Emigrants in their thousands streamed away from western Upper Canada. The best and most progressive settlers of the preceding decade are said to have been carried off. The rebellion thus reinforced the American Revolution in creating a conservative and even reactionary province.

Chronology

1817–19　Robert Gourlay in Upper Canada.
1821　　Bank of Upper Canada.
1824　　The Canada Conference of the Methodist Church instituted.
1825　　Reform majority in Assembly.
1826　　William Lyon Mackenzie's printing office wrecked.
1828　　Separation of Canadian Methodist Church from that of United States.
1829　　*Christian Guardian.*
1831　　First Expulsion of Mackenzie from the Assembly.
1832　　Mackenzie takes Grievances petitions to London.
　　　　Union of Canada and Wesleyan Methodists.
1834　　Reform majority in Assembly.
1835　　The "Seventh Report on Grievances".
1836　　Disagreement over nature of Executive Council.
　　　　General election gives Tories majority in Assembly.
1837　　December 5-7, Rebellion.

Additional Reading

Craig, Gerald. *Upper Canada: The Formative Years, 1784-1841.* Toronto, 1963.

Dunham, Aileen. *Political Unrest in Upper Canada, 1815-1836.* London, 1927.

Ewart, Alison and Julia Jarvis. "The Personnel of the Family Compact, 1791-1841." *CHR,* VII (Sept., 1926), 209-221.

Kilbourn, W. *The Firebrand: William Lyon Mackenzie and the Rebellion in Upper Canada.* Toronto, 1956.

Lindsay, C. *Life and Times of William Lyon Mackenzie.* Toronto, 1862. 2 vols.

Patterson, G. C. *Land Settlement in Upper Canada.* Toronto, 1921.

Sissons, C. B. *Egerton Ryerson, His Life and Letters.* Toronto, 1937-1947. 2 vols.

Sprague, G. W. "John Strachan's Contribution to Education, 1800-1823." *CHR,* XXII (June, 1941), 147-158.

Talman, J. J. "The Position of the Church of England in Upper Canada, 1791-1840." *CHR,* XV (Dec., 1934), 361-375.

CHAPTER 19

Liquidating the Rebellions

The rebellions may have been small affairs from a military standpoint and in the lives they cost, but the blood spilt in '37 was sacrificial blood, accomplishing as bloodshed often does, what years of talk could not have done. It sapped the vitality of privilege and rendered reform imperative. The rebellions gave to the French, after an interval, the control of their own province and to the Upper Canadians opportunity to work out a compromise between exploitation and settlement. The revolt of the French was more successful than that of the Upper Canadians, for it represented the movement of a people against their masters, and had not a fortunate conjunction of statesmen with events halted the revolutionary process at the stage of provincial autonomy, it might well have carried New France into the channels in which Ireland and India later found themselves. In Upper Canada, where the abuses in government that usually cause revolt were more serious, no such fate threatened and the settlement hardly had the same satisfactory clarity. Had the rebellion gone farther, the aftermath might have been a clearer appreciation of self-government, a firmer establishment of democracy, a more decisive rout of privilege, than actually occurred.

The fact that the rebellions had not been primarily against the British connection made them the more difficult for the Imperial government to understand. What was it the Canadians wanted? Reasonable concessions the British authorities were ready to accord. Their difficulty was that they did not imaginatively grasp actual colonial conditions. Canada was far away and not overly important in the British scheme of things. To many of the supporters of the Melbourne ministry (1834-41), it was the place from which came inferior timber at high prices, a colony that had succeeded in imposing its will, through the differential timber duties, upon the mother country. But even easy-going Melbourne had to do something when rebellion broke out.

1. Durham, "Lord High Executioner"

No other solution to colonial ills being in sight, the Imperial authorities resolved to try, for the second time, the usual procrastinating device of a Commission of inquiry[1] and the Durham mission was the result. Lord Durham,[2] son-in-law of Earl Grey, the previous Prime Minister, immensely rich, an aristocrat of the aristocrats, a man of first-class abilities, an experienced politician, well to the left in his views, was one of the uneasiest political bedfellows of the nineteenth century. "Radical Jack", as he was nicknamed, had been one of the principals in forcing through the Great Reform Bill. Lord Melbourne[3] had for a time solved the problem presented by such a troubler in Israel by inducing him to accept a special embassy to St. Petersburg,[4] but now Durham was back again, perhaps looking to the Whig leadership. What more natural than to get him out of the way again? Characteristic as the solution was, the easy-going Melbourne was no doubt not moved entirely by political expediency; everyone recognized Durham's abilities and when Melbourne offered him the high-sounding post of Governor-General and Lord High Commissioner of British North America, with unparalleled authority, the arrangement met with general approval.

Both in personality and ability, Durham was fitted for the difficult task ahead. A man of unbounded self-confidence, nothing could have suited him better than the chance to order the affairs of an entire world, even if one of the small dimensions of the St. Lawrence colonies. He was an intellectual who was fond of pomp, as witness his elaborate stage-entrance to Quebec, where on landing, he mounted a great white charger, and his retinue behind him, rode in solemn state to the Castle of St. Louis. Whether this made the expected impression on the natives is not recorded. In him eccentricities were coupled with high intellect;

---

[1] The Gosford Commission, 1835-39, had been the first.
[2] 1792-1840. Governor, May 20-Nov. 1, 1838. His famous *Report* submitted 31 Jan., 1839. The best life of Durham is Chester W. New, *Lord Durham* (Oxford, 1929).
[3] Whig Prime Minister, 1834-41.
[4] 1835-37.

his was the first outstanding English brain to occupy itself with the affairs of British North America. His character combined great rectitude with an attractive but difficult personality. An anecdote will illustrate this. Durham hated tobacco. On his voyage up the St. Lawrence to Upper Canada, strict instructions were given that no one on board must smoke. Once late at night, a whiff of tobacco smoke penetrated the Governor's cabin. Immediately orders were given to search the ship for the culprit. Finally he was discovered, squatting in hiding behind one of the boats. It was Vice-Admiral Sir Charles Paget, snatching a furtive cigar before turning in!

Perhaps it was imperiousness of temperament that led him to surround himself with certain men that a more tractable judgment would have rejected. Such were Thomas Turton,[5] who had been divorced, and under peculiarly malodorous circumstances, and above all, Gibbon Wakefield,[6] the man who had served a term in jail for abducting a young heiress. Wakefield had repented, but the fact that he had given more and better thought to colonizing than any other man in England was not sufficient to obliterate his lurid past. Although he came out privately and had no official connection with Durham, everyone knew that they were close, and he never ceased to be the object of bitter and uncharitable attacks by such journals as *The Church*. Charles Buller, the principal secretary, was too clever and too funny to meet with the approval of ordinary men. The Durham mission came to shipwreck on these rocks of personality and character, but it was the unconventional ability its members possessed that produced its spectacular results.

Durham began well by avoiding the invariable mistake of his predecessors: he refused to be taken into camp by the oligarchical clique. Keeping them at arms' length did not increase his popularity with the "best people". He spent the summer of 1838 in close investigation of the situation in Lower Canada, both personally and through various "Commissions" under his secretaries while at the same time he carried on the day-to-day tasks of administration. His evident desire for justice at first attracted French confidence. Then towards the end of the summer he appointed to the Commission on Municipal Institutions and as personal adviser, Adam Thom, editor of the *Montreal Herald*, a Scot who had only been in the country a few years but who had become one of its most reactionary Tories, a man unrestrained in his hate and con-

---

[5] A first-class lawyer, drafted Reform Bill of 1832.
[6] Wakefield (1796-1862) was the chief writer of his time on problems of settlement. He had marked influence on British colonial policy. The latest book on him is Paul Bloomfield, *Edward Gibbon Wakefield, Builder of the British Commonwealth* (London, 1961).

tempt of French-Canadians. Was he, after all, falling into the snares of the Chateau Clique? The French reserved judgment.

Durham's largest immediate problem was what to do with the political prisoners in the province, men who had taken part in the rebellion but whom no French-Canadian jury would convict, and whose very conviction would have widened still further the gulf between the races. To release them unconditionally was dangerous. Durham, never troubled too much by any sense of the limitation of his powers, decided to banish them to Bermuda, an island not within his jurisdiction. When the news got back to England, Lord Brougham, a man as difficult, as brilliant, and more unstable than Durham,[7] with whom Durham was not on good terms, attacked his action and secured considerable support in the Lords against it. To the everlasting dishonour of Melbourne, he weakly yielded and refused to uphold Durham's conduct. Durham himself first heard about his disgrace through the press. He acted characteristically in issuing a proclamation that almost suggested to the province that it would only get its abuses remedied by fighting again, resigned, and went home.[8]

2. The Durham Report and Its Reception

On the voyage back, the Report which was to be so formative in the future of Canada and the British Empire was put together. Much of it must have been prepared before the party left Quebec for it was published in a journalistic "scoop" by The Times just a few weeks after the frigate Inconstant landed Durham at Plymouth. It was formerly a favourite controversy of historians to quarrel about the authorship of the Report, some wishing to give the chief credit to Gibbon Wakefield. Wakefield as leader of the group of "systematic colonizers", had been in close touch with Durham for some years and their ideas must have been familiar to each other. Wakefield's was the more original mind: his efforts and his analysis of problems relating to immigration, settlement and land policy place him along with Richard Hakluyt and William Penn in the extension of the English race overseas. South Australia and New Zealand are his monuments. But Durham was still the "Radical Jack" of the Reform Bill, his mind was still fertile in generous political ideas. The Report was probably a composite, for it reflects the ideas and style of the two men, if not of others of the party too. The important thing is not its authorship since, after all, the leading reform idea in it, Responsible Government, belonged to Robert Baldwin, not to this group.

[7] Brougham had been Lord Chancellor and was at the time in opposition.
[8] He was in bad health and died within two years.

But in its extraordinary incisiveness, and its bold constructive proposals the Report to this day remains the best and most readable book on the Canada of the 1830's.

On this trip to Upper Canada, Durham had had a short conversation with Baldwin, who sent on to him a memorandum on his central concept, Responsible Government; this appeared as one of the two leading recommendations of the Report—self-government in internal affairs. Only three or four subjects—the constitution, foreign relations, colonial trade with foreign countries, the public lands—really concerned the Imperial government: all else could be better looked after on the spot. Thus, quite incidentally, the important federal principle of the division of powers found itself incorporated in the Report. For local self-government there appeared only one recipe, the equally important idea of Responsible Government: let the governor follow the advice of those who could get popular support behind them, as reflected by a majority in the Assembly. Then Crown, advisers, legislature, and people would be brought into line, and harmony instead of discord would result.

The other recommendation was not so happy. Durham's energetic and "progressive" nature did not lend itself to understanding a people with so different a view of life as the French; he saw their indifference to material progress, their primitive dwellings and farming methods, he noted their indifference to education, and he searched in vain for French-Canadian literature, for a single French-Canadian book.[9] Their very language was not the French that he knew. He concluded that this simple peasant people was sunk in apathy and that the greatest kindness to them would be to initiate them into the blessings of English civilization by gradually making them into Englishmen. This need not be done by force. Who, when given such an opportunity, would refuse it? His position was not much different from Pitt's 48 years before, when he professed to believe that the very image and transcript of the British Constitution then given to the Canadians would make them hasten to abandon their old institutions and culture. The gate to "anglification" was to be opened by the simple device of the union of the two Canadas: the powerful contagion of English example would then do the rest. As a result, few good words have ever been said for Durham in Quebec. French-speaking Canadians recognize his sincerity and his magnanimity in other directions, but they find it hard to forget that he said they had no culture or language worth preserving and that what little they had they ought to be content to lose. The Report, by the emotion it stirred

* His search would have been even more barren in English Upper Canada.

up among the French, must be considered one of the principal instruments making for the preservation of French nationality.

The supreme excellence of the Report, aside from its recommendation of local self-government, consists in the extraordinary penetration of its analysis. Who is there who does not know those classic phrases: "I expected to find a contest between a government and a people: I found two nations warring in the bosom of a single state. I found a struggle not of principles but of races". Englishmen had little in their own experience to enable them to understand the racial situation in Lower Canada, though they could have found it across the Irish Sea, and this failure to understand had been a large part of the trouble. Durham put his finger on the difficulty at once. Further, he described in exact terms the natures of the two struggling civilizations. All the more wonder, then, that he failed so signally to understand one of them. But apparently he was imbedded too far in the individualistic, Protestant commercialism of the time to be able to see virtue in medievalism.

Yet he had no sympathy with the narrow commercial group in Lower Canada that had succeeded in getting so much power into its hands and had been so kind with public favours to its members. A Whig oligarch himself and the son-in-law of a Whig oligarch, Earl Grey, he and his father-in-law had fought through into law the bill which went far to destroy English oligarchy; he was not likely to have much sympathy with the rather shabby version of oligarchy that he found on the banks of the St. Lawrence. Nor did he have any more regard for the great gentlemen who composed the Family Compact at Toronto, and brief as his sojourn in Upper Canada was, he subjected them to as severe an exposure as their opposite numbers in Lower Canada received.

Political analysis was the area in which he might be expected to excel. But the public land situation was laid open with the same sharp scalpel, though since this was Wakefield's special interest, this section of the Report was most likely worked up by him. Methods of land-granting were reviewed and its abuses[10] brought to light. Robert Gourlay's concern received abundant justification. Wasteful granting, fraudulent grants, the difficulties the ordinary settler had in getting title, all these were condemned. No exception was made for the Clergy Reserves. The Report took the position that most fair-minded English officials (invariably Anglicans themselves) arrived at when they saw the situation with their own eyes. In a country where Anglicans were in a minority, a country which cherished social equality and hated the idea of establishments of religion, it was not only idle but wicked for a little group of

[10] See p. 190ff.

wilful men to attempt to barricade themselves behind the privileges of Anglicanism. The Simcoes, the Maitlands, the Strachans, in their narrow insistence on denominational privilege, were not advancing the interests of their church but retarding them.

Durham drew a sharp line between ecclesiasticism and religion; his condemnation was reserved for the former. For ministers of religion, wherever found, he had nothing but good words. He praised the priests of French Canada as men devoted to their people, pious, earnest and moral. For the intolerance that, especially in the upper province, made a virtue of Catholic-baiting he had words of condemnation, words which fell with biting emphasis upon the professional Protestants, the rowdy, intolerant, power-seeking Orangemen.

The Report covered every other important public subject: immigration, education, local government, legal institutions, hospitals, finance. On each one of these, its words were trenchant and its views incisive. They all sprang from the same soil, that of liberal and cultivated English minds, from the great English Whig tradition whence had come the American Revolution (and indirectly the French Revolution), whence had come the Reform movements in British North America. The Report constituted both in spirit and in letter, the complete answer to Toryism. It spoke, in different terms, the same language as the elder Pitt, Edmund Burke, or Thomas Jefferson. In time to come its spirit was to be reborn in the conduct of Lord Elgin, the utterances of Sir Wilfrid Laurier and President Wilson, or the dicta of the Balfour Report of 1926. It is as a great liberal document that it takes its place as one of the foundation stones of the modern English-speaking world.

In both Great Britain and Canada the Report had a mingled reception. Upper Canadian reformers welcomed it warmly. The French saw in it an instrument for their extinction: the "anglification" suggestions blinded them to the more positive proposals and they remained suspicious and sulking. It was, however, among the loyalest of the loyal that the greatest storm arose: Tories everywhere cursed it. Durham's proposals, they averred, were merely rewards to rebellion. To put them into force would be to encourage the King's enemies and betray the friends of government. The Melbourne Government, which was becoming weaker every day, was only too glad to take refuge in the confused state of domestic politics and postpone action.[11] So 1839 dragged on, with only stop-gap governments in the affected colonies.

---

[11] In 1839 Melbourne resigned; Peel took office, then resigned, and Melbourne returned.

3. American Attitudes

In the United States, it was the rebellions rather than the Report, which got attention. The Report could only impress the educated few but nothing was better calculated to draw the excited interest of the many than what seemed like a second edition of the American Revolution. The rebellions renewed all their old revolutionary antipathy to the British and permitted all the old slogans to be trotted out and dusted off: "who would be the subject, or slave, of a king when he could be a free man and a citizen?" The period makes it easy to understand where Charles Dickens got the nonsense he put into the American chapters of *Martin Chuzzlewit*. Talk leading to action, it was not long before bands of sympathizers began to form which soon contemplated nothing less than liberation of the Canadas from "British tyranny". Rebels, who had escaped over the line, joined and encouraged these bands. Within six weeks after the outbreaks the border was in a state of complete unrest, and the Canadian authorities were preparing to resist the attack. Many American sympathizers had formed themselves into "Hunters' Lodges", secret societies of invasion and liberation. In the fall of 1838 attacks began on border points such as Prescott, and although these were easily repelled, sporadic violence, degenerating into isolated and criminal acts, continued until the early 1840's. Only the correct conduct—correct, but dilatory and possibly lukewarm—of the American government and its resolute attempt to control its citizens, after an initial period of laxity, prevented the strife from widening out into a dangerous international rift.[12] One is reminded of the United States and Cuba in the 1960's.

American sympathizers had badly miscalculated the situation. They believed that the rebellions indicated a desire to end the connection with Great Britain. This was not the case: the movements had been directed against privilege within the colonies, not against the Imperial tie. The bulk of the colonists had no desire to separate from Great Britain only to become the objects of American frontier expansionism. Canadians could easily see that the incentives to intervention were the old republican hatred of the British monarchy and the complex of motives usually given the name "Manifest Destiny". The disturbances received no support of consequence from the more responsible classes in the United States: their major result was to renew in Canada the old Loyalist distrust and dislike of the "Yankee".

[12] For this topic, see A. G. Corey, *The Crisis of 1830-42 in Canadian-American Relations* (Toronto, 1941).

4. The Province of Canada and its First Governor, Lord Sydenham

Meanwhile provision had to be made by the Imperial government for the situation forced upon its attention by the rebellions. After Durham returned, Melbourne was successful in finding another man of first-class abilities to succeed him. This was Charles Poulett Thomson[13] who had held office in his ministry. Thomson was associated with the "Philosophic Radicals" or left wing of the Whig party, sharing their doctrines of *laisser-faire*, especially as to free trade. Like some others of this group he had a direct family interest in the Baltic timber trade, the great foe of the preference accorded Canadian timber in the British market, and his free trade views were not devoid of relation to his business connection and its interests. In Canadian lumber and timber circles, the influential mercantile circles of Quebec and Montreal, his appointment as Governor-in-Chief was received with suspicion: the enemy was being handed the keys of the fortress. He, however, soon convinced the timber trade of his ability to keep private and public interests separate. It was soon recognized that he had the welfare of the colonies at heart.

Thomson's task was to set the colonies on a new course. This involved securing their acceptance of the policy that the Melbourne government, through its Colonial Secretary, Lord John Russell, was working out. The policy contained only one major structural change, the union of the Canadas. Otherwise it evolved along with Russell's thinking on the subject. In deciding on Union, the Imperial government was accepting one of Durham's leading recommendations, but not, however, without change. Durham had dismissed a federal solution and had suggested Union on a basis of representation by population in the Union Assembly, but although "Canada East", as Lower Canada now officially became, had the larger population, the Act of Union gave to each half of the new province of Canada equal representation. In this provision there lies an interesting historical sequence. The abortive Canada Union Bill of 1822 had provided for equal representation from each province, although at that time Lower Canada was much the larger. The object was plain: the English of Lower Canada plus the English of Upper Canada would outnumber the French. The project of 1822 was a reflection of Montreal commercial interests, whose object it had been from the beginning to bring in the English of the upper river and lakes to redress the French balance. Montreal merchants had expected this solu-

---

[13] 1799-1841. Vice-President of the Board of Trade in Grey Cabinet of 1830-34. Governor of British North America, 1839-41. Created Baron Sydenham, 1841.

tion in 1791 but had been given separation and a permanent minority position instead.[14] Their bill of 1822, which would have restored to them the English of Upper Canada, failed. Thereafter they never ceased their agitation for the annexation of at least Montreal Island to Upper Canada. Now in 1840, the Colonial Office dragged out the 1822 plan again, urged on by the Governor, on whom much of the responsibility for the scheme of representation must rest, and no doubt by the mercantile group's friends at court, and when the Union Act came down, it was found to contain provision for equal representation: the English of Canada East, whose nuclear centre was the mercantile group in Montreal, were to be allowed to join with the English of Canada West and "swamp the French". The Act of Union, as passed, represented not Durham's victory but his defeat.

Alas for the best plans of mice and men! Not long after the union was consummated, some of the English of the Upper province were to form what must have seemed to Montrealers a strange and unnatural *mésalliance* with the French: its outcome, the Baldwin-Lafontaine ministry, was to deal Montreal Tories, with its Rebellion Losses Bill, a blow severer than any they had received from Louis Joseph Papineau. Montreal, nevertheless, did not give up its struggle to escape from its narrow French prison and when in 1858, one of its prominent residents, A. T. Galt, entered the ministry on condition that it endorse his scheme for Confederation,[15] its new approach became discernible. Nine years later on, 1867, Confederation was an accomplished fact and Montreal business men had open to their economic vision a hinterland extending as far as the eye could see.

If the Act of Union was one episode in the long struggle of Montreal to control its hinterland, it was from the French point of view, another in the long series of attacks on their existence as a people. French Canadians took it to mean that Durham's "anglification" was about to begin. Equality of representation was a point of friction from the first, and after 1851, with population situations reversed between Lower and Upper Canada, it became an ulcer on the body politic of such malignity as to threaten its dissolution. The grievance at the time of its creation was the greater in that the Assembly of Lower Canada had been suspended. Thomson had little difficulty in securing assent to Union from the appointive Council that had taken its place. He also managed to carry the proposal through the Assembly of Upper Canada, and the Imperial Parliament in consequence passed the Act, 1840. Upper

[14] See pp. 156, 225.
[15] See p. 317.

Canada and Lower Canada ceased to exist and the Province of Canada was created.

Thomson was quite aware that it would be difficult to sustain orderly government against the antagonisms proceeding from both extremes. Like many another man at the head of Canadian affairs he found in practice that he had to walk a path with deep ditches on both sides; one false step and he was off. His difficulties were not lessened by the rapidly evolving conception of colonial government that kept coming to him in his Minister's despatches.

Russell had been a companion-in-arms of Durham's in the fight for reform of Parliament; his fundamentally liberal outlook was not in question. He was also a man of logical mentality, and like many another Imperial minister, unable to appreciate imaginatively the colonial point of view. At first he categorically dismissed the idea of responsible or ministerial government. If the Governor had to take the advice of his ministers, he could not take the orders of the State Secretary for the Colonies: the Crown would have two sets of advisers, one in the colonies, one in Westminster. Since the advisers at Westminster were the superior, their advice would prevail and the colonial governor would have to refuse the advice of his counsellors: therefore, there could not be ministerial government in the colonies.

However, even before Thomson had sailed, Russell had begun to modify his position. On September 7, the Governor would naturally seek the advice of those who had the confidence of the community.[16] How these persons were to be ascertained, he did not state. Then he went further: by October 16, officials were to be given to understand that they could not expect life tenure of their offices. They must retire when the public interest seemed to require it. Put these two together and ministerial government was not far off, for how could it be determined what men had the confidence of the community save by a vote of confidence in the Assembly of the community? It is probable that the evolution of Russell's ideas was hastened by the Open Letters addressed to him by the rising young journalist politician Joseph Howe from Nova Scotia,[17] who had already acquired a local reputation as a radical. His "Open Letters" were to make him known throughout British North America and in England as a constitutional reformer. Howe's dialectic,

[16] The despatches are in W. P. M. Kennedy, ed., *Statutes, Documents and Treaties of the Canadian Constitution, 1713-1929,* 2nd ed. (Toronto, 1930).

[17] In September, 1839. Reprinted in Kennedy, *op. cit.* Joseph Howe (1804-73) had been editor of *The Novascotian* for some years. His successful defence in the libel suit brought against him by the magistrates of Halifax had vindicated freedom of the press and secured his election to the Assembly.

as logical as Russell's own and psychologically far sounder, put an unanswerable case for colonial self-government. The letters refuted imputations of disloyalty and charges that self-government was a step towards independence. They showed that little conflict of jurisdiction between Imperial and local governments need arise. They refused to accept for Englishmen overseas a smaller degree of freedom than Englishmen at home possessed: if Englishmen in England could govern themselves, so could people of English stock abroad. Only by means of self-government, they asserted, could overseas communities of English speech be kept within the Empire.

Thomson, or Lord Sydenham, as he became on the passage of the Act of Union, at once found himself between the two fires that Russell had referred to. He had to take his orders from the Colonial Secretary but those very orders made it difficult for him to resist the clearly expressed will of the Canadian Assembly. In this difficult position he had recourse to finesse. In the first elections under the Union Act he displayed an adeptness in "practical politics" which indicated he had nothing to learn from any colonial expert in that art and apparently secured a favourable majority for the first session.[18] As he himself said, his idea was to keep the Assembly busy with specific and constructive measures, designed to prevent it from debating theoretical issues. His District Councils bill, which gave to Canada its first satisfactory system of local government, was an example of this. His trump card was the promise of the Imperial government to guarantee a large loan for the completion of the canals.

He did contrive to get much useful business through the Assembly, managing things from behind the scenes, but he could not avoid the theoretical debate. Quite convinced that the old government-by-clique had to go, he had given a post to Robert Baldwin, but the latter, on discovering that his ideas of responsible government did not coincide with Sydenham's, resigned, and on the first opportunity brought in six resolutions affirming the principle. This move the Governor countered through his mouthpiece, Harrison,[19] by a counter-set of four resolutions that, by a judicious choice of words, obscured but did not deny the principle. These resolutions carried. The Governor thus secured a tactical victory. But it was a victory that depended upon a vote of the

---

[18] See J. C. Dent, *The Last Forty Years: Canada Since the Union of 1841,* I. O. D. Skelton in his *Life and Times of Sir Alexander Tilloch Galt* (Toronto, 1920), p. 127, calls Thomson "corrupt", *tout court!*

[19] An English lawyer who had come to Canada a few years previously. Private secretary to Sir George Arthur, last governor of Upper Canada. M.P.P. for Kingston, 1841. Provincial Secretary under Sydenham. Moderate Reformer.

House. If the House chose to vote the other way, expressing no confidence in his officials, what would he do? This was an issue he never had to confront, for shortly afterwards[20] he suffered an accident from which he never recovered. The problem was left to his successors.

Sydenham's governor-generalship may be taken to have ended the immediate period of the rebellions. He had not established a new form of government in Canada; neither had he adhered to the old. His regime had been one of compromise between antagonistic forces. The rebellions had been revolutionary movements, but they had not been revolutions. They had not swept the old order away, but they had made it abundantly evident that room must be found in the state for the new. Canada thus entered on the next phase of its existence under the banner which it still reluctantly sees waving over it, that of compromise. The French soon put an end to the political domination of their province by a small group of English but proved willing to co-operate with the English in its government. The English of Upper Canada let in the fresh North American air. But it did not fill the room as fully as in the United States; Canada reflects some of the monarchical and aristocratic life of England as well as the wide, free democracy of the republic.

Everything considered, the Imperial structure had come out of the rebellions very well. Another American Revolution might have occurred if there had been a Tory Lord North in England at the time, instead of Whig Russells and Durhams. But as it was, the colonies had had a house-cleaning and also re-hardened their hearts against the Americans. For them all, the Maritimes included, the rebellions had struck a blow at privilege from which it was never to recover, and had opened the doors to the freer play of those continental forces of equality and liberalism which time has revealed as our very life-blood, the stuff by which we live and for which we fight. The rebellions were blessings in disguise. Until the rise of French *Séparatisme* they were the corner stones of Canadian nationhood.

Chronology

1830–41 Whig Governments in England, under Prime Ministers Grey and Melbourne.

1838   May 29—Nov. 1. Lord Durham Governor of British North America.
September. Joseph Howe's "Open Letters" to Lord John Russell.
Nov. 11. American sympathizers invade Canada near Prescott. "Battle of the Windmill".

1839–41 Charles Poulett Thomson, Lord Sydenham, Governor.

1839   Jan. 31. Lord Durham's *Report* submitted.

[20] September, 1841.

1840   The Act of Union passed by Lord Melbourne's Government.
1841   First meeting of the Parliament of the Province of Canada, at Kingston.
          First Parliamentary Executive.
          Robert Baldwin's Resignation from the Executive on the ground that he
              lacks confidence in some of his colleagues.
          September. The Harrison Resolutions.

Additional Reading

Houghton, Walter E. *The Victorian Frame of Mind.* New Haven, 1957.
Lucas, C. P., ed. *Lord Durham's Report on the Affairs of British North America.*
     London, 1912. 2 vols. (There are several editions of this all-important
     Report.)
Martin, Chester. "Lord Durham's Report and its Consequences." *CHR,* XX
     (June, 1939), 178-194.
New, Chester. *Lord Durham.* London, 1929.
———. "Lord Durham and the British Background of His Report." *CHR,* XX
     (June, 1939), 119-135.
———, *Life of Lord Brougham,* Oxford, 1961.

CHAPTER 20

A Revolutionary Decade: The End of the Old Colonial System, 1839-49

1. British Free Trade and Colonial Self-Government

The British colonial system had evolved in an empire of dependent colonies: it had suffered its greatest failure when former colonies had refused to remain dependent any longer. Now, in the second Empire, the wheel had come full circle: an accumulation of abuses had led to rebellion, and methods of reconstruction either had to be worked out or the Empire would be broken up once more. Was the colonial relationship consistent only with dependence, or could some other relationship be found? Durham had pronounced a decided affirmative, Sydenham had made the first tentative experiments, but the main test lay ahead. Would there be enough flexibility in British governing circles to meet it?

The new forces in colonial life met new forces emanating from Great Britain; the vast changes that lay ahead came only in part from the colonies, and if they had not themselves required a renovation of their institutions, one would soon have been forced upon them by their mother country. For the Great Britain of the 1840's was in full tide of the industrial revolution, at the top of its form in power, energy, self-confidence and inventive skill, and entertained a growing impatience with systems of government and economics that did not stand the test of practical common sense. The new men who had been making themselves felt since the reform of Parliament, represented not the landed, financial, and shipping interests but the new power industries that were leading the world in all the processes of production; they had no intention of allowing themselves to be hampered by the deadwood of a previous era, dependent colonies included.

Such men saw life simply: there was abundant opportunity everywhere for anyone of industry and intelligence, and every man could "get on". It was the British era of the self-made man, of *laisser-faire,* of each for himself and the devil take the hindmost. Looking at the world with such eyes, English industrialists saw an Empire that seemed to exist on huge preferences and high prices in the home market. They saw British aristocrats entrenched behind their Corn Laws; the Cape of Good Hope's artificial wine industry behind duties on French wines; the artificial sugar industry of West and East Indian planters behind duties on foreign sugar; and the artificial timber industry of British North American colonials behind the "differential duties" on Baltic timber. The conclusion was easily drawn that England was better off without aristocrats and colonies, that colonies were parasitic and, through the vested interests in the mother country which secured the various differential duties, sources of public corruption. "Buy in the cheapest market and sell in the dearest" was the battle cry, and so much the worse for the colonies that could not meet this test of manhood.

The pressure of the new elements for a tariff house-cleaning had been mounting since 1819. In 1821 some modifications of the timber duties had been obtained; in 1825 a consolidation and revision of the collection of archaic tariff acts had taken place. Some reciprocity treaties with other commercial states had been made, and then financial reform had stopped. The Whig governments of 1830-41, after one or two unsuccessful attempts at revision, had left the tariff alone. At last, weakened by their financial incapacities and by the leanings of their left-wing elements to tariff reform, they had gone down to defeat at the hands of the Tories under Sir Robert Peel.

Peel's ministry of 1841 opened the way for the re-introduction of the Tory policies of the 1820's. In the ministries that had effected the first reforms of that period, Peel had been second only to Huskisson in his progressive attitude. The commercial depression that had been hanging about since 1837 gave driving force to his new programme, the first instalment of which was a drastic reduction of the "differential duties" on Baltic timber (1842). Thereafter each budget saw some reduction or revision of duties. Peel himself was plainly thinking in terms of the new industrial England and overseas markets, no surprising state of mind in a man whose own fortunes derived from the cotton industry. Finally came the fateful year 1846, when England's division between the two sets of interests, urban and rural, industrial and agricultural, stood clearly revealed. A natural calamity of that year, the Irish potato famine, decided Peel, and his epoch-making budget initiated what was virtually a free trade regime: duties were to come off foreign wheat and nearly all duties off foreign timber and sugar. Thus at a stroke the three great monopolist interests were to be destroyed.

England had decided for free trade. This meant not only the weakening of the great vested domestic interest of "the land" but also the possible destruction of the two leading "colonial" interests, timber and sugar. In reality these were both just as English as was "the land", for the timber merchants in Liverpool or Quebec, the sugar importers of Great Britain, and the ship-owners whose vessels met with no foreign rivalry in these trades, were metropolitan rather than colonial. The only genuine colonials concerned in the trade monopolies were sugar planters and the lumbermen of British North America, who were actually engaged in felling and floating timber from forest to ship.[1] The traditional English colonial system had been forged by Englishmen for Englishmen, and now it was Englishmen who had ended it.

Once mercantilism and the concept of the closed commercial empire collapsed in Great Britain, it could no longer be maintained for the colonies. As a consequence of Peel's budget of 1846, British America was in that year given a large measure of control over local tariffs, and colonial autonomy in trade began. The whole weight of British feeling in the 1840's was that every pot should stand on its own bottom. This was a point of view that must be thoroughly grasped by those who would understand the way in which a dependent empire changed into a self-governing empire, for it goes a long way towards explaining the ease of the transition. Once Great Britain adopted free trade, she could not logically deny trade and tariff freedom to her colonies, and once freedom of action had been accorded in the sphere of trade, political freedom could not long be withheld: freedom was indivisible. The economic and political aspects of the colonial relationship were two parts of the complex which, in terms of colonial autonomy, receives the name Responsible Government.

The logic of the reform movement as it affected the colonial system[2] was not seen as clearly at the time as it can be now: every forward step was bitterly fought, especially in British North America, and when the process was completed, the usual minority united in agreeing that the

[1] To them should be added Canadian farmers, who had had a preference on wheat.

[2] After 1815 England faced a great international trading future with the institutions of a small agricultural state; she took just a generation to give herself institutions and laws adequate to her new position (1815-49).

sun of England's glory was set and her Empire broken up. It is hard today to grasp how completely the two conceptions of Empire and trade were at that time bound up together. If England and the colonies did not form one trading unity, then, it seemed to follow, there could be no political connection. Both in England and the colonies there were comparatively few who grasped the deep realities of blood, and in England there was virtually no one who had the same sentimental attitude towards the colonies, which might be considered parts of a greater England overseas, as had the average colonist towards the mother-country. To the English, colonies were markets, customers, empty lands, or at best strategic areas to be controlled by sea-power; imagination as to their future was lacking. The bonds of Empire down until the twentieth century were knit up almost exclusively by the colonists. To English Tories, the outer Empire meant dominance and a chance of jobs for younger sons, to English Whigs and Radicals it meant trade, and if trade could be done with other countries to better advantage, the Empire became a nuisance. There was only the occasional Durham or Wakefield. Everything considered, colonists having repudiated the Tory political view of Empire and the metropolis having repudiated the traditional mercantile conception, it was not surprising that the home government was willing to concede both fiscal and political autonomy.

2. The Riddle of Colonial Freedom and Imperial Control

The years of experiment from Sydenham to Elgin (1839-1849) have been the subject of more writing than has any other period except that of the Conquest. The outcome of the experiment turned on the personalities of relatively few people, on two Secretaries of State for the Colonies, five Governors, and three colonial statesmen. The Colonial Secretaries were Lord Stanley (1841-45), a Conservative, and Lord Grey (1846-52), a Whig. The governors of Canada were Sir Charles Bagot (1842-43), a moderate Conservative, Sir Charles Metcalfe (1843-45), a High Tory by nature though not a party man, and the Earl of Elgin (1847-54), a moderate Conservative. Two lieutenant governors of Nova Scotia complete this group of five: Sir Colin Campbell (1834-40), and Viscount Falkland (1840-46). The three colonial statesmen were Robert Baldwin from Upper Canada, the classical proponent of the idea of Responsible Government; Louis H. Lafontaine from Lower Canada, the natural successor to Papineau as French-Canadian leader; and Joseph Howe from Nova Scotia.

Lord Stanley, Peel's Colonial Secretary, was a Tory of less than ten years standing. He was not illiberal but his advice to Sir Charles Bagot,

Sydenham's successor, to stick to the Family Compact men as the real Loyalists, the only dependable element, showed that he did not understand the local situation, for his advice if taken might have destroyed the colonial relationship. His Whig successor, Lord Grey (son of the former Prime Minister), as a complete believer in free trade and almost a doctrinaire individualist, was in some respects the embodiment of the spirit of the times. Consonant with such doctrines was his conviction—which time was to prove correct and which he shared with Lord Elgin, than whom no governor contributed more to the solving of the Canadian riddle—that colonial autonomy, far from loosening the bonds of Empire, was the one thing that would make them hold. He went further and saw in colonial federation the building of a colonial nationalism which would be the antidote to centrifugal forces. He was thus a true liberal, sharing with great statesmen such as the later Gladstone the secret of the Empire vouchsafed to few political opponents. The Colonial Office had usually been regarded as well down the list of desirability in Cabinet appointments and had rarely before attracted men of prominence or ability; this had been no small factor in colonial misgovernment. Grey, while not a statesman of the first rank, was conscientious and above the average of competence. His five-year tenure of office was also much longer than had been usual for colonial secretaries. He possessed another great advantage in his close personal relations with Lord Elgin, the Governor during the critical period of transition to Responsible Government.

Of the strategic governors, three—Bagot, Metcalfe and Elgin—served in Canada: two—Campbell and Falkland—in Nova Scotia. These were the only two colonies in which growing pains were severe enough to cause crisis. To Bagot goes the credit for discerning the simple major premise of Canadian life, the fact that stares one in the face but to which so many of English speech have been blind: "You cannot govern Canada without the French", to use his own words. Since the rebellion the French had been sulking. In it most of their responsible leaders had committed themselves to a greater or less degree (Cartier had been "out" in 1837 and Lafontaine, having been in close sympathy down to the last, had found it prudent to leave the province until the amnesty proclamation was issued), and they all felt that the whole Durham-Sydenham programme had as its main objective their subordination and assimilation. They had hung back, refusing to work with such genuinely good measures as Sydenham's District Councils Act, which provided the system of municipal government that the Colonies had so sorely lacked; and appended to every one of their own who showed any signs of cooperation the epithet of ultimate infamy—un vendu. Bagot himself did some hard bargaining before he surrendered to the two men, Louis H. Lafontaine and Robert Baldwin, who could command a majority in the Assembly, but his acceptance of the inevitable was an act of statesman-ship whose importance grows with the years. When Lafontaine took office on his own terms, that constituted co-operation in government which could not be interpreted as selling out. It also was a testimony that the days of Chateau Cliques had gone forever: Lafontaine, even if he had wished it, was not to have the opportunity of becoming a Papi-neau. Office imposed responsibility, and there could be no more declamation against an arbitrary and over-riding power.

Yet how much responsibility did office impose? That was the question. Both Baldwin and Lafontaine regarded their being in the executive as tantamount to the accomplishment of self-government, and there began to be heard talk of "ministers". It would, however, be wrong to regard the advisers of Sir Charles Bagot as constituting a ministry. They worked peacefully with him, Bagot invariably taking their advice, they maintained a majority in the Assembly, and there was a large measure of collective responsibility among them; but Bagot was still governor, and many issues could have arisen that might have required him to refuse their advice and seek other counsellors. The embarrassment of such a situation he, like Sydenham before him, escaped by death.

Probably a tussle between governor and advisers had to come any-way, but no one more likely to precipitate it could have been chosen than Bagot's successor, Sir Charles Metcalfe. His previous experience had been in India and Jamaica, both of which posts called out whatever instincts of dominance a man had about him, and he came to Canada as he had gone to Jamaica, a sahib who took it for granted that the job of the governor was to govern. To come up against a Parliamentary system in which members of a conquered race, who a few years pre-viously had been in arms against their sovereign, were playing a leading part and actually making the decisions in the name of the Crown, must have been a severe shock to him. What is more, the people whose minds naturally marched with his, the "natural governing class", the Tories, were impotent. In those days, principles were not quite as clear as they afterwards became; they tended to be obscured by the details of the day. What was painfully apparent to the Tories was that they no longer enjoyed the sweets of office. Appointments were going to their enemies, or as they would have said, to rebels. Nothing could have gored more deeply a group of men who had been accustomed to regard the good things of the province as theirs by a kind of divine right; here was the ultimate bitterness of revolution: to be on the outside and see your enemies on the inside.

Metcalfe soon became aware of the situation; he heard plenty of tales of woe from men more to his taste than the persons he found on his Executive Council. When these latter made it clear to him that even he, the Governor, could not be allowed to change it, his relations with them became difficult, and when a test case arose, a trifling appointment which Metcalfe made without consulting his council, Baldwin and Lafontaine resigned. Metcalfe tried in vain to form another administration, and for over a year the province was without one.

The Governor felt that in driving the Reformers out of office he was saving the colony for the Crown. It was ridiculous that a set of men, lately "rebels", should suggest that the Queen's representative should not govern the Queen's colony except insofar as he was willing to demean himself by subordinating himself to his own subordinates; and it was shameful that the "loyal" people should be debarred from all recognition on the part of their sovereign, that rogues should flourish and honest folk droop because a given group of men was able to rally a majority of a popular assembly to their side. Such an attitude showed how blind he was to the realities of colonial life. He could not see, nor would he have admitted, the principle that the Assembly was the only device for discovering the will of the people and that in a white colony whose people were heirs of the English tradition (whatever might be the case in India and Jamaica), the only possible basis for government was the will of the people. He therefore fought in Canada that same losing battle which had been fought by the forces that had brought on the rebellions, or in England by the Crown in the seventeenth century, or in Ireland by the English government down to 1922. In fact, he fought the battle of "colonialism" as against "anti-colonialism", a fight the last stages of which the modern world is still witnessing.

Yet as a man of great sincerity and as the Queen's representative, he wielded much power, and when the inevitable election was forced on him, he was by no means without support. Like Sir Francis Bond Head before him, he seems to have been sure that "the people", as distinct from their representatives, were "loyal", and he only awaited the opportunity to show that the whole sad business of pretended ministerial government had been a mistake. Tories rallied to him, of course. But the determining personage was the same man who had swung Sir Francis's election of 1836 for him, Egerton Ryerson. Ryerson never seems to have penetrated the mysteries of Responsible Government, and when this second crisis arose, his primary instincts of Loyalism and conservatism came to the fore as they had in the first instance, and he entered the lists on the side of things as they were. His support brought a large Methodist vote with it; the result was that Baldwin and Lafontaine failed to secure a majority.[3]

But the necessity of the election had itself been sufficient acknowledgement of the principle of government by the consent of the governed, and the fact that it was won by the same flag-waving devices as in 1836 did not in the least mean that the methods of governing India were going, in the future, to be applied to Canada: in his victory, the governor was defeated. For him personally, the triumph was short-lived, for he too, like both his predecessors, was fated to die after a short term in office, leaving the question of sovereignty in Canada still unsolved.

Lord Elgin, who succeeded him, was Lord Durham's son-in-law; his wife was a niece of Lord Grey, the Colonial Secretary. This snug little family circle would be sure to produce a pooling of knowledge and opinion, of which people of much more than average ability and experience would make good use. Like his father-in-law, Elgin had a first-class brain, and the results were obvious in his governorship. The Grey-Durham-Elgin family connection, with its contribution of as much ability to colonial affairs as all the rest of governors and colonial secretaries put together, saved the British connection. It did not take Elgin long after his arrival to size up the situation in Canada, and when the next election had been held (1848), with its anticipated return of a Reform majority for Baldwin-Lafontaine, Metcalfe's *tour de force* was quietly ended. The old councillors, after a futile attempt to induce the French to work with them, stepped down on proof being forthcoming that they could not command a majority, and Baldwin and Lafontaine took over. Correspondence between Elgin and Grey was constant and intimate. When Elgin said he was determined to work with his councillors and give them his confidence as long as they could command the confidence of the Legislature, he was using the same language as Grey in his well-known despatches to Lieutenant-Governor Harvey of Nova Scotia[4] by which he virtually ordered the setting up of ministerial governments. After Baldwin and Lafontaine had taken office, as possessing the confidence of the Assembly, the end of the evolution had been reached, and Responsible Government had come into existence. It would have been impossible to turn back the hands of the clock to the old type of Crown colony administration without provoking further outbreaks, for if the period from 1791 on had made anything clear, it was that the evolution in colonial politics could not stop short of self-government. Although Elgin understood this readily enough and knew that

[3] See George E. Wilson, *Life of Robert Baldwin* (Toronto, 1933), p. 206ff.
[4] 3 Nov., 1846, and 31 March, 1847.

self-government was the only alternative to another American Revolution, there were many people in the colonies themselves who did not. Their actions were, within a year or two, to provide the occasion for a rigorous test of the new system, in the form of the Rebellion Losses Bill,[5] a test severe enough to prove its affirmation.

The other two governors who need consideration—Sir Colin Campbell and Lord Falkland, both in Nova Scotia—are not persons of prime importance. Campbell was of the old military type, a man who found it hard to understand that anyone except "the proper people" should conduct public affairs. But he had the misfortune to come up against a man of much greater capacity than himself, Joseph Howe, then a member of the legislature, and got the worst of it. Howe's arguments, addressed both to the people and to the Colonial Office, secured Campbell's recall (1840) as an official who did not enjoy the confidence of his people. His successor, Lord Falkland, was also ill-advised enough to enter into a personal controversy with Howe, who was again editing his old paper, the *Novascotian*, and who used his advantage rather shamelessly to hold the governor up to ridicule. The point at issue was whether a council should be formed consisting of men of different political leanings, who did not enjoy each other's confidence, even if they enjoyed the governor's. Howe naturally had to oppose such a suggestion, for the essence of Responsible Government was the corporate nature of the Council (or Cabinet, as we would say today) in its dependence upon the confidence of the Assembly. A non-corporate Council simply meant heads of departments dependent upon the governor (which had been the system of government of George III before the loss of the American colonies, or the system of Lord Sydenham in Canada). Falkland became the second scalp in Howe's belt, and his successor, Sir John Harvey, was instructed by the new Colonial Secretary, Earl Grey, in the despatches mentioned above, to accept the collective advice of his councillors, which made them his responsible advisers, his ministry. Nova Scotia thus had the honour of leading Canada by a few months in the establishment of a clear-cut Responsible Government.

It is rather astonishing how few men in the colonies or out of them actually seemed to divine the nature of the change that would be necessary if the colonies were to obtain government which their people would accept. Among the colonists neither Papineau nor Mackenzie did so. Nor did Egerton Ryerson. If any Family Compact Tories did so, they could only see in the device a sure road into political oblivion. Moder-

[5] See p. 277.

ates like J. W. Johnstone in Nova Scotia or William Hamilton Merritt in Canada may have understood intellectually, but they did not evince their conviction of the overriding importance of the device. It was left to Baldwin, Lafontaine, and Howe to fight the cause through, and it is proper that with their names this greatest of peaceful revolutions should be principally associated.

Robert Baldwin[6] has often been called "the man of one idea", but his one idea was the one thing needful. He had stuck to it through thick and thin since the late 1820's when his father had worked it out and he had embraced it. He had been tempted neither by Mackenzie left-extremism nor by the fleshpots that he could easily have enjoyed through Tory relations and friends. He had given Sir Francis Bond Head's offer an honest trial in 1836, and in accordance with his conception of the correct procedure, had resigned when that governor showed he had no intention of committing himself to his councillors. In the years of rebellion, although loose charges of being associated with the rebels were hurled at him, he had kept squarely in the middle of the road. He had gone through with Sydenham practically the same experience as he had with Bond Head. He had convinced Bagot that the only road to stable government was through working with the majority in the Assembly that he and Lafontaine possessed, and had thus constituted under that governor something close to a responsible ministry. He had fought against Metcalfe's reactionary position and had followed his principles in working with the governor as long as he had his confidence, then retiring. Finally, coming back to office again after the Reform victory in the elections of 1847-48, he had found himself in agreement with Elgin on the content of the term Responsible Government and had been a leading spirit in its accomplishment. If the will of the people, as represented by a majority in the Assembly, led to Rebellion Losses bills or Secret Societies bills,[7] he followed the will of the people. Throughout it all, he retained intact his Anglicanism, his colonial aristocratic attitude[8] and his attachment to the Crown. No such middle-of-the-roader could be overly popular: he was too cold, too correct, too consistent, and like Aristides, too just, for popularity. But it is to him more than to any other one man, Durham and Howe not excepted, that Canada owes self-government in the form of "Responsible Government".

Upon Louis Hippolyte Lafontaine had descended the mantle of

[6] The standard life of Baldwin is Wilson, *op. cit.*
[7] A bill introduced by Lafontaine to forbid all secret societies in the province (except the Masons). It was directed at the Orangemen and reserved by Metcalfe for the pleasure of the Crown.
[8] He had inherited some 50,000 acres of land.

Papineau. But Lafontaine was far from being a Papineau. Like the other generous-minded, freedom-loving young men of his race, he had been fully in sympathy with Papineau, but he was not an ideologue as Papineau tended to be, nor did he feel that his race was suffering intolerable wrongs or that no cost could be too great to match the setting up of a French republic in North America. When he realized that the rebellion had failed, he had no difficulty in having recourse to normal Reform constitutionalism, especially when Bagot showed his disposition to work with the French. Once Lafontaine had accepted office under the Crown, he had committed his people, through his followers in the Assembly, to constitutionalism. Lower Canada, thanks to him, did not become a precedent for Ireland. No aspirations towards the widest possible future for the race were to be abandoned, but in future these were to be realized at the polls and through debate, not through gunpowder. If trouble were again to arise, it would have to be on issues other than the form of government. This was Lafontaine's contribution: his good sense in accepting something repugnant to French mentality, a compromise, and in putting it on a working basis. Lower Canada was to remain French; but in doing so, it was putting itself in the harness of English institutions.

The most attractive figure of the period, the most vital personality, not excluding Durham, was Joseph Howe. He was a man, in every sense of the term. The son of a Loyalist, but outside the sacred circle of the well-born Halifax Anglicans who disposed of Nova Scotia's destinies, he did not see why being a colonist and a Loyalist should deprive him of those rights of self-government that he would have possessed as an Englishman. In him, and in his encounters with official-dom in his province, the old eighteenth century colonial contests were relived. He was not long in grasping Baldwin's idea of Responsible Government, and he became its most effective exponent in the rebellion period. It was, he said in his open letters to Lord John Russell,[9] absurd to think that a citizen of Liverpool was any less an Englishman because he had self-government than he would have been if governed direct from Westminster. The statement revealed both Howe's strength and weakness. He was determined to have all his rights as an Englishman, a member of an Imperial organization, but these extended no further than local self-government. Self-government, in his version, had nothing whatsoever to do with independence. That was also true for Baldwin, but the larger scale of the Canadas was to ensure that sooner or later all the other aspects of self-government would have to be brought under local control, too.

* See p. 257.

Nova Scotia, as a small community not likely to expand much, could safely be trusted, as was soon discovered, with local self-government, because it was unlikely that it would ever wish to have anything beyond provincial status. Canada was more of a question, because its politics were turbulent and there were many problems whose solutions might carry the province into unforeseen decisions. If it had not been for the Canadas, it may well be that ministerial government would have been accorded earlier than it was, for there were no rebels in the Maritimes and the Imperial government did not evince any desire to make them safe for the small cliques that controlled them.

After the open letters to Russell, Howe's contributions were somewhat of an anti-climax. They consisted mainly in his personal duels with Campbell and Falkland, already alluded to, and in providing in himself a centre for a party to rally about: the Reformers roughly corresponded to the group of the same name in Upper Canada, their opponents being known as Tories and, later, Conservatives. Once, however, Responsible Government was secured, the names hardly signified enough differences of principle to give a secure framework for the new device.

A period that saw the destruction of the Old Colonial System, a legal and political edifice over two centuries old, buttressed by innumerable statutes, treasured as a means for providing the basis of sea-power, and defended by great vested interests, and a radically new experiment in empire, the grant to the senior overseas provinces of local self-government—such a decade deserves to be called revolutionary. The second empire had sprung up on the ruins of the first, but it had been a new empire mainly in a physical sense as consisting in new territory, for the spirit of the old empire had lived on, and a new empire in a real sense was not born until the 1840's. The empire consisting of a metropolitan centre and white colonies attached by ties of sentiment rather than dominance, in which the centre was prepared to concede autonomy as a father concedes it to a son coming to manhood, that empire—the third empire, it might be called—did not come into existence until the 1840's had destroyed its predecessors. By the combined experiences of Great Britain and her colonies, concentrated in the personalities of a relatively small number of men, and by "the whiff of grapeshot" of 1837, a secret had been stumbled on that was to give to the new political edifice relative immortality.

Like all political movements of importance in Canada, before and since, its nature was essentially that of a compromise. Impatient Manchester men in England would have completed the English revolution from the British Empire by throwing the colonies overboard. Hard-crusted Tories would have insisted on dominance and forced them into real revolution. Colonial doctrinaires like Mackenzie and Papineau would have gone far beyond the mere remedy of abuses; reactionaries like Sir John Beverley Robinson (Chief Justice of Upper Canada), Metcalfe, Haliburton,[10] and Uniacke[11] would have stood on their privileges and had their hands forced. It was the middle-of-the-road men, the compromisers, the idealistic realists, the Baldwins, Durhams, Greys, Howes, Elgins, and Lafontaines, who saved the British Empire of the 1840's and gave it another century of life.

Chronology

1841–46 Sir Robert Peel Prime Minister.
1842 First of Peel's reductions in Colonial Preference.
       Sir Charles Bagot, Governor.
1842–43 The Lafontaine-Baldwin Executive Council.
1843–45 Sir Charles Metcalfe, Governor.
       Resignation of the Baldwin-Lafontaine Council.
1844 Montreal becomes the capital.
1846 Repeal of the English Corn Laws, and further steps towards free trade.
1846–52 Lord Grey, Colonial Secretary in Lord John Russell's Whig Ministry.
       November 3: Lord Grey's despatch to Sir John Harvey enjoining the principle of Responsible Government.
1847–54 The Earl of Elgin, Governor.
1848 Baldwin and Lafontaine form the first Responsible ministry in Canada.
       The Uniacke-Howe Ministry in Nova Scotia.

Additional Reading

De Celles, A. D. *Lafontaine et son temps*. Montreal, 1907.
Glazebrook, G. P. de T. *Sir Charles Bagot in Canada*. Oxford, 1929.
Hodgetts, J. E. *Pioneer Public Services; An Administrative History of United Canada, 1841-1867*. Toronto, 1956.
Kennedy, W. P. M. *Lord Elgin* (Makers of Canada Series, Vol. 6). London, 1926.
Leacock, Stephen. *Mackenzie, Baldwin, Lafontaine, Hincks*. (Makers of Canada Series, Vol. 5). London, 1926.
Longley, R. S. *Sir Francis Hincks*. Toronto, 1943.
McDougall, D. J. "Lord John Russell and the Canadian Crisis, 1837-1841." *CHR*, XXII (Dec., 1941), 369-388.
Monet, Jacques. "*La Crise Metcalfe* and the Montreal Election, 1843-44." *CHR*, XLIV (March, 1963), 1-19
Morison, J. L. *British Supremacy and Canadian Self Government, 1839-1854*. Glasgow, 1919.
Ryerson, Egerton. *The Story of My Life*. Toronto, 1883. 2 vols.
Shortt, A. *Lord Sydenham*. London, 1926.
Turcotte, L. P. *Le Canada sous l'union, 1841-1867*. Montreal, 1871.
Wilson, G. E. *The Life of Robert Baldwin*. Toronto, 1933.

[10] T. C. Haliburton (1796-1865), the well-known author of *Sam Slick*, etc.; a decided Tory.
[11] R. J. Uniacke (1753-1830), Attorney-General of Nova Scotia, 1797-1830. Not to be confused with J. B. Uniacke, Reform Premier of Nova Scotia, 1848.

CHAPTER 21

Reaction and Reconstruction, 1849-1854

---

1. Depression

Responsible Government was no sooner attained than it had to meet the hardest of tests in a severe business depression. When men saw ruin staring them in the face and their enemies standing in the place of power, they were not slow to associate the two. To many in 1846, Responsible Government and depression must have been twin calamities. If the passions smouldering from the period of rebellion, kept going by the uneasy fear that the rebels and the French were going to triumph after all, had not been fanned into fresh flame by this new and scorching wind, it would have been a miracle.

The depressions of the early nineteenth century originated in the logical place, the metropolitan centre of an exploitive world economy, London, spread outward from there first to New York and thence to the British provinces. Colonial economy depended upon the price of wheat, timber, and new ships in the British market, and upon the readiness of English exporters to grant long credits. High prices in the British market induced the production of large supplies in British North America; a subsequent collapse, or even a considerable fall, in British prices brought everything to a halt in the colonies. Agriculture retreated to a subsistence level, few men went into the woods, no new ships were laid down, and men without work quickly got out for the American west. Wholesalers pressed the retailer, who under the customary system of long credits and high prices could never turn debts into cash quickly, and the chronically over-expanded merchandising position of Canada contracted to the noise of failures great and small. The delicate mechanism stretching from London across the Atlantic up the St. Lawrence to the farthest fringes of exploitation was easily thrown out of gear.

The depression following the Napoleonic Wars (1816-1821) had caught the colonies in a state of distended war prosperity. On its collapse, it was only the resources that had been accumulated out of the War of 1812 that tided them over. In the early 1820's trade picked up in England, most of the oversupply of shipping hanging over from the Napoleonic wars disappeared, and orders for timber and new ships came pouring into Canada and New Brunswick. The usual delayed post-war boom resulted, lasting until 1825-26, when collapse in England brought collapse in America and a few years of deep depression. It was New Brunswick, a province entirely dominated by an economy based on wood, that suffered the most heavily. By 1830, moderate prosperity had returned. The height reached this time was not so giddy; consequently when reaction came, it was as a recession rather than a sharp crisis. But coinciding as it did with the political troubles of the times, it accentuated them, and, coupled with crop failures, prepared the ground for the rebellions of 1837.

Again a slow recovery followed; the Act of Union was launched on a mild return of prosperity in 1841. After that the trend was rapidly upward. In England there began the great period of railroad building, which induced an orgy of speculative activity and also heavy demands for Canadian timber. The railway mania reached its peak late in 1846, and then the boom broke. Before the news arrived in Canada, everyone who could scrape a few dollars together had gone into the bush for the winter (1846-47) to make timber, in expectation of still heavier English demand and still higher prices. Instead, when they came out in the spring, and got their wood down to Quebec or Saint John in the late spring, they found it unsalable. There it just piled up, as heavy an incubus over the timber market and the return of prosperity as oversupplies of Canadain wheat have sometimes been in our own day.

It was also in 1846 that Sir Robert Peel's last and most revolutionary budget turned England into a virtually free-trade country. Colonial timber thereafter would have to compete against timber from the nearer Baltic countries without most of the huge preference it had previously enjoyed. The new conditions of competition made necessary a drastic readjustment in the Canadian timber industry. Hitherto, exporters had been able to unload almost any rubbish they wished, and producers could be slipshod in its manufacture. In future, back-woods rough-and-ready ways would find difficulty competing with Baltic precision.

Peel's budget and the collapse in England brought calamity not only to the colonial timber trade (which in those days supported from a third to a half of the economy) but also to the second item in colonial life, wheat. Wheat had never become the staple that timber was, partly because it had had to compete with home-grown English supplies and had, therefore, never secured the favoured tariff position of timber; but it was the natural pioneer crop, and in Upper Canada the settlers had come to depend upon it as the source of most of what little cash they saw. Upper Canada was good wheat country but no better than other parts of the same region, and now it had to compete with the well-established agriculture of New York or Ohio. In 1843, Sir Robert Peel had allowed flour shipped from Canada to enter Great Britain under a preference, regardless of the origins of the wheat from which it was made. Under this arrangement it would pay to import American wheat into Canada and ship it out as Canadian flour, and numerous flour mills were erected along the Welland Canal in consequence. These had just been completed when free trade caused the advantage to disappear, ruining the builders. Upper Canadians felt strongly that Peel had acted unjustly and that before he destroyed the whole structure he should have used free entrance into the British market as a bargaining lever with the United States. But Peel was Prime Minister of Great Britain, not of Canada, and colonials did not understand how minor their interests were in British eyes.

All this was bad enough, but it was not the whole story. That very year, 1846, the Americans made a substantial increase in their own tariff, rendering more difficult the limited trade that had been going on across the borders. They also passed acts that, in the long run were to be of great advantage to Canada but at the time seemed to cut at the heart of the well-being of Canada's metropolis, Montreal. These were the Bonding Acts, by which goods passing through the United States on their way to or from a Canadian port of entry, could be sealed up and go through "in bond" without paying American duty. Toronto merchants could now import from London via New York. The move was a shrewd bid for traffic on new American railroads, and Montreal felt that it was aimed at itself, for apparently it cut off at a stroke its Upper Canadian hinterland.

The dreadful immigration experience of 1847,[1] when the unfortunate Irish victims of the potato famine arrived to die, spreading disease and

See p. 186.

filth wherever they went, put an additional burden on an already over-taxed people. As usual when times were bad, men began to leave for the States. These depression exoduses reduced public provision for relief, but they also drained off energy and left the Canadian community discouraged and stagnant.[2] Emigration, coupled with a general débâcle such as occurred in 1846, meant abandoned homesteads, unpaid debts, empty houses, and unrented stores, unsalable stocks, and bankrupts. So severe was the economic storm of the 1840's that in that decade the population of Montreal actually decreased by some thousands of people.[3] Lord Elgin's letters, in commenting on the hardships of the times, frequently observe that men's fears for their property and their future were bound to have political repercussions.

2. Tory Treason

These duly came. In the session of 1849 the Rebellion Losses Bill was introduced. It proposed to compensate those in Lower Canada who had suffered property losses from the rebellions. This was the last straw. Its opponents immediately shouted treason and made the charge that many among those to be compensated had aided the rebels or actually been in arms against the Crown. Ministers who had already antagonized Upper Canadian Orangemen by their Secret Societies Bill[4] and the Anglican Church by taking from it the control of the public university, could hardly expect much support from Montreal mandarins fearful for their businesses, when they proposed legislation to subsidize people who, in their eyes, were not only rebels but also contemptible. Yet there was no possibility of the bill being defeated in the Assembly and little likelihood that the Governor would refuse to sign it. The alternative was to accept it quietly or to attempt to frighten the Governor by a show of violence. The crisis had blown up too suddenly to give the Tory opposition a chance to organize mass resistance, even if there had been enough popular sentiment in the country to back them up, which there was not. Instead there occurred the sudden thunderstorm of the spring riots of 1849, the burning of the Parliament buildings and the rotten-egging of Lord Elgin. The disturbances were not spontaneous. "The whole row is the work of the Orange Societies, backed by the commercial men who desire annexation and the political leaders who want places."[5] "Almost all the leaders in the commotions are bankrupts—

[2] See also pp. 395, 409.
[3] From 64,897 in 1842 to 57,715 in 1851.
[4] See p. 270.
[5] Lord Elgin to Earl Grey, 30 April 1849.

desperate men who are looking to annexation as a last resource. Sir Allan MacNab. Cayley and others of the political clique are also ruined men."[6] "I have not the least doubt that MacNab (who will swear in England that he disapproved of the riots) actually got them up to produce effect at home."[7]

The riots had the twofold result of preventing Montreal continuing as the capital and confirming the principle of Responsible Government. Lord Elgin refused to accept the advice of those who were not his ministers and who could not command a majority in the Assembly (even if it were driven home with rotten eggs), so the obnoxious bill became law, "rebels" were compensated, and after a debate in the Imperial Parliament, the British government refused to disallow the Canadian act. Violence from the right had failed, just as violence from the left had previously failed. The old trick of appealing to the Imperial government[8] had failed. The Tory opposition, gentlemen and bullies alike, was put in the painful position of having to accept the will of the people.

A majority vote seems today self-evidently conclusive. In those days, this was not at all the case. "Democracy" to many was a word of evil import, something practised by repulsive republicans and repudiated by all proper British subjects. Sir Francis Head had inveighed against it, Sir Charles Metcalfe fought against it, John A. Macdonald disapproved of it. The comments in Conservative London dailies were bitter against the principle, and Elgin's conduct was viewed as "degrading subordination to the absolute will of democrats" or to "a tyrannical democracy". Yet the measure was carried in the Assembly by 47 to 29, and of these there were 23 English votes for and only 18 against leaving 24 French votes for and 11 against. Here lies the inner significance of the Rebellion Losses vote: it constitutes a specific turning point in Canadian political theory, away from old semi-monarchical conceptions, where the Assembly was but one element in government along with others, to the new ideas of North America, the continent where privilege had been swept away, where one man's vote was as good as another's and where the will of the majority was the ultimate sanction.

The logical conclusion of the events of April, 1849, was delayed until October of the same year, when the Annexation Manifesto appeared. The charge of treason lay much more fairly against this pronouncement than against the Rebellion Losses Bill. It was signed by a curious combination of Montreal Tories and *Rouges*, but mainly by Tories, mem-

---

[6] Lord Elgin to Earl Grey, 5 May 1849.
[7] Lord Elgin to Cumming Bruce (father of his second wife), 10 June 1849, in Elgin Private Papers. References kindly furnished by Prof. D. C. Masters.
[8] As exemplified in the MacNab mission.

bers of the mercantile aristocracy of the city,[9] who now saw themselves ruined by the policy of the British government and forced under French domination by the conduct of its representative, the governor. At last they were making the threat that Lord Durham had foreseen: they were proposing to remain English at the expense of being British. It must be admitted they had considerable provocation. The Imperial government, through the Tory Sir Robert Peel, had cast off the colonies like old shoes, and all its fiscal legislation had unintentionally favoured the elder American son. Defection from the Empire evidently paid.[10] But so nakedly and unashamedly to exhibit the truth of the saying that where the treasure is there is the heart also, to turn against all their British past, they who had shouted themselves hoarse in their denunciation of "traitors" and "French rebels", put these loyalest of the loyal in a sorry light. The Montreal variety of Canadian Toryism, no longer able to wring profits from the country it had brought to the verge of revolution, amply demonstrated that its "patriotism" was exactly equivalent to self-interest and forfeited forever any special character as a "loyal" element.[11]

The actual Annexationists, it is to be said, were mainly confined to Montreal; up-river Toryism, expressing itself in such organizations as *The British American League*, had kept its skirts clean. The two groups represented a real line of division. The Tories of Montreal were and are the merchant group, the bearers of the commercial state of the St. Lawrence. Their "loyalty" was geared to their pocket books: they had been ready to make a quick jump during the American Revolution, but on Canada remaining in the Empire, had soon acquired a large voice in the control of the province, which paid handsome dividends. With the destruction of their regime by the coming of Responsible Government, it seemed natural to men accustomed to judge of right and wrong by the columns of a ledger to urge the course that would bring back their prosperity. With the up-river Tories, however, the bonds of Empire were sentimental as well as commercial.

3. Prosperity and Reciprocity

The Annexation squall blew out as rapidly as it had blown up, and for the same reason: hard times had brought it on, and returning prosperity

---

[9] Among the signatories were A. T. Galt and several of the Molsons.

[10] A colony can be counted upon, a foreign country cannot; it is therefore the independent power that will be courted.

[11] Yet in 1937 the Montreal *Gazette* denounced the Governor-General of the day, Lord Tweedsmuir, much as it had denounced Lord Elgin, because, according to its notions, he was not "loyal". See p. 544.

dispersed it. Like other depressions, that of 1846-47 ran about three years and then improvement set in, slowly at first but with mounting rapidity. The tide turned in 1849, in 1850 there was a slight stir of business activity, in 1851 there was moderate prosperity, and in 1852 "good times" had returned. By 1853, the pace was becoming rapid, and had it not been for the outbreak of the Crimean War in 1854, there might have been another collapse. Instead, the war, reciprocity, and imports of capital postponed that until 1857.

The return of prosperity was hastened not only by recovery in England but by demand from the United States. This was something new in Canadian experience. It was a reflection of American growth. Great centres like New York and, after 1850, Chicago were insatiable in their demands on the territory contiguous to them for anything that could be usefully consumed. New York at first drew down to itself the products of its Hudson valley. Then with the building of the Erie and Champlain canals, it secured those of the territory directly tributary to them. It reached across Lake Ontario from Oswego in the 1830's and across Lake Erie from Buffalo in the 1840's, capturing the Canadian white pine on those lakes. This process of the great consuming centre pulling into its own market all the products of its hinterland has already been alluded to in previous chapters in the case of London and the Atlantic.[12] Now, as new settlement built up larger and larger American urban centres, the United States began to change from its earlier simple economy of supply to a more mature one of demand, subjecting British North America not to one pull, as previously, but to two or more. Great Britain would continue to draw through the St. Lawrence, but New York would exert a tug felt from Nova Scotia to Detroit, and soon Chicago, through the lakes, would begin to try to capture the western settlements, not to mention lesser attempts to secure a portion of the Canadian hinterland by cities like Boston and Portland.

As the new half-century began, it was becoming plain that there was a good deal of geographical predestination about the trade relationships of Canada and the United States. It reinforced the determination of various influential men in Canada, after the drastic experience of the 1840's, to see that all the eggs should not again be put into a single basket. There must be a second market, and the United States must supply it. Here lay the genesis of the Reciprocity Treaty of 1854. Lord Elgin was convinced that nothing but entrance to the American markets could save Canada for the Empire. Canadians like William Hamilton Merritt, who had had the bitterness of seeing the magnificent St.

[12] See p. 201ff.

Lawrence canals completed only to remain idle because of the competition of American railways and Atlantic ports[13] abetted by the unrepealed remains of the Colonial System,[14] were convinced that with no favours to either side the St. Lawrence would come into its own again. Maritimers were suspicious because it was their trump card—the right under the convention of 1818 to keep Americans out of the inshore fisheries—that would be used to lever open the American market for Canadian products. Americans were indifferent; British America had almost been forgotten. It was only when the colonies began to enforce the Fisheries Convention by seizing American vessels that they realized its presence. Then they became annoyed and a dangerous international situation resulted, with both British and American naval vessels on the fishing grounds to enforce national rights.[15] Yet without the actual threat of war that the fisheries protection service stirred up, it is questionable if there would have been a Reciprocity Treaty. In the United States, the prospects of a treaty were related to the growing rift between North and South. It is often said that the Southerners were opposed, as believing that Reciprocity meant Annexation and, since all the colonies were opposed to slavery, a dozen more Senatorial votes against them: it is a sounder view that they were convinced by Lord Elgin in his celebrated champagne-drinking mission to Washington in 1854[16] that only Reciprocity, and therefore prosperity, would keep them out. At any rate, the Treaty was passed, and Elgin proved right. The colonial infant had made its first toddling steps beyond its own doorstep.

4. The First Canadian Railway "Boom"[17]

Meanwhile pre-Reciprocity prosperity joined to the energy that came with self-government had been prompting accomplishments in other directions. It was disappointing to see the canals lying idle because New York, after having stolen one march with the Erie a generation before, had now stolen another in the form of a railroad paralleling it. It was disappointing to reflect on the long winter closing of the St. Lawrence, with the northern colonial metropolis hibernating for half of every year

---

[13] See p. 207ff.
[14] The Navigation Acts, or what was left of them, were repealed in 1849.
[15] See p. 443.
[16] It was said at the time, somewhat in overstatement, that "the Reciprocity Treaty was floated through the Senate on champagne". See O. D. Skelton, *The Life and Times of Sir Alexander Tilloch Galt*, p. 288.
[17] The latest standard work in Canadian railroading is G. R. Stevens, *Canadian National Railways*, I, *Sixty Years of Trial and Error (1836-1896)* (Toronto, 1960).

and the southern republican port wide open. Why could the colonies not avail themselves of the new invention as well as the States? There had been talk of railways in Canada for a quarter of a century: why could there not be some action? The little portage road from Chambly to Laprairie,[18] a mere fifteen miles, was not much to show for so much talk.[19]

It was natural that the first substantial project should reach out from Montreal in an attempt to overcome its gravest defect, the winter closing. The closest point on salt water to that city is Portland, Maine, only 300 miles away, and Portland, like other American coastal cities, was anxious to reach up into the interior by railroad in order to secure for itself a hinterland that nature had not given it. The joint scheme of the *St. Lawrence and Atlantic* and *Atlantic and St. Lawrence* lines to connect the two cities would give Portland a hinterland (a light in which Montreal had probably not thought of itself) and Montreal a winter port. Among the leaders from Montreal was Alexander Tilloch Galt, then President of the British American Land Company, across whose territories around Sherbrooke in the Eastern Townships the proposed line would run. Galt signed the Annexation Manifesto at approximately the same time as he was negotiating the railroad; the son of a novelist and a poet, he turned out to be a typical "big" business man of the type that Montreal necessarily produces. He may be taken as the very embodiment of the forces that were at work building up larger political structures for economic motives.

The first piece of ambitious railroading in Canada, like much of the rest, was an attempt on the part of Montreal business men to extend the territory tributary to their city. In the end, Portland's attempt to tie in Montreal led to its own subjugation: it became merely the winter port of Montreal, which thus laid a good part of Maine under tribute.

The southern rival, New York, having reached Lake Erie, looked for more territory to conquer, saw the easy gradients and rich pine forests lying north of Lake Erie, and welcomed the lines that were pushed across the southern peninsula of Upper Canada to tap lower Michigan: these were completed in the 1850's and became the Great Western Railway.[20] Meanwhile, the Oswego Canal, the Erie's Lake Ontario feeder, was carrying off the pine growing north of Lake Ontario, in

[18] Opened 1837, to shorten the connection between Montreal and New York.
[19] For pre-Confederation railway development and its related subjects, see R. G. Trotter, *Canadian Federation, Its Origins and Achievements* (London, 1924) and G. P. de T. Glazebrook, *A History of Transportation in Canada* (Toronto, 1938).
[20] There was continuous rail connection from New York to Windsor on the Detroit River by 1855.

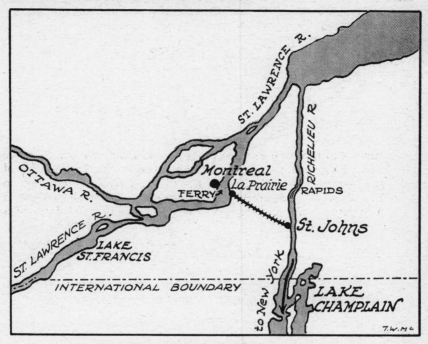

EARLY PORTAGE RAILROADS: THE CHAMPLAIN
AND ST. LAWRENCE RAILROAD, 1836

which territory every stream was being used to bring timber down to such ports as Trenton and Port Hope. But since the height of land was not far from the lake, the amount of forest that could be tapped by stream-driving was limited. The situation called for railroads, and several, such as the Rice Lake Railway, were built. The chief of these was the Northern, north from Toronto, which was to tap the dense pine forests of Simcoe County, to bring down the agricultural produce of the settlements to the north and eventually to reach across to Georgian Bay at Collingwood. This road reached Lake Simcoe in 1853 and Georgian Bay in 1855. It duplicated and extended Upper Canada's Yonge Street. By the lands it opened up between Toronto and the upper lakes, it gave the province a little breadth (about 90 miles) as well as length. but its chief result was somewhat unexpected. The western centre of Chicago was bounding ahead, buying every board and scantling that could be got on the upper Lakes. All the Canadian side tended to

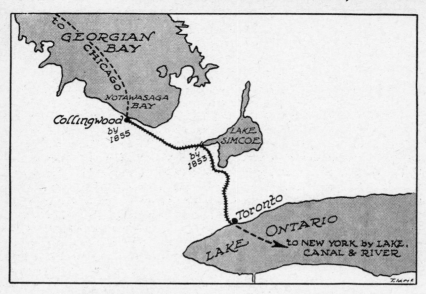

EARLY PORTAGE RAILROADS: THE NORTHERN RAILWAY
OF CANADA

become tributary to Chicago and the Northern soon found itself serving
a port from which schooners and steamers were leaving for the distant
Lake Michigan. It became a portage road across from Lake Ontario to
the Georgian Bay and somewhere along it emerged as the "watershed"
between the two rival pulls, that of New York and that of Chicago.

These were all lines built to reinforce the commercial ascendancy of
particular cities,[21] but now projects of a different nature were coming
up. Talk was heard about a railway to unite all the British provinces,
and another to link up all the country from salt water clear through to
Lake Huron, or even beyond. There was even the occasional forecast of
a line in some distant future to the Pacific Ocean. These were all projects greatly exceeding in ambition any hitherto undertaken, and they

---

[21] Boston interests, for example, attempted to capture the trade of a region as
distant as the Upper Ottawa. Boston capital built a line connecting with
Ogdensburg. From that point, Boston projected and helped to finance a line to
Bytown—*The Prescott and Ottawa*—which was to cut off the freight, mainly
lumber, of the upper river at that point and carry it down to Boston. As a rule,
these early projects overweighted the technical ability of the railroad and
underweighted the waterways, which latter did not give up the struggle easily,
and in heavy freight are still on top.

were prompted not only by economic motives but also by political. In them, especially in the project for linking the lakes with the sea, the Atlantic-St. Lawrence pull of metropolitan Great Britain was asserting itself and fending off the challenge coming up from the growing urban centres of the United States.[22]

The maritime colonies were completely isolated from the pair on the St. Lawrence. Yet the British connection, when added to their mutual uneasiness in the presence of a gigantic and assertive neighbour, was strong enough to keep all of them loosely together. In addition, Halifax and Saint John, especially Halifax, were beginning to believe that they too could reach back into the interior, as New York and Boston were doing. Why could they not get the winter trade of Canada? A line joining the provinces together would open up new territory in all of them, it would provide an all-British route for passage of mails and troops, especially in winter, and it would be a link in a vast British chain reaching out from England across the Atlantic into the recesses of North America and some day, perhaps, to the Pacific Ocean and the Orient.

There was no chance of the colonies being able to build the new road for themselves. In 1851, however, British assistance proved forthcoming when Lord Grey, that architect of empire, agreed to a loan of £7,000,-000. The line was to follow what was then considered the strategic route away from the international boundary, along the north shore of New Brunswick and thence to the St. Lawrence.[23] The move was an extraordinary one, for the amount was large and loans were not to be secured from a realistic Imperial government for the mere asking. Conditions were attached, the principal one being that no change was to be made in the route without Imperial consent. Here was the reef on which the whole project was wrecked, for the eternal rivalries of Halifax and Saint John became involved. Saint John at the time was becoming interested in another ambitious Portland project, the *European and North American* line, which was to run from Portland east to Saint John, thence up through to Halifax. Grandiose talk was heard of a jump to Newfoundland, across it, and thence steamers to fill in the gap between St. John's and Galway, Ireland, whence the railroad would begin again, on its way to London. It was hinted that this speedy route would run the trans-Atlantic steamship companies out of business and that Portland would take the place of New York. Saint John business men saw the future of their city in this link with Portland and thence with

---

[22] For the general subject, see A. R. M. Lower, *The North American Assault on the Canadian Forest* (Toronto, 1938).

[23] Following the "Robinson Line", surveyed, 1848.

the American railway net. The north shore of New Brunswick, not being on the route, stood for the other or "intercolonial", and there was much pulling and hauling between the two sections right down until Saint John, with its American love, was overborne and the north shore shoved the province into Confederation.[24]

This local jealousy in New Brunswick ruined the project, for the Saint John interests succeeded in having the government of New Brunswick demand that whatever road was built on the guarantee should run through Saint John. The Imperial government pointed out that the only justification for its loan was the strategic, which meant keeping to the northern route. The whole project, therefore, collapsed. The weak and scattered colonies had lost a magnificent opportunity of Imperial aid.

Meanwhile Nova Scotia bravely began to push a line of its own back from Halifax, but it could not find much capital and as late as 1864 it had only got as far as Truro. On Nova Scotian efforts alone Halifax could never have had its chance at the trade of the interior.

Still more fateful for the project was Canada's loss of interest in it, thanks to the greater opportunities that were opening in the west. The story of railroading in the decade of the 1850's is a tangled skein and its connections with politics close: in fact, as old Allan MacNab said, "railroads were politics". Montreal, having got its connection with the Atlantic, was now looking to the west again. Upper Canada was looking eastward towards the sea and for freight rates low enough to enable its wheat to go to England. Into all this there was released a bomb in the shape of the proposal of an English firm of railway builders to undertake a road from salt water to Toronto—or beyond! This was Peto, Brassey, Betts and Jackson, who had been building railways in all parts of the globe and now, possessed of vast experience and of huge supplies of navvies and machinery, were looking for new worlds to conquer. Their projection into Canadian life marks what might be called the conception of the Confederation movement, as contrasted with the various ideas about such a project that, in themselves, would never have flung the spark of life into it; once English interests were engaged on a dollars-and-cents basis, they were bound to see that a political framework which could give some security to their investments was erected.

There were various other factors present. There were the local ambitions for trade and the exploitation of local resources. There was a politician anxious to make a name for himself and a future for the

---

[24] See A. G. Bailey, "Railways and the Confederation Issue in New Brunswick, 1863-65," *CHR*, XXI (Dec., 1940), 367-83. See also his "Basis and Persistence of Opposition to Confederation in New Brunswick," *CHR*, XXIII (Dec., 1942), 374-97.

colonies, Francis Hincks.[25] There was the novelist's son, Alexander Galt, with his head full of big schemes about the development of Montreal and its surroundings, and his heart by no means immune to the charms of opulence. There was a Toronto group that was already looking forward to seeing their city becoming a rival metropolis, especially on the western end of the province being opened up. It was represented by such men as Casimir Gzowski, the wandering Pole, who lived to become a rich man and one of the "best people" of Toronto, and David Lewis MacPherson, later on to be again the opponent of Montreal in the struggle with Sir Hugh Allan over the Pacific Railway.

Then there was the incidence of metropolitanism, as just suggested, in the form of the firm of railway contractors. Behind them stood the two London banking houses, Glyn, Mills and Co., and Baring Brothers and Co. Few financial houses have had such wide-ranging interests as the Barings and exerted more direct control. They were influential on both sides of the boundary, keeping some of the states on the same leash of loans as Canada. They married and inter-married with Americans— Lord Ashburton, who was one of them, had an American wife—and through their members, such as Ashburton, or later, Lord Cromer or Lord Revelstoke, they became the custodians of Imperial policv and the disposers of the Imperial domain. With these two banking empires interesting themselves actively in the railroad—mainly, ic is to be presumed, to safeguard their own interests as loaners-in-chief to the provincial government—English metropolitanism took a new lease of life in Canada: the day would come when the necessary political dispositions would be engineered.

The only obstacle to English domination lay in the native capitalistic ambitions of the Galts, MacPhersons, Holtons, and Gzowskis. Galt and the Montreal group, interested in the *St. Lawrence and Atlantic,* were jealous of the new project extending up river and at one time threatened to duplicate it. Gzowski and the Toronto group clung tenaciously to their western Ontario plans. Eventually, under the auspices of government itself, all were brought together into one concern, *The Grand Trunk Railway,* whose name sufficiently indicated its nature: it was to be a great connecting thoroughfare; no mere collection of little portage roads, but the most ambitious and longest railway yet to be undertaken on North American soil. To help effect the consolidation of interests and in view of its guarantee of £3,000 per mile, the government of Canada was to name half the directors. In this way, at this early stage,

---

[25] 1805-85. Of Irish birth. Editor of the Toronto *Examiner,* a Reform party organ. In public life from 1841. Inspector-General under Baldwin, and his successor as Reform Leader. The standard life is R. S. Longley, *Sir Francis Hincks* (Toronto, 1944).

occurred that marriage of railways and government, promoters and politicians, that was never dissolved.

The game—played many times since—was to form the company, keep a controlling interest in its stock, float that portion of it in public which could be floated, and then award fat construction contracts to the "insiders". In this way, various members of the group got rich.[26] Characteristically, in the first scramble in Canadian history for the luscious fruit of railroad contracts, the primary purpose of the road tended to become obscured. Built extravagantly and unwisely as a "Grand Trunk", it was going to render the waterways obsolete, its proponents declared, so it ostentatiously steered a course three or four miles distant from each of the lake and river ports along its route. Similarly, it would show up all its rivals, so it was built with a wider gauge than other lines and could not interchange traffic with them. Later on, its gauge had to be standardized and its cast-iron rails had to be replaced by steel. But its worst handicap from the first was its colonial-jobber and old country-promoter management. The effects of this combination were never overcome, and although it had the best territory in the country, the Grand Trunk Railway, until the day (65 years later) of its absorption into the Canadian National, was never a financial success.

The money dumped into Canada by the orgy of railroad building in the 1850's has been estimated at as high as one hundred million dollars. Nothing remotely approaching it had ever occurred before in the country's history, not even the British expenditures during the War of 1812. Much went to promoters and contractors; a little, but no impressive amount, to the English financial interests, who in general found themselves outdone in their own area by the smart colonials; and a great deal in actual costs of construction. English methods were expensive, unnecessarily elaborate, and not well-fitted to the country. The English interests had themselves to blame for their financial woes. Between all these groups, the money was shoveled out, making every little point near which the railway was to come think of itself as likely to become a great city. The real-estate promoter, that familiar figure on the Canadian landscape, profited accordingly. This expenditure, together with the profits drawn from the Crimean War and the buoyancy attributable to Reciprocity gave Canada a positively hectic three years of prosperity from 1854 to 1857, and incidentally some railroads. It was the first of

---

[26] Gzowski and Co. secured the contract for the section from Toronto to Sarnia, and "the members, Galt, Holton, MacPherson, and Gzowski, all made fortunes" (Trotter, *op. cit.*, p. 167).

other similar experiences, to be repeated each time a new major project was undertaken.[27]

5. The Liberal-Conservatives

The political events of the period were rather overshadowed by all these dizzy railway jobs, but the two, of course, are organically connected. The transitional period from Downing Street domination to colonial self-government had been definitely completed with the Rebellion Losses Bill, and from that event onward, the province had its fate in its own hands. The so-called "Great Ministry" of Baldwin and Lafontaine (1848-51) reflected this, enacting many useful measures. Of these, apart from the Rebellion Losses Bill, the University of Toronto Act was perhaps the most enduringly important; others effected useful administrative changes, very necessary in a community where public affairs had been managed in slip-shod, antiquated fashion for half a century, but did not embody outstanding principles. The ministry's third year saw its locker empty of legislative shot. Mere lack of measures to enact would not have affected the avidity of the ordinary Canadian politician for office, but both Baldwin and Lafontaine were tired of the obloquy that had been consistently hurled at them from the right and which was now beginning to come from the left, too. The great Canadian compromisers had given their country an example of the kind of understanding partnership between the races that should always exist at the top in Canada and under which alone the country can be at peace with itself. Now, still in the prime of life (Baldwin was 47, Lafontaine 44), both made the decision to retire.

They left administration in the hands of lesser men, men who were not Olympians, not capable of piloting the boat through the rapids but quite equal to the stretch of rather sordid railway politics upon which it was now entering. Among these the most prominent at first was Francis Hincks, who became the English head of the province's second double-barrelled administration, the Hincks-Morin[28] ministry. His job was financial, and in his efforts to secure the Reciprocity Treaty, he deserves well of his country. Whether the same can be said of his connection with the Grand Trunk is not so certain. His day of prominence was not long, for there was one greater than he in the background who was to seize the stage and then hold it for many a long year.

[27] As the C.P.R., the National Transcontinental, Grand Trunk Pacific, and Canadian Northern.
[28] Morin, 1803-65, was able and respected, but not strong enough to be the successor of Lafontaine. One of the authors of the 92 resolutions of 1834.

This was the rising Kingston lawyer, John Alexander Macdonald, who was also that rather rare phenonemon in Canada, a Scottish and Presbyterian Conservative. It is probably not fair to call him a Tory[29] for Scottish Toryism is something else again, a compound of impossible loyalties and romantic traditions, which cherishes loves, hates, and status but has little relationship to reality. With the exception of the native-born Sir Allan MacNab, no really Tory Scotsman in Canadian public life comes to mind. Bishop Strachan would be the nearest, though it is to be suspected that with him it was mainly that through Toryism there lay *le moyen de parvenir.* The characteristics proper to Scottish Tories Macdonald did not have, though he had the Highland fire and dash that often goes with them. He was a kind of imaginative realist, a clear-sighted, cool-headed boon companion who at one and the same time could both be "one of the boys" and bend all "the boys" to his own purposes, a born manager of men. But as might be expected of a young man who had known too much of the *res angusta domi,* he was rather too given to the main chance—not for himself in a monetary sense, but for his party and himself in the sense of immediate success—rather too much a stranger to a broad philosophy and to those enduring principles that characterize the greatest. But he was affable, attractive, and mag-nanimous—a man sure to succeed.

It was Macdonald who combined in himself the perspicacity which saw that a time for a rearrangement of political groups had arrived and the gift of manipulation necessary to bring it about. He had a good case. The old feuds were over: Responsible Government was no longer an issue, the French were co-operating, and Upper Canada had settled one of its difficult questions with the establishment of the provincial university. Hincks was unable to get rid of the ancient millstone of the Clergy Reserves, and Morin in his half of the province could not dispose of that outmoded inheritance from New France, seigneurial tenure; these were both pressing. If moderate-minded men could get together, they would be able to form a stable administration and secure for them-selves a long lease of power. Let them concentrate on practical tasks, such as railway building, which did not divide the country on funda-mentals. Leave that to the violent young fellow running *The Globe,* George Brown:[30] it would serve to keep him out of office. His associates,

---

[29] Elgin spoke of him as "one of the Tories who is becoming reasonable".

[30] 1818-1880. Came to Canada, 1840's. Editor and owner of the Toronto *Globe.* Identified himself with the "Clear Grits" about 1854, and shortly became Upper Canadian Liberal leader. His doctrine of "Rep. by pop." contributed greatly to bringing about the deadlock of 1864 and his agreeing to form a ministry with Macdonald at the time, opened the way to Confederation. See J. M. S. Careless, *Brown of "The Globe",* 2 vols. (Toronto, 1959, 1963).

the so-called *Clear Grits*, the agrarian radicals from western Upper
Canada, who represented the left wing of Reform, would share his fate.
Their agitation for annual parliaments, in imitation of the English
Chartists, or soft money and universal suffrage would only serve to
frighten the men of property without securing anything for the
farmers. As for the French, their coming man, Georges Etienne Cartier[31]
had been solicitor for the G.T.R. for some years and saw things almost
in the same commercial terms as the English. In a new political combination he would realize his own personal ambitions and be able to look
after the interests of his people. The extreme Tories were discredited
and would have to go along whether they liked it or not.

Just how many of these considerations occurred to Macdonald, it is
naturally impossible to say. Probably a good many, for it was in this
practical calculation of odds that he was most at home. Whatever the
arguments he used, they were successful, and his new combination was
duly formed. A good deal of life had gone out of the Hincks-Morin
administration, which was under fire from both sides. The Reformers,
in accomplishing Responsible Government, had completed their programme, and a Reformer with a completed programme is a Conservative.
There was, therefore, not a great deal to keep Conservatives and Hincksite Reformers apart. The new elections of July and August, 1854, had
given no party a clear majority,[32] and if Hincks and Morin were going
to carry on, they would have to fall back on personal combinations of
groups. A coalition with the Tories would command a good working
majority.[33] Sir Allan MacNab, High Tory Leader, took office along with
Morin[34] though Macdonald and Cartier were the energetic young men

---

[31] 1814-1873. A nominal rebel in 1837. Cartier moved to the right during the
1840's, and after he was appointed solicitor for the Grand Trunk, he came
close to the Montreal commercial group. Since he was also becoming the
acknowledged leader of the majority of French Canadians, this double capacity
and his own gifts made him a key man during the 1850's and up to Confederation. See John Boyd, *Sir Georges Etienne Cartier, Bart: His Life and
Times* (Toronto, 1914).

[32] On Sept. 5, 1854, the Hincks-Morin Ministry, meeting Parliament after the
elections, was beaten in a vote on the speakership, 62-59, and a little later, on
another vote by 61-46.

[33] Its composition was, approximately: French Canadians following Morin, 46;
Conservatives, formerly Tories, 32; Hincksite Reformers, 22; total, 100. This
left in opposition 30 members, of whom about 19 were "Rouges" and 11,
"Clear Grits".

[34] 1798-1862. See p. 278. No one hunted rebels with more vim in 1837 than the
super-Loyalist MacNab. Yet in 1854, he took office with a man who had been
identified with rebellion.

behind the scenes, and the most effective and lasting manoeuvre in Canadian party history was thus consummated.

The new Liberal-Conservative combination took in everybody from the extreme right to all but the extreme left, the only groups left outside being the little band of *Clear-Grits* and the *Rouges.* Yet at first it was considered no more than a coalition, not a party; it was only gradually that the different elements in the coalition grew together into a party. The ministry itself was described at the time as consisting of "Ultra Romanists" from Lower Canada with four Tories of the deepest die from Upper Canada and "one lonely Reformer".[35]

The new group was essentially one of action. It did not base itself upon ideas, though it possessed prejudices. As such it suited the Canadian people, who as pioneers in a new land, were unreflective but carried on the complex of emotions, loves, and hatreds handed down to them by their fathers. Everything matched so perfectly that, with the exception of an interval or two,[36] the new party governed Canada until 1896. As long as it did so, serious racial cleavage was avoided, for the party rested on both races and both religions, together with the north and south poles of British connection and French indifference thereto. It was unbeatable, and Macdonald was its prophet.

Chronology

1847   Collapse of the Timber "Boom".
1847–50 Depression.
         Tentative attempts at Reciprocity.
1848–51 The "Great Ministry" of Baldwin and Lafontaine.
1849   The Rebellion Losses Bill.
         The Annexation Manifesto.
1851   Times begin to improve.
1851–54 The Hincks-Morin Reform Ministry.
         Opening of the St. Lawrence and Atlantic Railway.
1853–60 Grand Trunk Railway under construction.
1854   Reciprocity Treaty.
1855   Northern Railway open, Toronto to Georgian Bay.

Additional Reading

Allin, C. D. and G. M. Jones. *Annexation, Preferential Trade and Reciprocity.* Toronto, 1911.
Careless, J. M. S. *Brown of the Globe.* 2 vols. I: *The Voice of Upper Canada,*

[35] See J. P. Macpherson, *Life of the Right Hon. Sir John A. Macdonald* (Saint John, N.B., 1891), I, 276.
[36] 1862-3; 1873-8.

1818-1859. Toronto, 1959. II: *Statesman of Confederation, 1860-1880*. Toronto, 1963.

Currie, A. W. *The Grand Trunk Railway of Canada*. Toronto, 1957.

Skelton, Oscar. *The Life and Times of Sir Alexander Tilloch Galt*. Toronto, 1920.

Stevens, G. R. *The Canadian National Railways*. 2 vols. I: *Sixty Years of Trial and Error, 1836-1896*. Toronto, 1960. II: *Towards the Inevitable, 1896-1922*. Toronto, 1962.

Walker, F. G. *Catholic Education and Politics in Upper Canada*. Toronto, 1958.

CHAPTER 22

Nationalism on the Horizon

A Fair Trial for Union and Self-Government, 1854-64

1. Self-Government

With the formation of the Liberal-Conservative ministry of 1854, the local autonomy of the province of Canada passed out of the experimental stage. Government became visibly more efficient. New departments, such as Agriculture, were established, and men of high calibre found employment in the Civil Service. It seemed also as if union were going to work. Reciprocity had been secured, railway building was proceeding apace, settlement was going forward, the population of cities and towns was increasing, their local institutions were working well, the lumber trade was flourishing, with two outlets now instead of one, schools were being opened, and the various institutions of higher learning were beginning to get on their feet. All statistical tests showed progress. Less than ten years later, by 1864, the sky had clouded over, and it seemed as if the united province had come to the end of its tether; despite substantial material progress, its institutions simply would not work.

In 1854, the first job of the new government was to deal with the ancient problems of Clergy Reserves and Seigneurial Tenure. The Reserves question no longer occasioned its former bitter dissensions, and when government proposed to secularize, after making provision for clergymen who depended on revenue derived from the Reserves, the measure went through rather easily.[1] So with the Seigneurial Tenure, which, although an economic handicap of even greater magnitude, had never provoked so much antagonism. Opportunity was now offered for *censitaires*, if they so desired, to commute their payments, capitalized at six per cent interest, and get clear titles. Church lands, said to be one-quarter of the whole, went untouched. The seigneurs did very well for themselves in that the ungranted lands, for which under the Arrêt of Marly (1711) they had been only trustees, became theirs in outright ownership; they also were voted a collective compensation of five million dollars for cancellation of their other rights. The next year (1855), a more contentious measure was passed, giving the Roman Catholics of Upper Canada, in expansion of the Act of 1843, their own separate schools, a measure of justice that nevertheless provided new sources of division.[2]

2. The End of Good Land: Expansive Forces

The first regular Annual Report of the Commissioner of Crown Lands (1856), in an excellent survey of the lands still remaining to the Crown, drew attention to a condition that was to be of primary importance in the succeeding forty years. The simple statement was made that there remained in the whole province of Canada very little more good land available for settlement. There were still small parcels here and there in the form of bush land held for private sale. But everywhere from the Saguenay to the Georgian Bay, the settlers were now in contact with "the rough country", "the lumbering counties", by which terms was meant the Canadian Shield. Into this, settlement could not enter with any degree of success. Government was aware of the problem and was sending out survey parties every year to look for new areas of good land. In the "Huron-Ottawa Tract", lying between the Upper Ottawa and the Georgian Bay in the county of Renfrew and the district of Muskoka a certain amount was found. Some fair townships were known to lie around the western end of Lake Superior. But these latter were out of range at the time, and farmers' sons never thought of them. Instead, they headed out to the American west, to Iowa and Minnesota. For the first time, Canada was feeling a sense of spatial limitation.

[1] Carried, 70-33.
[2] The latest references on Catholic Separate Schools are F. G. Walker, *Catholic Education and Politics in Upper Canada* (Toronto, 1958); C. B. Sissons, *Church and State in Canadian Education* (Toronto, 1959); and Margaret Prang, "Clerics, Politicians, and the Bilingual Schools Issue in Ontario, 1910-1917," *CHR*, XLI (Dec., 1960), 281-307.

Government drove roads from "The Front" and from the Ottawa, into the Huron-Ottawa Tract,[3] hoping to divert the stream of farmers' sons from the States. But to no avail. Young men who, after the custom of the time, had spent a winter in "the camps" knew well enough that under the pines there lay sand or rock, not good loamy soil, and it did not tempt them. Resort was had to immigration. There had been a certain amount of public effort made to promote immigration as early as the 1830's, when Dr. John Rolph was sent to England to lecture on the attractions of Upper Canada; now in the late 1850's, a Bureau of Immigration was set up. Its propaganda abroad set the tone for Canadian immigration methods, and it was not a melodious tone: the literature sent out pictured Canada as a kind of earthly paradise.[4] Naturally when the immigrant arrived, finding not gold in the streets but hard work and rough conditions, he would be disappointed and often leave for the States. Many of those induced to come were themselves unsuitable. At the end of the 1850's, considerable numbers of Irish and Germans were brought to Canada and settled on the new colonization roads. These newcomers, complete strangers to "the bush", would slash down the best of the pine for the nearest lumber company, and when they came to the sand, they too often "got out". Their inexperience often resulted in forest fires that burned in a season as much wealth as they would have produced in a lifetime. This programme of immigration gave Upper Canada the little German settlements near Pembroke and west of Renfrew and the scattered Irish in the back townships of the St. Lawrence counties; where the soil gave them half a chance, some of these people made good, but the others remained sunk in apathy, typical "hill-billies"—of whom Canada has more than its share!

Lower Canada welcomed no immigrants but made strenuous attempts to divert the stream of its own people from urban New England to colonization projects. The same difficulties were encountered, but they were more successfully overcome, for the French, since they did not expect very much from life, made better pioneers than immigrants who came under the impression that fortune lay ahead. The French had developed a sensible and systematic mode of attacking the wilderness. They made their colonizing efforts in groups, organized around their priest, who was leader-in-chief. He kept them together, and if the women could have their church and the consolations of their religion, the men found bush life not uninteresting; so things went fairly well on a humble basis.

[3] The Bobcaygeon Road, the Ottawa and Opeongo, etc.
[4] This deceptive type of immigration advertising obtained as late as the 1920's.

The system had been used in the establishment of new parishes along the St. Lawrence, but it was at the period under discussion, the end of the 1850's, that it was given its first prominent trial against the Canadian Shield in the interior.[5] In this early penetration of the Shield, the settlers had their first clash with the lumbermen, who soon became loath to see them coming among their pines: settlers often meant the ruthless destruction of the forest, regardless of what was underneath. In the eyes of the colonizing priests of Lower Canada, the increase of mankind was to be considered before lumbermen's profits. The struggle between exploitation and settlement thus entered another phase, waged not so much in the legislative hall as in the backwoods.

The end of good land had much to do with the first piece of Canadian expansionism, the determination to secure the British west. It was about 1855 that a group of Torontonians, including William McDougall,[6] who was to be the first unfortunate Canadian governor of Rupert's Land, and George Brown, began to interest themselves in "The North West Territories". The government sent out an exploring party in 1858 that reported favourably on the agricultural possibilities of "the fertile belt" lying from Red River along the North Saskatchewan to the mountains and containing, it was estimated, some 64,000 square miles of land.[7] Its importance was soon to be heightened by the discoveries of gold on the Pacific coast. About the same time a few Canadians drifted into Red River.

The big problem was how to terminate the sovereignty of the Hudson's Bay Company over the North-West. Under the Company's regime, Great Britain had lost the Oregon country, and now, with the approach of American settlement to the 49th parallel, it was possible that she would lose the North-West also. The British government was awake to this danger, and in consequence, it put the whole question into the hands of a Parliamentary Committee of investigation. Canada sent as her representative before the Committee her chief justice, W. H. Draper; his main point was that "the boundaries of Canada must be determined". The people of Canada, speaking through their legislature, if not the government, were saying that these boundaries should extend

---

[5] Mainly up the valley of the St. Maurice.

[6] 1822-1905. Associated with George Brown on the Toronto *Globe* from 1857. Entered coalition of 1864. A "Father" of Confederation. There is no published biography of McDougall, but a good M.A. thesis on him is in the Queen's University Library; see D. E. McFee, "The Honourable William McDougall" (Queen's, 1953).

[7] In 1961, about 100,000 square miles were occupied in the three prairie provinces.

to the Pacific Ocean. But the Committee refused to recommend a delimitation of the boundary and left the whole issue open for further negotiation. Although London would make no precise disposition of the question, the inquiry had the result of committing the British government to the thesis that a large, fertile area could not remain under a commercial company but must sooner or later come under the control of Canada.

3. Commercial Distress Once More

The impulse towards territorial expansion was reinforced by the course of business. In 1857 a sharp commercial depression, marking the deflationary aftermath of the Crimean War, came into the colonies. It was combined with poor harvests. It is significant that just as its worst effects were being realized Alexander Galt drew up his memorandum of a Confederation scheme, entered the Cartier-Macdonald government on a Confederation plank, and a little later brought in the first confessedly protective tariff (1859). At the time there was much complaint of the emigration going on from Canada, especially from Lower Canada, where Galt's British American Land Company still had homesteads to dispose of. A man of his clear-sightedness would see in a larger union the remedy for many of these economic ills. When he, as a minister of the Crown, put his weight behind a Confederation scheme, it became more than an idle fancy.

The depression was relatively short-lived. Railroad building was still going on, and as long as it continued, it was bound to blow away any depression, however severe. However, recovery was equally short-lived, for the outbreak of the American Civil War brought so much uncertainty that business once more came to a stop. The war had the usual effects on trade: first, dislocation, then a slow recovery as people got their second wind, then a rush of war orders, and finally high prosperity as Northern demand swept away Canadian stocks. The period closed in 1864 as it had begun, ten years earlier, on a note of "boom".

By that time, a different Canada had emerged. There was now relatively good railway connection throughout the province. A large increase in population, especially in Upper Canada, had taken place. Wealth had increased greatly; the young barrister Oliver Mowat, was making several thousand pounds a year at his law practice in Toronto. There was a consciousness of strength about. John A. Macdonald could say in 1861 that the province was becoming an ally rather than a dependency of Great Britain. Industry was growing up, especially around Lake Ontario, thus creating a new vested interest that was to have strategic political affiliations. The province was making not only material progress, but progress in the arts, in self-consciousness and self-confidence. The decade of the fifties was the best period Canada was to experience down to the 1900's.

Growth brought its problems and experiments. It was within these ten years that provision was made for gradually introducing the elective principle into the Legislative Council: at Confederation the experiment had not been completed. In 1858 occurred the roundly-abused manoeuvre of the Conservatives, known as the "Double-Shuffle".[8] It was a piece of sharp practice, but was accepted by the Governor, Sir Edmund Head,[9] who, by refusing a dissolution to George Brown, gave a dubious and misleading precedent for Byng in 1926. A few months later, Galt's tariff, already mentioned, became the occasion for a considerable extension of autonomy. British merchants found themselves facing the same protective duties in the Canadian market as foreigners, and protested to their government. The British government of the day was loath to see one of its colonies going in for protection when it held to free trade, but Galt met its objection by the argument that if Canada was to govern itself, its responsible ministers in its Legislature must be the only judges of the kind of taxes that were to be imposed. The British government did not carry interference any farther, and Canada took entire control over its tariff.

Autonomy, Canadians were to learn, carried with it corresponding responsibilities. The threatening nature of American relations during the Civil War prompted the British government to press measures for defence on Canada, but when the Cartier-Macdonald Government introduced these in the Militia bill of 1862, they were conclusively defeated.[10] A good many Lower Canadians deserted their leader, Cartier, to vote against the bill. British newspapers were loud in their expressions of disgust and decided that Canadians were not manly enough to defend themselves. The explanation of the defeat of this bill is complex: Canadians, especially French Canadians, did not deem that

[8] Macdonald and Cartier were defeated on the floor of the House. Brown was called on to form a ministry. Accepting office, he had to resign his seat. His followers could not secure a vote of confidence for him in the House; after two days in office, he had to give up his attempt to form a government. The former ministers came back, took different portfolios, and thus under a law of the time, avoided having to face election. Within a short time they resigned and resumed their old offices. This was "the double shuffle".

[9] 1854-61. See D. G. G. Kerr, *Sir Edmund Head, A Scholarly Governor* (Toronto, 1954).

[10] The vote for the bill: Upper Canada, 32; Lower Canada, 21. Against: Upper Canada, 24; Lower Canada, 37. Total: for, 53; against, 61.

the bad blood between England and the North was their business;
Canada was passive in the quarrel; the amount to be expended frightened members; and the spirit of party was so bitter as to cause party
advantage to be placed before public necessity.

The rejection of the bill helped confirm in English minds the impression already strongly fixed there that, while colonies in general were
probably undesirable, Canada in particular was just a plain nuisance
and should be encouraged to take itself out of the Empire as soon as
possible. It was a parasite stuck to its parent's body (no inhabitant of
the British Isles had any idea how firmly it was anchored there!).
English official support of the Confederation movement, when it came,
derived in part from the hope that it would be easier to get rid of one
large colony than of several smaller ones.

4. Sharp Tension Without and Within the Country

The most significant aspect of the period lies not in specific measures
but in the play of forces that eventually caused the wheels of government to stop. These consisted in sharp tensions within and without the
province and in vigorous personalities driving their own opinions and
interests to the limit.

Sharp tensions without arose from the American Civil War. All
British North Americans were against slavery, but since President
Lincoln carefully avoided identifying the war with slavery, they became
puzzled. Their sons enlisted in Northern Armies,[11] but the people at
home were unable to avoid yielding to long-standing prejudices and
soon became frank in their appreciation of Northern difficulties.[12]
Celebrated diplomatic passages such as the *Trent* Affair, which concerned Great Britain alone, were matched by border incidents which
gave Northerners the chance to accuse the Canadians of not acting
neutrally.[13] These culminated in the St. Albans Raid of 1864.[14] Relations between the Anglo-Saxon peoples, bad enough in the previous
decade, became worse. The curious thing was that the colonials refused

---

[11] Some 40,000 it is said, though the figure has been challenged. See R. W.
Winks, "Creation of a Myth: 'Canadian' Enlistments in the Northern Armies
during the American Civil War," *CHR*, XXXIX (March, 1958), 24-40.

[12] A column of American news in the *Acadian Recorder* of Halifax, which had
formerly been headed "United States", now became "Disunited States".

[13] These are detailed in L. B. Shippee, *Canadian-American Relations, 1849-1874*
(Toronto, 1939), Chap. 7.

[14] Made by Southerners from a point near Montreal on St. Alban's, Vermont.
Little more than a plundering expedition.

to get alarmed: later on they were much more excited and frightened by sporadic "Fenian Raids" than by the possibility in 1864 of the armed might of the United States being turned against them.

Sharp tensions within were many and varied. One of considerable significance was set going by the development of industry and the appearance of industrial capitalism. During the 1850's industries secondary to lumbering, such as axe factories, came into existence, and in the Toronto area especially, agricultural implement factories, foundries, and works auxiliary to the railways sprang up. New and pushing men appeared, men impatient of the old would-be aristocratic elements in Canadian life, men who often were not within the old Anglican, Tory framework.[15] With their appearance arose the demands for "protection for home industries" that have never since ceased to be heard.[16] Pressure from such groups, together with their own views, resulted in Cayley's tariff of 1858 and Galt's of 1859 with their resort to what they termed "incidental protection", but what was, without subterfuge, protection. The rise of industry provided a new sharp antithesis in Upper Canada, flinging an urban protectionist group against the radical, agrarian, free-trade "Grits", who in their turn represented a protest movement against commercialism—that is, against the mercantile and forwarding interests in Montreal and other river and lake ports.

Since mercantile and industrial groups both had natural affiliations with Conservatism in politics, they tended to divide the English wing of that party, leaving the Quebec "Bleus" as the determining element in it. This split was accentuated by the association of commercialism primarily with Montreal and by the growing primacy of Toronto and neighbourhood in industry. It was also reinforced by geography, for the country immediately tributary to Montreal extended into Upper Canada as far as Kingston. John A. Macdonald, several times in the course of the "Rep. by pop." controversy, used the argument that the Union could not be resolved into the original two provinces again and that either everything as far west as Kingston would have to be included in Lower Canada or three provinces be erected. He was fond of speaking of eastern Upper Canada as "Central Canada". But it was from the

[15] The founders of the firms of Massey-Harris or of Gurney Stoves, or the new financial men, such as William McMaster, first President of the Bank of Commerce and founder of McMaster University, furnish examples.

[16] Isaac Buchanan organized his "Association for the Promotion of Canadian Industry" in 1858, consisting largely of Toronto and Hamilton manufacturers. See D. C. Masters, *The Rise of Toronto: 1850-'390* (Toronto, 1947).

western part of Upper Canada that the most dynamic impulses proceeded, as the rise of the "Clear Grits" and of industrialism indicate.

Both groups in western Upper Canada maintained the traditional hostility of the interior to Montreal. The Montreal business men found their chief interests then, as always, in wide-ranging schemes of transportation. They had, it is true, to share the great project of the time, the Grand Trunk Railway, with the business men of a still greater metropolis, London,[17] but though the Englishmen predominated, the Montrealers never entirely lost their grip. Georges Etienne Cartier, a Montrealer, at an early date became solicitor for the road and remained so until late in his life, whether Premier or not. A. T. Galt was close to the Company throughout the period. Western Upper Canadians in general and the "Grits" in particular identified the Grand Trunk not unfairly with Montreal exploitation; they thought of it as another tentacle of the strategically placed metropolis that ever since its founding in 1642 had been trying to "hold the gorgeous west in fee". Toronto and "The Grits" were not far wrong when they equated the railway, the city, and the Conservative ministries of Cartier and Macdonald.[18]

This fresh tension between east and west might have been released had there been available a new programme of public enterprise comparable with the original main job of railway building (whose completion is marked by the construction of the Victoria Bridge across the St. Lawrence in Montreal, opened by the Prince of Wales in 1860). But there was none, and efforts to frame one failed. If Maritimers and Canadians could have agreed upon the building of an intercolonial railway, a new period of material achievement would have opened that might have eased not only sectional strains but the more serious political strains arising out of them. Two unofficial interprovincial conferences, held in Quebec in 1861 and 1862, to see if something could be worked out, had little result.

In the organization of both of these interprovincial gatherings, the Grand Trunk Railway was prominent. The interest of the railway in seeing the British provinces flourish was plain. Mr. Thomas Baring of Baring Brothers and Co. had been its interim president. Holding the sword of finance above the head of the Canadian government, his own firm and Glyn, Mills and Co., were able to give "advice" that would not be misinterpreted. Thomas Baring was succeeded in the presidency of

---

[17] See p. 287.
[18] "The Grand Trunk Railway Company governs Canada at the present moment. Its power is paramount. The Ministry are mere puppets in its hands. . . ."— *The Globe*, Toronto, April 22, 1857. Quoted in Masters, *op. cit.*, p. 65.

the railway by Edward Watkin,[19] a busy and energetic English railroader, who had gained the confidence of the Duke of Newcastle, Colonial Secretary (1859-1864), though not of the permanent officials of the Colonial Office, and through him had a channel of influence upon all colonial governments. The G.T.R. group probably expected to construct, with handsome contracts, and operate, the intercolonial railway of which there was so much talk; such a line might make their unproductive extension to Rivière du Loup worth something. The Civil War, particularly American threats to terminate the Bonding Acts, had shaken their attachment to Portland, Maine, as the one railway outlet for Canada, and apparently they were ready for an "All-British" line from Montreal to Halifax. To business motives in this politico-railway complex there is to be added genuine Imperial sentiment on the part of men like Watkin, who had made up their minds that the scattered colonies should not fall into the lap of Uncle Sam.

Yet not all the influence of the G.T.R. and its friends would make the pieces in the jigsaw puzzle go together and no agreement could be reached. At one time the Imperial government would not guarantee the necessary loan, at another Canada would not take on itself as large a share of the cost as the other provinces wished, at still another a change of government required all negotiations to begin over again. The conferences of 1861 and 1862 had proved encouraging but abortive. Perhaps their chief value had lain in enabling Canadian and Maritime public men to get acquainted. One of the main difficulties was the Grand Trunk itself. John Sandfield Macdonald's[20] Reform ministry of 1862 viewed the inter-colonial scheme as a Grand Trunk project aided and abetted by their political enemies, the Conservatives. The Reformers' relations with the Grand Trunk were not good, the railway not finding it as easy to get what it wanted out of them as out of Tory ministers who were also "company men". The Reform ministers reacted strongly against the superior Englishmen who were running the Grand Trunk in Canada, especially the General Manager C. J. Brydges.[21] Tories were more amenable. The Grand Trunk Railway, like the Canadian Pacific later, a "Conservative baby", was somewhat unjustly regarded by Reformers as a political device of their opponents for keeping in office; when they themselves got in, their attitude was hostile.

[19] His book on the period is valuable: E. W. Watkin, *Canada and the States, Recollections, 1851-1886* (London, 1887).
[20] 1812-72. Glengarry Gaelic-speaking Catholic Reformer. Advocated the "double-majority" principle. Premier, 1862-4. Premier of Ontario, 1867-71.
[21] C. R. W. Biggar: *A Biographical Sketch of Sir Oliver Mowat* (Toronto, 1905), I, 116.

This attitude contributed to the failure of the intercolonial scheme in 1863 and later was to delay the Pacific Railway in Alexander Mackenzie's ministry. It was an unfortunate reflection of the extreme partisanship of Canadians and this, in turn, of the sharp antitheses of the country.

5. Racial Cleavages and Party Groupings

Geographical and economic tensions in Canada were and are deep enough, but they are pale in comparison with the violent antitheses of race and religion. In the period under review, these primary antitheses were, to some extent, correlated with industry and transportation but it was the expansive buoyancy of Upper Canada and the nature of the new political machinery of the Union that threw them into the harsh relief that eventually broke down the structure. By 1861 Upper Canada had several hundred thousand more inhabitants than Lower, but only the same number of representatives in Parliament. The men of that day could not be expected to foresee that the two curves of growth were not likely to continue at their current rate of divergence: they looked forward to a constantly increasing discrepancy between the English and French. The discrepancy in wealth was greater still. Upper Canada's contributions to the revenue were rated at four or five times those of Lower Canada, yet the recurring charge was that most of the public moneys were spent in Lower Canada. Upper Canada had had to accept Separate Schools Legislation, carried against the wishes of a majority of its representatives by Lower Canadian votes.[22] Whether the situation was unjust or not is hardly the question; most Protestant residents of Upper Canada were convinced that it was, and the more extreme among them were prepared to go to almost any length to end it. In a deliberate attempt to "swamp the French" the Act of Union had given equal representation to each province. After Upper Canada swung from having a lesser population than Lower to a greater, the French held, rather justly, that it was not sporting of the Upper Canadians to wish to change the basis of Union into one of representation by population. The Act of Union, therefore, which by almost any judgement, had been conceived in sin, stands high in the list of causes of breakdown.

Ministerial government itself accentuated the difficulty: it had been accorded to all the provinces without their having the clear-cut party

[22] The main Separate Schools Acts were passed 1843, 1855, 1863. The latter was introduced by Richard (later Sir Richard) Scott of Ottawa, a Catholic, during the Reform administration of J. S. Macdonald. It was passed with only a half-dozen Upper Canadian Reform votes, all Catholic, J. S. Macdonald's included.

system which alone enables it to work well. In Canada, there never was a period that brought forth more ability or more vigorous personalities, and there were plenty of matters large enough to give ministries and assemblies vital work to do. But political forces came to be in such nice balance that the wheels of government finally refused to turn. When in 1854 the Liberal-Conservative coalition was engineered, it was expected that stable government would result, the groups left outside being small. Just the contrary was the case. It is true that from 1854 to 1864, every ministry except three[23] was drawn from what was loosely called the Liberal-Conservative party, but a little examination of the politics of the era shows that what in reality was happening was the formation and dissolution in rapid succession of group governments, based only in part on party affiliation and just as much on personal loyalties and racial groups.

The original MacNab-Morin ministry of 1854 combined English Tories with "Reformers" and French Moderates. These latter, in the course of a year or two, became *Bleus* and to their fellow-racialists of more leftish tendencies was left the term *Rouges*. *Les Rouges*, as political descendants of Papineau, were "Red Republicans", "socialists", anti-clericals, and atheists; their tenets were those of European Liberalism. The *Clear Grits* in Upper Canada were by no means their opposite numbers; coming mainly from west of Toronto, the newest part of the province, they were a characteristic North American frontier and agrarian group, born naturally on Canadian soil but consciously influenced by American precedents. They were "excessively devoted to the elective principle": they would have elected all officials from the governor down. That is, they were typical pioneer democrats, and it was largely through them that the tone of political life in Canada shifted from its old oligarchic and monarchic note to that of the democracy taken for granted and eulogized today.

The mere fact of being in opposition together was not sufficient to make *Clear Grits* and *Rouges* into a political party. They had certain general ideas in common,[24] but on the pressing practical matters of the day, they could not agree. "Representation by population", the great Grit cry, sprang not only from the feeling that Upper Canada was being discriminated against but also from the good pioneer thesis that one man is as good as another, that one man should have one vote. But no *Rouge* could accept "Rep. by pop." unless he wished to commit

---

[23] The abortive Brown-Dorion two-day ministry of 1858 and the two ministries of Sandfield Macdonald, 1862-64.

[24] As, for example, "the sovereignty of the people".

political suicide, for it was a racial programme. Nor could *Rouges* and Grits agree on the equally divisive subject of separate schools.

The groups furnishing the "Liberal-Conservative" ministries exhibited a similar degree of division. English Conservatives themselves shaded all the way from the ultra-violet of Sir Allan MacNab to the pale blue position of former Baldwinites or Hincksites who continued to think of themselves, rather vaguely, as "Liberals". Among the French, the word "Bleu" did not necessarily mean "Conservative": Georges Etienne Cartier insisted on calling himself a "Reformer" as late as 1857, three years after the coalition. Within each racial section, sub-groups might appear at any moment, followers of some strong man: Joseph Cauchon was credited with having had in the Parliament of 1854-57 a personal following of 18 members, sufficient to enable him to force on the ministry the North Shore Railway policy[25] and accompanying extravagant land grants.[26] The defection of 18 votes would have defeated nearly all of the ministries under the Union.

A collection of groups based partly on race, on regionalism, on political doctrine, on personalities, and least of all on a common political programme, cannot be called a party system. Under the Union there seems to have been little party organization and less discipline. Private members were far more independent in speech and vote than they are today, and the House of Commons was correspondingly freer. The tradition of the day was against coercion on the part of the executive. Ministers did not interfere in local elections. When the elections had been held and until Parliament assembled, they did not know what support they would get; when the House met, the test usually came on the election of a Speaker, but its results could easily be upset by defections. It is no wonder, then, that ministries were invariably short-lived.

The disintegrating effects of a system of groups were accentuated by the mode in which parliamentary life was conducted. Ministerial government was a new game, and everybody seemed to get the utmost enjoyment out of playing it in punctilious adherence to the rules. A modern Canadian minister is almost impossible to dislodge, but his prototypes under the Union resigned with amazing frequency. Ministers seemed to be coming and going all the time, either because a certain vote had indicated the withdrawal of the confidence of the group that they represented or because they had quarrelled with a colleague, or because the Premier of the day thought he could see a few more seats

[25] A line along the north shore of the St. Lawrence from Montreal to Quebec.
[26] Biggar, *op. cit.*, I, 66.

in a cabinet rearrangement.[27] Whatever the reason, retirements and reconstructions were invariably accompanied by full-dress speeches, in which everyone set out at length, and with the most extreme parliamentary nicety his position and his reasons. Very often when changes had been made in heat, these debates were the occasion for personal passages of a most unrestrained nature. After John Sandfield Macdonald had dropped D'Arcy McGee from his cabinet of 1863, the latter burst out against his leader to the effect that "if he followed any man, it would be one with steady principles and courage, and not a piece of dough which was moulded in one shape today and another tomorrow".[28] In these interchanges between late colleagues, presumably of the same party, no holds were barred. The contrast with the ironclad solidity of the party ties and attitudes of today is sharp.

Looseness of political organization required the Crown's representative to act very differently from today, when his duties have become nominal and ceremonial. If no one knew who could form a cabinet with a fair chance of securing a vote of confidence, it was evidently the Governor-in-Chief's duty to make the best selection he could. When the Macdonald-Cartier ministry resigned in 1858, Sir Edmund Head sent for A. T. Galt to form another. Galt was a man with no personal following and no ministerial experience: he failed to secure support, whereupon the Governor sent for George Brown, and on his failure for Cartier. Today, our inflexible party allegiances and our formally chosen party leaders, with the logical by-product, an official "Leader of the Opposition" in receipt of an official salary, give the Governor-General virtually no freedom of action.[29]

This analysis of the political situation under the Union brings to mind the France of the Third Republic, with its multiplicity of party groups and their doctrinal differences, with its ministries formed by powerful personalities out of the circle of *ministrables* and drawn from the party groups in such a way as to command an immediate, though precarious, majority on a vote of confidence. The Third Republic, like Canada under the Union, was in constant political crisis because it could get no government with a chance to endure until it had worked out its policies.

[27] When J. S. Macdonald dropped McGee and Sicotte for Dorion and Holton, just before the election of 1863.

[28] J. P. Macpherson: *Life of the Right Hon. Sir John A. Macdonald* (Saint John, N.B., 1891), I, 453.

[29] Though with four parties in a more or less evenly balanced House, as in the Parliaments of 1962 and 1963, these views may need some modification, especially since the electorate has become more flexible in its party allegiances than in the old days.

In the twenty-seven years of the Union there were eight parliaments, innumerable ministries or re-constructions of ministries and some ten persons who could have been designated "premier". The main basis for what stability there was was the political ingenuity of John A. Macdonald after 1854, which succeeded in keeping a fair-sized group of members from Upper Canada (though these followers were steadily lured away from him as the province went over more and more to the "Grits") attached to the large *Bleu* bloc from Lower Canada under Cartier. This combination gave enough parliamentary votes to maintain a small majority provided that matters of too controversial a nature did not arise.[30]

So many involutions and evolutions occur in the period that all the familiar correlations of Canadian life were thrown into disorder; all the wires became crossed. Montreal Tories, who had scorned French Canadians for ninety years, found themselves in 1854 working in the same ministry with them. Orangemen who had chased "rebels" in 1837 and had cheered for the Tories at every subsequent election found themselves swinging in behind George Brown and the Grits. They could not long refuse adhesion to any man shouting, as vehemently as only George Brown could, such battle cries as "No denominational schools", "Rep. by pop.", and "No Popery". But the followers of Brown were Reformers who might actually have carried a musket with Mackenzie in 1837 and who ever since had been bitter opponents of nearly everything that Orangemen stood for. They, and those Orangemen who followed them, staunch Imperialists though they were, had to work with the "Red Republican" *Rouges*. The situation grew still more complex in 1863 when the Catholic Glengarryman, John Sandfield Macdonald, became Reform leader.[31] John Sandfield abandoned the device he had talked about so much, the "double majority"[32] and voted against his Upper Canadian Protestant supporters for another Separate School bill.

Matters rose to a pinnacle of contradictions during the visit of the Prince of Wales in 1860. When Orangemen erected arches at Kingston and Belleville, the Prince, under the advice of the Colonial Secretary, the Duke of Newcastle, refused to land unless the insignia of a group

[30] As the Militia bill of 1862, in which many of Cartier's *Bleus* "bolted".
[31] There has always been a place for Catholics in English-Canadian Liberalism, simply because Canadian Toryism has been so imperialistic and so close to Anglicanism. Canadian Liberalism has usually consisted of a smallish group somewhat to the right of the Tories, and a large group to their left.
[32] Sandfield Macdonald had advocated the plan of requiring ministries to secure a separate majority from each half of the province on important legislation.

hostile to the religion of so many of Her Majesty's subjects were removed; it was not, and the towns did not have the royal visit. Similar incidents occurred at Toronto, where Orangemen stuck up their insignia over the doors of St. James Cathedral while the Prince was attending a service there: he outwitted them by leaving through the vestry.[33] This large and powerful group of rabid Protestants, which constantly proclaimed its "loyalty" and its attachment to all things British, had insulted the heir to the throne; yet John A. Macdonald, loyal British subject and second in Her Majesty's Canadian Ministry, was shortly afterward to make a long and apologetic speech to them, explaining how wrong Her Majesty's Colonial Secretary had been to give such advice to the Prince! The reasons for ministerial instability during the Union are not far to seek.

6. The Men Concerned

Upon this exceedingly tangled situation there played a number of forceful, able personalities, nearly all in the prime of life. In 1860, J. A. Macdonald was 45, Cartier, 46, Galt, 43, Brown, 42, J. S. Macdonald, 48, A. A. Dorion,[34] 42, L. V. Sicotte,[35] 48, D'Arcy McGee,[36] 35. These eight men, of varying personalities, all strong, of widely different temperaments, diverse interests, creeds, and origins, were constantly thrown together in the intimacy of the old Parliament of Canada. They were in and out of the ministries of the day, sometimes serving together, at other times in opposition. Each one pressed his own point of view hard, was unsparing of his opponents in his words and not overly influenced by considerations other than his own. Together they drove the Union coach down hill at top speed.

It was little wonder that at last it went into the ditch. Galt had become identified with Montreal high finance and the Grand Trunk Railway; he was anything but popular with Upper Canadian agrarians. Cartier, for the same reason, shared this unpopularity, and his intransigent stand for the interests of the French increased it. Dorion, as a *Rouge*, was anathema to the French clergy, but could not work effectively with George Brown, who had incurred for himself the bitterest of all the hates of the period. It was Brown, more than any other man, who

---

[33] Masters, *op. cit.*, pp. 85-86.
[34] Became *Rouge* leader in the 1850's. Opposed Confederation. Minister of Justice, 1873-74.
[35] A French-Canadian *Rouge* leader, 1860-64.
[36] Irish Nationalist, later Canadian Nationalist. The orator of Confederation. Assassinated by a Fenian, 1868.

by his unrestrained vehemence, which loosed the strongest passions of
Protestantism, destroyed the Union. D'Arcy McGee was a newly-arrived
Irish Catholic, suspected of disloyalty to the Crown. Although he sat
in a Reform ministry, not all his eloquence could render him acceptable
to Protestant and British Upper Canadians. Sandfield Macdonald, the
only non-French native-born of the group, was one of the weaker
characters, but in control of the Catholic wing of the Reform party,
which was not so much Liberal, as anti-Tory. There remained only
John A. Macdonald, great reconciler of differences, skilful manager of
men, to keep ministries together and win votes in the House. He himself,
who knew so well how to be all things to all men, had faults of character
of which his opponents did not fail to make the most. That he was a
procrastinator, leaving difficulties to settle themselves if possible, was
well known, though he had not yet earned the nickname, "Old Tomorrow". Worse than that, while a good Presbyterian himself and a
loyal subject of the Crown, he associated with and seemed to favour
French Catholics, ready, apparently, to sacrifice his own province to
Lower Canada. Privately, it was said that he was a complete opportunist, laughed cynically when topics such as "patriotism",[37] were mentioned, and would stop at nothing merely to stay in power. During the
period 1858 to 1863, his tenure of office depended on Cartier's Lower
Canadian majority: he could not count on more than half of the Upper
Canadian Conservatives. His prestige, not added to by the very dissipated life he was leading, was never to be so low again; he was not far
from being a discredited politician. Yet as he himself later remarked, if
he had chosen to identify himself with the racial feud, he could have
had all Upper Canada behind him. He was not given credit for something that may account for a good deal of his conduct, a determination
to keep the experiment going as long as possible in the hope that some
unexpected turn of events would bring it out all right.

All the tact of "John A." would have failed in the end: the two
halves of the province were uneasy bed-fellows, the two races could not
forever be driven in double harness. That was becoming increasingly
clear. The election of 1861 had given the Cartier-Macdonald ministry
a majority in both provinces, but within a year it had been shattered
by the vote on the Militia bill. Sandfield Macdonald, compromise leader,
had carried on for another year, only to receive a vote of want of confidence at the end of it[38] and, in the ensuing elections, an impracticable

---

[37] Biggar, op. cit., I.
[38] May 8, 1863. Vote against government, 64-59. Upper Canada: for, 31;
against, 28; Lower Canada: for, 28; against, 38.

majority of two or three.[39] This was the ministry that was to resign in
the winter of 1864, leaving the task of government to whomever was
strong enough to undertake it.[40] Sir Etienne Taché was persuaded by
the Conservatives to come out of retirement and have a try at it. After
having attempted to induce various Upper Canadian Reformers to join
him, along with Cartier "Bleus" and Macdonald Conservatives, he
formed a party administration which, on May 14, 1864, received a
majority of two. A month later, June 14, it found itself in a minority of
two. Two elections and four ministries in three years! Everyone recognized that it was impossible to go on. Out of the impasse came that
coalition which, by bringing John A. Macdonald, Cartier, Galt and
George Brown into the same cabinet, was to open a way—a way not to
be closed, as it proved, until Confederation was reached.

Chronology

1854   The Liberal-Conservative Coalition.
          Seigneurial Tenure and Clergy Reserve Acts.
1857   The Parliamentary Committee of Inquiry on the Hudson's Bay Com-
          pany.
          Commercial Crisis.
1858   Decimal Currency.
          Ottawa chosen Capital of Province of Canada.
          The "Double-Shuffle".
          The Galt and Head Plans for a Confederation.
1858–62   The Cartier-Macdonald Ministry.
1861   Outbreak of the American Civil War.
1862   Defeat of Cartier-Macdonald Ministry on the Militia Bill.
1862–64   John Sandfield Macdonald's Reform Ministry.
1864   "Deadlock" and the Macdonald-Brown Coalition.

Additional Reading

Biggar, C. R. W. *A Biographical Sketch of Sir Oliver Mowat.* Toronto, 1905. 2
     vols.
Cornell, P. G. *The Alignment of Political Groups in Canada, 1841-1867.* Tor-
     onto, 1962.
Creighton, Donald G. *John A. Macdonald.* I: *The Young Politician.* Toronto,
     1956.
Kerr, D. G. G. *Sir Edmund Head, A Scholarly Governor.* Toronto, 1954.
Lewis, J. *George Brown.* London, 1926.
Lower, A. R. M. *et al. Evolving Canadian Federalism.* Durham, N. C., 1937.

[39] The approximate party complexion in the Parliament of 1863 at first, was
     Upper Canada: Liberals, 41; Conservatives, 24; Lower Canada: Liberals, 24
     or 25; Conservatives, 40 or 41.
[40] It had carried a vote of confidence on August 8, 1863, by 63-60.

Masters, D. C. *The Reciprocity Treaty of 1854*. New York, 1937.
———. *The Rise of Toronto, 1850-1890*. Toronto, 1947.
McFee, Dougal Edgar. "The Honourable William McDougall." (Unpublished M.A. thesis, Queen's) 1953.
Pope, J. *The Memoirs of Sir John A. Macdonald*. Ottawa, 1894. 2 vols.
Shippee, L. B. *Canadian-American Relations, 1849-1874*. Toronto, 1939.
Thorburn, Hugh, ed. *Party Politics in Canada*. Toronto, 1963.
Underhill, F. H. *In Search of Canadian Liberalism*. Toronto, 1960.
Watkin, E. E. *Canada and the States, Recollections, 1851-1886*. London, 1887.
Wheare, K. C. *Federal Government*. New York, 1947.

CHAPTER 23

The Miracle of Union

1. Political Unions

Making one political body out of two is among the most difficult of human tasks. The difficulty increases as the square of the number to be united, so to speak. It took centuries to unite England and Scotland, more centuries to form Italy or Germany. But here on this North American continent two political miracles have occurred: thirteen American states peacefully united to form the United States of America, and then three British provinces equally peacefully formed the Dominion of Canada. How is this mystery to be explained? Very few achievements in state-building have been peacefully accomplished. As a rule larger political structures have been built by conquest, by dynastic marriages, or in areas with some self-government, by bribery. France was put together by the conquests and marriages of Philip Augustus and his successors. Scotland and Ireland were brought into the United Kingdom by mixtures of consent and bribery. Rarely, if ever, have small entities submerged themselves in greater out of pure political conviction.

If we introduce overmuch idealism into explaining the formation of either of the North American polities, the record of mankind is against us. So is our own history. The thirteen colonies came together not primarily because of the joy in making a great free American community, but because disintegration stared them in the face and men of substance saw in union salvation for their fortunes. It is no reflection on

British North Americans that they too made their union under duress. Goldwin Smith's sneer that "the Father of Confederation was said to be Mr. So-and-so, or Mr. So-and-so, but that the real father was deadlock", may be passed over. To make a large political structure out of smaller ones is such a supreme achievement that it requires every device and pressure known to man, and no one need be ashamed if these go beyond a heroic blowing of bugles.

After all, the marvellous element in Canadian Confederation was the smoothness and ease with which it was accomplished. There was not much in the way of precedent: the United States and, more remotely, England and Scotland, or England and Ireland; possibly Switzerland. Canada is the second in the world's great federal structures. The task was not as great, the solution was not as original, as that of Annapolis in 1789, but it was a good second and has worn well. Both instances speak volumes for the political capacities of the people making them: two political miracles from one continent is a very good record.

2. Large Factors in Confederation

Canadian confederation depended upon three large or "remote" factors: a sense of British North American unity never wholly obscured; the forces of continentalism working through mechanical advances in transportation: and the emulation, jealousy, and fear of the United States.

The framework of union was the over-riding British allegiance, which threw the colonies together in a potentially hostile world. At the Montreal interprovincial banquet of 1861, Joseph Howe exclaimed, either in a burst of after-dinner good feeling or because he meant it, that if the public men of the various colonies could only get together as they were then doing, they would discover what excellent fellows they all were and the barriers between them would soon go down: "Oh, if you fellows would now and then dine and drink with us fellows . . .". Here were men drawn together not because of the common social traditions, which in the case of some of them were closer with the Americans than with their fellow colonials, but because of a common political loyalty. Nor did the official aspects of the British connection have much to do with it. As Howe said, in the same speech, "We have done more good by a free talk over this table tonight than all the Governors . . . could do in a year, if they did nothing but write despatches". Confederation was not a matter of official British despatches but of the British memories in the hearts of the colonists—a tribute to the force of history.

Yet just as the most loving family memories do not prevent daughters from losing touch with each other if they remain apart too long, so the common allegiance of the colonies probably would have become less significant as they found their individual roles in the world, had not devices appeared which could bring them together. The eighteenth century British Empire had been cradled in the ocean world of the North Atlantic. A generation or two after the eldest daughter went out of her mother's house, slamming the door behind her, she had turned her face inland, devoting her energies to the exploitation of the internal riches of a continent. Without slamming the door, Canada, especially Upper Canada, did the same; the destinies of the St. Lawrence colonies lay in the interior. For the Maritime provinces, however, the ocean remained the highway: they belonged to that string of island or peninsular colonies running all the way down the coast from Newfoundland to Trinidad. To them the interior hardly existed. Their Atlantic position was emphasized by the ridges of the Appalachians, row on row, between them and the St. Lawrence, practically eliminating communication by land. What little intercourse there was with the St. Lawrence went on by sea, around the end of the Appalachian Barrier where it entered the Gulf at Gaspé. Nova Scotia from Halifax to Yarmouth, New Brunswick from Chignecto to the Maine border, remained within the hinterland of Boston. Even so, by mid-century, on a basis of "flour down, coal up", the St. Lawrence had begun to attract the northern and eastern parts into its orbit again, as they had been in the old French days. Oceanic forces towed the Maritime colonies out to sea; continental forces split them in two.

This balance of forces was affected by each successive improvement in transportation. A good road across the mountains would at any time have drawn a part of New Brunswick into the St. Lawrence orbit. Ocean steam navigation strengthened the position of the American ports: Halifax, lying on a great circle from New York to the English Channel, became a port of call for Samuel Cunard's steamers; the St. Lawrence, off at right angles to the route, had to furnish its own separate line. Destined to be more potent than ocean navigation was the railway, the technical instrument that led to the triumph of continentalism in North America, tying the whole continent together in one tight geographical unit. That stage, however, was preceded by the efforts of individual ports to extend their separate hinterlands.[1]

The railway development, which was such a powerful factor in Confederation, was a reflection of these efforts of individual ports and of national, or political, conceptions. A railway to bind the British colonies together had been a favourite plan for a generation. It had been shoved

[1] See p. 282.

aside by the prior interest of Canada in roads more immediately useful, and complicated by the scheme for the *European and North American Railroad*. But with the Grand Trunk built through to Rivière du Loup and ambitious men seeking fresh worlds to conquer, the scheme revived again. There were strong sectional arguments for it: it would give the St. Lawrence a British American winter outlet; it would, so it was thought, give Halifax a continental hinterland; it would—and here was the talking point for securing Imperial assistance—a route for troops from one colony to another, if the Americans attacked. A railway to the Maritimes was regarded by the Canadians as a somewhat expensive luxury, but the assurance that Confederation would bring it went far to secure the adhesion of Nova Scotia and northern New Brunswick to the Quebec Conference scheme.

The third general factor, jealousy and fear of the United States, has been interfused with every incident of Canadian history; it and the British tradition have been opposite sides of the coin. In the Confederation period, for scattered colonies just becoming self-conscious, the American federation constituted a standing challenge in political accomplishment with benefits, despite the Civil War, plain for all to see. Colonial jealousy of the Americans was an old story: it took the form of superior airs—an attempt to ascribe undesirable characteristics to the successful neighbour and to oneself indefinable qualities of refinement, breeding and moral excellence—the habitual escapist refuge of the weak in the presence of the strong. At bottom it was mainly a simple human lust for the luxuriant fruits just over the garden wall. There had been so many occasions for fear: boundary disputes, quarrels over the fisheries, memories of the War of 1812, and now the bad relationships growing out of the Civil War. At the time, the American attitude was emphatically not that of the good neighbour. After 1865 there was a whole catalogue of reasons for fear: an unemployed Northern army, Fenianism, and the pronounced unfriendliness of the government of the United States.

3. Intermediate Causes

Those causes of Confederation that grew specifically out of the conscious motives of men may be termed intermediate. Four of them may be named: metropolitan finance, prospects of new areas of exploitation, personal ambitions, and the appeal lying in a big job of political construction.

British financial Imperialism, which had followed the trader and the soldier, was well represented in North America. The two great London

banking houses associated with the Grand Trunk Railway held over the
Canadian government, through the London money market, all the power
of St. Peter to bind and loose. Through Peto, Brassey, Jackson, and
Betts, they had become deeply involved in the Canadian railway
situation, and through Francis Hincks, they had become deeply involved
in the provincial government. Neither party seems to have foreseen that
A. T. Galt and other natives would show so much prowess in securing
a share of the good things. When peace was restored between the two
groups, the railway turned out to have become a project that might
prove beyond Canada's strength. A situation might arise in which, not
for the first or the last time in history, bankers and bondholders would
have to dictate political policy.

It may be a mere coincidence that it was at that juncture that Galt
worked out his Confederation scheme (1858), and as the price of his
becoming their Minister of Finance, succeeded in getting the Cartier-
Macdonald group to accept it as an official (if at that time rather
academic) plank in their platform.[2] A union of all the provinces would
give a larger credit base for financing provincial liabilities and the railroad would profit indirectly if not directly. When in 1860, E. W.
Watkin was persuaded to attempt the thankless task of straightening out
the Grand Trunk's affairs, a primary condition of his acceptance was,
according to his own account, the large Imperial consideration of a
union of the colonies, followed eventually by a railway from coast to
coast. He convinced the somewhat surprised London bankers that while
the Grand Trunk might be put in better order, only by some such bold
scheme would it actually pay returns.

Watkin became active in political circles in Canada. The intercolonial Conference at Quebec in 1861 was a piece of his stage-
management. Given the entrée he had to the Colonial Secretary, the
Duke of Newcastle, it may be that the Prince of Wales' tour in 1860 was
another. To start on his Pacific scheme, he brought together a group
in London to buy out the Hudson's Bay shareholders and then persuaded Sir Edmund Head, ex-Governor-General, to become the new
Governor of the Company. Meanwhile he kept in the confidence of the
Duke of Newcastle, whom he says he found in deep sympathy with his
ideas. This mixture of London and colonial finance, empire-building
enthusiasms, railway operation, colonial politics, and large Imperial
interest was potent in bringing about Confederation.

To Watkin and the London group the North West Territories came
in as valuable in themselves but still more valuable as a route to Asia.

[2] See p. 298.

To Canadians, they were of more immediate importance. As long before as 1851, George Brown had "discovered" the West. He had failed to wrest it from the tenacious grasp of the H.B.C., but had won recruits as interested as himself, notably William McDougall. The North-West must belong to Canada. Not only would the pressure of population, caused by the approaching end of arable public land, be relieved, but out in the west a counterbalance could be built to French Canada. Neither Brown nor his associates seem to have taken the Hudson's Bay claims very seriously, a state of mind that Watkin, after he had put his money into the old company, found to his distaste. Montreal capitalism in the pre-Confederation era was not much interested in acquiring the West. When it came to building a railway, it popped up at once, but the dreamers of Toronto and London were chiefly responsible for the master-strokes that opened the way for a dominion from sea to sea.

From pure egoism the Confederation movement was relatively free. There was no towering figure bestriding the narrow British North American world in the 1860's. There were many men with "a good conceit of themselves", but there were no Napoleons. One wounded soul there was, however, whose absence from the Charlottetown and Quebec Conferences of 1864 was to affect deeply the future of Canada, Joseph Howe. Of all the Fathers of Confederation, it was a fellow Nova Scotian, his young rival Charles Tupper, who possessed the largest measure of self-appreciation.

For ordinary ambitious men, the appeal that lay in a large job of political construction must have been potent enough. The colonial stages had been small, and upon them the limits of a career were soon reached. The governorship of a small British colony was preferable in dignity and responsibility to that of a colonial premiership. A new union would bring a larger life, greater responsibilities, bigger rewards. It would powerfully beckon leaders of men. More than that, the task of building something, always in the forefront of men's motivation, was a challenge, especially the engrossing task of building something so intricate, so difficult, so spectacular, as a new state.

4. Immediate Circumstances, Internal and External

Direct occurrences and influences that manifest themselves in the period just preceding the culmination of a historical movement may be denominated "immediate" causes. The "immediate" period of Confederation began in 1858 when A. T. Galt's sponsorship, as that of a senior statesman, hauled the idea down out of the clouds and made it semi-practical politics.[3] As more sand got into the machine of government, a change of some sort became imperative. The idea, in the two years 1862-64, came closer to reality. Two solutions were being suggested: one, the more practical because the easier, a federalization of the two halves of the province of Canada; the other, still apparently far off, a union of all British North America. Only with the political deadlock of the spring of 1864 did the larger plan triumph. From that time on until 1867 was its period of gestation, during which on several occasions it seemed about to miscarry. On July 1st, 1867, its birth took place.

In this interval of three years, opinion and action differed from province to province. In Lower Canada, the proposals evoked no burst of enthusiasm. That province had done very well under the Union, and the new arrangement was the subject of considerable suspicion. Was it another up-river device like "Rep. by pop.", for putting French-speaking Canadians at the mercy of an intolerant Protestant majority? There were those who said it was. Calmer voices like Cartier's assured the people that their rights would be safeguarded and that in the area dearest to them, the intimate things of every-day life, they would be safer than before, for they would have provincial home rule. The attitude of the church turned the scale: pronouncements by the bishops approved the scheme. Most of them took the view that Confederation was the only alternative to eventual annexation, than which nothing could be worse.[4]

In Upper Canada, there was, on the contrary, a discernible warmth in the reception accorded the new Dominion. But only secondarily for its own sake. Through it Upper Canada was escaping from prison. No longer would it be legislated for and taxed by French Papists. For Upper Canada, Confederation meant provincial home rule, too. Nor need it have any fears of the general Government, for it was the largest and strongest of all the provinces. Only among the few of wide vision and tolerant minds did pulses beat a little faster than before at the distant prospect of nationhood.

In Nova Scotia, active opposition, led by a group of Halifax merchants, soon began. It received a spokesman in Hon. William Annand, proprietor of the *Morning Chronicle*, Joseph Howe's old paper, and shortly afterward, a still more formidable protagonist in the person of Howe himself. Most of the opponents were genuinely convinced that union with Canada would be detrimental to the interests of their

---

[3] See p. 298.
[4] Robert Rumilly, *Histoire de la province de Québec* (Montreal, 1940), I, Chap. 1.

province: they pointed to the possibilities of direct taxation,[5] to the adoption, now that the Reciprocity Treaty was disappearing, of a licensing system for foreign fishermen in the inshore fisheries instead of their exclusion, and to the protective tariff of Canada, just then being raised still higher.

Howe's attitude is harder to explain. He had placed himself on record at various times as in favour of a union, sometimes in emphatic terms. And now he was rousing the province against it, expounding rather thin arguments such as that the province was safer in its isolated position than if linked up with regions so open to American attack as the Canadas, flinging out visionary schemes of a tight British state with a central constitution and universal conscription. Howe had been invited to Charlottetown and Quebec but his duties as British Commissioner of Fisheries had seemed more important to him at the time than conferences that could be foreseen as historic occasions. Or did he absent himself because he would not appear on the same stage as the pushing and arrogant Charles Tupper,[6] who had already taken the old hero's measure at the polls? Howe, with all his qualities, was a great egotist, and the sight of a successful rival may have been too much for him. Or was it that, despite his earlier work for Responsible Government, he was no more than a colonial who preferred the crumbs that fell from the rich man's table in England to the promise of North American nationhood? As he put it himself, what was Ottawa, that distant backwoods town, to him, contrasted with that greater and more glorious capital, London—a capital where, if he would have confessed it, he had licked a good many boots in vain for that preferment in British Colonial Service which his colonial status prevented him from obtaining. London, with its halo of tradition and its metropolitan impressiveness, perhaps captured the romantic Howe, who in this crisis of his life turned to the past and could not catch the vision that lay in the backwoods capital.

Probably beneath these attitudes, beneath his jealousies, a still deeper sentiment determined him: that which, common to every Nova Scotian, has continued to make the province an uneasy partner in the Canadian state—devotion to a peninsula set off in the ocean by itself, with enough history behind it by 1867 to make it already an incipient nation. Nova Scotia disliked Confederation as New Englanders disliked western expansion, because it meant absorption in a larger whole whose dynamic

[5] The first direct taxes in the history of the province had just been provided for by Tupper in his Educational Act of 1865.
[6] 1821-1915. Became Conservative premier of Nova Scotia, 1863, after defeat of Howe in election of that year. In Dominion politics until 1900. Prime Minister, 1896.

centre was elsewhere. To this day the people of Nova Scotia, some of them, are in Confederation but not of it, Canadians according to the law but in their heart of hearts men by themselves, Nova Scotians.

Neither in Nova Scotia nor in Canada were the people called upon to vote upon the proposal. The fact has often been made much of, but in 1866 no responsible public man would have agreed that every important issue had to be put to a popular vote. The people elected their representatives (on a property franchise), and it was the representatives' duty to take decisions. This was the form of government that had been established in the 1840's, not popular "democracy".[7] Hence public men in those days were not overly perturbed by public agitations got up by political opponents; if ministers could secure a favourable vote in the Assembly, that was the sanction they looked for, and this Tupper had done.

In New Brunswick, Premier S. L. Tilley,[8] a strong supporter of Confederation, did go to the polls, was soundly beaten and as soundly criticized by John A. Macdonald for poor tactics. Not until an intricate series of manipulations had been made, extending from Fredericton to Ottawa, from Ottawa to London, and from London back again to Fredericton, was the reverse repaired. The recall of a governor unfavourable to the union was secured; his successor virtually forced an election on his advisers, and when the election was over, Tilley was back in power. He had risked Confederation, not on a grand gesture towards the popular will, but on a mistake in generalship. Yet the election gave a sanction that had not been obtained elsewhere, and New Brunswick, the crucial colony, found itself within the gates. The reasons for its reversal of attitude are not entirely clear; New Brunswick politics rarely are.[9] It has been asserted, with good show of proof, that just as American money had been judiciously distributed to secure the consent of the province to the Reciprocity Treaty of 1854, so money from the Secret Service Fund of Canada changed from mysterious hand to mysterious hand prior to the election of 1866.[10] There would be nothing surprising if this were the case, for Canadian annals have been littered with instances of corruption. Bribery is a form of consent, and the alternative to consent is force.

Another factor in the New Brunswick reversal was the Fenian danger.

[7] Not a single supporter could be found for universal suffrage at Quebec.
[8] 1818-1896. Conservative. Minister of Finance, 1873, 1878-85. Lieutenant-Governor of New Brunswick, 1873-78, 1885-93.
[9] See Hugh G. Thorburn, *Politics in New Brunswick* (Toronto, 1961).
[10] G. E. Wilson, "New Brunswick's Entrance into Confederation," *CHR*, IX (March, 1928), 4-24.

An invasion was supposed to be imminent. The peril was capitalized rather openly, and the alarm of the public expressed itself in votes for a union that could defend itself. Still another explanation lies in the realization by the people of the North Shore that without Confederation there could be no railway for them. Bankers and business men of Saint John feared absorption into a greater metropolitanism than their own, as did their friends in Halifax, and fought the proposal. But the people of the North Shore had no metropolis of their own and favoured union. The achievements of Peter Mitchell, a North Shore man of property and a practical politician of outstanding accomplishments, had a good deal to do with the result. New Brunswick's decision seems to have been made by local sectional groups, as was to be expected in a province which, in contrast to Nova Scotia, was not knit together into a genuine community.

After the three provinces—Canada, Nova Scotia, New Brunswick—had expressed their approval of the proposals made at the Quebec Conference, 1864, all that remained to be done was to put these into shape and embody them in a bill to be submitted to the Imperial Parliament. Representatives of the lower provinces crossed to London in the summer of 1866, but those from Canada, either through unavoidable delays or from John A. Macdonald's unerring tactical sense, did not arrive until late November. If the delegates had worked at the scheme in the summer, Parliament would have been adjourned by the time they had it ready. It would then, by one channel or another, have leaked out, and there would have been several months for its opponents to attack it. Under such treatment a revision might have been required. All this would have entailed endless delay, hard feelings, and perhaps failure. Macdonald's idea was to meet in London, perfect the bill, then have it passed through Parliament before there was any opportunity for objection. As he said, it must be carried *per saltum*. This was done, and the colonists on March 29, 1867, were confronted with the British North America Act.

It would have been impossible to bring the colonies together unless the Imperial government had given its blessing. In the earlier period before 1860, Colonial Secretaries held that initiative must come from the colonies themselves, and some were not convinced that Union would be a blessing; they shared with governors and some colonials (among whom was Robert Baldwin) the fear that union would mean separation. Misunderstanding and procrastination accounted for much: official circles, while inundated with despatches from colonial governors, never really seem to have penetrated beneath the surface of colonial life. Well-informed, they were not understanding. The Colonial Secretaryship itself continued to suffer from lack of continuity[11] and policies were apt to change as often as the occupants of the office.

However at last, probably because of the reports brought back by men of reputation such as Sir Edmund Head,[12] more still, perhaps, through the weight of financial interests, the British government changed its attitude. To this change the royal tour of the colonies in 1860, on which the Duke of Newcastle, as Colonial Secretary, accompanied the Prince of Wales, may well have contributed. The Duke's policy began to favour union; if not the larger federal union, at least a union of the Maritime provinces among themselves. Edward Watkin claims for him the foremost place in the whole movement. Since he was Secretary for five important years, 1859-64, there may be weight in the claim. At any rate the alteration of official attitude in England from negative to positive during his secretaryship was all-important.

American influences were manifest in a dozen directions: in the series of alarms arising out of the Civil War, in Fenianism, in unconcealed unfriendliness to the colonies, and in the approaching end of the Reciprocity Treaty. Here was a strong factor in Canada: a larger market had to be obtained somehow and if the United States would not provide it, perhaps the Maritimes would. In Nova Scotia, the loss of Reciprocity did not seem so important; there were still the fisheries and now, under the treaty of 1818, Americans could be kept out of them. In this Nova Scotians did not display their usual hard realism, for they might have known that no British government would risk war with the United States by insisting on the letter of the law in the grievance of a minor colony. It was becoming plain to far-seeing men that if the colonies hoped to retain their rights against the United States, in fisheries as in other matters, if they hoped to retain their very existence, they must cease to depend on Great Britain and find their strength in unity.

5. The Place of Personalities

When all the impersonal factors are set out, a large gap still remains, for history, after all, consists in the interaction, not of blind forces, but of human beings. It is the role of individuals which is of ultimate significance. Since so much depends upon unrecorded conversation and upon likes and antipathies, this is also the most elusive. Yet as the movement was not a great ground swell of popular feeling but proceeded from logical necessity, the number of persons concerned in it is relatively small and a few dwarf all the others.

Among Englishmen, Newcastle, Head, and Watkin occupy the high

[11] Seven men, six of them in seven years, occupied the office between 1855 and 1867.
[12] Term ended, 1861.

places. Head, as Governor-in-Chief, had been in the authentic liberal Imperialist line of Durham and Elgin. Newcastle, one of the major figures to hold the Colonial Secretaryship in the nineteenth century, was a clearing house for ideas and influences; whether his part was as great as claimed for him by Watkin is debatable, but it was large. Watkin brought men together, but there is some evidence for believing that he suffered from not being personally popular. He was a central figure, though it would hardly be possible for him to have been as central as he himself seemed to think he was.

Of the British North Americans, there were some dozen who were prominent enough to require some mention, either as advocates or opponents of Confederation. Of the opponents, A. A. Dorion and L. H. Holton,[13] both Lower Canada Liberals, were outstanding. As a way out of the impasse of Union, Dorion had formerly approved the smaller scheme of a federation of the two halves of the Province of Canada, but now he and Holton found themselves unable to accept the larger plan.[14]

Among those who worked for Confederation, Tilley, McDougall, Morris[15] and Mowat[16] were secondary figures who require but passing mention. D'Arcy McGee, the Irishman who carried over his feelings for nationhood from Ireland to Canada, is intermediate; his eloquence was persuasive, his zeal unremitting.[17] Attention should centre on Cartier, Brown, Macdonald, Galt, and Tupper.

Among these five, Cartier has earned his place in history as the man who persuaded French Canada to accept the new arrangement. The worthy successor to Papineau and Lafontaine in the confidence of his people, he alone was capable of allaying their suspicions and removing from Confederation any suggestion of coercion. Conservative ministries from 1858 had rested on the majority he had been able to bring from Lower Canada. His power over his own people was plain but he was no narrow racialist. He had been so close to the Grand Trunk from its inception that he was more or less assimilated to the English commercial

---

[13] 1817-1880. Liberal. One of the native group that forced its way into the G.T.R. project. Minister of Finance, 1863-64. Representative of Protestants of Canada East.

[14] See p. 334.

[15] Alexander Morris, 1826-89. Contributed a good deal to public and literary discussion, his pamphlet, *Nova Britannia* (Montreal, 1858), having had a wide influence. A principal agent in bringing Macdonald and Brown together in 1864. Later, Lieutenant-Governor of Manitoba.

[16] 1820-1903. In J. S. Macdonald's Cabinet, 1863. Strong power in Liberal circles. Premier of Ontario, 1872-96. Minister of Justice, 1896-97.

[17] E. R. Cameron, *Memoirs of Ralph Van Sittart* (Toronto, 1924) considers McGee of leading importance in the movement. An interesting biography of McGee is Josephine Phelan, *The Ardent Exile: The Life and Times of Thomas Darcy McGee* (Toronto, 1951).

way of life, and his association with the railway brought him within the London circle that was working for a union. He formed a link between the races and between metropolitanism and colonialism. To a man of his discernment it must have been plain that sooner or later something would have to be done to meet Upper Canada's demands for "Rep. by pop.". He may well have believed that between the sea-faring people of the lower provinces and those of Lower Canada there would, in a larger union, be common interests enough to overbalance their racial differences. There is no reason to think that he saw Confederation with the eye of a prophet; it was an expedient, a political device to meet practical conditions. But once having accepted its necessity, his share in bringing it to pass, by securing the adhesion of his people, was major.[18]

To George Brown goes the credit appropriate to a destructive force: he was the man who brought the old machine of Union lumberingly to a stop. His agitation for "Rep. by pop.", based on all that turbulence of race and creed with which Canada is so familiar, made government impossible and change inevitable. A man of passion and conviction, he rendered a great service to his adopted country when in 1864 he consented to join in coalition with men whom he had been denouncing for years and at least one of whom, John A. Macdonald, he regarded as a personal enemy. The public accepted his position—it was no mere "sell-out" for office—but once the crisis was past and the Conferences over, Brown seemed to have little more to offer. Confederation for him was an expedient by which to secure the rights of Upper Canada. Like other Liberals, he would have preferred the smaller Union, but was willing to accept the larger for the sake of reaching a solution. His does not seem to have been a constructive mind. He was an uneasy colleague, soon left the administration in a huff (thereby committing political suicide and giving his arch-rival Macdonald his big chance), and though remaining a power behind the scenes in the Liberal party, did not thereafter contribute anything of note to the building of the Canadian nation, except critical editorials in *The Globe*.

Charles Tupper of Nova Scotia, a relatively young man like the rest,[19] should stand high on the list of "Fathers". His motives probably could be called Imperialistic: that is, he wished to ensure that the British Dominions in North America would not be absorbed by the United States but would remain indefinitely an outpost of empire. The best way to secure that goal seemed through their union, for it was strength against the Americans that seemed most needed in the 1860's. No doubt

[18] On Cartier's "conversion" to the idea of Confederation, see W. M. Whitelaw, *The Maritimes and Canada before Confederation* (Toronto, 1934), p. 124.

[19] He was 46 in the year of Confederation and his fellow Maritimer, Tilley, was 49, so they were of the same age group as all the other leading figures.

he had other motives. Union, if effected, promised more scope for the very ambitious Dr. Tupper. Whatever his motives, by bringing the old proposal of Maritime union down to earth, where few politicians had ever intended that it should be deposited, he forced action and paved the way for the Charlottetown Conference. Again, his conduct in keeping his legislature in session and yet avoiding a vote against the proposals was adept and courageous. He risked his political life by his actions during these two years. This pushing and persistent physician from Nova Scotia contributed with professional skill to the successful delivery of the infant.

Alexander Tilloch Galt had been a strategic figure in Canadian financial and political affairs from the 1840's. It was his plan of 1858 that formed the backbone of the Quebec proposals, as of the later Act, so that in this direct way he deserves to be ranked as the immediate legal "Father". He had the vision of an empire-builder but was no visionary. A sound and cautious Scot, his feet were solidly on the ground, and it was probably as the biggest of his promotions that he saw the new state. At the Quebec Conference, he was the financial wizard who worked out all the accounts. It is not to his discredit that later he felt compelled to resign from the Macdonald ministry in an effort to protect the educational interests of his fellow Protestants in the Eastern Townships. Galt is the only one of the group who had not been a strong party man; he had been regarded as an independent until he accepted office under Cartier in 1858. He might be termed the accountant of Confederation.

Lastly there was John A. Macdonald, a man long since famous for his qualities, loved by political associates, cursed but not hated by his foes. Where the opportunist stopped in Macdonald and the statesman began, who is to say?[20] Unwilling to admit that the Union was a failure

---

[20] This is the central problem as to Macdonald. Though it never can be entirely solved, his stand with respect to the race question was consistent throughout his life, whatever the cost to himself. It has been noted above that he refused to raise the race cry at a time when he was in low political water. His words to Brown Chamberlain, the editor of the Montreal *Gazette*, further clarify his attitude: "The trouble is that you British Canadians can never forget that you were once supreme, that Jean Baptiste was once your hewer of wood and drawer of water. . . . You struggle for *Ascendancy*. If a Lower Canadian Britisher desires to conquer, he must 'stoop to conquer'. He must make friends with the French. Without sacrificing the principle of his race or lineage, he must respect their nationality. Treat them as a nation, and they will act as free people generally do—generously. Treat them as a faction and they become factious." (Courtesy Mr. Blair Fraser). Wise words, the beginning and the end of our Canadian puzzle, but by few indeed taken to heart! Can the man who wrote them and who lived them be accused of having been "a mere opportunist"?

(it gave him ten years of office) he would have nothing to do with Confederation as long as it remained an academic project, but when it became "practical politics" he seized on it at once. He was a man who was not much interested in general schemes or broad ideas. It was the clash and din of battle that appealed to his Highland blood; he was the commander in the field, not the distant general preoccupied with wide-ranging strategical conceptions. It would be unfair to him, a man who had been in and out of ministries for years past, to suggest that he entered into the coalition with Brown merely to prolong his tenure of office. The Queen's government must go on, he would have said, and the coalition with its agreed goal of federation was the best hope that it would peacefully do so. As early as 1861, he had expressed the opinion that the larger scheme of the two was preferable, and now, in 1864, he insisted on it.

Once he had taken his stand, his place in the movement was decisive. He made friends everywhere in the Maritimes, leading the people there to believe that it would be no ill wind that would blow them good in the person of such a leader as he. At the conferences, he persuaded, cajoled, and convinced. He was the great reconciler of differences, the adept at smoothing out the wording of a clause to suit the general sense, the supreme tactical expert who knew by instinct just the right step to take at the right time. He was the practical man who brought other men's ideas to fruition. Macdonald was the pilot of Confederation.[21]

And so on July 1, 1867, after a troubled three years on the stocks, the good ship *Canada* was launched. She had been built because the weather was bad and smaller craft unseaworthy. Her builders and her crew were reasonably satisfied with her but she had not engaged their deep affections. For that she would have to prove herself on future voyages. But there was in this man and that a quiet feeling of confidence that she would carry her canvas handsomely. Colonial British America had no poets to celebrate the event but there was the occasional versifier, usually bad, to grace the occasion and to suggest that the people thus united were not without just a little touch of what might now be properly denominated National Pride.

> Through the young giant's mighty limbs, that stretch from sea to sea
> There runs a throb of conscious life—of waking energy
> From Nova Scotia's misty coast to far Columbia's shore,
> She wakes—a band of scattered homes and colonies no more

---

[21] The most recent biography of Macdonald is Donald G. Creighton's in two volumes: *John A. Macdonald: The Young Politician* (Toronto, 1952) and *John A. Macdonald: The Old Chieftain* (Toronto, 1955).

But a young nation, with her life full beating in her breast,
A noble future in her eyes—the Britain of the West.[22]

Chronology

1864   Charlottetown and Quebec Conferences.
1865   Tilley's Defeat in New Brunswick.
          United States decides to terminate Reciprocity Treaty.
1866   Tilley successful in second election.
          Fenian Raids.
1866–67   Westminster Palace Hotel Conference, London.
1867   March 29: British North America Act passed.
          July 1: The Dominion of Canada.

Additional Reading

Boyd, John. *Sir Georges Etienne Cartier, Bart.* Toronto, 1914.

Canada. *Parliamentary Debates on the Subject of the Confederation of the British North American Provinces.* Quebec, 1865.

Canada. *Confederation Debates in the Province of Canada, 1865.* P. B. Waite, ed. Carleton Library No. 2. Toronto, 1963.

Canada. *Royal Commission on Dominion-Provincial Relations.* Vol. I, Appendix 2. Donald G. Creighton. *British North America at Confederation.* Ottawa, 1940.

Chisholm, J. A. *Speeches and Letters of Joseph Howe.* Halifax, 1909.

Grant, W. L. *The Tribune of Nova Scotia; a Chronicle of Joseph Howe.* Toronto, 1915.

Groulx, Lionel. *La Confederation canadienne, ses origines.* Montreal, 1918.

Kennedy, W. P. M. "The Terms of the British North America Act," in R. Flenley, ed. *Essays in Canadian History.* Toronto, 1939. 121-131.

Saunders, E. M. *Three Premiers of Nova Scotia.* Toronto, 1909.

Stacey, C. P. *Canada and the British Army, 1846-1871.* London, 1936.

Whitelaw, W. M. *The Maritimes and Canada Before Confederation.* Toronto, 1934.

[22] "Fidelis" as quoted in J. P. Macpherson, *Life of the Right Hon. Sir John A. Macdonald,* II, 89. "Fidelis" was Agnes Maule Machar, daughter of the Principal of Queen's University, Kingston, and as such, no doubt in friendly association with John A. Macdonald, brother-in-law of one of her father's colleagues.

CHAPTER 24

July 1st, 1867: The First Colonial State

1. The Bonds of Union

It is not recorded that there was any crashing of bands at the launching of the new ship of state. Canadians welcomed the first Dominion Day with customary restraint. Certain great men had been talking about a new nationality forming under Her Majesty; but common people, while they might be affected by the inconveniences and the pettiness of the old colonial arrangements, did not take much stock in new nationalities: they would judge Canada as a new experiment on its merits. The farthest they are on record as going was participating in some processions, speeches, and the rare display of fireworks.[1] If a few years before, the question had been put to a vote as to whether to continue as British colonies with a moderate amount of self-government, to seek annexation to the United States, or to demand virtual independence as a new nation, the poll almost certainly would have gone in the order named, with a very small count for the last.

No popular patriotism, no revolutionary faith, brought forth the new creation. The life of the new Dominion was at first as drab, as empty, and as devoid of great ideals as had been that of the struggling provinces. Only the eye of faith, and the great visions of its few founders, kept it together. Only by tediously slow degrees did the loyalty and love

[1] P. B. Waite, *The Life and Times of Confederation, 1864-1867* (Toronto, 1962), 322-29.

of its inhabitants show indications of centring on it, rather than on the far-off motherland. Compared with the United States, *élan* was lacking. Yet it might be said of that country, too, that no great popular wave of feeling had greeted its union. It was July 4, 1776, not September 17, 1787, that was celebrated in the republic—the revolutionary idea, not the tame job of constitution-making. Canada was to wait another 64 years for its "Independence" day, and when it came,[2] it stole in so quietly that few people were aware of it, and fewer still would think of celebrating it. Some peoples are born nations, some achieve nationhood, and others have nationhood thrust upon them. Canadians seem to be among these last.

What, then, kept the new entity together? In general, the pressure that lay in fear and jealousy of the United States, the larger trading unit Confederation afforded, the common British political allegiance and common traditions in law and society. Colonial society was still something of a cross between English and American, deriving from the one a semi-aristocratic tone and from the other, or from a common environment, its instinctive democracy. Aristocracy, however, was already a lost cause, the prestige of British institutions and traditions serving to preserve it only in a few limited areas; the destiny of the new polity was to become more and more democratic as time went on, conforming to the norm of the continent. The Protestantism and the Puritanism that had radiated out from New England had powerfully reinforced that which already existed in English-speaking Canada and here, too, was a bond of union. Common puritanism, the common language, the natural weakness of class lines, these—even though they knew no international boundary—were supports to the union of the English-speaking provinces.

Institutions of law and government were as significant as social traditions. All the provinces had representative institutions, although in the Maritimes these were almost non-existent in the municipal area. All had been cast in the same legal and political mould. The significant field of the criminal law had been the same everywhere, French Lower Canada included, and in the French community the civil law as well had developed towards a uniform model. This removed friction about fundamentals and gave large areas of parliamentary activity in common.

But the strongest bond was from without, the over-riding attachment to the motherland, so deep that few could have conceived its absence. It carried with it strong habits of political obedience. When Joseph Howe, failing to get the Imperial government to annul or alter the

---

[2] With the Statute of Westminster, Dec. 11, 1931.

Confederation arrangement, was faced by Charles Tupper with the logical consequence of persistence—disobedience to the Crown—he gave in. Confederation probably could have been imposed on all the provinces by the British Government more easily than it was achieved by their own decisions. As British statesmen of the time well knew, colonials in their obedience to British authority displayed a kind of "Catholic" attitude, contrasting sharply with the pronounced individualism of their religious and secular Protestantism. "Papa locutus est. . . ." —"When the Pope speaks, the faithful have only to obey".[3] Nothing approaching their fervency of subordination (which rested on their need for protection) could be found in Great Britain itself.

This very intensity of colonialism was possibly useful, for it helped to tide the British North Americans over to a time when they might find themselves a people.

In 1867 this they emphatically were not. The name "Canadian" was automatically extended to cover New Brunswickers and Nova Scotians; but to these latter it was something not a little repugnant, and they clung to their own. In the old province of Canada itself, it was not allowed by the French to *"les Anglais"* and on many among the latter it sat uneasily, for they still talked of "home" and preferred to think of themselves as Scottish, English, or Irish. It was to be years before the name Canadian outside of Quebec came to have content and to be worn proudly.

2. The Framework of Union

If spiritual bonds among the colonists were few, legal and constitutional bonds were made explicit and strong. Federalism was in reality no new thing, for the whole Empire as early as 1848, if not from 1791, had been quasi-federalized. After the Revolution, Parliament had ceased to enact colonial legislation except for major purposes.[4] This division—by which the Imperial government enacted general legislation and the colonial local, continuing for many years after 1867—made the federation of that year a federation within a federation. The British North America Act, involving the performance for several colonies of that which they themselves could do neither singly nor collectively, was a good example of the use of the overriding Imperial power for a wide purpose.

[3] This precise maxim was quoted and acted upon at the Washington Conference of 1871, when Macdonald was virtually told he had to obey orders—and did! See Goldwin Smith, *The Treaty of Washington* (Ithaca, N.Y., 1941), p. 79.

[4] See Helen Taft Manning, *British Colonial Government after the American Revolution, 1782-1820* (New Haven, 1934).

The Act was also the first of the great federal constitutional acts of the Empire.[5] As such it was to some degree experimental, both in detail and conception. As emanating from Westminster it reinforced the legal doctrine of Parliamentary Supremacy, but as conferring almost sovereign powers on a large political creation it took from Parliament most of its jurisdiction over an important part of the royal domain.

The Act is often referred to as the Canadian Constitution. This is hardly correct. It is the formal instrument of union and contains explicit definition of large areas of Canadian government, but legally it is only one act of the British Parliament and, except through precise reference or "by necessary intendment", did not repeal previous acts relating to the British North American colonies, many of which continued in force until the Statute of Westminster, 1931. It therefore left a door open by which much of the older British constitution could come in. It did not give the clean, neat break with the past represented by the American Constitution. Rather, it was one branch, albeit the main branch, in the legal tree sprouting from Westminster.

This conception of Westminster as the final seat of authority, which rests upon the still more traditional conception of the Crown as the ultimate source of power, disposes of that heretical view of the Confederation arrangements, the so-called compact theory, according to which Confederation was a treaty between the provinces. Like other treaties it could, according to this thesis, be abrogated at the will of the signatories, and could not be changed without their consent. Exponents of this view forget that only three provinces made the original "pact" (one of which, Canada, promptly committed suicide, to be reborn as two separate entities, Ontario and Quebec) and that now ten are governed under it. By some biological sleight of hand, those who hold the compact theory make children into their own parents, for if they are right, the prairie provinces, which have been carved out of the Dominion, are also antecedent to it and parties to its creation. Their case is weaker than the corresponding States' Rights theory of the American Constitution, for British doctrine, in contrast with American, does not admit of action proceeding from "The People". What happened in 1867 was that the Crown, in the fullness of its wisdom, decided to rearrange its administrative areas in British North America. It wiped out its old provinces of Canada, New Brunswick, and Nova Scotia and created in their place four new provinces, Ontario, Quebec, New

---

[5] Among the others being the Commonwealth of Australia Act and the Union of South Africa Act, though the latter was only semi-federalizing.

Brunswick, and Nova Scotia.[6] All were cast into the crucible of Imperial omnicompetence and came out remelted, shining, new, and fused. Old institutions were continued as a matter of expediency until the new authorities saw fit to change them. There can be no question of "consenting parties" or a treaty; there were no consenting parties and there could be no treaty: the Crown rearranged its domains. But, according to the genius of the English tradition, it did not do so until it knew that its act would be acceptable to those of its subjects who were affected. These, however, had no corporate character; they, therefore, could not make a treaty with each other.

The Compact thesis, held strongly in Quebec, is not consistent with federalism, for it would dissolve the state. It was abolished, once and for all, by the American Civil War. Once allow it, and the right of one of the federated divisions to secede is also allowed. If it be the right of one, it is the right of all. A structure in which members may withdraw (and the provinces of Canada are not "members" of the Canadian Federation) may be a League, but it cannot be a federation. The end of all Leagues of partners is the same—disruption. But no federation is put together on a basis of limited liability. The intention in all of them is not a *mariage de convenance*, but one "until death do us part". This is not to say that there can be no flexibility in the federal form of government; on the contrary, flexibility is its great virtue. Every federation is constantly in process of adjustment to the balance of political forces within it. If particularism be strong, the general government will be weak. If the centripetal forces gain, as during a war, then the general government takes on added authority. In a federation there is a constantly moving point of balance between centralization and decentralization, and the direction of the movement depends upon the nature of the forces at work. Mechanical transportation, for example, has infinitely strengthened central authority, but the violent recrudescence of particularism might greatly weaken it, as it threatens to do in Canada as this is written (1963).

In the Canadian type of union, there are two distinct and separate ideas, and the interfusion of these gives to it its unique interest:[7] they are the American idea of federalism and the English tradition of parliamentarianism.

In the making of the American constitution, Alexander Hamilton represented everything that tends to draw society up around a centre:

[6] See Sections 4, 5, 6 of the Act.
[7] No attempt is made in this book to give a close analysis of Canadian federalism; only a wide interpretation can be offered.

strong government, with minimum diffusion of power; a ruling class, complete, if possible, with monarchy; the power of centralized finance; industrialism and urbanism as against agriculture; their concomitant, a tariff nationalism; the brittle bourgeois view of "progress" as against a rural contentment with life and living. The line of his descent is clear, through Federalists and Whigs to Republicans. Thomas Jefferson stood for the complete opposite: dependence on the small and nearby authority where a man could be an individual, as against the distant, in which he was only a unit—on the county against the State and on the State against the Union; popular conceptions, such as the sovereignty of the people, the election of all officials and for short terms; universal suffrage; democracy of the widest sort, with no class lines; hatred of the tyranny of finance, manifesting itself in opposition to central banks; soft money as against hard; agriculture as against industry, hence free trade; life as against "progress" and efficiency. He comes down today through men like Andrew Jackson and F. D. Roosevelt, in slogans such as "the common man", or "the forgotten man" and in the great hold-all, the motley, easy-going, Democratic party.

In Canada the two schools of thought (without the names) have been as clearly delineated as in the United States. The Conservative party has been Hamiltonian, and the Liberal pretty largely Jeffersonian. In shaping the Federal Constitution, it was mainly Hamiltonianism that prevailed. John A. Macdonald had read, marked (with comments in the margin), and inwardly digested Alexander Hamilton's *Federalist*. A. T. Galt was the representative figure for the financial side of Hamiltonianism: the Bank of Montreal in its original charter (1817) had strongly reflected Hamilton's ideas for the first Bank of the United States, and Galt was nothing if not the embodiment of Montreal finance. Inborn Jeffersonians like A. A. Dorion, instinctively afraid of Leviathan, formed the heart of the Liberal opposition to Confederation. Their position, though more and more impracticable in the crowded modern world, was one which all who love liberty must respect. Other Liberals like Brown and Mowat proved Jeffersonian to the extent of first favouring the small confederation (Upper and Lower Canada only) and then later on standing up, like later Calhouns,[8] for Provincial Rights.

The heart of federalism, the great secret of the federal idea, its power as reconciler of the centre and the circumference, the large and the small, lies in the device termed the division of powers: that is, in the attempt to divide sovereignty into two more or less equal halves, the one

---

[8] The great protagonist for the "States Rights" (in the period 1815-40) view of the American Constitution.

in the control of the general government, the other under the local.[9] The American union was fighting a civil war while this division was being worked out at Quebec, and the lesson most of the men there drew was that the war arose because the power of individual states was too great: the American Constitution gave the residuum, or unnamed remainder, of power to the States "or to the people". By the British North America Act, the Crown gave to certain classes of its subjects specific guarantees, beyond the reach of either federal or provincial legislatures (neither of which in consequence were fully sovereign bodies). It placed the specific powers in the hands of the provinces, reserving all the rest to the Dominion. Unfortunately it then went on with the subsection of Section 91, beginning "and for greater certainty . . .", which names 29 specific powers that were to inhere in the Dominion. The result has been that history, with some valuable assistance from Oliver Mowat and the British Privy Council, has pretty well stood the Act on its head, awarding the residuum not to the government plainly named in the Act as having it, that of Canada, but to the provinces. As the Canadian constitution departed from its original principle of strong centralization of power, the American, mainly through judicial interpretation, came closer to it, so that now each finds itself more or less in the other's shoes, and Canada, apart from wartime centralization, faces the *impasse* in which the United States found itself before the Civil War.

A few gains, however, survive from the efforts of the far-seeing "Fathers". The lieutenant-governors are officers of Canada and their duty is to submit all provincial legislation to the Governor-in-Council; he may, and sometimes does, exercise his right of disallowing it. The criminal law is one throughout Canada, not fifty-one as in the United States. Particular works in a province may be declared for the benefit of Canada as a whole (such as the Welland Canal). In contrast, property and civil rights, which under Section 92 are given to the provinces and were clearly intended at the time to reflect the meaning of those words as used in the old French "laws of Canada", where they referred only to personal property and the individual and family rights connected with it,[10] have become the lean kine that have systematically swallowed up the fat cattle of Dominion enactment. This misinterpretation of *droits*

---

[9] The sections of the Act dealing with the division of power are 91 and 92, and also 59, 65, 93, 94, 95, 132.

[10] See Hon. C. H. Cahan, *The British North American Act, 1867* (address to the Canadian Club of Toronto, Sept. 15, 1937). See also *Report of the Royal Commission on Dominion-Provincial Relations, 1940*, I, 32 (the "Rowell-Sirois Report").

civils is a standing monument to the lack of legal historical training marking the judges of the Privy Council and of the Canadian High Courts alike.

The feature of the Canadian Act which sets it off distinctly from the American Constitution lies in the traditional and legal concept of the Crown as the source of power. Government proceeds from the Crown, flowing into fresh receptacles at its behest. There cannot therefore be an absolute division of sovereignty as in the United States, where the People of the State may set up one set of institutions and the People of the United States another:[11] all the courts are the king's courts, all justice the king's justice; the lieutenant-governor is the king's representative (and incidentally his appointment by the governor-general-in-council constitutes a declaration that provincial "sovereignty" is something very much thinner than state sovereignty), and provincial as well as Federal legislation runs in the King's name.

The unique American contribution to government, federalism, finds its counterpart in the unique English—parliamentary government, or limited monarchy. In Canada (and the later dominions), the two are dovetailed together, giving a structure unlike that possessed by any other states. All these broad foundations of the Canadian state are enunciated in the first sentence of the British North America Act, which proclaims that the provinces have expressed their desire to be united federally into one dominion under the Crown of the United Kingdom and with a constitution similar in principle to that of the United Kingdom. But it may well be asked what the constitution of the United Kingdom is. It is so hard to describe, so much a matter of usage and convention; it is English history. No other country may, therefore, take over the English constitution in its entirety. When Canadians desired a constitution similar in principle, they did not bargain for an established church, a hereditary peerage, or a local monarchy complete with King, Challenger and Norrey-King-at-arms. These are aspects of the English constitution, which is a seamless garment. What they had in mind were, to change the metaphor, what might be called the bold headlands of the English constitutional coast: the monarchy (*in absentia*), a council (or "cabinet") to advise it, a parliament of two houses, the law courts, and the Common Law.

In England where they have grown up, these "bold headlands" rest on tradition, not on enactment. In Canada, they had to be made to rest on enactment. Yet so severe is the logic of the English legal mind that it has been possible for a new state to bud off the old stem without the

---

[11] As two sets of courts.

symmetry of the conception being disturbed. The myth is that all government radiates out from the person of the monarch.[12] The personal monarch of the middle ages has been built up by the lawyers into the impersonal monarchy! Today "the king reigns but does not govern"; "the king can do no wrong"; "the king" never even dies. "The king" has become "the crown".

The British North America Act maintained the elaborate stage play. A Privy Council for Canada[13] was set up, but no mention was made of the cabinet, and the prime minister continued to be a legally non-existent person. The Act will be searched in vain for direct reference to what everyone knows to be the heart of the system, Responsible Government. Canada, therefore, has a conventional constitution plus a legal constitution specifying certain outstanding portions of the law of the English constitution.

If much of the Canadian constitution is not within the British North America Act and if Canada yet exists by this act, then the Act in itself transcends its own words. It is the symbol of a new start and a new state. It endowed the people of the uniting provinces with a new political structure, through which the most ample provision for government by consent was afforded. It made a new people and placed on them responsibility for their own fate.

Did it therefore represent a turn from monarchy to democracy? Most of the "Fathers" were anti-democratic; none were for universal suffrage, and most were for property qualifications for senators. Macdonald would have gone farther and had a seven year term for the commons. He had little interest in arithmetical politics; let the cities represent numbers, he used to say, but the counties property. Yet of necessity the Act symbolized that which had been settled in principle twenty years before, government by the people, and opened the door to a democracy seemingly based on majority rule; its spirit rather than its words liquidated the bad, old inheritance of privilege which had caused so many Canadian woes.

Similarly, the spirit of the Act removed all distinction of status between French and English. Confederation obliterated the English conquest. The Act symbolized an agreement between the races to live and let live and gave a formula for the solution of the antagonisms that had brought the wheels of government to a stop. French-speaking Canadians could only point to one or two specific clauses in hard legal support of their "rights",[14] but their claim would be that these were but

[12] The people are "his people"; the army, "his army", etc.
[13] Section 11.
[14] Sections 93, 133.

"the evidence of things unseen", the crystallization into law of understandings reached behind the scenes, of the compromises and mutual confidence which alone could have brought forth Confederation. In Confederation, English and French, after a stormy courtship, took each other for better or for worse, and whether the marriage had much prospect of being happy or not, it must, like other marriages, create a reasonable degree of equality between the contracting parties.

The sections of the Act making the financial arrangements also symbolize more than they express. If it was a union among equals, an approximate equality would have to be maintained. If Canada was to be a family, it would be a poor kind of brotherhood on the part of the fortunate that allowed one's flesh and blood to go in rags. If the central provinces used their numbers to get what they wanted relentlessly (as through a protective tariff), there could be no genuine basis for a nation. The economic clauses, with their arrangements for subsidies, debt assumptions and an intercolonial railway, were admissions of a parental responsibility on the part of the general government for all its provincial children. The union was to be strong enough to maintain its constituent parts in that estate in life to which they were accustomed. This surely was the spirit of Confederation, borne out by Galt's invitation to each province to submit its bill.[15] Canadians must sink or swim together.

Linguistic, religious and sectional rights being guaranteed in the fundamental instrument, Canada thus came into existence with constitutional provisions of the same solemnity as those affirmed in the American Bill of Rights, although not called by that name and guaranteeing sectional or minority rights, not the traditional freedoms of the "individual". The British North America Act is fundamental law, and it contains a Bill of Rights, later to be added to by the Diefenbaker Ministry, in the shape of a formal *Bill of Rights.*

Before the legislation of 1949, which terminated appeals to the Privy Council and ensured the eventual transfer of the power of amendment to Canada, narrow legal views had gone far to destroying the effectiveness of the federating act. The Judicial Committee had interpreted the Act as a mere administrative statute, not (except in three cases) as the vehicle for a nation's growth. If the Act is the vehicle of a nation, then the broadest construction must be put on it in order that under it all parts of the nation may have adequate life.

The instrument fashioned at Confederation was wise and far-seeing:

---

[15] The derisive "sold for eighty cents a head, the price of a sheepskin" was part of Howe's attack on the Confederation agreement, but its origin was simply Nova Scotia's own estimate of its needs.

correctly interpreted, it would have served as a vehicle of nationhood. Most of the "Fathers" would have been dismayed could they have foreseen what niggling lawyer's work would do to it. They would have been gratified by the repairs of our own day, for they were inspired by the vision they did so much to bring about—building out of scattered and parochial colonies a great continental nation.

3. Canada in 1867

In 1867, the great continental nation was still a vision. Only three provinces of the six had come together and their combined strength and resources were not overly impressive. Still, there was hope ahead, for had they not all sprung from next to nothing within a lifetime? Were

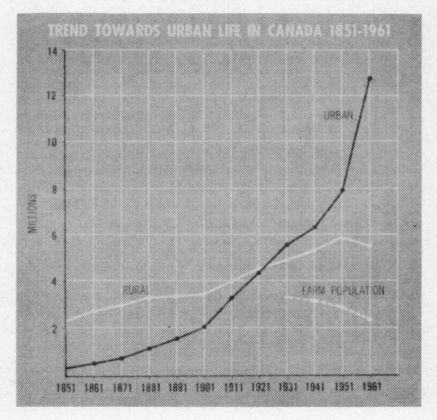

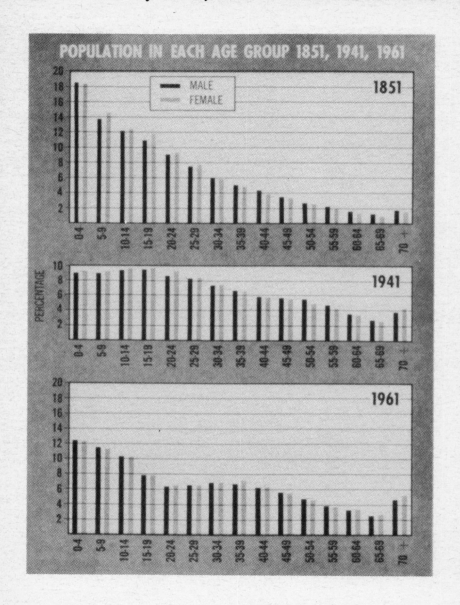

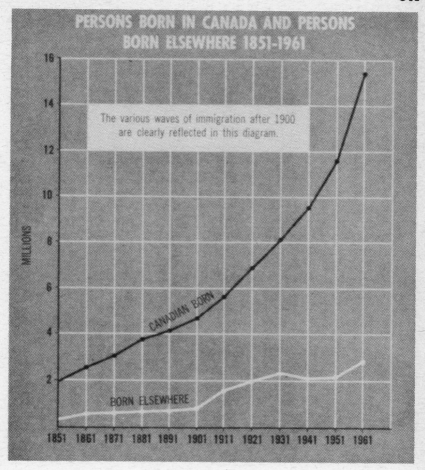

PERSONS BORN IN CANADA AND PERSONS
BORN ELSEWHERE 1851-1961

The various waves of immigration after 1900
are clearly reflected in this diagram.

CANADIAN BORN

BORN ELSEWHERE

they not just taking their most imposing strides? Though the pace had lately become more moderate than a few years previously, no one foresaw a future less robust than the past and all lived in the atmosphere of the exuberant fifties.

In the year of Confederation the people of Canada numbered about 3,300,000, of whom nearly 50 per cent lived in Upper Canada, which then had about half a million more inhabitants than Lower Canada. The two provinces between them contained 80 per cent of the total.

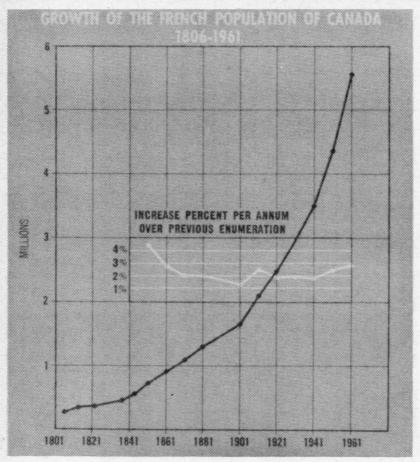

Upper Canada was still moving ahead at a fair rate,[16] but the people of Lower Canada were streaming off to the United States, and the province was almost stationary,[17] its total increase in the decade having not been much more than that of Nova Scotia. All the provinces were overwhelmingly rural[18] but the balance was beginning to swing, and there were signs of that urban development that has since contributed most of

[16] 16% increase for the decade 1861-71.
[17] 7.2% increase or 80,000 people in the ten years.
[18] 82% approximately. See diagram.

Canada's growth. Nova Scotia was least urbanized,[19] Lower Canada most.[20] The population at that time was not the collection of greybeards which for some time it threatened to become: there were many children and young people.[21]

Confederation occurred about twenty years after the peak of nineteenth century immigration: in consequence there were still a good many people who had been born outside the country, mainly in the British Isles. But in every province their number decreased greatly between 1861 and 1871, indicating that there was little more immigration coming in and that the original immigrating generation was now dying off.[22] The population was steadily becoming more "native", and continued to do so until the new immigration of the twentieth century. At Confederation it was also very "local": at most there were only a few hundred people living in any of the Maritime Provinces who had been born in the Canadas and very few Maritime-born living in the central provinces. Even as between Nova Scotia and New Brunswick, there was not much interchange.

In racial origin, the population was then more "British"[23] than later. In 1871, French-speaking Canadians formed 31% of the total, a proportion that remains about the same, but those of "British" descent were 60.5% as against about 43.8% in 1961.[24] Only about eight per cent were of other origins, and of these latter many were Loyalists of remote German or Dutch descent. Among the "British", the Irish predominated. In those days the province of Quebec was much more English in speech than nowadays, with over 20 per cent of its rural population and 30 of its urban population "British" in origin.[25]

---

[19] About 17%.

[20] 22.6%.

[21] Percentage of the total population below fifteen years of age, 1851, 1901, 1941, 1961: (See diagram, p. 340).

Age:	0–4	5–9	10–14
1851	18.5	13.8	12.1
1901	12.1	11.4	10.9
1941	9.14	9.89	9.73
1961	12.8	11.4	10.17

[22] See diagram, p. 341.

[23] A term that includes Celtic and Saxon Scots, Protestant and Catholic Irish, English, Welsh, and in general all those who have forgotten their ancestry, is not very scientific; it may practically be equated to "English-speaking".

[24] See diagram, p. 428.

[25] In 1961 these percentages were 6.25 and 12.3. To these should be added those persons who spoke English but did not put themselves down as of "British Isles" descent. The percentages would then become rural, 6.8; urban, 15.4.

PRINCIPAL RELIGIOUS DENOMINATIONS
OF CANADA 1851-1961

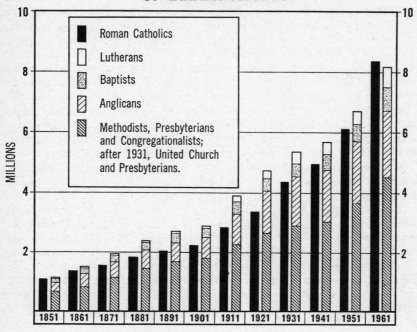

At Confederation the denominational complexion of the community was not greatly different from today.[26] Roman Catholics numbered about 42 per cent in 1871, as compared with 46 per cent in 1961; of these some 11 per cent of the total population or 385,000 people were non-French as compared with some 2,800,000 in 1961. The non-French Roman Catholics in 1871 were about 20 per cent of the Protestant population and in 1961 about 28 per cent. The leading Protestant denominations in those days were Methodists, Presbyterians, and Anglicans, all approximately equal in number, followed at a considerable distance by Baptists and Lutherans. This held true for all the provinces except Nova Scotia, where the Baptist church was strong, a reflection of the pre-Loyalist New England origins of many of the people. In religious demeanour, however, the age was centuries removed

[26] See diagram.

from our own. It witnessed the peak of Victorian piety. Doubt had not entered, fervour abounded, the practice of church-going was universal. Every mother prayed that her son might become a minister. Here was an area of contrast with the neighbouring republic, where "godlessness" and "Sabbath-breaking" had begun to disrupt the ancient puritanism.

The economic foundations of the new Dominion rested on its primary resources and the extractive industries based upon them—the forest, the fisheries, and the farm. Of these, the forest from the beginning had been the mainstay of the country and was only then beginning to be surpassed by agriculture. The country had a forest flavour to a degree now hard to appreciate. Rafts of timber or booms of logs floated on every bit of navigable water, mills were everywhere, the smell of wood was constantly in the air. New railways were being built to tap new forests, and new towns were springing up as saw-mill centres. The characteristic Canadian figure was the lumberjack or raftsman. He and his songs and his brawls gave the country a local colour of its own, a "folk" element that no other class of men supplied. Closely bound up with lumbering was ship-building, Canadians in those days being among the leading constructors of wooden ships. It was the coincidence of the decline of the wooden sailing ship with Confederation that stamped on many Maritime minds an association between Confederation and misfortune.

The forest had furnished to British North America a "get-rich-quick" industry, something like mining: the trees, men held, were there to be cut down. It was the soil which was to form the more permanent source of wealth. The amount of land occupied[27] had steadily mounted from about eighteen million acres in 1851 to nearly twenty-four million in 1861 and was to be over twenty-seven million in 1871.[28] There were corresponding increases in production, except in wheat which, as in other areas of the continent passing out of the pioneer stage, was declining. Only in the last frontier counties of Huron and Bruce was wheat still the main reliance. In the older sections of Ontario, on many of the farms, the characteristic brick houses of the countryside were going up in place of the old frame or still older log cabins. Eastern Ontario had already equipped itself with those handsome, well-proportioned stone houses still to be seen in large numbers in the triangle between the St. Lawrence and the Ottawa.

Farm machinery was coming in. The Massey family had been making implements for twenty years, and their reapers, rakes, and mowers were beginning to be well known. The "Bingham plow" had just taken

[27] See diagram, p. 346.
[28] The increase 1851-61 was 32%; 1861-71, 14.4%—another test proving 1851-61 to have been the most flourishing decade before Confederation.

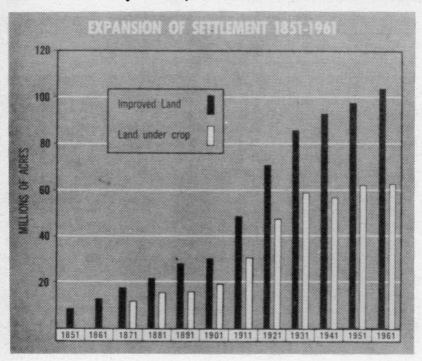

prizes at the Paris Exhibition. Ontario, if not Quebec, was making much of its advantages, and in an intelligent way. There were Boards of Agriculture scattered throughout the province, Fruit Growers' Associations, a Provincial Agricultural Association dating from 1847; and that familiar feature of Ontario life, the Fall Fair, was well established. A Chair of Agriculture had been set up in the University of Toronto and a veterinary college founded.

The urban accompaniments of a successful economy were coming to be much in evidence. There were a good many chartered banks (most cities of some importance containing the head office of one or more), and in Montreal and Toronto there were insurance companies and embryo stock exchanges. The banks were safer than American banks but had not reached their later stable character, and there had been a few bad failures, one of the most serious occurring just before Confederation. That masterpiece, the Canadian Bank Act, was not yet on the books. Foreign trade was running about one hundred million dollars per year, having nearly doubled in the decade. Imports, as might be expected in a debtor country, had exceeded exports in all but two of the sixteen years preceding Confederation. Trade was almost entirely confined to Great Britain and the United States. Industries had been started here and there; many of the little factories of the time were in villages or the countryside, and there was no marked concentration of industrial control. It was contended that industrial development had been marked after the tariff increases of 1858 and 1859. While industrialists were already powerful enough to exert pressure for further protection, most establishments were still small, and all of them together bulked less than lumbering alone.

The Canada of 1867 could boast few urban centres of much importance. Montreal was a smallish city of about 100,000. The wealth of its close-knit merchant group was considerable, the gaiety and good manners of its upper class French, conspicuous. Quebec, which actually decreased in the decade, numbered about 60,000, Toronto 50,000 and Halifax 26,000. Other cities such as Hamilton and Ottawa maintained their previous relative places. Kingston, with 12,000 people, a university, and a garrison, was then more important than it is today. For the city of Quebec the crisis of its economic existence was approaching: in the year 1864 the largest number of ships on record had entered its harbour, the largest number that ever did enter, and the peak of the old square timber trade had been reached. Decline was not yet in evidence, but growth had stopped. It had already lost its place as capital to Ottawa. The third distinct age of the old city was ending, the fourth not begun.[29] Toronto had acquired its sentimental appellation of "the Queen city of the West"; it bubbled over with energy, was full of churches, bar-rooms, crusty old Tory families, rising merchants, ardent western Grits, strong Anglicans, devoted Methodists and turbulent Orangemen—a tempestuous kind of place then as now.

In contrast with the previous generation, the cities were large and imposing, their level of comfort and civilization high. They had been equipping themselves with sidewalks and a few paved roads. Gaslighting had been in for some years. In 1861 the first street-railways, horse-cars, made their appearance in Montreal and Toronto. Some houses had bathtubs. In physical equipment, Canadian cities were taking their places with those of the rest of the continent in the march of material comfort, though in showiness and movement lagging well to the rear. None of them were built on the generous lines marking so many

[29] The first, as capital of French America; the second, as capital of British America; the third, as leading lumber-export port; the fourth as industrial centre and capital of French Canada.

American cities; their streets were narrow, and there was little provision for open space. The centre of Toronto lay along narrow, ugly Yonge Street; the "Queen City" was already distinguishable by an un-Queenly dinginess. Montreal with its earlier French squares (such as the Place d'armes), Halifax with its Common, were pleasing, if partial exceptions. Contrasted with American, Canadian cities exhibited the mark of the timid and narrow colonial mind.

Architecturally, they may have gained a little advantage over their American neighbours by reason of their comparative poverty. Canadian cities were not wealthy enough to build the worst eccentricities of nineteenth century ugliness, and in most of them there still remained houses and some public buildings from an age when taste had been purer. Kingston contained the finest Georgian architecture in Canada. Though its citizens, it would seem, would like nothing better than to get rid of it, much of it remains to this day to put to shame the gaudy contraptions erected in wealthier places. Halifax may be added for its dignified old *Province House* and Ottawa for some of its pleasant old limestone residences. That recent capital was, like Washington, "synthetic", not being a centre in its own right. Unlike Washington, it was not planned; Government merely took over the old Crown reservation, Barrack Hill, and began the erection of the new Parliament Buildings. These were described as being in "The Italian Gothic Style". Sir John A. Macdonald, who was not without discernment in such matters, is said to have called the attention of a friend one evening to the tower on the West Block. "Do you know what it looks like?" he asked, and went on, "Just like a cowbell!" It was unfortunate for Canada that its national capital was being adorned with the Parliament Buildings at the height of the cowbell style of architecture.

The people of Canada, however, were not much worried over questions of architectural taste. Yet they were willing to make great efforts to equip themselves with the educational facilities which determine taste. By 1867 most people outside Quebec were more or less literate. Towns and cities had quite fair school systems for the age, and in country districts the "little red school-house" had already become a feature of the landscape. In Nova Scotia there were in 1861, six "academies"; in Upper Canada there were 86 "grammar schools"[30] with 4,766 pupils. Since there were only 111 incorporated places in Upper Canada in 1871, nearly every town or village must already have had its grammar school. Such schools, however, were still for the select few, as

---

[30] i.e. secondary schools.

were the private schools, of which there was reported the surprising number of 300.

In higher education, all the larger colleges and universities of eastern Canada had been founded with the exception of Western Ontario and McMaster. Some of these institutions, such as Queen's, already had several faculties. Both Queen's and Victoria had Faculties of Medicine, and there was also a medical school in Toronto. Queen's had 18 professors and 180 students; Victoria had 200 students; Trinity seven professors; University College, Toronto, nine. Every institution in the country, with the exception of Toronto and Dalhousie, was denominational, and there was about them all, as there was about every school, a strong religious flavour. The University of Toronto was rarely mentioned except to be damned with faint praise, and Dalhousie's successful operation was delayed for years from denominational rivalry. The church watched secularism advance into education with regret, which is not to be wondered at in an intensely religious age and an atmosphere of colonial conventionalism not open to new ideas. Yet the church colleges with their libraries and museums[31] were themselves opening doors that could never be closed.

In addition to colleges, the new Dominion boasted at least two observatories, several normal schools, and various other evidences of social growth, such as the Canadian Institute at Toronto, or that then new institution, the Y.M.C.A. Every town had its newspaper, and the larger towns had several: Halifax in the early 1860's boasted thirteen! Most of these still consisted of four sheets, with much of their news extracted from American or British journals. They were not great capitalist undertakings, and it was relatively easy to begin one. There were few dailies and no sensationalism. The advertisements were small and talk of "freedom of the press" therefore still made sense. The newspaper served as an *omnium gatherum* for the literary efforts of the day, with political debates interminably spun out in letters to the editor, descriptions of travels through the provinces, and the efforts of budding poets.

These were almost the nearest approach to a literature that the colonies possessed. French Canada had had its Garneau and was beginning to find itself in its poets[32] but English Canada, with the honourable exception of Nova Scotia, was virtually devoid of anything that could be remotely described as original culture. In Nova Scotia, a sense of

---

[31] The largest library in the country appears to have been that of the University of Toronto, with 15,000 volumes.

[32] Such as Octave Crémazie (1827-79) or Louis Fréchette (1839-1908).

community and stability built on a New England foundation brought forth a provincial literature[33] that did the small province credit. To produce even one written work of merit argues a certain intensity of intellectual life in a large circle adjacent to the author, and Nova Scotia produced several. Possibly there were similar circles, but less intense, in other provinces: in the Toronto of the 1850's, Alpheus Todd, the Librarian of Parliament and his brother were writing to friends describing their musical evenings, where they played Mozart sonatas together. And some of the celebrities of the day came up from the south occasionally to appear before Canadian audiences.

Why was there little native cultural development if educational facilities were good and the people alert? Apart from the impossibility of an original culture growing up in a colony, that is, in a derivative community, Canadians in general were not interested in that side of life. Many of them had backgrounds of philistinism, depending on which parts of the British Isles they had come from; many moved from the fringes of British civilization to the fringe of civilization in British North America; they were twice colonial. Nearly everyone, as is perhaps unavoidable in a pioneer country, was utilitarian in outlook. That clarification of vision and enlargement of soul which liberal education brings would have been of little interest to all but a microscopic proportion of the generation of 1867.

Liberal education itself in its higher areas was rather unreal; nearly all professors were Old-Countrymen, who did not provide much relationship between their teaching and the circumstances of the new country. With some exceptions in the ministry, the educated tended to be an exotic class, pale imitations of those of the mother country, and "good society" was marked by stiffness of behaviour and old-fashioned opinions. In the countryside, most of the folk-arts of the older world, which provide a genuine culture for the people, had been left behind, and society had had to begin again; consequently along with the most generous hospitality and a true sense of neighbourliness, typical pioneer crudity was still much in evidence. It was often accompanied by an ugly and vicious intemperance, which explains the "prohibition movement", the first piece of native social reform. Consonant with this kind of conduct were the free fights at elections, the broken heads on the Twelfth of July or Saint Patrick's Day, and the bombast that too often was (and still is!) heard from public platforms.

It was, it is evident, neither a powerful state nor a brilliant society that had been put together in 1867. For a cultivated metropolitan,

---

[33] Of which Haliburton's *Sam Slick* is the best known example.

acquainted with the latest achievements of the human spirit, to live in it must have required grace and faith; it is no wonder that the occasional wanderer of that description such as Goldwin Smith[34] recoiled rather violently from it. Canada in its first days was narrow and shabby: few of the great bracing winds roaring in the south blew through it. Yet it was an immense improvement on the struggling individual colonies, it expanded the vision of its best citizens, it called out the best energies of many of its sons, and for those who wished quiet homes in a God-fearing environment and in surroundings of natural beauty, for those who wished a modest competence, if not wealth, it promised much. There was hope ahead in those days, and if the ordinary man had not caught the vision, many of the leaders had: they were in no doubt as to what they had done; they had laid the foundations for a national structure which they were determined to provide with a future and in whose future they believed.

Additional Reading

Rumilly, Robert. *Histoire de la province de Québec*. Montreal 1940 —. 33 vols. published to 1961.

Trotter, R. G. *Canadian Federation*. Toronto, 1924.

Waite, Peter G. *The Life and Times of Confederation, 1864-1867*. Toronto, 1962.

[34] 1823-1910. After a brilliant academic career in Oxford, Goldwin Smith had come (1866) to the United States to help launch the new Cornell University. He retired to Toronto (1872) where he lived the rest of his life. An uncompromising *laisser-faire* Liberal and anti-Imperialist, he was hardly popular in the best circles of that city, which nevertheless could not avoid accepting him socially.

CHAPTER 25

A Mari Usque ad Mare, 1867-1878

1. The Impact of Canada Upon British North America. A National Spirit?

Confederation represented to a considerable degree the impact upon the British possessions in North America of the relatively prosperous and energetic community lying between Montreal and Lake Huron. If the colonies contained a dynamic centre, there it was. There was the region from which had come the determining pressure for Reciprocity in 1854 and for Confederation in 1864. At the Charlottetown Conference, its representatives had appeared with precise proposals: the Maritimers, holding mainly watching briefs, had accepted them. At Quebec it had been the same: the detailed blueprint of Confederation was the work of the English Canadian politicians; the main contribution of the Maritimers was discussion and reshaping, and the proper insistence on voting in the Conference by provincial units, while that of the French was the safeguarding of their rights. English Canada also contributed nearly all the "fathers" of constructive initiative, Tupper being the only Maritimer to rank with them: he rates as an almost first-class figure, but Tilley, from New Brunswick, hardly does. Cartier was French Canada's only representative of high calibre. The politics of this interior region were stormy and unstable, its orators too vehement and vindictive for calmer Maritime tastes, but its very storminess indicated life.

The dynamic region, like all such, was expansive. It expanded westward by migration and both westward and eastward through financial and commercial control. Expansion westward became a race between Toronto (in association with western Ontario) and Montreal. Montreal won the fight for the Pacific Railway. Its railway and financial control of the West became almost complete, but western Ontario took the surer way and sent out its men to occupy the land: Ontario projected itself all along the main line of the Canadian Pacific right through to the coast, though in diminishing strength westwardly, and today Manitoba and south-eastern Saskatchewan are its colonies. Throughout the West, the influence of Ontario people and their descendants is potent, a blood tie to the east and one of the bonds of the modern nation.

The extension of financial control was marked by the action of the chartered banks of the central region, which rushed to establish branches everywhere,[1] without much effective competition from the outlying banks. Today all but one of these has disappeared, the Bank of Nova Scotia, and though it holds a symbolic annual meeting in Halifax, its head office has been moved to Toronto. Other phases of metropolitan finance, such as insurance companies and trust and loan companies, followed the banks in the race to east and west. This semi-subjugation of hitherto autonomous communities by an expanding metropolis was to contribute heavily to Maritime resentment against Confederation.

The churches also obeyed the same law. Within six or seven years after Confederation all the Presbyterian bodies had come together in the Presbyterian Church of Canada and all the Methodist in the Methodist Church of Canada: these two became genuine national churches, with the same organization obtaining from coast to coast, but with a disproportionate number of their leaders, clerical and lay, domiciled in Ontario-Montreal. The rising churches of the west more often than not were staffed by young men from this central region.[2]

Another and highly significant example of the impact of Canada

---

[1] The extension of Montreal finance is indicated by the dates at which branches of the Bank of Montreal were opened:
Bank founded, 1817.

Quebec branch opened,	1817		Halifax branch opened,		1867
Kingston " "	1818		Saint John "	"	1867
Toronto " "	1818		Winnipeg "	"	1876
Ottawa " "	1842		Regina "	"	1883
London " "	1844		Calgary "	"	1886
			Vancouver "	"	1887

[2] A famous example was "Ralph Connor", the Rev. C. W. Gordon, who was born and educated in Ontario, but passed most of his active ministry in Winnipeg.

upon British North America was the expansion of the Conservative party of the old province into the Conservative party of the Dominion. It was most important that parties should not become sectional, racial, or worse still, religious. The example given in the first elections by Nova Scotia's solid phalanx of secessionists was not a happy one, and the country owes a debt of gratitude to Macdonald and Tupper for their adroitness in inducing the leader of the malcontents, Joseph Howe, to accept office in Macdonald's cabinet, thus breaking secessionist ranks and transforming them into harmless Liberals. In a similar way Macdonald succeeded in preserving the old alliance with the French; the politics of the first twenty-five years of the Dominion turned on it. Macdonald's selection as first Prime Minister, to the exclusion of men like Cartier, who had contributed to Confederation even more than he had, gave a chance to mould the new material while it was still fluid. Of this he took full advantage by attracting men from all parties into his ministries.

Macdonald called his first cabinet a coalition, but it was under the firm control of a Conservative Prime Minister, even though it contained former Liberals like W. P. Howland and William McDougall and later on, Joseph Howe. It was a favourite jibe to remind Sir John of the monster's cave to which all the footsteps pointed inward, none outward. His ability to "devour" opponents, makes the analogy not unfair, but the "devouring" built up a party representing many sections and interests. While there was something in the charge that he manoeuvred to bring new provinces in as party assets with over-weighted representation, his letters show that he sedulously set out to influence and instruct (usually wisely) their local administrations. He looked on all provinces and especially the small, new ones, as minor political units, to be carefully shepherded by Ottawa. This yielded direct party advantage, but it also pushed a national party into each new province and fostered a general, as opposed to a parochial, point of view. The Liberal party, in contrast, had little of this wide outlook: it was constantly being divested of good men by coalitions which became Conservative and, consisting as it did in a collection of negative units—Nova Scotian secessionists, Quebec Rouges, Ontario followers of Brown or Blake—it could muster little unity. No fusion of importance could occur until a national programme was worked out, and that did not occur for many years. To Macdonald Conservatism must go the honour of acting at a crucial time as a strong piece of national cement.

The new Dominion, it is plain, soon acquired national organizations, but did national organizations make a nation? The answer must lie in the negative. There was much talk of Canada and of Canada's interests in the press and by public men;[3] among them an expansion of view and vision had occurred, with here and there some of that real emotional stirring without which merely political structures are brittle. But a few swallows do not make a summer, and there is no evidence for the penetration of such feelings far downward. The Dominion of Canada was to reach the Pacific without the inner concept *Canada* having been born.

2. Expansion Eastward

A stipulated condition of Confederation had been the long-discussed intercolonial railroad. It was at once taken in hand as a public work and was completed by 1876. Its route followed the original northern line, along the St. Lawrence and then across to the north shore of New Brunswick,[4] thence to Halifax, with a branch to Saint John. The Intercolonial did not make Halifax into a great port, commanding the commerce of the interior, but partially converted it into an out-port for Montreal, as Portland was and as Saint John was to become. Nothing could overcome the strategic situation of Montreal, a seaport tucked hundreds of miles inland.

The Intercolonial repeated the experience of the S. S. *Royal William*, which had been put on the Quebec-Halifax run about 1830: not much traffic developed. It was built partly as a strategic railway, mainly as a bond of union. It became and remained a political railway. As Sir John Macdonald later said, "the men that are put on the railroad from the porter upward become civil servants. If one of these men is put on from any cause whatever, he is said to be a political hack; if he is removed, it is said his removal was on account of his political opinions; if a cow is killed on the road, a motion is made in respect to it by the member of the House who has the owner's vote and support . . . it is impossible for the government to run that railroad satisfactorily".[5] The Grand Trunk had been a reflection of the "promoting" type of capitalist: the I.C.R. as it was run, was a reflection of the small, grafting politician. Its economic problems have never been completely solved. But during the two world wars, it abundantly justified its strategic concept: the port of Halifax came into its own as a great naval base, and the Intercolonial became the invaluable feeder from a wartime hinterland. Without it, Canada would have been infinitely handicapped.

[3] "If we wish to be a great people, if we wish to form a great nationality. . . ."— John A. Macdonald in his Confederation speech, Feb. 6, 1865.
[4] This is actually only about 40 miles longer than the later route direct to the St. John at Edmundston and then on to Moncton, N.B.
[5] Hansard, Jan. 18, 1881.

The Intercolonial was a boomerang for Nova Scotia, although it took many years before the fact became patent. But in another area the province began its struggle against engulfing metropolitanism at once. Its secessionists were really Nova Scotian nationalists, as the bitter cry "Sold to Canada at eighty cents a head" indicates. Yet being in the water, they might just as well swim. Thus began the long game of extracting the utmost from "the purchasers". The first results were the "better terms" devised for Nova Scotia in the initial parliament of the Dominion: these consisted in larger annual grants, which were not, however, equal to the revenues the province had surrendered to the Dominion. It was placed in a difficult financial position from the beginning, a condition accentuated by the downfall of the sailing ship economy.

Railways represented the forces of continentalism: they had drawn the continental provinces into Confederation, and six years later they attracted one of the two Atlantic island colonies. One of the conditions of Prince Edward Island's entrance was the guarantee of good ferry connection with the railway system of the Dominion. Another lay in the Island's financial difficulties in building a railway for itself, and a third in the financial aid to be afforded in buying out the absentee proprietors, the curse of the colony since its beginning.[6] The other island colony, Newfoundland, still formed part of the Atlantic world, where its trade connections mainly lay. After nibbling the bait, it refused to bite, and until 1949, remained outside. Newfoundland is at the point of balance between three sets of forces: those coming across the Atlantic, those coming out of the Gulf of St. Lawrence from one side of the Appalachian Barrier, and those coming up the Atlantic coast, from New York, Boston, and Halifax on the other. In 1867, the political and traditional association with England was supported with economic ties, but economic ties with the St. Lawrence were relatively weak. The forces of continentalism were not to prevail until 1949, and Newfoundland remained outside Confederation.

3. The North West: Montreal's Old Hinterland Restored

It was in the west that the dynamic continental nucleus of British North America made its plainest impact. To secure the Hudson's Bay Territories had been one of the large objects of Confederation: provision had been made in the Act for this purpose, and in 1869, the deal was

---

[6] The whole area of Prince Edward Island was granted away to a few court favourites shortly after the Conquest of 1763; settlers could never obtain freehold tenure from these absentees.

closed. The Company, no longer under the direction of the old fur-trading hands, but of a quasi-financial, quasi-imperialist group in London,[7] was bought out for a reasonable amount. This included its retention of lands on a generous scale as private property. That Edward Watkin did not do so badly in his combination of patriotism and profit is evidenced by the Company's subsequent successful financial history. The purchase was the first step in the restoration of the old hinterland of Montreal.

The Canadian impact on the west in terms of persons took the shape of a noisy and tactless frontier movement that alienated the little community at the confluence of the Red and Assiniboine rivers upon which it impinged. Canadians from Upper Canada had been out in Red River since the late 'fifties where, in 1859, two of them had begun the first newspaper, *The Nor' Wester*. These men, by aggressive demeanour and speech, had made themselves unpopular enough to give Canada a bad name. Now on the eve of taking over the territories, the government sent out parties to lay out a road from Lake Superior, the well-known Dawson Road, and begin working out the general land survey system. The surveyors with equal lack of tact alarmed the *Métis* by carrying their lines across their Red River lands (which were loosely arranged on the Quebec model of narrow river frontages and long depths). There is some evidence for believing that the surveyors not only trespassed but also talked boastfully about Canada taking over, making suggestions that the *Métis* would then have their lands taken away from them. Here was a major cause of the so-called Red River "Rebellion" of 1870.

For a generation after the union of 1821, the Red River settlements had been peacefully governed, directly or indirectly, by the Hudson's Bay Company. Then towards the end of the 1840's, the outside world began to crowd in on them, and their long isolation was quickly over. The Red River *Métis* began carrying furs and buffalo hides southward to the traders who formed the American outriders of settlement. This was infringing the Company's legal monopoly. A test case made in 1849 resulted in the release of the offender from the Company's custody by a mob, whose leader was Louis Riel, father of a more famous son. This event broke the Company's power, and thenceforth trading went on without much interruption. In 1859, when a steamboat was put on the Red River to connect with St. Paul, the approach of the American frontier was confirmed more emphatically. Ominous possibilities of "Manifest Destiny" were suggested by bills introduced into the Legislature of Minnesota and into Congress itself[8] for annexation, by consent,

[7] See pp. 302, 323.

[8] The text of this bill (1866) is printed in Watkin, *Canada and the States*, 227ff.

of all the British provinces. There was also some Fenian penetration into Red River, and propaganda from that source had something to do with the outbreak of 1870. How loose things were becoming in the territories is evidenced by the remarkable conduct of one Spence, a resident of Portage la Prairie, who one fine day in 1869 came out with a modest proclamation announcing that he had set up the Republic of Manitoba. The "Republic" did not become more than a proclamation, but the incident was merely one among others indicating that the point was being reached where only decisive action would preserve the North West as British territory.

In the affair of 1870 very few reputations came out enhanced. William McDougall, whose long interest in the West entitled him to the post, had been made governor, but his attempt to assert his authority before actual word had been received of the transfer from Great Britain to Canada earned for him exclusion from his prospective domain by Louis Riel's followers: until the territory was actually Canada's, he was a purely private person. Riel[9] himself might have become another "tribune of the people" if he had known how to act temperately, but his "execution" of the Ontario Orangeman, Thomas Scott, was exactly the kind of deed required to set that particular heather on fire. In retrospect, the death of Scott looms as the most determinative specific political incident between Confederation and the Great War, for by leading more or less directly to the execution of Riel in 1885 and thence to the Mercier-McCarthy troubles[10] and the conflict over the French schools of Manitoba, it dug up the hatchet that was supposed to have been buried in 1867 and opened once more a gulf between the two races. It is difficult to prove Riel's "Government" legal, and the execution, at best of dubious necessity, thus must come close to having been a murder.

Among others concerned, Bishop Taché, in his emergency trip back from Rome and his arrangement of terms with the inhabitants, displayed statesmanlike qualities. Donald A. Smith[11] managed to calm the troubled waters a little. The allegation was frequently made, and as frequently denied, that he gave Riel, at Macdonald's suggestion, a large sum of money (which was not repaid, something that one Scot would find hard

---

[9] 1844-85. French half-breed. Leader of both the Red River and the North-West risings.

[10] See p. 390ff.

[11] 1820-1914. Began life as Hudson's Bay fur trader in Labrador and rose to the top of the Company's service. Member of first Canadian Parliament. Later, leader in building of C.P.R. High Commissioner to London, 1896-1914. Created Lord Strathcona and Mount Royal.

to forgive in another) to make himself scarce and remove an embarrassing case from Canadian courts.

Macdonald himself came out badly. He wrote sensible letters to McDougall, but he surely could not have discussed the whole situation thoroughly enough with that official before he left, nor did he seem apprized of its details in anything like proportion to its importance.[12] It would have been quite easy to lose the whole west at the time. No one had surer vision than Macdonald of what it would mean in the future, and yet his approach was fumbling. A thorough canvassing of the situation followed by sharp action was not forthcoming. He was inclined to be not statesmanlike, but legalistic. His conduct in bribing Riel to keep out of the way while he was shouting to the roof-tops that he was trying to catch him was, if the allegation is true, discreditable.[13]

Recent studies[14] have refused to see in the movement a rebellion at all. Macdonald himself seemed to have been of this opinion, for he wrote to McDougall that, after the Company had given up and before the Imperial Government had transferred the territories to Canada, their inhabitants were in a state of nature and had the right, according to the law of nature, to provide themselves with a government. This may have been good political philosophy in the school of John Locke but was it good law? Is not the authority of the Crown all-pervading and ever present? In a British possession can there exist "a state of nature"? The legal attributes of the Crown in respect to its possessions surely are those suggested in the scriptural exclamation, "If I fly to the ends of the earth, lo! thou art there". Louis Riel was no more in a position to exact obedience to his "government" than was Spence. Though a provisional government that exercises coercive powers is not necessarily a rebel government, its members must be responsible as individuals for their acts. So that if Riel escapes the charge of being a rebel (and there is no suggestion that he intended to resist constituted authority when, in the person of Colonel Wolseley, it arrived) he would come in for the murder charge. Whatever the legal situation, it was

[12] He never really did know the west well.
[13] Col. G. T. Denison, *The Struggle for Imperial Unity* (Toronto, 1909), Chaps. 2-4, maintains that it was only the pressure of the Ontario agitation over Scott that made Macdonald take action. The allegation that Riel was bribed to leave was widely accepted when Riel actually did go.
[14] A standard work is G. F. G. Stanley, *The Birth of Western Canada: A History of the Riel Rebellions* (London, 1936; Toronto, Canadian University Paperbacks, 1963). Stanley's *Louis Riel* (Toronto, 1963) is the definitive biography. It discusses all the above points in detail.

unfortunate in the extreme that the inclusion of the North-West in the Dominion should be marked by the tragic transfer there of the passions that inflamed Ontario and Quebec.

Riel's outbreak had as its objective, provincial standing for the settlements of his people in "Red River". This it secured, Manitoba being the first "colonial province" carved from Canada's own imperial domain, the North-West Territories. Without it, Red River would not have obtained provincial status so soon. The new province was decided upon as the result of a bargain struck with the inhabitants, who had drawn up their "bill of rights" to protect themselves against the encroaching "English". It was given legal validity in The Manitoba Act, a Canadian law later confirmed by the British Parliament and different only in necessary details from the British North America Act. Manitoba began almost as a second French province. In educational control, the use of French or English in the legislature, and in the possession of a legislative council, the province was modelled on Quebec, and for a few years its politics were controlled by persons hailing from Quebec.

4. British Columbia: The Pacific Railway

In the Far West the same initial mistakes were not made; the agreement with British Columbia was apparently reached easily. It was drastically censured by men like Edward Blake and Richard Cartwright, who were convinced that it could never be carried out and that it had its origin in a typical Macdonald move to get the public attention off the Riel affair and secure a few more Conservative seats. The important point was that British Columbia's inclusion in the Dominion rested clearly on consent. Luckily for the British connection, the California gold miners who had flocked in to the Fraser gold "bars" in the late 1850's had gone away again almost as fast as they had come, and when in 1866 a movement for annexation had been begun, it did not receive much support. Nevertheless it indicated for the Pacific coast, as well as the Prairies, that to keep the northern half of the continent within the Empire, action would have to come soon. This was supplied by the dominating group in British Columbia, which was strongly Federationist and British in its sympathies and which, in such a loose-jointed community, did not have much difficulty getting its way. It would have brought British Columbia into Confederation without Macdonald's audacious promise of railroad connection with Canada within ten years, but the promise more than turned the scale, which was pressed firmly down by the decision of the San Juan boundary dispute in 1871 in favour of the Americans.[15]

It is difficult today to realize how big the railway decision was. There had been casual talk about a Pacific railway for years, but it had never got to the stage of specific proposals, and still less of plans. In the 1850's, Walter Shanley, the Canadian engineer, had lent his prestige to the idea, and then in the 1860's Watkin's London group, by purchasing the Hudson's Bay Company, had removed a major impediment. Most of the country along the route was quite well known, but much of it was enough to dismay the stoutest heart. For two hundred miles from Montreal the valley of the Ottawa provided good farm land. Then the granite rocks of the Laurentian Shield closed in on the river, and from that point[16] west for eleven hundred miles there was little but rock ridges, muskeg, rivers, and lakes, making some of the hardest country ever faced by the engineer. The thousand miles of prairies presented no difficulties, except supply, which all had to come from "end of steel" at Winnipeg, but when the mountains were reached, six or seven hundred miles more of almost impregnable wilderness lay ahead. The main northern pass, the *Tête Jaune* or *Yellowhead*, was not difficult, but the canyons of the rivers flowing into the Pacific presented problems indeed. Along the whole three thousand miles, some twelve hundred at most could be counted as fair agricultural land that would one day be settled: it was as plain as anything could be that the rest could never be more than timber and mining country, and most of it would remain forever a wilderness.

If technical means of construction had been as advanced then as they are now, the job would have been formidable enough. But they were far from that: the dynamite and power drills which today make quick work of the rock-cuts had not arrived. Or if the country proposing the road had been populous and wealthy, the feat of construction, while great, would not have been superhuman. The United States had just completed its Union Pacific (1869) across to San Francisco, but it was a country of forty millions, and even for it the Union Pacific was a notable piece of construction. Canada was a little country of four millions, with annual revenues of less than twenty million dollars and a credit standing in London that had to depend on Imperial guarantees for reasonable rates of interest. In 1871 the decision must have seemed either magnificently bold or just plainly silly.

[15] For British Columbia see F. W. Howay *et al, British Columbia and the United States* (Toronto, 1942). The most recent book is Margaret A. Ormsby, *British Columbia: A History* (Toronto, 1958).
[16] A little above Pembroke, Ont.

Why it was made has never been completely explained. Are we to dismiss all practical considerations? Had any assurance come from the Watkin group that assistance would be forthcoming? If we can judge by Watkin's own memoirs, he was devoted to securing the northern lands to the Empire and the railway was the condition of their retention, for if one was not built on British territory, the Northern Pacific was ready and waiting to supply connections with American centres. What we know for certain is that the agreement with British Columbia included a promise to build a railway through to the coast within ten years. It was the Macdonald ministry that made the bargain. Whatever the exact allocation of the parts in it may be, he was the captain of the ship. To him goes the credit for the pertinacity that secured completion of the railway. On it, as firmly as on his share in making Confederation, rests his fame as the architect of his country. To this most practical of politicians must be allowed an imaginative vision, a boldness—or a wanton recklessness—that leave lesser men gasping.

It is evident from his utterances that once Sir John had put his hand to the Confederation plough he never looked back. The task to him was plain, and he spoke of it repeatedly: it was to build a great and prosperous nation. That, in the thinking of the day, meant physical accomplishment in the fields of transportation, settlement, and industry. It seemed a materialistic goal, but it was guided by impulses other than the merely materialistic. Opponents of "the old man" repeatedly alleged that the chief of these was the provision of means for keeping himself and his party in power. But what the bounds were between national good and party advantage, or between right and wrong, in that subtle mind, who is to say? Macdonald probably saw in a Pacific Railway a great coup that would keep him in office indefinitely and enable him to reward his friends magnificently. He also probably saw in it national opportunity. He is a man to be praised and to be damned in the same breath. The simplest explanation of his conduct is the best: the prize of the Pacific coast, so vital to the future of the new country, was only to be secured by a railway, and so a railway, by hook or by crook, must be built. Macdonald's half-poetic Highland spirit, not unduly tied down to the practical small change of life, not conspicuously afflicted with the accountant's mentality, must have had in it something of the gambler, and so he threw the dice and won.

The decision itself was the big thing: it was so big that it alone would have raised Sir John Macdonald to the highest eminence among men. Once he had made it, there were plenty of people ready to associate themselves with it and to join in the enterprise. But the decision itself was so breath-taking that almost necessarily its execution could not go smoothly.

The immediate task was to find a group ready to have a fling at construction. One condition was fundamental: the road must go north of the lakes, entirely through Canadian territory, and the Americans must not be allowed to have anything to do with it. The group that was building the Northern Pacific would have been only too glad to come into the project, for it would have given them access to the Atlantic, but they would have carried the line south of the lakes and would have used the prairies as "feeder" territory for their own main line.

Yet, the Rubicon once crossed, the Prime Minister seemed to relapse into his customary indecision, for when two groups appeared, ready to undertake the task, the government, anxious not to incur anyone's hostility, attempted to turn away wrath by giving a soft answer to each of them, in the form of a company charter authorizing them to build. Sir Hugh Allan of Montreal, Canada's richest man, headed one group, and D. L. MacPherson, from Toronto, the other. The issue crystallized the rivalry of these two cities—the old metropolitan centre and the western town that was beginning to achieve metropolitan proportions. Which, by becoming headquarters for the railway, was to command the West? A tussle ensued in which government tried to get the two companies to unite, but they fell out over Allan's requirement that he should be president. Meanwhile the first Parliament of Canada had been dissolved, and in the elections of 1872, the Macdonald coalition, which had now absorbed its Liberal elements into Conservatism, was again returned. Before the second Parliament assembled, the Ministry had succeeded in forming a new company to construct the railroad. The new one was suspiciously similar to the old Montreal organization, with Allan at its head. It agreed to begin work within a year and was to have a subsidy of thirty million dollars and fifty million acres of land, an amount not far short of the total arable area available.

5. Rapids in the Stream: The Pacific Scandal; The Mackenzie Regime

It was this reorganized company which came to grief in the "Pacific Scandal" of 1873, the episode that also destroyed Macdonald's government. L. S. Huntingdon, a Liberal M.P. from Quebec, in the spring following the election of 1872, made most serious charges of corruption against Macdonald and of bribery against Sir Hugh Allan, who was alleged virtually to have bought the new charter from the Conservative government in return for campaign funds. The whole incident was

unsavoury and no one emerged from it with increased stature. Huntingdon refused to appear before the Royal Commission of Inquiry (the
means by which he had come into possession of his knowledge would
probably not have borne investigation), and the Opposition as a whole
proved itself small and shortsighted. Though the victim of blackmail by
the unscrupulous ex-Canadian go-between McMullen, though he may
have cleared himself of the charge of treasonable relations with American capitalists, and though in his contributions to Sir John's campaign
funds, he may have felt he was not acting contrary to whatever it is that
passes for ethical conduct in the world of business, Sir Hugh Allan had
sailed close to the line of rectitude. Donald Smith, whose speech it was
in that memorable session of November 5, 1873, that finally brought
down the government, was not talking from such a height of pure
principle as his words might have led his hearers to believe. There had
been a stormy scene with Sir John not long before. The Prime Minister,
one of his intimates later affirmed, had been resorting to his favourite
"tactical" device for keeping himself, with the aid of an all too familiar
friend, *incommunicado* until the storm had a chance to blow itself out.
He was, therefore, not in as lucid or good tempered a state as he might
have been, so instead of trying to win Smith over, he had merely "cursed
and sworn" at him.[17]

What of Sir John himself? No one ever suggested that money stuck
to his fingers. But he had few scruples when it came to finding the
sinews of war. He did not deny that he had secured large amounts of
money from Allan. He did not deny the authorship of the "I must have
another ten thousand" telegram. He merely said that his opponents
were dishonourable in the way in which they had come into possession
of such knowledge and that no promises were made to Allan by which
election contributions would be turned into bribes. In his private letters
to the Governor-General, Lord Dufferin (1872-78), he contended that
elections were always fought in such a way in Canada and that his
conduct was no exception to the rule. Rather meanly, even though
privately, he suggested that Cartier, who had died in the interval, by
his obduracy in contesting a difficult and expensive Montreal riding
when he might have been elected elsewhere by acclamation, had
occasioned some of the necessity for the heavy drafts on Allan.[18] An
onlooker from England at the time was Hon. George Brodrick, Warden

[17] See A. L. Burt, "Peter Mitchell on John A. Macdonald," *CHR*, XLII (Sept.,
1961), 209-227—an extraordinarily revealing document, known to the author
when writing the above, but not then available for publication.
[18] Canadian Archives, Macdonald Papers, Macdonald to Dufferin, Oct. 9, 1873,
'Railways' Vol. V, 1873, 278.

of Merton College, who wrote a long letter to *The Times*, commenting on the episode. He should have been reasonably impartial and his opinion of weight:

> After following the evidence with some care . . . I feel bound to acquit Sir John Macdonald of having actually sold or conspired to sell the Pacific Railway contracts, either to foreign capitalists or to Sir Hugh Allan himself. . . . Nor was any attempt made to show that any part of these large funds was expended in bribery. What is proved, or what is acknowledged by Sir John Macdonald himself, is that, being Prime Minister and trustee of a grand public undertaking, he not only accepted but solicited contributions for electioneering purposes from a man then seeking to obtain control over that undertaking, and who could not but look for his reward in an advantageous charter.[19]

A fair verdict would be "Not guilty but don't do it again!" Sir John's honour was precariously saved at the expense of his judgement. The incident revealed some of the weak spots of the man: he was not fastidious, never particular about the means that would serve his ends, willing to sail close to the wind for the sake of party advantage and personal triumph.

Under the circumstances it was fitting that the public judgement in the ensuing elections should be pronounced vigorously against him. It is difficult to believe that Canadian consciences were then any more sensitive about such things than they have been since or than was Sir John's, and it is only too probable that the election result depended as much on Orange offence over an unpunished Louis Riel as on the wounded honour of the community. However, it could always be quoted as the just punishment meted out to wrongdoers and so was a useful milestone in the road.

When Macdonald resigned, the Governor-General called upon Alexander Mackenzie,[20] formally chosen leader of the opposition in the previous year. Among prominent Liberals Edward Blake, Premier of Ontario, would have seemed the more likely man,[21] but his interests

[19] Quoted in H. H. Ardagh, *Life of Sir James Gowan* (Toronto, 1911), p. 97.
[20] 1822-92. An Upper Canadian follower of George Brown, he had been relatively inconspicuous but became prominent after Brown dropped out of public life and Mowat confined himself to Ontario. The latest and best biography of Mackenzie is Dale C. Thompson, *Alexander Mackenzie, Clear Grit* (Toronto, 1960).
[21] 1833-1912. Entered public life about 1867 as Ontario Reformer. Second Premier of Ontario, 1871-72. Minister without portfolio, 1873-74. Minister of Justice, 1875-77. Leader of the Opposition, 1880-87.

appeared firmly anchored in his native Ontario, and the Ottawa field had been left to Mackenzie. The new Prime Minister was another Scot; there were few Ontario public men who were not. He was a man of the people, a stone-mason who had reached the heights of great men by "climbing upward in the night". Like William Lyon Mackenzie and like George Brown, he derived from the Scottish Liberalism of the early nineteenth century, that product of Calvinistic theology, the individualism of self-made men, and the fight against the corrupt oligarchy of pre-Reform Scotland. He tended to see Canadian life through Scottish eyes, and that perhaps explains why his administration was unable really to come to grips with the problems facing the country. Men of the Mackenzie school were honour personified compared with their opponents, but they were essentially timid, quailing before the immensity of the problems raised by nation building. They were men of intellect, but not men of vision. Like liberals everywhere, they were temperamentally antipathetic to grandiose schemes.[22] Like nineteenth century Liberals, they overdid the practical approach, were too much afraid of the impossible, too fond of casting up accounts and refusing to act if the monetary balance came out on the wrong side.

Mackenzie had trouble in forming a ministry. Brown had written himself off by his resignation in 1865, though he still remained the *eminence grise* behind the Liberal throne. Edward Blake, that man of massive intellect[23] but uncertain course, refused at first to join, then became a minister without portfolio, and later resigned. Blake seems to have spent much of his life resigning: he became minister of justice in 1875 only to resign before the elections. Richard Cartwright said that he was constitutionally incapable of serving loyally under anyone, and he also was a failure as a leader. Yet it was Blake who has perhaps left the most enduring memorials of the Mackenzie regime in his success in having the Supreme Court Act approved in London and in his restriction of the powers of the Governor-General through the revision by the Imperial authorities of the official "Instructions", particularly in the matter of the pardoning power. As minister, he seemed inclined to take an advanced nationalist position, if he is to be judged by his well-known Aurora speech of 1874, but sixteen years later, prompted by his concern for the British connection, he ended his Canadian career in refusing to subscribe to the Liberal Reciprocity programme of 1891. He was a conundrum, no small factor in destroying Liberal chances of success in their first term of office.

[22] See p. 333.
[23] A quality reflected in his face: no one could fail to be impressed by the ability and poise mirrored in the portraits of Blake.

Mackenzie, on taking office, did not dissolve but waited to see what his support in the House would be. Such a course of action indicates how loose party ties were at the time. Not enough of Sir John's late supporters coming over to him, he went to the people, and in the beginning of 1874, received a good majority. His chances seemed good. In contrast with his predecessor, he was the most open and honest of men, and his ministry was above suspicion. Yet honesty in itself was not a very hearty recommendation to the electorate of those days, and in the case of Mackenzie it was more than counterbalanced by political ineptitude of a high order. The Prime Minister used to pass some fourteen hours a day in his duties as departmental head and had no time or energy left for building up his party. The very rectitude of his conduct destroyed his chances. He offended public works contractors by depriving them of the easy pickings they had had under Sir John. He offended the liquor interests by supporting the Scott Act, a prohibition measure. He offended the Orangemen by his amnesty to Riel's followers and his failure to bring to justice the men who killed the Orangeman Hackett in a Twelfth of July parade in Montreal, 1877.[24] He inherited the bad finance of his predecessor, and his able Minister of Finance, Richard Cartwright,[25] never was able to shake himself free of it. He inherited Sir John's civil servants, who in a partisan age, worked against him in a dozen subtle ways. More especially, he inherited a railway programme with which he was out of sympathy, and to crown all, he inherited a first-class depression.

Mackenzie's railway policy, of going ahead slowly, building links between the waterways and not attempting to finish within ten years, almost lost British Columbia to Canada. Edward Blake actually invited the province to take itself off. Few incidents in Canadian history bring out more clearly that difference in party psychology which rests ultimately on differences in human types. "Grits", as individualists, concentrated on the problems under their noses; Tories, as men of action rather than thought, took readily to these wide-ranging schemes. In the difficult situation precipitated by Mackenzie's delay, with British Columbia clamouring for the Dominion to honour its engagement, the Governor-General persuaded both parties to agree to an arbitration and rearrangement. This eased the situation, and before it became acute

[24] See p. 373.
[25] 1835-1912. Minister of Finance, 1873-78; of Trade and Commerce, 1896-1911. Of Ontario Tory background, he became an uncompromising *laisser-faire* Liberal. One of the ablest—and most caustic—men in Canadian public life—a verdict amply borne out by his *Reminiscences* (Toronto, 1912).

again, Mackenzie had been defeated and Macdonald was back with his new railway syndicate.[26]

The other great issue, the tariff, the ministry also handled badly. Like its prototype in England, Canadian Liberalism stood for free trade. Mackenzie himself, a faithful colonial reflection of Cobden and Bright, was a doctrinaire on the subject. His Minister of Finance, the pugnacious Richard Cartwright, was steeped in the inheritance of Adam Smith and John Stuart Mill. The situation was made ironical by the deep depression that in 1873 came into Canada and sat on the empty chest left by Macdonald, for as it got worse it forced this free-trade Liberal government to increase the tariff in order to get revenue. Indirectly this depression was caused by the termination of the Reconstruction "boom" in the United States, and, directly, it marked the reaction which followed the Franco-Prussian war. For the Mackenzie Government it was "the old man of the sea": "bad times" sat upon the shoulders of the administration at its birth and clung to them until its death. Not until a few months before the election of 1878 did they begin to give way, and then it was too late for ministerial fortunes to benefit. Few governments can survive hard times. Mackenzie's was foreordained to defeat.

Canadian Liberalism in the 1870's did not succeed in making itself a real force in the land. It no longer had the crusading fervour that comes from abuses to be ended: there was no "Rep. by pop." agitation to be conducted, no battle against a family compact to be waged. Maledictions of Sir John Macdonald for his corruption or his adroit political footwork were no adequate substitute. Liberalism really had no programme: bold construction—state-building—was outside its orbit. Doctrinaire *laisser-faire* and the English type of individualism would not work in Canada, where strong individuals had to be linked with the state in a combination none too powerful for the projects that must be undertaken if Canada was to become a nation. Mackenzie and his men gave the country honest government, but uninspired, and with the exception of Blake's constitutional accomplishments, unconstructive. They were not in the main current of Canadian history; they were rapids in the stream, and they had to be swept out of office before its majestic course could be resumed "from the sea even unto the sea".

---

[26] Behind the Governor-General stood the Colonial Secretary, Lord Carnarvon. Carnarvon, who had attempted to unite South Africa in 1858 and was to do so again in 1878, and who had had something to do with Canadian federation, evidently regarded himself as a connoisseur in the subject, the proper physician to prescribe for federal ills. Mackenzie resented his interference in Canadian affairs, but because of the larger stake involved, accepted it. See Marquis of Dufferin and Ava, *Dufferin-Carnarvon Correspondence, 1874-1878*, ed. C. W. de Kieweit and F. H. Underhill (Toronto, 1955).

Chronology

1867   The First Ministry of the Dominion: another Liberal-Conservative Coalition.
1869   The Hudson Bay Purchase.
1869-70 The Riel Affair in Red River.
1870   The Manitoba Act creates Canada's first Prairie province.
1871   British Columbia enters Confederation.
1872   Second Dominion Election: Macdonald victorious.
1873   The Pacific Scandal; Resignation of Sir John Macdonald. Alexander Mackenzie Liberal Prime Minister.
        P.E.I. enters Confederation.
1873-78 Severe Commercial Depression.
1874   Third Dominion Election: Mackenzie victorious.
1875   The Supreme Court of Canada established.
        Edward Blake Minister of Justice.
1878   Fourth Dominion Election: Defeat of the Liberals on the issues of the Pacific Railway and the Tariff.

Additional Reading

Creighton, D. G. *John A. Macdonald.* II: *The Old Chieftain.* Toronto, 1955.

Morton, W. L. *The West and Confederation, 1857-1871.* (*CHA* Booklets No. 9) Ottawa, 1958.

———, *Manitoba; A History.* Toronto, 1957.

Ormsby, Margaret A. *British Columbia: A History.* Toronto, 1958.

Rumilly, Robert. *Mercier.* Montreal, 1936.

Skelton, Oscar. *General Economic History of the Dominion, 1867-1912.* Toronto, 1914.

Smith, G. *The Treaty of Washington, 1871.* Ithaca, N.Y., 1941.

Stanley, G. F. G. *The Birth of Western Canada.* London, 1936. (Canadian University Paperbacks, 1960.)

———. *Louis Riel.* Toronto, 1963.

Thomson, Dale C. *Alexander Mackenzie: Clear Grit.* Toronto, 1960.

Underhill, F. H. "Edward Blake and Canadian Liberal Nationalism," in R. Flenley, ed. *Essays in Canadian History.* Toronto, 1939.

CHAPTER 26

The Dominion of Macdonald, 1878-1885

1. Driving a Six Horse Team: Sir John's Political System

> Trade revived, crops were abundant and bank stocks once more became buoyant, owing to the confidence of the people of Canada in the new administration. A citizen of Toronto assured me that his Conservative cow gave three quarts of milk more a day after the election than before. . . . —"John A."[1]

The Conservative victory of 1878 represented a combination of hard times, special interests, and political skill. It brought back the men of architectural instincts and uninhibited temperament. It restored to power a politician who had touched pitch but could get things done, a quality of powerful appeal in new countries. It implied the completion of the state edifice that had been begun in 1867 and all necessary subsidiary measures. If, however, the Conservative cow was to go on giving her additional three quarts of milk a day, the dairyman would have to be more assiduous than ever. So deep and bitter were the divisions of the times that the very continuance of the Canadian show depended on the day-to-day success of the chief juggler in keeping all his numerous balls in the air at once.

[1] E. B. Biggar, *Anecdotal Life of Sir John A. Macdonald* (Montreal, 1891), p. 98.

After the Pacific Scandal, Sir John had offered to resign the party leadership, but having been asked to carry on, he soon discerned, with that unequalled eye of his, the weak spots in the opposing line. The depression of 1873 was a gift of the gods. Having selected new fighting ground, at the right moment he announced his policy. If the United States had been willing to make a new reciprocity agreement, he would have been in favour of it, but under the circumstances, with American manufacturers dumping their unsold goods on Canada as a "slaughter market", he was for protection. Protection would give Canadian industrialists their own home market and keep Canadian labour in Canada. It was the old, familiar story, dignified by the name of "National Policy". D'Alton McCarthy[2] then rising to prominence as one of Macdonald's lieutenants, was to assert a few years later that the policy launched in 1878 with such protestations of profound statesmanship had been frankly opportunistic: "If the Grits had come out for protection, we would have come out for free trade", were the words, uttered well after the event. That was unnecessarily cynical but attempts to prove Sir John a protectionist on principle fail. He was an opportunist on principle and probably, as a man of few fixed ideas, believed sincerely enough at the time that protection would be good for the country. At any rate, it might be good for an electoral victory.

The plan of campaign comprised, as a leading manoeuvre, a vast series of "political picnics". A shady grove, the "neighbours" gathered in their thousands from the utmost range of horse and buggy, merry and ample open-air meals, "visiting" all round, some sports for the boys and girls, all accompanied by minglings with the crowd, interminable hand-shakings, and "recognitions", more or less genuine, of "old friends"; and then, an outpouring of Macdonald eloquence! At this sort of thing Sir John was unbeatable. Mackenzie was defeated on the picnic grounds of Ontario. Add to the picnics, the closed factories. No successful argument is possible with a closed factory. So when Alex. Mackenzie looked up from his desk in the department of Public Works to find out the result of the election, he found that he was in a considerable minority. "We have lost five years," said Sir John in taking over the reins again.

The election ushered in the triumphant consummation of Macdonaldism. Macdonald had made the Dominion, and now he was to finish it: it was to be the Dominion of Macdonald in very truth, made in his image, reflecting his merits and his blemishes. He piped, and Canadians,

---

[2] 1836-98. A fighting North of Irelander from the heart of Orangeism, Simcoe County, soon to achieve prominence as a "hammer of the French".

at least Tory Canadians, danced. He had begun as a politician; he was to end as an institution.

The victory stamped his methods with approval. The system of politics of the period was in a unique way his. He had never been fastidious and had always loved power. Not made out of whole cloth himself he did not expect other men to be. He did not quite echo Walpole's words "all these men have their price", but he knew that nearly all men, if they cannot be bought, can be cajoled. Careless with his own income, he could be careless with that of the public, or with the public domain; of that, evidence exists. But not much: Sir John was careful of what he put on paper and what he said before witnesses.[3] His system of government might be described not unfairly as one of amiable venality joined to concern for material progress.

His alliance with the French continued unbroken but was becoming a little more difficult. Sir Hector Langevin,[4] who stepped into Cartier's shoes without filling them, drew much of his support from the extreme, or ultramontane, wing of the church and people, which at that time reflected the resurgent and intolerant Catholicism set in motion by the great Vatican Council of 1870.[5] Macdonald quietly offset his influence in 1882 by inviting into his cabinet the leader of the moderate "Bleus", Adolphe Chapleau. At the time of his appointment there was raging in French Catholic circles a domestic controversy of extreme bitterness over the effort to found in Montreal, then the centre of ultramontanism, a new University, free of Laval at Quebec. Such a foundation would symbolize the independence of Montreal as a French centre, under its doughty, die-hard Bishop Bourget and the Jesuit Order. Chapleau represented Quebec, Laval, and moderation. His appointment was, therefore, a body blow to extremism, widening the gap in the Conservative party in Quebec. In October, 1882, the appearance of the pamphlet *Le Pays, Le Parti et le Grand Homme,* signed by one "Castor" and constituting a bitter indictment of Chapleau and his affiliations, was followed by the right wing of the French drawing off as a sub-group at Ottawa, known as *Les Castors.* Extreme racialists and Catholics, they were the expression in French terms of the spirit which had its English counterpart in extreme Britishism and Protestantism: D'Alton McCarthy

---

[3] See the Campbell and Mitchell correspondence in the Macdonald Papers, among others, P. Mitchell to Macdonald, Nov. 12, 1877. See also the document from Mitchell "explaining" the Pacific Scandal, referred to on p. 364n. above.
[4] 1826-1906. A member of most of Macdonald's cabinets.
[5] This was the Council that promulgated the dogma of Papal Infallibility. See for the period in general, Skelton, *Alexander Tilloch Galt,* Chap. 15.

and Bishop Bourget were just opposite sides of the same coin. Extremists, necessarily purist, dwelt uncomfortably in the great, easy-going camp of Macdonald Conservatism.

Quite as important as the alliance with *Les Bleus* was the understanding effected with the Orange Order and marked by the inclusion in the cabinet of 1878 of its Grand Master, Mackenzie Bowell.[6] Thenceforth for the rest of his life, Macdonald governed Canada by a tacit alliance between Protestant extremists and Roman Catholic zealots. The understanding seemed to be that each would leave the other alone and supreme in his respective spheres. The Biblical prediction of days when the lion and the lamb would lie down together had come to pass. Orangeism in its appropriation of a special quality of "loyalty" to itself, was naturally Conservative.[7] Yet it had found it difficult not to range itself behind a man like George Brown, and still more difficult to tolerate Macdonald's failure to exact Papist blood for the murder of Thomas Scott. Such considerations delayed its consolidation behind Conservative banners until the middle seventies.

In 1877 a Twelfth of July parade was held in Montreal, apparently for the express purpose of provoking trouble with the Catholics of that city. In the fracas resulting, an Orangeman, one Hackett, was beaten to death. The episode was parallel to Oswald Mosley's Jew-baiting parades in the East End of London before the Nazi war broke out: both were turbulent demonstrations designed to cause civil commotion for factional ends; to both the word "Fascist" in its most invidious sense is to be fairly applied. Unfortunately the members of the opposing mob who actually caused Hackett's death could not be discovered: this was attributed to Alexander Mackenzie's desire to see Papists escape and was used to swing the Order in behind Conservatism.

The atmosphere of religious hatred prevailing in the Canada of the 1870's and 1880's accounted for political changes to a greater degree than did National Policies; in many an Ontario rural riding, the real issue of the day was the battle of the Boyne. The Orangemen were supposed to have about 2,000 lodges and some 100,000 members. Since the approximate total of all voters for Ontario was about half a million, the weight of their power can easily be judged. It was lucky for

---

[6] 1823-1917. Born in England. Senator, 1892. Prime Minister, 1894-96.
[7] "A veteran Orangeman in *The Sentinel* . . . lays it down expressly that a true Canadian Orangeman must be a Conservative. . . . Yet Orangeism goes to the polls hand in hand with the religious power against which William of Orange fought, in order to keep a Tory government in place."—*The Week,* Toronto, Oct. 29, 1885.

Canada, perhaps, that the two rival fanaticisms managed to come to an understanding.

It was from this period of the 1870's that the alliance between Conservatism and industrialism, still existing, also took its rise. Industrialists are necessarily less firmly attached to party than are religious partisans: they often find it wise to back both horses. Yet apart from the natural correlations with wealth, an instinct for control (such as the average factory owner must have if he is to be successful), and Conservatism, the so-called National Policy of the Conservatives necessarily ranged behind them those who stood to benefit from protective tariffs. As the Canadian Manufacturers' Association developed, without ostensibly taking sides, it usually put its weight on the Conservative side. That weight, expressed in pressure on employees and in campaign funds, was heavy. Many of the leading financial institutions tended to be closely associated with Conservatism: this was particularly true in Montreal, where close connections existed between the Bank of Montreal, the Canadian Pacific Railway, and Conservative administrations.

A significant subsection of industry and commerce which was firmly attached to Macdonald Conservatism was the liquor trade, wholesale and retail. Liberals from an early period had shown tendencies to espouse the temperance doctrines then being urged so vigorously and in some cases to favour total prohibition. The Scott Act had been approved by Mackenzie's government, and both Mackenzie and Oliver Mowat of Ontario were strong temperance men. This threw the liquor interest into Conservative arms. That position seemed congenial to both parties. There was little room for saloon keepers in the great Protestant churches—Methodist, Presbyterian, and Baptist—which constituted the backbone of Liberalism, and it is no accident that the Carlings, the Gooderhams, the O'Keefes, were Conservatives in politics and Anglicans or Catholics in religion.

Another important sector of interest lay in the outlying provinces. Manitoba, British Columbia, Prince Edward Island—all at first were over-represented and since these provinces would wish to get as much as possible from the Ottawa Government and would, therefore, support the powers that were, by returning "Ministerialists", his enemies invariably charged Sir John with purchasing additional support by this device.

Still another considerable section of public opinion, the Irish Catholics, Sir John cleverly succeeded in dividing. Most of these, as a reaction against Conservative Imperialism, if left to themselves, would have voted

Liberal, but Macdonald adroitly kept the Irish Catholic hierarchy on his side and thus got a good proportion of the lay voters.[8]

The votes of all these groups added up to a large majority in 1878 and to majorities of descreasing size in the three subsequent elections of 1882, 1887, 1891. The aid they afforded was supplemented by campaign methods of a type that Canada knows too much about. Large amounts of money were usually available, and they were expended both legally and illegally. One favourite device was to bring back persons who had gone to the United States but whose names were still on the lists, a trick that could be freely played under the law as it then stood: it has been alleged that many an election was turned by this "foreign vote". The "foreigners" when bought, contrary to the usual experience, stayed bought; "an expensive article, but prime" one party heeler of the time said of them.

Another tactic was the election petition. This was an appeal to the courts alleging irregularities under the "Controverted Elections Act" in an election in which the vote had been close, as in those days of small electorates, it often was. If the courts sustained the allegations made in the petition, the election would be voided. The Liberal opposition rarely had much money: it was good generalship to open petitions against them wherever possible, in order to exhaust their funds and be able to propose bargains in cases where they had themselves lodged counterpetitions; this device came to be known as "the saw-off". A surprising number of elections was constantly being voided in this way, particularly after the very strict "Controverted Elections Act" passed by the Mackenzie Government, which made it easy to find grounds for unseating. By this Act the Liberals found themselves "hoist with their own petard".

●

                                                                     Oct. 20, '85
My Dear Lord:
    I have not forgotten your stained windows but as by law I find the duty is collectable, we must try to arrange the matter without breaking the letter of the law.
    Will you therefore make a written application for the windows to Mr. Hamilton the Collector of Customs, *subject to appraisement*—but without stating the values, Mr. Hamilton will thereupon deliver the windows to you. Mr. Bowell, the Minister of Customs, will see to the future proceedings. What he must of course avoid is a question or motion put in Parliament next session —charging him with a breach of the Customs Laws.
                                          Believe me, My Dear Lord
                                          Faithfully yours
                                          John A. Macdonald.
From the Macdonald Papers, Letter Book 23, 331. See also Macdonald Papers, Bowell Correspondence, 377.

A third device was the familiar one of expenditure on public works. This was pushed so far that it sometimes threatened the budget itself. It led to protests from within, to which John A. piously assented, but of which he took little notice.[9] Probably, if he could have had the field to himself, he would have preferred other methods but when it came to the good, that is, the success, of the party, ethics had little weight. Some of his colleagues ably seconded him—to such an extent that after the Langevin scandals of 1891, English newspapers could remark that "a more sordid spectacle of corruption has never been presented to a free people. . . . It is abundantly clear that the cancer of corruption has eaten deep into Canadian institutions", or that "For twenty-three years, Sir John and his party had maintained themselves in power . . . by a colossal system of bribery. . .".[10] It was this type of conduct, a direct sequence of the original lapse of 1872, which drove home Laurier's charge that Macdonald permanently lowered the level of Canadian public life.

A more legitimate aspect of his methods lay in his personal contacts. In the course of a long career, he came to have acquaintances by the thousand. There was hardly a riding where he did not personally know scores of men, with an incredible number of whom he kept up a personal correspondence. To this the volumes of his correspondence, row on row, bear witness. Men who remembered Parliament in his day used to tell of him sitting there listening to the debates with one ear, so to speak, and throwing out an interminable stream of little notes to the page boys;

[9] Sir Alexander Campbell, Macdonald's Minister of Justice, wrote to Macdonald Sept. 9, 1885: ". . . Let me say how much I hope that we may get on without this eternal yielding to everyone who has, or thinks he has, control of a few votes . . . the country is impoverished by consenting to expenditure which is unnecessary and fruitless. In Lower Canada at the demand apparently of a score or less of members from the Quebec district we have wasted a million of money in forcing an unnecessary transaction with the Grand Trunk and the C.P.R. Railways—and in the Lower Provinces another million in constructing a rival line to the Intercolonial . . . and in a ship railway which could only have been warranted pecuniarily, had we the business of two continents to transport. . . . The constant giving way to truculent demands and our delays and the irritation and mischiefs they produce are in everybody's mouth. . . ." Macdonald's reply (Macdonald Papers, Campbell Correspondence, 480): ". . . You are right in stating that we have yielded too much to certain influences, but I think there will be an end to all that when the North Shore matter and its consequences are closed. . . ."
That is "just this once, then I'll repent".

[10] See the collection of quotations from the English press in Cartwright's Reminiscences, pp. 391ff.

each just a few words, but probably enough to keep some one somewhere in line.

So divided a country is Canada that a Canadian prime minister must
be continually walking a tightrope. Macdonald performed his act
superlatively well. Herein lay the real genius of the man: he was a
perfect master of equilibrium; he could reconcile the irreconcilable.
With steady rein year after year he drove his restless, ill-assorted six-
horse team. Perhaps only he could have kept the Confederation structure
going. And for that perhaps he considered easy political morality a
cheap price.

His opposition was never a match for him: neither in men nor in
organization did the Liberals approach him. Until the advent of Laurier
they hardly constituted a genuine national party. Mackenzie, Blake,
Cartwright, and Mowat were men of honesty and large abilities, but
Mowat confined himself to Ontario (where he was very successful),
Mackenzie was inept and Blake pursued his own eccentric orbit, as
often a liability as an asset. Liberalism laboured under the political disadvantage of too much virtue. The weight of its support came from
Ontario and lay in substantial Scottish farmers and townsmen who had
followed George Brown and read "the Scotchman's Bible", *The Globe*,
men who took seriously the injunctions of their religion. As one dear old
lady is reputed to have said to Mackenzie, "we don't expect much from
John A., you know, Mr. Mackenzie, but you are a Christian man, Mr.
Mackenzie". Liberalism rested on the very flower of middle-class
respectability and decorum. In Quebec, until Honoré Mercier came
along to acquaint the party with the methods of Sir John, Liberalism
centred on the old *Rouge* group, who were pure but anti-clerical and
therefore few. A Liberal victory against Sir John would have been
difficult to achieve.

The period after 1878 saw public interest in party government at its
highest. Sir John, to his delighted followers, was the wizard who always
came out of every situation, no matter how difficult, by smilingly dis-
comfiting his opponents. Political meetings, banquets, and picnics furnished the average man with that zestful interest in life for which the
modern radio and movies essay their mournful substitutes. It was the
era of the Gladiators, and there was always the prospect of a good fight.
There were giants in the land, too, to do the fighting: in the debate on
the execution of Riel, Blake led off with an indictment of government
that took seven hours to deliver, but Sir John Thompson replied in a
speech of eight; men were made of stern stuff in those days.

The period constituted the very pitch in Canada of pure partyism.
The old issues that had previously divided society to the point of armed

rebellion had been cleared up, and now party rested only on economic differences and traditionalism. The result was a partisanship that dominated every soul and invaded every walk of life, public and private, even the courtships of youth. Society was divided into two factional camps, each concentrated mainly upon power and office, hating each other not quite as much as armed enemies (though they referred to each other as "the enemy"), but with the bitter pseudo-hate drummed up between the supporters of rival hockey teams. Having little more satisfactory spiritual sustenance, with no great cause before them and no native culture at their side, men lived in a tribal frenzy of excitement against the opposite party. "A most *violent Grit*", "A violent Rouge Grit", "A brawling Grit", are some of the appellations Mackenzie Bowell appends to his political enemies.[11] Yet he, Grand Master of the Orange Order, could at the same time be making suggestions to help Bishop Cleary deviously get his stained glass windows in free[12] or telling Sir John that he ought to attend a Roman Catholic picnic where "You could make an anti-Huxley Speech, similar to that delivered at the Methodist dedication in Kingston the other day, with a slight sprinkling of politics . . .".[13] On the Conservative side, there was a free-and-easy atmosphere about all this, contrasted with the rather self-righteous tone of the "unco guid" Reformers.

> See the faces of the Grits,
>   Grizzly Grits,
> What a woe-begone expression at present o'er them flits.
> They are thinking, thinking deeply
> How to run this country cheaply
> And they wonder
> How in thunder
>   It is going to be done.
> But the people—they who vote—of their twaddle take no note,
> For they know the dismal, dreary, direful dole
>   Of the Grits
> Of the moribund, morose and melancholy Grits,
>   Grits, Grits, Grits.
> The greedy, grubby, garrulous old Grits.[14]

That strikes the authentic note!

[11] Macdonald Papers, Bowell Correspondence, p. 33.
[12] See above, p. 375n.
[13] Macdonald Papers, Bowell Correspondence, p. 37.
[14] *The People's Almanac*, Supplement to the *Gazette*, Montreal, 1891.

2. The Agencies of Exploitation: The National Policy

The Macdonald ministries, so carefully geared to party needs, contained in a more complete way than any administration has since done, the elements in the community that could in any way be labelled conservative: French *Bleus*, English Tories, industrialists, Roman Catholics, Orange Protestants, the upper layer of society and the bottom. They could supply traditionalism, energy, corruption, "push", achievement, violence, shining reward—all qualities associated with the right rather than with the left. All elements could work together in "opening up the country" and sharing the profits, all (*Bleus* included) accepted the exploitive attitude. The period lines up with the contemporary era in the United States, the gilded era of robber-baron capitalism.

The National Policy, in its frank creation of vested manufacturing interests living on the bounty of government, illustrates the point. A system of tariff protection is a kind of capitalist socialism. The National Policy established this conception of social propriety in Canada: it was an element in the state that was being built. With a magnet of the power of the United States alongside them, the British colonies had been forced into union to prevent absorption. Once having set their feet in the way, they had to go on. Confederation sketched out a rough design for a nation: a railway to the Atlantic coast, and the inclusion of the west. The bargain with British Columbia assured a transcontinental line to bind the whole together. The National Policy put up a fiscal fence around it all. All these were parts of a national policy in a wider sense, of a nation-building policy. In this way the Dominion of Canada represented a planned society. It was never the negative *laisser-faire* state of the individualist doctrinaires, but a positive state from the beginning—a semi-socialistic state, the top layer of whose society was the beneficiary rather than the bottom.

In the first days of the Dominion, the complications of economic interests which afterwards arose were not present. There was only one staple trade of importance, lumber. As exporters, the men engaged in it should have stood for free trade, but they did not seem to feel that tariff policy vitally affected their interests, and their political affiliations varied. The farmers of Ontario and Quebec were also divided, for their relationships to an export market were not very clear, and urban expansion gave many of them direct home markets. Eastern Canada with certain exceptions (such as the fishing industry in the Maritimes) was not badly adapted to the practice of a semi-self-contained economy. It was only later with the rise of the west and its international staple, wheat, that the great complication set in.[15] Meanwhile, with Tupper and Tilley there in parliament to officiate at the altar, that natural international trade area, the Maritime provinces, could without much qualm, be sacrificed to the growing metropolitanism of the St. Lawrence valley.

Macdonald's way of imposing the new tariff was simple: he just invited anyone who wanted a duty to come to Ottawa and ask for it. In subsequent Canadian politics the fortunes of economic nationalism and internationalism have varied, but on balance economic nationalism must be considered the victor. A tariff is like the sailor's tattoo—"easy on, hard off". While some of the industries behind the Canadian tariff have grown healthily, many others, decades afterwards, find themselves infants of advanced years, still howling lustily for the mother's milk on which they live.

3. The Hinterland Tied In

In boldness of conception the second great project of the Macdonald administration far surpassed the National Policy. The Canadian Pacific Railway, after the false start of the early seventies, was brought to a remarkably efficient conclusion. The government carried on with the Mackenzie programme of public construction until 1880, when it found in the group of men associated with the Bank of Montreal—George Stephen,[16] R. B. Angus, Donald Smith, and a few others—capitalists willing to undertake the task. It is significant that both the Bank of Montreal and some of the capitalists, notably Smith, were representative of the old North West Company fur-trading tradition and that what they did eventually was to bind together both coasts with steel and link them through steamships with the opposite sides of the Atlantic and Pacific oceans, as the North West Company had formerly done through the canoe and the sailing vessel. They formed themselves into the famous Syndicate, which, as the Canadian Pacific Railway Company, ultimately completed the line. Terms to it, both in cash and lands, were generous, but perhaps not too generous. They were bitterly assailed by the Opposition, which saw in the organization a gigantic monopoly to which the west was being handed over and which would have its hand in the public treasury for an indefinite future.

---

[15] The Canadian Pacific itself, which as the outlet to the west might have been expected to favour free trade, stood, in the person of its president, Sir Wm. Van Horne, staunchly by the National Policy.

[16] 1829-1921. Montreal Scot and chief force behind completion of the C.P.R. Later Lord Mount Stephen.

This time there was no hesitation: Montreal would be the head-quarters of the new company and its eastern terminus. The St. Lawrence metropolis had won against Toronto, reasserting its rule over the west. When in 1885 the railway reached Winnipeg, the Laurentian Barrier had at last been breached, and Canada could flow out on to the western plains. When in 1886 the line was opened through to the West coast, there was attained "the consummation and the poet's dream", and Canada stood on the shores of the Pacific. It was an epic feat, fought through against time, against financial stringencies, aaginst nature, and against the former Conservative standby, the Grand Trunk.[17] It must have been a proud day in Sir John's life, when at last, having made his first trip across the continent he had welded together, he stood on the shores of Burrard inlet, "from Canada by rail".[18]

The railway finished, men might well inquire what had been built. A colonization road? A national artery that would keep the Yankees and their Northern Pacific out of the west? "Steel of Empire", or an English route to the Orient? Whatever it would turn out to be, one thing was certain, a huge railway corporation had been built. It has been remarked that "the kingdom of Prussia was in reality an army in search of a state". So huge, so influential, was the Canadian Pacific to become in Canadian life, that with equal truth it might be asserted that "Canada has been a railway in search of a state".

4. Mowat v. Macdonald: Provincial Rights

The completion of this Leviathan, the C.P.R., represented the high-water mark of the Macdonald view of Confederation: a great semi-federal state, whose distant regions were bound together by railways and whose constituent parts were deftly but wisely controlled by the supreme genius presiding at Ottawa, all these working smoothly together in loyalty to that band of brothers, the Conservative party. Yet there has always existed another view of Confederation, and at the period under discussion it was being put forward with persistence and skill. Macdonald had made no secret of the position he designed for the provinces: they were to be magnified counties. The protagonist of the

[17] The G.T.R. had been offered a chance at the building but would not go north of Lake Superior. Instead of cooperating, it preferred to try and sabotage the Dominion and its new road from its vantage point in London, as instance the bitter attack on Canada in the London paper, *Truth,* Sept. 1, 1881.

[18] July 24, 1886. As Alexander Mackenzie had stood nearly a hundred years before him, July 22, 1793, chalking up his "From Canada, by land". See p. 148.

other view was Oliver Mowat, premier of Ontario. 1872-1896.[19] As a Liberal, he was a Jeffersonian, a "States' Rights" man. His instincts were against great over-riding political structures, and they were reinforced by the circumstances of the times. Ontario had not come out of the tribulations of the Union merely to pass once again under French domination disguised as federalism.[20] To Mowat, Ontario was what it has never succeeded in becoming:—an integer, a political community, with a soul of its own. In fighting for that "soul", he uncovered again the sources of Liberalism, for once more the faithful could be summoned to repel the hordes attacking the citadel.

Rationalized, his position was that the Confederation instrument set up two organs of sovereignty, the Government of Canada and the governments of the provinces: these were not in the position of superior and inferior, but co-ordinate; each sovereign in those areas that the British North America Act had allocated to it. The problem was first to win recognition of the principle, then to establish the delimitation in the law courts. In any federation these questions must be worked out, but the personal and political contrasts of Mowat and Macdonald carried them forward rapidly in Canada and set going a battle that raged as long as their two careers overlapped—long after, indeed, for it is still going on, and Quebec nationalism drives it to the logical limit in advocating "independence".

The first of the law cases, the Escheats case,[21] arose in the 1870's. Mowat's act was disallowed by the Canadian Government, but he fought it through the courts, losing each appeal until he came to the Privy Council, where he was successful. Other battles royal, all of which were won by him, were the *Insurance Case*,[22] *Hodge v. the Queen*[23] (arising out of the *Crooks Act* for licensing taverns), the controversy over the *Rivers and Streams Act* (1881-1884) and the Ontario-Manitoba Boundary Case (1884). It was *Hodge v. the Queen* that established the sovereignty of the provinces within their spheres, upsetting the old Austinian conception of its indivisibility. The provinces "are in no

---

[19] For Mowat, see Biggar, . . . *Sir Oliver Mowat*. For the details of the constitutional struggle, see, Lower, Scott, *et al, Evolving Canadian Federalism* (Durham, N.C., 1958).

[20] "It was supposed that Confederation had secured Home Rule for Ontario . . . but the ruthless encroachments of the Ottawa Tory leader have demonstrated the necessity of stronger safeguards. Until the veto power is abolished —and the appointment of Lieutenant-Governors made in some other way the province will not be safe from an unscrupulous leader at Ottawa."—*Canadian Post,* quoted in *The Week,* Toronto, July 10, 1884.

[21] 8 Appeal Cases, 767; see Biggar, . . . *Sir Oliver Mowat,* I, 243.

[22] Parsons v. The Citizens Insurance Co., Parsons v. The Queen's Insurance Co.

[23] 9 Appeal Cases 117, 1883.

sense delegates of or acting under any mandate from the Imperial Parliament. . .". The British North America Act . . . "conferred authority upon them as plenary and as ample—within the limits prescribed by section 92—as the Imperial Parliament in the plenitude of its power possessed and could bestow. . .". This judgement made the provinces into states. How the Privy Council managed to concentrate so intently on section 92 and ignore the many limitations on sovereignty elsewhere in the Act, such as the Lieutenant-Governor, a Dominion official, or the Dominion's right of disallowance, has never been explained. The language of section 91 was even wider than that of section 92, but though it embraced the extremely wide area of the peace, order, and good government of Canada, the ingenuity of the court invariably enabled it to cut down Federal sovereignty rigorously, by extending that of the provinces. From its wording nothing could be plainer than that the British North America Act set up an integral scheme of federalism, in which circumference and centre were all parts of a whole, not a number of independent bodies joined together only by the quasi-diplomatic tie of a refereeing court.

The other cases expanded, by interpretation, the area of section 92, as similar decisions continued to do, until at last the Privy Council accomplished the handsome feat of virtually taking away the residual power from the body to which it was expressly given, the Parliament of Canada, and awarding it to those which had by the Act been deprived of it, the provincial legislatures. This was done mainly by a continuous expansion of the content of the sub-section on "property and civil rights",[24] whose extensible boundaries are sufficiently obvious, once the words are given legal priority.

That Canada through the Privy Council had entailed on it many of the worst consequences of the doctrine of States' Rights is no accident, for its application to Canada seems to derive from the area of its American assertion, the Southern States. One of the Confederate Secretaries who found it convenient to leave the South at the end of the Civil War was the Attorney-General, Judah P. Benjamin. He went to England, where he soon became a leading counsel, and was interested in some of the Canadian cases. A young man trained under him later achieved distinction as Lord Watson, the Privy Councillor who became the author of so many of the judgements enlarging the sphere of Provincial Rights. The Civil War issue, after having been settled in the land of its origin, continued to be fought out over the rather mangled body of Canada.

Mowat himself never seems to have had any qualms. He was premier

[24] B.N.A. Act, Section 92, 13.

of Ontario and therefore bent on securing as large a responsibility as he could. He was a lawyer and therefore bent on pushing the interpretation of the law as far in his own direction as he could. He was champion of the God-fearing Protestant people of his native province against corrupt and over-riding Conservatism with its tail of French and Irish Catholics. With him local loyalties dominated, and when he needed a larger one, he looked to "Britain". He often used to say that no sufficient sense of nationality had as yet developed to weld the Canadian people together and that their main link was the British connection. He probably did not realize how much he himself was doing to place the Dominion between the hammer of the Empire and the anvil of the provinces.

Perhaps his most famous victory was in the Boundary award. His claim was that the boundary of Ontario on the west arose out of the Treaty of 1783, which gave a line due north of the source of the Mississippi River. Macdonald, and Norquay of Manitoba, stood on the Quebec Act, which gave a line due north of the confluence of the Ohio and the Mississippi, or just west of Fort William. The dispute went on for several years, leading to conflict of jurisdiction and disturbed conditions in the territory affected and even to a limited resort to force.[25] Mowat fought the case through as if hostile troops were on his soil, and when he returned from his great victory at the Privy Council, he was received as a conquering hero. His attitude evinced no conception of a Canadian interest as contrasted with a provincial and no feeling for Canada as over against Ontario. Partisanship entered here, as everywhere at that time, and it was easy to view Macdonald's attitude as a deliberate attempt to weaken Ontario, and the Grits politically, by strengthening a more dependent province, Manitoba. But to include the territory between Lake Superior and the Lake of the Woods in Ontario meant handing it over to the jurisdiction of a distant imperial power at Toronto. After Mowat's day, Toronto regarded it as little else but a political melon, slices of which were periodically handed around among friends. It would have been more easily and probably more honestly administered from Winnipeg, which is its urban centre.

Sir Oliver Mowat is worthy of regard as a man of integrity and Christian principles but it is hard to admire his achievements in weakening the structure of the Dominion. To this he himself would have had a strong answer. In addition to judicial decisions, it simply would have been that he, not Macdonald, represented the views of the majority of the people, that the people were for their provinces first and for Canada second. The stepmother, Confederation, had not yet been reborn as the

---

[25] At one time the Ontario authorities arrested a Manitoba official at Rat Portage, and a company of soldiers was sent down from Winnipeg.

mother, Canada: curiously enough there was more hope of that transmutation coming about out of the constructive corruptions of Macdonaldism than out of the legalism and righteousness of Mowatism.

Mowat laboured under the disadvantage of walking upon a narrower stage than Macdonald and of being a simple, unpretentious man. As an actor "John A." was in a class by himself. Full of his tricks, a master of tactical skill, never failing in resource and *bonhommie*, with an unlimited store of masculine stories and unlimited thousands of acquaintances, he had by the 1880's become more than a national hero. He was a legend, a kind of folk-figure to his supporters and, if reprobated, not really disliked by his opponents. He had been in public service for a period longer than the lives of most of those who supported him: he had been at the making of every important decision in Canadian affairs. He was the party and the party was he. It could almost be said that Macdonald was Canada and Canada was Macdonald.

> Thou linnet in thy green array
> Presiding spirit here today
> Dost lead the revels of the May
> And this is thy Dominion.

In the 1880's the Dominion of Macdonald it veritably was.

Chronology

1878   Sir John Macdonald returned to power.
        The "National Policy" Tariff.
1880   C.P.R. Contract signed.
1882   The first Gerrymander.
1882   Sir John's third victory.
1883   *Hodge v. the Queen*: Privy Council decision establishing the "sovereignty" of the provinces.
1881–84 The Rivers and Streams controversy.
1884   The Ontario-Manitoba Boundary award.
1885   "Last Spike" of the C.P.R. driven, Nov. 7.

Additional Reading

Creighton, Donald G. "Conservatism and National Unity," in R. Flenley, ed. *Essays in Canadian History*. Toronto, 1939.

Fowke, V. C. "The National Policy—Old and New." *CJEPS*, XVIII (August, 1952), 271-286.

Innis, H. A. *History of the Canadian Pacific Railway*. London, 1923.

MacDermot, T. W. L. "The Political Ideas of John A. Macdonald." *CHR*, XIV (Sept., 1933), 247-264.

Pratt, E. J. *Towards the Last Spike*. A Verse Panorama of . . . the First Canadian Transcontinental . . . Toronto, 1952.

Underhill, F. H. "The Development of National Political Parties in Canada." *CHR*, XVI (Dec., 1935), 367-387.

CHAPTER 27

The Disintegration of Macdonald Conservatism, 1885-1896

1. The Limits of Opportunism

In the 1880's, Liberals, unavailingly toiling to break the hold of Macdonald on the country, might have consoled themselves with the text "Be sure your sins will find you out": they had little other hope, for Sir John outgeneraled them at every turn. Yet the character of his regime was such as to give them considerable confidence in the prediction. The assault against Macdonaldism was made on every possible front. Provincial premiers attempted to cut down the powers of the Canadian government. The Mercier nationalists in Quebec tried to dislodge the old *Bleus* and *Castors*. In the federal area the Liberals under Laurier and Cartwright, in an effort to find a prosperity programme of their own that would offset the national policy and the railway policy of the Conservatives, reintroduced the reciprocity question; they saw in it an issue broad enough to defeat the combination of financial and industrial interests, railroads, Orangeism, Roman Catholicism, and plain corruption by which, as they alleged, Macdonald ruled Canada. But the assaults did not succeed in dislodging him. Sir John fished a precarious victory out of the election of 1887, when his reputation was at its lowest, and went on to his smashing apotheosis of 1891.

The statutory redistribution of seats after the census of 1881 had been made the occasion of the first of the Canadian gerrymanders, ridings being sliced up in such a way as to ensure that marginal seats would receive accessions to the party in power from neighbouring ridings which either had votes to spare or would elect the opposition anyway. Sir John had often expressed his belief that the county was the appropriate district for representative purposes, but he showed no scruple in cutting across county lines if a political advantage resulted. Liberal partisans contended that the gerrymander, which was ready for the election of 1887, was felt for another twenty-five years, especially in Ontario, but later students have offered some evidence to indicate that it was not of major effect. At the time, so crude were Canadian political morals that Sir John's *coup*—"hiving the Grits", he called it—was greeted with shouts of joy by his followers as a clever move against the "enemy".

Yet one of the sins was already beginning to descend on "The Chieftain's" head. It grew out of his political indecision rather than his political corruption, from his desire to be all things to all men, rather than from his lust for power. In 1870 he had bungled the Red River affair; in 1885, he was to do the same with the North West. Ironically enough, the selfsame man whose leading political principle it was to keep the Conservative party in power by an alliance with the French was the very one who by his neglect and his hesitations was to drive between the two races a wedge that has never been withdrawn. "Old Tomorrow", the prince of opportunists, was at last to find the limits of opportunism.

The grievances of the Métis upon the Saskatchewan were similar to those of their brethren previously upon the Red. Again a small group on the edge of civilization had been overtaken by the advancing frontier of the English Canadian, again they were worried for fear they would lose their lands, again delay, ignorance, and mismanagement on the part of government intensified their fears, until at last they fought. Louis Riel returned and put himself at their head, but the effective fighting leader was Gabriel Dumont. Riel developed peculiar religious views which lost him the support of the priests upon the scene and later of the hierarchy of the Church. Some help was received from the Indians, and at one time it looked as if the whole West might be in flame. Over the still incomplete C.P.R. government sent out a large force of militia, including some French units. These troops, after losing nearly all the skirmishes to the rebels, crushed them by sheer weight. Dumont fled, and Riel surrendered. As a military affair it was a minor rebellion put down by amateur soldiers under leadership that was far from brilliant. But the extremists of Ontario remembered Tom Scott, and since they had not before had sufficient outlet for those combative qualities with which they were so liberally equipped, the rebellion gave them a much appreciated taste of blood.

Most of the people of Quebec were at first agreed on the necessity of restoring law and order in the West, but they soon convinced themselves that the onus of the rebellion did not lie on the rebels. "Le sang canadien a coulé en expiation de la criminelle négligence de nos gouvernants".[1] Riel might be a heretic, he might be insane, but he was a Frenchman. He had led a tiny people struggling for their rights. And now Ontario Orangemen were roaring for his blood. Soon demands for clemency began to be heard, and long before the last shots were fired, sentiment had come over to the rebels and their leader. Riel surrendered, casting himself on the mercy of General Middleton. As the cries for blood mounted higher from Ontario, the determination of the French that Riel should not die became firmer. Once again the two irreconcilable peoples were at daggers drawn. Attempts to prove him insane failed, and the English-speaking jury brought in a verdict of guilty, with a recommendation of mercy. A date was set for his execution. As it drew near, efforts to save him were redoubled from Quebec, demands for his death from Ontario steadily increased in fury. Caught between the two fires, the Macdonald government temporized. The execution was postponed, postponed again—and finally, amid a breathless hush in the whole country, carried out.

Nothing could have been more inept than the way in which the government had handled the situation. There was neither swiftness nor certainty: justice *limped* to its end. It was fairly plain that poor Riel was of secondary consequence. It is hard to avoid believing that the final decision not to interfere with the course of the law did not represent justice so much as political expediency, the view of the cabinet on the balance of political forces in the country.[2] In fairness, it must be said that a popular agitation against the hanging of a man guilty of high crimes and misdemeanours is hardly reason for interrupting the course of justice, and the Cabinet may have been sincerely convinced that Riel deserved to die. But though the execution may not have been a political act—French Cabinet Ministers concurred in it—given the Prime Minister's own culpable record with respect to the Métis and North West, it carried that suggestion and so cast an unfortunate cloud upon Canadian annals.

It is remarkable that two men, Scott and Riel, the one with no claim to fame and the other with little, should have become in their deaths decisive figures in Canadian history. To the Orangemen and most other English-speaking Canadians, Scott's death had been a political murder,

[1] Quoted from *L'Electeur* in Rumilly, *Histoire de la province de Québec*, V, 32.
[2] Yet see p. 390n4.

as Riel's became to the French. To Orangemen it symbolized popery, Catholic tyranny, French domination. Riel in 1885 symbolized to Frenchmen the blood lust of Orangeism, its determination to take away from French Catholics all their rights, to oppress and destroy them. The execution took on a highly representative character: a whole people was on trial. It was taken as a direct challenge to the whole French race, just as Scott's execution had been a challenge to Protestantism. Wherever justice lay, from the deed the curse descended once more upon Canada, the curse of division and of racialism.

Riel executed, everyone understands, means the triumph of Orangeism over us.

The judicial murder they are undertaking to commit signifies that in future the English majority does not intend to allow any claim on the part of the French. It will make injustice reign arbitrarily.

At the moment when the corpse of Riel falls through the trap and twists in convulsions of agony, an abyss will be dug between the province of Quebec and the province of Ontario.

The scaffold of Regina will grow, grow, grow. . . . Always the image of this poor fool's corpse, hung for miserable party ends, hung to maintain men in power, hung in hatred of the name French-Canadian, will be there, balancing itself between earth and sky.

The hatred was well expressed by the Toronto *Mail*:

If the downfall of the cabinet should result from the withdrawal of French influence . . . in that case, we British subjects believe that we shall have to fight again for the Conquest; and Lower Canada can be sure of this, there will be no new treaty of 1763. This time the conqueror will not capitulate.[3]

These quotations are representative. An abyss had been opened. It has never since been closed, though at times a surface may have formed over it.

The execution gave opportunity for a rising *Rouge* politician, Honoré Mercier, to assail the French members of Sir John's cabinet. Having invited M. Chapleau to put himself at the head of a national movement of protest and having had no notice taken of it, Mercier went about organizing an agitation in the province. It was not so much political as

[3] Quotations are from newspapers of the day, translated from Rumilly, V, 97, 117.

national, as proved by the adherence to it of a large group of *Castors*. At a great meeting in the Champ de Mars, Montreal, on November 22, 1885, many orators of both parties harangued the crowd, and resolutions were passed condemning the execution as political and asking that Sir John be opposed by every constitutional means. The *Castor* wing called for a "national movement", the Mercier wing a national party. Thus was launched that nationalist idea in Quebec which, under various leaders and after many births and rebirths, has never since ceased to be a prime factor in Canadian life. A little over a year later (January, 1887) Mercier won the provincial election against the official Conservative party: in his campaign great play was made against "les pendards", the French members of the federal Cabinet, who had consented to the execution.[4] The ministry which he formed, he insisted on calling a national government.

As a gesture to the Church, which suspected him as a *Rouge*, and as a mark of gratitude towards the Jesuits at whose hands he had been educated, Mercier proceeded to bring in the famous "Jesuits' Estates Bill", by which it was proposed to compensate the Order for the estates that had been confiscated from it after the English Conquest. The Church was to receive the sum of $400,000, to be divided among the Jesuits, Laval University and the Ecclesiastical Corporations. The measure was bitterly denounced in the federal Parliament by D'Alton McCarthy and a little group of Ontario Protestant Conservatives, close to the Orange Order. These men—they received the name from their admirers of "The Noble Thirteen"—tried to get Macdonald to disallow Mercier's measure, but the old tactician was not to be caught so easily, and nothing was done. Thus at the same time that the extreme French Catholic wing of his party was casting off its allegiance to him because he had allowed Riel to hang, the extreme English Protestant wing was doing the same because he would not coerce the provincial government of Quebec.[5]

In Quebec, the results of the federal elections that followed within a short time of Mercier's victory (February, 1887) were a virtual vote of censure on Sir John's government. In the previous parliament he had had 50 supporters from Quebec, as against 15 *Rouges*: this number fell to about 32, as against 33. It had been the attitude of the heirarchy alone that had prevented a worse defeat. The bishops saw the political agitations getting out of hand: Riel had been a notorious heretic and

---

[4] To Chapleau, the most important "hangman", the decision was an agonizing one but arrived at in full conviction that it was just.
[5] Compare Mackenzie King and the Conscription issue of 1944-45.

would not do as a "national" figure; racialism carried to an extreme could but come into conflict with religion. The ultramontanist Bishop Laflêche of Trois Rivières, unable to overcome his distrust of a *Rouge*, whatever the cause might be, and Bishop Taché of St. Boniface, who knew the western situation so intimately, counselled support of the government. It was not the last time that the hierarchy opposed itself to popular tendencies, and not the last on which it was to be flouted. In Ontario, the gerrymander transmuted a precarious Conservative popular majority of some 3,000 votes into a majority in the House of some 14 to 18. Thus the Riel affair, though it did not defeat the government, seriously weakened it and marked the beginning of that shift from Conservative to Liberal in Quebec that when completed was to be the key to Canadian politics for many years.

Yet Macdonald did win the election of 1887, and the Liberals did lose it.

This second failure under his leadership brought about the resignation of Edward Blake. Always cold and aloof, he had lately taken to making extremely lengthy speeches from voluminous notes, going into every nook and cranny of the questions he discussed. In the great opportunity given to him by the Riel decision, he had failed completely: what the occasion called for was sharp denunciation; he had supplied a tedious legal brief. He was fast becoming "the dinner bell of the House". In his place was chosen a diffident but pleasant and amiable young lawyer from Quebec, one Wilfrid Laurier. By 1887, Laurier had already made a reputation for charm and culture and for skill as a speaker. Without the frigidity of Blake, and as amiable as Sir John himself, he was a man with a future.

Laurier had associated himself with the movement to save Riel, but he was not to be caught in the nationalist extremes to which Mercier seemed inclined to go. Shortly after he formed his government, the latter politician issued invitations for a Dominion-Provincial conference at Quebec. Ottawa declined sharply, but four of the six provinces invited accepted. Nova Scotia's W. S. Fielding had just won an election on a frankly secessionist programme. Oliver Mowat was still in the midst of his legal quarrels with Macdonald. Norquay of Manitoba was waging his own warfare against the Dominion in an attempt to overcome the monopoly clause of the C.P.R., which prevented other railways being built between the American border and its main line. The deliberations of such a group could lead in only one direction, towards proposals for weakening the central government. These were duly made, in resolutions which proposed to take away from the Dominion various important rights. It was proposed to put the suspending and veto power over provincial legislation into the hands of London again. Since London had virtually ceased to use it as against federal legislation, it would not, it was supposed, be used against provincial. The proposal was therefore equivalent to removing any control by another body over provincial legislation, putting the provinces in the position of American states. Ottawa was also to be required to give up the power to declare specific public works as being for the general advantage of Canada. Provincial legislation was to be made harder to attack in the courts.

Never before or since has Canada reached so low a state; never has there been so little evidence among its people of national spirit. Here were four provincial premiers and their colleagues calmly proposing alterations to destroy the federation. They proposed, not to go forward as the fathers of the American Union had done in 1787, but backward to something resembling the ramshackle old Continental Confederation. They represented the extreme position that, if pushed to its logical limit, leads to attempts at secession and thence to civil war. These wise men— Fielding, Mowat, Mercier, Norquay—put their feet on the road which would have led to the reduction of the great Canadian edifice to its former miserable little group of provinces. They were not a generation ahead of the Fathers of 1867, but a generation behind.

Probably they were accurate representatives of their people. Provincials could not rise to national stature. Nova Scotians were parochial and unfriendly, the French wanted to keep to themselves, and the people of Ontario were waging their fight for "home rule". Canada in very truth was a league of provinces. To these perhaps unavoidable tendencies in a young and scattered country[6] were joined a common distrust and dislike of Sir John Macdonald and his associates which seemed to justify any measures to oust him from power. Norquay of Manitoba, a Conservative himself, was afraid he would be doublecrossed in the railway matter. Mowat disliked Macdonald for his corruption and his former irregular way of life. Mercier hated the "vieux pendard", who had become in his eyes the enemy of his race. There was a great deal of pure partyism in it all, but so far had partisanship been carried that many a man would cheerfully have dissolved the Dominion to gain a party end. For the future the problem was to be whether the structure erected in 1867, which was proving anything but rainproof, would completely fall down.

---

[6] The point has often been made that until the Civil War, the Government of the American Union was really that of a league of sovereign states, not that of a nation.

2. Depression and Unrest Again

Not only did the family (perhaps "roomers" is the better word) seem intent on smashing up the happy home, but the big, bad wolves outside began to huff and puff also. The insecurity within was reflected by schemes that would have robbed the country of whatever independence it had managed to acquire. From the one side came the proposals of the Imperial Federation League, which would have chained Canada to an empire far beyond local control, and from the other suggestions for "unrestricted reciprocity" and "commercial union", which would have made it a satellite of Washington. Both were the work either of expatriates or of persons who were deliberately attempting to offset one metropolitan pull by emphasizing the other.

"Imperial Federation" sprang from the same roots as those renewed sentiments of empire whose pressure had persuaded Disraeli to change his sentiments of 1853 ("These wretched colonies are millstones round our necks") to those of the Crystal Palace Speech of 1872, in which he discoursed upon a great systematic Imperial edifice. Before 1870 nothing could have been more marked than English indifference to the self-governing colonies, amounting in the case of Canada to enmity, but when great new military powers appeared in Europe and the overseas "land-grabbing era" began, Great Britain became imperially-minded once more, and though most of her expansive energy was directed to "native" areas, some sentiment was left over for the white colonies. About the same time a little knot of ex-colonials came together in London, and with the true zeal of pilgrims gathered at the centre of the faith, began to whip up enthusiasm for the common Imperial religion.[7] The new ideas of Empire found expression in the historians Seeley and Froude, in the politician Sir Charles Dilke, and in John Ruskin's mystical Oxford enthusiasms, which produced the most mystical Imperial mystic of them all, Cecil Rhodes.

In Canada such sentiments were sure to find ready response, for a large and powerful body of opinion still saw itself purely as part of a common "British" nation. "Canada is my home, the Empire is my country", a slogan invented later, describes this point of view. Oliver Mowat continually spoke of himself as a Canadian, but of "our nation", meaning the English-speaking peoples minus the United States. The Imperial Federation League had been organized in England in 1884, and a few branches were founded in Canada. Its object, not too plainly put, was quite simple, to get the colonies to contribute to Imperial

[7] See C. A. G. Bodelsen, *Studies in Mid-Victorian Imperialism* (Copenhagen, 1924) for an account of this.

defence. It might not have made much impression in Canada had it not been for the appearance of the project for "Commercial Union". "Commercial Union" meant throwing down all trade barriers between Canada and the United States and the adoption of a common tariff. Such a tariff would have been the American high protective tariff, directed against Great Britain as well as other countries. When discrimination was made against British goods, Canadian loyalists preferred to make it themselves rather than have "the Yankees" make it for them. The "Commercial Union" project gave them the finest kind of fighting ground.

It led directly to the formation in Toronto of a branch of the Imperial Federation League. The man who successfully kept Canada out of the Yankee maw, according to his own account, was Col. George T. Denison of Toronto,[8] who seems to have included a genuine Canadian patriotism in his over-riding idea of "loyalism". His group persuaded D'Alton McCarthy, who had become associated with it, to move an approving resolution in the Commons, with a suggestion that the self-governing parts of the Empire should give tariff preferences to each other. This inaugurated the long struggle to resurrect some kind of Imperial trading unit, a struggle that achieved a doubtful kind of success in the Ottawa trade treaties of 1932,[9] but which at the time rendered ineffective the English branch of the Imperial Federation movement: Great Britain was completely committed to free trade and had no intention of injuring her international position for the sake of relatively unimportant colonies. The situation reinforces the view that the British Commonwealth derived from the expatriated English groups rather than from the home of the race.

"Commercial Union" represented continentalism; "Imperial Federation", the old oceanic world. The one is to be identified with the metropolitan pull of New York, the other with that of London. From 1887 to 1892, the two forces, identified with two specific political camps, fought another of their innumerable battles. In all these battles, the Conservative party has been the repository of tradition, whereas the Liberal has been more susceptible to the forces of continentalism. Liberalism has, however, never been of one mind but has been divided into right and left wings, the right favouring tradition, the left continentalism.

By the 1880's, Conservatism and traditionalism having once again secured almost as strong a place in Canadian life as before the rebellions

---

[8] See his *Struggle for Imperial Unity* (London, 1909), a book that sheds a piercing, if unconscious light, on some of the roots of Canadian life.
[9] See p. 512ff.

of 1837, it had become heresy to propound a course of action that involved any considerable deviation from the established order of things. Yet upon Liberalism rested the onus of finding an innovation of sufficient individuality to assure prosperity to the country and office to itself. After Laurier became leader of the Liberal party in 1887, the question had to be "what programme would turn Macdonald's flank at the next election?" Within a year or two, the left wing, of which Sir Richard Cartwright was the principal member, had won, and it was decided to adopt a modified form of the "Commercial Union" project. This was known as "Unrestricted Reciprocity", a phrase which meant that if the United States would open its markets to Canada, Canada would open hers to the same extent to the United States. Cartwright himself always made the argument that such a policy would so increase the prosperity of Canada that her imports from Great Britain would increase. But the party was divided. Outstanding members like Mowat and Blake distrusted the policy and were emphatic in affirming their affection for the British connection. As for the Conservatives, their cue, upon which they at once acted, was to identify Commercial Union with Annexation, and "Unrestricted Reciprocity" with both. The extreme Tory Loyalist group, nowhere more strongly marked than in Toronto, quite simply equated Liberalism, Laurierism, Unrestricted Reciprocity, and treason: what had been legitimate for Tories in 1849 became criminal for Grits in 1889.

3. The Old Man, The Old Flag, The Old Policy

In the late eighties, the brief upswing in business resting on an increase in the lumber trade and on the building of the C.P.R. had come to an end. The railway seemed a failure, for after the first initial rush, people by the thousand were abandoning their homesteads in the West. So heavy did the outgoing flood of emigrants to the United States become that some localities were permanently weakened and others almost deserted. These were the days, according to Sir Richard Cartwright, when the Dominion which "began in Lamentations, seemed to be ending in Exodus". Macdonaldism, with its high tariffs and its railway monopolies, was becoming bankrupt.

By 1891 another severe depression had descended, bringing with it the usual loose talk about annexation. Although such talk did not become widespread until the severity of the depression had greatly increased, that is, not until after the election of 1891, discontent was piling up so rapidly that Sir John, now an old man of seventy-five, was convinced that the sooner he tried for a new lease of power, the better. Colonel Denison assured him, *tout court*, that the issue would be, simply,

"Loyalty". That probably seemed to the old warrior a very good issue: whatever his private feelings on the subject, he seems to have spared no pains to make it the issue. He brought the elections on suddenly in the winter of 1891, catching the Liberals in their usual state of disorganization. Every possible effort was made on behalf of the government to besmirch them as the party of disloyalty. One especially famous incident began with Colonel Denison obtaining, by methods of dubious honesty, proofsheets of a pamphlet being printed by Edward Farrer, a newspaper man loosely rooted in Toronto:[10] this gave, for American benefit, advice on how to exert pressure against Canada in order to bring her into the Union. It was handed to Sir John and used by him with great effect in Toronto at a huge meeting with which he began the campaign. Farrer was more or less of an irresponsible and was no spokesman for the Liberal party, but his private views on how to seduce Canada made a good stick for beating the Liberal dog. Nor did the Prime Minister of the country scruple in availing himself of stolen goods.

No political party in Canada that had got itself branded as "disloyal" would have had a dog's chance with the electorates of the English-speaking provinces, and when to that were added internal divisions (Blake was restrained only with difficulty from coming out against the party's programme just a few days before the election[11]) the result was a foregone conclusion. "The old man, the old flag, the old policy!" "A British subject I was born, a British subject I will die!" Here was Canada's first sloganeering election. It was a spectacular success, and the Liberals were defeated for the fourth consecutive time. As Sir Francis Bond Head and Sir Charles Metcalfe had found out before him, and as Sir Robert Borden was to find out after him, so Sir John now knew that the simple recipe, deftly enough made up, with which the Toronto colonel had furnished him—the loyalty cry—would always carry the day.

Sir John literally paid for his victory with his life. He died within three months of the election into which he had thrown his every resource and trick. He had saved "the party"; probably he was convinced that he had saved Canada. And most likely this complex character would have deemed his own life well lost for the cause. His death places an emphatic period in the text of Canadian history. For thirty-seven long years he had been the great reconciler of opposites. No issue of principle had ever come home to him in such a way as to require him to take a

[10] Denison, according to his own account, conducted a spy ring in New York, which enabled him to know every move about to be made by "the enemy" and put much private correspondence in his hands; see his book, p. 110.
[11] See F. H. Underhill, "Edward Blake, the Liberal Party, and Unrestricted Reciprocity," CHA Annual Report for 1939, 133-141.

THE BOW OF ULYSSES

clear-cut stand upon it. Decision could be postponed, some men would retire, others die, still others could be bought by office or more directly. In a country fiercely divided he had taken a leaf out of the book of Queen Elizabeth and had trusted in "tomorrow". Compromising ability such as this would of itself give a man a place in history.[12]

For such a place Macdonald had many other and greater claims. In the old Union he had been powerful; in the Dominion he was supreme. He had been one of the principal figures in its birth and had a principal share in the plan according to which it had been built. His record was written not only in the centralizing clauses of the British North America Act, in the National Policy, and in the Canadian Pacific, but in speeches that had moved men, in innumerable confidential anecdotes lingering in their memories, in thousands of acquaintances in every riding of the land, few of whom had not been to some degree touched by his friendliness or directed by his counsel, and most of all in that great political church of which he had been the chief apostle, the Conservative Party! His services to Canada were great. Were his disservices greater? His political opponents did not hesitate to say so. When the critic sees two pictures of the same man, one painting him as a devil, the other an angel, he is safe in taking a middle view and believing him neither. He was a sea of good and ill, and from those ocean depths the lead brings up to this day conflicting evidence.

4. The Bow of Ulysses

A short time after Sir John's death, some of the most unsavoury scandals in the not overly fragrant political history of Canada were exposed. A relative newcomer, Israel Tarte,[13] began the revelations, and before he had finished, the reputation of Sir Hector Langevin was gone and perhaps only his death had saved that of Sir John. The scandals were of the usual type: contracts awarded at high figures, fat percentages of which had to be turned over to the party chest. Canadian loyalists had writhed a year before when the New York *World* had written that "nobody who has studied the peculiar methods by which elections are won in Canada will deny the fact that five or six million dollars, judiciously expended . . . would secure the return to Parliament of a majority pledged to the annexation of Canada to the United States . . .".[14] In that Canadians have never proved willing to sell their

[12] W. L. M. King's qualities were much the same.
[13] 1849-1907. At first a *Bleu,* then supporter of Laurier and Minister of Public Works (1896-1902). Quarrelled with Laurier and drifted once more to the Conservative side.
[14] Denison, p. 108.

birthright, the *World* was wrong, but it was correct in its estimate of the methods by which elections were won. After the exposures, severe comments also appeared in English papers of every party, and not even Macdonald's memory was spared. Politics are coarse and often corrupt in every pioneer democracy; Macdonald had done nothing to raise their tone.

The exposures went far to undermining the hold of the Conservatives, but in Quebec the Liberal, Honoré Mercier, had been playing the same game, and he and his cabinet were dismissed from office by the lieutenant-governor (one of the few cases where the Crown in Canada has exercised that power). The victors could now say *tu quoque* and rejoice in the corruption of both parties. Canadian public life had reached a low ebb. The Dominion was sick.

There was no one left, strong enough in power or guile, to bend the bow of Ulysses. Men to essay the task were many: there were four prime ministers in as many years. None of these was able to pull the situation together and the Conservative Government, assailed with internal dissensions, a severe economic hurricane, and a religious cyclone, at last went down in the epoch-making election of 1896.

Sir John Abbott, the immediate sucessor of Macdonald, was a frank compromise. He did not wish the Prime-Ministership. He was a senator, and the Senate is not a happy place from which to carry on the government of a democracy. He was not entirely free of the associations of the old Pacific scandal, and having been for many years leading counsel for the C.P.R., he represented the quintessence of Montreal big business. As a young man Abbott had been one of the Tory signers of the Annexation Manifesto of 1849. This youthful misdemeanour he was not allowed to forget. He himself solved the problem of his leadership within a few months by resigning (1892).

There succeeded him Sir John Thompson from Nova Scotia, Macdonald's Minister of Justice. Thompson was a man of unquestioned probity and ability, but he had one very prominent political defect: he was a Roman Catholic convert from Protestantism. Nor had he the temperament, it was said, of a politician; he had resigned from the Bench to enter the government, and it was as a judge that he would have found himself most at home. He had to encounter the full weight of the depression.[15] However by his sudden death (1895) he, too, was

[15] The population of Ontario increased only 68,000 from 1891 to 1901, most of this after 1896. This meant that practically all the net natural increase was lost by emigration. From 1891 to 1896, the population of Toronto increased by about 7,000 only. There were thousands of vacant houses in that city. Other areas were much the same.

freed of his embarrassments before they overwhelmed him and his party.

The new leader was the chief political "fixer" of the old Macdonald administrations, Sir Mackenzie Bowell. Bowell had been Grand Master of the Orange Order: Conservative leadership certainly could not be charged with lacking variety. He also sat in the Senate. His abilities and personality were second-rate. He inherited from Thompson not only the depression, which showed few signs of breaking, but one of the thorniest racial problems in Canadian history, the Manitoba Schools Question.

The main factors in the Manitoba Schools Question may be briefly set out.[16] Manitoba had been founded amid the high hopes of the French that they could make it a second French province. But before many years English immigration, mainly from Ontario, had placed them in a small minority. The English, carrying out with them their dislike of the Catholic religion and the French race together with belief in efficient and democratic schooling, soon found the educational system to their distaste. The Manitoba Act had provided that "no law on education made by the Province should prejudicially affect any right or privilege with respect to denominational schools which any class of persons had by law or practice in the province at the union" with Canada. The provincial government, containing men of strong Protestant convictions and Ulster background (or, as with "Fighting Joe" Martin, simple desire for notoriety), and urged on by the Ontario crusader D'Alton McCarthy, began about 1890 to establish a system of public state-supported schools and to take away from other schools the right to the taxes of their supporters. Law cases ensued which went to the Privy Council and were there decided in favour of the Province.

Unfortunately for the Dominion Cabinet, on the second of these cases the Privy Council held that if an injury had been inflicted, under Section 22 (2) and 22 (3) of the Manitoba Act, it lay within the Dominion's power to remedy it. The French and Catholics of Manitoba, headed by their bishop, at once appealed to the Dominion for "remedial legislation". The ex-Grand Master of the Orange Order, Mackenzie Bowell prepared to coerce the Protestants of Manitoba in the interests of French Catholicism. His conduct in so doing has often been criticized by the practical politician, for he could have resorted to delaying tactics until the elections arrived, or have covertly taken the Protestant side: this need not have alienated the masses of his supporters. However it is to the honour of the "practical politician" Bowell, that he decided to follow the arduous path of duty.

[16] For fuller accounts, see O. D. Skelton, *Life and Letters of Sir Wilfrid Laurier*, 2 vols. (Toronto, 1921); J. W. Dafoe, *Sir Clifford Sifton in Relation to his Times* (Toronto, 1931).

He first passed an order-in-council (March 21, 1895) requiring Manitoba to restore the rights of the Roman Catholic minority. The Province refusing to obey, a Remedial Bill was introduced in February, 1896. Conservatives were lukewarm, but Liberals saw in it a heaven-sent opportunity at last, and fought it with all the resource in their power. One fine morning a few weeks before, the country had awakened to find that seven Cabinet Ministers had resigned. That looked like the end of the government but proved in fact to reflect domestic dissension in the shape of dissatisfaction with Bowell's leadership, rather than difference in policy. The deserters soon returned, under the impression that Bowell had given a pledge to make way later on for the old war horse, Sir Charles Tupper. Tupper agreed to enter Parliament again at once and fight the Remedial Bill through. But all his efforts proved unavailing. At one time he kept the House in continuous session for over four days without breaking the Liberal filibuster. Finally the legal life of Parliament expired, and there was nothing to do but to face the country.

The Conservative regime was ending with a display of stubborn honesty; it was a welcome if unusual sight, and it cost the party office. Bowell had offended the Orangemen. Several extremists such as D'Alton McCarthy and Colonel O'Brien[17] left the party at this juncture, throwing over, for the sake of curtailing Catholic privilege in Manitoba, the leadership of an old Orangeman for that of a French Catholic. Nor did the Conservatives have anyone in Quebec to conserve to them the allegiance of their French followers. Instead, by far the most brilliant and popular of French Canadians, Wilfrid Laurier, was leader of their opponents. And Laurier was ably seconded by the irrepressible J. Israel Tarte. Liberals, moreover, could argue that no government had a right to introduce crucial legislation such as the Remedial Bill in the last weeks of the last session of Parliament. The only support the old party could rely on was that of the Catholic hierarchy, which saw in the Remedial Bill a measure of simple justice.

For once the Liberal party showed some practical political skill. On the question of the tariff, it abandoned its former free trade attitude, together with all hankering after "Unrestricted Reciprocity". On the separate school controversy, Laurier was at first in doubt whether he should support his co-religionists in Manitoba or not. Finally, acting, it is claimed[18] on the advice of J. S. Willison of Toronto, then editor of *The Globe*, he decided to come out unreservedly on the traditional

[17] 1831-1914. Another Simcoe County Irishman, neighbour of McCarthy's and one of "The Noble Thirteen" of 1888.
[18] A. H. U. Colquhoun, *Press, Politics, and People, The Life and Letters of Sir John Willison* (Toronto, 1935), p. 40.

Liberal position of support for provincial rights, making the claim that he would be able to do more for French Canadian rights in Manitoba by conciliation, by "sunny ways", as he put it, than by conflict. He risked his political future, for the power of the official church was solidly against him.

Sir John's dictum that "elections are like horse races, you can tell more about them after they are run" was never illustrated more clearly, than by the election of 1896. Wilfrid Laurier secured 118 supporters in a House of 213.[19] Ontario, centre of belligerent Protestantism, gave the party which proposed to coerce the Protestants of Manitoba 43 seats out of 92. But it was Quebec, stronghold of the faith and the French language, that provided the sensation of the election. Of its 65 seats, 49 went Liberal. Laurier and Liberalism had been denounced from every pulpit. A man who spoke as Laurier did, so the indictment ran, was a rationalist; he had formulated a doctrine entirely opposed to Catholicism. Under the circumstances no Catholic, except under penalty of committing a grave sin, could vote for such a leader. The faithful had been explicitly directed to vote for candidates who promised to favour a remedial bill acceptable to the bishops. The hierarchy had done its best; the Church had spoken—but the faithful had not obeyed. The prospect of having a native son as Prime Minister of Canada had prevailed over indignation against the treatment of the French minority in Manitoba and over the injunctions of the spiritual leaders of the race. Henceforth on more than one occasion the clergy were to be reminded of their own favourite text "render unto Caesar the things which are Caesar's; and unto God the things that are God's".

As for Manitoba, that "victim" of a tyrannous central government, its electors showed themselves so completely unconcerned about the "real" issue, the "burning" issue, of separate schools, that they returned a majority of Conservatives![20]

Elections such as 1896 make it difficult to believe that the results turn chiefly on the issues discussed in Parliament and press. There are so many local complications that as often as not the main points of contention are lost sight of. Elections are not referendums. Their significance in national history often becomes clear only after minute study. In 1896 what stood out beyond dispute was that the old allegiance, on which the half-century of Macdonaldism had been built, had been that of Quebec to the Conservative party and that a new Cartier had arisen

[19] 88 Conservatives were returned and seven independents, most of whom voted with the Liberals.
[20] See the unpublished M.A. thesis (University of Manitoba, 1943) by E. G. Cooke, "Manitoba in the Election of 1896".

in the person of Laurier, who would build the government of the country upon a bloc of French Liberals rather than upon a bloc of French Conservatives. A slightly ironical byproduct of the situation was that the "Grit" premier of Ontario, Oliver Mowat, heir to George Brown's "Rep. by pop.", "home rule for Ontario" philosophy, would shortly become his colleague and Minister of Justice.

Once again, it is obvious, all the wires were crossed: a re-alignment of political forces had taken place that was to serve as the basis of Canadian life for another half-century. What 1896 signified, it would seem, was the termination of an era: the old provincial Dominion was ending with the old leaders, a new generation was taking over and facing a new century that would bring a new world.

Chronology

1884   The "Imperial Federation" League.
1885   The Dominion Franchise Act.
        The North-West Rebellion.
        The execution of Riel.
1886   Nova Scotia's Secession Election.
1887   The Mercier Government in Quebec.
        The Interprovincial Conference.
        Resignation of Edward Blake as Liberal Leader: Laurier as successor.
1887–91 The "Unrestricted Reciprocity" Movement.
1888   The Jesuit Estates Act.
1891   Sir John Macdonald's last election and death.
1891–92 The Langevin-McGreevy Scandals.
1891   Downfall of Mercier.
1891–92 Sir John Abbott, Prime Minister.
1892–94 Sir John Thompson, Prime Minister.
1894–96 The Manitoba School Question in Dominion Politics.
1895–96 Sir Mackenzie Bowell, Prime Minister.
1896   Sir Charles Tupper, Prime Minister.
        Liberal electoral victory: Wilfrid Laurier, Prime Minister.

Additional Reading

Clark, Lovell C. "The Conservative Party in the 1890's." *CHA Annual Report 1961.* 58-74.
Landon, Fred. "D'Alton McCarthy and the Politics of the Later 'Eighties." *CHA Annual Report 1932.* 43-50.
Stanley, G. F. G. *Louis Riel, Patriot or Rebel?* (*CHA* Booklets No. 2) Ottawa, 1954.
Tupper, Sir Charles. *Recollections of Sixty Years in Canada.* London, 1914.

CHAPTER 28

A Generation of Confederation: The Dominion at the End of the Century

1. Canada, 1867-1900

The loose-jointed body that had emerged in 1867 under the name of Canada had made visible growth by the end of the century. The new central institutions had been "shaken down" and were working with reasonable smoothness. Parliament in 1900 might have been centuries old rather than thirty years old, so fixed were its forms, so traditional its atmosphere (a condition that could not have obtained had it not been for the ancient political heritage standing behind the new institutions). It said a good deal for the political sense of Canadians that they had been able to draw up a paper scheme and as a piece of machinery, have it work fairly well from its inception.

It was in the area outside Parliament that political instincts seemed least dependable: elections continued to be fought with a maximum of sound and fury, involving every type of "dodge"[1] and corruption. The "election petition" was a recognized device for continuing the battle after the voting had taken place. Sir Richard Cartwright in his

---

[1] There is a story still extant which tells how "John A." who was to address a late autumn meeting in Prince Edward County, across the Bay of Quinte from Belleville, found that the night before it was to be held "the Grits" had stolen all the boats to prevent his party getting across. However, nature came to the rescue: that very night the bay froze over; the heroes tackled the thin ice with planks and got safely over to the Prince Edward shore.

Reminiscences pays a tribute to the good sense and high principles of the farming population of Ontario in the period, and with some qualification, it is well deserved. Partisanship, however, often overruled good sense and sometimes principles. Nor did local knowledge carry very far beyond local interests.[2] It was true then, and it remains true today, that the average Member of Parliament was above the average level of his constituents in education and talent, in application, and often in character. The weakness of Canadian democracy has lain not so much in its leaders as in its followers.[3]

At the top of the governmental structure there had come into existence a well-recognized way of putting Cabinets together. From the first the Canadian Cabinet had to include representatives of the various major interests in the country—provinces and sections, religion and races. This federalized cabinet worked with a certain amount of creaking and groaning, limiting the Prime Minister's freedom of choice and sometimes excluding men of ability (as Charles Tupper in 1867), but it did work. Contrasted with the essential anarchy of Washington, Ottawa was the seat of strong, decisive government.

In 1867 the Crown, through the Governor-General, was a major factor in Canadian government. With the diminution in the personal exercise of the Royal prerogative, effected mainly by Edward Blake when Minister of Justice, 1875-78, the Governor-Generalship receded in importance. If at any time it came to life again, as it did under Lord Minto during the Boer War,[4] that was behind the scenes. The passing of power away from the Governor-General was an indication of the swing to popular democracy. Here was a trend that could not be blocked. When Macdonald in 1882 attempted to institute a Dominion franchise in Dominion elections, he took his stand on the looseness of the provincial franchises. His idea was a property suffrage. But he was on the losing side, and after his death manhood suffrage rapidly gained the day. By the end of the century, although Canada was not as wide-open a democracy as the United States, it had come to be a country in which the "will of the majority" was accepted as the principle of government. In one respect it had gone farther than the United States, for

---

[2] Sir Richard elsewhere qualifies his admiration by remarking very severely on the worthlessness of "public opinion".
[3] In the elections of 1962 and 1963, it was frequently alleged that the working class areas of cities showed the lowest percentages of votes cast to total electorate; in other words, the suggestion was that there was a correlation between such factors as economic standing, education, and political interest.
[4] On Minto, see H. P. Gundy, "Sir Wilfrid Laurier and Lord Minto," *CHA Annual Report for 1952*, 28-38.

that country had incorporated in its constitution a formal Bill of Rights which as the fundamental law of the land, protected minorities, or the individual, against the tyranny of majorities: as safeguard Canada had only the limited guaranties of the school rights of Catholic or Protestant minorities and of the French language. For such rights as freedom of speech or freedom from arbitrary arrest it depended on its inheritance of the Common Law and of certain British statutes (such as Habeas Corpus) re-enacted in the British North American provinces.

Towards the end of the century it also looked as if Confederation had been more or less successful in remedying the ancient racial wrongs. Both Quebec and Ontario had passionately striven for home rule, in order to escape from the "tyranny" of the other. Each now could run its own show in its own way. The English in Quebec, having obtained special safeguards in the British North America Act, settled down to that pleasant materialistic existence which by the end of the century had been far more successful than overt French aggression in removing them from the scene. From the countryside, their young people streamed off to the attractions of urban life, and the French just moved in and bought the farms from the old people. In the cities, they kept to themselves, developed their own institutions[5] and, except for a few members of Parliament and a very small quota of aldermen, retired from public life to business. There they found another source of power, and strange things sometimes happened in the provincial government of Quebec as a result.

Ontario showed its joy in its freedom by keeping the Defender-in-Chief of Provincial Rights, Oliver Mowat, as its premier for 24 years (1872-1896). Mowat minded his own Ontario business but extremists led by such men as D'Alton McCarthy, Colonel O'Brien, and N. Clarke Wallace[6] had no intention of allowing the French in the neighbouring province to do as they liked. The majority in both provinces showed strong tendencies to act on the old saying that "what's yours is mine, but what's mine is my own". From Ontario had come the cries for the blood of Riel and for the disallowance of the Jesuits' Estates Act (1888). Similarly when New Brunswick in 1872 abolished denominational schools, the French people of Quebec clamoured for Dominion interference, and in 1896, the hierarchy of Quebec (but not the people) sought the coercion of Manitoba.

Quarrels were invariably the work of extremist minorities: the masses

[5] The city of Westmount, completely surrounded by Montreal, being a conspicuous instance.

[6] 1844-1901. An Orange chief. Controller of Customs, 1892-95. Resigned in protest against Bowell's Remedial Bill.

did not show much concern. Ontario men had to be roused to cry for revenge for Scott;[7] and the French of Quebec in 1896 showed more desire to ensure a French Prime Minister than to protect the school rights of their brethren in Manitoba. In Parliament, racial relations were cordial: members of both races took part good-humouredly in the cut and thrust of debate, met in the clubs, and founded important friendships; Parliament was the most successful agency of understanding in the land.

2. The Communities of Canada

Canadian nationalism was formed from the top. The farther down the scale one went, the less consciousness there was of the whole country, the more of the local community. It was first of all a man's own home that commanded his loyalty, then his church, after that town or province, and on full-dress emotional occasions, the Empire. Variations in this scale of loyalties (in which one note was conspicuously silent) must be made for Nova Scotia, Prince Edward Island, and Quebec. In the two former, genuine local communities had been achieved. Prince Edward Islanders were intensely in love with their island home. Over in Nova Scotia, people were sympathetic with those who had not the good luck to be Nova Scotians, and throughout the peninsula, from North Cape to Cape Sable, whether a man were Highlander, Lowlander, New Englander, German, or Acadian by descent, he was first and foremost a Nova Scotian. "Upper Canada", as he termed it, was a distant country to which his Parliamentary representatives went to stand up for Nova Scotian rights. In Nova Scotia, the local, the racial, and even the religious loyalties had been subordinated to the provincial.

In Quebec, the first loyalty was to the race and to the church. If a choice had to be made between the two, as the election of 1896 shows, the race would be put first. French Canadians were so peculiarly a band of blood brothers, they had come through so much since the Conquest, were so conscious of the hostility of the English, that there is nothing surprising in this devotion to "the race". It was devotion stimulated by every possible device in order to assure to the French what has always seemed to them the one thing needful, "la survivance".

Of the other provinces, New Brunswick had not succeeded in achieving much integration. It was still a "river-valley" province, and the people on the various rivers did not have a great deal to do with

[7] So says Col. Denison, *The Struggle for Imperial Unity*, pp. 24-27.

each other. Superimposed on the local communities was the major division between the North Shore and the Bay of Fundy. By the end of the century, this lumber-jack province had cut all its pine and was making a large impression on its spruce. What it would do when its wood was gone was a worry for the future. Nearly all young people moved away on growing up, leaving the province little more than an area of exploitation for the mill-owners. New Brunswickers, not living on a peninsula thrust out into the ocean, as did the Nova Scotians, were more "continental" than their neighbours and for that reason, as also because of the absence of *esprit de corps*, rested more easily in Confederation. Their political life continued to be their own mystery.[8]

Ontario, so far beyond all the others in wealth and the kind of progress that the continent understood, was fast losing the sense of community that "Clear Grit-ism" and the George Brown crusade against "French Domination" had given it. The old fanaticisms were waning under the allurements of material developments, and the province was drifting into amorphousness; a congeries of localities but not a community. The significant Ontario community was to be sought in the small town, which as a comprehensible unit, often situated in surroundings of natural beauty, showed great ability to rivet upon itself the loyalty of its citizens, present and past. A partial explanation for amorphousness lay in mere size. Outlying territories from whose forests or mines much public revenue was derived, were in some cases over twelve hundred miles from the provincial capital. The government of Ontario was ruling a kind of empire within an empire, and its own citizens were lost in this approximation of province to Dominion. Mowat had made such strides in autonomy and expansion that had it not been for the lack of cohesion among Ontario people, Canada would have existed on this province's sufferance. Like Prussia within the German confederation, or England within the British, so also had Ontario almost become within the Canadian.

In the West, new Anglo-Saxon groups were working out a new way of life for themselves in surroundings as different from anything in their past as well could be imagined. People who had lived in the mild climate of the British Isles before they came to the relatively similar environment of Ontario now found themselves in mid-continent, hundreds of miles from the water, on flat and sub-humid plains. The job of adaptation was great, but no greater than that called for by the Pacific coast, where they had to face the mountains and the sea. While natural difficulties did not daunt them, they did not take to the sea, nor did they

[8] For politics in New Brunswick, see Thorburn, *Politics in New Brunswick.*

become plainsmen as the Indians had been, or mountaineers, as the Swiss are mountaineers. Rather, their effort was to shape their surroundings to their memories of the old home, under the technical methods and the way of life they had carried west with them.

Neither on the plains nor at the coast could genuine communities be said to have appeared in the nineteenth century. Everything was in such rapid flux that no one had a chance to become rooted. Everyone was here today and gone tomorrow. Western cities were the real estate agent's paradise. New districts built up so quickly that what was "the best neighbourhood" yesterday became half a slum today. Such instability was unavoidable under the rapid growth experienced, but it prevented a genuine sense of community from developing. The very freedom from local attachments, however, and the admixture from all parts of Canada left room for the conception of a common country to develop. But first, the sameness of the prairie environment and the vast wilderness lying to the east of it called forth regionalism: "The West" came to think of itself as one, in contrast with "The East".

By the end of the century the communities of Canada still had to become the community of Canada. The over-riding conception, a Canadian nation, was still vague. Yet there was something on the credit side of the ledger, too. A sense of Canadianism was developing, and already there was much difference between Vancouver Island as part of Canada and Newfoundland, a remote British colony. Youngsters might let off their firecrackers on "the twenty-fourth of May", but young men had their sports on Dominion Day. Even if old Mr. Blackadar down in Halifax did insist on printing his *Acadian Recorder* in "mourning" on the First of July, the concept "Canada" was more of a reality in 1900 than it had been in 1867. Every election testified that in a large, rough way, Canada was becoming a political community. If that had not been so, it could not have stood: if a section had been so alienated that it could not regard itself as part of the whole, it would have tried to fight its way out. But that did not occur. Nova Scotia began Confederation under protest, but Joseph Howe entered the Dominion cabinet. In 1886 W. S. Fielding could win a provincial election on the frank issue of secession, but ten years later, he, too, was in the Dominion cabinet. Canada existed on genuine government by consent.

3. The Disappointments of the Censuses

Secession talk and other phenomena of disintegration proceeded either from economic disappointment or its by-product, partisan sniping. Of the former there was much, and it was graven deep in the failure of the country to grow. Hopes were high in 1867, and the immediate past had been bright. But the generation of Confederation was to know a succession of disappointments. A population of some three and a third million in 1867 had in 1900 increased only to about five and a third, as compared with the growth of the United States from forty million to seventy-five. This was far below the legitimate hope of a young country. New countries with unlimited land have more or less regularly doubled their population every twenty-five years, but from 1881 to 1901 Canada was only gaining at a rate[9] that would have required sixty years for doubling. Between 1871 and 1881 the country had maintained a fair annual increase;[10] but then for two whole decades it fell off to slight proportions.[11] If Canada had retained all the persons born in the country or coming to it as immigrants in 1881-1901, there would have been in 1901 a population of between seven and eight million. Instead there was one of 5,371,000. There had been a leakage of over two million, not counting the children born to Canadians in the United States.

Where had all these people gone? The answer stared Canadians in the face. Everyone had relatives and friends in the States: that was where they were, just over the border, in New England or Michigan. There were so many Maritimers in Boston alone that today most of its people must have some Canadian blood. There were almost as many Canadians in a little New York border city like Watertown as there were Americans. Canadians had left their own country to settle just over the border, at first on the land in the border states and later in the border towns. None of them had gone very far afield. New England, Michigan, and the immediate northern border would have included all but a small fraction of them.[12]

All the old provinces had suffered from this loss of blood, but some more than others. From 1881 to 1891 New Brunswick and Ontario increased only by microscopic proportions. For the Maritime provinces growth had virtually stopped about 1880, and Ontario and Quebec were not much better off. Only in the west, in Manitoba and British Columbia, did it go on rapidly, in accordance with what had come to be regarded as the norm of the continent. Everywhere else the pace of life was sluggish. In the Maritimes, wooden ship-building faded away before

[9] 1.2% per annum.
[10] 1.72%.
[11] 10%.
[12] See map in L. E. Truesdell, *The Canadian Born in the United States; An Analysis of the Canadian Element in the Population of the United States, 1850-1930* (Toronto, 1943), p. 31.

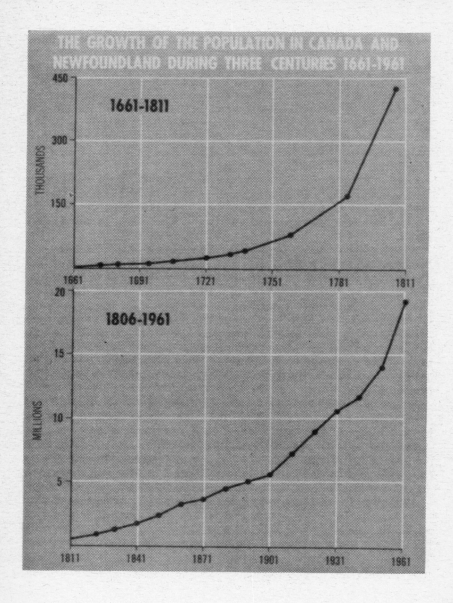

THE GROWTH OF THE POPULATION IN CANADA AND NEWFOUNDLAND DURING THREE CENTURIES 1661-1961

1661-1811

1806-1961

the rise of iron and steel elsewhere, and the passing of the age of sail turned a leading sea-going people into a minor one. Hill farms were deserted and began going back to forest. Villages shrank, and the chief cities barely held their own. In Quebec, whole countrysides took themselves to the United States, leaving behind abandoned farms and houses with doors and windows boarded over. From that province the people, smitten by what used to be called "la fièvre aux Etats-unis", went to the industries of New England. From Ontario, they went to the farmlands of the west.

This general slowing-down could not fail to be without its psychological and therefore political results. The latter have been examined, in the movement for "Commercial Union" and the elections of 1891 and 1896. The former remain to this day in the Canadian subconsciousness. The continental optimism, its belief in unlimited progress, Canada shares with the United States, but she has had far less reason for optimism and not nearly as much progress. Canadians have shared, or copied, their neighbours' exuberance but they have had to live with their own realities. The result has been a certain artificiality in outlook. Just because Canadians have always been looking over their neighbours' fence, they have tended to exaggerate the point of view they have borrowed from him. They have been small-town people giving themselves big city airs.

Owing to the country's failure to grow, colonialism, already deeply ingrained, was deepened, but it received a second direction, the United States supplying the new metropolitan fashion. Those who survive of the generation which was brought up in small Canadian towns in the nineties, know how desperately everyone struggled to put off rusticity, to acquire urban manners, to be "up-to-date", to be anything but themselves. That attitude was general in a continent where the approved social type was rapidly changing from pioneer to townsman, but it stuck out in Canada, where the social process did not entirely warrant it—especially in the small-town backwaters, the majority of whose young men and women left as soon as they had finished their schooling, to return as visitors later on with an air of American prosperity about them.[13] Those at home might emulate the air, but they could not share the prosperity, and as often as not both parties would be glad when the visit was over. The imparting of some spurious aspects of the American

---

[13] "I go on Les Etats-Unis, I go dere right away
An' den mebbe on ten-twelve year, I be riche man some day,
An' w'en I mak' de large fortune I come back I 'spose
Wit' Yankee femme from off de State an' monee on my clothes."
     W. H. Drummond, "The Habitant" (New York, 1900).

"go-getting" spirit, a deepening of envy, and therefore dislike, on the part of the stay-at-homes, and perhaps most important of all, a decrease of energy, ability, and initiative—these comprised the psychological heritage of this period of stagnation. The restless or enterprising spirits going to the United States,[14] whither others were streaming from all over Europe, heightened the spirit and daring of that country: the blood-letting that Canada suffered lowered its temperature, made people more "set in their ways", less imaginative, less creative. It and the colonial dependence upon Great Britain combined to give Canadians that uncreative, secretarial type of mind which is so good at detail but so conspicuously lacking in the higher ranges of initiative. The stolidity of the national character owes something to this period, and the marked difference of intellectual and cultural level between the older sections of the two countries is related to it. Heavy inroads cannot be made on the best blood of any community year after year without the bill coming in.

4. Land and Production

The stagnation of the times could most conveniently be blamed on the government: Liberals attributed it variously to the National Policy, the building of the C.P.R., or the corruptions of Sir John Macdonald. Few people seem to have been aware of the explanation: namely, that the country stood between two distinct economies—one, which was passing, based on a large measure of subsistence agriculture or fishing and on a technique in which wood was the principal material; the other, hardly ushered in, based on new and highly productive staple areas, on metallurgy and electricity. Until the end of the century the country was mostly rural,[15] yet except in the West there was no more land of consequence. People were forced to get out. Prince Edward Island, hardly larger than some Ontario counties, followed much the same course as they did, filling up rapidly as long as new land remained to be taken up and then falling off as the young people grew up and went away.[16]

[14] This still continues. In 1944, the Canadian air hero, Beurling, as soon as out of uniform, announced that he was going off to the United States. He "liked the set-up of that outfit", he said (according to newspaper report). In the decade 1950-60, over 40,000 persons classified as "professionals" left the country. Of course these were more than balanced by immigrants, but the immigrant has the factor of adaptation to reckon with. Enough "professionals" emigrate to drain off the larger share of the first-class brains entering life year by year. See *The Migration of Professional Workers into and out of Canada, 1946-1960*, Professional Manpower Bulletin 11, Economics and Research Branch, Dept. of Labour (Ottawa, 1961).

[15] See diagram, p. 339.

[16] Counties in Quebec formed no exception.

Until the new industrial era came in, with its secondary consequence of local markets, the countrysides of the old provinces had to decrease.

Nor were the towns yet ready to receive many of the farmers' children. Toronto was not much larger in 1901 than it had been in 1891. The only area where expansion was still going on at the old rate was in the lumber industry: that had been greatly stimulated by new railroad building (and had occasioned some) which opened up regions of virgin timber. As the wasteful old square timber trade began to decline in the 1880's, ending shortly after 1900, the sawn lumber industry rapidly filled the gap and, requiring large amounts of capital in the form of mills, tugs or camps, gave more employment. The pine forests of Ontario and Quebec still seemed "inexhaustible" (those of New Brunswick were already exhausted), and there was a market for all the lumber that could be cut. Extensions of the frontier depended mainly on lumbering. In Ontario, settlement went into Muskoka, Manitoulin, Parry Sound, Nipissing, Sudbury, Thunder Bay, and Rainy River; in Quebec, into the Lake St. John district, the Appalachian area, the country north of the Ottawa, and along the railway north from Montreal to Mont Laurier. This latter, Labelle County, was the colonization region of Abbé Labelle, of which so much was made by French nationalists. Some of these districts had ephemeral growth based upon the timber, or upon mining, permanent settlement depending on whether any soil was found underneath the trees. It was easy to raise a little hay and oats to supply the neighbouring camps, but when the timber was cut off and the camps closed, that was another story—colonization and settlement in the Canadian Shield has never been easy.

The forested area was so large and the original forest so rich that quite substantial progress could be made at many specific points. This was reflected in the prosperity of the larger centres. Ottawa was the "hub" of the Canadian lumber industry, but other regions were not far behind. Between 1871 and 1901, the rich pine forests on the Northern Railway and on the watershed of the Georgian Bay were being exploited. On them there grew up Barrie, Orillia, Midland, Gravenhurst, Parry Sound, and many of the Georgian Bay ports. These towns were linked by rail to Toronto, which profited from this extension of its hinterland. While Montreal was looking to the west, through the Canadian Pacific, Toronto looked to the north.

It was the combination of North and West with technical invention that made modern Canada: of timber, minerals, pulp and paper with wheat and meat; of hydro-electricity with the chemistry which showed how to extract metal from difficult ore or paper from spruce trees. The nineteenth century saw only the beginning of all this. In the early

1890's, the Riordons were making wood pulp and newsprint in the Niagara peninsula, and about 1895, the first steps were taken in harnessing Canada's water power for electricity. Discoveries of minerals had been rare and not very satisfactory. The very rich mine at Silver Islet, near Port Arthur, was typical, working out in a few years. The Klondike gold rush, which was to induce its thousands to follow "the trail of '98", had mounted quickly to sensational heights only to fall off as quickly. The most impressive find had been that of nickel at Sudbury, destined to be of primary importance in future Canadian metallurgy. There was already a coal and iron industry of some size in Cape Breton. But the really big movements were still in the future.

In the West, the end of the century did not see much more than the experimental stage over. People had been coming in from the end of the seventies, but there too the big jump came later. By 1900, Manitoba had about a quarter of a million people, and what are now the two other provinces each had a good deal less than a hundred thousand. The colonizers still were nearly all Anglo-Saxons, mostly from the east, with smaller groups of Icelanders and Mennonites; as late as 1901, there was no such phrase as "new Canadian". The earlier settlers had had trouble with frosts, but a lucky chance had given them a wheat (originally from the east of Europe) which proved satisfactory, Red Fife. From it the later wheats, which have marched northward over the prairies, have been bred.

The West was so far away from a market that it looked at first as if persons going there would have to be content with mere subsistence-farming, a prospect that had little attraction and which retarded the growth of the country. The first western land boom broke in 1883, after a great rush to take out homesteads and just as sudden an abandonment, leaving Manitoba as flat as nature had made it. Achievement had to wait until the requisite technical devices had been satisfactorily worked out. These were the grain elevator, the special type of grain-boat on the Lakes, the appropriate financial mechanisms such as the grain exchanges, and a system of grading the wheat so that the buyer knew what he was getting without seeing it. The small quantities of western wheat exported before the end of the century had already made so good an impression on buyers in the Liverpool market that the term "Manitobas" had become well known. When the grading system was perfected, "Manitoba No. 1 hard" became the synonym for the best wheat in the world. By the end of the century, the West was ready for the enormous expansion that was shortly to come.[17]

[17] The standard work on the grain trade is D. A. MacGibbon, *The Canadian Grain Trade* (Toronto, 1932).

5. The Growth of Communications

A substantial railway foundation had been laid for the new age. In addition to the two major jobs of the period, the Intercolonial and the Canadian Pacific, by the end of the century branch lines reached nearly every part of Ontario and Quebec. The longest south-north line in Canada was still that from Toronto to North Bay, but the province of Ontario was just on the point of extending this into "New Ontario" where it would open up districts then thought of as the remotest wilderness.[18] In the early nineties the C.P.R. built its short line across Maine to Saint John, giving it a winter outlet on the Atlantic and tying New Brunswick still more firmly into relationship with Montreal and into Confederation. In the west, a couple of obscure Ontario farm boys named Mackenzie and Mann had formed a railroad partnership that was to take them to dizzy heights as founders of the Canadian Northern. By 1903 the chain of transportation on which Canadian wheat was to depend was crowned with the deepening of the St. Lawrence canals to 14 feet, and the making of a correspondingly deep channel from Montreal to salt water.

The period had amply demonstrated that there could be no Canada without railways: without them British Columbia would have fallen away and perhaps Nova Scotia too. Of Manitoba and the North West Territories the same is true; the North West Rebellion of 1885 was put down with reasonable speed because the force sent out could travel by the almost completed Canadian Pacific Railway. Canada in the first half of the nineteenth century was the child of her waterways; in the second half she became no less truly the child of her railways.

6. Achievements in Civilization

At the end of the nineteenth century English-speaking Canada was well on the way to the middle-class, commercial state: the old typical figures of the settler, the lumber-jack, and the fisherman were giving way to that of "the business man". Urban values were fast replacing rural. Yet urbanism, despite its inevitable scepticism, had not greatly affected that sensitive barometer of social change, the church. Protestants in 1900 were still assiduous in their church-going and in their fidelity to the old "fundamental" type of religion, which had not been touched by the acid of historical criticism that had gone far in more intellectually advanced countries. In those days not only the sons of poor men or of clergymen went into the church; it was still strong enough to attract recruits for

[18] The line now extends to James Bay, and has become "The Ontario Northland Railway".

its ministry from every walk of life. All classes of society were equally prominent in church-going[19] and in good works. Canadians were being schooled in that discipline of organized charity that has made them outstanding in their susceptibility to altruistic appeals. The church was in tune with the life of its day, and its leaders were the genuine leaders of their society.

Consonant with the prominence of religion, manners were strict: one great church forbade its members to play cards or dance, and frowned on the stage. Young women who equipped themselves with "bloomers" to ride the new pneumatic-tired bicycles were apt to be considered "fast". The temperance movement, now two generations old, was making great headway, drying up pioneer thirstiness in every neighbourhood: all the churches were behind it except the Anglican and Catholic, and a good many of the clergymen of these denominations gave it their blessing. Already Canada was a more decorous country than it had been a generation before, which in itself reflected the growth of the bourgeois ideal.

Europeans have always been surprised (and shocked) at the freedom between the sexes in North America. Until today there has been no occasion for their being shocked, for freedom is simply a reflection of pioneer simplicity and equality. They might well be surprised, for the reverse has been true in older countries, where woman has had no scarcity value. In 1900, Canada, a country where men outnumbered women, had not remotely approached the stage of sophisticated relationship between the sexes. Pioneer democracy expressed itself not in sophistication but in a greater degree of legal equality than in older countries. It had never occurred to anyone to have anything else but co-education in the public schools, and in the 1880's, this was introduced into the universities. Sir John Macdonald in 1882 would have been quite prepared to give the vote to women owning property in their own right: and about that time, single women and widows actually did acquire it in municipal elections. "Married Women's Property Acts" made their appearance, well before they became the law in England. In Canada no such "feminist movement" as later developed in England could get under way, simply because there was not the requisite resistance to it.[20]

---

[19] In one of the early numbers of the *Queen's Quarterly*, there was an article by the great engineer, Sir Sandford Fleming on "The Efficacy of Congregational Prayer"! It is many years since either the *Queen's Quarterly* or an engineer published another such.

[20] The province of Quebec, with its Latin and Catholic outlook, has been an exception to some of these statements, but in most matters relating to "women's rights" has finally fallen in line.

In higher education the church still was powerful, most heads of institutions and many professors being clergymen, but there was little suggestion of illiberalism in its attitude. In all institutions the new studies of the age were being given recognition. Science was advancing: Canada had produced one outstanding geologist in Principal Dawson of McGill, a Nova Scotian. As early as 1873 the School of Practical Science had been built on the campus of Toronto, and by the end of the century other universities had their schools of engineering. In the liberal studies, the classical core had given way: Latin (and to a lesser degree) Greek were still prominent, but they did not dominate. The University of Toronto had established chairs of English and of Political Economy in the 1880's, and in the early nineties had appointed its first Professor of History. By 1890 the denominational rivalries that had cursed Ontario for three quarters of a century had been eased by the federation of the university. Victoria moved up from Cobourg, St. Michael's, the Roman Catholic college, entered, and the low church wing of the Anglicans was represented by Wycliffe Theological College. When in 1903 Trinity College also entered, the great modern institution represented nearly all creeds and outlooks.

The universities were still somewhat out of the main currents of Canadian life. As late as 1890, their staffs were mainly old-country men who regarded themselves as "exiles" in Canada; Canada's own able young men, under the weight of the older and stronger culture, were only slowly winning footholds in the higher education of their country. Student bodies were larger, but not much larger than they had been thirty years before. Universities were for the education of persons who took education seriously and expected to go into a profession: the great modern movement of mass education had not begun. The same was true of the high school: it was still mainly for "promising youths" and had not yet become an institution for keeping young people off the streets. Standards varied from province to province. In Ontario, where the "honours courses" of the universities exerted an influence present nowhere else, high schools gave a sound education and had already built up their courses to five years for "senior" matriculation. In the other provinces, little was attempted beyond junior matriculation,[21] university standards being in proportion. Most provinces had compulsory elementary education, and everywhere nominal illiteracy was decreasing quickly.

In what might be denominated "culture", the young country had no exciting accomplishment, but the apparatus of scholarship was being

[21] Grade XI.

elaborated, and in the social process scholarship seems to precede cultural achievement. The Royal Society of Canada had been established in 1882: it became a useful clearing house for many disciplines and also a gathering point for the *litterateurs*. For many years it remained the only national vehicle of scholarship.

Quite a few literary periodicals had appeared from time to time. Some of them, like *The Canadian Monthly* (1872-82) and *The Week* (1884-1896), both of Toronto, were of a high order, but since they did not pander to popular prejudices, they did not live long. To last they needed backing. This Queen's University gave in 1893 when it established its *Quarterly*. The *Quarterly* was at first concerned mostly with theological subjects, together with a little political comment, mostly relating to Great Britain, "the government" in those days meaning the British Government. There were occasional references to the Canadian scene, but the prevailing tone was "colonial" in the sense that it found its world of ideas and interests abroad. A marked change dates from the days when the young Adam Shortt, first of Canada's native-born economists, began to write on Canadian subjects: he saw life through native eyes, like the Canadian painters later. Within a few years after the turn of the century, thanks to him and others like him, *The Queen's Quarterly* had become a different periodical.

By the end of the century, daily papers were numerous: there were six in Toronto alone. The increasing influence upon them of business became more and more marked as the day of the old editor-politician passed away. In 1900 there was not an editor in the country of great political significance; Willison of the *Globe* was influential, but no more than influential. Editors had descended to the second level: there were none left of the calibre of Ryerson or Mackenzie, Hincks, Howe, or Brown.

For the most original and creative expression of the Canadian life of the period, we must go to the little group of poets who appeared about 1889.[22] Curiously enough it was the sterile soil of New Brunswick which bred the Roberts family and their relative Bliss Carman. The publication of Charles G. D. Roberts'[23] *Orion and other Poems* stimulated the foremost member of what might be called the Ottawa Valley School, Archibald Lampman,[24] encouraging him to believe that, contrary to the colonial ideas in which upbringing and education had saturated him, something fine and original might after all be done on Canadian soil.

[22] The best account of Canadian poetry of that period is E. K. Brown, *On Canadian Poetry* (Toronto, 1943).
[23] 1860-1944.
[24] 1861-99.

The prospect of a new nation that had inspired the *Canada First* group in the early 1870's passed over to these young men and although it luckily did not take the form of "patriotic" poetry, it became the spiritual dynamic that gave them power. Both groups, as was natural under the circumstances, wrote mostly nature poetry, but some very good nature poetry. They suffered, as who could avoid suffering in the Canada of the 1880's and 1890's, from the half-light of provincialism. They are not to be blamed because there did not lie behind them the complex social process out of which great poetry must come. They had no great themes (such as Confederation might have been had it been forged rather than carpentered), no severity of social clash to inspire them. In order to be themselves and not write as if they were Englishmen having a holiday in Canada, they had to write of the nature round about them.

At the end of the century, it must be admitted, Canada was culturally still backward and provincial: it was a land, Canadians hoped, with a future, rather than a past. That seemed to entitle them to be philistine about everything not of an immediately practical nature. Good poetry, like good manners, would come in time. When there was more leisure and more wealth, these things, which every proper society ought to have handy somewhere, would sneak in unobserved. In the meantime, not many people regretted their absence. Possibly in sticking to the immediate task in hand and getting the practical jobs done, they were right. But at the pace of the last quarter of the nineteenth century, a future, philistine or cultured, did not seem imminent. Canada was a comfortable but static country, a poor relation in the Anglo-Saxon world, a case of arrested development, where it would hardly have been logical to look for significance in any field. Canadians were wise in looking to the future, for they did not have a great deal else to look to. Few people dreamed of what was "just around the corner", and no one foresaw the strong nation of a half-century onward. Though they might have been kindled, the nineteenth century did not see the fires blazing.

Additional Reading

References to the topics of this chapter are almost all indirect. The author's own *Canadians in the Making* may be consulted for a more direct type of treatment. The following indirect references are useful.

Bezanson, A. M. *Sod-Busters Invade the Peace*. Toronto, 1954.
Burton, C. L. *A Sense of Urgency*. Toronto, 1952.
Coburn, John. *I Kept My Powder Dry*. Toronto, 1950.
Cragg, K. C. *Father on the Farm*. Toronto, 1947.
MacPhail, Sir Andrew. *The Master's Wife*. Montreal, 1939.
Riddell, Rev. J. H. *Methodism in the Middle West*. Toronto, 1946.
Sharp, Paul. *"Whoop-Up" Country*. Madison, Wisc., 1955.

CHAPTER 29

A New Leader and a New Canada, 1896-1911

---

1. 1896, Annus Mirabilis: "Canada's Century"

In the year in which Laurier Liberalism gained power, Canada was born again. Beginning in 1896 such a dramatic change took place in her fortunes that a new country was the result. There occurred a most extraordinary change in the material situation, which within a few years completely transformed her, giving her two new provinces and more new people than had been added in a generation. These newcomers fundamentally altered the character of the Dominion, for many of them were of alien extraction. The new life was felt everywhere. Cities east and west began to shoot ahead in population and wealth. Canada at last seemed to have its feet on that endless road of prosperity and growth which its American neighbour had so long been treading.

The new Liberal ministry, being human, did not hesitate to take full share of the credit, but the explanation, of course, lay deeper than a mere change of government. However, Sir Wilfrid Laurier began well. He put together one of the ablest cabinets that has ever governed Canada, a cabinet containing giants like Mowat, Fielding, Cartwright, and Clifford Sifton.[1] Sifton represented that promoting energy and

---

[1] 1861-1929. Previously in the Manitoba ministry. Laurier's Minister of the Interior, 1896-1905. Broke with him over the school issue in the two new provinces, 1905. Opposed reciprocity, 1911. An architect of union government, 1917.

exploitive ability which had hitherto been more familiar in Conservative than in Liberal ranks. This westerner, who possessed the natural business abilities of his Ontario Ulster stock, gradually edged the party away from the traditional, somewhat academic position of Laurier, towards the big business attitude of "exploiting our vast natural resources". Yet Liberalism never became mere transformed Toryism; the specific programme of the two parties might approximate, but the political attitudes behind these remained distinct.

Laurier's first job was to get the Manitoba Schools Question settled. He had proclaimed his belief in good will and compromise; this he was now to try. He was successful. Once they saw that no direct attack was premeditated, the Manitoba ministers were not too unreasonable, and Laurier's figure of the Conservatives as the north wind and himself as the sun proved accurate enough. A settlement was arrived at by which the French Catholics retained a certain modicum of rights in the public schools although they could not get a separate school system. The settlement was not unacceptable to the Catholic laity of Quebec, but the hierarchy declared total war on it and for a few months French Catholicism was in danger of being torn apart. The more extreme bishops insisted on authority over their flocks in matters religious and political alike. Some denounced voting for Liberals as mortal sin; others required the press to conform or be stripped of its readers. Laurier became a kind of anti-Christ, a re-incarnation and more of the old, atheistical *Rouges*.

In this crisis, no one showed himself a more faithful servant of his church or a better Christian than the Prime Minister. He could see that disruption would be easy if persons of extreme tendency rallied too aggressively to his defence. Managing to keep them in check he, as a good Catholic along with other Catholics, took the step of appealing to Rome for a settlement. Over the introduction into Canadian affairs of "Papal domination", he had naturally to risk drawing the fire of Ontario Orangeism, which duly came. But he contended that the appeal, made through private channels, was a purely denominational step, an attempt to secure peace in the Catholic household. The upshot was that in carefully guarded language, the Pope enjoined his bishops to quiet down. The election of 1896 had been a blow against hierarchical domination; the papal encyclical was a harder one. The two together ended the attempt to make French-speaking Canadians subservient subjects of a clerical ruling class. To Laurier the church owed deepest gratitude, for the fate of an ultra-clerical Quebec, arrayed religiously and by party against the rest of the country, would not have been a pleasant one. The incident must have impressed on the Prime

Minister what he already no doubt knew, that it is not easy to govern a country part of whose people are more British than the king and part more Catholic than the pope.

It was the British side of the house with which it was Laurier's next task to deal. The diamond Jubilee of Queen Victoria (1897) was made much of in displaying to the world and the colonial premiers the panoply of Empire. As an aspect of the festivities, Mr. Laurier reluctantly accepted a knighthood. He probably was rather bowled over by it all: it was his first trip abroad, and he was lionized everywhere. It has never been an easy thing for a simple Canadian to be plunged into the shining world of British aristocracy and keep his head. Perhaps Sir Wilfrid did momentarily lose his balance. He made a few speeches that for him seemed to go rather far in the direction of Imperialism; these did not increase his popularity in Canada, for French Canadians did not like them and many English Canadians assumed that he was not sincere. However, he returned home to a heart-felt welcome comparatively unscathed, having resisted the wiles of a gentleman at the moment engaged in building a vaster empire than had been, Mr. Joseph Chamberlain, who would have liked to capitalize the emotions of the time into some kind of centralized Imperial machinery of government. His visit paid Great Britain dividends in that it was followed by the enactment into Canadian law of the system of "Imperial Preference", by which Canada gave goods coming from the mother country (which maintained free trade with all the world) a substantial reduction in her regular tariff rates.

At home, relative harmony prevailed between the races. By a strange turn of events, the arch-disturber of the peace, D'Alton McCarthy, who had crusaded against the Jesuits' Estates Act, and toured the west to whip up ex-Ontario men against French papists, who had fiercely fought his leader Mackenzie Bowell, when this ex-Grand Master of the Orange Order, in his Remedial Bill, had proposed a measure of justice for Roman Catholics—this same D'Alton McCarthy, Protestant of the Protestants, now found himself a follower and even an admirer of the French Catholic, Wilfrid Laurier.[2] When his nephew Leighton[3] inherited his seat in Parliament it was as a Liberal. But such unexampled amity was almost unnatural. The political weather was too good and other storms based on race, if not on religion, lay ahead.[4]

---

[2] Laurier offered him the Ministry of Justice.
[3] Canadian Minister to Washington, 1941-44
[4] Of these the Boer War, to be discussed in the next chapter, was to prove the most serious.

2. The New Canada Beyond the Lakes

The prairie west and the Pacific coast, which furnished the physical basis for the new Canada, contained tens of millions of acres of usable soil, the richest of forests and of fisheries, unlimited coal and other minerals—all the requisites, apparently, for a great future. Though shortcomings in climate and rainfall reduced its effectiveness, there was more than half as much arable land as in a great country like France. Of the resources other than soil, all spoken of as "inexhaustible" by those who wished to exhaust them as quickly as possible, the only really "inexhaustible" were the coal measures of Alberta. But however much there was of each, there was a great deal—enough for quite a large, if scattered, society, though not for the unlimited visions of many of the people of the day.

In 1896, this whole vast area, stretching fifteen hundred miles from Winnipeg to the Pacific, was peopled only along the lines of railway then built; Winnipeg, Vancouver, and Victoria were little cities, but other places such as Calgary were only small towns. It had been expected in the 1880's that once the C.P.R. was built there would be a great migration to the new lands. That did not occur; there was fair progress, nothing more. Dozens of explanations can be given for this, but without much question the single most significant condition lay in the course of prices. After the American Civil War a long decline had begun: from 1865 to 1896, producers might normally expect to sell for a little less than they had bought for. In the United States, industry, thanks to new techniques applied to unlimited natural wealth, avoided the worst consequences of deflation, but with the farmer, American or Canadian, it was a different story. If when he bought his farm, wheat was selling at one dollar a bushel and ten years later at seventy-five cents, he had to raise four bushels to pay his mortgage interest where previously he had had to raise only three. Fresh new lands, well situated in good climates, were able to stand this, but a generation of falling prices stripped the people off the hill farms of Massachusetts and Nova Scotia alike, and injured the morale of those on the good soil of old communities like New York and Ontario.

To falling prices many other adverse factors were added: the barrier of the Canadian Shield preventing that continuous westward movement which had been so marked in American settlement; the milder climate of the American states and their better lands, with more timber and more rainfall; better economic conditions in the United States, with the lack of worry about distant overseas markets; the cheaper prices of American manufactured goods and their better quality compared with

those made in Canada behind a tariff: better conditions of transportation and absence of the railway monopoly in control of the Canadian
west; the greater taxable value of local communities, reflecting itself in
better schools and roads; the hopeless partisanship and generally grubby
conditions of Canadian life; the freer and more democratic atmosphere
of the United States; insofar as European immigrants were concerned,
the preference for a great nation rather than a mere colony (and one
whose lands of settlement had lately been disturbed by armed uprising).
The list becomes so impressive as items pile up that one wonders why
anyone went to the Canadian North-West. In the early days, persons of
a marked type must have gone—those who had a more than average
emotional attachment either to their Canadian homeland, or what is
more likely, to the British tradition. We come back, by another route,
to that highly selective process which from 1870 to 1896 was making
Canada a more and more conservative country.

The blunt truth was that the Canadian west had to wait until the
American west had filled up; this did not occur until the 1890's. As
soon as the last good boundary state, North Dakota, had been settled,
the condition had arisen for diversion of the stream to Canada. The
settlement of the Canadian west is an aspect of the general "westward
movement" of the continent.

It was in the period 1893-1896 that the spectacular gold discoveries
in South Africa began to halt the long decline in prices. In 1893 the
lowest price for wheat since the fourteenth century[5] had been recorded;
thereafter there was a steady rise until 1920. As prices trended upward,
gradually until about 1908 and then a little more sharply in the years
before the First World War, the economic situation at last moved more
in favour of the future.

Coincident with rising prices, other favourable factors appeared. The
lands south of the border, after a number of years of steady cropping,
were falling off from the pitch of their fertility. The long chain of
technical devices between grain field and ultimate market was now
satisfactorily functioning.[6] Early frost danger had been overcome, and
"Manitoba No. 1 hard" had won its reputation. Men saw profit ahead.
Therefore, they began once more to go west. Their needs worked back
to the east, keeping factories busy. Thus the snowball started. As it
rolled, it was made larger by the new immigration and by the new
railway building programme, both of which were to bulk so large in the
Laurier regime. All these factors, set in a world that was bounding

[5] 64¼ cents per bushel. Since exceeded by the low price of December, 1932,
39⅜ cents.
[6] See p. 414.

ahead in every continent under the same impetus, gave to Canada the most spectacular growth she has experienced.

Spirits rose accordingly, there was a feeling of buoyancy in the air, and Canadians began to add to the adaptiveness of pioneer people a self-confidence which they had not hitherto possessed. Business leaders and other authorities of equal incompetence began to make those astronomical predictions of future population which no amount of scientific calculation has yet been able to dispel.[7] Politicians began ringing the changes on the phrase "Canada's vast natural resources". Every citizen began translating the future into riches for himself. "The twentieth century", proclaimed the new Prime Minister, "will be Canada's".

The attitude was an aspect of the commercial civilization that was then carrying all before it. The Republican McKinley's victory over W. J. Bryan for the American Presidency in 1896 had been more than a party triumph. In that contest American ruralism had gone down before the onrush of the heavily armed troops of industry and finance. Urbanism had won. Henceforth the continent was to leave the rural life, with its simple piety and frugality, far in the rear and devote itself more and more to the bustle, the cleverness, the atomism, the pleasure-seeking of city sophistication.[8] Commercialism engulfed agriculture. The old conception of the settler as a man identified with the soil gave way to middle-class cupidity in the exploitation of nature. In the past the exploitive urge had been applied in directions that threw into high relief its essential antagonism to settlement—in the fur trade, in lumbering, ship-building, and especially in the Montreal complex of forwarding and finance (to which was later added industry), the two representing the quintessence of urbanism. But in the Canada beyond the lakes, there developed a certain identity between settlement and exploitation. The western prairies lent themselves to large-scale working, especially as power-machinery came in, and where conditions were favourable, "bonanza farms" sprang up. These, in their range and methods, were just rural factories, or mines, for extracting the wealth from the soil. They had little in common with traditional farming. They were, however, exceptional, for there were too many immigrants, and they were too much on a level to permit of anything like a plantation system developing. The west, like the east, became a country for the

---

[7] Even Sir Richard Cartwright talked airily of "a population of fifty millions". Lesser lights shoved it up cheerfully to one hundred.

[8] It was about this time that derisive terms began to appear for the farmer: he became a "rube" or a "hick".

average man, who nevertheless was closer to the urban middle class in the west than his father had been in the east.

The very nature of the country pressed commercial standards upon him. Nearly the whole of the prairies was fitted for wheat farming, and ten million acres were fitted for nothing else. Wheat was a great international commodity which had to be grown with one eye on the financial pages of the daily press. The unforested prairies did not turn every man into a lonely pioneer with an axe in his hand; rather, they induced him to join a local society for getting a railroad built and launched him into business associations. The speed with which the country was opening up and the vital necessity of railroads produced a commercial attitude towards land values not common among the pioneers of the east. Many a man homesteaded not so much to make a home but because he expected a railroad to come along and pick out his homestead as a "townsite".[9] The western settler, in contrast with his eastern parallel, who originally had been closer to the peasant type in his attachment to the soil and his relative independence of a money economy, was, if an Anglo-Saxon, almost as much a business man as a farmer.[10]

By 1900 there was no doubt about it: in the west and its wheat Canada had another string to her bow. The country had flourished on fur; it had flourished on lumber; now it was to flourish on wheat, the third of the great staples. All staples are similar in that they must be obtainable in large quantities, be of fairly uniform quality in dependable grades, and arise in response to a large demand. Wheat met these requirements perfectly, and in addition it was easily transportable because it was almost a liquid—it could be poured and pumped almost like oil. All great staples have thrown up high-coloured exploitive societies like wildfire and have rapidly subjugated all the country fit for producing them.[11] Wheat was to be no exception to the rule. It called for men and for railroads, and it soon got both.

The west was pioneered from Ontario; it was settled by people from the ends of the earth. Canada had been inviting the immigrant for decades, but of the not inconsiderable number who came, nearly all had

---

[9] "The Macdonalds were hurrying to The Elbow to 'squat' on land in anticipation of its being required for townsite purposes. . . . Ultimately 'the line' passed fifty miles south of The Elbow."—W. B. Cameron, "The Trail of '81," *The Beaver* (March, 1943), p. 45.

[10] As times have become harder in the west and the Anglo-Saxon has receded before the European, the land has been claiming its old toll again, and country values, despite "progress", have perhaps become stronger than they originally were.

[11] The best example is cotton in the American south.

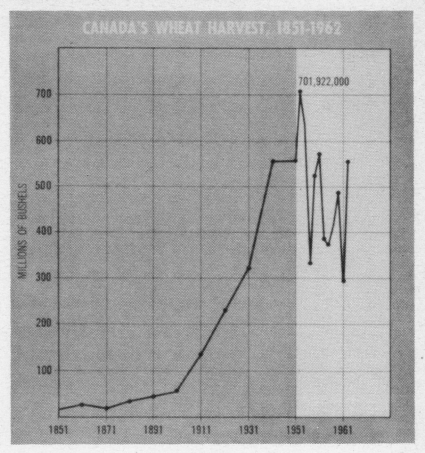

CANADA'S WHEAT HARVEST, 1851-1962

701,922,000

passed on to the greener fields of the south. The only immigrants who had been coaxed into the west by 1896, in addition to easterners and some old-country people, were a few Icelanders up near Lake Winnipeg and a few thousand Mennonites in southern Manitoba. It was Clifford Sifton who was first successful in diverting a part of the stream from American ports. By resorting to an intensive campaign of advertising and soliciting, by inducements to steamship companies, by a most extraordinary system of European agents and others financially interested, he caught the attention first of people in Great Britain and then of more and more remote Europeans. He seems to have had an eye

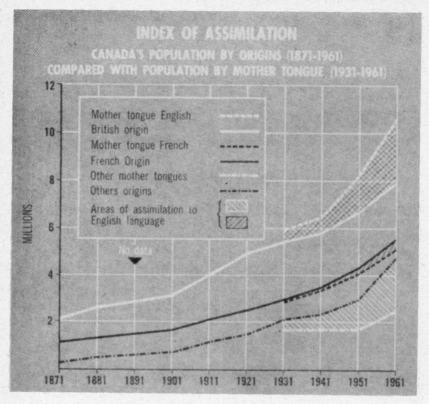

fixed solely on the task in hand—"filling up the country"—and to have been indifferent to the problems of assimilation, social, political, and religious, that he was entailing on posterity. "I think," he said, "a stalwart peasant in a sheep-skin coat, born on the soil, whose forefathers have been farmers for ten generations, with a stout wife and a half-dozen children, is good quality."[12]

Whatever else there is to be said about Sifton, he did get people moving into western Canada. The stream continued to flow long after he resigned. It was interrupted by the Great War but resumed in 1920 and continued until 1930. During this thirty-five years some five million people[13] entered Canada as immigrants. Austrians, Bohemians, Bul-

[12] Quoted in Dafoe, *Clifford Sifton*, p. 142.
[13] Canada Year Book, 1932.

garians, Lithuanians, Poles, Russians, Serbs, Slovaks, Ukrainians, Swedes, Danes, Norwegians, Magyars, Germans, Finns, Italians, Roumanians—all had come in by the St. Lawrence and marched across Canadian soil. Winnipeg and other western towns had become veritable Towers of Babel, with scores of languages spoken on their streets. No nation can accuse Canada of having acted like a dog in the manger: her gates were open wide, the only condition being that one take off his coat and work. These millions of strangers constituted a cheap labour force of the largest dimensions. They built the railroads and they bought the farms, good or bad, that smart real-estate men sold them; they bought tickets on the railways to come and they bought more tickets when, being no longer needed, they obligingly took themselves off again. Of the vast army of them there remained in 1931, the year after Prime Minister Bennett closed the gate, less than one-half.

Within a page or two it is impossible to do justice to such a theme as the second great Canadian wave of immigration. It is a subject that invites volumes, one full of high colours, of human hopes and tragedies, of good intentions and sordid selfishness. Out of it all, when the hurly-burly was over, there emerged another Canada, a Canada a fifth of whose people were of recently arrived alien stock, most of them Catholics, Roman or Greek, who looked at the older hands, the civilization they had built, and the political ties they kept up, with hard alien eyes. These newcomers had not been received into the bosom of the family. If they were Protestant in religion and Scandinavian, Dutch or German in origin, if they learned to speak English reasonably well, then they stood a chance of being taken in. If not, they quickly discovered that Canada was no United States, where all were equal and all engaged in building the republic. English Canadians had despised the French and used their strength against them when they could; they were not now disposed to admit "Bohunks" and "Dagoes" into any degree of intimacy. The newcomers were shoved off by themselves and settled in colonies or flocked into the slum areas of the cities.

Not until the foreigner had been on Canadian soil for a generation or so was there much disposition to accept him. There was though, much censure of him for his failure to assimilate, and when he did, he had to conform to the Canadian norm. But little by little the new blood and the old began to mingle—kindred stocks first, and slowly, very slowly, the rest. For the third time since the English conquest, an old society had been swamped by newcomers, and the job of building another had to be begun all over again. Ukrainians and Hungarians, Poles and Germans, all had to be ground through the mill of the public school, taught English, and painfully and roughly trained in that English tradition of law and government that was not understood too well by the natives themselves. As a result of it all, by mid-century a new people had been begun in the West, neither "British" nor "foreign", simply Canadian.

New railroads both preceded and followed the new people. Those celebrated financial wizards, Mackenzie and Mann, had been constructing short roads in the west "on a shoe string" as early as 1896, but few people realized that the remarkable pair were building up a system that would one day reach transcontinental proportions. They worked quietly, and the source of their money was a mystery. One thing was certain: they did not supply it themselves.

Their efforts were soon overshadowed by the soaring project brought down to the Commons by the Liberal ministry in 1903, which was nothing less than a second transcontinental road, complete with seaports on either coast. The old Grand Trunk, seeing what a good thing the west was becoming, began to think that it had "missed the boat" when it had turned down the offer taken up by the C.P.R. Syndicate and decided to try to get in before it was too late. It had a line to Chicago. By building in the west, it too might eventually reach from sea to sea. The government did not give it the chance but countered the Grand Trunk Pacific scheme with a more ambitious one of its own: the company to build west of Winnipeg, the government east, the whole to be made into one system operated by the Grand Trunk, a system that would outweigh the C.P.R. itself. Though the terms were easy, the Grand Trunk accepted reluctantly, and Canada's greatest railway boom began.

There was some opposition within the party, but the "bigger and better" spirit was in full possession, and the "pessimists" were swept aside. The reasons for the government's proposal have never been made entirely clear. Basically they were simply responses to the optimism of the age. In detail, the promoters, the contractors, and all who could smell money, may have had a good deal to do with it. The Conservative party had had their transcontinental (which had "come across" handsomely at election times) ; why should the Liberal party not have theirs? Such reasoning was not shouted from the roof-tops, and it was not what appealed to Sir Wilfrid, who had his own reasons, which were honest but not very sound ones. He believed a new transcontinental was imperative for the development of the west—that Canada's hour had struck, as he phrased it. He believed what he was told when they said that the new line would, by taking a northerly route, approximating a great-circle course, be able to bring grain down from the west at low figures and that it would make the city he had represented for so many years, Quebec, once more into an ocean port. He did not realize that the amount of grain brought down to Atlantic ports by an all-rail route would in very truth "not pay for the axle-grease" of the cars containing it and that it is the St. Lawrence and the lakes stretching into the heart of Canada which has brought grain flowing out from it. He was not at home in these practical matters, with their need for endless calculation. The only figures he ever understood, it used to be said, were figures of speech.[14]

Laurier was not ceasing to be master in his own house, but the Liberal party had been some years in office and was fast gathering round it the inevitable barnacles; to be "in on" spending several hundreds of millions was too good an opportunity to allow party labels to stand in the way. Sir Wilfrid was not the first Prime Minister to be embarrassed by his own success. The new railway was built to a high standard of construction and built extravagantly. Contractors did well out of it. But major profiteers, if there were any, must have covered their tracks very carefully, for no resounding scandal such as had almost sunk Macdonald was unearthed by a vigilant opposition.

The National Transcontinental was hardly well under way when Mackenzie and Mann again were heard from. They had followed the astute policy of building short lines on a low standard and then getting provincial governments involved in their completion, usually by guarantees of bonds. So successful had they been that, by this method and in the English market, they had raised many millions of dollars. At last they felt strong enough for the master stroke, a line across the north that would connect their western and eastern networks. Well before the Liberals went out of office in 1911, a third transcontinental was being shoved across above the lakes and through the mountains. No one asked whether it was necessary. Everyone, from the highest officials and the most expert engineers down, was quite convinced that "this is a great country" and that it would need all the railways it could get. After all, the United States had a hundred million people! Never were such huge projects undertaken with so little fundamental study. Americans built railroads to develop their country, Germans for purposes of war, but Canadians apparently just for the fun of building them.

However, the country was proving more and more productive, and foreign loans were rolling in by the hundreds of millions of dollars. The new bout of railway building differed from those of 1854 or 1881 in that prosperity preceded it and tended to engender it. Yet once it was under way, it was the same old story of money rolling out everywhere by the

[14] See the quotation from the speech in which he introduced the proposals to the House, given in Skelton, . . . *Sir Wilfrid Laurier*, II, 190—a most unusual note, to say the least, in Canadian politics for this kind of measure.

barrelful. The most gorgeous spending spree in Canadian peace-time history resulted. New elevators sprang up like mushrooms. A space on a map yesterday became a village today and got a new railway tomorrow. City lots sold faster than they could be put up for sale and good citizens of Winnipeg went about to each others' houses, admiring the resulting booty of silverware or oriental rugs, in what were termed by the cynical, "gloating parties". Immigrants coming in with cash were sold land, the farther away the better; those coming without were put to work. New farmers were everywhere; new totals for wheat were being made every year; new towns were springing up with the speed of light;[15] new fortunes were ubiquitous. If you were "broke" today, you might be worth a million (in unsold real-estate) tomorrow. "The sky was the limit" and "if you couldn't boost, you mustn't knock".

At last, in 1913 when the loans were all spent, the inevitable happened, and Canada prepared to sober up. But by that time the European shadow was beginning to stretch across the country, and next year the economic crisis was swallowed up in war. Hectic though the dozen years had been, the opening of the west not only had given Canada two new provinces and two million more people, but also it had established her firmly as a second continental power, integrated by the railroads she had acquired, having, in no uncertain way, "Dominion from Sea to Sea".

3. The Downfall of Laurier Liberalism

There were two outstanding political correlations to the rise of the west: one was the creation of the two new provinces in 1905, the other was the attempt at Reciprocity with the United States in 1911. The North-West Territories had been governed first of all by a council, then by a partially elective body and lastly by a legislature with responsible government; in 1905 it was decided to bring in that portion south of 60 degrees north, as two provinces. Saskatchewan and Alberta were therefore constituted by the Acts of Parliament bearing their names. There was not the slightest vestige of a "compact" in these two cases. There was no entity preceding them that could make a contract, as there had been in British Columbia; there was not even the unofficial understanding between a half-organized group and the Crown, as there had been in the case of Manitoba. The two provinces were aspects of the sovereign will of Canada: its children, not in any sense its parents. Yet they were endowed with all the powers of a province, no matter how wide those might prove to be.

In their creation the perennial Canadian ghosts, race and religion,

[15] Calgary and Edmonton jumped from 4,000 each in 1901 to about 40,000 in 1911.

walked again. The first draft of the bills would have opened the way to a school system somewhat similar to that of Quebec, where Catholics and Protestants each have their separate establishments. This caused a fierce commotion in Protestant ranks, especially in Ontario, where "denominational schools" came in for their usual denunciation. Sir Clifford Sifton, who was away holidaying, does not seem to have seen the offending clause until it became public: in consequence, he resigned, though it has been suggested that the resignation really rested on much more personal grounds.[16] Mr. Fielding's resignation was also rumoured, but timely discussions and an amendment making the school system similar to that of Manitoba's (that is, national public schools with minority privileges) saved further defections. The popular agitation soon died down but the Prime Minister had received a blow. His leadership had faltered, and he had made enemies among the extremists of both peoples.

The new west, a primary producer for the international market, did not take long in realizing, with a clarity that no other section of Canada has ever achieved, where its economic interests lay. They lay in free trade, the widest possible measure of it, for since the wheat grower had to compete in the world market without a single stitch of protection, his consumption goods—his food, clothing, lumber and implements—must be as cheap as possible. To buy from Canadian industries existing behind a tariff wall was simply to pay them toll. The western farmer from the beginning was forcefully and vocally a free-trader. To him anything was welcome that would get his products over the American tariff wall, or American manufactured goods over the Canadian.

Reciprocity[17] had been the Canadian dream ever since the abrogation of the treaty of 1854, and Conservatives, in embracing the National Policy or fighting "Commercial Union", had never repudiated "reasonable reciprocity". Not that there had been any chance of getting tariff favours from the hardboiled Republican business men who ran the United States after the Civil War! In 1908, when W. H. Taft was elected President, no more interest than previously was being displayed in the subject: two years later, however, the President, to the great surprise of the Canadian government, seemed ready to take the initiative in making an offer.[18] Laurier and Fielding grasped at the golden opportunity and shortly presented to the surprised country a Reciprocity

[16] Skelton, *Laurier*, II, 236.
[17] For this topic, see L. E. Ellis, *Reciprocity, 1911* (Toronto, 1939).
[18] Rising prices in the United States, the current battle against "the trusts", the need for some piece of legislation that would appeal to the voters, a discernible swing to the Democrats, are all given as his reasons. Perhaps his summers at Murray Bay in Quebec as neighbour and friend of the historian George M. Wrong had been a predisposing condition!

agreement actually made, awaiting only parliamentary ratification. Here were two Santa Clauses filling Canadian stockings with the gifts of free entry into the American market for primary products and for a wide range of manufactured articles. No wonder that when on January 26, 1911, Mr. Fielding introduced the proposals in Parliament, the Opposition were "stumped". For some time they wavered, undecided what their line should be. Gradually voices began to make themselves heard against the agreement. The manufacturers and the railroads had been taking stock of their position and began to protest against being "sacrificed to the Yankees". Soon the perennial loyalty cry was added. Should Canada cast off her connection with Great Britain, to marry herself to Uncle Sam? With this the Conservatives had found their line: they prepared to fight to the death for the British connection.

Sir Clifford Sifton, westerner and Liberal, came out against the agreement; to the Conservatives his support was worth a battalion. A group of Toronto Liberals revolted from their party. Someone coined the slogan "No truck nor trade with the Yankees". In Parliament, the Opposition staged a filibuster against the agreement, and at last Sir Wilfrid, unable to get on with it, dissolved. The campaign raged during the summer of 1911. The Conservatives steadily gained ground in Ontario, and the winning cards were put in their hands by Americans who tactlessly spoke of the agreement being "the parting of the ways" for Canada and of its making her "an adjunct" of the United States. It was 1891 over again—the same "sloganeering", the same flag-waving.

The Liberal ship might have had some chance of weathering the reciprocity storm had it not been for an entirely distinct tempest that burst in the province of Quebec. Discontent with Laurier had been smouldering since the Manitoba Schools controversy. It had been increased by his apparent surrender to Imperialism in consenting to sending Canadian soldiers to the Boer War. That war produced Henri Bourassa,[19] a most intelligent, well-educated, young politician and journalist of oratorical gifts. He took the "nationalist" point of view that Great Britain's wars were not Canada's business and won for himself a reputation and a following. Three or four years later, a formal Nationalist movement was organized, the direct successor to that "national party" of Mercier's which had come out of the execution of Riel. It might have faded as Mercier's had, if the European situation had not presented it with an issue. In Canada the "German peril" (the much-used phrase of the day) crystallized in Laurier's Navy Act of 1910.[20]

[19] 1868-1952. See p. 448.
[20] See also next chapter, p. 453.

Conservatives vigorously opposed this act: a Canadian navy, according to them, would weaken ties with the Empire. French "Nationalists" opposed it too, but for different reasons. They protested that Canada had no need of a navy, that innocent young French Canadian boys would be wrested from their mothers' knees and sent abroad to fight England's battles on British ships under Protestant captains for causes that were none of theirs. As the elections approached, old tales of the press-gangs began to circulate about the countryside. Mr. Bourassa and his young lieutenant Armand Lavergne drenched the province with oratory, and, so it is said, men in the uniforms of British naval officers appeared at farm-houses to inquire how many sons the family had.

When the smoke of battle cleared away, the Liberals had suffered the fate of Alexander Mackenzie: they had been in a majority of 45; they were now in a minority of 45. Outside Quebec, they had 50 seats, the Conservatives 106; inside, 38 as against the Nationalists' 27. Even rural Manitoba had spurned the Liberal gift of free trade.[21] Once again, in this second slogan election, as three times before, the party which had succeeded in identifying itself with "the flag" whether Union Jack or fleur-de-lis, had ridden triumphantly to victory. When such fundamental passions are engaged, Canadians vote according to their ancestral urges. But it is rarely that the heaven-sent opportunity comes of combining all the ancestral urges on one side with all of those on the other in order to smite a foe who stands midway between the two. The Liberals had been beaten by an appeal to "loyalty" in English-speaking Canada and to "disloyalty" in French.

Canadians thus threw Uncle Sam's offer in his face. That they lost a good trade bargain no one would deny, except the manufacturers and their dependents whose protection would have gone. Had they gained something more precious, their own soul? That was not the point the case had rested on; they had preserved the British connection, the victors claimed. Yet it may be that the self-confidence which inspired the decision and which resulted from it, the feeling that now they could "paddle their own canoe" and tell the Americans to go about their business, came close to that. Canadians for decades had been suppliants first in John Bull's house, then in Uncle Sam's. Their rejection of the Reciprocity agreement signified their confidence that they could get along by themselves.

Sir Wilfrid took the defeat hard: for him it represented disapproval of a French Canadian and a Catholic as Prime Minister. That was not so: he was and remains a figure probably more respected in English

[21] See diagram, at back of book.

Canada than in French. He had suffered the fate of most honest men who stand in the middle, fired on by both sides. In a country every page of whose history bears evidence of vehement unwillingness to see the other man's point of view, he had devoted his career to the Christian virtue of tolerance. No people are more legalistic in their attitude towards their rights than his own, demanding the uttermost farthing, and compromise is not a virtue that the French learn easily. The English, for their part, have been Puritan rather than Christian, certainly Puritan rather than liberal: they have admired the stern virtues—manliness, strength, steadfastness, efficiency—but they have had too strong a sense of "right and wrong" to have given them much insight into the essential Christian ideal of charity and love. To the French, compromise has appeared as treason to their race, to the English as sinful. Such extreme attitudes have not been universal, but agitation has always been able to send the fire through most of the moderates too. Sir Wilfrid was a victim of his life ambition to act as a Christian should.

In retrospect the man thus defeated bulks higher and higher. The years have revealed few flaws in him. His life-work of compromise, tolerance, and the reconciliation of the two partners in Canadian life had been Sir John Macdonald's before him. But how differently the two espoused it! What a contrast in intellectual distinction, in range, in fastidiousness, in simple honesty, between the two men! The comparison is all in favour of the French Canadian. He was a giant in character.[22] Politically, his Liberalism was that of Gladstone, rather Whiggish, built on the great English tradition of freedom. It was free from the doctrinairism of the Benthamites or the extreme practical individualism of Cobden. It had enough of Conservatism in it to enable it to embrace far-ranging concepts, but it had about it nothing of the continental Liberal with his anti-clericalism and his atheism. In few fields was Laurier's service to Canada greater than in convincing his people and their clergy that Liberalism was a respectable political creed to which a good Catholic might commit himself, for it enabled him to build another great national party, cutting across creeds, races, and sections, just as Macdonald's Conservative party had previously done. It was thanks largely to him that his overly diverse country found itself with two national parties into which all men might go and thus continued to be able to work its system of Confederation and self-government.

[22] A minor incident illustrates Laurier's devotion to toleration. When the Salvation Army first appeared on the streets of Quebec, it met with a rowdy opposition, and its parades were stopped. Sir Wilfrid said that the "Army" must be allowed to march, that the civil authorities must protect it, and that "if need be, he would march at the head of their procession with them".

Laurier Liberalism had to pay the price for such catholicity. At the beginning of his leadership, "the Grits" and *Les Rouges* had been hopelessly in the wilderness: they were a Gideon's band, who thought much and kept themselves close to the basic philosophy of liberalism but had little hope of office. Success opened the gates to all, and Liberalism lost a good deal of its meaning. Such is the fate of parties. They start out like the early Christians, a chosen band of devotees. But no doubt as soon as Constantine gave official recognition to the Church, many prominent pagans turned up at mass. Still, for the Church there always remains a Christian nucleus, and for a political party, a tag of its original philosophy. By 1911 Liberalism had, as it were, become a universal church.[23] In that year, too, it was to suffer the loss of a number of its members over Reciprocity, in one of those splits which parties of the left are always experiencing: its right wing took itself off to the great hold-all, the Conservative party, the ultimate political home of all whose interests or sentiments are trampled on by a marching world.

Sir Wilfrid's ministry had begun auspiciously and for eight years had gone from triumph to triumph. He had found what Mackenzie and Blake had never been able to come upon—a programme. It had consisted, in essence, in an extension of Sir John's: a national policy, not called such, of moderate protection, railway building, immigration. Both men lived to see the main lines of their systems worked out, but whereas Canada was at the bottom of the curve when Sir John died, Sir Wilfrid's regime coincided with the best days the country had ever known. In office he had few rough seas to meet. How would he have weathered the storm that in 1911 lay just up ahead? On that he was not tested in office. Was he then a fair-weather sailor? It would be unfair to say so. Perhaps if he had been in a strategic place, his character and the confidence that men had in him might have enabled him to avoid the tragic rift of 1917. Or was it practical administrative capacity, rugged endurance, common-sense judgement, and dogged drive that the country needed most at that trying time; not the poetic talent of the humanist but the hum-drum efficiency and fair-mindedness of the Nova Scotian lawyer who was about to succeed, Robert L. Borden?

4. The New Conservatism: Sir Robert Borden

Mr. Borden's ministry was a strange amalgam. It contained fire-eating Imperialists like Sam Hughes, the Minister of Militia, and representatives of the anti-Imperialists of Quebec such as F. D. Monk, proved men

[23] See also p. 453.

like George E. Foster, and "practical politicians" of too subterranean abilities like Hon. "Bob" Rogers. Founded on the most opportunist bargain in Canadian history, the Liberals could feel justified in calling it an Unholy Alliance. Here was a coalition, the first in history, between the old Papineau-rebel-*Rouge* tradition and the Tory-Loyalist. Papineau-ism, mixed in a strange amalgam with Castor Ultramontanism, had come full circle: once on the extreme left, it was now on the extreme right. Of genuine French Conservatives, men in the Cartier tradition, there were few left, and many of these were now to be found in the Liberal ranks.[24] Quebec had moved not along lines of social progress but merely along those of racial assertion, and now found itself bound to a government utterly alien to itself in outlook.

During the three years given to Sir Robert Borden (as he became in 1911) before the war of 1914, his conduct of affairs, being concentrated on similar developmental policies, showed no great divergence from that of his predecessor. Sir Robert, like Sir Wilfrid, was a man of sterling personal qualities; between the two of them much was done to break the bad, old tradition of public corruption. Canadian politics have often been crude and raucous since, but they have never fallen to the depths of the previous period. Sir Wilfrid had made a start at introducing the merit system into the Civil Service; Sir Robert carried this further. He saw the National Transcontinental through to its completion and continued the immigration and settlement policy of his predecessor.

His sharpest alteration was in the naval proposals of 1912, when he brought down a bill to give Great Britain $35,000,000 to build three dreadnoughts. He forced the bill through the Commons by the new expedient of the "closure", carrying with him all but four of his Nationalist collaborationists. But the Liberal Senate refused to accept the Commons' bill, and the Borden naval programme thereupon ended. There was some Conservative talk of an appeal to the people, but appeals to the people cost individual members even more than battleships, so the issue was allowed to fade away and gradually die. As in 1862, when the Conservative Militia Bill, also introduced at English instance, was defeated in a time of danger, the government of the day compromised by doing nothing at all.

It was in the year after the great debate on naval policy, that the

---

[24] Sir Adolphe Chapleau, leading representative of the Cartier tradition, had, towards the end of his career, swung into the Liberal orbit. But since the above lines were written, it has been called to the author's attention that most of the French ministers under Borden were, nevertheless, in the *Bleu* tradition. However, Bourassa and Armand Lavergne, his principal lieutenant, were certainly in the tradition of Papineau, and they were key figures in Laurier's defeat.

western land boom "broke". There had been something unreal to the average Canadian in all this talk about distant Europe: the country was full of people who were trying to get away from Europe and the natives were far more concerned, as someone said at the time, "with box cars than with battleships". When good times disappeared, many of the newcomers went with them. With the spending of the railway money, activity dampened down everywhere. Then, whether they liked it or not, Canadians saw Europe rear its ugly head once more, this time breathing the flames of war. Sir Robert's pre-occupation with the domestic affairs of his country had ended; thenceforth he was to devote his time to being Canada's first war minister.

Chronology

1896 Sir Wilfrid Laurier, Prime Minister.
Understanding reached with Manitoba with respect to Catholic Schools.
1897 Ensuing struggle with the Hierarchy of Quebec.
The British Tariff Preference inaugurated.
1900 Laurier's Second Electoral Victory.
1901 R. L. Borden, Leader of the Opposition.
1903 A Second Transcontinental undertaken.
1904 Laurier's Third Electoral Victory.
1905 Creation of Saskatchewan and Alberta.
Resignation of Sir Clifford Sifton from the Laurier Cabinet.
1908 Laurier's Fourth Electoral Victory.
1911 Laurier's Defeat on the Issues of Reciprocity and a Canadian Navy.
1911 The Borden Conservative-Nationalist Ministry.

Additional Reading

Borden, Henry, ed. *Robert Laird Borden: His Memoirs*. Toronto, 1938.
Colquhoun, A. H. U. *Press, Politics and People: The Life and Letters of Sir John Willison*. Toronto, 1935.
Dafoe, J. W. *Clifford Sifton in Relation to his Times*. Toronto, 1931.
——. *Laurier, A Study in Canadian Politics*. Toronto, 1922.
O'Connell, M. P. "The Ideas of Henri Bourassa." *JEPS*, XIX (August, 1953), 361-376.
Sissons, C. B. *Bilingual Schools in Canada*. Toronto, 1917.
Skelton, Oscar. *The Life and Letters of Sir Wilfrid Laurier*. Toronto, 1921. 2 vols.
Weir, G. W. *The Separate School Question in Canada*. Toronto, 1934.
Willison, Sir John. *Reminiscences, Political and Personal*. Toronto, 1919.

440

CHAPTER 30

The World beyond our Doors

1. The Legacies of the American Revolution

Until the twentieth century, Canadian external affairs can be equated to the unfinished business of the American Revolution. Canada in itself represented the main item of that business: she represented the degree by which the Revolution had failed, she constituted an unwelcome reminder to the Americans that it had never been quite completed, the hated British never entirely put in their place. Consequently a strong current in American thinking was directed at the very existence of the British colonies. The dynamics of American westward expansion were expressed in such phrases as "Manifest Destiny", talk of "our continent" and a more or less avowed policy of North America for the Americans. As General Cass of Michigan put it, "Americans had an awful swaller for territory". It was such conceptions which lent power to their diplomacy in all the tussles to get the unwelcome stranger out of the house, while the British were propelled mainly by the vested interests involved, among which the colonial was only one.

Most of the disputes which involved British North America arose out of the vagueness of the Treaty of 1783.[1] That treaty had described the boundary in terms which could not be traced upon a map, and it had created an impossible situation with respect to the Atlantic coastal

[1] See p. 85.

fisheries. Controversies on subjects other than these two nearly all resulted from civil disturbances in the one country and their repercussions in the other, especially from the rebellions of 1837 and the Civil War. It being quite impossible to draw a line from "the most north-western point of the Lake of the Woods and from there in a due west course to the Mississippi River", a compromise was effected in 1818 by which a line was projected from the "north-west angle" of that lake south to latitude 49° N. and thence along that parallel to the Rocky Mountains. This gave the United States the major part of Lord Selkirk's rich Red River valley, and in exchange Great Britain got the sage brush, cactus, and rattlesnakes of what is now southern Saskatchewan and Alberta.

The next border dispute concerned the boundary between Maine and New Brunswick. Here again, little could be made out of the words of the original treaty, which talked about "the north-west angle of Nova Scotia", "the highlands", and other such obscurities. Arbitration in the 1820's had failed, and in the 1830's local rivalries for the pine timber of the tract under dispute almost led to bloodshed and war: in fact a New Brunswick-Maine war was on the point of breaking out in 1839[2] when it was stopped by the good sense of the two metropolitan authorities. Three years later a joint commission concluded the Webster-Ashburton Treaty, which defined the present boundary. At the time it was unsparingly condemned by colonials as sheer British surrender, but more recently it has been considered that under the unfortunate terms of 1783, Ashburton got as much as could have been expected.

The Atlantic end of the boundary was no sooner settled than domestic American agitation rendered necessary the determination of the Pacific, after nearly a generation during which sovereignty over the regions between Russian and Spanish territory had been exercised jointly by the United States and Great Britain. The conquest of California, the annexation of Texas, and the battle cry of the presidential campaign of 1844, "Fifty-Four Forty or Fight", must all be considered aspects of the same wave of "Manifest Destiny" which, having accomplished these great feats of expansionism, reached its crest in the 1840's. The "Oregon Question" was settled by the Treaty of 1846, which extended the line of 49° N. (in 1818 this had stopped at the mountains) through to the coast and thence around the southern tip of Vancouver Island. Although the Americans had formed a small settlement near the mouth of the Columbia, they had no claim by occupancy to anything north of that spot. But they were determined to secure a port on Puget Sound and

The so-called Aroostook, or Lumbermen's War.

their truculence frightened into acquiescence the old woman who had so many colonial children that she didn't know what to do.

The Oregon Treaty had left undetermined the exact channel through the Gulf Islands, which lie between Vancouver Island and the mainland. By the Treaty of Washington, 1871, this was submitted to the arbitration of the German Emperor: the American claim was confirmed, depriving Canada of a satisfactory channel to the open sea. Four years before, the American purchase of Alaska had also cut off the northern interior from the coast, down to 54° 40′.

This rather successful effort to restrict the access of a British colony to the Pacific ocean had its logical completion in the settlement of the Alaska Boundary dispute in 1903.[3] The dispute arose out of the interpretation of the original Anglo-Russian treaty of 1825, which left it uncertain whether the boundary of the Alaska "panhandle" was to be based on a given distance from the open sea or from the heads of inlets. After a good deal of manoeuvring, it was agreed to submit the case to a judicial tribunal, to meet in London. Great Britain appointed a British judge and two Canadian lawyers. The United States appointed the Secretary of State, Elihu Root, Senator Henry Cabot Lodge, a notorious Anglophobe, and Senator Turner from the state of Washington, whose chief city, Seattle, represented the main American vested interests in the territory in dispute, which in essence was Skagway, the port of entry to the Klondike gold fields. The "court" was divided up to the last moment, on national lines of course, and then Lord Alverstone, the British member, gave way. The British government had been told confidentially, but plainly, by Theodore Roosevelt, then President of the United States, that if the "verdict" did not correspond with his desires, he would draw the boundary according to them anyway.[4] Alverstone therefore obligingly changed his judicial opinions, and a four to two finding against the Canadians was brought in. The Canadian representatives may not have been any more impartial than the Americans, but whether they were or not, the Canadian government surely revealed weakness in accepting such a tribunal. At best all that could have been expected was disagreement, and the record of previous boundary negotiations must have made the actual result little of a surprise. "The completeness of the victory is amazing; all that 'poor Canada' got by the decision was the title to two small islands."[5]

The Alaska Boundary Dispute ended that particular and dangerous type of contention. The controversy arising out of the fishery clauses

[3] Very fully discussed in C. C. Tansill, *Canadian-American Relations*, Chaps. 5-9.
[4] See Tansill, p. 258.
[5] U.S. Secretary of State, John Hay, quoted in Tansill, p. 263.

of the Treaty of 1783, was more amenable to arrangement, though interminable in the time it took for liquidation. In 1783, the United States had obtained the right to fish along the British coasts. The British at Ghent (1814) holding that this right had been abrogated by the War of 1812-14, a new arrangement was effected under the Convention of 1818: by it, American fishermen were given the privilege of landing and drying their fish on unsettled shores in Newfoundland, but lost it in the other provinces. Their vessels could only enter harbour for water, wood, and necessary repairs; that is, they had no right to buy bait, ice, or supplies, or to load and unload. Whether bays whose headlands were more than six miles apart were closed waters or not remained in dispute. Matters went along comparatively smoothly on a basis of covert mutual interest (Maritime bait and port facilities in return for American smuggled goods) until, in the late thirties, the provinces began strict enforcement of the terms of the Convention. Then seizures of trespassing American schooners soon engendered a serious situation, which was not ended until the Reciprocity Treaty of 1854 gave their former privileges back to American fishermen, on a reciprocal basis and allowed the free entry of colonial fish into American ports.[6]

On the abrogation of the Treaty, the Convention became the law again, and once more friction arose. The new Canadian government began, not to exclude the Americans, but to charge them a tonnage duty. This the American fishermen, many of them former Nova Scotians who had moved down to Gloucester, resented and tried to evade. The resulting seizures, which were really few in number, as every schooner was given two warnings before action was taken, were made much of by the Americans, and the subject was put down on the agenda for the Washington Conference of 1871. Out of this conference, to which Sir John Macdonald was appointed by the British government as one of the five British commissioners (and virtually in a representative Canadian capacity), came the Treaty of Washington, 1871, one of the most significant international statutes of the nineteenth century. Settling most of the dangerous points of friction between the United States and Great Britain which had arisen as a result of the Civil War, it might well be called the third treaty of peace between the two nations.[7]

Canada was interested in two major subjects: claims for damages resulting from the Fenian raids, and some resolution of the fisheries difficulty. Careless preparation both in England and Canada resulted in the Fenian claims being left off the agenda, and Macdonald's efforts to get them discussed met with no success. On the fisheries question he had

[6] See p. 281.
[7] See Goldwin Smith, *Treaty of Washington, 1871*.

little support from his British colleagues. According to him, their sole idea was to get a settlement of the British points (such as the "Alabama" claims) and, regardless of Canadian interests, return to England as quickly as possible. He had to come to the verge of withdrawing from the conference before he could secure much attention to the Canadian fisheries case, and the most he was able to get was that in return for the former privileges accorded for a period of twelve years or longer, the United States would pay a cash compensation, the amount to be determined by an arbitration commission. Macdonald was bitterly criticized on his return home for having "betrayed" the Canadian cause, but he revealed no hint of what had actually gone on and urged acceptance of the Treaty in the general interests of the Empire.

As it turned out, the award of the Arbitration Commission in 1877, from a money point of view, was in Canada's favour.[8] Later on, in 1885, the United States exercised its right to terminate the arrangement, and once more the Convention of 1818 became the law. A *modus vivendi*, based on tonnage duties, was, after some difficulty, again worked out, and eventually in 1910, this running sore, becoming less significant because of the relative decline of the fisheries interests, was healed by reference to an arbitral tribunal drawn from the Permanent Court at the Hague. The points at issue for 127 years were decided mostly in accordance with the traditional British interpretation.

The two periods of internal disturbance[9] in some respects were more dangerous to the peace than boundary and fishery disputes. In 1837-38 American raiders repeatedly committed crimes of arson and murder; the American authorities, although "correct" throughout the period, were for some time lax in their efforts to restrain them. Canadians had to swallow their indignation as best they could. The Civil War disturbances originating on Canadian soil, against which the Canadian government acted with a fair degree of energy, were greeted by torrents of indignation from Americans, and for a time the situation was most acute. The Fenian Raids, in which again there was laxity on the American side, were much more formidable but again Canadians had to make the best of the situation. It was clever tactics on the part of the Americans to keep the Raids off the agenda of the Treaty of Washington, but in that kind of nimble footwork, the British were no match for the Yankees.

In these episodes Canadian indignation was not directed against the

[8] Tansill, p. 12. The U.S. paid about eight times as much as the fish caught by Americans were worth. Tansill gives a very complete discussion of the later stages of the fisheries controversy.
[9] Discussed at pp. 254, 300, 322

United States, which was only playing its cards well, so much as against the mother country, which invariably let Canada down. After repeated demonstrations, it was slowly beginning to dawn upon Canadians that British policy was not based upon sentimentality but upon hard realism, and that the mistake would never be made of sacrificing the major consideration, correct relations with the United States, to the interests of a mere colony. The United States was the only power against which Canada was likely to need protection, and by the twentieth century, it had become evident that against the republic Great Britain could not afford protection. If Canadians wished to get justice in their American disputes, they would have to get it for themselves. As they began to manage their own business, relations improved, and eventually became cordial. In the period after the First World War, when the United States for the first time was able to discern Canada as a personality in her own right, free of the stigma of being a British colony, they reached high peaks of friendship and, for Canada, of justice.

2. The Canadian View of "The British Connection"

Jealousy and fear of the American, that estranged and too successful elder brother, lies in the very origin of the English-speaking Canadian, but for Great Britain he has had all the affection of a child for its mother. This filial attitude evolved in much the same way as that of individuals. At first there was hardly any sense of a different identity, then the irresponsibilities of the small boy manifested themselves. Next came the uncertainties and sudden antagonisms of adolescence, followed by the growing confidence of early manhood, not without over-sensitiveness at any display of the parental authority just ended. Lastly the separate establishment of married life entailed growing concern in one's own family affairs. Thanks to the War of 1812, French-speaking Canadians too were partly caught up in the relationship. While they never shared the sentimentalism of English Canadians towards that emotionally supercharged concept "Britain" and never forgot that they had been conquered into the British Empire, they did come to give their political allegiance to the British Crown. As Sir Wilfrid Laurier used to say, France had given them their life and their culture, but Great Britain had given them freedom, so, with few exceptions, they were correctly loyal British subjects. For both the Canadian peoples, the British connection has been a constant conscious counterweight against the power of the magnet to the south. To the English Canadians, it has been emotionally heightened by the concept of Empire: they have pictured themselves as part of a ruling race, whose mission it was to carry "British and Christian civilization" (in the late nineteenth century the two words were equated) to the ends of the earth.[10]

It is not surprising, then, that Canadian attitudes towards the outside world should always have been so heavy with emotion as to hinder the growth of a native Canadian patriotism and, as a rule, exclude rational discussion. In all debate on foreign relations, whatever the immediate issue, there has been an *arrière pensée*:—"will this proposal take us closer to (farther from) Britain?—the States?" Canada is perpetually divided between the forces of history and geography, tradition and environment. All the public symbols, such as flag and king, represent tradition. Those, therefore, who have wished to accept the environment and allow the forces of history to take care of themselves have invariably insulted the public conscience and incurred the ready accusations of treason and sedition. Yet so strong is environment that native forces have not failed to make themselves felt. In Canada the intersecting influences of the two older and more powerful communities have greatly retarded the process of building a Canadian community with a life and personality of its own.[11]

The relations of Canada to the world beyond her doors illustrate the foregoing generalizations. Not until the Reciprocity Treaty of 1854, negotiated by the Governor-General on behalf of the British Government, did the colonies have official relationship with the country next door to them. When "John A." went to Washington in 1871, it was legally as a British commissioner, not as Prime Minister of Canada. Similarly, Sir A. T. Galt later on had little success in securing for himself, as Canadian "High Commissioner" to London, any recognition other than that of a colonial agent, and the trade treaties made during his own and his successor, Sir Charles Tupper's, incumbency of the post, had (at first in fact, though afterward in form) to be negotiated by British diplomats. At this there is no occasion for surprise, for even as late as 1914 few English Canadians thought of themselves in any other

---

[10] "I do not believe the British Empire is an accident. I believe the miracles of this war are indeed miracles and that we have survived and will continue to do so because we have a divine mission to rule the world."—Lord Bennett, formerly Rt. Hon. R. B. Bennett, Prime Minister of Canada, 1930-35, as reported in the *Winnipeg Free Press,* Dec. 16, 1943.

[11] "You [Canadians] are so busy proving to the English that you are not Yankees and proving to the Yankees that you are not English that you have no time to be yourselves at all."—quoted in Judith Robinson, "Canada's Split Personality," *Foreign Affairs,* XXII (Oct., 1943), 70. This idea might be expressed in other terms by the statement that Canada consists in the intersection of the east-west British axis and the north-south American, but that the intersection of two lines is a point and a point is that which has position but no magnitude!

light than that of British subjects overseas. Since autonomy in foreign relations would have meant independence, it could hardly even be contemplated, and the small groups that from time to time thought in that direction, such as the "Canada First" movement of the seventies, the independence groups of the eighties, or John S. Ewart and his few followers in the twentieth century, had little effect on public opinion.

On the contrary, it was in the eighties that the "Imperial Federation" movement arose, whose purpose was to bind the Empire together in a federation that would have cancelled the autonomy that had already been secured.[12] A. T. Galt leaned toward this, but no other responsible statesman favoured it, and it eventually proved abortive. In 1885 Sir John Macdonald took a decided step away from centralization when he made it clear that, since "Gladstone and Co." had got themselves into a mess in the Sudan over General Gordon, they could get themselves out without expecting any aid from Canada. But perhaps in few fields were statesmen less representative: the fundamental emotions of the English-speaking wing of the Canadian people, rarely exhibited except in periods of public excitement, were simply and automatically "British"; with the events in the next decade centring around the Diamond Jubilee and the Boer War, this was made abundantly clear.

When Rudyard Kipling began to write of lesser breeds, Cecil Rhodes to talk Germanic nonsense about the divine mission of the Teutonic races, and Doctor Jameson to conduct his private invasion of the Transvaal, many English-Canadian hearts bounded in accord: here were the roles that they could not play in peaceful Canada but to whose performance abroad they might thrill in vicarious ecstasy. When the Jameson Raid (1895) was capped by Diamond Jubilee (1897), their pent-up urges were unstopped and the country poured itself out in demonstrations of jingoistic rejoicing. All that was needed was a foe, and that the Boers soon obligingly provided. Laurier, the Frenchman, might hesitate as to whether aid should be given to Great Britain, but the English-speaking people of Canada did not hesitate, and if Lord Minto's[13] and General Hutton's[14] efforts to make Laurier commit himself and Canada had been made publicly known, they would have been cordially approved.

The Boer War (1899-1901) raised once more the whole issue of race. To the French it constituted the price, but to the English the pride, of Empire. These latter saw themselves as young lions, bounding to the aid

[12] See p. 393.
[13] Governor-General, 1898-1904.
[14] A British Major-General, in command of the Canadian Militia, 1898-1900.

of the old lion without inquiring the cause or justice of his quarrel. But the French saw the Boers as another small people of alien speech attacked as they had been attacked and by the same foe. "There but for the grace of God, go I," they might have exclaimed. They were especially fearful of contributions of men; for that seemed to them to lead to the whole dreaded Imperialistic programme of English foreign wars fought on colonial manpower. Henri Bourassa and the Nationalist movement in Quebec[15] were the results. The Boer War was a touchstone—"Are you for England and the Empire or are you for Canada?" was the question it asked, and for the most part it was answered in racial terms.

Despite French opposition Canada did contribute a considerable force to the British armies and the men sent gave a splendid account of themselves. French Canadians had no objection to English Canadians going off to the wars if they wished, especially if they did not return, but they did object to having to pay the bills and to seeing established the precedent which Joseph Chamberlain made no secret of considering more important than actual aid. The divisions generated out of the Boer War were to be reproduced with singular fidelity and with greater intensity in the First World War, and in much the same fashion in the Second. It was hard to align the viewpoints of two peoples, one of whom its history and connections had accustomed to think outward all over the world, wherever its kin were scattered, and for whom its metropolitan centre had the bright colours that only the distant scene possesses; the other of whom had little memory of anything but a parochial existence on the banks of the St. Lawrence which was its entire world, possessed almost no interests outside of its own parishes, and was possessed by the complete absorption in itself that characterizes the French race.

3. Sir Wilfrid Laurier's View of External Policy

Sir Wilfrid had come into office with hope of carrying out the task to which his life was consecrated, bringing harmony between the two races. His, too, it seemed, was to be the privilege of leading Canada into the promised land of twentieth-century achievement. History played him an ironical trick when it plagued him from his first official day to his last with distractions from abroad. No sooner had he stood off Chamberlain's centralizing ambitions at the Diamond Jubilee than he had to conduct the country through the passions raised by the Boer War.

[15] See p. 434.

Thereafter at each Imperial Conference he had to take the lead among the colonial prime ministers in avoiding military and political commitments which would have cut deep into autonomy. That would have been hard enough for an English-speaking statesman; it was doubly hard for a French, for the epithet "disloyal" lay constantly in wait for him from both sides.

Laurier's position had been enunciated once and for all in the debates on Canada's contribution to the Boer War.

> While I cannot admit that Canada should take part in all the wars of Great Britain neither am I prepared to say that she should not take part in any war at all. . . . I claim for Canada this, that in future she shall be at liberty to act, or not to act, to interfere or not to interfere, to do just as she pleases.[16]

Sir Wilfrid, however, by no means meant that Canada was at liberty to be neutral while Great Britain was at war. In a still more famous passage, he used the words "When Great Britain is at war Canada is at war".[17] Long before the First World War he foresaw the necessity of distinction between secondary conflicts and those in which the very existence of Great Britain was at stake,[18] and of these latter he recognized that Canada neither could nor should keep out. What he meant by his original pronouncement was that Canada must be the judge of the degree of her participation. Passive belligerency was possible in secondary wars because there was little concern as to the ultimate outcome and because the enemy could not injure Canada, but this reasoning could not apply to major wars.

Sir Wilfrid's position has stood the test of two major wars. When he defined it, he probably had in mind the embarrassing English efforts to influence him into sending troops to South Africa for the sake of precedent. His formula was a declaration of independence—from English pressure; it was not a declaration of independence. As the First World War approached, he saw clearly how unavoidable participation would be, and loyally played his part as Leader of the Opposition in seconding the Government's efforts. Canada's actions were in line with his doctrine: the extent of her participation was a matter for her own judgement, and the British Government, acting with perfect propriety, in contrast with the Boer War, made neither request nor exhortation. In the Second World War, the position had advanced still further and

[16] February, 1900. Quoted in Skelton, *Laurier,* II, 105.
[17] In the Naval Debate of 1910.
[18] As, for example, the speech of March 29, 1909. Quoted in Skelton, II, 321.

Canada asserted for a symbolical week her right of neutrality. Sir Wilfrid's position was that which every Prime Minister of Canada, whatever his words, has in practice taken and must take: the guiding principle in Canadian action outside the country as well as inside must be not colonial sentimentalism but the best and highest interests of Canada.

4. A Distant World, The Orient: Relations with Japan, 1893-1913

Canadians have always thought backward across the Atlantic, rather then forward across the Pacific: they still refer to the western shores of the Pacific as "the Far East". Yet when they began to live on the west coast, they had to discover sooner or later that something more than water lay over the horizon. It was during the two decades before the First World War that the Orient began to impinge upon Canada.

Even before its completion the Canadian Pacific Railway had begun to arrange for steamer service across the Pacific. Most of the British Columbian sections of the road had been built by Chinese labour, and that experience had decided British Columbians that the Asiatic was not going to be allowed to crowd into their province and swamp its white population. Against the Chinese, Canada built up such defences as the "head-tax",[19] but after the British in 1894 made their Treaty of Commerce and Navigation with Japan, official discrimination against the Japanese became impossible. Then in 1902, the Anglo-Japanese Alliance was concluded. Of this Japan availed herself in 1904, in her attack on Russia. Russia being seen by Canadians only through British eyes, and Japan having become "our gallant ally", her stock went up in Canada to rather fantastic heights. The Japanese were the heroes of the hour.

After the war, the heroes began to arrive in British Columbia. This was quite another matter; the heroes being most appreciated at a distance, an agitation arose to keep them out. As a result, one of Sir Wilfrid's ministers, Mr. Rodolphe Lemieux, travelled to Japan and there negotiated the celebrated "Gentlemen's Agreement" of Dec. 23, 1907. The Japanese Government gave a letter in which it indicated its willingness to restrict emigration and stated that it did "not contemplate that under existing circumstances the number of emigrants who will go to Canada as household servants and agricultural labourers will exceed four hundred annually".[20] It yielded none of its right under the Treaty

[19] The head tax was increased at intervals from $50 to $500.
[20] Canada, House of Commons, Sessional Paper No. 126J, July 17, 1943, p. 3.

of 1894, but the Canadian Government had substantially obtained its object. What was perhaps more, after the sharp lesson taught by the Alaska Boundary award of the futility of relying on the British Government, it had gone directly to its mark and had negotiated the arrangement itself.

"The Gentlemen's Agreement" is the first important Canadian essay into independent diplomacy and a successful one: the limitation which, as a *modus vivendi*, worked fairly well for 34 years, could not possibly have been negotiated by the British allies of Japan. Yet Canada succeeded in cutting down Japanese immigration to relatively small proportions and not disturbing the military alliance which was to prove so significant at the outbreak of the First World War. The proof of this lay in the renewal in 1911, by Great Britain, of the original Treaty of Navigation and Commerce, and Canada's adherence to it two years later. On the approach of war, Canada's western gateway proved to be politically, if not navally, well secured.

5. The European Shadow

During the Boer War the people of practically all the great powers (including the United States) had been hostile in feeling towards Great Britain. Their governments had been officially correct, no government more so than that of Emperor William II of Germany. But the Emperor's previous tactless speeches, with such phrases flung about as "Our future is on the sea", "The trident of Neptune must be in our hands" were not forgotten by the British. Nor did Germans fail to read the lessons of the war: that nation which would grasp the trident of Neptune must have a powerful navy. Joseph Chamberlain's courtship of Germany failed, for German officials saw that England needed her alliance more than she needed England's. England then turned to Japan and later to France. When she buried the hatchet with the French and in the Convention of April, 1904, liquidated sources of friction the world over (such as the "French Shore" of Newfoundland), she had for practical purposes ranged herself on France's side against the central powers. The two great groups were solidifying—France, Russia and England on the one side, and Germany, Austria and a doubtful Italy on the other; Europe was balanced against itself, and it was becoming plain that mastery could be decided only by the arbitrament of war.

Few Canadians either understood or were interested in what was going on. Everyone was absorbed in the opening west and in the golden future. The Boer War had been quickly forgotten, and the Alaska Boundary award had given the necessary douche of cold water to the jingoism associated with it. Backs had been turned on the bad, old world, and Canada was becoming more and more concerned with her own domestic evolution. Rumours were heard from time to time of a projected increase in the German navy being matched by a greater one in the British. There was mild applause when Sir John Fisher brought out the first "all big gun" ship, his *Dreadnought*, but not enough knowledge to understand the naval implications of a boomeranging innovation that at a stroke gave the Germans a fair chance of naval equality. To most Canadians in the happy 1900's, God, that is, the appropriate British authorities, seemed to be in his Heaven and all to be right indeed with their own particular world.

The first awakening did not come until 1909, and even then it was not complete. On March 29 of that year, Hon. George E. Foster, the outstanding orator of the Conservative Opposition and a typical New Brunswick Loyalist-Imperialist, moved a resolution in one of his powerful speeches advocating a Canadian navy and, if the Prime Minister desired, an emergency gift to Great Britain of a dreadnought. The speech really marked the public crystallization of a campaign that had been waged ever since the Boer War by Imperialistic groups in Canada, to implement Chamberlain's plans for a centrally defended empire. During periods of international quiet, the public in Canada has quickly lost interest in foreign and imperial affairs, but the centres which harbour this specific inheritance, such as Toronto and Saint John, have kept their propaganda going: they have organized fresh militia battalions and Empire Clubs and have gained possession of Canadian clubs. Their testifying to the official faith of the country could not very well be objected to, but when nationalist elements which, as little more than protest groups, have never possessed much organization, have lifted up their voices in dissonant accents, charges of dissent and heresy have always been available. When emotional stress was engendered by an international situation in which Great Britain was concerned, the ancestral war-drums could be heard sounding, awaking response in the dormant impulses of the English-speaking people.

Among French-speaking Canadians, precisely the same gamut is run through but in the opposite direction: among them, it is the French racial cause that is kept hot by the few, and when the pressure goes on, it is racial and anti-English sentiments that come to the top. Each crisis therefore sees the two races go in opposite directions.

So it had been between the Boer War and 1909. Toronto Tories on the one side had been matched by the Bourassas on the other, and now with Mr. Foster's speech, the issue had been flung to the general public. The winter (of 1909) had seen a strong British agitation for a great dreadnought building programme, based on the calculation that by 1912 Germany would have more dreadnoughts than the United Kingdom. This had been transferred to Canada and formed the principal staple of the campaign. The prediction turned out to be inaccurate, but the situation was admittedly fraught with peril, and although it was only one aspect of the total European picture, it was the one most easily grasped in Canada. Left to himself the native Canadian, English or French, would not have concerned himself much with the defence problems of his own country, let alone those of others. But the ordinary man has rarely been left to himself. He has been orated at, and being an ordinary man, he has responded to oratory. In the Canada of 1909 and 1910, imperialistic orators were stirring up the English, and nationalist orators the French. The Government of the day was in the middle, looking for the course that would antagonize the fewest people. This also was a logical position for a party that had outlived its crusading days. Laurier Liberalism had come of age:[21] it had the tolerance that sometimes comes with maturity, but beyond the ideal of Canadian harmony and its general adherence to the freedom of the *laisser-faire* state, it had no positive social programme. It, therefore, was fated to do that which offended most men the least. In Laurier's opinion, this meant, at that specific time, setting up a Canadian navy. Such a programme would take away from the English press the opportunity of renewing the former jibes against Canada as lacking in self-respect. Since the Canadian fleet could be put under British command in time of war, it would help meet the emergency, and should thus satisfy the Canadian imperialists. It would be a national effort and as such should appeal to the patriotism of a budding nation. All the arguments seemed to support the Laurier policy of a Canadian navy. Even the Opposition appeared to approve.

But when the issue got into the press and on the platform, quite another situation developed. It became the subject of one of the usual bitter Canadian dogfights. That is, Bourassa's Nationalists from Quebec accused Laurier of betraying his race, while Tory imperialists poured scorn on the very conception of a national navy. It was Premier Roblin of inland Manitoba who first dubbed the Canadian navy in advance "a tin-pot navy". Other Conservative provincial leaders came out for direct and permanent contributions to the Royal Navy. The Government was attacked from both flanks.

It nevertheless persevered with its scheme. The Federal Opposition under R. L. Borden proved more responsible than the Conservatives

outside the House; Mr. Borden approved the idea of a Canadian navy,
but he was for meeting "the emergency" by a direct money contribution
for dreadnoughts. The Liberals held this to be the negation of Responsible Government. They pushed ahead with their programme, which was
really a considerable one: five cruisers and six destroyers were proposed,
to be stationed on both coasts. A naval college was to be established.
Provision was made for naval personnel. In an emergency the governor-
general-in-council might place the Canadian navy under Admiralty
control, but Parliament must be called upon to approve as soon as practicable. If this programme had been implemented, Canada would have
had in the First World War a respectable navy instead of two floating
death-traps and the motley collection of yachts and fishing vessels that
she actually possessed—a "tin-pot navy" in bitter truth—and her sons
who fought at sea would not have had to go abroad to serve in the ships
of another country.

Sir Wilfrid carried his proposals through Parliament, but it was
evident that the battle had only started. Mr. Bourassa and his men,
Mr. Monk, lieutenant to R. L. Borden in the Commons, and many
other Conservatives vigorously continued the campaign. The combination of Anglo-Canadian imperialist and French-Canadian nationalist which finally defeated him had begun to form.[22] A by-election in the
riding in which lay Sir Wilfrid's own old home, Drummond-Arthabaska,
November 3, 1910, gave them their opportunity. Every effort was made
to defeat the Liberal candidate.[23] Canada hung on the result, for his
defeat would be tantamount to a vote of want of confidence in Laurier
by his own people. The Liberal candidate was defeated. By some
strange logic, Ontario Conservatives interpreted the Nationalist success
as a victory for their views.

Sir Wilfrid was not dismayed by the result, but he saw clearly what
store of trouble it meant for Canada. A year or two earlier he had
given an excellent statement of his political *credo* in a letter to an
Ontario friend.[24] Severance of the British connection, he admitted,
would "do more to assure our safety than building of warships". But he
considered that the benefits of the connection outweighed its liabilities.
Moreover, no "happy, free, content and prosperous" people would ever
move to change its political condition. Canada, in any case, was a nation
and must assume a nation's responsibilities, among which was self-
defence. As a nation "it is the most anomalous that has ever existed".
Consequently no statesman could ever follow the ideal policy; every

[22] See p. 434.
[23] See the summary of the arguments used in Skelton, II, 338.
[24] Skelton, II, 331.

course must offend some section or group to a greater or less degree, and therefore the only way was to follow the course which made the greatest appeal to the greatest number. Here was his doctrine of harmony, of the golden mean, of conciliation—one of the most characteristic marks of the Liberalism of his time.

Just over a year elapsed between the passage of the Laurier Naval Act and the defeat of the Liberal Government on Sept. 21, 1911. It then fell to R. L. Borden's unique crew of Imperialists and anti-Imperialists to take over the ship. Mr. Borden had himself apparently not taken a highly centralizing view of empire until pressure began to mount from the former of these two groups. He then began to swing to the tide. His government did nothing to implement the Laurier programme and it soon became apparent that the goal was contribution to the Royal Navy and the abandonment of the idea of a separate Canadian navy. To this there began to be added the suggestion that Canada (and the other Dominions) should share in the direction of British foreign policy. The schemes for some kind of Federation now seemed about to be revived, this time with Canada as their sponsor.

Sir Robert Borden went to England in the summer of 1912 and there he was advised by the Admiralty that the most effective aid he could give Great Britain would be some of "the largest and strongest ships of war which science can build or money supply". Sir Robert was not so immune as was Sir Wilfrid to metropolitan influences, and so he came back with any ideas for a Canadian navy laid aside and the scheme for contributing to Great Britain $35,000,000 to enable that country to build three extra dreadnoughts.[25] The debate on that measure brought out every shade of opinion in the country on the relationship of Canada to Great Britain, the Empire, and the world, but amid such abundant clarification there was little novelty: Canadians still were divided into French Nationalists who wished to do nothing whatever, Tory jingoes who were ready to sacrifice their all on the altar of Empire (especially, as Sir Wilfrid said, if there were good prospect of high posts and senior commissions), moderate Conservatives who wished to aid Great Britain if she were in peril, without much concern over abstract questions of autonomy, centre Liberals who differed from them only in degree of their concern for Canadian self-government, and those Liberals, who embraced a full-fledged policy of national autonomy and responsibility.

Sir Robert several times cited, as his guiding star, the opinion and advice of a young man, not so well-known then as he afterwards became, the First Lord of the Admiralty, Mr. Winston Churchill, who

* See p. 452.

kept sending him bolstering arguments during the course of the debate. "Mr. Churchill demonstrated that Canadians could not build battleships, that they could not and Great Britain would not, man their cruisers, and that they could not maintain a navy in efficiency. His naively frank argument for the perpetual use of British rather than Canadian shipyards and for permanent Admiralty control, 'the most irritating document from authority in Britain since the days of Lord North'. . ." intensified national feeling in Canada and stiffened Liberal opposition.[26]

After the Senate's rejection of the Borden proposals, the country more or less forgot the issue. It was always glad to forget the defence issue, for one of the aspects of colonialism, which state of mind had barely begun to dissipate, is irresponsibility. Sir Robert seemed relatively pleased to forget it, too: his days of colonial-mindedness had passed their zenith; thenceforth he travelled closer and closer to the goal of nationhood. Meanwhile in Europe, the furious Balkan blood-lettings of 1912 and 1913 seemed to give a certain relief to the patient, and the period from the middle of 1913 to the middle of 1914 was one of relative calm. The thoughts of all North Americans, Canadians included, were far away from the Old World when the news of the assassinations at Sarajevo came out. But they, too, seemed no more than additional examples of Europeans' normal mode of conducting their affairs.

Then suddenly, six weeks later, Europe was ablaze and for Canadians, though they did not know it at the time, their accustomed course of life, that interesting and happy life of rolling back the wilderness and building a civilization "from the ground up", was forever changed. For the first time since the great wars of the eighteenth century, they were to be launched into the bottomless sea of European discord, there, with the aid of like-minded peoples, either to impose their own ideas of decency and neighbourliness upon nations that had little conception of such things, or to remain forever involved in Europe's endless civil wars.

Chronology

1842	The Webster-Ashburton Treaty (New Brunswick-Maine Boundary).
1846	The Oregon Treaty.
1871	The Treaty of Washington.
1892	The Bering Sea Arbitration.
1894	The British Treaty of Commerce and Navigation with Japan: 1906 adhered to by Canada.
1897	The Diamond Jubilee of Queen Victoria.

[26] Skelton, II, 409.

1899–1902 The Boer War.
1902   The Anglo-Japanese Alliance.
1903   The Alaska Boundary Award.
1907   Dec. 23: The "Gentlemen's Agreement" with Japan.
1909   The Joint International High Commission.
1910   The Laurier Naval Act.
1912   The Borden Naval Bill.
1914   August 4: Great Britain declares war on Germany.
1887, 1894, 1897, 1902, 1907, 1911 Colonial and Imperial Conferences.

Additional Reading

Amery, Julian. *The Life of Joseph Chamberlain.* Vol. 4. London, 1951.

Dewey, A. G. *The Dominions and Diplomacy.* Toronto, 1929.

Jebb, R. *The Imperial Conference: A History and Study.* London, 1911.

Neatby, H. Blair. "Laurier and Liberalism." (*CHA Annual Report 1955*), 24-32.

Ollivier, M., ed. *The Colonial and Imperial Conferences from 1887 to 1937.* Ottawa, 1954. 3 vols.

Sinclair, K. *Imperial Federation, 1880-1914.* London, 1955.

Stacey, C. P. *The Military Problems of Canada.* Toronto, 1940.

Thornton, A. P. *The Imperial Idea and Its Enemies.* London, 1959.

Tucker, G. N. "The Naval Policy of Sir Robert Borden, 1912-1914." *CHR*, XXVIII (March, 1947), 1-30.

——. *The Naval Service of Canada.* Ottawa, 1952.

Wallace, W. S. *The Memoirs of the Rt. Honourable Sir George Foster.* Toronto, 1933.

Woodward, E. L. *Great Britain and the German Navy.* London, 1935.

CHAPTER 31

<hr>

The First German War

<hr>

The first German war might with some logic be regarded as having begun with the victory of Bismarck's Prussia over France in 1871. "Europe has lost a mistress and gained a master", it was said at the time. No words were to prove truer. The German Empire grew swiftly in industrial power, in population, and in technical achievement, but not in self-government. Boding more ill for the world than the lack of interest in self-government, however, were the ideas that informed German minds. At the end of the eighteenth century, German philosophers had turned their backs on the rationalism of the west and proceeded to create for themselves a cloudy edifice of romantic idealism. Out of it came the cult of the hero, reflected in England by that Victorian Nazi, Thomas Carlyle, and symbolized magnificently in Germany by Wagner in his operatic dramas, with their gods and supermen strutting about the stage.

To it was joined a misapplication of Darwin's theories about the survival of the fittest. Darwin's "those who survive must be the fittest" was twisted in Germany into "we are the fittest and therefore we have a right to survive". The doctrines of the warped and difficult philosopher Nietsche brought the edifice close to completion. It awaited only the appearance of such men as the historian Treitschke, with their Hegelian teachings, to popularize the idea of the completely sovereign, irresponsible, amoral state, beyond law because complete in itself, as God is beyond law. The cult of the hero, the dark mystery of the racial blood, the twisting of Darwinism in its Nietschean doctrines of "The Lords of the Earth", the amoral state as a vehicle of power for these concepts, and a strong people "drenched in army worship"—all these were portents of the tempest that was to break on Europe. German idealistic philosophy and its perversions touched action at every point, from soldiers to business men, giving a belief in power and a conviction of destiny that, joined to the capacities of the German people, could have had no other result than a world explosion.

The explosion, as is invariably the case with events long expected, took men completely by surprise. Yet German philosophy had been heavily reinforced by growing German commercial and naval rivalry with England, and this alone perhaps might have sooner or later produced such another duel as England and France had fought years before. In addition, the balance of power built up against just such an eventuality as a general war, ended in so delicate a poise that little was needed to tilt it one way or another. The obscure events in the Balkans supplied that little, and by August, Europe was aflame.

1. The Canadian Response

In that placid summer of 1914, Canadian thoughts were far away from Europe. It is true that "times had become bad", but no one believed the check to expansion to be more than momentary. Canadians had gone at the subjugation of nature with a frenzy of efficient energy. Great physical tasks, requiring not abstract thought or social wisdom but concrete planning and vigorous execution, requiring the engineering mind, had revealed them at their best as bold, courageous organizers of accomplishment.

Suddenly the outbreak of the war called on humanity for just these qualities. Canadians responded to the call as if they were building a new railroad. The qualities that had served them well in their fight against the wilderness could now be directed into the making of war. Men who were familiar with life in the bush, who could use firearms and shift for themselves in the open, were soldiers, whether they knew it or not. Canada's war effort might be described as frontier energy in the trenches.

"He could imagine nothing less likely," Lord Morley had once said, in commenting upon the distance growing up between the new world and the old, "than men from some American country such as Canada fighting for the neutrality of Belgium." Yet in August, 1914, such men were so fighting. Few of those enlisting, we may be sure, did so out of intellectual conviction but rather because their ancestral feelings had been aroused for Great Britain. In that summer of 1914, with work camps shut down everywhere, Canadians were psychologically ready for war. All that energy of accomplishment, suddenly dammed up, had to spill over somewhere: what more natural than that it should divert itself into the new channel? Canadians might profess to be peace-loving people, and except for the few to whom it was an avenue of social prestige, they were not fond of "soldiering", but it does not take much to rouse the fighting instincts of a people strong in accomplishment. To the more jingoistic among them, the Boer War had been a little *hors d'oeuvre*, and now the real banquet was at hand. English Canada rushed to war with enthusiasm.

Men from Great Britain were among the first to go. Numbers of recent immigrants were left without work when the western "boom" broke, and many of these, in addition to their desire to fight for England, were glad to move into the army. But the native-born, though more secure in employment and status, soon began to leave their jobs and enlist, and succeeding contingents showed larger and larger proportions of them. To those longest away from Great Britain by descent and farthest away from the world influences of the times, to men, for example, on distant farms where their fathers had been born before them, the European struggle must have seemed remote, and they developed the least interest in it; the great and continuing wonder is that such an amazingly high proportion of the population should take such an immediate, personal interest in a distant struggle waged for purposes not well understood.

Before the war had ended, Canada had enrolled nearly three-quarters of a million men. She began with one division, under the command of a British general, and ended with a corps of four divisions, plus supporting troops and reinforcements, under the command of one of her own sons, Sir Arthur Currie—a general who was in no respect more typically Canadian than in that before the war he had been a real estate agent. In addition to her army, Canada formed a small coast-guard navy, sent some men into the British navy, and contributed a large proportion of the flying personnel of the entire British air force. If she had wished to prove to herself that she was a fighting nation, she could not have acted more convincingly. There was no form of fighting in which her sons were not outstanding.[1] It was her troops that encountered and withstood the first shock of the Germans' pleasant new wrinkle, gas warfare. Her sons died by the thousands in the mud of Flanders, they captured Vimy Ridge, broke the Hindenburg line, and

---

[1] Some 65 Victoria Crosses awarded to Canadians bear testimony to this.

led the advance into Germany. Canadians became intensely proud of their fighting men, though, characteristically, they took little interest in their generals. They believed "their boys" combined the steadfastness of the English with the ingenuity of the Americans. To men on the spot, it was a matter of observation that they had not quite that embarrassing degree of individualism which possessed the Americans or Australians and that they were not afflicted by the Englishman's unwillingness to be thorough. Along with the fighting qualities of their breed, they carried with them into the battle line the precision and the teamwork of North America.

It was perhaps in the new service, the air arm, that Canadians most effectually found themselves. Quickness of physical reaction, the individualism that did not take kindly to the mass discipline of armies but responded to the thrill of running one's own show aloft, mechanical aptitude, the delight in sheer physical sensation, the absence of reflective qualities, these characteristics gave to Canada thousands of able airmen and a number who distinguished themselves before all the world. Canadian boys took to the air as the *coureur de bois* had taken to the woods. That was to count in the opening up of their own country after the war was won.

It is all rather ghastly to recall now—the shooting down in flames (no hope of parachute escape in those days), the losses at sea, and above all the mud and blood of the Flanders bog, swallowing men by the tens of thousands. People speak of the second German war as more horrible than the first, but do those who do so know the first? Canada left some sixty thousand of her men in Flanders fields, those tributes to mediocrity in high places[2]—as many as the whole vast United States— and brought back three times as many wounded. The toll such a bloodletting took on the young nation can only be revealed by the patient tracing of the sociologist, and that has not yet been done.

Yet people stood up to it well. In Canada itself it was only in casualties that the direct effects of the war were felt: there were no hardships, no restrictions of importance, little discomfort. Just the reverse: the productive processes set going by the war, which greatly accelerated the pace of Canadian industrial development, the neverending demand for supplies, called forth another vast display of activity. It was 1900-13 over again. Everybody had a job and at high wages. The prices of wheat and other food stuffs rose steadily. Even the farmers began to admit that times were not too bad. Women whose men were overseas received allotments of pay and other allowances often in excess

[2] See among others Alan Clark, *The Donkeys* (London, 1961).

of anything they had had before. Such material prosperity assuaged much grief. It enabled English Canada to support the war to the end with almost unabated zeal; not until afterward did the spiritual hurt begin to make itself felt.

Joined to prosperity, as a support for a people at war, was pride in the accomplishment of the fighting men: Canada had entered the war a colony, a mere piece of Britain overseas; now she was forging visibly ahead to nationhood. It was good to be a Canadian. It was good to read each day of victories won or gallant resistance offered, of promotions gained and honours awarded. It was good to know that "our boys" could meet the best that the most experienced military nation of Europe could send against them and have something to spare. The "boys" were "making good" in Flanders just as they had "made good" in the west. Yet good as the "boys" were, both as individuals and as a fighting team, Canada's contribution to victory lay mainly in the subordinate areas of the war: she provided fighting men who were soon singled out as "shock troops", she provided generalship up to the divisional and corps level, which proved competent rather than brilliant, and she provided large masses of war supplies. She did not question the competence of the incompetent British high command. She provided neither military genius nor dynamic statesmanship; the great tasks of initiative (such as the conception of the League of Nations) were for more original minds. Canadians proved themselves steady, reliable, and sensible, but not conspicuously endowed with the gift divine, creative imagination.

There could have been few families from English-speaking Canada that did not have members or close relatives in the fighting forces. That, however, did not prevent the less worthy aspects of human nature from asserting themselves. Talk about peace will always be unreal as long as there are numerous people to whom (though they would probably deny it) war is more desirable than peace. War is the making of many a business man. To many in a subordinate and meaningless job, war offers release from boredom. It offers adventure to those chafing under the mechanical routine of urban life, prospects of promotion and the life of gentlemen to the misfits of civil life, release for many from familial complications. War offers the importance of the uniform.

Canada had nothing like a military caste when the war began and did not have a very impressive military hierarchy when it ended, but for many not in uniform the war was to prove a boon. Large prospects of profit soon opened out. After the usual year or so of commercial dislocation, war orders began to pour in, and a war boom resulted. It would have been asking too much of human nature for advantage not to be taken of it. The country was inexperienced and the only way it could get on with the war was to follow the *laisser-faire* methods it knew. There had been no previous necessity for the management of society: finance, taxation, administration of the economy as a whole, were uncharted seas, and politico-economic navigation had to be by rule of thumb. War contracts were let as seemed best at the moment, prices were set to encourage production, wages rose, all prices rose. Canada had never been a country of fastidious conduct, and it had become almost a tradition that in dealing with Government, the Eighth Commandment did not apply. The wonder is not that there were so many scandals but that there were so few.

For maintaining a reasonable measure of public virtue, credit must go to Sir Robert Borden. When two Members of Parliament, in accordance with the orthodox standards of the age, "got in on" contracts involving fraudulent practices, he read them out of his party and out of public life. The example was salutary, and joined with his efforts in other directions (as in curbing the spoils system in the Civil Service), may have marked a turning point in Canadian public ethics. Nevertheless, huge profits, often no doubt quite honest profits, were made, new millionaires appeared on every hand, and the term "profiteer" was added to the language. Perhaps few by-products of the war have had more importance, for much of the social conflict of the succeeding years, much of the determination to secure social justice, and, specifically, the successful efforts made during the Second World War to prevent another edition of the type from emerging, go back to the unpleasant spectacle of undue and often ugly wealth, side by side with the wounded and the broken and against the dark background of the slain.

There were other deep effects on Canadian society also. Canadians had had the virtues and the defects of a pioneer people, among the latter of which were limited experience and narrow-mindedness. As an Englishman writing on his pioneer days in Manitoba remarked, settlers from Great Britain had at least known two countries, but the natives had only had the circumscribed experience afforded by the one. The war was to change this for some hundreds of thousands of men. For them the old parochialism was broken by their experiences overseas of more mature cultures than their own. Their influence went far, and joined to the "spirit of the times", it produced a new Canada, a Canada which for better or for worse tore itself loose from the simplicity, the Puritanism, and even the religion of the nineteenth century. The more rigorous Protestant denominations could no longer maintain their taboos. The disruption of manners which a war always brings, the excitement and exhilaration that it produces, especially among young women, joined to contacts with the sophistications of the Old World, swept away most of the social landmarks of pioneer Canada and opened the gates for the period of paganism that was to follow.

But there was many a man for whom the brief moment of exhilaration was followed by years of depression. Of the third or more of the expeditionary force that had returned wounded, many were incapacitated permanently, and although no country exceeded Canada in efforts to salvage the human wreckage of the war, the broken soldier became a familiar sight. Not only that, the spiritual wounds that many men received were as serious as the physical. Many old veterans found it hard to settle down again to humdrum civil life, were hard to please or resentful of employers who had stayed comfortably at home. Civilians began to use the term "returned man" as signifying a difficult, unadjusted, barely respectable individual. That cut. It was a good number of years before authority officially admitted the situation and made provision for "burned out" veterans. The phrase was graphic and the condition behind it real enough: during the late twenties and early thirties the deaths of ex-service men in their forties were reported with inescapable frequency. The veterans had not been entirely reabsorbed into civil society by the beginning of the Second World War, and the Veterans' Guard formed at that time enabled them to recapture, after a fashion, the days when, a generation before, they had really lived.

Another by-product of the war had made itself manifest even before the army returned. At its end many men had been away from home three years or more. Cut off from family ties, they had become rootless. Little wonder that as their thoughts went back to Canada, it took on all the greenness of the far-off field. It was so easy to contrast its virtues with the evident failings of the French and English strangers among whom life had to be lived. That, joined to the *esprit-de-corps* natural to military units, which so often is a reflection of comparisons (the more odious the better) with other units, called forth the consciousness of "belonging", or to use sociological jargon, of the "in-group" and the "out-group". Once the Canadian Corps had received a Canadian commander, once its men had fought and died together, it could only be a matter of time until national pride took possession of it. In the trenches of France and Flanders, the spirit of Canadian nationalism was born. It was carried back to Canada in the knapsacks of Canadian troops and there, taking firm hold, hastened the slow processes by which a community comes to self-consciousness.

2. A House Divided

Unfortunately Canada's cursed heritage of race had also once more been thrust forward by the war. Where there is so much dynamite lying around, explosions must be frequent. It would have been miraculous if the tense emotions of war time had not acted as detonators.

The experiences of the previous quarter of a century had only served to confirm the French in the attitude which might have been expected from a conquered people. The execution of Louis Riel in 1885 had been taken by many of them as a deliberate blow in the face, and it had hardly been carried out before the suppression of the Catholic public school system of Manitoba renewed the conviction that the English were determined to humiliate "les Canadiens". The Boer War gave opportunity for further bickering, and for the first time depicted in colours that no one could mistake the general French attitude on "Imperialism" and on British wars. It was re-emphasized in the Bourassa agitation of 1910-11 over the Laurier Naval Act and in the subsequent defeat of Laurier in 1911. Yet when war came, most of the French Nationalists, who by that time had become half-digested Conservatives, preferred party and power to previous principles, and no longer possessing moral authority, stuck shakily to Sir Robert Borden. It was left to Sir Wilfrid to define the attitude of French Canada, and this he did in terms that might have been expected of him. This was no ordinary war: it was a great world conflict for existence and for freedom itself. Canada, already legally at war on the King's declaration, must therefore take an active part. Sir Wilfrid pledged all reasonable cooperation with the Government, and during the war his attitude never wavered.

At first French newspapers seemed as fervid as English, and French Canadians seemed almost as ready to enlist as English. The momentary fusion of emotions was too good to last, and long before the war had been won, the two peoples had fallen back into their old hostile attitudes. War enthusiasm mounted in English Canada and waned in French. Here was the primary cause of friction. But there was nothing strange about it. English Canada was full of people born in Great Britain. English Canadians as often as not had parents who had been born in the old country. There was not a community in the land where old-country people were not prominent: they and their associates were the deciding minds everywhere. The traditions of English-speaking Canada were wholly British, and English Canadians fought not out of knowledge of European conditions but because they were "whelps of the lion". French Canadians were not whelps, and they had little knowledge of European conditions. It was unreasonable to expect their legal acceptance of British institutions to carry them as far as the strong sense of filial love was to carry the English Canadians, and their sense of duty, the Protestants.

This difference in attitude towards the war was the rock on which the two peoples split. The English, ever ready to suspect the worst of the French, soon discovered that not many of them were enlisting. Notes of abuse began to creep into the press. The French have never been slow to reply in kind when it comes to verbal abuse, and so the good old-fashioned racial controversy was soon raging again.

The French attitude can be simply explained: they were a people of the New World, and the war for them as for the Americans was a "piece of work entirely out of their line which seemed to bear no relation to the normal course of their national life".[3] They were less interested in Europe than the Americans, for the United States as a great world power has to take its place in world affairs, but the little world of the St. Lawrence, sheltered for generations under the protection of great metropolitan states, has had no such responsibility. The true comparison is not to the United States but to some isolated Catholic state of South America such as Ecuador or to Eire in the Second World War, where hatred of England was more powerful than fear of Germany. If French Canada could have had its way in both wars, it would have been neutral too. The most tactful of governments and the most tolerant of majorities could not have persuaded the French to throw themselves into war as the English did.

But tact and tolerance are the very qualities that have invariably been in short supply among the English of the New World, and so the situation was handled badly from the first. No attempt was made by government to educate the French as to the nature of the war. English was the language of command in the army, and no one dreamed of making a concession on that point. Moreover there seemed in certain quarters deliberate design to humiliate the French. Sir Sam Hughes, the energetic and erratic Minister of Militia, was of fighting Ulster stock, with all that that meant in the way of anti-Catholic and anti-French antipathies. Stories survive, which may or may not be true, and it is to be hoped that they are not, of his appreciation of the opportunities for coercion that the war would give. Sir Sam's views later became rather broader, but that such stories could circulate indicates the attitude which certain groups of English can take toward the French in times of excitement. Many of the French seize on these pieces of "evidence", make more of

J. T. Adams, quoted in F. H. Soward, *Twenty-Five Troubled Years, 1918-1943* (Toronto, 1943), p. 116.

them than they probably deserve, use them as excuses for not co-operating with the English, and end up by holding back and sulking.

Another type of provocative incident consisted in the forays of certain English-speaking recruiting officers into the countryside of Quebec. Imagine the consternation on all sides, especially among the priesthood, when some of these men turned out to be Protestant clergymen. Here, it[4] would appear to them, was a direct attempt to seduce French youth from their religion by sending them off among the English to die in England's wars.

It was an unhappy chance that projected into this troubled situation one of the perennial disputes over education. In the French sections of Ontario, investigation had revealed, English was taught either badly or not at all. Counties in the Ottawa valley were becoming virtual extensions of the countryside of Quebec. The Government of Ontario decided to attempt to improve the situation by making English the principal language of instruction, while allowing for the subsidiary use of French.[5] Two factors aggravated the situation and brought back to French minds the persecutions of Manitoba. The first lay in the city of Ottawa. Instead of coming to a federal district (as in the United States), federal civil servants from Quebec found themselves in a city subject only to Ontario law, which to them seemed to be framed with the object of Anglicizing their children. They found arrayed against them fellow-Catholics of English speech and Irish descent. The two factions in the Ottawa Separate School Board convulsed the country. The other factor was the Irish Catholic Bishop Fallon of London, Ontario,[6] who in a famous interview with a provincial minister some years before[7] had declared war on bilingual schools and French clerical agitators.

There were half a dozen regional facets of the bilingual question in Ontario. There was the Ottawa city situation. There was the situation in the western peninsula and at other scattered points, where it was against the interests of the community and of the small French groups that children should have no English. In parts of Northern Ontario, the French formed almost the sole population. In the Ottawa valley, there was an unadmitted struggle for the soil, and if the English could succeed in imposing their language on the French (many of them immigrants from Quebec, possibly aided financially by agencies of colonization

---

[4] Think of the uproar that would have occurred had the Government sent French priests into the Protestant countryside of Ontario.

[5] The famous "Regulation 17".

[6] Bishop Fallon had lived in Ottawa, and in his diocese of London were the French communities around Windsor.

[7] The Provincial Secretary, W. J. Hanna, May 23, 1910.

linked to the Church), they would have a better chance of heading off the invasion. But it was unfortunate that at the very time when race relations were particularly tender on account of the war, this secondary controversy should also have grown steadily more bitter.[8] It may be that certain French leaders saw in the bilingual school question an opportunity to muddy the waters and a justification for their attitude towards the war. It was easy and popular to assert, as did Henri Bourassa (who always claimed to be a Canadian Nationalist, but whose words and deeds often suggested that he was little more than a French-Canadian Nationalist), that there was no need to go to Europe to fight Prussianism when the Ontario government was itself giving the worst exhibition of that spirit.[9]

In addition to all this agitation, to the loss of two suits over the question before the Judicial Committee of the Privy Council, to an encyclical from the Pope himself taking a rather cool view of their position on language rights,[10] there was presented to the French fresh evidence of the iron determination of the English to carry the war effort to the uttermost limit. Closely coinciding with the Ottawa disorders over bilingual schools came Sir Robert Borden's announcement (made directly and not in Parliament) that the Canadian army would be raised to 500,000 men. The French saw in this, despite Sir Robert's assurances to the contrary, an indication of conscription, the most dreaded measure of all. By the summer of 1916, a National Service Board had been set up, and a National Registration of man-power taken. Demands began to be heard for a coalition government to unite all parties behind a greater war-effort. All these were straws in the wind.

Sir Robert appears to have returned from the Imperial Conference of 1917 convinced of the necessity of conscription, put into force if possible by a Union Government, if not, without it. In his attempts to form such a government he met with little success, for Sir Wilfrid Laurier saw clearly enough that if he entered it, he bound himself hand and foot. He believed sincerely that conscription would do more harm than good. If he consented to it, he would simply hand Quebec over to Nationalist extremists. Meanwhile Sir Robert went on with his efforts. The life of Parliament had already been extended once, by a year, and it was evident that there was little support for a second extension. An election would therefore have to be held. At this juncture, one of the Prime Minister's young lieutenants, Mr. Arthur Meighen, came forward with two bills designed to influence the result, The Military Voters Act and the War Time Election Act. These denied the franchise to conscientious objectors, to those of enemy alien birth or those of European birth speaking an enemy alien language and naturalized since 1902 (for example, a German-speaking immigrant from Russia naturalized, say, in 1903). They gave the franchise to all on active service and to the wives, widows, and other female relatives of servicemen overseas. The opposition denounced the bills as "Kaiserism",[11] but they undoubtedly found favour with Canadians and were easily carried. Given the temper of English-speaking Canada, they were hardly necessary as election-winning devices and constituted gratuitous affronts to many naturalized Canadians, forcing upon them the memories and loyalties of their European past.[12] Mr. Meighen's first conspicuous contribution to Canadian public life was like too many of his subsequent actions, provocative and divisive.

On June 11, 1917, the long-impending blow fell: a Conscription Act was introduced.[13] The Liberal opposition was split, many members, especially those from the west, supporting the bill, others remaining true to the old chief, Sir Wilfrid. During its passage and after, much behind-the-scenes manoeuvring went on, and on October 12, the Prime Minister announced the formation of a Union Government. As might have been expected, only English-speaking Liberals went over. Few, indeed, remained behind, and Sir Wilfrid found himself head of a rump party consisting mainly of his own French followers. The Conscription election followed on December 17, 1917. The Canadian people were in a frenzy of excitement. The French found their worst fears being realized. The English looked on the election as a solemn act of renewed consecration in a holy war. Press and pulpit rang with exhortations to duty and sacrifice. All the missionary fervour of nineteenth century Protestantism reasserted itself. That powerful church which had been foremost in the social and missionary crusades of the past generation, the Methodist, was now logically foremost in insisting on the Christian duty of its people to prosecute to the limit the war against the German barbarian.

[11] At the poll held at Dunkirk, France, in the conscription election, of which the present writer was an eye witness, the number of voters who turned up calling themselves "Canadian" was distinctly surprising.

[12] The disfranchisement provision may have constituted, among other things, a Conservative attempt to offset the previous organization of the immigrant in the Liberal interests; the high fervour of the conscription election may not have lacked low party manoeuvring.

[13] Passed August 28.

The results had not been uncertain, and when the returns were in, they proved drastic. The Union Government secured 153 seats (85 Conservatives and 68 Conscription Liberals) as against the Liberals' 82, all but some twenty of whom were from Quebec. The most hopeless and the most feared of all Canadian situations had arisen: party, race, and issue had coincided. How could a country of two races continue to exist under such circumstances?

The wonder is, and it is a considerable testimony to the strength Confederation had acquired in fifty short years, that it did. There was a certain amount of trouble over the enforcement of the Conscription law, some harsh pursuit of draft evaders, and some open rioting in Quebec city. But there was nothing resembling a rebellion, and when J. N. Francoeur introduced in the Quebec Assembly his motion suggesting that Quebec "would be disposed to accept the breaking of the Confederation Pact of 1867 if, in the other provinces, it is believed that she is an obstacle to the union, progress and development of Canada",[14] his proposal got a sympathetic and intelligent debate, but no support. A partial explanation lies in the failure of the Conscription law to attain its objects. Innumerable exemptions were allowed, and thanks to this, the number of conscripts enrolled in the Canadian army was not large. Of those enrolled, those of French origin would not reach any impressive total and few could have got within gunshot of the enemy.[15] The most determined opponents of conscription probably avoided conscription.

It seems unfortunate that for such meagre results there should have been introduced into Canadian life a degree of bitterness that surely has seldom been equalled in countries calling themselves nations. Lord Durham's classical description had once more come to apply, and again Canada, to its sorrow, presented the spectacle of two nations warring in the bosom of a single state. Yet given the characters of the two peoples and the overwrought emotions of the war period, probably no other result could have been expected. The English Canadians exhibited, in combination with a good deal of sheer malice, all the qualities that go with an exalted sense of duty in a great cause: concentration, determination, ruthlessness, intolerance, and a complete lack of ability to see the other party's point of view. These qualities of theirs, never far below the surface, the war brought into full evidence.

Most of the French do not seem to have been ready to see the issues

---

[14] Jan. 17, 1918.

[15] In finding ways around the draft law, it is said that the countryside of Ontario was just as adept as that of Quebec. Yet during the war some 200,000 volunteers came from Ontario, but only some 50,000 from Quebec, and of these latter, large numbers were English-speaking.

at stake at all. The plight of France could not move them, the entrance of the United States did not change them. To them, the great struggle to hold in check a power whose victory would have changed the face of the world was just another British "Imperialist" war. While few among them would have said outright that Canada should withdraw from the war, still there were also few who were not appalled by the unlimited sacrifice of blood and treasure; a deeply conservative and rural people could not gaze on the immense flux of life without deep dismay. The French, even in peace, have been like men trying to keep up to others constantly outpacing them, with all the out-of-breath resentment that the effort entails. But in time of war, they are like horsemen trying to keep up to motorists. The association of English and French is like that of a badly mated man and woman. When trouble comes—and when does it not?—the woman sulks while the man bullies. It is as a very womanly woman that such a feminine people as the French should be treated; such a one could be wooed, but all the English Canadian can do is to shout. In their attitude towards each other, the Great War displayed the two peoples at their worst, and the healing of the wounds was to be a long and painful business.

3. The Price of Victory

After the high colours of the racial strife, other domestic aspects of the war must come like anticlimaxes. Yet they were by no means without importance: some of them, indeed, were of the highest importance. Of them, four may be mentioned: the National Debt, railway nationalization, the effect of the war on freedom, and the effect of casualties.

The public debt, modest at the beginning of the war, had soared continuously and at the end was, for the time, astronomic.[16] In a day of orthodox finance, people thought in terms of its eventual redemption, but the initiate must have seen that the best that could ever be hoped for would be refunding at lower interest rates. This was what was done later on and to lower interest rates there was added another standard cure-all—currency inflation. Canada had joined the large collection of countries that keep pushing ahead of them a heavy National Debt; all the best countries have unredeemable national debts.

The second matter, railway nationalization, was an accidental by-product of the war. There had already been certain conspicuous examples of public ownership, among which the Hydro-Electric Power Commission in Ontario was outstanding, but the subject had invariably

---

[16] Nearly three billion dollars, or rather over $300 per capita.

been approached quite without reference to first principles. Yet the country was a product of nineteenth century *laisser-faire*, and though great enterprises like railways had received much state aid, the normal assumption was that they would be privately owned. It took every last ounce of energy the country could summon to build the railroads and when they were built, more often than not they did not pay. The Grand Trunk never paid. The Canadian Northern had not really become a system and never got within sight of paying. The Intercolonial did not pay. The Ontario Government's Temiskaming and Northern Ontario was marginal. Only the C.P.R. paid, and that partly by reason of the generous assistance it had formerly had from the state.

War traffic and the winter of 1917, which was particularly severe, disorganized the Grand Trunk, and the territory dependent upon it suffered some hardship. Its western extension, the Grand Trunk Pacific, was in worse straits, and by 1917, the Canadian Northern had reached the end of its resources. After public inquiry, a recommendation was brought in that it, the Grand Trunk Pacific, the Intercolonial, and the National Transcontinental (which had never been taken over by the Grand Trunk, despite the original agreement) should be consolidated under a Board of Trustees. Here was the pattern for the subsequent Canadian National System. The immediate necessity was to do some-thing about the Canadian Northern. That road, it has been alleged, was heavily in debt to one of the large banks, and if it had been allowed to go into receivership, the bank also would have failed and Canada would have faced a financial crisis of the first magnitude in the middle of a war.

Whatever the truth, government decided to take over the Canadian Northern. The Dominion now had on its hands the bits and pieces of a transcontinental railway, together with many of its bonds and some of its stock, although this had been declared worthless by the Drayton Com-mission. Later (1919) the Grand Trunk Pacific and the parent line, the Grand Trunk, were also nationalized. The Board of Arbitration, which decided that the common stock of the latter company was valueless, came in for much criticism at the hands of the English holders, some of whom seem to have had it in the family for three-quarters of a century without getting any return on it, surely a good proof of its worthlessness. The railway, run from London, had been mismanaged from the first,[17] often to the dishonest profit of those within its inner circle. Through the dislocations of war, Canada found herself involved in a major adventure in "public ownership" or in plain words, socialism.

[17] See pp. 287ff., 302ff. See Stevens, *Canadian National Railways*, 2 vols.

THE PRICE OF VICTORY

Attracting far less attention than the status of railroads but far more vital in the long run was the structure of law that grew out of war's emergencies. During the special session of Parliament held at the outbreak of the conflict there was enacted under section 91 of the British North America Act[18] the War Measures Act. This little statute was short and to the point: it simply handed over to the government (that is, the cabinet) all the powers of Parliament. Parliament in passing it, superseded itself and so far as the words of the Act go, committed suicide. The parliamentary tradition still being strong, Parliament continued to be called and to vote taxes, but the surrender of power was so complete that a strong government might have found that in practice[19] it actually could do without Parliament.[20] The Canadian War Measures Act was the most complete surrender of parliamentary power made in any English-speaking country (except Newfoundland) since 1540 when Henry VIII persuaded Parliament for a brief period to allow him to legislate by proclamation. The result was that both during the first German War and the second, Canada had, not parliamentary government, but "Order-in-Council" government.

During the first war, government felt its way to power slowly and issued special "War Regulations" having the force of law (against espionage and similar dangers) as they were required, but by the end of the war, these regulations had come to apply to innumerable situations in which the subject was deprived of his civil rights. It speaks volumes for the immaturity of Canadian society and the weakness of Canadian traditions of freedom that these Regulations went virtually without protest. The War Measures Act was not repealed at the end of the war but remained lying forgotten in its lair in the statute book, ready to spring out once more at the opening of the Second World War and at that time to father an even more stringent and arbitrary set of "Defence of Canada Regulations". It was to do grave injury to the structure of Canadian democracy.[21]

Lastly, there was the question of the casualties. Some 60,000 men had been killed, and perhaps as many more of those who had been wounded were to die prematurely. These men on enlisting were among the best the nation had to offer, both in brain and brawn. They were

---

[18] "It shall be lawful . . . to make laws for the peace, order and good government of Canada. . . ."
[19] It could call Parliament; then prorogue at once.
[20] No attempts to get any action taken under the War Measures Act declared *ultra vires* by the courts succeeded.
[21] When Prime Minister Diefenbaker succeeded in passing his Bill of Rights through Parliament in 1960, he left the War Measures Act intact.

preponderantly Anglo-Saxon in race. Their loss must have weakened a young country of less than nine millions which needed all the man-power, and especially all the ability, it could find. Not only this: the hard times following the war drove thousands of "returned men" to the United States, where they were lost to Canada. Again, the call to service had brought many men into the ranks from the farms. Many of them did not go back, and in western Canada the family farm often passed into the hands of some of the immigrant newcomers. The older Canadian, or Anglo-Saxon, population of the western countryside began to give way, and there commenced in the west the same kind of displacement which set English against French in the east.[22]

4. The War and Constitutional Evolution

Canada entered the war a colony; she emerged from it close to an independent state. The effects of the contributions she made were reinforced by the attitude of her war Prime Minister. The heavy responsibilities imposed upon him—responsibilities that lay first to the country of which he was the head—made large changes in his outlook. He soon came to see that Canada must have a place in affairs com-mensurate with her weight. For him this took the form of belief in a group of British nations, each co-equal with the others, working out their destinies together.[23] Although Borden never overtly went beyond that point, both events and the honest openness of mind which was perhaps his finest characteristic were driving him during the last few years towards the full nationalist position. That would seem to be a fair conclusion from his own *Memoirs*,[24] various passages in which show clearly enough that he had a mind of his own and had no disposition to follow the authorities in London too complaisantly. His sharp intimation that if London's means of informing him on the conduct of the war were not improved "Canada would have to reconsider her entire position" is a case in point.[25]

For two years, Canada's part in the war involved mainly domestic issues, but when the crisis just referred to came up and Borden found the Imperial authorities casual in accounting for Canadian aid though

[22] The Second World War was to accentuate this process: the original Anglo-Saxons of Canada were tending to become an urban people whose numbers by 1941 seemed not far from stationary, though this trend was reversed in subse-quent years.

[23] See his *Canada in the Commonwealth* (Oxford, 1920), p. 88.

[24] H. Borden, ed., *Robert Laird Borden: His Memoirs*, 2 vols. (Toronto, 1938). See especially II, 622.

[25] Private information substantiates this view and carries its inference further.

ready enough to accept it, this, joined to heavy casualties, caused a review of the whole situation. The immediate result, hastened by Lloyd George's displacement of Asquith in England, was the arrangement of the winter of 1917, by which the five members of the British "War Cabinet" and the Prime Ministers of the self-governing Dominions met as an "Imperial War Cabinet", while concurrently the Dominion ministers and the Colonial Secretary met in an "Imperial War Conference". The War Cabinet examined general questions. This was a far cry from the old attitude in Great Britain. Yet the direction of the war effort of the Empire, it may be assumed, was not allowed far out of the grasp of the five men composing the British inner circle. The significance of the Imperial War Cabinet lay in its symbolic rather than its practical aspect.

The chief duty of the Imperial War Conference was to consider readjustment of constitutional relations within the Empire, upon the assumption that some systematic form could be given to them. This was the original Chamberlain programme. At all Imperial Conferences where it had been offered, some tactful way round it had been found, and that of 1917 was no exception. Sir Robert and General Smuts drafted a resolution, since become well-known, stating that the development of constitutional relations was too important and intricate a subject to be dealt with during the war, recommending its consideration at a special Conference as soon as hostilities had ceased, and affirming the principle of Dominion autonomy, with the right of a voice in foreign policy and the obligation of consultation and action based upon consultation.[26] Once more what began as an effort towards centralization brought more local autonomy. In 1917 evolution had not yet gone so far as to demonstrate the incompatibility of nationalism with mere autonomy and the compatibility of nationalism with co-operation. It was still possible to be a Canadian nationalist and a believer in an organized Empire.

5. Sir Robert Borden, Canada's First War Minister

When R. L. Borden became leader of the Conservative Opposition, he was a relatively unknown Halifax lawyer. His first efforts captured the imagination of neither his party nor his country, and his task was not made easier by his defeats in 1904 and 1908. But this period in opposition brought out some of his characteristic qualities, among others his determination, his ability to stand adversity, and his dependability. Plots against his leadership failed, and in 1911 he had his reward.

Like many other Prime Ministers, Borden was not entirely in control

[26] Text in Borden, *op. cit.*, II, 91, and numerous other publications.

of his cabinet. Circumstances had virtually forced upon him Sam Hughes, his first Minister of Militia, but by the time that gentleman became impossible (he seems to have been afflicted with delusions of grandeur) and Borden required him to resign (November, 1916), there was no longer any doubt as to his being master in his own house. Thenceforth, even more than before, he could be considered Canada's War Minister just as Lloyd George was Great Britain's.

Since Canadians were not under the same pressure as were the English, Borden did not have Lloyd George's hard task of sustaining the morale of his countrymen. Nor would he have been equal to it, for he had no gifts of eloquence or of picturesque or passionate speech. He was a plain, blunt man who could state a case effectively, who saw things clearly, whose judgement was good and whose spirit tolerant. As such he gradually won the confidence of most of the country. On the whole its trust was justified. He made many mistakes, of course. A more imaginative man might have handled the problem of Quebec somewhat more successfully, and a man less inclined to give wide scope to his subordinates would have moderated Arthur Meighen's extremist statutes of 1917. But these situations represented defect of capacity rather than of character, and most people were ready to admit that Borden was doing his job according to his best abilities and under deep conviction. Even at the height of the Conscription disturbances, he was able to secure a hearing at a crowded meeting in Montreal.

Borden grew steadily in stature as a Canadian, which task has invariably been difficult for anyone with the semi-independent tradition of Nova Scotia behind him. With little of the passion and intolerance of the Ontario Tory about him, he yet came to Ottawa a colonial. But long before the war ended, he had become a Canadian. Of that, his books are ample proof. His external policies had to be forged under great pressure but the key to them is the same as to those of Macdonald, Laurier, and King—the safeguarding and extension of Canadian autonomy. The effort has invariably been made in Canada to convict anyone stressing national sentiments of being "anti-British". Of none of these four men could it be said that he was "anti-British", for all found it possible to entertain respect and admiration for Great Britain while devoting their careers and their hearts to their own country. It is more than accidental that these are also the four outstanding names in the role of the Prime Ministers.[27] Each of these great men has had qualities

---

[27] But what is to be said of St. Laurent? The present writer feels that it is still too soon to attempt anything but a tentative estimate, though it is evident St. Laurent had the great gift of a reconciling, healing character and that under him the gulf of racial distrust was temporarily narrowed.

of his own. Borden did not have the lovable magnetism of Macdonald, the incomparable personality of Laurier, or King's extraordinary characteristics as the highest common factor of the many terms in the Canadian equation. He did have his own steadfast honesty and a largeness of mind which causes his stature to increase as the years go by.

Chronology

1914 Great Britain declares War on Germany, Aug. 4.
1915 Canadian stand at Ypres against the first gas attack.
1917 Capture of Vimy Ridge, April 9.
      Imperial War Cabinet.
      Canadian Northern Railway taken over by the Canadian Government.
      Union Government, October 12.
      The Conscription Election, Dec. 17.
1918 Armistice, Nov. 11.
1919 Peace Conference at Paris, January.
      Canada signs the Treaty of Versailles, July.
      Canada a Member of the League of Nations.

Additional Reading

Armstrong, E. H. *The Crisis of Quebec, 1914-18.* New York, 1937.
Cook, Ramsay. "Dafoe, Laurier, and The Formation of the Union Government." *CHR,* XLII (Sept., 1961), 185-208.
——. *The Politics of John W. Dafoe and the Free Press.* Toronto, 1963.
Dawson, R. M. *William Lyon Mackenzie King.* Vol. 1. Toronto, 1958.
Graham, R. *Arthur Meighen.* Vol. 1. Toronto, 1960.
McGregor, F. A. *The Fall and Rise of Mackenzie King, 1911-1919.* Toronto, 1962.
Morley, P. F. *Bridging the Chasm.* Toronto, 1919.
Nicholson, G. W. L. *Canadian Expeditionary Force, 1914-1919.* Ottawa, 1962.
Prang, M. "Clerics, Politicians, and the Bilingual Schools Issue in Ontario, 1910-1917." *CHR,* XLI (Dec., 1960), 281-307.

CHAPTER 32

Canada Enters the World, 1917-1932

1. Canada as Party to the Peace Treaties and as a Member of the League of Nations

The Canadian blood poured out in France filled statesmen and troops alike with a consequent sense of national destiny, whose reflection was to be seen in the results of the Peace Conference. At this gathering the self-governing Dominions under the leadership of Sir Robert Borden acquired a unique position, for they were members of the British Empire delegation and also members of the Conference in their own right.[1] This double-barrelled arrangement nonplussed not only foreigners but the British themselves. It was from certain Americans that the most decided opposition came (Secretary of State Lansing, in particular) but others, such as Colonel House, President Wilson's confidential adviser, saw that there was no need to worry about a sixfold British representation, for the step really meant that Great Britain was abandoning control.

Meanwhile, until the logic of the position should have developed, the Dominions were favourably situated:

[1] For the dramatic way in which separate representation was achieved, see J. W. Dafoe, "Canada and the Peace Conference of 1919," *CHR*, XXIV (Sept., 1943), 233-248. For a general and competent discussion, see G. P. de T. Glazebrook, *Canada at the Paris Peace Conference* (Toronto, 1942).

For the representatives of a small power the Canadian delegates exercised perhaps as much influence as any, partly because of their added status in their empire delegation, partly because of their own exertions. They played a rôle about midway between that of the three leading great powers, who were obliged to consider the settlement as a whole, and other delegations like those of Japan, Italy, and many small states, who troubled themselves hardly at all with anything but their own well-defined ambitions.[2]

They were in fact too favourably situated. They had their cake and ate it too: they were both "British" and themselves. While such an anomalous status might be indulgently accepted at the time, in view of their great military contributions, the day would come when they would have to decide whether they were speaking in their parent's right or their own. Perpetual adolescence is the lot of no one. Although Canada is tantalizingly slow in growing up, a dozen years after the peace conference, she had, at least legally, come of age.[3]

The new status arrived at in Paris, whatever it was, was confirmed by separate signature of the Treaty of Versailles, which was debated and accepted by the Canadian Parliament, and by the right not only to membership of the League of Nations but also, on election, of its Council.[4] Here again, there was objection, and in the case of the signature of the Treaty, the position was blurred in that British representatives signed for "The British Empire" and the Dominions signed separately under this heading, there being, despite Canadian endeavours, no separate signature for "The United Kingdom of Great Britain and Ireland". Arthur Sifton, the most nationalistic of the Canadian delegates, complained bitterly of the humiliation put upon his country, which in this or similar ways he saw being reduced to a status below "Portugal, Cuba, Uruguay, Liberia."[5] The answer to him, though it does not appear that anyone made it, was to suggest that if Canada wanted the status of an independent state, she should become one. This, of course, she would not have done, for whatever the constitutional evolution, her people were still far from being psychologically ready for independence.

As it turned out, after the United States "walked out", other states were only too glad to have Canada at Geneva. It was easy for Canada to explain the general attitude of America, for it was never far from her

[2] Glazebrook, p. 86.
[3] By the Statute of Westminster, 1931.
[4] As also of the International Labour Office.
[5] Glazebrook, p. 127.

own. Nothing brings this out more emphatically than the problem posed by Article X of the League Covenant. At Paris, before its adoption, this article, which offered a virtually unlimited guarantee against territorial aggression anywhere, was strongly contested by the Canadian delegation, and as strongly insisted on by President Wilson. Seeing that it was mainly fear of this unlimited responsibility which kept the United States out of the League, the Canadians at Paris evidently reflected American sentiment rather better than the President himself. They objected to becoming involved on the orders of some remote authority in distant wars for the sake of a cause of which they might know nothing. As Senator Dandurand was later to say, at that time they lived in a fireproof house and could not see why they should be expected to pay high insurance premiums.[6]

There are suggestions in some of the memoranda made at Paris that the Canadian delegation attached more importance to recognition of the country's *status* than to its interests and functions in the new world order,[7] probably because Canada had no direct interests of her own to serve. Her interest was simply the common interest of mankind—peace and order. Few peoples have ever fought so bloody a war for so disinterested a purpose. This was recognized in part, and the position of detachment it conferred gave to the erstwhile colony a certain moral authority it would not otherwise have had. Consequently when the League of Nations was launched on its career, Canada played a fairly large part at Geneva. But not a particularly constructive part. She devoted her efforts towards those practical problems of administration upon which Canadians are most at home and towards attempting to secure some revision of Article X.

Thanks to French opposition and the rule of unanimity, which reduced the Assembly to the level of the ancient Polish Diet, a synonym for organized anarchy, Article X was not revised. But an "interpretative resolution" was carried, by which a state's obligations were admitted to be somewhat in proportion to its proximity to the scene of disturbance. Canada might have got further if her representatives from year to year had not often been ministers who liked to combine some intriguing interest in affairs with a European tour. Knowing little of what their predecessors had said at previous meetings of the Assembly, they were inclined to confine themselves to sonorous sentiments about the duties of man, the excellent way in which the two Canadian races got along with each other, and the blessings of peace, so much so that "the

---

[6] For the Canadian fight against Article X, see Glazebrook, 67ff.
[7] See e.g. Arthur Sifton's letter of April 2, 1919, Glazebrook, p. 78.

Canadian speech" came to be received each year with a certain amused boredom.

Yet it was not long before Canada was elected a member of Council, where she served usefully. Canadians might not have many constructive ideas, but it soon became plain that they took no orders from the British, a circumstance most pleasing to the French, who found these arguments within the British group very much to their taste: "ça goutte, ça", said a Frenchman after one particularly sharp interchange. This readiness to hold their own line was a great service to the League, for it showed that the British nations made up no closed intra-League group, carefully facing outward against all comers, but were prepared to argue out issues on their merits. This surely provided a very essential element in international cooperation.

2. Canada and Japan, 1918-1939

In the inter-war period, 1918-1939, it was in respect to Japan that Canada was to make two of its infrequent sallies into high policy. By the close of the First World War, a tangled skein of events had brought American-Japanese relations into tender condition. Japan, thanks to her conduct against China during the war and the difficulty of getting her out of Siberia after it, was drifting into the position of inevitable enemy. She on her part had little reason to feel well-disposed to any of the white nations. The latest example of what, to the Japanese, appeared as their arrogant superiority had come at Paris, where a proposal to enunciate a doctrine of racial equality in the peace treaties had received no support,[8] not even from the country still her formal ally, Great Britain. The Anglo-Japanese alliance had originally been intended to safeguard mutual interests against Russia and Germany but now both these countries were out of the ring. Certain Americans began to see in it a combination against the United States. It was never that, but if Americans thought it was, the very suspicion would be dangerous to Canada, for a breach between the two senior English-speaking countries would be intolerable.

The Imperial Constitutional Conference that had been proposed in 1917 not having been held, it was decided in 1921 that instead there should be a meeting of the Prime Ministers of the Empire. For Canada, where the storm-warnings being flown at Washington were plainly discernible, Anglo-American relations were of dominating importance. Whether Arthur Meighen, who had succeeded Sir Robert Borden in the previous year, was indirectly in touch with important personages at

[8] Because it might have prevented discrimination against Japanese immigrants.

Washington, is not known, but nothing could have been easier than for him to descry how the land lay. About that time he was receiving advice from certain acute Canadian observers in England, among whom Loring Christie, later to be Canada's ambassador to Washington, was conspicuous, to the effect that Europeans were beginning to find some satisfaction at the approaching falling-out of the English and Americans over the Japanese question. Whatever the background, one thing is plain: Meighen went to London to do his best to secure the abrogation of the Anglo-Japanese alliance.

It was an embarrassing mission. Suggesting abrogation of a well-tried alliance with a loyal friend must have come as a shock to British statesmen, while to Australians, such a gesture of enmity seemed madness. Even Canada had felt the value of the alliance during the earlier part of the war, when Japanese ships undertook patrol duties on the British Columbian coast, then open to threat from Von Spee's squadron still at large. Mr. Hughes of Australia dubbed Meighen "the American ambassador", thereby giving that ultra-Imperialist a strange role. Nevertheless he played it and thereby helped to change British policy. While the Prime Ministers were arguing over what should be done, an invitation arrived from Washington to take part in a general conference on naval disarmament and Far Eastern affairs. The proposal offered a way out of the British family debate and was accepted. Thus was initiated the movement that led to the Conference of December-January, 1921-22, so large in its decisions that it has often been called a second peace conference.

At the Washington Conference, the Anglo-Japanese alliance, the only subject which directly concerned Canada, was politely buried in the striking measure of naval disarmament for which the Conference is mainly remembered[9] and in the general body of Pacific legislation comprised in the "four-power", the "five-power" and the "nine-power" treaties.[10] These treaties, signed as guarantees of the rights and interests of the Pacific powers (and therefore virtually crystallizing the *status quo*, as had the League Covenant) were held to supersede the necessity for ordinary bilateral alliances. Thus with the disappearance of the Anglo-Japanese alliance disappeared the immediate danger of Anglo-American friction.

Meighen had acted forcefully in the very highest sphere of high

[9] The celebrated "5-5-3" ratio in battleship tonnage. This was, as far as the writer knows, the only internationally agreed-upon measure of disarmament that history records—with the exception of the Rush-Bagot Agreement of 1817 for disarmament on the Great Lakes.

[10] So called from the number of states signing them.

politics. He had fought to protect Canada's interests by preventing a gulf developing between Great Britain and the United States. This must always be the ultimate objective of Canadian diplomacy and if by reason of awareness of American conditions, Meighen did prevent such a gulf, then not only does Canada owe much to him but in his person she was acting in the role for which she has so often rather meaninglessly been cast, that of "interpreter", "bridge" or "linchpin". She was acting thus by reason of acepting her position as one of the British family, persuading the head of the house by domestic argument around the family table.

Vast political changes began to make themselves manifest after Washington. The Japanese, looking at the geographical, commercial, and power situation in the Pacific, came to realize that their erstwhile ally was not their natural friend at all but the chief obstacle to their southern expansion, the commercial rival which held most of the prizes in the Orient that they would like to have, the only power whose naval strength and geographical advantages might challenge them. The Washington Treaties did not produce this situation but they and that deduction from them, the Singapore naval base,[11] caused the scales to fall from Japanese eyes. Alliance or no alliance, sooner or later the Japanese would have turned against the British in the Orient. If Meighen claimed for Canada an influential voice in deciding British policy towards this heaving eastern world, he surely pledged his country to its share of responsibility. When, ten years later, the implications of Washington worked themselves out, and the Japanese defied the League authorities, neither the Canadian people nor Meighen's Conservative successor, R. B. Bennett, were inclined to assume any responsibility at all.

In the interval between the two events, Canadian relations with Japan were confined to lesser matters. Two more "Gentlemen's Agreements" were negotiated, in 1924 and 1928, by which Japanese immigration was still further pared down to eighty per year, without any rude blow between the eyes such as the United States delivered in 1924 with its Japanese Exclusion Act. In 1929 the Canadian legation in Tokyo was opened. Separate diplomatic representation, decided on by Sir Robert Borden but not put into practice, had been inaugurated by Mackenzie King two years before, when Mr. Vincent Massey was sent as Canadian minister to Washington. There had been a good deal of opposition on the usual ground that the unity of the Empire would be destroyed. This was renewed in Parliament on the proposal over the Tokyo legation, in a debate that echoed the "tin-pot navy" derisive

[11] Built, partly on Australian insistence, in the 1920's.

colonialism of nineteen years before, the new Conservative leader, R. B. Bennett, taking occasion to ridicule Canada's presumptuousness. How could she defend her citizens when disturbances abroad forced them to flee to the shelter of her legation, he asked; what notice would Japan take of ultimatums delivered by a country as weak as Canada? A year or so later, as Prime Minister, Mr. Bennett was vigorously defending the necessity of having a legation in Tokyo, so quickly had it become evident that legations are not primarily citadels abroad from which the old flag flies, but business offices, where innumerable matters of detail are daily ironed out.

In 1931-32, with the Japanese seizure of Manchuria, an issue of an entirely different order of importance was precipitated: would the League act to prevent aggression against one of its members? Would the unlimited guarantee of Article X come into effect, and would the members live up to their contract? It was plain that the only powers that could really do much towards coercing Japan, the great naval powers, England and France, were reluctant to act. The English knew that coercion limited to economic sanctions might mean Japanese seizure of Hong Kong and of other British areas, and they were not assured of support from the United States. In addition, their policy was in the hands of men unfriendly to this new-fangled conception, the League. To such men, the general principle of the rule of law in international relations did not make much appeal. They thought in terms of national interests, the balance of power, or, in the case of the foreign secretary, Sir John Simon, narrow legal rights. Therefore in the sessions of the Assembly devoted to finding some solution to Japan's law-breaking, where the Japanese were almost universally condemned, the British spoke up in their favour.

To the amazement of nearly everybody in Canada, Canada in the person of her representative, C. H. Cahan, also spoke, if not exactly in favour of Japan, certainly not against her. As a reporter of the day remarked, "Canada, in a curious oration, spoke strongly on both sides". At home there was much indignation displayed at his attitude, for feeling against aggressive, unjust action and in favour of the principle of law had been growing strongly in Canada since the war: Canadians had been taught that they had fought Germany because of her unprovoked and illegal attack on Belgium. Now Japan was doing the same thing to China, and Canada's representative abroad seemed to be condoning her action. As a matter of fact, Mr. Cahan was in a difficult position. It has been said that he had no specific instructions from his government, but it has also been asserted that he did have such instructions and disregarded them—at least until he came to the second half of his speech, which was what presumably gave it its curious ambivalent quality. He knew the gap between righteous indignation and Canadian willingness to act. He himself said European powers kept urging, "you in Canada are right next door to the trouble: you will of course be ready to send an army". Canadians, far from viewing the other side of the Pacific as "right next door", thought of it, he knew very well, as on the other side of the world and would hardly be willing to send fifty men, let alone an army. He therefore acted on his own responsibility and advised caution in the treatment of Japan.

The great naval powers were only too glad to be cautious and any suggestion of coercion faded out. As between upholding the law and consulting their own interests, they had consulted their own interests. Their retort might have been that lesser powers, not having to act, could afford to be sentimental about the rule of law. The counter-retort might just as well have been that in the long run (which meant Pearl Harbour, December 7, 1941) the great naval powers would have to fight the lawbreaker: why not give a blow rather than take a kick?

As for Canada, her governments, both Conservative and Liberal, after the first unfortunate foray into the muddle, kept discreetly out, confining their relations with Japan to an attitude of diplomatic correctness. So correct were they that almost up to the final oubreak of war with Japan, crucial war metals like nickel and scrap iron were going across to Japan. The people of the country, as apart from its administrations, were divided. The east was lukewarm. The west and certain groups such as the evangelical churches and political radicals manifested indignation but were never able to compel national action. Attention was gradually diverted, so that the Japanese attack on China in 1937 became not much more than another war in distant foreign parts. As for the government, it may be said in its extenuation that it could not single-handedly take an unfriendly attitude toward Japan, for that would have precipitated matters: Japan would probably have broken off relations. Canadian action, it could have been said, had to accord with that of Great Britain and the United States. But would courage in high places have influenced those countries? As it was, it was left to little New Zealand almost alone to hoist the banner of principle aloft and place an embargo on scrap iron shipments to Japan. In Canada the only banner waved aloft bore the motto "appeasement".

3. The Road to Independence

Once the victory of 1918 had been won, Canadians rapidly lost most of the interest the war had given them in the affairs of continental

Europe. The debates on the peace treaties (September, 1919) contained remarkably few references to the problems of foreign politics and a colossal number to the position and status of Canada. This self-centred attitude was not confined to Canada by any means, but it indicated how little prepared the country was to play its part on the international scene; it was still the call of the blood, not knowledge or direct interest, that furnished the main constituent of Canadian action across the Atlantic. Until the Second World War became imminent, the vital aspect of external relations was not foreign policy but the extension and completion of Canadian autonomy. The participation of Canada in international affairs was limited to the role she had assumed at Geneva, to membership in various international conferences of second rank, to minor variations on the theme of British relationship with Russia, and to the negative task of contracting out of certain obligations assumed by Great Britain. Canada did not act when Mr. Lloyd George invited assistance against the Turks in 1922, in the so-called Chanak affair; she repudiated any responsibility for the final peace treaty with Turkey, that of Lausanne, not having been a party to the negotiations; and she contracted out of British obligations assumed under the Locarno Pact of 1926.

Towards Russia it was difficult to find a satisfactory policy. The Russians were trade rivals in the British market, especially in timber and furs. Lumber and fur interests in Canada tried to get the government to influence the British to discriminate against Russia.[12] It was not edifying to see "hard-boiled" business men working to get Russian timber or furs excluded from English markets by emphasizing the "godless" nature of the Bolshevik regime. However, such action met with support from the French and Catholic people of the country. The result was that Canada hesitated in accepting the *rapprochements* which Great Britain made with Russia but was prompt in following when relationships were broken off.

In international gatherings, with the exception of the fight against Article X, the Canadian role had no particular individuality. For the most conspicuous of such gatherings before 1931, that which met to sign the Paris Peace Pact of 1928,[13] Canada's representative, Prime Minister King, made a special trip to Europe. Whether his tongue was as firmly in his cheek as those of many other representatives at that ceremonious and highly farcical proceeding is not a matter of record. Probably it was not; in such sentimental ritual Mr. King found himself at home. Of

---

[12] See p. 514.
[13] The Peace Pact was an agreement to abandon war as an instrument of national policy, which was equivalent to the individual abandoning sin.

course, to him it was also another occasion to emphasize Canadian autonomy, a repetition of the separate signatures at Versailles in 1919.

In 1928 no one was disposed to dispute Canadian claims to autonomy. The intervening decade had virtually completed the evolution, and all that remained was to work out the details. In external affairs here was the significant development of the period. The Imperial Conference resolution of 1917 had declared for a revision of the constitution of the Empire when time permitted. The Prime Ministers' meeting of 1921, owing to its preoccupation with the Japanese alliance and to the gathering sentiment in Canada and South Africa against giving fixed form to inter-Imperial relationships, did not undertake the task. If Arthur Meighen was not prepared to work out a constitution for the Empire, Mackenzie King could hardly be expected to be, and since it was King who was in office for most of the period, the evolution of imperial relations, if it bears the imprint of any one personality, must bear his. What would be expected of him would be stress on Canada's separate legal personality, that is, on autonomy, and that is exactly what occurred.

The indirect refusal to assist Great Britain over the Chanak incident (1922) was the first notice given that Canada would make up her own mind about foreign affairs. It was followed by the still more emphatic show of independence involved in the way in which the Halibut Treaty of 1923 with the United States was signed. No Dominion had previously claimed complete diplomatic independence, and treaties, if negotiated by Dominions' representatives, had been signed by the appropriate British diplomat as the King's plenipotentiary. But in 1923 Mr. Ernest Lapointe went to Washington furnished with full powers from the King, and when the British ambassador, Sir Auckland Geddes, turned up to sign the treaty, he was politely informed that that would not be necessary. The name of the King's Canadian plenipotentiary alone appeared on the document.

The manner of signing the Halibut Treaty practically established diplomatic autonomy, although a rearguard action was fought by certain constitutional metaphysicians who contended that since the King had to furnish full powers to the Canadian representative and since he must act on advice and this advice must be that of his British ministers little change had occurred.[14] If the British nations were to remain together, the position attained had become impossible. The Halibut

---

[14] The Conference of 1923 agreed that each self-governing state should have the right to negotiate treaties affecting itself, informing the others if the treaty were likely to affect them.

Treaty had been accepted by the American senate only with many objections, for that body could not discern Canada as an independent state. In the Imperial Conference of 1926, therefore, an attempt was made to straighten the matter out. Mackenzie King went to London with memories of Lord Byng's refusal of dissolution fresh in his mind and the Jacksonian democratic ideas of his grandfather in his family tradition: to him it was intolerable that the representatives of the people should be interfered with by a pale shadow of that Crown which had long since been deprived of its arbitrary authority. At London he met men as jealous of the autonomy of their Dominions as himself— Hertzog of South Africa and Cosgrave of Southern Ireland. The result was the re-arrangement of Imperial affairs embodied in the famous Balfour Report:

> They are autonomous communities within the British Empire, equal in status, in no way subordinate one to another in any aspect of their domestic or external affairs, though united by a common allegiance to the Crown and freely associated as members of the British Commonwealth of Nations.

In these rather rhetorical words the new conception of Empire as worked out by the Conference was set forth. The Report went on to say that while all were equal in status they manifestly could not be equal in function, for there was one of the self-governing communities which was much more experienced and much more powerful than the others, Great Britain. On Great Britain, therefore, must for some time to come rest special responsibilities, with correlated necessity for freedom of decision. As to the Governors-General they were no longer to be mere Colonial Office appointees but the representatives of the King himself, with duties, privileges, and limitations comparable to those of the King himself. They really became viceroys. Correspondence was no longer to go from Governor-General to Dominions' Secretary but direct from government to government. This part of the edifice was made logically complete when Canada and Great Britain exchanged High Commissioners in 1928, thus establishing a thinly-disguised form of diplomatic relationship between the two governments.

The Conference of 1926 solved the great problems of inter-Imperial relationships in principle but left a good many details to be worked out. This process was completed at the next Conference, in 1930, but previously heavy pressure had been put upon the Prime Minister, Mr. R. B. Bennett, by Howard Ferguson, the Conservative premier of Ontario, to secure consultation before the Committee's report was accepted. Mr. Ferguson's case was based upon that specious conception, the Compact theory of Confederation. Mr. Bennett yielded, and the proposed constitutional and defining statute was changed to prevent any possibility of its being made a basis for altering Dominion-Provincial relations as defined in the British North America Act. With this modification the act was passed in 1931 under the title of The Statute of Westminster.

The Statute of Westminster abolished the doctrine of "repugnancy", that is, no Dominion legislation could in future be held *ultra vires* because it happened to be *repugnant* to legislation of the Parliament of the United Kingdom.[15] The further consequence of such abolition was that the Parliaments of the United Kingdom and of the other self-governing countries became co-ordinate bodies and the Crown in Great Britain lost its right to withhold consent to "Dominion" legislation. 1931 had drawn abreast of 1775,[16] and the old struggle over Parliamentary Supremacy was laid to rest.

The statute also solved the question of extra-territorial legislation. As long as the British Parliament was the over-riding authority for the Empire, no local parliament could legislate for its own citizens beyond the three-mile limit. Canadian citizens automatically became "British subjects" three miles off shore, and Canadian ships "British" ships. There were many acts of the Imperial Parliament in this field[17] and all these remained to be re-enacted: one of the first big jobs, for instance, of the Parliament of Canada in its new status was to pass a Canadian Merchant Shipping Act. Thus the long road of responsible government, begun in the 1840's with internal legislation, was at last cleared of all obstacles and Canadian control completed over the entire field, within and without the state.

The Statute of Westminster came as close as was practicable without revolutionary scissors to legislating the independence of the "Dominions". There is good ground for holding December 11, 1931 as Canada's Independence Day, for on that day she became a sovereign state. It was still possible to make a debating contention that the authority which had enacted a statute must be superior to those existing under such statutes, that the British Parliament having constituted Canada by the British North America Act and clarified its position by the Statute of Westminster, must be a superior body to the Canadian Parliament and that under certain circumstances it could prove its superiority by repeal-

[15] The doctrine was specifically written into the Colonial Laws Validity Act of 1865, which the Statute of Westminster repealed.
[16] See p. 77.
[17] e.g. acts respecting wrecks.

ing these acts. But the British Parliament had also long ago passed an act acknowledging the independence of the United States: could it reduce the United States to a group of colonies again by repealing that act? The only means by which independence could have been more sharply defined would have been a declaration of independence from the people of Canada themselves. Since there was no machinery for such a declaration, it would have been revolutionary and would have precipitated a completely new situation, changing the institutions of the country. There was no hint of desire for such a course; Canadians followed the road to which they had become so thoroughly habituated, the well-tried road of legal tradition.

If the Statute solved the problem of independence for Canada, it created an anomalous situation for the Crown. If the Governors-General were viceroys, ministers in advising them were advising the Crown. If there was no difference in status between the self-governing countries, all His Majesty's ministers were coordinate, and he might find himself in the difficult position of accepting different advice on the same subject from all seven of them.[18] In 1931, the position had not developed to the point where doctrines of the divisibility of the Crown were acceptable. The King was not regarded as a personal monarch in the sense that he wore a separate crown and was a separate person in each of his self-governing kingdoms; he was one person, wearing one crown, with all the attributes of unity of personality. Yet he ruled over seven separate states. Yet since they had a single ruler, they were one state. What had happened was that the Commonwealth had evolved a metaphysical position exceeding in complexity, as seven exceeds three, the metaphysics of the Trinity. Surpassed was mystic One in Three and Three in One: God in three persons was outnumbered by the British King in seven persons, the Septennity.

Chronology

1919   The Conference of Versailles, January-July.
        First Meeting of the League Assembly.
1921   Meeting of the Prime Ministers of the Empire, London.
1921-22 Washington Conference, December-January.
1922   The "Chanak Affair".
1923   The Halibut Treaty.
        Imperial Conference.
1926   The Locarno Agreements.
        Balfour Report presented to Imperial Conference.

[18] Five and eight years later this is what occurred in the abdication of Edward VIII and in the declaration of war.

1927   Separate diplomatic representation instituted.
1928   Briand-Kellogg Peace Pact.
1931   The Statute of Westminster, December 11.
1932   League Assembly for determining policy on Japan's seizure of Man-
        churia, December 6.

Additional Reading

Carter, Gwendolen M. *The British Commonwealth and International Security: The Role of the Dominions, 1919-1939*. Toronto, 1947.

Dawson, R. M., ed. *Constitutional Issues in Canada, 1900-1931*. Oxford, 1933.

——, ed. *The Development of Dominion Status, 1900-1936*. Oxford, 1937.

Glazebrook, G. P. de T. *Canada at the Paris Peace Conference*. Toronto, 1942.

——. *A History of Canadian External Relations*. Toronto, 1950.

Hancock, W. K. *Survey of British Commonwealth Affairs*. I: *Problems of Nationality, 1918-1936*. Toronto, 1937.

Soward, F. H. *et al. Canada in World Affairs: The Pre-War Years*. Toronto, 1941. (*Canada in World Affairs* is a series by various authors, one volume for the most part dealing with one year. It will not be cited under authors' names, but under the general title.)

CHAPTER 33

Domestic Interlude, 1919-1930

1. The Reconstruction Period

Far from history swinging back to normal after 1919, which was what most people seemed to think had happened, it swung sharply away from the past, away from the nineteenth century's *laisser-faire* individualism, towards the twentieth's ideas of community. The old parties, the old religions, the old institutions, the old ways of thought were all drastically affected by this climactic change. The first dozen years or so of the inter-war period were the last in which talk in the old nineteenth century terms of peace and progress could still make a little sense. The depression which began in 1929 emphatically signalled the new road humanity was to follow, and the political upheavals which it quickly produced as clearly indicated that the victors of 1918, far from having solved the problems that had led to the world war, were merely living on the capital of their victory.

Canada's efforts towards mending the immediate ravages of war were greatly affected by the large changes wrought in her economy by the struggle. Canadian external trade had increased by leaps and bounds up to 1917. In the west, new cultivation had gone forward at such a rapid pace that Canada became the largest wheat exporter in the world. In industry new plants had been built and tens of thousands of people trained in new forms of skill. Lumber production had risen to vast heights, and even the depressed areas dependent upon codfisheries had experienced a wave of prosperity. In finance Canada had almost completed a change from debtor to creditor country, for the war loans had nearly all been raised internally; capital had, indeed, flowed out in the form of war supplies to Great Britain and France, with which countries Canada had established credit balances. All these evidences of an expanding economy had been subject to some degree of control and management by the federal government. While Canadian business men and farmers remained sturdy individualists who assumed they were running their own show, some of the experience gained during the war in managing the national economy continued to be utilized in such controls as The Canadian Wheat Board (1919-1920) and still more was to be drawn on when in 1939 the second war broke out.[1]

The beginning of the reconstruction period was marked by a high level of prosperity, attained as a result of the war. Canada in 1914 had been a flourishing country, but in 1919, even though the saying "easy come, easy go" could properly be applied to much war-time wealth, it was close to being rich. This was particularly evident in the cities, where new residential quarters, larger and more elaborate shops and long strings of automobiles in the streets testified to war-time prosperity and to the rapidity with which urbanism was gaining the ascendancy in a country hardly beyond the backwoods stage. In such a society, few dreamed of revolutionary measures. All that appeared necessary was quiet recuperation, during which the disbanded troops would be reabsorbed and war production would change to peace production. That done, things would hum along again. Reconstruction, therefore, took such forms as schemes of hospitalization, pensions, and insurance. A special department, Soldiers' Civil Re-establishment, was instituted, and an ambitious resettlement programme, the Soldiers' Land Settlement arrangement, was put into operation. Only a fraction of the "returned men" availed themselves of it, and over a quarter of those who did eventually abandoned their land, but it was as successful as most large-scale colonization plans of the sort have been. It indicated the direction Canadian thoughts were still taking: the attack on the land was still the accepted norm of behaviour. "Reconstruction" consisted in binding up wounds, and then letting people look after themselves. The aim of public policy was still negative; the government was not trying to create a society of any particular type. Its aim was not socialization, still less "socialism"; it was still, in the best nineteenth century style, developmental.

[1] See p. 533.

2. Another Phase of Immigration and Settlement

After the war, it being given to few to see that the previous age had ended, efforts were made to resume one of its most prominent features, mass immigration. In 1919 few people understood that the great *Völkerwanderung* of the nineteenth century was drawing to a close; most thought that the war had only interrupted a flow that would eventually give Canada a much larger population. It was not realized that the supply of good land in the west was, like others of Canada's "inexhaustible" resources, not far from exhausted; there were no fresh Saskatchewans.

Interested parties would not accept such a view and throughout the period there was a great deal of pressure to remove all restraints on importing immigrants. This came not only from the railways and land companies but from industrial interests that wished to repeat for Canada the American experience of cheap factory labour. The docility of poor foreign immigrants has made them desirable "hands", and upon their semi-slave labour much North American industry has flourished. During the period after the war, efforts seem to have been made to bring in, not persons from the British Isles, who were too soon at home and too independent for these purposes, but peasants from eastern Europe, who would be least acquainted with Canadian conditions. Farm labourers and servant girls were still the official foundations of the state, but somehow or other after arriving they frequently got transmuted into factory hands and by 1931, sixty per cent of the new arrivals lived in cities. There was little knowledge of the problems of population, and not until the end of the 1920's were scientific studies available to guide public policy. By that time the movement was working to a close. Considerable agitation against it was developing for racial and religious reasons, and shortly after the great depression set in, Prime Minister Bennett intervened, and immigration virtually ceased.

This last wave of immigration had proved much like all previous ones. At the end of the period two-thirds of the "immigrants" could not be found. Not only that but there was a heavy emigration of the native born to the United States. If Canada had retained all her own natural increase during the period and all the immigration which came to her, she would have had a population in 1931 of about 11,622,000. Instead she had one of 10,377,000. There was a "leakage" of 1,245,000.[2] An "immigration" of persons born in the United States of 85,000 only succeeded in decreasing the American-born population of Canada by 30,000. Meanwhile the Canadian-born population of the United States

[2] Census of 1941, I, 147 diagram.

had increased at a rate that suggested an emigration of the native born
from Canada of about 300,000, a figure which included too many young
people of energy and good education. To replace them within a single
generation called for too great a step in adaptation on the part of the
children of recently arrived immigrants, however good these latter might
be intrinsically. Immigration was proving as injurious for the quality of
the population as it was ineffective for the quantity.

The man who will work for a low wage will always drive out the
man who has become accustomed to a higher: to a clergyman from
England or a carpenter from Poland, Canadian pay seems high. But it
is lower than American. Consequently, other things being equal, the
clergyman or carpenter will come to Canada, and the Canadian clergyman or carpenter go to the United States. Sir Richard Gresham, in the
days of good Queen Bess, formulated the rule that "cheap money drives
out dear", a sound monetary maxim. Just so will "cheap" men drive
out "dear", an equally sound sociological principle. If the movement of
population were completely free throughout the world, there is little
question who within a few generations would inherit the earth: it would
be a class of man not much liked in Canada, the only human being who
seems able to stand heat and cold, hunger and thirst, the Arctics and
the tropics, who will work cheerfully from dawn to dusk on wages on
which other men would starve, and who seems to have more disease-
resistant anti-toxins in him than any other known specimen of the
human animal—the Chinese coolie. The men who demand least from
life drive out the men who demand more. From 1921 to 1931, the
increase of Canadian-born professionals in the United States and of
European-born peasants in Canada indicated how inexorably this
"Gresham's Law of Immigration" was working.

The immigration of 1921-31 created serious stresses and strains in
Canadian society. Labour opposed it because it was pretty sure of its
deliberate cheap wage aspects. The French opposed it because they
objected to foreigners being aided to settle in the west while the native-
born had to depend on their own resources and because immigrants
assimilate to the English group. The Protestant churches came to oppose
the new immigration, for it was heavily weighted towards Catholicism.[3]
English-speaking western farmers opposed it, for the European immigrant was steadily driving them off the land. But none of this opposition
was of sufficient strength to countervail the influence of "the interests"
(of which the railways were the chief) with a government such as Mr.
King's which, its leader apart, had no social ideas of its own and

[3] Roman Catholics of non-British, non-French origin increased in Canada, 1921-
31, by about 100%.

responded to the strongest pressure. It took the largest depression in history to end an influx that was rapidly becoming socially injurious.

3. A Renewed Struggle for Hinterlands

The competition between developing metropolitan centres during the period expressed itself in the familiar struggle for hinterlands. Cheap industrial labour and new settlement were but two factors in this competition, which, as in previous periods, went on mainly between Montreal and Toronto, with Winnipeg as an outpost of Montreal and Vancouver quickly developing as a centre in its own right, and beyond the two larger Canadian centres standing the great external conurbations of London and New York.

Montreal's position at the conjunction of water routes had made it the focus of the commercial system of the St. Lawrence, and thanks to railway building, it had become the focus of the commercial and financial system of Canada. Already the headquarters of the Canadian Pacific, after the war it became the headquarters of the Canadian National too. The rapid extension of the western grain area plus some very large harvests also made it the world's largest grain-shipping port. As a great centre of international trade, Montreal should have been a free trade city but transportation that could bring goods down would also take them up, so its manufactures (which had quickly expanded after the inauguration of the "National Policy" in 1879) came to outweigh its commerce, and Montreal became a stronghold of protection. Not only could it take toll on western grain passing through its port, but it could also require western grain growers to buy its manufactured products at high tariff prices. It could comfortably say "Heads I win, tails you lose".

Originally even more interested in the opening of the west than Montreal, Toronto had not been able to secure an equal share of the profits involved. It had made a financial penetration of the prairies with its banks, its trust and loan companies, and it had found there a large market for its manufactures,[4] but it did not secure satisfactory rail service until the C.P.R. built its Toronto-Sudbury line (joining its main line at the latter point) about 1907. Even then none of the grain routes passed near Toronto. That city's hold of the west, as has previously been pointed out,[5] lay in the personal and family connections that arose out of the mass migration of Ontario people, a relationship which was to give its growing cultural predominance added significance.

Toronto looked naturally to the north, which its railroads enabled

[4] Especially farm implements.
[5] See p. 353

it to lay under tribute.[6] North Bay, the junction of the Northern Division of the Grand Trunk (later C.N.R.) and the main line of the C.P.R., had by the end of the century become a flourishing "jumping-off point" for the land that lay beyond. Attention turned to "New" or Northern Ontario in the late nineties but it was not until the province of Ontario began to build its Temiskaming and Northern Ontario Railroad (about 1902) that northern minerals started to pour southward, and it was upon these (silver, cobalt, gold) together with the nickel and copper mines at Sudbury[7] that the growth of the north first was based. To them were added lumber and the rapidly expanding pulp and paper industry, while at the same time settlement began in the large areas of arable land north of the Shield known as "The Clay Belt". In Northern Ontario a new community, with a life and outlook of its own, was growing up.[8]

But to grasp where one of the principal beneficiaries of it lay, it was only necessary to walk along University Avenue in Toronto and see the large office buildings housing the companies developing the resources of the north. The expansion of Toronto in the 1920's, both in wealth and population, was largely based on Northern Ontario. The northern interests did not stop short at the provincial boundary but laid northern Quebec under tribute too. Perhaps the crowning evidence of Toronto's dominance lay in its feat in pushing a branch line up from the T. and N.O. to the newly discovered copper deposits around Noranda, Quebec, thus cutting them out from the hegemony of Montreal, to which they had already been connected by the northern line of the Canadian National. But Toronto itself had to acknowledge a superior, for its gains had to be shared with the metropolis that stood at the other end of the north-south axis. Just as New York a century before had drawn down the pine timber of southern Ontario to itself,[9] in the twentieth century it drew down the cash proceeds from the pulpwood and minerals of Northern Ontario.[10] If Winnipeg was an outpost of Montreal, Toronto was a kind of suburb of New York.[11]

The countryside of "old" Ontario was markedly affected by the

[6] See p. 283
[7] Begun in the early 1890's.
[8] Population 1921: 256,423; 1931: 349,374.
[9] See p. 282.
[10] The dominating interests of Dome Mines were in New York, the head office and chief refinery of International Nickel not far away, at Bayonne, N.J. The Toronto Mining Exchange was closely tied in with the New York Exchange and with New York finance.
[11] This north-south axis in North America may first be recognized in the 17th-century efforts of Albany fur-traders to cut the French lines of communication with the west.

presence of the rapidly expanding centre. Toronto threw out outliers
such as Oshawa, a considerable automobile manufacturing centre.
Hamilton, too, and indeed the whole industrial area of the Niagara
Peninsula and the western peninsula of Ontario were tied into Toronto
metropolitanism. This urban development, which brought about a
relatively large concentration of population in a relatively small area,
turned an exporting agricultural province into a local food demand
region: by 1960, Ontario was said to be no longer capable of feeding
itself. The economic interests of the Ontario farmer changed from free
trade to protection, and with modern devices of communication, he himself ceased to be a farmer in the old sense, having an independent life
and folkways of his own, and, subject chiefly to his distance from
Toronto (or other large centres), passed over into a modified kind of
suburbanite.

As the older rural areas became subjugated to their urban centres,
newer regions opened up into which the settler penetrated, hoping, like
his breed from time immemorial, to establish a new world for himself,
far from the crowds and corruptions of "effete" civilization. In Northern
Ontario the pioneer did not long escape mechanized civilization, for as
soon as the first highways were opened, he had to face competition from
the earlier products of southern counties, delivered by truck to the very
doorsteps of the mining and paper towns. In contrast, the newer
northern areas of the west were far enough away to allow the settler to
enjoy some of his self-contained life. The Peace River country, one of
the chief of these, separated by a broad band of wilderness from the
nearest settled region, was an area of primary production, like the rest
of the prairies. The northern prairie frontier generally continued to
expand without much consciousness of metropolitan pressure, save
where it joined in with the general prairie agitations against the Winnipeg Grain Exchange, which for the western farmer symbolizes metropolitanism even more directly than "St. James Street".

Although the frontiersman longs to get away from civilization, he
never fails to press for improved communications. It was the pressure
of settlers which produced another railroad programme, a small one consisting mainly in branch line construction. Farmers have understood well
enough how the branch line ties them in to the general system, and
their fear of urban domination has been reflected in demands for
alternative outlets: thus the Peace River district has never ceased to
agitate for a direct rail outlet to the Pacific coast, and as early as the
1880's Saskatchewan and Manitoba were pressing for a railroad to
Hudson's Bay.

The only piece of through line in the programme was the Hudson Bay Railway, completed in 1931. It should have re-established the old dominance of "The Bay". Churchill should have become the modern York Factory. Despite a large saving in distance,[12] this did not occur. The explanation lies partially in the opposition of the shipping and insurance interests of the east, partially in the short season, partially in the established shipping routes of the east ("liner" traffic, to which grain is just good ballast, or availability of tramps, especially at New York). If Churchill were ever to be freely used, it could be no more than a way-station on the route to Liverpool, and all the problems of Canadian urban domination would repeat themselves in English terms. What in practice has happened of recent years is a certain modest growth in Churchill's place as a military base for the defence of the north, with American predominance.

Contrasted with pioneer settlement, non-agricultural northern expansion was an integrated aspect of metropolitanism. The most striking mineral finds (in the Flin Flon area of northern Manitoba) were developed by capital from Boston, and controlled from New York. To it the Province of Manitoba surrendered all royalties, showing the tightness with which its mines were wedged into American metropolitanism. Winnipeg was repeating the experience of Toronto and, for mining at least, becoming an outpost of New York. Similarly the expanding oil industry of Alberta was dominated by eastern capital, mainly The Standard Oil Company, through the Imperial Oil Company, which also reached down into the remote north and secured oil rights at Fort Norman on the Lower Mackenzie, where considerable deposits had been found. The Mackenzie river is a great artery of transport at whose head stands the city of Edmonton; whether despite its rapid growth and considerable size that place will develop in its own right or remain an outpost, a larger North Bay, is still undetermined. It is significant that the radium found on Great Bear Lake, the most showy result of the scurrying about in the north made possible by that unique Canadian type of air transport, "bush-flying", is refined on Lake Ontario.

In the country beyond the mountains, after the original railroad penetration, eastern influences continued strong in finance, religion, and education, but the diversity of wealth on the coast enabled local interests to grow too: relatively small amounts of capital were needed for lumbering, salmon canning, fruit farming. This quasi-independence was strengthened with the construction of the Panama canal, for then at a bound Vancouver became a great sea port, sending the products of its

[12] About 1,000 miles to Liverpool as compared with the route via Montreal.

hinterland not only to the Orient but to Europe. Vancouver began to draw wheat from as far east as mid-prairie. Lumber it obtained from the whole stretch of coast north to Alaska. Its sea connections, together with the excellent interior railway net (built mainly by the people of Canada as a whole), gave Vancouver possession of a rich hinterland several hundreds of thousands of square miles in extent. As a result it grew rapidly but by the end of the period under review, 1930, it had not developed the ultimate attributes of metropolitanism—financial control and a cultural life of its own. Nor, thirty-five years later, had it yet done so.

The application of a cultural test robs all Canadian cities of the metropolitan status, though Montreal for French Canada and Toronto for English, have gone a certain distance towards it. Canada has had little independence in culture: its theatrical and literary centre was originally London, later New York, which city has become almost the sole continental focus of original, creative work in most arts: attempts in Canadian centres at literary or dramatic production, at local symphony orchestras and so on (like those of similarly situated American cities) wear a slightly *démodé* air.[13] Canadian literature (in either language), though creditable, has not advanced far and a Canadian music, a Canadian drama, are just beginning. As these words are written (1963), Canada stands, as it were, on a knife-edge: she could easily slide down the American side of the knife, and lose all cultural distinctiveness; or she may advance some distance in the direction of a cultural life of her own. Towards this, an indisputable metropolitan centre would greatly help.

4. The Post-War Business Cycle and Its Political Correlation

The secular economic disturbances set going by the great wars of the modern industrial age seem to have similar rhythms. They work through small pulsations within a decade or so after the peace up to heights of speculative prosperity and tumble with a crash that has broken not only the business structure but political edifices also.[14]

After the Armistice of November 11, 1918, there was a brief hesitation and then early in 1919 a short burst of "replacement" activity; this was followed by a lull and then a "boom" based on reconstruction optimism. Commercial optimism, as always, overshot the mark and by

---

[13] Painting forms a partial and distinguished exception. And now signs which give ground for optimism increase (1963).

[14] The period after 1918 has many resemblances to that following 1815.

the fall of 1920, a serious depression had begun. This deepened for a year or two, and there was a rapid fall in inflated war prices.[15] Three years of "bad times" followed, but by 1924 recovery was again evident. By 1926 the pace was becoming swift, and during 1927 and 1928 it became frantic. These years witnessed the most unbridled "boom" in history. The climax was reached amid a frenzy of excitement in 1929, and in October of that year, "the props fell out".[16] The biggest and most calamitous of depressions was at hand.

The vagaries of the business cycle were at once reflected in politics. In Canada, a country where the economic aspect of life has a dominating place, the connection between politics and economics must be close. The broad results of their interactions during the period were the decay of the old party structure and much loss in the prestige of the old institutions of government. These results first became visible in agricultural circles.

The rapid rise in farm produce during the war had not been an unmixed blessing to the farmers, many of whom unwisely bought additional land at high prices. The average man, with no experience other than the stability of the previous generations, had come to regard the new level of prices as permanent, and when it collapsed after the war, serious social consequences had to follow. Men were first puzzled, then dismayed, then angered, and at that point political action ensued. No farmer was going to stand by watching high interest rates and capital costs eat up the diminishing revenue from his crops, especially when, to his mind, the cause was plainly visible in the greed of vested interests, in the bankers and mortgage holders who were devouring him and the eastern manufacturers who were holding him to ransom. From such causes sprang the new agricultural revolt which was to rumble on in greater or less intensity for many years. In tariff matters the two traditional parties seemed to have come to differ only in detail. A new political grouping, therefore, emerged as soon as the wheat farmers realized how closely their interests were tied up with free trade. Early in the century their weight had begun to be felt at Ottawa, and when Sir Wilfrid embarked on his long-delayed tour of the west in the summer of 1911 "the farmers began whetting their axes for him on the rough edges of long-delayed hopes".[17] His attempt at meeting western pressure by reciprocity failed, and shortly afterwards the war, with its high prices for wheat, obscured political grievances. Union Government in 1917,

[15] Wholesale prices 1920=100; 1921=71.
[16] C.P.R. common stock stood at 250 in June, 1929, but later on had sunk as low as 5.
[17] L. E. Ellis, *Reciprocity*, p. 20.

which received the enthusiastic support of the west (only three Liberals were returned out of 55 members), had the important effect of loosening traditional party ties, rendering the developments that were to come that much easier.

After the Armistice, government attempted to wind up its special war controls as quickly as possible, among them the Canadian Board of Grain Supervisors, which from 1917 had been in charge of the marketing of Canadian wheat. Western agitation succeeded in extorting a continuation of control, the new authority being the Canadian Wheat Board, which was given power to market the crop of 1919. But in August, 1920, free-trading reopened on the Winnipeg Grain Exchange. This return of the interests to power, together with the precipitous fall in prices, gave the impetus that carried western farmers into political action. In Ontario also, and even in the staid province of New Brunswick, where new-fangled ideas do not quickly penetrate, the fall in prices was a major factor in calling organized farmers' parties into existence. An election taking place in Ontario in the fall of 1919, a farmers' slate of candidates was put up (the "U.F.O." or United Farmers of Ontario) and to everyone's surprise it swept the province. Mr. E. C. Drury, a farmer and the son of a farmer, a Liberal and the son of a former Liberal provincial minister, became premier.

The victory in Ontario gave encouragement to the rural interests everywhere. By the beginning of 1920 they had been brought together into the National Progressive Party, under the leadership of T. A. Crerar, also a former Liberal and an ex-member of the Union government. In July, 1921, a farmers' government was elected in Alberta, and in the Federal election of December, 1921, the new party carried 65 seats, making it the second largest in the House[18] and giving it the right to become, if it wished, the official opposition. A farmers' government was also returned in Manitoba.

At last, it seemed a movement of agrarian revolt had come to the threshold of power; would it succeed in putting into effect its new national policy of free trade, thereby turning back the hands of the clock, mastering vested urban interests, and making Canada into a country not for the privileged commercial and industrial few, but for the rural many, a land of sturdy yeomen, not of city factory hands and "bloated plutocrats"? Where Bryanism had failed in the United States, would Progressivism succeed in Canada?

Alas, the gates of Paradise, though standing well ajar, were never to be entered. The Farmers' movement had risen on price discrepancies, the tariff, and especially on the cooperative movement. It had blossomed

¹⁸ L: 117; C: 53; P: 65.

into a political party almost overnight but had neither the leadership nor the programme for permanence and was handicapped from the first by the individualism of the farmer, his suspicion and jealousy of his own leaders. From the first it was vindictively assailed as a "class party", "a sectional party". All too easily, men versed in the sharp corners of politics and backed by the resources of those who fully realized that their power was at stake managed to use some of the leaders and, in Ontario, to compromise them. In that province, by 1923 the United Farmers' government had foundered, and by the same year the Federal Progressive party was definitely in decline. It had made a fatal mistake when its leader, T. A. Crerar, failed to claim the place of official Leader of the Opposition: this indicated to all and sundry that the Progressives were just a group in Parliament for the furtherance of their own interests, not a party which aspired to the government of the nation. The void they left was at once filled by Mr. Meighen and his fifty-three Conservatives, an action which may have saved that party from destruction. Within a year from the election Crerar had resigned. With the leadership in weaker hands, Progressive influence slumped, and in the election of 1925, the party secured only 25 seats. In the election of 1926, the Progressives disappeared as a formal party, falling back, like other rural protest movements before them,[19] into the Liberalism from which they had mainly arisen. Only a few members, mostly from Alberta, remained, now definitely no more than a sectional group.[20]

Ruralism had failed; urban forces could once more take over control (tempered by concessions), as in the United States after 1896. Industry and commerce were overbalancing agriculture, the population of cities and towns that of the countryside. If a successful movement of revolt was to appear, it would have to be built, not on the failures of 1919-26, but on new conceptions.

The pattern of these new conceptions had already begun to unfold. At the end of the war, the prompt discontinuance of munitions-making and the ensuing depression created unemployment and labour unrest. Curiously enough it was in a centre far from major industrial developments that there occurred the event which was to stamp on the subsequent period a character of its own. This was the Winnipeg Strike (1919). New regions are invariably more volatile than old: they gather to them men from all points of the compass, many filled with a spirit of adventure, many with half-assimilated sophistications brought with them from older societies, while nearly everyone has something of the "try-anything-once" attitude. Under the leadership mainly of men who had

[19] e.g. The Patrons of Industry in the 1890's.
[20] For the Progressive party, see W. L. Morton, *The Progressive Party in Canada* (Toronto, 1950).

had their views formed in British leftwing Labour circles, with cooperation from some who through Methodism had been deeply moved at the
spectacle of social injustice,[21] the Winnipeg Strike went further than
ordinary labour agitation. By 1919, thanks to the heavy immigration of
previous years, Winnipeg had become a labour centre of the old-country
type (as, for another generation, it was to remain) : although it was easy
for men of this schooling, in reaction to the passion displayed against them
by their opponents, to be carried beyond their original objects, it is difficult to believe that they were possessed of serious revolutionary intentions.

Before the episode was concluded, the Federal government had rushed
through Parliament the infamous "Section 98" in amendment to the
Criminal Code, by which a man could be found guilty of most serious
offences on the weakest of evidence.[22] This was a demonstration to many
of how feeble the English tradition of freedom was when compared
with the fears of the ruling classes; it weakened Canadian liberalism,
and many years were required before its repeal could be effected
(1936). "Section 98" and the travesty of justice constituted by the trial
of the Winnipeg strike-leaders struck deep into western society and had
a good deal to do with the subsequent emergence of radical movements.

It was almost by accident that the leading Methodist humanitarian
of his day, Rev. J. S. Woodsworth, a man whose career had been
passed in the service of the underdog, became associated with the
strike.[23] Once he had put his shoulder to the wheel, Woodsworth was
not the man to turn back. He himself received a flick from the whip of
authority in the form of prosecution for seditious libel, based upon pub-

[21] Most of these latter trained in Wesley College, Winnipeg, the Methodist Arts
and Theological foundation in the University of Manitoba, a college which took
the teachings of Christ seriously enough to father a remarkably large share of
the movement for social justice in Canada. J. S. Woodsworth (see p. 517)
was among its best-known graduates.

[22] Section 98 consisted in five subsections. The first defined in very wide terms
an unlawful association. The second gave power to seize property "belonging
or suspected to belong to an unlawful association". The third provided imprisonment for not more than 20 years for any officer or member of such an
association, or for anyone wearing any badge or emblem suggesting that he
was in anywise associated with such association. The fourth enacted that if
anyone had attended meetings, spoken publicly, or distributed literature of an
unlawful association "it shall be presumed, in the absence of proof to the
contrary that he is a member of such unlawful associations".—That is, he was
guilty until he was proved innocent.

[23] Woodsworth, the son of a pioneer Methodist minister in the west, devoted
himself to working among the immigrants in North Winnipeg, whence he wrote
his book Strangers within our Gates. Later on, he thought his way out of the
church, abandoned the ministry, and found work as a stevedore in Vancouver.
This experience strengthened his interest in labour problems, but it was little
more than a chance visit to Winnipeg which involved him in the strike and
thus in politics. See K. W. McNaught, "J. S. Woodsworth and a Political Party
for Labour, 1896 to 1921," CHR, XXX (June, 1949), 123-143, and his more
recent biography of Woodsworth, A Prophet in Politics (Toronto, 1959).

lication, *inter alia*, of passages from the prophet Isaiah. But shortly afterwards the people vindicated him, as they had William Lyon Mackenzie before him, and in the election of 1921, he was returned to Parliament. There, this man with the burning urge to justice for his fellow man in his heart, but with no formal doctrinaire philosophy, found himself at the head of a little Parliamentary group which stood in opposition to both old parties. It was sheer power of personality and a character of singular integrity that brought Woodsworth to the leadership of the dissidents and in 1932 to the headship of a new national party, the "C.C.F.".[24]

Canadian history is full of rural protest movements but not until the inter-war period did a corresponding urban movement arise, and then it was weak. After the Winnipeg Strike, labour took no very active part in politics, and men like Woodsworth were not, in a strict sense, Labour members. Rather, they were intellectuals and humanitarians who had the interests of labour at heart. Labour cooperated with them luke-warmly. There are many reasons for the political backwardness of labour. Canada has been mostly rural. When industry did develop, it was in relatively small units, far apart. Labour struggles were sporadic and dispersed. Most of the older unions were affiliated with the American Federation of Labour, which did not permit direct political action. When in the twentieth century big industry did develop in Canada, much of it was situated in Quebec, where it found docile work-men, cut off from labour elsewhere in the country. Leftwing contentions are that Quebec has been ruled by a tacit alliance of English Protestant finance and the French Catholic hierarchy:[25] French-Canadian nation-alist movements have represented in part a cover for the connection, but in greater part the irritation of French intellectuals at English business domination. French labour, in its turn, has been divided between the call of race and church through the Catholic Unions and the pull of economic interest represented by the "International Unions". It remains to be seen whether the capitalist-hierarchic alliance or French labour will triumph in the end.[26] In the meantime the Canadian labour move-

[24] See p. 517.
[25] Various branches of the church in Quebec are believed to have large holdings of industrial securities.
[26] A possible way out might well be an ambitious programme of provincial state-socialism which would take economic control from the English and transfer the struggle into purely French terms; the expropriation in 1944 by the Godbout Liberal government of the Montreal Light, Heat and Power Company was a first step in this direction. The preceding words of this note were written in the 1940's. They were prophetic, for in the 1960's certain ministers in the Lesage government were strenuously advocating large extensions of public ownership, with the expressed objective of putting economic control into the hands of French Canadians. The expropriation in 1962 of most of the private companies generating electricity was an expression of this. In the interval, the Duplessis government had talked Nationalism but played into the hands of industry.

ment as a whole is divided and weakened by the racial question, in addition to the lesser factors which in this area, as in all others, make cohesion in Canada difficult.

5. The Course of Politics, 1921-30

Canadian politics in the pre-depression portion of the post-war period cannot be said to have lacked variety. Not only did new parties wax and wane, but there were between 1921 and 1930 four Prime Ministers, four elections, and five years during which the life of the government of the day hung by a thread. Underlying the whole period, as has already been noted, was the secular change in the basis of politics from individualism to collectivisim which would eventually force a major realignment of party allegiances. One age had gone, another was struggling to be born.

For the new age, the war was a midwife rather than a parent. The new forces in national life would in any event have sought political expression; the war hastened this process. As is so frequently the case, the government that had conducted the war was discarded at the first opportunity after the peace: however good its record the war government accumulates all the unpopularity that springs from the necessary coercive measures. Sir Robert Borden's Union Ministry began to show signs of disintegration not long after the Armistice. The death of Sir Wilfrid Laurier in January, 1919, stirred old associations among many Unionist Liberals, and by 1920, now that the Union Government had dealt with the only issue on which it had been formed. the successful conduct of the war, most of them had returned to the fold. When Sir Thomas White, the war-time Minister of Finance, retired and then in the summer, Sir Robert himself, for reasons that were given as ill-health, it was clear that the Conservative party's tenure of power was limited.

Sir Robert's successor, nominated rather than chosen, was Arthur Meighen, associated in the public mind, especially the French mind, with the most invidious war measure, conscription. Meighen exhibited all the faults and virtues that characterize the men of Ulster descent: he was loyal to his friends, loyal to his prejudices, admirable in his family life, but ridden by his hates, full of vituperation in speech, and unrelenting in his personal antagonisms. Meighen has been described by those who knew him well as a charming and kindly person in private life, yet wherever he went he left a trail of enemies. No more divisive spirit, no man more loved and hated, has appeared in Canadian life.

No greater contrast could possibly have been presented to him than the man who was chosen as Sir Wilfrid's successor, Mr. William Lyon

Mackenzie King. The two recall the sentiments of Shakespeare's Julius
Caesar:

> Let me have men about me that are fat,
> Sleek-headed men, and such as sleep o'nights.
> Yond Cassius has a lean and hungry look.
> He thinks too much, such men are dangerous.
> ... Seldom he smiles, and smiles in such a sort
> As if he mocked himself, and scorned his spirit
> That could be moved to smile at anything. ...

We are told by psychologist and biologist alike that the "lean and
hungry" type tend to be intellectuals: like Cassius they think much.
This hard analytical approach—they "look quite through the deeds of
men"—makes them prefer principle and philosophical scheme to warm,
human relationships: that is, they are typical nineteenth century Liberals. It is the jovial, fat men who are the natural Conservatives. The
lean and hungry Cassius of a Meighen should therefore have been a
Liberal, the short, stout man who looked as if he slept o'nights, a Conservative; in this case, the scientists were wrong. It was the man who
smiled seldom, and smiled in such a sort as if he mocked himself, who
speciously bore all the earmarks of the introvert, that was the Conservative; it was his opponent, who appeared the extroverted type, that
was the Liberal. Canadian politics, intensively down to 1926 and inter-
mittently thereafter until 1943, were to be a duel between these two.

Mr. Meighen did not fare well in the only session of the expiring
Parliament in which he acted as Prime Minister, that of 1921. The government's war record, plus the depression, plus skilful attack by a reviving Liberal opposition, caused it to achieve a height of unpopularity
rarely reached in Canadian annals. The election of December 9, 1921
registered the obvious verdict. Meighen was swept from office. Quebec
had emphatically expressed its disapproval of the man responsible for
conscription, who to it was the embodiment of English Canadian
imperialist extremism. But the west and parts of Ontario were caught up
in the agrarian movement, as already described. The result was a three-
cornered division of the Commons, with Mr. King having the largest
group, 117 out of 235, or one short of a majority over the other two
combined. However, Progressivism was so much closer to Liberalism
than to Conservatism that he had reasonable assurance of being able to
carry on.

King's first ministry thus proved fairly stable. Parliament lived out
its natural term and the next elections occurred in 1925. On the two
large issues of the day, finance and the railway difficulties, the govern-

ment's record was very fair, and on the eve of the elections it attempted to strengthen its appeal to the west by making some reductions in the tariff. There were few clouds on the horizon, near or remote, and consequently no sharp issues. It was natural to expect that Liberalism would prove, as in other such cases, the residuary legatee of the dissolving Progressive party, whose original parent it was. This would give a solid majority and restore the two party system.

The people did not speak in that way. King's support fell from 118 seats (at dissolution) to 101, that of Meighen increased to 116, leaving 28 dissidents in a House now standing at 245. This confused situation was the basis for one of the hottest constitutional disputes since Confederation. The King government, dependent on the independents for its day-to-day existence, harassed by the Conservatives, who successfully disinterred some major scandals affecting certain of its ministers, faced the loss of Progressive support in the spring of 1926. King asked the Governor-General, Lord Byng, for a dissolution. The latter, convinced that Meighen could obtain enough independent support to enable him to carry on, refused. Mr. King had no course but to resign. Meighen, becoming Prime Minister, found he could not command the independent support upon which he had reckoned. He had the option of forming a cabinet whose members, having in those days to seek re-election on acceptance of office under the Crown, would be absent from the Commons, thereby leaving his party in a minority, or of attempting to govern by some make-shift expedient of dubious legality. He chose the latter. He himself, having accepted office, had to resign his seat, but his prospective cabinet remained in the House. Liberals vigorously contended that these men were private members and had no right to act as departmental heads. A threat of refusal of supplies was held out and then after three days of office a vote of want of confidence in Prime Minister Meighen was carried. He had no alternative but to ask in his turn for a dissolution, which was granted.

Oceans of ink have been spilled to prove that Lord Byng (a) had, (b) did not have, the right to refuse dissolution to King.[27] The only pertinent precedent was Sir Edmund Head's refusal of dissolution to George Brown,[28] and that did not throw much light on the situation. Apparently the Governor-General honestly believed that there was an alternative government in the House. Yet under the principles of Responsible Government, should he not have taken the advice of his Prime Minister? Whatever he should or should not have done, the fact

---

[27] See Eugene Forsey, *The Royal Power of Dissolution of Parliament in the British Commonwealth* (Toronto, 1943). See also the interminable controversy between Forsey and J. W. Dafoe in the *Winnipeg Free Press* during the winter of 1942.
[28] See p. 299.

remains that the Governor-General represents the law of the constitution and that if he refuses a dissolution, though it may be contrary to all precedent and against the custom of the constitution, it is perfectly legal —as King's prompt resignation indicated. Refusal of dissolution, the incident showed, was not quite as dead as the royal veto, which, too, would be perfectly legal (though perhaps, revolutionary) if it were resurrected.

The ensuing election vindicated King, for Conservative seats dropped to 91. Unhyphenated Liberals alone numbered 119 and various brands of Liberal-Progressives, Progressives, United Farmers, Labourites and Independents, most of whom could be counted on to vote with the government against the Conservatives, accounted for the remaining 35. Mr. King was able to form a stable ministry, which lasted out the term of Parliament, or until 1930. A great effort had been made to base the campaign on the constitutional issue, but the experience indicated clearly how difficult it is to carry abstruse constitutional issues to the public at large. King won because distrust of Meighen in Quebec was still strong, because he reaped further gains from the dissolution of western agrarianism, because he had become identified with "good times" and because he had made substantial reductions in the duties on imported motor cars. To all this there may have been added tinges of hostility against interference in Canadian affairs by an English Governor-General.

In 1926, it seemed as if the threatened disintegration and re-arrangement of parties had passed over. Four years more of stable government by King and three years of high prosperity confirmed the impression. Notwithstanding the replacement of Meighen, who realized that success had become impossible to him, by a new Conservative leader, R. B. Bennett, this time in open convention, nearly everything went well for the government. Then the world was flung into the depression of 1929 and all became uncertain again. Bennett saw his opportunity, enhanced, as it was, by the hostile heights to which the Americans were building their tariff wall,[29] and began advocating a reversal of the King government's mild tendency towards lower tariffs. A pompous and explosive individual, he talked, somewhat ridiculously, of "blasting his way into foreign markets". King decided to dissolve rather than go on to the end of his term, when the depression would presumably have deepened. That was acute strategy, for if he were defeated, it would leave his opponent to carry on through stormy times, saddled with the responsibility for them. That was exactly what happened.

[29] In the Hawley-Smoot tariff, as worked out April, 1929—June, 1930.

In the election campaign of 1930, Mr. Bennett produced the old Conservative cure-all: a higher tariff. No truckling to the Yankees, but stalwart national self-sufficiency! The old bogeys of Americanism in their various forms were once again trotted out, but with a marked lack of the stampeding effect they had had in 1911. However, the deepening flood of depression, the severe unemployment that accompanied it, and a certain lack of campaigning vigour on the part of a ministry that had never had any spectacular attributes, nothing more than solid respectability (and not always that!) to commend itself to the public, proved too much for King's government, which found itself in a substantial minority. Only fifteen labour and farmer dissidents (mostly from the west) remained, and what was more remarkable, Bennett had carried 25 seats in the province of Quebec! He was able to form a ministry representative of all provinces and the dangerous coincidence of race and party seemed to have disappeared. Insofar as the political situation alone went, the barometer in 1930 stood high for R. B. Bennett.

Chronology

1919 Death of Sir Wilfrid Laurier.
      Winnipeg Strike.
1920 Retirement of Sir Robert Borden: Arthur Meighen, Prime Minister.
1921 General Election:
          W. L. M. King, Prime Minister.
          Progressive Party takes 65 seats.
          J. S. Woodsworth, Labour M.P.
1922 Sir Henry Thornton, President, Canadian National Railways.
1925 General Election: King in minority.
1926 June 28, Lord Byng's refusal of dissolution to King. Meighen, Prime
          Minister.
      July 2, Meighen government defeated in Parliament.
      Sept. 14, General Election: King, Prime Minister.
1928 Largest wheat harvest on record.
1929 Post-war boom ends in crash of Oct. 23.
1930 General Election: R. B. Bennett, Prime Minister.

Additional Reading

Britnell, G. E. *The Wheat Economy.* Toronto, 1939.
Masters, D. C. *The Winnipeg General Strike.* Toronto, 1950.
McHenry, D. E. *The Third Force in Canada: The Cooperative Commonwealth Federation, 1932-48.* Berkeley, Calif., 1950.
McNaught, Kenneth. *A Prophet in Politics: A Biography of J. S. Woodsworth.* Toronto, 1959.
Morton, W. L. *The Progressive Party in Canada.* Toronto, 1950.
Sharp, Paul F. *The Agrarian Revolt in Western Canada.* Minneapolis, 1948.
Underhill, F. H. *Canadian Political Parties.* (*CHA* Booklets, No. 8) Ottawa, 1957.
Wood, L. A. *A History of Farmers' Movements in Canada.* Toronto, 1924.

CHAPTER 34

The Internal Crisis: The Bennett Regime, 1930-35

1. The Great Depression

The great depression of 1929 was one of the most important factors in modern history. In itself an absorbing economic phenomenon, its effects in every sphere began to be felt not long after it commenced and reached their culmination in the Second World War. In the perspective of the depression the history of the nine or ten years between its onset and the opening of the war, internal as well as external, assumes a fearful unity. After October, 1929, when the great Wall Street crash occurred, times got steadily worse. In the summer of 1931, Great Britain "went off gold", which was almost tantamount to bankruptcy. At home, American exchange went sharply against Canada, and several large brokerage houses failed. The price of wheat began tumbling to "an all-time low", and unsold western grain surpluses, which grew larger year by year, came to constitute one of the severest problems of the day—this despite seven lean years of crop failures, 1931-37, occasioned by drought of catastrophic proportions. In urban areas unemployment mounted until at its peak in the beginning of 1933, approximately one out of every two wage earners was out of work. Cities were full of beggars. In 1933, occurred the general closing of American banks.[1] Suicides rose sharply. Chaos seemed at hand.

[1] No Canadian banks got into difficulties.

However, the American bank-closing occurred at the darkest hour, and the gigantic depression, after having hung over the world like a poisonous fog for some four years, gradually began to lift. By 1937 another peak had apparently been reached, for in that year the so-called "recession", which was just a shallow depression, took place. Things were again beginning to pick up when the war clouds came. It remained for the Second World War to bring back that prosperity which peace could not provide.

The "bad times" following 1929 were so cyclonic in force that they not only brought governments tumbling down constitutional stairs but helped to sweep strategic countries like Germany into revolution and the world into war. In September, 1931, Japan, taking advantage of the confusion to go into Manchuria, began that defiance of the established public law which was to destroy collective security. By 1933 economic confusion and unemployment on a colossal scale had put Hitler's Third Reich in the place of the Weimer Republic. The story of the descent to Avernus is only too familiar. The dynamics of acquisition, upon which the English-speaking society of the nineteenth and twentieth centuries had been mainly built, gave way to the dynamics of power, upon which German society had been mainly built, and there could only be one conclusion. It was the approaching war which after 1933 dominated every scene, domestic as well as foreign.

Although Canadian political institutions proved strong enough to weather the storm, deep changes were wrought in them. Political dissent revived, manifesting itself in the strengthening of the old rural forces, in a further phase of industrial radicalism and in the initial phenomena of Fascism.[2] The Federal government, upon which the main economic burden fell, soon had to finance the weaker provinces. It had also the duty of finding and applying nation-wide remedies, a task which led it into uncharted seas, away from the *laisser-faire* courses of preceding generations on to the unknown routes of the "positive state". Since unemployment was universal, the effects were felt by the whole country, but since it was Saskatchewan which owing to drought had suffered more than any other area, that province was the logical source of the drive towards institutional change.

2. The Imperial Economic Conference of 1932

In the election of 1930, R. B. Bennett had campaigned against Mackenzie King on quite a simple platform: he undertook, by applying

[2] See p. 516, 528ff.

the old-fashioned remedy of protection, to "end unemployment". Mr. Bennett, while Leader of the Opposition (1927-30) and for the first three years or so of his term of office, seemed to be quite unaware of the deep ground swell of the age and began battling the worst economic storm in history with the old-fashioned equipment of his youth. For the boy in New Brunswick, steeped in the Loyalist tradition, the dominating issues of the age had been the proposals of the 1880's for Imperial Federation and for the young law student in Halifax, the Chamberlain conception of empire of the 1890's; in these devices the man still saw the means by which the mighty united empire of Loyalist dreams could be re-established.

Mr. Bennett's first move after becoming Prime Minister was to call a special session of Parliament and secure from it a greatly heightened tariff. That done, his second was to put before the Imperial Conference of that fall his proposals towards an Imperial *Zollverein*. This was the idea that had been realized after a fashion in the mercantilist empire of the eighteenth century, the background of Loyalist traditions. Destroyed in 1846, it had remained in the memories of colonials, if not of Englishmen.

When Mr. Bennett put his *Zollverein* proposals before the Imperial Conference, they got the reception that might have been expected: the other Dominions thought they were excellent, and Great Britain, to whom would fall the trifling task of paying the shot, characterized them, through the Dominions Secretary, J. H. Thomas, as "humbug". Next year conditions were different. Labour had been unhorsed. Mr. Ramsay MacDonald was still Prime Minister, but Stanley Baldwin, the Conservative steel magnate, was "Mayor of the Palace": he represented the new, industrial Conservatism which ruled England for most of the period between the two wars. This new Conservatism could not shock the four corners of the world as had its nineteenth century predecessor: rather it looked for a fortress and apparently found a safe one in the Empire. One of its guiding spirits was Neville, son of Joseph Chamberlain. The son, like the father, became a supporter of neo-mercantilism. Mr. Bennett's proposals found a receptive hearing from such men and another conference was agreed on. To Canada's pride, the meeting place was to be Ottawa.

On Ottawa there duly descended Prime Ministers, ministers, secretaries, experts, and newspapermen from all over the Empire. It was a gala occasion. For Canadians the glitter of decorations and the exotic Indian ladies in their *saris* constituted something new and piquant, and the crowded and gay evening receptions showed that not even statesmen believe in all work and no play. For a time all went well: at the public sessions sentiments were voiced on the warm fraternal feelings existing among the British family of nations. But as the Conference went on, a jarring note began to make itself heard. Its nature could not be clearly distinguished, until one day the rumour went about that Mr. C. H. Cahan, the Canadian Secretary of State, was threatening to resign. This was followed by suggestions that the Conference might break up with nothing done. As Mr. Cahan was member for one of the Montreal seats, it was not difficult to piece together explanations. Among the sickest of British industries was the cotton trade. But cotton was the very ground into which the vested interests created by the National Policy had most securely burrowed, and Montreal was their centre. It is a fair deduction that the men behind the cotton mills, traditionally Conservatives, were reading the riot act to the Secretary of State. Canadian manufacturers were quite willing to have Great Britain grant Canada preferences but drew the line at the drastic step of giving something in return.

The textile corner was for the moment turned, and the Conference went on to embody its conclusions in bilateral agreements. No general customs union, or anything approaching it, had been reached: just a series of trade treaties between nine different countries. The British had proposed working downward from the existing tariffs, but the Canadians had stood out for working upward. The Canadians won, and considerably reinforced those currents of economic "autarchy" which were bringing nations closer and closer to the breaking point.[3] The Canadian-British agreement proved a victory for the textile interests, those old veterans who had never lost a tariff battle in all their two generations of existence on the public bounty. British cottons received certain nominal privileges in the Canadian market, dressed up with various face-saving devices such as a tariff commission to adjudicate on production costs. Canadian primary products, especially timber, received some assurance of protection against "dumping" of Russian timber in Great Britain. In two or three years both parties to the bargain had managed to find ways of avoiding its implications: the British failed to get into the Canadian textile market, and the Canadians failed to prevent the Russians getting into the British timber market. It was an embarrassed and harassed group of British delegates who met in that last classical plenary session to sign the documents and make the conventional speeches: they had been beaten, and they knew they were beaten. As a demonstration of Imperial unity, to say nothing of brotherly love, the Conference was not exactly a success. But it was a

[3] See Sumner Wells, *The Time for Decision* (New York, 1944).

splendid demonstration of the hard bargaining of which the Canadian right is capable when it comes to business deals: on such occasions it reserves its affection towards the mother-country for the next election campaign.

3. Hard Times and Political Heresies

No tariff arrangement could affect the drought in Saskatchewan, which had begun before the Conference and got worse after it,[4] reaching its extreme low level in 1937, when only thirty-seven million bushels of wheat were produced in the entire province (as compared with 321 million in 1928). Whole areas of the countryside were wrecked. The very soil blew away in the terrible dust-storms of the period. People began trekking from the devastated regions to find new homes in the wooded areas of the north. In these years nature dealt a blow as heavy to a once prosperous province as an invading army might have done. In some years half or more of the farmers had to go on relief, and those from the worst areas literally became refugees. The wonder is that morale stood up so well. Saskatchewan was well served by the indomitable spirit of a pioneer people. When the extent of the calamity began to become known, it also received willing aid from outside. The Protestant congregations of the east especially distinguished themselves in this good work, but the weight of the task had to be taken by government. Saskatchewan itself would have soon become bankrupt had it not been for the aid of Ottawa. Even so, to meet these burdens and those caused by mere economic dislocation, the Federal government for several years in succession had to carry on by deficit financing, raising large loans on the general credit of the country, not for developmental purposes as in the old days but simply to keep bodies and souls together.

In former days "bad times" had simply meant that the floating population had taken itself off to the United States in sufficient numbers to restore equilibrium, but now American doors were closed, and Canada, for the first time in its history, had to "consume its own smoke". Not only did unemployment mount to fantastic heights, but young men, leaving school, could find nothing to do. "Why are you looking for a job when your father's got one?" came to be an ordinary question. These were the days when such young men, finding nothing to do at one side of the continent would strike out for the other, begging food and stealing rides on freight trains to get to their "destina-

---

[4] Average yield of wheat per acre, Saskatchewan: 1900-1938: 14.7. 1930: 14; 1931: 8.8; 1932: 13.6; 1933: 8.7; 1934: 8.6; 1935: 10.8; 1936: 7.5; 1937: 2.7; 1938: 9.6 bushels.

tion", and on arriving there, finding nothing to do, would begin the long weary ride back again. It was not uncommon to see forty or fifty men together riding on the roofs of the box-cars in those days.[5] Many of these box-car boys were not absorbed into useful occupation until war broke out. For many of them enlistment then meant not duty but food.

The amount of civil disturbance that followed these hardships was remarkably small, bearing out Francis Bacon's observation that "revolution is not made from the belly". What did occur was, in some cases, the result of attempts by Canadian Communists to exploit the situation and in others, of provocative action by the authorities. The methods resorted to focused attention on the threat to traditional liberties and caused thoughtful people to wonder whether the cure might not be worse than the disease. In 1931, an Ontario court ruled that under Section 98 of the Criminal Code the Communist party was unlawful, and sentenced five of its leaders to jail. During the previous King administrations seven votes for the repeal of this dangerous invasion of freedom had been secured in the Commons but vetoed in the Senate, which still had a Conservative majority. Under Bennett, there was no prospect of repeal. Not until King's next ministry, once more bringing liberal principles into play, was the objectionable section repealed. As for the imprisoned Communists, an incident in Kingston Penitentiary, when some of them were fired upon (but not hit) by excited guards, gave them all the glory of martyrdom without its usual disabilities. They made the most of it on their subsequent release and secured some increased adherence among the foreign born.

They got still more advantage out of some of the disturbances. One of these occurred at Regina in the summer of 1935. A "march on Ottawa" was initiated in Vancouver, and several hundred unemployed made their way eastward. At Regina, where they secured transient accommodation, they were holding a public meeting in the open when the Mounted Police, on instructions, it is said, from Ottawa, interrupted proceedings by arresting one of their leaders. This unwise and perhaps provocative act set off a *mêlée* in which some life was lost. Nothing better could have been asked by those anxious to bring traditional institutions into disrepute. Fortunately, the difference in political principles between the two leaders was so marked that when King returned to power reactionary attitudes were moderated and Communism sank back into a minor expression of political dissent.

It was in the summer of 1932 that the more moderate dissenting

---

[5] The railroads at first attempted to stop this but later gave up.

elements organized themselves into a national party. At Calgary in that year there came together representatives of several groups: rural dissent in the persons of the Albertans who still upheld in Parliament the tradition of the former Progressives: similar non-parliamentary elements from Saskatchewan; one sitting member from Ontario of the same outlook; left-wing humanitarians and representatives of labour, especially those that derived from the Winnipeg Strike of 1919, and men who had brought with them from Great Britain the traditions of the Labour party, tinged by Fabianism or possibly Marxism. From the meeting arose a party whose strange name reflected the demands which had been pouring out of the Prairie provinces: the Co-operative Commonwealth Federation ("C.C.F."). Co-operation in grain-growers' associations, in wheat pools and as United Farmers had long been familiar to westerners: it was not surprising that the co-operative idea should be carried over into politics and that well before the party itself had been formed, the term "co-operative commonwealth" should have come into use. An ideal realized over a portion of life, the marketing of grain, could surely, so went the thoughts of western farmers, be realized over much more of it.

At Regina in 1933 the new party adopted a rather advanced programme based largely on the ideas of The League for Social Reconstruction, a group headed by some of the younger social scientists from eastern Universities.[6] There could only be one leader, the indomitable idealist, J. S. Woodsworth. Woodsworth was neither foreigner, Jew, Marxian philosopher, trade union organizer, nor farmer. His people had been in Canada for generations, and he was typical of a wide section of Canadian life, for as a Methodist minister and the son of a Methodist minister, he was steeped in humanitarian and social doctrine. It was an easy transition for a man of well-trained mind endowed with a sensitive imagination to pass over to doctrines of social justice. His doctrines, however, did not derive from the neat categories of an intellectual system, but were passionate affirmations of a faith, a faith to which he testified in outspoken language and in a spirit of unconquerable courage. Courage, faith, and an almost complete indifference to the material side of life marked Woodsworth. He was a Saint in politics!

The new movement, drawing together so many sections of dissent and rather top-heavy with ability which did not run in the usual channels of acceptability, provided a vision of a brave new world that neither of the older parties could offer and attracted many young people

---

[6] See League for Social Reconstruction (research committee), *Social Planning for Canada* (Toronto, 1935).

who, unlike their fathers, were not rooted in the Liberal or Conservative faiths. It met Canadian yearning for efficiency by propounding "a planned society". It was at once assailed as "socialist" (which, in a loose sense, it was), and efforts were made to identify it with "Bolshevism" (which it was not). Such charges certainly frightened the persons making them. But they did not frighten the western farmers who were told that the new socialist party they had formed would end up in socializing their land. It is not to be forgotten that the C.C.F. movement originated on the western farms. If socialism, it was a new Canadian brand—rural socialism. Elsewhere, workers' and farmers' movements have broken down on the different interests of the two classes, but in Canada some kind of fusion, based on the highly co-operative nature of western Canadian agriculture, seemed realizable. If the new party succeeded in understanding that parties, to gain power, must water down their doctrines,[7] then there was no reason why the alliance could not go on, just as similar alliances went on inside the older parties. A collectivist movement of some sort there was bound to be, for the march of history could not be halted indefinitely. The immediate questions were how far would the new party succeed in capturing a place for itself in national life, how closely did its tenets correspond with the needs and aspirations of the country, and whether its pressure, like that of the Clear Grits in the 1850's, would eventually telescope together the two old parties.

Another type of political dissent with a somewhat different economic basis found expression through the Honourable H. H. Stevens, Minister of Trade and Commerce in the Bennett cabinet. In 1934 Stevens secured a searching parliamentary investigation into conditions in retail trade; this came to be known as "The Price Spreads Inquiry". A multitude of depressing facts was brought out on such subjects as hours of work and wages; in face of them it was hard to see how Canada could retain its claim to being a country with a high standard of living.[8] The chief targets for the attack were the big chain and department stores. Mr. Stevens was a kindly, honest man genuinely concerned over such hardships. He was English born and had been brought up a Methodist: it is not hard to see the same kind of social ferment working in him as in Woodsworth. Finally his feelings apparently got the better of him, for at a private meeting, he "spilled over" so emphatically that his censures

[7] See pp. 437, 453. "Watering down" did not officially begin until the 1950's.
[8] Some "wages" ranged down to $1.50 for a 75-hour week. The worst examples of exploitation were from Quebec. A good article on Stevens is J. R. H. Wilbur, "H. H. Stevens and R. B. Bennett, 1930-34," *CHR*, XLIII (March, 1962), 1-16.

almost immediately became public. They constituted a severe indictment of the whole system of individualist exploitation of wealth. "Unscrupulous financiers", "starving producers", "sweated workmen" were phrases that fell startlingly from the lips of a Conservative minister of the Crown. No severer indictment of capitalism could have been made by J. S. Woodsworth himself.

A man cherishing such sentiments could hardly stay in the Conservative party, let alone in a Conservative ministry. In October, 1934, he resigned and freed himself for a campaign in the spirit of his original speech. It was apparent that either the Conservative party must disown him or must itself seek to do something about the situation, beyond handing out doles. But few there were who anticipated the startling form such action might take. In January, 1935, it was announced that the Prime Minister would deliver a series of radio addresses on the state of the times. They were keenly anticipated. When, however, people heard coming over the air a forcefully pronounced burial service for "the capitalist system", they could hardly believe their ears. Was this a Conservative Prime Minister speaking, a millionaire many times over? Was this Satan rebuking sin? Bennett had always been regarded as incalculable: he had never shown so clearly how correct the description was. Who would ever have imagined that they would some day listen to a Bennett bull roaring in the capitalist china shop? Industrialists who had been offended at the Prime Minister in 1932 for his attempt to give British manufactures a part of the Canadian market now were thoroughly alarmed. Was some kind of communist revolution to be staged with this Tory Trotsky leading it?[9]

Mr. Bennett followed his talk by characteristic action. In the following session, he introduced a number of acts designed to implement the findings of the Price Spreads Commission. Low wages and long hours were to be struck at through a Wages and Hours Act. Unemployment Insurance was to be introduced. Dominion control over prices and marketing conditions, already initiated under the Natural Products Marketing Act, was to be extended and tightened. Farmers were to be given relief from excessive debt through the Farmers' Creditors' Arrangements Act. Evaders, unfair advertisers, and other persons who followed unfair practices, were to be dealt with not as ordinary civil offenders but as criminals. Companies were to be required to publish fuller statements, and an attempt was to be made to deal a blow to swindling "promoters". Appropriate boards and commissions were to be

---

[9] Is it too far-fetched to imagine that something of the creed in which Bennett had been brought up was beginning to work in him after many years' overlay by "worldly" considerations? That creed was Methodism!

set up to administer the new legislation. Most of the individual acts constituted evident invasions of provincial rights under the "property and civil rights" clauses of Section 92 of the British North America Act, as interpreted by the courts, but an attempt was made to outflank that enactment by basing them on Section 132 of the Act.[10] Canada had been a party to the labour and other conventions negotiated at Geneva through the International Labour Office (such as the Eight Hour Day Convention). These she had never enacted into the law of the land. Mr. Bennett now took them up and his legislation asserted that since it was made pursuant to a treaty, it was within the competence of the Parliament of Canada. It was a characteristic way for the Prime Minister to proceed. He consulted no one; he mollified no interests in advance; he asked no province to co-operate. "Blasting" seemed Mr. Bennett's favourite operation, and having failed to blast his way into markets abroad he was now about to attempt to blast "capitalism" and provincial rights at home. The Liberals were only too glad to shout "ultra vires" without having to show their hand.

The programme, while not as hair-raising as the radio talks, was to the old-guard stalwarts of the Prime Minister's party, horrible enough. If not communism, it was "New Dealism", inserted into the northern capital from the southern by the inside route: was not William Herridge, Mr. Bennett's brother-in-law and Canadian Minister to Washington, known to be on intimate terms with President Roosevelt? As a Canadian version of "The New Deal", did it not merit the epithet so freely used in those years of changing conceptions? Was it not "regimentation"? "Regimentation" it was, of course, just as are fines for exceeding the speed limit. The world has become used to a good deal more regimentation since then, and we are in a somewhat better position to see what the Bennett legislation really signified. Some of it, such as the Wages and Hours Act and the Unemployment Insurance Act simply brought Canada approximately into line with countries industrially more mature. Other statutes apparently did propose a considerable measure of control over the whole national economy. Now, while individuals or groups have for many years controlled the Canadian economy after a fashion and in their own interests through such devices as the tariff, never had a government sought to impose a broad conception of social justice to be attained by specific regulatory measures.

---

[10] "The Parliament and Government of Canada shall have all powers necessary or proper for performing the obligations of Canada or of any Province thereof, as part of the British Empire, towards foreign countries, arising under treaties between the Empire and such foreign countries."

The importance of the Bennett legislation lies not in its details, some of which (such as provision for marketing control) had little clarity of aim and were probably impracticable, but in the sharp turn it indicated as having been reached in the economic and social road. The *laisser-faire* state was coming to an end; the period of a controlled, a planned, society was beginning. Some form of socialism, under whatever auspices, was at hand.

Bennett's efforts projected the new issue into Canadian politics with more force than the young Co-operative Commonwealth Federation could summon, and produced wide party rearrangements. These received quantitative expression in the election of 1935. From the beginning of the campaign it was evident that the two party symmetry, so recently recaptured, would once more be disturbed.

The severe conditions in the most politically volatile of the provinces, Alberta, had produced still another expression of rural revolt in the "Social Credit" movement. Every frontier in America at one time or another has produced cheap money doctrines. The weapons of the possessing classes have traditionally been "hard money" and the banks. In rural America, from Atlantic to Pacific, banks have been hated as symbols of "the interests" of "the money power". "Hard money" has checked the inflationary process so beneficial to those who, like farmers, have things to sell and obligations to meet. The battle of hard and soft money has echoed through Canada ever since old Jacques de Meulles, the intendant of New France, took packs of cards and scribbled money denominations upon them in the year 1685. Nova Scotians in the eighteenth century had their struggle with their "provincial notes", another form of unredeemable paper. The original English shilling had shrunk to about twelve and a half cents by the time it reached Upper Canada as the "York shilling" of eight to the dollar, introduced from New York state. Upper Canada was to become a monetary museum, with a circulation of worn-down coins from the ends of the earth and of tattered bank-notes that might or might not have some kind of bank remotely behind them: these constituted "cheap money" with a vengeance. In our own day, soft money has had its last stronghold on the last frontier, Alberta. The contest of the 1930's between the Social Credit government and the bankers was only one in the long series between east and west, city and country, banker and farmer, hard money and soft money, which had been going on ever since those early days when absence of hard cash forced resort to mooseskins,[11] merchants'

[11] New France.

I.O.U.'s.[12] or pieces of leather with holes in them.[13] The Albertans fought the "St. James Street gang" as dauntlessly as the people of Upper Canada, a century before, had fought the "Montreal shavers".[14]

Many Albertans had come from those western American states which forty years before had been devoted to W. J. Bryan and the cheap money doctrines of his time.[15] They were profoundly democratic in the Jacksonian sense, profoundly distrustful of "the east" and its "money barons", and religious in an old-fashioned way. Hard times seem to turn people's thoughts to soft money and "the old-time religion". In 1935, the people of Alberta produced not only a doctrine, in the form of the inflationary monetary theories propounded by an Englishman, Major Douglas, but also a prophet in the person of William Aberhart, a remarkable individual who combined the duties of High School principal in Calgary (and a very good one, it is said) with the exposition of a hot-and-strong form of revivalist religion in a church of his own founding and over a broadcasting station under his own control.

Through their farmers' organizations and through countless "study groups" the Alberta farmers, hopeless of a solution from Ottawa, had set out to find their own cure for their ills. The movement rolled up. Mr. Aberhart's mellifluous accents rolled out from the radio station of the Prophetic Bible Institute into the tired hearts of the farm women of Alberta. To an eminently practical people the promised land he talked of must not only be a heaven beyond the skies, it must also consist in a Utopia actually present on the foothills of Alberta. Mr. Aberhart's religion and Major Douglas's theories seemed to meet all requirements. To make straight the way, members of the old Progressive party, who had been prominent in public life, by an unwise "self-denying ordinance" stepped back into private life. The result, registered in the provincial election of August, 1935, was a resounding victory for the new version of the farmers' old political faith. The new party chose Mr. Aberhart as premier, assembled a cabinet of indifferent quality and then went on to new fields of conquest in the federal elections of the succeeding fall.

For Alberta, one more piece of political experimentalism was all in the day's work. It was much more surprising when people all over the country began to display interest in a movement known as the "Reconstruction Party" sponsored by Mr. Stevens, on the basis of the revelations of the Price Spreads Inquiry. Its attractions were evident: it spoke up for a "new deal" for youth, decent wages, public housing pro-

[12] Upper and Lower Canada.
[13] P.E.I. See Innis and Lower, *Select Documents in Canadian Economic History*, II, 432, for lively descriptions of this old "currency".
[14] See p. 210. The non-sterling "shillings" were "moneys of account" only, not actual coins.
[15] See p. 425

grammes, for low interest, and against the monopolistic few. It found ready response in the *petite bourgeoisie*, who saw their little businesses threatened by the chain stores or taken over by the banks, and their sons and daughters forced to work for the triumphant combines at low wages and long hours. Mr. Stevens, without knowing it, was appealing to the same classes and against the same conditions as another politician on a greater stage, Adolf Hitler in Germany. The insecure little people of the towns and cities who have so much to lose in a status that is so dear to them, their independence and their respectability, who in the nature of things must have narrow outlooks, are the people who will always follow vigorous leadership, unaware of constitutional considerations, but susceptible to the atmosphere of the times; not isolated, but awake to the day-to-day situation—the class upon which popular and reactionary dictatorship can readily rest.

4. Unemployment Ends Mr. Bennett

Mr. Bennett went to the country in the fall of 1935. So many points of view made for a confusing campaign but the results were practically a foregone conclusion. The Liberal party plastered the billboards with the legend "It's King or Chaos". The people had had enough chaos. To "The Old Man, The Old Flag, The Old Party" (1891) and "No Truck nor Trade with the Yankees" (1911) which had won elections for the Conservatives, was now to be added "It's King or Chaos", which was to win the election of 1935 for the Liberals. When the votes were tallied, it was found that Mr. Bennett's Conservatives had shrunk to a corporal's guard of 39. The Social Credit party had swept Alberta and had 17 seats. The C.C.F. had only seven. Mr. Stevens' "Reconstruction" party distinguished itself by losing every contest it fought except one, his own; it disappeared as suddenly as it had emerged. The Liberals had behind them the first of those huge majorities which were characteristic of other countries at the time, 171 seats out of 245. Here was the great centre group which had received into its ample bosom frightened Conservatives from one side and those who could not go as far as C.C.F. socialism on the other. The victory was not a tribute to Mr. King, it was not a proclamation in defence of Liberty, it was not even a pronouncement on the issues of the day. Liberalism, as it emerged in Canada after 1935, was the counterpart of Baldwin Conservatism in Great Britain, of *Le Front Populaire* in France, and of Rooseveltian Democracy: it represented the huddling together of frightened people, uncertain of their way in a chaotic world. Since those days, the huge majorities often enjoyed by the government of the day, whatever its political label, have continued to represent much the same thing.

Mr. Bennett had come into office promising to "end unemployment". Now unemployment had ended Mr. Bennett. He had given the country five exciting years and it had pronounced its verdict upon him. Here was a man with great force of character, with rugged sincerity, with the concern for his fellows characteristic of his Methodist traditions, and with the deep irrational prejudices of a Loyalist background, yet a man whose love of dominance reduced his ministers to nonentities and vitiated his career. Had Mr. Bennett been able to triumph over mere prejudice as Sir Robert Borden had done, he might have had a considerable place in history, for his energy would have carried him far. As it was, the scales began to fall from his eyes too late in life. Apparently he had realized at last that Canada would have to make reductions in tariff if she were to play fair with Great Britain, but his protectionist orthodoxy and his party loyalties prevented him from accomplishing the stroke that might have made the Imperial Economic Conference of 1932 a factor in world stability instead of another milestone on the road to ruin. While he was alienating Conservatives with his thunders against the failures of capitalism, he was estranging democrats by arbitrarily reintroducing the granting of knighthoods into Canada. He alienated the bankers with his new central Bank—the Bank of Canada—and he won no friends for this greatly needed forward step because he made the bank a private institution. He omitted few opportunities to make enemies.

Nor could he be called a friend of freedom. He took executive power over the tariff to such an extent as to constitute a blow at the parliamentary right of taxation. He instituted the system of blanket appropriations (for unemployment purposes) which resulted not only in a huge waste of public money but also, more seriously, deprived Parliament of its ancient right of appropriating definite sums for definite objectives. He greatly increased the expenditure on the Mounted Police, which he moved some distance in the direction of those Ogpus and Gestapos of which the world has heard all too much. The attitude of his government towards annoying heretical groups such as the Communists had something in it of persecution. Mr. Bennett's regime embodying, as pronouncedly right-wing regimes must, a considerable element of will, as opposed to constitutionalism, drove several nails into the coffin of Canadian liberties.[16]

[16] Mr. Bennett's personal tendencies to domination became a byword. This chapter has given several examples of administrative action distinctly illiberal in nature. For the political theorist, the general point may be noted that right-wing regimes tend to rest on will, left-wing on ideologies; either one, if of extreme degree, is hostile to constitutionalism, which represents a balance of wills.

Chronology

1930 General Election: R. B. Bennett, Prime Minister.
1932 Imperial Economic Conference, Ottawa.
     C.C.F. formed at Calgary.
1934 Hepburn Liberal Premier in Ontario.
     The Price Spreads Inquiry.
1935 Social Credit Party gains power in Alberta.
     Rise of the "Reconstruction Party".
     General Election: Bennett defeated.

Additional Reading

Irving, J. A. *The Social Credit Party in Alberta*. Toronto, 1959.
Macpherson, C. B. *Democracy in Alberta*. Toronto, 1953.
Mann, W. E. *Sect, Cult and Church in Alberta*. Toronto, 1955.
Thomas, L. G. *The Liberal Party in Alberta: A History of Politics in the Province*. Toronto, 1959.
Tyre, Robert. *Douglas in Saskatchewan: The Story of a Socialist Experiment*. Vancouver, 1962.

CHAPTER 35

The Internal Crisis: The Third King Administration, 1935 and After

1. The Depression and the Rowell-Sirois Commission

Luck was with Mackenzie King: he took office when times were on the mend again. Yet grave problems confronted his government. The unemployed still rode the box-cars. Western harvests were still failing. Deficits were still astronomical. Under these circumstances, the questions before the country wore two aspects—one financial, the other political. Depression had carried the financial question beyond loans for provincial relief, beyond provincial political experiments, to the very structure of the federation itself. In the field of politics, the stresses it set up encouraged the emergence, within the two largest provinces, of tendencies of an ugliness theretofore unknown, arbitrary and in certain respects almost Fascist in character.

There was still little to show for the deficits arising from unemployment. The relief camps had not succeeded in maintaining morale, as had the American "C.C.C.", nor had they paralleled the energetic road-building programme of the American scheme. Here and there, as a work of relief, a public building was erected, and there was little more. The huge deficits of the Canadian National Railway constituted a serious national problem in themselves, one which R. B. Bennett had energetically tackled in his appointment of the Duff Commission.[1] The Com-

---

[1] Chairman, Rt. Hon. Sir L. P. Duff, Chief Justice of Canada.

mission had recommended against the amalgamation of the two lines but had suggested ameliorative steps, such as cooperation. Bennett's government, though no enemy of the C.P.R., had repudiated "Amalgamation" as a policy, for public opinion was too evidently opposed to a railway monopoly so powerful as, if private, to threaten the state itself, and if public, to threaten the nation through lethargy and perhaps corruption. The King government had no sympathy with amalgamation but had little else to suggest. The Second World War, taxing the capacity of both railroads, at long last enabled the C.N.R. (whose deficits had been owing mainly to bonded indebtedness and to interest on government loans) to show good profits. The railway problem was thus temporarily shelved.

The most contentious area of finance was the division of revenue between the Dominion, which had unlimited power of taxation, and the provinces, which only had the right of "direct taxation within the province . . . for provincial purposes". Since the courts in their wisdom had greatly expanded the area of provincial powers, the provinces found themselves with more and more duties but no corresponding expansion of revenue. Weaker provinces had found it hard enough to carry on in normal times: now if they were to remain solvent a rearrangement of the whole tax structure of the country was necessary. Accordingly in 1937 the King government appointed a Commission, whose searching investigation became that grand inquest into the financial aspects of Canadian federalism which from the names of its successive chairmen is known as the Rowell-Sirois Commission. The Commission toured Canada from end to end, heard interminable evidence, and hired scores of experts to conduct studies. As never before, the country had recourse to its trained brains, most of the memoranda being written by the economists and political scientists of its universities and two of the Commissioners themselves being professors of Political Science. The result was a most systematic and intelligent attack on the problems investigated. The Rowell-Sirois Report was the most exhaustive and most valuable state paper since Lord Durham's documents of a hundred years previously.

The recommendations of the Report were, briefly, that the provinces should abandon certain taxes (such as income tax and succession duties) which the Dominion government was already levying or was in a more strategic position to levy, and that in return, the Dominion should assume responsibility for the rapidly mounting expenditure on social services. The Report conspicuously omitted direct reference to the tariff and its differential effect as between the sections. It showed clearly that Canada consisted in "have" and "have not" provinces—

Ontario, Quebec and British Columbia forming the "haves"—and by inference showed that the "have" provinces benefited materially by national policies, especially the protective tariff. The problem posed was how to find some device to compensate the "have-not" provinces, the victims of Canadian metropolitanism, for national policies which sucked their wealth out of them. This, the Report suggested, could be accomplished if the Dominion assumed responsibility for the social services. It was left to government to find means of putting the recommendations of the Report into effect: that this could only be done by mutual agreement with the provinces was plain.

The next step was to call a conference of provincial governments in the hope of securing their cooperation—no easy task. Mr. Aberhart's government in Alberta had boycotted the Commission, and Mr. Duplessis in Quebec had barely recognized it. But few people were prepared for the scene that actually occurred. The Conference met at the capital in January, 1941. All the provincial premiers were present, but it was left to one of them to act. This was Mitchell Hepburn who in 1934 had overthrown the Conservative government of Ontario, which had become involved in questionable financial complications. Mr. Hepburn who, during his seven years in office, kept hurling insults at Mr. King, now, in a cheap and slangy speech, virtually told the Dominion authorities, if it be permissible to use such a phrase in a book of this character, to "go to the devil". However history will eventually apportion the responsibility, the Conference came to a sudden end, with predictions on the part of the Dominion members that the provinces sooner or later might find themselves forced to accept such terms as were offered. These predictions were subsequently borne out in part when Mr. Ilsley, Mr. King's competent Minister of Finance, managed to negotiate with each province, for the duration of the war, agreements similar to those proposed by the Commission, leaving it to the future to mend, or end, the financial anarchy produced by the existence of ten (since become eleven) taxing and borrowing authorities in a country whose economy cries aloud for central direction.

2. Movements to the Right

In industrial communities, employers have habitually met "bad times" by discharging employees and dumping the responsibility on the local municipality. Employees in attempting to protect their existence have often been pressed into violent or imprudent action. Every major industrial dislocation contains a potential civil war. In Ontario and

Quebec, here in the field of labour, was the basis of politics during the depression.

In Ontario, Premier Hepburn had found it no bar to office to be cast in the role of honest young farmer, waging war against the corruptions of "the great"; after the elections the part seemed equally useful against labour. In the Oshawa Automobile Workers' strike of 1937, depiction of the strikers as better off than the farmers (farmers toiling from morning to night while motor mechanics "pulled down" their five and seven dollars a day), opened the class line between farmers and labour in Ontario almost as successfully as the C.C.F. had closed it in the west. In the Oshawa strike the premier of Ontario took astute advantage of the workmen's desire to join a union affiliated with the American C.I.O., denouncing "foreign agitators" (this although the strike was against a company of foreign ownership, the General Motors Company) and flourishing about such words as communism. A body of police was specially organized for the occasion on military lines, "Hepburn's Hussars", as they were dubbed. But the strikers refused to be intimidated, received support from an influential Toronto newspaper of the premier's own party, *The Star*, and behaving themselves moderately, won recognition and improved conditions from the company.

A short time previously, Hepburn had cancelled certain contracts between the province and a large American electric power company with plants on the Ottawa river. A little later his relations with American power interests apparently changed. His handling of the Oshawa strike had provided a demonstration against radicalism effective enough to win additional rural support, and in the elections of 1937, he carried seventy-five per cent of the seats. New contracts, not unacceptable to the power interests, were negotiated shortly afterward. Meanwhile, the power interests of New York seem to have been pressing for the right to import into the United States a good share of the power to be developed on the Canadian side of the St. Lawrence, through the proposed canalization scheme. The Federal government would allow no export of power. At this juncture Hepburn made an attempt to influence the terms of the treaty which was then being negotiated between Canada and the United States, covering the whole St. Lawrence waterways situation. He seemed to be ready to assert that Ontario should make its own international arrangements, and, in support of his position, hurled at Mr. King letters which were markedly at variance with the canons of Canadian public behaviour. Mr. Hepburn's deportment suggested a lack, not only of good taste but of something more serious: he seemed a typical product of that period of gay abandon between the two wars when so many young people,[2] freed from the restraints of the previous generation and with few of its religious convictions, drifted from their moorings. It was unavoidable that many of these would see life in simple terms of a struggle for power, "with no holds barred". Here, though few of them would have perceived or admitted it, was the spiritual root of Fascism.

In Quebec, Liberal administrations had been in power for many years. The hierarchic succession had descended from the Merciers to the Gouins to the Taschereaux, the well-born representatives of a cultured, intelligent, and almost hereditary élite who gave moderately good government to the province without forgetting their own family circles.[3] Sir Lomer Gouin had regarded his province as a great seigneury, to be developed as a careful estate. Under him had been consummated that understanding between administration and industrialists which had given to Quebec the special character of its modern development. Mr. Taschereau had carried on the tradition, but under him the connection perhaps became too intimate: it seemed too easy for the corporations to secure the good things of the province—the waterpowers, the timber limits, the pulpwood. English industrial concerns found too little interference with long hours and low wages. Quebec labour gained a reputation throughout the continent for being docile and cheap. Quebec had become the employers' paradise.

Such a situation was ripe for trouble when bad times came. It had been remarked by Lord Durham that everything in the province tended to be translated into racial terms. Nothing could be truer than this when applied to the difficulties arising out of the new industry. If employees were inefficient, it was because they were French; if bad times came and the factory had to lay off hands, it was because the English were the managers and naturally the French were the sufferers.

The person in the best position to see what factory industry was doing to his people was the parish priest. He might confine himself to his religious duties, and find the local company a generous contributor to his church funds; he might put pressure on it through his influence over the employees and become a kind of co-conspirator with it; or he might understand what industry really meant for his people, in which case the local Catholic Labour Syndicate would find its hands strengthened. The experience of the parish priests, whatever it was, passed

---

[2] He was still in his thirties when he became premier.

[3] Gouin was a son-in-law of Mercier's, Taschereau of a family whose members as early as the French regime had held prominent official posts and which after the Cession had included innumerable judges and other high officials. It also included Cardinal Taschereau, 1820-98.

about among the French and was supplemented by such direct knowledge as young professionals could acquire. Among these two classes, whose members often knew at first hand what it was to be treated as second-class citizens by the superior and arrogant English, opinion gradually took shape against the English control of industrial life. Why should the French be such simpletons as to work for starvation wages for a lot of rich English? A new nationalism emerged, adding to the old determination to preserve language, faith, and institutions, the new animus against English capitalism. To "notre langue, notre foi et nos lois" was added "à bas les trustards".[4]

The provincial election campaign of 1936 gave French-Canadian economic nationalism its first chance to put its case, and then the issue, as usual, was not simple. Liberals could point to the rapid development of the province and its continuous increase in population. Opposition was divided. Paul Gouin, son of Sir Lomer, a generous-minded young man, sure that something was wrong with Taschereauism, organized a group around himself (*L'Action Liberale Nationale*) and succeeded in virtually forcing the resignation of Mr. Taschereau, whose majority had been reduced to six in the elections of 1935. Mr. Godbout succeeded him. But a cleverer and more realistic politician than Gouin now appeared in the person of Maurice Duplessis, a man of Conservative, that is, old *Castor*, complexion. There was much dickering between the two but the result evidently was that the Duplessis cat had swallowed the Gouin canary. Some semblance of union was kept up during the campaign, but after Duplessis's victory of 1936, which gave him 76 seats out of 90, Gouin practically dropped out of public life.

Duplessis took office as head of *L'Union Nationale*. This group, which could hardly be called a party, contained some *Rouges* who had not left when Gouin did, but it consisted mostly in the conservative forces of Quebec: that is, it derived its oratory from the *Castor* tradition, its funds, it is to be suspected, from the Montreal English *trustards*, and most of its votes from simple country people. Duplessis, like his opposite number in Ontario, belonged to a generation on whom the old restraints sat lightly. The ultra-*Bleus* of Langevin's time had been gentlemen, and they had lived in the mighty shadow of Victorian England when the traditions of parliamentary self-government were at their strongest. Since those days democracy had watered down parliamentary government, and the tradition of the gentleman had almost disappeared. Still more significant, French conservatism had not been tempered by the long constitutional tradition that helps to hold English conservatives

---

[4] See Everett Hughes, *French Canada in Transition* (Toronto, 1943).

in check. Reaction in Quebec had fewer barriers to break in its destruction of liberty than it had elsewhere in Canada. There was also the authoritarian tradition of the Roman Catholic church to provide an initially favourable setting.

Duplessis's three years of office (1936-39) were stormy. Many English Canadians were committing treason against their own institutions in those days by using the bogey of Communism for reactionary purposes, so it is not surprising that French Canadians should use it too, especially when they had a motive that was weak among the English, in the strong determination to preserve their religion against the threat of Communist atheism. Urged on by many among his own people and by strong pressure, it may be assumed, from certain circles in the church, and nothing loath himself, Mr. Duplessis enacted, in 1937, the notorious "Padlock Law". Under its authority the Attorney-General could, without court action, close for one year premises suspected of being used to propagate "communism" (the word was not defined). In effect the authorities took arbitrary discretion to harry persons suspected of "communism" (political heretics, in other words), by searching their domiciles, seizing their books and papers, and, through the "padlock", turning them out of their very homes. So far did this go that policemen at times pushed their way into private meetings in McGill University, ready to make note of "dangerous thoughts".

The injustice of the Padlock Law was evident: persons attacked could get no redress unless they proved themselves innocent. Open accusation and a fair trial in open court were denied them. It must be admitted that few of the English people of the province showed concern: the satisfaction of "business" and its satellites in seeing "Communists" persecuted exceeded solicitude over abstract questions of liberty, of which there was perturbingly little.

Efforts to test the act in the courts failed, thanks to the complete sovereignty of the legislature: there were no bills of rights in Canada. Nor would the federal government intervene. Mr. Lapointe, the Minister of Justice, had no hesitation in disallowing Alberta measures which infringed on the sacredness of property, but he allowed this gross interference with the rights of the subject to pass unchecked. Yet had he disallowed the Padlock Law, he (and Mr. King) would have been represented as the friends of atheistic communism, the enemies of true religion and of Quebec. Perhaps he acted in accordance with the proverb "Give the man more rope and he will hang himself". That is exactly what for the time being Duplessis did, when in 1939, he decided to challenge the whole King-Lapointe thesis for Canadian participation in the war; the good sense of Quebec, Mr. Lapointe's heart-felt appeal, and the prospective resignations of its federal ministers if the province voted against Ottawa—all combined to defeat a man who, whatever his thoughts, acted as if his sympathies lay with Nazi demagogues, and to install once more a Liberal administration at Quebec under a very different man, the tolerant and fair-minded Mr. Godbout.[5]

3. The King Administration During the Second World War

The Second World War descended upon Canada when depression was still the chief public topic. For a time business hesitated, but the war expenditures soon began to make a difference, and the "blitz" campaign of the spring of 1940, when European countries toppled over like ninepins, changed the entire complexion of things. English industrialists had expected a comfortable war, fat contracts, and a semi-monopoly of supply but after the fall of France, their country faced Hitler almost unarmed and made frantic efforts to procure wherever it could the armaments that should have been ready long before. Jealously guarded blueprints now came streaming over to Canada, which within a year or two was turned into one of the largest armaments-manufacturing nations in the world.

From the outset, strict regulation was undertaken. Once more (as in the case of the Rowell-Sirois report), trained brains were called upon, and professors and their former students soon were occupying a large place in the direction of affairs. Controls were instituted over foreign exchange, over profits, and eventually over the whole range of prices, wages, and employment. With extremely high taxation, the payment of a high proportion of expenditure out of revenue and huge war loans, with rigorous surveillance over civilian production and some commodity rationing, Canada by the middle of the war had a tightly regulated economy. The government took over the marketing of wheat and other agricultural products, it closely prescribed the conditions of war contracts, and it set up numerous public production companies. The circumscribed area of the Canadian economy left to private initiative had by 1942 or 1943 given the country a regime as socialistic as that for which the C.C.F. had been campaigning. The main lines of the achieve-

[5] The Duplessis administration also exhibited highly authoritarian traits in its labour legislation; these cannot be discussed here. Nor can the tide that ran throughout the province for "The Corporate State". The Liberal victory having been won not only by "heart-felt appeals" but by less innocent devices also, it might be argued that subsequent elections in which such devices had been even more prominent, just as accurately reflect Quebec opinion.

ment were struck out with splendid ability: on the financial, economic, and administrative side of the war programme Canada led the world.

As the war went on, the benefits of the controls became increasingly clear: prices, wages, profits, and taxation maintained stability. No huge fortunes seem to have resulted, no one starved. Otherwise, the Canadian war experience was what it had always been in previous conflicts: an initial period of hesitation, followed by the most intense activity for everyone, with nearly everyone sharing in the general prosperity and the standard of living attaining levels which peace could not produce. During the Second World War, Canadian diet and health were better than in peace. So was morale, for the stir and change of war, its satisfaction of the sense of accomplishment, just suits the English-Canadian temperament: it is hardly too much to say that, except for those who lost relatives or dear friends as casualties, except for the women whose menfolk were in danger, and except for the very trying period of the fall of France, English Canadians found in the Second World War, not fear and terror, but exhilaration.

The French Canadians were different. They were still not much closer to understanding the issues abroad than they had been in the first war. They were still filled with apprehension at the dynamic movements of the age.[6] Above all, they were still immovably opposed to conscription for overseas service. They did much better, however, on a voluntary basis than they had before (six times as well, it has been calculated) and they made a large contribution to the industrial effort. Sharing the prosperity that resulted from it they experienced its social effects. Unionization of labour increased but of this the international unions were greater beneficiaries than the Roman Catholic Syndicates. Here was an indication in Quebec of an increasing secularism which explained the sharpness of the nationalist note sounded by young intellectuals and by certain groups among the clergy. A notable point in this sequence was reached when a Jewish Communist, Fred Rose, "le petit Fred", was elected to the House of Commons for a Montreal riding (August 9, 1943), partly by the votes of the French "submerged tenth", who had evinced one of the characteristic features of urbanism by drifting away from the Church. As the war ended, the old and the new struggled against each other in Quebec, and no one could foresee the outcome of the complex situation.[7]

[6] See p. 471
[7] The provincial election of Aug. 8, 1944 did not resolve the situation. The Duplessis *Union Nationale* elected the largest number of members, though not a majority over all the other parties combined. In few ridings did the elected member have a majority of the votes cast.

The innumerable episodes of the war period, the dozens of interesting phenomena to which it gave rise, must be omitted. It must suffice to say that the war greatly hastened the pace of Canadian industrial development, decisively shifting the balance from ruralism to urbanism, that it greatly weakened *laisser-faire* and strengthened communalism, that it disclosed a wealth of professional and technical ability for the service of the state, though not an increase of ability in those elected, and that it avoided, though by a narrow margin, the open racial clash of the first war.

When the changes in the Canadian way of life and the revolutionary expansion of governmental activities are taken into account, only one verdict can be given: any administration which could pilot the boat through such storms with such a high degree of efficiency (not overlooking many mistakes) and with freedom from the besetting Canadian sin of corruption, deserves high praise. Rarely had there been a ministry with so much administrative talent, never before had so much ability been concentrated in Ottawa, and never in Canadian history had administrative careers (on the basis of appointment, not election) been so open to talent. At last Canada began to use her gifted young men instead of shipping them to the United States, and the results were discernible in policies not only of competence but, as noted, in certain areas, of brilliance.[8] Whatever his own personal contribution to the result, the head of such an administration should have his country's gratitude; he must have imparted to it some of his outlook and his spirit, for the personality of the leader is communicated by a kind of osmotic process to all ranks beneath him.

4. The Character of the King Administration

The country was, it may be agreed, fortunate in the men in power during these years of internal stress. There was, it is true, nothing of Henry V about William Lyon Mackenzie King: no one can imagine him leading his dear friends once more into the breach or closing the wall up with his Liberal dead. He was cautious, patient, supple, courteous, and tolerant, but not bold or decisive. In his determination to preserve the unity of Canada, he was a true disciple of Laurier, and of a family tradition and education steeped in Liberal democracy. Of this, he had, it would seem, his own conception. To him, Liberalism was

---

[8] Much of this rested upon the decline of parliamentary power and prestige through the use made of the War Measures Act. The war saw a brilliant bureaucracy grow up in Ottawa, but it did not strengthen parliamentary, that is, representative government.

close to humanitarianism, democracy meant "government by the people", and an election was a device for ascertaining the will of the people. He disliked the Senate because it represented privilege, because it was a survival from days when other orders in the state contended for mastery with the people. As his readiness to appeal to the electorate against Parliament shows, his democracy was Jacksonian.[9]

Democracy, pinning its faith to a majority vote as the revelation of the voice of God, harbours an unsuspected but innate antagonism to liberalism. The old English Whig party, the guardian of the Revolutionary tradition of 1688, looked to the supremacy of Parliament, which to it meant the supremacy of the constitution, that is, of law; the new Whigs came to look to the Rousseau-istic "general will" as determined by popular vote. But time has amply demonstrated (as in the plebiscites for the first and second Napoleon and for Hitler) that the voice of the people may also be the voice of Satan. Today we have been forced back, not to the uninstructed voice of the people, but to a set of first principles, to something like the natural rights ideas of the eighteenth century. We have fought two wars, not on majority votes, but in defence of our conviction that man is an individual, with a unique value, that he must not be deprived of his natural dignity as man or of his fundamental human rights; we have fought for the Christian conception of man, with which the English-speaking peoples have closely bound up the concept of freedom and the traditional guarantees they have worked out to safeguard it. Freedom transcends democracy. Would King have shared such views? Verbally, yes, but to judge from his career, though he talked much about freedom and little about democracy, he would appear to have believed in the infallibility of the people's verdict (in office he may have identified this with the strongest pressure group) rather than to be guided by the ethic of freedom, which is the essence of liberalism. His democratic convictions may well have outweighed his liberal ideas.

There have been few passages more ironical in Canadian history than that it should have been the fortune of this great democrat, this eminently peace-loving man, to carry his country through a great war, during the course of which his government was to act in a manner so opposite to its leader's expressed convictions. The government, which had been coming more and more to represent all that was left of the old *laisser-faire* philosophy, had to regiment the Canadian economy with a multitude of controls that could hardly have been exceeded by a doctrinaire socialist administration. A Liberal government, which had always stood

[9] As in his surprise dissolution of 1940. Note also one of his speeches later on: in the face of obstruction, he would not hesitate five minutes, he said, in appealing to the people.

for the utmost freedom to the individual and for the maintenance of all his traditional civil rights, was the government that cut into freedom and abrogated civil rights to a degree not equalled in any other English-speaking nation. The man whose faith was in the voice of the people, having directly consulted that oracle in respect to conscription[10] and having received a weight of evidence from it that its voice was in the affirmative, had by indirect shifts and devices to find a means of not obeying the voice. The great parliamentarian, whose phrase "Parliament will decide" had become a household word, had to bypass Parliament and bring in much of his important legislation by order-in-council. King found Canada a parliamentary country and went far towards destroying the prestige of Parliament. He found Canada a free country; his administration went far towards destroying the basis of that freedom.

Did King and his ministers then commit the unpardonable sin? Knowing light, did they choose darkness? It would be unfair to make such a charge. They had a great crisis to meet, and they met it as best they could. Lucky is that state which can fight two great wars within a generation and retain its liberties. So much may be granted. What may not be granted is the necessity of so complete an invasion of Canadian liberties as occurred. King might have justified many of the episodes by saying that "the people demanded it". "The people", in this collective sense, at times of public excitement are frequently intolerant to the point of cruelty, and the voices that chiefly make themselves heard cry out for dark measures. But was there necessity for such an entire surrender of liberty, so complete a plunge into the police state of European type, as the War Measures Act and the Defence of Canada Regulations effected? Freedom-loving citizens achieved amelioration of a dangerous and unjust situation[11] only by long effort. Government itself seemed to be indifferent: it had struck at the fundamental right of the citizen, and it did not seem anxious to give up its power.

There was not much more to be said for its treatment of Parliament. Important and complex legislation rushed through by order-in-council while Parliament was actually sitting, or immediately after it adjourned, robbed the Commons of its ancient rights, and turned it into a Reichstag, a debating society. The most lenient verdict that may be pronounced upon King is that because of their urgent nature he permitted many things which his better judgement may not have approved of, or that to colleagues he amiably committed powers which they used more arbitrarily than he himself would have done. The kindliest thing

[10] In the plebiscite of 1942; see p. 559.
[11] In particular, Regulation 21, giving the power of arrest and detention without trial.

the historian can say about the King war administration is that it consisted of men most of whom were too thoroughly saturated in Liberal principles to take advantage of the arbitrary powers they had assumed. Despite Defence of Canada Regulations, despite the neglect and supersession of Parliament, Canada remained a free country, her press remained free, and her citizens substantially retained their freedom of speech and their representative institutions. The men charged with government had not within their breasts the spirit of the despot, and although they erected a machine for war which, along with the other qualities of a fine mechanism, had all the powers of the despotic state, they could not bring themselves to harness it to the ways of despotism. For this it may be that they themselves did not deserve too much credit. There is such a force as tradition in society—tradition and accepted usage. No one can escape this. Men are bound by it, seemingly, against their will. It is probably fair to assert that our freedom was maintained, not by the individuals in whose care it was, but by long tradition and strong customary habits.

Chronology

1935 Mackenzie King's third administration.
1936 Duplessis *Union Nationale* premier of Quebec.
1937 "Bennett New Deal" *ultra vires.*
     Duplessis Padlock Law.
     Rowell-Sirois Commission.
1939 Sept. 10. Canada declares war.
     Godbout defeats Duplessis in Quebec.
     Economic War Programme of King government inaugurated.
1940 King government returned to power.
1942 Conscription Plebiscite.
1943 Liberal government defeated in Ontario: C.C.F. the official opposition.
1944 C.C.F. carry Saskatchewan Provincial Elections.
     Duplessis again Premier of Quebec.
1945 June 11: General Election: King Ministry returned.

Additional Reading

Canada. *Report of the Royal Commission on Dominion-Provincial Relations.* Ottawa, 1940 (reprinted 1954), 2 vols.
Fowke, V. C. *The National Policy and the Wheat Economy.* Toronto, 1957.
Lamontagne, Maurice. *Le Fédéralisme canadien; évolution et problèmes.* Quebec, 1954.
Mallory, J. R. *Social Credit and the Federal Power in Canada.* Toronto, 1954.
Stacey, C. P. *The Canadian Army, 1939-1945.* Ottawa, 1948.

CHAPTER 36

The External Crisis, 1931 and After

1. Factors and Points of View

It took the intense atmosphere of the decade preceding the Second World War to bring the subject of foreign policy to the notice of the general Canadian public. Until the first war, Canada had looked out mainly through the eyes of the mother country: she had not begun to build up her own conceptions until the inter-war period. Even then, except for the broad aspects of relations with Great Britain and the United States, the subject hardly became one of wide popular interest. The course of events in the 1930's, however, forced attention to the outside world: the Canadian people underwent a few years of intensive education. The process was by no means complete in 1939, but by that year, most of the main problems had been publicly discussed (though certainly not settled), and the circle of persons conversant with them had widened. The discussions, often acrimonious, at least brought some understanding of the basic factors in Canada's international position. These lay in her geographical situation, her blood-ties, and her traditional attachment to Great Britain.

Geographically, Canada shared a private world with the United States, friendship with which power had to be taken for granted since enmity would be suicidal. From it Canada's forces were free to sally forth when the motherland found itself at war, but that war might come to them, in their own homeland, was a notion remote from Canadian

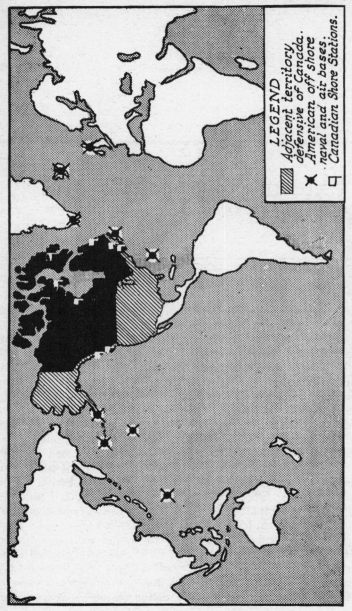

CANADA'S ISLAND-LIKE POSITION.

(Period of the Second World War).

minds. Thousands of miles of ocean, with the legendary British navy on the other side of it, seemed to show that there was little need in time of peace for an army, still less for a navy. In addition, those who had studied the situation were impressed with the strength of the inland position, with its hundreds of miles of wilderness and mountain on both coasts. Canada was no Poland, open to every army that cared to march across its borders. On the contrary, it was, for purposes of defence, the most invulnerable of all configurations of land: Canada was an island. It was a very large island, it is true, but an island nevertheless, an island surrounded by wide and stormy oceans on three sides and on the fourth by the strong and friendly barrier of the United States, a medium even more impenetrable than water. Given the command of the sea in friendly hands, Canada had nothing to worry about. Given its loss, although Nova Scotia was exposed and the weak island of Newfoundland, the stopper in the St. Lawrence bottle, had no defences of its own, she was still in a relatively favourable position. Until 1940, however, few Canadians worried over command of the sea.

The development of air power after the first war only altered the position in detail, for to make air power effective against North America, an enemy would have first to secure bases through sea power. The possibilities in air warfare did not shift most Canadians from their sense of geographical remoteness, and the efforts of the right wing to make their flesh creep had little result.

In Canada, racial memory, the next factor in external relations, constantly struggles with geography. No English Canadian can forget that he is a member of a cultural group extending in space and time far beyond the limits of his own homeland and consisting in two great powers as well as several smaller ones. If he has found it difficult to accept the high-handed attitude of the United States towards British colonies and its repudiation of the British tradition, he has always remembered not only the long peace along his borders, but his own unhappy state of mind when the two older countries were on bad terms. Any prospect of misunderstanding between them has destroyed his inner harmony at once, rendering him puzzled and distressed. Paradoxically enough, English Canadians never were more at peace with themselves than when fighting the Second World War, for then the common purpose of English and Americans bridged for a time the ancient cleft in the race.

The traditional attachment to the British Isles has clearly been one of the dominant themes in Canadian history, it having determined nearly every major issue and postponed for decades the emergence of Canada as an international person. When in September, 1939, the country entered the war "by its own act and of its own volition", was it not the relationship to the motherland—historic, sentimental, and social—that produced both the act and the volition?

To French Canada, "the call of the blood" has not applied, and in external affairs, that has been the rock on which the two peoples have split. French Canadians, removed from Europe by conquest and a revolutionary gulf, have been for taking advantage of the country's geographical isolation. Their attitude has been almost the same as that of the Americans, also cut off from Europe by a revolution. But the United States is a great power, and Americans have been compelled by their status to enter world affairs, whereas French Canadians have only been compelled by their English-speaking fellow-citizens. When in 1867-68, their own metropolitan centre, Rome, was involved in its "struggle for existence" against the secular Italian state, the feelings of many of them were engaged much as those of English Canadians when German bombs began to fall on London, and the result was the rather comic-opera expedition of the "Papal Zouaves".[1] The English and French attitudes in foreign affairs have been so different that the country, when at war, has only by the narrowest margin preserved its unity.

European affairs and ideologies in themselves have been of minor importance in Canadian external relations: providing Great Britain was not engaged, the whole of Europe could probably be utterly destroyed without English Canadians feeling called upon to intervene. And French Canadians would not have felt the same deep anguish of soul at the overwhelming of France as English Canadians with respect to the British Isles. When France was overrun in 1940, French Canadians, it is true, felt it keenly, but not sufficiently to evoke the irresistible urge to action that marked English Canada at the time. Towards Asia, especially towards Japan, Canadians, before the Second World War broke out, had begun to manifest a certain independence of interest, which, however, did not carry close to the point of independent action.[2] Towards the League of Nations, with its implications for a new kind of world, most of them were lukewarm. The League was out of the course of their experience. To the masses, it was just a term; it was neither fish nor flesh, British or American, only a thin ghost with no blood in its veins. The realities were, for French Canada: itself; for English Canada: Great Britain and the United States.

The schools of opinion that arose from varying combinations of the fundamental factors ran from the jingoistic Imperialism of many

---

[1] A corps of which name set out from Montreal after the Battle of Mentana, 1867, amid scenes of delirious devotion, but failed to do much for the Pope.
[2] See p. 481ff.

English-speaking Tories to the extremes of isolationism encountered among the French, with many gradations in between. In Canada, the political attitude of a man or a group depends not so much upon reason as upon family tradition, racial descent, religious denomination, and economic interest. Persons of North of Ireland descent, for example, Anglican in religion and of substantial property, are virtually certain to be Conservative in politics, strong Imperialists in peace time, and zealous advocates of "all-out" measures in time of war, whereas if they are of Presbyterian background, the equation, though remaining the same in its other terms, may read "Liberal" in domestic politics. At the time of the Second World War more than a century of mixture had not destroyed the original affiliations, and to know the primary terms in the equation was often to know the answer.

The Tory colonial group, as it may be called, was most numerous among established families in old United Empire Loyalist districts, among Anglicans, persons of the upper age groups, and in the Maritime provinces. Its members tended to regard Canada as a colony with its real government still at Westminster. Tory colonialism was not identical with Imperialism, though having much in common with it. The word "imperialism" in Canada has not had its European sense of expansion and domination but has rather connoted strong belief in "Britain" and in the unity of the British peoples. The Canadian imperialist has been strong in his monarchical and aristocratic sentiments. He has dreamed of a day when Canada might hold the leading place in the British Empire and he has had no rooted objection to Canadian autonomy. In this he differs from the Tory colonial. The loyalties of both these schools towards London have usually outweighed their loyalties towards Ottawa.

Under the label "autonomist" a wide variety of people could meet, for by the time of the Second World War most Canadians had come to agree that Canada should govern itself. The logic of autonomy has been legal partnership with Great Britain, and since this involved no basic alteration of the sentimental relationship, it was easily attained. The right wing, nevertheless, usually fought autonomy every inch of the way.[3]

The word "interventionist", often used in the thirties, gives another cross-classification. In the inter-war period, many groups for one reason or another, were ready to take a hand in Europe's troubles. The right wing of Canadian opinion thought that Britain should give the law to lesser breeds and would have been ready to rush to her support at any moment.[4] Humanitarians were wounded by the cruelties of aggressor

[3] See pp. 264, 454, 483, etc.
[4] Meighen, in a speech at Toronto, proclaimed that Canada's response to the British appeal for troops in the Chanak affair should have been "Ready, aye, ready".

nations and advocated boycotts or other measures that might have
brought about armed intervention, a type of action to which they were
at that time fervently opposed. Believers in the League of Nations, who
hoped to preserve the structure symbolized by Geneva, wished to uphold
the public international law. Catholics wished to intervene on behalf of
the Church in Mexico; Communists wished to intervene in Spain. Jews
wished a declaration on the Palestine problem, Ukrainians wished an
attempt to succour their minorities in Poland. Interventionists agreed
only in that they wished to use the power of the state for their own
purposes. Among them, to borrow a figure from Stephen Leacock, they
would have had Canada "galloping off in all directions".

A sub-species of interventionists, who might be called "internationalists", consisted in the small groups of intellectuals who supported the
League of Nations, whether because they saw in collective security the
only device that would hold together the British Empire or because the
League held the ultimate problems of Canadian sovereignty in suspen-
sion, or because they believed that an international order which would
avoid war could be achieved through the League. A variant of inter-
nationalist was to be found in the earnest people who filled the ranks of
League of Nations societies. Inspired by the ardent evangelical traditions that had produced great movements, such as that for prohibition
or the foreign missionary movement of the previous generation, they
conceived of the League as a kind of great international church.

Some contrast was offered to all the foregoing by persons who might
properly have been called nationalists. They were those who had succeeded in completely transferring their centre of reference to Canada
and who therefore met Lord Tweedsmuir's requirement that "a Canadian's first loyalty is not to the British Commonwealth of Nations but to
Canada and to Canada's king . . .",[5] a sentiment that would seem
obvious but which, by the amount of resentment it stirred up in certain
limited but vocal quarters, indicated how far the process had to go
before the bulk of the inhabitants of English Canada became, in a vital
sense, Canadians.[6] Nationalists found no inevitable identity of interests
between Great Britain and Canada and did not judge British policy on
the usual sentimental basis. Canadian nationalists were persons to whom
the British connection did not have the original emotional appeal. They
considered Canada an independent nation that should furnish forth
from within itself the springs of its own life and forge its own foreign
policy.

[5] Speech to Canadian Institute of International Affairs, Montreal, Oct. 12, 1937.
  The Governor-General was soundly rebuked for such "disloyal" sentiments by
  the editor of the Montreal *Gazette*.
[6] See p. 279.

Another school of opinion consisted of those, often dubbed "isolationists", who wished to keep out of all European entanglements and were ready to cut the British connection, if necessary, in order to do so. Most French Canadians were isolationists; the vast majority of English Canadians were not, although there was a considerable and influential isolationist element in English Canada. Few isolationists, however assuredly they argued for neutrality in the case of Great Britain being engaged in war, believed in the possibility of maintaining neutrality: the most they probably expected was to delay impetuous action.

A school prominent in the United States was hardly present in Canada at all, the isolationist pacifists. In Canada, those who echoed the cry "I didn't raise my boy to be a soldier" became zealous League of Nations supporters. True pacifists, who are willing to endure the uttermost consequences of their creed, are rare. Most of those dubbed "pacifists" are simply well-meaning people seeking to avoid the terrors of war. Such persons could not find within Canada itself a world sufficiently large and safe, so they turned to what seemed the best hope of safety, the League. In the United States, which seemed sufficient in itself to give safety, they retreated from reality and simply hoped that their country could somehow or other keep out of war.

There was in Canada hardly a trace of the common European attitude towards international affairs. Machiavellian policies, based on hard, realistic thinking, divorced from ethical considerations, with the state conceived as an end in itself, or balance of power conceptions, were almost entirely absent from Canadian minds, nearly all of which, professional and lay, took their point of departure from some sentimental or idealistic conception. Each school of thought merged with its neighbours, but the extremes were poles apart. All these opinions diverged so widely that the emergence of a unified Canadian point of view seemed impossible. Under the circumstances, the supreme task of statesmanship was to avoid enunciating a foreign policy. Opportunism came to be one of the heroic virtues.

2. The Completion of Autonomy

After the Statute of Westminster was passed, relations with Great Britain became diplomatic rather than constitutional. Yet one clause in the Statute provided for constitutional eventualities in that no act of the British Parliament could extend to a Dominion except with the Dominion's consent. To the surprise of most, it was not long before the clause became operative. In December, 1936, occurred the abdication of Edward VIII. Since the Canadian Parliament was not in session, the government requested the British Parliament to include Canada in its Abdication Act, which thereby became law in Canada: on December 11, George VI became King in Great Britain, Canada, Australia and New Zealand.[7] But the Parliaments of Ireland and South Africa passed their own Abdication Acts: in South Africa George VI became King on December 10, 1936, and in Ireland on December 12. There were three days during which two kings reigned over one empire. What had become of the unity of the Crown? It could hardly be maintained that Edward VIII and George VI were wearing the same crown. The unity of the Crown had given way to an unadmitted personal union. This became more explicit in the coronation oath of George VI, which read in part: "Will you solemnly promise and swear to govern the peoples of Great Britain, Ireland, Canada, Australia, New Zealand and the Union of South Africa . . . according to their respective laws and customs?" When in the spring of 1939, the King personally visited Canada, he came unaccompanied by any member of his British government, and as King of Canada held his high court of Parliament and from his throne in his Senate chamber ceremonially signified his assent to Acts of the Canadian Parliament.[8] In February of the same year a member of the Canadian Parliament, J .T. Thorson, had introduced into the Commons a bill stating that Canada should become a belligerent only on a declaration of war made by the King on the advice of his Canadian government: the principle involved, that Great Britain could not automatically commit Canada to war, would have left to Canada the right of neutrality. The resolution was not put to a vote but when war came in September of that year, the Canadian declaration did not occur for a full week after that of Great Britain. During that week the United States treated Canada as a neutral country, and the German consular service also carried on its duties. On September 10, the King of Canada made his separate declaration of war. Canada had achieved the last test of legal sovereignty, the right of war and peace, and after that, whatever their legal form, the so-called "Dominions" were in practice sovereign states. Except for certain anachronisms that rested on the conservatism of the Canadian people and the divisions among them (the appeal to the Judicial Committee of the Privy Council, the amendment of the British North America Act by the British Parliament, the failure to have a national flag), the process of achieving autonomy had been completed.

[7] For the debates on the Canadian parliamentary confirmation of the Abdication Act, see Hansard, Jan. 19, 1937.
[8] The Royal Assent, pronounced by the Clerk of the Senate in both languages, ran "His Majesty the King doth assent to these Bills".

3. The Course of Foreign Policy After 1931

Autonomy was one thing, the definition of relationships to other powers and to world problems another. The completion of autonomy had been certain from the day when the first settlers of English speech came to Canadian soil, and it had little effect on the "British connection", which depended on something much deeper than constitutional points. But the definition of political relationships with other countries and towards world problems necessarily meant their definition towards Great Britain. Political definition involved psychological definition: in relating themselves in a new fashion to the outside world, Canadians were having to examine the secret places of their hearts. Little wonder, then, among a people who very conspicuously do not wear their hearts on their sleeves, such discussion as there was was bitter and acrimonious, concerning itself not with concrete issues but with the burning issue of a shift in deep political allegiances.

Discussion went on over the radio, in the periodical press, in books (of which there was a surprising stream in the years after 1933), through local study clubs, and especially in the branches and annual conferences of the Canadian Institute of International Affairs. Although the argument was not always in good temper (how could it be, when it touched, as it did, the fundamental nature of the state?), the general effect was to bring home to Canadians the nature of their country and help them define their attitude towards it. Parliament did not make the contribution that might have been expected of a national assembly. Not only did its members as a body prove less able and more poorly informed than some of the laymen who were conducting the extra-parliamentary debate, but also Prime Minister King frowned on discussion of current international topics as too dangerous.[9] That what was said in Canada would have brought war nearer, may be doubted; that such discussion was divisive internally, is evident. The policy of Mr. King, who so frequently told Parliament that "it would decide", that "we had no commitments", seems to have been to avoid the necessity of public decision by avoiding public reference to the matter to be decided. The subject of Canada's participation in the war about to come was an explosive one, and it has always been difficult to reconcile the sharp differences in Canadian life; it may be necessary for the man who

[9] An attitude called by John MacCormac in his *Canada, America's Problem* (New York, 1940) "Deaf-mutism as a foreign policy", "thirteen years of tiptoeing around the sick-room". There is no reason to change the judgement made above on the M.P.'s of the 1930's in applying it to the M.P.'s of the 1960's.

would retain the office of Prime Minister and maintain the unity of the country to risk charges of hypocrisy by resorting to a logic-chopping dialectic. That, however, does not bring admiration to the person who bows to the necessity.

In practice it was impossible to keep consideration of Canada's foreign relations out of Parliament and foreign relations formed the subject of some discussion every year, and in some of the last years before the war, a good deal of discussion. But it was discussion that rarely went beyond academic debate. "The illusion that Canada has something to do with the conduct of foreign affairs," a distinguished official, Loring Christie, in what was probably an overstatement, once said to the writer, "is sustained by a considerable show of paper study and chatter about 'parliament will decide' . . . and by occasional polite essays in full-dress clothes solemnly read to a bored House of Commons —essays which are not part of a course of conduct or action or decisions . . .". Canada, through ministers and officials, has at times had decisive effect on international affairs, but nothing confirms the unrealities of Parliamentary debate more plainly than their own nature. Mr. Bourassa in his eloquent oration of April 1, 1935, after argument for Canadian neutrality in time of war, occupying 13 pages of Hansard, was able to put a motion in general, nebulous terms, coming down strongly on the side of peace and good will, and have it carried unanimously! If there had been the slightest likelihood of the resolution actually entailing neutrality in Canada during a British war, not a corporal's guard of English-speaking members would have had anything to do with it. As it was, they approved Mr. Bourassa's admirable and eloquent sentiments.

The most formal and considered exposition of Canadian foreign policy, an exposition that to some degree escaped the charge of being "a polite essay in full-dress clothes", was probably that of Mr. King on May 24, 1938. It may be briefly summarized. Mr. King defined foreign policy as the sum of one country's dealings with another. Canada's direct dealings with other countries were simple: it was the indirect connections through the League and the Commonwealth that presented so much complexity. Of direct relations, those with the United States were immeasurably the most important and had fortunately reached a state of cordiality that facilitated agreement on specific issues. In general terms, Canadian policy was one of peace and friendship. It took account of the complexities in Canadian life, such as traditional relationships, geography, population, race, and economic development. It could not therefore be "a spectacular headline policy". There was no likelihood that Canada would, of its own motion, intervene in other people's affairs. Nor was there much greater likelihood of an aggressor troubling Canada, given distance and the other prizes more tempting to him. In so far as indirect complications went, Mr. King took the stand that the League should be a body for conciliation, not "an international war office" (a position he had put at Geneva in September, 1936). He could not accept for Canada the theory of automatic commitment through League action.[10] He could not admit that she could be saddled with responsibility for wrecking the "universal policeman" view of the League for, as a secondary state, her influence was limited. He repudiated participation in foreign troubles on an ideological basis.[11] Fascists, Communists and others must fight it out among themselves: he would have nothing to do with "the democratic countries firmly and unitedly calling a halt". In so far as Great Britain was concerned, he recognized the overwhelming complexity of the conditions she had to meet but dismissed out of hand the view that Canada should accept any policy adopted by the British government of the day. As to the idea of giving Great Britain advice, he pointed out its impracticability in that the Dominions might not all give the same advice, that policy is not a matter of formulation at a moment's notice but the result of a slow accumulation of decisions and that Great Britain's ministers must be responsible to Great Britain and would, therefore, take their own advice. He then dismissed any notion of a declaration of neutrality in advance, for this would be a policy of commitments and in so far as participation in war was concerned, he said, "we may take the position that parliament will decide upon our course when and if the emergency arises, in the light of all the circumstances of the time".[12]

Here was the policy of "no commitments", assailed by the Tories as "disloyal" to England and by the French as a hypocritical device for engaging Canada in Imperial wars. King invariably stood between the devil and the deep blue sea. He was the person who divided Canada the least. However strong one's preference for a bright and shining blade, his clumsy weapon of hair-splitting verbosity at least kept the internal foe, disunity, at bay.

[10] But see p. 551.

[11] But see p. 555. What did Mr. King mean by the word "ideological"? The writer uses the noun, "ideology" as a rough equivalent of "way of life"; an "ideology" comes close to a philosophy or even to a religion, without being as systematic as the former, while lacking the historical overtones of the latter.

[12] The speech contained its own neat summary. See Hansard, May 24, 1938, p. 3450.

Commendable though his intentions were, Mr. King's position was open to serious criticism. In the first place his own speeches make it clear that he was a believer in what was called "appeasement" and it is hard to grasp what his limits of tolerance were.[13] In the second place, "Parliament will decide" was little more than a procrastinating phrase. Thirdly, "no commitments" was a specious device: Canada might have no legal commitments but English Canada, anyone could see, was determined to be committed in the event of Great Britain's going to war, and so was Mr. King—committed by his heart, whatever his head was saying, as were ninety per cent of his fellows.[14] "No commitments", "Parliament will decide" and similar phrases were not far from being mere, half-honest, rhetorical subterfuges.

As contrasted with her interminable debates, there were three occasions in the period 1931-39 when Canada acted, and in a decisive if negative way. The first consisted in Mr. Cahan's intervention in the Manchurian question, already discussed,[15] the second arose out of the sanctions imposed on Italy after she invaded Ethiopia and the third consisted in Mr. King's declaration in the Assembly of 1936 against a League based on force.

In September, 1935, Sir Samuel Hoare at Geneva had made a resounding speech on the Italo-Abyssinian dispute, indicating that Great Britain was about to come down on the side of public law. That autumn, the League for the first time tried to coerce a great power, Italy. The government of Canada, under Prime Minister Bennett, and through its representative at the Assembly, Hon. Howard Ferguson, took a strong affirmative line, not only supporting sanctions but proposing additional measures.[16] But it so happened that when the arrangements were being worked out, the Canadian government was in process of passing from Bennett to King, and Mr. Riddell, the Canadian Advisory Officer at Geneva, was for an unfortunate moment, left to act on his own discretion. Receiving no answer to cables for instructions and assuming that the new government would continue the policies of the

[13] "My visit to Germany in 1937 had as its objective to make it perfectly clear that, if there was a war of aggression, nothing in the world would keep the Canadian people from being at the side of Britain." Hansard, Aug. 11, 1944, p. 6420. A very typical statement! What about the steps that preceded a "war of aggression"?

[14] See Hansard, *op. cit.*, especially p. 6419, and the speech of Aug. 11 as a whole.

[15] See p. 484ff.

[16] For the oil sanctions incident, see Gwendolen M. Carter, *Consider the Record: Canada and the League of Nations* (Behind the Headlines pamphlet series, Vol. I, No. 6 (Toronto, 1942), p. 19ff. See also one of Mr. Riddell's own books, *Documents on Canadian Foreign Policy* (Toronto, 1962).

old, he carried out the steps begun by Mr. Ferguson and proposed, among others, the crucial sanction on oil.

This action precipitated a sharp division in Canadian opinion. English-speaking Canada was solidly against Italy (though not unanimously in favour of coercion), for on such an issue its various groups coincided, the imperialists seeing in the Italian proceedings defiance to British majesty; the humanitarians, a cruel aggression against a weak people; and the internationalists, a violation of the law. French-speaking Canada was quite indifferent over what happened to the Abyssinians, except in that an Italian conquest would give opportunity to reclaim them for Roman Catholicism (with Protestant missions eliminated, as they afterwards were).

Mr. Riddell's oil sanctions proposal consequently became a *cause célèbre*. French Canadians and other Catholics pressed for disavowal, and to their efforts were joined those of some of the English who, while disapproving of Italy, had no wish to see their country take a lead in coercing a great power. Counter-pressure could not have been as strong, for within a few weeks (December 2), Mr. Lapointe explained on behalf of the Canadian government that Canada did not intend to take the initiative in extending economic sanctions though she would accept the decisions made. This perfectly sensible position for a power of Canada's weight and detachment encouraged the Italians, strengthened the hands of those in England and France who did not favour sanctions, and met with the cordial approval of the French Canadian press. Objections to it from English Canada were buried in the avalanche of protest that a few days later overwhelmed the Hoare-Laval compromise by which Great Britain and France virtually agreed to what Italy was doing in Abyssinia. This cynical bargain at Abyssinia's expense, so emphatically repudiated by the people of England, also threw some light to those Canadians who had eyes to see on the type of men who were governing England.

The Italians duly completed their conquest of Abyssinia, not overly hampered by such sanctions as were maintained against them: at last these too were withdrawn. The King government's action in refusing to stand by Riddell's proposal had removed Canada from the list of those countries that were prepared to uphold the public law by force. When Mr. King spoke at Geneva on September 29, 1936, he relegated the League to a medium of conciliation. In September, 1936 "the League of Nations, with assurances of the most distinguished consideration, was ushered into the darkness by Mr. Mackenzie King".[17] This was the

[17] J. W. Dafoe, "Canadian Foreign Policy," in R. G. Trotter, ed., *Conference on Canadian-American Affairs, 1937* (Boston, 1937), p. 225.

third decisive Canadian action. Thereafter, Canada had no foreign
policy except a correct neutrality. Her voice was not raised in international affairs and she left it to the great powers to wreck the world as
they deemed best.

If Canada's policy abroad after September, 1936, was negative and
"correct", her attitude towards her neighbour was much more positive.
A few days after his victory over Mr. Bennett, Mr. King visited Mr.
Roosevelt. Shortly afterwards came the announcement of the completion
of the trade agreement between the two countries, negotiations for
which had been initiated by the previous administration: this was the
first Canadian-American trade agreement of significance since the Reciprocity Treaty of 1854-66. The visit that preceded it was by no means
the last, for much of the succeeding good understanding between the
two countries seems to have been built up on the cordial personal relations between the two men, King and Roosevelt.

In 1936, President Roosevelt's speeches, designed to rouse his country
to its dangers, began to include references to Canada. The first of these
he put into the Chatauqua speech of August 14, 1936, in which he
spoke of the readiness of the United States to defend itself and its
neighbourhood. Was this an explicit extension of the Monroe Doctrine
to Canada? Two years later, in August, 1938, when receiving an
honorary degree from Queen's University, the President made his reference more explicit: the United States, he said, would not stand idly by
and see its neighbour Canada attacked. A few days later, at Wood-
bridge, Ontario, Mr. King made the situation mutual: he promised
reciprocity in defence and this promise was duly implemented when in
December, 1941, Canada, first of all the western nations, declared war
against Japan. In the period between the British declaration of war and
the Canadian (September 3-10, 1939), the American authorities were
ready to give Canada all the benefits of neutrality. This meant that she
could have become a channel for war supplies between the United
States and Great Britain, an activity that would otherwise have been
forbidden by the American Neutrality Act. The coping stone to the
edifice was supplied by the Ogdensburg Agreement of August, 1940,
which set up a Permanent Joint Board on Defence for the two
countries. Their affairs, placed on a basis of complete equality by Mr.
King's determination that Canada would at all times pay her own way,
thereafter became more and more commingled as the war developed.
The American policy of the King government was an open book.

4. The Approach of the Inevitable

After 1931, when Japan went into Manchuria,[18] the world situation rapidly went from bad to worse. Every day provided its new shock. To defer speaking of Germany for the moment, there came in 1935 the Italian attack on Abyssinia, which revealed differences in Canadian attitudes towards the outside world deeper even than those which Anglo-Canadian relations had brought to light. Controversy over "the British Connection" was in the tradition of the American Revolution, which had not severed common ties of language and religion, but the Italo-Abyssinian incident, and still more, the Spanish Civil War, introduced into Canadian foreign affairs the country's racial and religious differences. For most of the French and English Catholics alike and almost unanimously, Franco was a crusader whose cruelties and whose Mohammedan soldiers were sanctified by the cause. Following the lead of the Papacy, they believed the struggle in Spain to be against the atheism of Bolshevism. To defeat this threat no help need be spurned and when German aviators experimentally bombed a Spanish town out of existence, the deed did not shake those who believed that the faith came before human suffering. The English-speaking Protestant world was divided and confused. While in Canada there was virtually no class sympathy for Franco and no important trade relations with the rebel regions of Spain, yet there was little inclination to fight in the cause of Spanish democracy.[19]

Faced with the deep division of race and religion in the country, the government steered a characteristically cautious middle course, endeavouring to prevent volunteering for Spanish armies by a Foreign Enlistments Act and to avoid all suggestions of bias by an embargo on supplies going to either side. As with the similar actions of Great Britain and the United States, this policy of "non-intervention" just meant acquiescence in the destruction of the elements of Spanish life favourable to the western cause. Yet could the government of Canada have done anything else? A positive policy, even had Canada been ready to take a line of its own and oppose the desires of England and the United States (and there was no sign that it was ready) would have divided the country to the roots[20] and might have plunged it into civil strife.

---

[18] See p. 484ff.
[19] The Communists raised a battalion which they managed to get to Spain, and with an imaginative touch that the government could never have supplied, called it "The Mackenzie-Papineau Battalion".
[20] 43 out of every 100 Canadians being Roman Catholic.

Nothing could have shown more clearly the internal divisions of the western world than the preliminary Italian and Spanish bouts. It almost seemed as if all that the toreador himself, Germany, would have to do would be to stride into the ring and administer the *coup de grâce*. Yet the German situation presented strong contrasts with the other two. Memories of the last war were fresh. In Canada, no Catholic or Latin sympathies gave Germany bonds with Quebec. No Canadian big business interests of consequence had to live with the Nazis. German sympathies in Canada were confined to immigrant groups.[21] Consequently when Hitler obtained power, still more when he withdrew from the League, most Canadians knew fairly well what was up. Yet at first what the Nazis did seemed remote enough. There was disapproval and disgust over the Jewish persecutions. There was dismay over the surrender of England's Baldwin government in the Anglo-German naval agreement of June, 1935. There was perturbation over the advance into the Rhineland in 1936. But when it came to letting slip the dogs of war again, most people, pugnacious old veterans included, recoiled. Yet as one event followed another, as the shrieking, half-mad voice of the German dictator poured out of the radio, lethargy began to dissipate. The seizure of Austria was taken as an indication of what was to come but it was not until the events centring on Munich in the fall of 1938 that Canadian feelings became deeply roused. Then emotions were rocked. Reactions to Munich were as diverse as Canadian opinion. All could see the danger, and few there were who could be like many Americans and calmly regard approaching events as just another European quarrel.

A typical example of emotional disturbance was furnished by the Toronto *Globe and Mail*. In the beginning of September, 1938, when the crisis was developing, it shouted vehemently against Hitler. For the moment, British Empire, League of Nations, instinctive Canadian hatred of despotism, all coincided. Then when Chamberlain's policy began to unfold, *The Globe and Mail* became confused. It shouted as loudly as ever, but to all points of the compass. Finally when Chamberlain's course became clear, it was off (with scarcely a day to catch its breath) in his wake as fervently as if there had never been a League of Nations. Canada at the time had no policy of her own but Canadian

---

[21] More especially to the confessedly Hitlerite group centring round the German Consul-General in Winnipeg and the newspaper which Hitler's government supported through him, *Die Deutsche Zeitung für Kanada*. This paper printed contributions from, among others, one of the prominent professors of the University of Manitoba.

emotions had to come out, and come out they did in a great variety of directions.

For most Canadians the die was cast when in March, 1939, Hitler seized the remainder of Czechoslovakia and Chamberlain gave his impossible guarantees to Poland and Roumania. For a year or two previously, debates in the Commons had been shifting over from the generalities of national defence: votes for the armed services had increased. The enthusiasm marking the royal visit in the spring of 1939 indicated that Canadians were swinging closer to their historic allegiance. Although dissatisfaction with British policy was widespread and, even in Conservative circles, there was lack of faith in Chamberlain, yet the official policy being "no commitments", there was no possibility of doing anything to avert the approaching fate. Thoughtful persons saw their country being dragged inexorably towards Niagara without their having the least power or right to take part in steering the boat. At last, in the tense August of 1939, the cataract was reached. German troops went on the march again, Chamberlain's guarantee to Poland came into play, and the vessel, her radio blaring out raucous speeches and confused voices in many languages, swept over the falls. The Second World War had begun.

5. The Second World War

In August, 1914, the Canadian people had gone to war in high fighting spirit. In September, 1939, they accepted the blow that fate had dealt them. Ten years of depression and twenty years' crumbling of old institutions and beliefs did not provide the soil in which buoyant, fighting spirits flourish. There was little jingoism, and Mr. Woodsworth's pacifist declaration of faith[22] was listened to with respect by the House of Commons. In the country at large there was neither jubilation nor active protest. Canadians reluctantly prepared to accept their fate.

Mr. King's objections to fighting for ideological reasons[23] promptly disappeared, and despite the extremity of coercion represented by The Defence of Canada Regulations, the struggle at once became officially a war for "freedom". That was perhaps as definite a word as could be used to cover the reasons which, from one motive or another, secured the assent of the diverse groups to entering the war. French Canadians reluctantly concurred, and the English in general accepted the duties of the blood relationship. A small and determined Tory group would

[22] Hansard, Sept. 8, 1939.
[23] See p. 549.

probably have been ready for civil strife rather than see the country remain neutral. Canadians began the war feeling vaguely or ruefully or violently, as the case might be, that they were on the side of right, and for that the word "freedom" would do. The conflicting political and religious creeds in the country had rendered it quite impossible for government, even had its members so desired, to associate itself with any one clearly defined way of life. But years earlier, as suggested above,[24] it had become plain enough that sooner or later an ideological war would have to be fought. It had become increasingly impossible for countries of the western liberal tradition, with its doctrine of the rights of man and its ultimate foundations in Christian teaching, to live in the same world with the calculated brutalities of Hitlerism.[25] Canadians, it is true, fought because of the call of the blood; they fought because of the tradition of "Flanders fields"; they fought to prevent the conquest of western Europe (which to most of them meant the British Isles) ; they fought to nail the hides of the Nazis to the fence before their own occupied that position. But all this meant that they fought a war for their traditional institutions of government, for their liberties as they understood them, for the basic principles of their religion, for that whole way of life which, notwithstanding so many misconstructions and so much overburden, may properly be called liberal and Christian democracy.

Such good reasons for fighting did not become clear at once. There

---

[24] See especially p. 485

[25] The modern world's disturbances reflect in the main the sharp turn from individualism to collectivism, but the tensions of the transition are heightened by the clashes of its major life-patterns. These may be termed "ideologies", or perhaps, since people passionately believe in them, religions. They are, or were, Latin (or Roman) Catholicism, Nazi-ism, Fascism, and related creeds of people or state, Protestantism, Capitalism, Communism, and the racism of the former colonial peoples. Catholicism takes its stand on an absolute, a traditional, unvaried conception of God and the universe. Nazi-ism and Fascism rejected this absolute, but as offshoots of German idealistic philosophy, found another in "The People" or "The State". All these doctrines are in essence mystical. Protestantism is a "Welt-Bejähung", an affirmation of life; it is dynamic and realistic. In its more evangelical forms, it can find liaisons and sympathies with Communism, which possesses its own evangelical social drive. Both Protestantism and Communism look forward to the bettering of man's fate on earth, whereas Catholicism looks forward to a mystical destiny for man. Capitalism is simply a pagan attitude towards power and pelf, and so may shelter with any of these creeds that seem as if they might be of use to it. Racism is always and everywhere present as a dividing and temperature-raising force. Distribute these basic concepts among the jarring elements and myriad situations of the modern world, and the result is the complex equation of our times.

was many a puzzled person in that first winter of "phoney" war. But the economic benefits of war had already begun to compensate for its other derangements; Canada was already playing its historic role of a secure supply base. Then suddenly in the spring of 1940, the country woke up. The Germans had seized Norway. They had defied British seapower. Their skill and their audacity compelled a reluctant admiration! They were playing Chamberlain's incompetent team off its feet. When as the spring went by, Holland, Belgium, France itself, were successively conquered, the current of Canadian life changed. As British soldiers crowded to the shores at Dunkirk, many a Canadian must have felt himself saying an unaccustomed prayer for their salvation; the inescapable bonds of blood were sealed again and when to them was joined the eloquence of Mr. Churchill, English Canadians, casting aside whatever elements of national individuality they had acquired, merged their fate once more with England.

The hard events of 1940, which touched the emotions of all, provided the first major domestic crisis of the war.[26] From the centres of the orthodox faith, the cry went up for conscription, as it had in 1917, and again it was echoed by much of English Canada. The internal disturbances, which hastily-applied coercive measures would probably have precipitated, were avoided for the time by the introduction of a partial form of compulsory service for a short term and within "the Western Hemisphere". This compromise, embodied in the National Resources Mobilization Act, surmounted this first internal crisis.

The second came some time after Japan struck at Pearl Harbour, December 7, 1941. It is hard to grasp how even the most obscurantist person could see the way after that event as anything but a struggle for survival. The vast majority of Canadians did so see it, and approved of their government's declaration of war on Japan. For many English Canadians the day of Pearl Harbour was almost a happy day, a day even of exaltation. The circle was complete: all the lines were drawn. "Now God be thanked who hath matched us with this hour", men could have said. Not only that; at last the great sister nation was embarked on the common task. Through blood and toil, ties would be knit up with her that would never be undone. There was a little waspish satisfaction in old anti-American quarters that "the Yankees were now getting it", but it was with undisguised relief that most Canadians saw the United States take her place alongside them. Here—with the immense productive power, organizing genius, and exuberant energy of the

[26] For the Quebec elections of 1939, see p. 532.

Republic at their side—was victory. Here, too, it might be, was the healing of the deep rift in the race.[27]

The entrance of the United States affected French Canadians rather differently. As a North American people, it became harder for them to contend that this world conflict, with the United States in it, was just another of England's wars. The sense of danger wiped out for the moment even the horror of Russia, the country of the uttermost blasphemy, the blasphemy against the Holy Ghost. "If the maiden is drowning," said a French priest, on the entry of Russia, "she does not ask the religion of her rescuer." Unfortunately the moment of fusion was not to last, and later on, as hope of victory reappeared, narrow racialism again asserted itself.[28] But by no means all the French were parties to it, nor had the English given the provocation they had in 1914-18. For that, the country owed much gratitude to Mr. King: whatever his short-comings, his life was consecrated to the stupendous task of holding the balance fair between two suspicious, jealous peoples ever seeking pretext of quarrel.[29] His failure of entire success was only to be expected, for not even the stresses and strains of two world wars were enough to reveal to either people the limitations imposed on its actions by the presence of the other. French Canadians might have been expected to realize that they could not live a comfortable, self-contained life without reference to the rest of the world, and English Canadians, that the country could not be taken into war solely on their terms. Both might have been expected to see that Canada was neither a small isolated state nor yet a world power. Many from both sides did understand such things, but the pressure of the Tories for conscription afforded French racialists their best rallying point, while the attitudes of these extremists nourished the wrath of the English jingoes. Unfortunately it was plain that despite the large centre group of people of good will on both sides, neither race had got far in the hardest of their lessons, those of compromise and tolerance.

As matters went from bad to worse in the Pacific, conscription seemed to be the only device of which a frustrated people, far from the battle, could avail itself; to English Canadians it became a symbol of consecration. As such, and apart from considerations of utility, which

---

[27] See p. 541.

[28] During the bad days of 1942, ships were sunk in the St. Lawrence itself. The diehards said that these were not French-Canadian ships, nor would they have been sunk if Canada had not been in the war.

[29] "M. King, c'est plus qu'un homme d'Etat. C'est un symbole. C'est la vivante incarnation du principe de l'unité canadienne. . . ."—*Le Canada*, Montreal, Nov. 22, 1944.

were weighty, it gained such force after Pearl Harbour, that it looked as if Canada, just at the moment when its maximum effort was required, might be reduced to semi-impotence through its internal divisions. To the jingoes, the conscription issue afforded the double opportunity of turning out the government and coercing the French. Once more it seemed as if, for this symbolic gesture, the country's war effort would be damaged, and once more the Prime Minister's extraordinary gift for face-saving formulae prevented that calamity. Mr. King's huge majority in the House constituted no blank cheque, for the authority which commanded his ultimate respect, the people, was making itself heard above the voices in Parliament. In obedience to it, he devised the Conscription Plebiscite of April 27, 1942, by which the voter was asked to state whether or not he was in favour of freeing the Government from its promise not to introduce conscription. This allowed the country to express its opinion, required all opponents to come out in favour of his plan and did not compel him to resort to conscription for overseas service except at his own discretion. The vote turned out to be in the ratio of 179 to 100 in the affirmative. The old English-speaking areas were as overwhelmingly for, as the French were against. Ridings and provinces with large numbers of persons of European descent were in between, registering the familiar facts of assimilation.[30] Someone remarked at that time that instead of the involved formula used, the question might just as well have been "Are you an Anglo-Saxon?"[31]

With freedom to conscript or not to conscript, King proceeded to nurse along a divided country. The war effort increased prodigiously and English Canadians rose to sombre magnificence in their devotion to a cause. From Quebec, the government won a high degree of cooperation in war production and in contributions to war loans. That province's contributions of men, while smaller than those of the rest of the country, were several times larger than in the previous struggle.

Whatever the contributions of Quebec, they could never have satisfied the English-Canadian extremists, and the third internal crisis of the war, the crisis over reinforcements in the autumn of 1944, bears this out. This was the greatest of all the crises, and as with the others, it is hard to assess the proportions in it of genuine patriotic concern and mere party manoeuvring. During the Quebec provincial elections of the summer of 1944, the *Union Nationale* and *Bloc Populaire* had deluged

[30] Ontario voted 518 to 100 for; Quebec, 264 to 100 against.
[31] The formula ran, "Are you in favour of releasing the government from any obligation arising out of any past commitments restricting the methods of raising men for military service?" In 1942, about 60% of the population was of Anglo-Saxon or cognate stock; the affirmative vote was 64%.

the province with flysheets manifesting the bitterest and most factious opposition to Canada being in the war at all. The campaign had revealed a divided province, a fair proportion of whose people were unwilling to follow the war lead of the English. In the autumn, Colonel Ralston, Minister for Defence, attempted to convince the Cabinet that infantry reinforcements, after the four months' campaign in France, could no longer be maintained by voluntary enlistment. The Cabinet was reluctant to impose conscription for overseas service, knowing what it might mean for the civil peace of the country.But a vehement demand for this very measure arose and spread all over English Canada. It was fomented by extremist groups, who stirred up the easily-aroused emotions of English Canadians. It is hard to see where an alternative administration could have been found, yet so divided within itself (to say nothing of supporters and public opinion) was King's ministry that its fall seemed very possible. The Conservative opposition in Parliament was taking every advantage of the emotional wave sweeping Canada. In order to prevent the country being torn in two, the Prime Minister did not bow to the storm until he had managed to convince his French colleagues of the necessity of the step. Even so, he had to face the resignation of two out of three of his defence ministers: Mr. Ralston resigned because Mr. King would not immediately invoke conscription, and Mr. Power, sitting for a French riding, because he was about to invoke it. The public spirit of neither was in question, but the two men took opposing views of the best method of conducting the war in such a country as Canada, and their resignations, coupled with Mr. King's continuance in office, mirrored exactly the disposition of forces in the country at large. French Canada could not resist English Canada, and English Canada could not coerce French Canada. The result was embittered compromise—and Mr. King.

King's solution of the impasse was typical of himself and of Canadian necessities. He agreed to send a given number of conscripts overseas and then he carefully blurred the issue in a flood of words. He satisfied few; few knew what had really been done. But in an emergency session of Parliament, he obtained, despite his desertion by a number of French Liberals, a majority of over two to one. The situation satisfied no one: it shelved, but did not solve, the problems which had occasioned it. With victory in sight, Canada remained, as it had been throughout its history, a house divided. Whether in the storms of peace, which no special discernment was needed to foresee, it could stand, remained for the future to reveal.

6. Reflections

When the fall of France made the possibility of the fall of England very real, strange currents began to course through English Canada: it was not merely the loss of naval control over the Atlantic which loomed up, but personal tragedy. The occupation of Great Britain would have been painful to contemplate, but more painful still was the apprehension of there being disrupted something that was infinitely deep: ways of thought, views of life, traditions, familiar associations, the whole framework of existence that proceeded from the unbroken continuity of English history. The children saw the death of a dear parent approaching and for the first time looked at life through their own eyes.

The moment passed; the parent recovered; English Canadians slid easily back into the attitudes of children. French Canadians, orphaned generations before, had long since learned self-reliance, and for them, however touched they might be by the fall of France, the psychological shock had not occurred.

When Japan attacked the United States, another high emotional moment presented itself. On the west coast everything was confusion, for once again the prospect of direct attack was opened. Canada's two mainstays, the two great world powers which overshadowed every aspect of her life, were wounded and bleeding. Half the American fleet lay on the bottom of the sea, and the British navy seemed to be rapidly following it. Colonies went over like nine pins: armies of white men surrendered to the Japanese. In the midst of it all came the dagger in Canada's own ribs: the news of the fall of Hong Kong, with the loss of two Canadian regiments.

Here were deep experiences shared by English Canadians in common, and partly shared by French Canadians too. Of such are communities made. Compared with the trials of many another people, they were slight enough and far from sufficient to impress on the inhabitants of Canada a common character. They did not do that for the English, and their influence was far weaker on the French. Yet through one medium or another, during the Second World War, a common character was emerging in English Canada. Whether there was any prospect of a general Canadian community or not, as the end of the war drew in sight it was plain that an English Canadian community with traits of its own, neither English nor American, was taking shape.[32]

[32] This community has since been more or less upset by the huge immigration of the 1950's, and as has happened more than once before, several generations will be required for building another one of close-knit character.

Unfortunately the government of the day, with all its good points, was singularly lacking in the creative imagination which might have given form, balance, and purpose to the English-Canadian people and encouraged both them and the French to understand their common destiny. No group of men could frame a better set of exchange regulations, but they could not rise to the height of a national occasion. No Churchillian speeches came out of Ottawa. No national symbols were born from that source, no national pageantry set going. The Prime Minister of a country of two languages would not even make a speech in French. When the Canadian navy received its first cruiser, instead of this being the occasion for a flourish which would have made her an object of pride to all Canadians, she was brought in with a trifling announcement on the back pages of the daily newspapers. An imaginative touch would have named her after one of the great provinces; instead of that she was accepted with her original English name and called H.M.C.S. *Uganda* "after the protectorate", as it was lamely explained. The real explanation no doubt lay in the higher personnel of the Navy, which could hardly distinguish itself from the British Navy[33] or possibly in departmental leadership of a colonial rather than a national turn of mind. Whatever the reason, the action was all of a piece with the general conduct of the government in such matters of national symbolism.

An outstanding opportunity for creative statesmanship was missed in the forces themselves. Nearly a million men were embodied in the land, sea, and air services. They constituted a magnificent expression of the country's will and as fighting men, like their fathers before them, were unsurpassed. The ability with which they were organized was splendid. Canadians were intensely proud of them. They were intensely proud of Canada. They could have been made the basis for a national feeling that would have stamped character and unity upon the country. As it was, it seemed as if the fighting services became Canadian almost in spite of the spirit of their organization and direction, which would have made them little more than subordinate branches of the British. If the spirit of colonialism could have been completely dissipated (the circumstances of war did make great inroads upon it), such men might have become the vehicle to integrate the Canadian community, French and English, curing it of those schizophrenic ills, that suicidal diffusion of loyalties, from which it chronically suffers. A nation might have been

---

*This is borne out by the Royal Commission report on the navy, tabled in Parliament, October, 1949.

forged from the fighting men but the government of the day would not have dreamed of initiating the project.[34]

Little criticism, however, was made of it on that score. Government was condemned in Quebec for contributing too much to the allied cause and it was condemned in Ontario for not contributing enough, but it was condemned nowhere for not being imaginatively and creatively Canadian. At the end of this long survey, that fact alone provokes the question whether, in the course of the century and three quarters since the Conquest of 1760, anything vital had been created.

French Canadians would have summed up by contending that they were a people in themselves, but that they were willing to keep the spirit of Confederation and agree to a frankly bilingual, bicultural state. They would have pointed to the numerous occasions on which the English had broken their faith and would have claimed that only by insistence on every jot and tittle of their rights could they hope to survive as a group. They would have rejected with horror the idea of assimilation. Clearly the first of Canadian problems was the last, and the primary antithesis of Canadian history remained largely unresolved.

Honest effort at a judgement forces the conviction that the heavier share of responsibility has lain with the English Canadians. They have been more numerous, but as a group, and with many honourable exceptions, they have not been magnanimous. They have been the stronger, but they have not hesitated to use their strength. They have been greedy and intolerant, and then have turned naïvely round and wondered why the French (under their command) would not enter their wars. They might have made at least a Switzerland out of Canada and they have created an Austria-Hungary.

Admittedly, the French, considered also as a group and with as many individual exceptions as among the English, have been a difficult people. Parochial, oversensitive, and self-centred, they have been so conscious of their rights within Canada that they have had no adequate sense of their duties towards Canada. In face of the defence mechanisms set up for the protection of race and creed, the very real efforts of many of the English to be fair, friendly, and just have gone unheeded and unappreciated. They have had before them innumerable examples of the fate of small peoples: if they had wished, they could have seen Ireland, Poland, or others of the miserable subject minorities of Europe; instead, they have seen mainly those legal privileges that they have not succeeded in

[34] This statement no doubt assumes that the government, that is, Mr. King, had clearly formulated ideas upon the direction in which it would like to see Canada go. A close observer has remarked that this was not the case, and that Mr. King merely reflected the ordinary views of the moment upon such matters.

attaining. Their conception of *race* has become an obsession and it has been carried to un-Christian and almost Hitlerian intensities.

But the English Canadians have been little fitted to deal with a sensitive minority: they are a dour and unimaginative folk. Having failed to find a centre in themselves, they borrow the heroes, the history, the songs, and the slang of others. With no vividly realized *res publica* of their own to talk about, they take refuge in silence, unable to formulate their loyalties, confused over their deepest aspirations. Yet they are surcharged with a sense of duty, and when the great occasion of war comes, their efforts seem to know no limit. They must surely have an intuitive faith in the unexpressed essence of their traditions, for few of them have a formulated creed.

Canada with its divisions of race presents no common denominator in those profundities which normally unite—in race, language, religion, history, and culture. If a common focus is to be found, it must come out of the common homeland itself. If the Canadian people are to find their soul, they must seek for it, not in the English language or the French, but in the little ports of the Atlantic provinces, in the flaming autumn maples of the St. Lawrence valley, in the portages and lakes of the Canadian Shield, in the sunsets and relentless cold of the prairies, in the foothill, mountain, and sea of the west, and in the unconquerable vastnesses of the north. From the land, Canada, must come the soul of Canada. That it may so come is not as fanciful as some might think. When in 1763 the experiment was begun in the northern wildernesses, no one foresaw the strong state that was to be. Canada has been built in defiance of geography. Its two coasts were bridged by a transcontinental railway almost in defiance of common sense. Canadian statesmen reconciled the irreconcilable when in the 1840's they joined dependence to independence. They accomplished one of the greatest acts of statebuilding in history when in 1867 they brought together scattered provinces and two peoples into one country. Though the extremists would more than once have wrecked it, the structure so built has never failed in crisis to rally to it the support of moderate men from both races. It has stood through the storms of two world wars. In every generation Canadians have had to rework the miracle of their political existence. Canada has been created because there has existed within the hearts of its people a determination to build for themselves an enduring home. Canada is a supreme act of faith.

Never was there greater need of faith than in the days when the second great world war reached its closing stages: it seemed as if the dream dreamed in 1867 would either be realized or the country would disintegrate. Perhaps victory would be accompanied by a renewal of the faith, something of that tolerance and magnanimity without which Canada could not continue. Perhaps the cleansing torrent of war would bring the self-knowledge and the self-reverence that would mean new strength for the country's institutions, for the freedom which alone could keep them sweet and clean, and for the faith upon which that freedom rested. Perhaps for the one great thing its two peoples have in common, this strange and difficult land itself, this maddening land, there might be at hand a destiny not less enduring for the slow and bitter travail of its birth.

> My roots are in this soil,
> Whatever good or bad, what vain hope or mighty triumph lies in you
> That good or bad, that destiny is in me.
> Where you have failed, the fault is on my head.
> Where you are ignorant or blind or cruel, I made you so.
> In all your folly and your strength I share
> And all your beauty is my heritage.[35]

Chronology, 1945-1963

1945 United Nations formed.
      August 6. Americans drop first atom bomb on Hiroshima, Japan.
1946 Feb.-July. Royal Commission on Espionage. Arbitrary arrest and examination *in camera* with finding that specific individuals appeared guilty of betraying Canadian state secrets to Russia raises fundamental question in civil liberties and the allegiance of the citizen.
1947 Spectacular new discoveries of oil, iron ore, and uranium ore begin to work radical change in the Canadian economy.
1948 Quebec adopts official provincial flag.
      Nov. 15. Resignation of Mackenzie King. Louis St. Laurent Prime Minister.
1949 March 31. Newfoundland enters Confederation.
1950 June 25. Korean War begins.
      August 22. General railway strike in Canada.
1952 Rt. Hon. Vincent Massey, first Canadian Governor-General.
1953 May 14. Television Broadcasting, CBC.
      First Shakespearian Festival, Stratford, Ontario.

---

[35] From the unpublished poem, "Oh Canada, My Country" by Gwen Pharis Ringwood.

1954 March 30. Canada's first subway, Toronto.

Nov. 21. H.M.C.S. *Labrador* completes the North West Passage.

1955 May 9. Formation of the Canadian Labour Congress.

Dec. 14. Canada takes initiative in admission of 16 new states to the United Nations.

1956 May-June. The "Pipe-line debate" in the Commons weakens the St. Laurent government.

Nov. The Suez Crisis. Canada's proposals for a United Nations "police force" accepted in the U.N.

1957 March 6. Supreme Court finds Quebec Padlock Law *ultra vires.*

June 21. John George Diefenbaker becomes Prime Minister.

July 31. NORAD (North American Air Defence Command) comes into operation.

1958 Bicentennial of Legislature of Nova Scotia, first Assembly in British North America. Centennial Year of British Columbia.

Jan. 16. L. B. Pearson chosen Liberal leader.

1959 June 26. Queen and President open St. Lawrence Seaway.

Sept. 13. 200th anniversary of the Battle of the Plains of Abraham.

Sept. 15. Major General Georges P. Vanier Governor-General.

1960 August 4. The Bill of Rights passes the House of Commons.

1961 March 8-17. Conference of Commonwealth Prime Ministers. South Africa censured for *Apartheid,* partly through Canada's action, and leaves Commonwealth.

July 12. Death of Mazo de la Roche.

December. *Séparatisme* in the province of Quebec becomes active issue.

1962 March 6. Sons of Freedom Doukhobors destroy important electrical installations in British Columbia.

1963 Feb. 4. Diefenbaker government defeated in the Commons.

April 8. General election. Liberals having the largest number of seats, though not a majority, L. B. Pearson becomes Prime Minister.

Additional Reading

Hutchison, Bruce. *The Incredible Canadian.* [W. L. M. King] Toronto, 1952.

Pearson, L. B. *Democracy in World Politics.* Toronto, 1955.

Pickersgill, J. W. *The Mackenzie King Record, 1939-1944.* Toronto, 1960.

Riddell, Walter A. *Documents on Canadian Foreign Policy, 1917-1939.* Toronto, 1962.

Index